DIE REVISION DER POSTMODERNE
POST-MODERNISM REVISITED

DIE REVISION DER POSTMODERNE
POST-MODERNISM REVISITED

IN MEMORIAM HEINRICH KLOTZ

DIE REVISION DER POSTMODERNE
POST-MODERNISM REVISITED

HERAUSGEGEBEN VON/EDITED BY
INGEBORG FLAGGE UND/AND ROMANA SCHNEIDER

DAM DEUTSCHES ARCHITEKTUR MUSEUM JUNIUS

ESSAYS

PROJEKTE / PROJECTS

Als vor über zwei Jahren die Idee entstand, eine Jubiläumsausstellung mit dem Titel »Die Revision der Postmoderne« zu veranstalten, lagen dem verschiedene Vorstellungen zugrunde, was ein solches Projekt leisten solle. Im Vordergrund stand, das zwanzigjährige Bestehen des Deutschen Architektur Museums DAM zu feiern. Dann wollten wir an Heinrich Klotz, den Initiator und Gründungsdirektor des Museums, erinnern. Auch die Architektur des Hauses selbst von Oswald Mathias Ungers sollte bei dieser Jubiläumsausstellung eine Hauptrolle spielen. Der Titel »Die Revision der Postmoderne« schien folgerichtig, weil er die Verbindung zur Eröffnungsausstellung von 1984 »Die Revision der Moderne. Postmoderne Architektur 1960-1980« herstellte. Mit diesen Parametern war aber der Inhalt der Ausstellung noch nicht umrissen. Denn wie sollte sich aus der Fülle der Möglichkeiten eine überzeugende Auswahl von Bauten ergeben, die nun einmal die Grundlage einer jeden Ausstellung und eines überzeugenden Buchs sind?

Doch zunächst zum Titel »Die Revision der Postmoderne«. Was heißt »Revision«? Was verstehen wir unter dem Begriff »Postmoderne«, der so eng mit der Gründungsgeschichte des DAM verbunden ist? Wie schon bei der Eröffnungsausstellung steht das Wort »Revision« für »erneutes Hinsehen«, »Zurückschauen«, »Prüfen«, »wieder Durchsehen«. Uns geht es also weder um die Rückkehr zu etwas Vorherigem, noch um den Abgesang auf eine Epoche, sondern um die Darstellung ihrer fortwährenden Erneuerung. Eine Neudefinition des umstrittenen und uneinheitlich verwendeten Begriffs »Postmoderne« wollten wir nicht leisten. In den Essays des vorliegenden Buchs wird das Phänomen jedoch von verschiedenen Standpunkten aus beleuchtet.

Unser Bestreben ist, Architektur zu zeigen, die sich ihren jeweiligen Aufgaben entsprechend autonom und immer wieder neu stellt. Diesen Anspruch verfolgte auch die Eröffnungsausstellung des DAM. Deshalb sieht unser Konzept vor, ausgewählte Projekte aus dieser ersten Schau mit neueren Architekturen der letzten zehn Jahre zu konfrontieren. Wir greifen also die Pole des Zeitraums von zwanzig Jahren heraus und vergleichen sie. Da sich diese Periode durch die Gleichberechtigung und das Nebeneinander unterschiedlicher Auffassungen auszeichnet, kam für uns nicht in Frage, eine lineare Entwicklung zu konstruieren. Auch hätte dieser Versuch den Rahmen des Projekts in quantitativer Hinsicht gesprengt.

Im Gegensatz zur Eröffnungsausstellung des DAM ist die Jubiläumsausstellung thematisch angelegt und nicht nach Architektennamen gegliedert. Wir orientieren uns aber an den Inhal-

Two years ago, when the idea of staging a commemorative exhibition entitled "Post-Modernism Revisited" was born, opinions differed about what a project of this kind should seek to achieve. First and foremost was the wish to celebrate the 20th anniversary of DAM, the Deutsches Architektur Museum or German Museum of Architecture. Secondly, we wanted to commemorate Heinrich Klotz, the initiator and founding director of the museum. The architecture of the building itself, the work of Oswald Mathias Ungers was also to play a principal role in this commemorative exhibition. "Post-Modernism Revisited" seemed the logical title, because it made the connection to the inaugural exhibition in 1984 "Die Revision der Moderne. Postmoderne Architektur 1960-1980" (Modernism Revisited. Post-Modern Architecture 1960-1980). But these parameters did not define the actual content of the exhibition. How were we to go about sifting through such a wealth of possible buildings to make a convincing selection, which after all is the basis of any exhibition and any convincing book?

But first of all, let us look at the title of the exhibition: "Post-Modernism Revisited." What do we mean by "revisited?" What do we understand by "Post-Modernism," a term that is so closely associated with DAM's genesis? As in the inaugural exhibition, the word "revisited" is used in the sense of "taking another look," "looking back," "reviewing," "re-appraising." We are not concerned with returning to something in the past, nor with penning a valediction to a bygone era, but with portraying its constant renewal. We did not set out to try and redefine Post-Modernism, a term that is both controversial and has no single definition. However, the essays in this book explore the phenomenon from different angles.

Our aim is to exhibit architecture that confronts whatever task it faces with autonomy and a fresh approach. This was also one of the aims of DAM's inaugural exhibition. That prompted the concept of juxtaposing selected projects from the first show with examples of new architecture from the last ten years. In other words, we have taken a period of twenty years and compared the works created at each pole. Since the main characteristics of this period were parity between and co-existence of different approaches, there was no question of attempting to construe a linear development. Also, an attempt to do that would have gone way beyond the scope of the project in terms of number of exhibits.

By contrast with the inaugural exhibition, the anniversary exhibition is organised by theme, not by architect. However, we

ten der Ausstellung von 1984, indem wir Themenfelder aus ihr abgeleitet haben, die wie Arbeitstitel formuliert sind. Damit soll der Eindruck vermieden werden, wir hätten einen Kanon intendiert. Die Themenfelder bilden die Struktur des Projekts. Wir handeln keine Typologien ab. Das Grundsätzliche, das wir zeigen möchten, nämlich wie vielfältig und unterschiedlich gute Architektur eine gestellte Aufgabe lösen kann, würde sonst aus dem Blick geraten. So beginnen auch im Projektteil dieses Buches, der die Ausstellung widerspiegelt, die verschiedenen Kapitel mit ausgewählten Projekten der Eröffnungsausstellung. Ihnen folgen neue Beispiele, die vergleichbare Eigenschaften mit den alten Exponaten aufweisen beziehungsweise aufgrund verwandter Qualitäten aufeinander bezogen werden können. Bei der Auswahl stand im Vordergrund, Bauten zu zeigen, die mit ihrer Architektur einer komplexen und von gesellschaftlichen Umbrüchen geprägten Realität Rechnung tragen und somit auf Zukunft hin orientiert sind. Ganz besonders haben uns Interventionen an Orten der Peripherie, in Industriebrachen, in zersiedelten Gebieten interessiert, die durch architektonische Eingriffe zu »Epizentren« von Entwicklung werden (sollen).

Die in der Ausstellung und in diesem Buch vorgestellten Projekte haben die Bedürfnisse der Nutzer im Blick und erheben den Anspruch, gestalterische und räumliche Architekturlösungen gegen Langeweile und Gleichförmigkeit anzubieten, Identität zu schaffen, Individualität und Gemeinschaft in Einklang zu bringen. Wichtig ist uns die ideelle Verknüpfung der verschiedenen Beispiele, die sich, obwohl in unserem Projekt einem Thema zugeordnet, diesem immer auch entziehen, also auch in anderen Zusammenhängen gesehen werden können. Bauten mit postmodernem Schnickschnack, von gleicher Mittelmäßigkeit und Banalität wie diejenigen Vorgängerbauten der Moderne, die zu überwinden sie antraten, werden in der Ausstellung nicht berücksichtigt; über ihre mangelnde Qualität kann bei denen, die dieses Buch zur Hand nehmen, kaum ein Dissens bestehen. Uns ist daran gelegen, positive Auswirkungen von Pluralismus und Komplexität zu zeigen, die sich – so hoffen wir – zu einem neuen oder anderen Bild von Architektur zusammensetzen.

Die verschiedenen Ausprägungen und Stadien der Postmoderne werden im Essayteil dieses Buches unterschiedlich beschrieben und kritisch behandelt. Hier wird auch den Vorwürfen nachgegangen, die während des gesamten Zeitraums, von dem unser Projekt bestimmt ist, in der Fachliteratur und im Feuilleton ausgiebig diskutiert wurden: mangelndes, einseitiges oder selektives Geschichtsbewusstsein, Kommerzialisierung,

have been guided by the content of the 1984 exhibition, in that we have based the topics covered on it. The topic headings read like working titles: to avoid creating the impression that we see them as immutable canons. The topics give the project its basic structure. We do not deal with typologies. That would detract from the fundamental thing we are seeking to illustrate: the very diverse range of responses good architecture can bring to the same task. For that reason, the different chapters of the project section of this book, which mirrors the structure of the exhibition, begin with selected projects from the inaugural exhibition. They are followed by new examples that have similar characteristics to the old exhibits or have related qualities that enable links to be drawn between them. In making the selection, we focused on showing buildings whose architecture adequately reflects a complex reality marked by social change and in that are future-oriented. We were especially interested by places on the city edge, brownfield sites, areas scarred by sprawling development, places where architectural interventions were intended to become "epicentres" that might stimulate further development.

The architectural projects presented in the exhibition and in this book focus on the needs of the user and set out to offer design and spatial solutions that can counter boredom and monotony, create a sense of identity, and reconcile individuality and community. We felt it was important to show the connections between the different examples, which, although assigned to a particular topic in our project, cannot be confined to a single theme, in other words can be seen in several different contexts. The exhibition does not pay any attention to buildings with Post-Modern trappings that are of the same kind of mediocrity and banality as the very buildings subscribing to the Modernist creed that they set out to supplant; surely no-one who picks up this book will disagree about their lack of quality. We were keen to show the positive effects of pluralism and complexity which—at least that is our hope—combine to form a new image of architecture.

The essay section of this book contains different descriptions and critiques of Post-Modernism's different expressions and stages of development. Here we look at the various accusations levelled at Post-Modernism during the entire period covered by our project, which were discussed at length both in architectural publications and in the features section of the press: lack of historical awareness or, at the very least, a one-sided or selective perception of history, commercialisation, kitsch, ignoring

Kitsch, Ausblenden negativer gesellschaftlicher Umstände und Strömungen, fehlender Glaube an geschichtlichen Fortschritt oder die Resignation vor der aktiven individuellen Einflussnahme auf den Lauf der Dinge. Die Beiträge in diesem Buch verharren jedoch nicht bei den negativen Entwicklungen, die sich aus einer postmodernen Ideologie ergeben, sondern machen den Versuch, Perspektiven für eine zeitgemäße Baukultur zu entwickeln.

Unser Projekt stellt exemplarische Lösungen vor; es versucht sich nicht an einem allgemeingültigen Programm oder einer grundsätzlichen Kritik. Die Botschaft der Ausstellung und des Katalogs soll die sein, dass es ein breites Spektrum innovativer Architektur gibt, auch wenn wir nur einen kleinen Ausschnitt davon zeigen. Ferner geht die Ausstellung davon aus, dass es nicht den einen Weg gibt, heutige Architekturpraxis zu beschreiben und zu bewerten, und dass auch die in der Gesellschaft vorhandene Dynamik von Gegensatz und Unterschiedlichkeit mit Hilfe von Architektur künstlerisch anspruchsvoll und sozial verantwortlich umgesetzt werden kann.

Das wichtigste Motiv für Heinrich Klotz, ein Architekturmuseum zu gründen war, die in Zeichnungen und Modellen festgehaltenen Ideen der Architektur vor der Vernichtung zu retten und einem größeren Publikum bekannt zu machen. Unbestritten ging es ihm dabei auch um die ästhetischen und künstlerischen Qualitäten dieser Darstellungen, die er in den Rang von Kunstwerken erhob. Viele Architekturausstellungen lebten fortan von dem Anspruch – und wurden daran gemessen –, solche Kunstwerke im Original zeigen zu können. Als wir mit der Arbeit an der Jubiläumsausstellung begannen, dachten wir, diese Tradition fortsetzen zu können. Natürlich waren wir darauf vorbereitet, dass bei jüngeren Architekten kaum noch Zeichnungen im klassischen Sinne hergestellt werden und auch für idealistische Darstellungen von Architektur inzwischen der Computer eine Hauptrolle spielt. Aber der unmittelbare Vergleich zeigt, dass die Diskrepanz zwischen einer mit der Hand hergestellten Zeichnung und einer Computergraphik oft noch größer ist als zunächst angenommen. Letztere wirkt meist überholt, wenn der Bau realisiert ist. Deshalb sind wir schnell davon abgekommen, die Computergraphik wie ein Äquivalent zur Handzeichnung zu behandeln; die Qualitätsunterschiede sind zu groß. Vielmehr haben wir bei realisierten Bauten auf Fotos zurückgegriffen, da sie in den meisten Fällen aussagekräftiger waren. Durch die hier vorgenommene Konfrontation von Alt und Neu wird einmal mehr deutlich, wie schnell sich ein wichtiger

negative social conditions and movements, lack of faith in historical progress or resignation and a sense of the inability of individuals to proactively influence the course of events. However, the articles in this book do not focus exclusively on the negative developments that result from Post-Modern ideology, but attempt to develop perspectives for an architectural culture that is appropriate for our times.

Our project presents schemes as examples; it does not attempt to put forward a universally valid programme nor to present a fundamental critique. The message both the exhibition and the catalogue intend to convey is that there is a broad spectrum of innovative architecture even if we are able to show only a small sample of it. Secondly, we wish to convey that there is no single way of describing and evaluating contemporary architectural practice and that the dynamics of contrast and difference in society can be given artistic expression by architecture that is both of high quality and socially responsible.

Heinrich Klotz's most important motive for establishing an architecture museum was to prevent the architectural ideas that were recorded in the form of drawings and models from being destroyed and make them available to a broader section of the public. There is no doubt that he was also concerned with the aesthetic and artistic quality of these representations, which he elevated to the status of works of art. From then on, the very legitimation for many architectural exhibitions was their claim to be able to exhibit works of art of that kind in the original—and they were judged by that yardstick. When we started work on the anniversary exhibition we thought we would be able to continue this tradition. Of course, we were prepared for the fact that younger architects no longer produce drawings in the classic sense and that the computer now plays a major role even in ideal architectural representations. But direct comparison shows that the discrepancy between a drawing that has been produced by hand and computer graphics is greater than we initially imagined. The latter on the whole seems to lose its value once the building has been completed. For that reason, we soon abandoned the idea of treating computer graphics as equivalent to hand drawings; the differences in quality are too great. Instead, we have used photos of the buildings that were realised since in most cases they were more informative. The confrontation between old and new we have sought to highlight shows all the more clearly how quickly an important motive for DAM's foundation has become obsolete: in the meantime

Beweggrund für die Gründung des DAM überlebt hat. Denn die traditionelle Architekturzeichnung ist inzwischen aus dem Architektenalltag verschwunden.

Die Beiträge zur Rezeption von Architektur, die das DAM seit seiner Errichtung vor zwanzig Jahren durch Ausstellungen, in Diskussionen und durch Publikationen kontinuierlich leistet, sind aus der Öffentlichkeit nicht mehr wegzudenken. Die Pionierleistung von Heinrich Klotz, vielen Menschen Architektur nahe gebracht und sie dafür begeistert zu haben, hat sich als unumkehrbar erwiesen. Architekturqualität in der Vielfalt zu erkennen, das Interesse an Architekturgeschichte zu vertiefen, für den Respekt vor historischen Bauten einzutreten, den Geist eines Ortes zu schützen, neuen Entwicklungen offen zu begegnen, all dies ist heute selbstverständlicher geworden, als es vor zwanzig Jahren war – und das DAM hat Anteil daran. Auch fällt die Kritik über die Architektur der achtziger Jahren inzwischen differenzierter aus, zumal wenn sie von den Bewohnern wider Erwarten angenommen und sorgsam behandelt wird. Dennoch, die Debatte, über das, was gute Architektur allgemein ausmacht, bleibt kontrovers; die Zukunft ist – für die Architektur allemal – ein offenes Buch.

Die Ausstellung und der Katalog hätten nicht realisiert werden können ohne großzügige finanzielle Unterstützung. Wir danken ganz herzlich: Stadt Frankfurt am Main, Ernst & Young, Hessische Kulturstiftung, Georg und Franziska Speyer'sche Hochschulstiftung, Gesellschaft der Freunde des Deutschen Architektur Museums e. V., ABG FRANKFURT HOLDING Wohnungsbau- und Beteiligungsgesellschaft mbH, Frankfurter Sparkasse und Herrn Architekt Dieter Köhler, Frankfurt am Main.

Ingeborg Flagge, Romana Schneider

the traditional architectural drawing has disappeared from everyday architectural practice.

It is not possible to imagine the relationship with architecture the general public has developed without the contributions that DAM has constantly made—in the form of exhibitions, discussions and publications—since it was built twenty years ago. Heinrich Klotz's pioneering achievement of making architecture accessible to many people and inspiring their interest in it has turned out to be irrevocable. Recognising architectural quality in all its diversity, deepening interest in architectural history, promoting respect for historic buildings, protecting the *genius loci* of a place, maintaining an open mind towards new developments: all this now taken for granted to a far greater extent than it was twenty years ago—and DAM had a part in that. Also criticism of the architecture of the 1980s has become more differentiated, particularly in cases where—contrary to expectations—the residents accept it and treat it with care. Nevertheless, the debate on what generally defines good architecture remains fraught with controversy: the future is—most certainly as far as architecture is concerned—an open book.

The exhibition and the catalogue would not have been possible without generous financial support from a number of sources. We would like to express our gratitude to the city of Frankfurt am Main, Ernst & Young, Hessische Kulturstiftung, Georg und Franziska Speyer'sche Hochschulstiftung, Gesellschaft der Freunde des Deutschen Architektur Museums e. V., ABG FRANKFURT HOLDING Wohnungsbau- und Beteiligungsgesellschaft mbH, Frankfurter Sparkasse and Mr. Dieter Köhler, architect, Frankfurt am Main.

Ingeborg Flagge, Romana Schneider

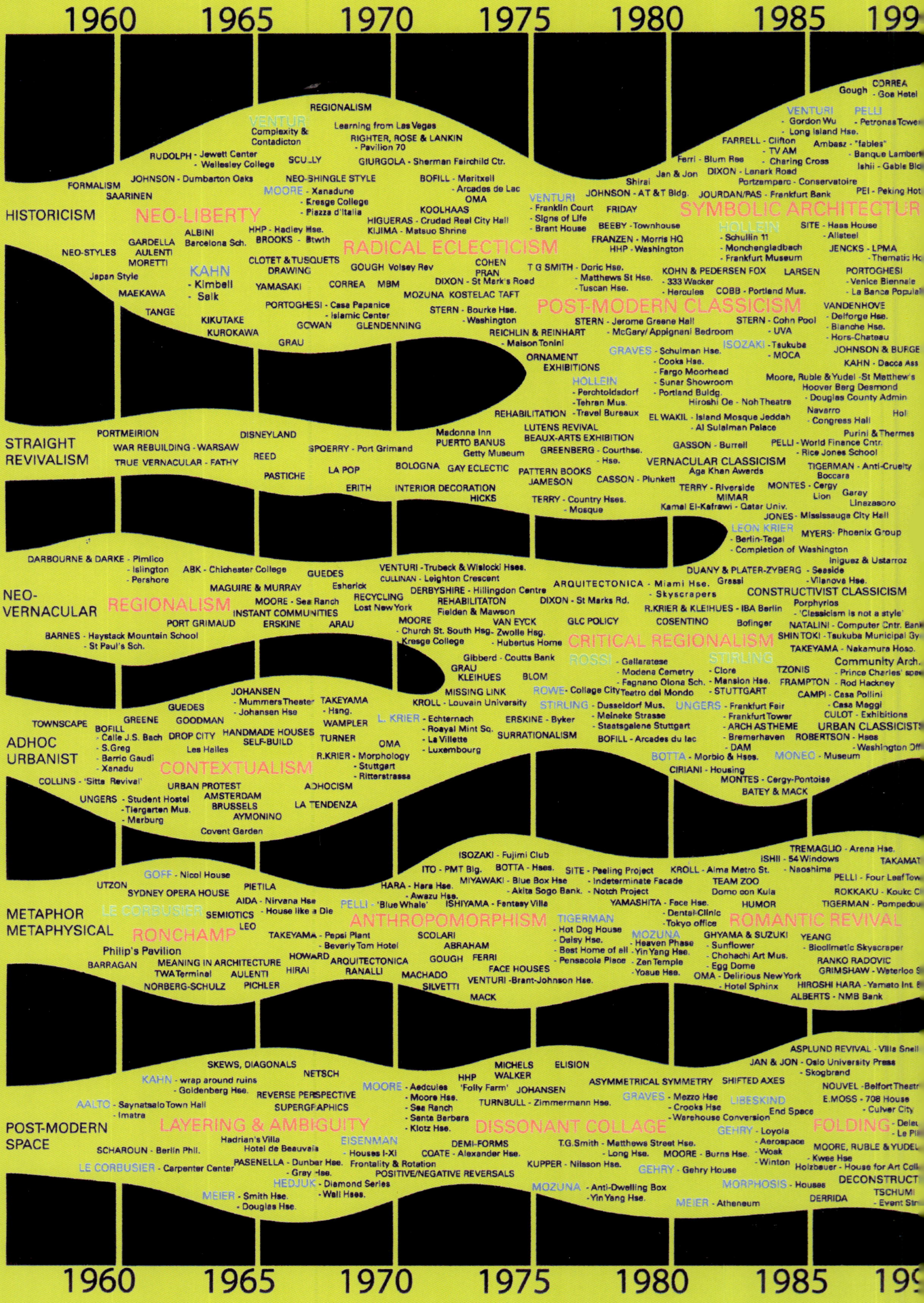

1960
1965
1970
1975
1980
1985
199
HISTORICISM
FORMALISM
SAARINEN
NEO-LIBERTY
NEO-STYLES
GARDELLA
AULENTI
MORETTI
Japan Style
MAEKAWA
TANGE
KAHN
- Kimbell
- Salk
RUDOLPH - Jewett Center
- Wellesley College
JOHNSON - Dumbarton Oaks
ALBINI
Barcelona Sch.
VENTURI
Complexity & Contadicton
REGIONALISM
Learning from Las Vegas
RIGHTER, ROSE & LANKIN
- Pavilion 70
SCULLY
GIURGOLA - Sherman Fairchild Ctr.
NEO-SHINGLE STYLE
MOORE - Xanadune
- Kresge College
- Piazza d'Italia
HHP - Hadley Hse.
BROOKS - Btwth
CLOTET & TUSQUETS
DRAWING
YAMASAKI
CORREA
MBM
KIKUTAKE
KUROKAWA
PORTOGHESI - Casa Papanice
- Islamic Center
GOWAN
GLENDENNING
GRAU
BOFILL - Meritxell
- Arcades de Lac
OMA
KOOLHAAS
HIGUERAS - Crudad Real City Hall
KIJIMA - Matsuo Shrine
RADICAL ECLECTICISM
GOUGH Volsey Rev
COHEN
PRAN
DIXON - St Mark's Road
MOZUNA KOSTELAC TAFT
STERN - Bourke Hse.
- Washington
REICHLIN & REINHART
- Maison Tonini
ORNAMENT
EXHIBITIONS
VENTURI
- Franklin Court
- Signs of Life
- Brant House
JOHNSON - AT & T Bldg.
FRIDAY
BEEBY - Townhouse
FRANZEN - Morris HQ
HHP - Washington
T G SMITH - Doric Hse.
- Matthews St Hse.
- Tuscan Hse.
POST-MODERN CLASSICISM
STERN - Jerome Greene Hall
- McGary/Appignani Bedroom
GRAVES - Schulman Hse.
- Cooks Hse.
- Fargo Moorhead
- Sunar Showroom
- Portland Buldg.
HOLLEIN
- Perchtoldsdorf
- Tehran Mus.
REHABILITATION - Travel Bureaux
Shirai
Jan & Jon
Ferri - Blum Rse
FARRELL - Clifton
- TV AM
- Charing Cross
DIXON - Lanark Road
Portzamparc - Conservatoire
JOURDAN/PAS - Frankfurt Bank
SYMBOLIC ARCHITECTURE
HOLLEIN
- Schullin 11
- Monchengladbach
- Frankfurt Museum
KOHN & PEDERSEN FOX
- 333 Wacker
- Hercules
COBB - Portland Mus.
LARSEN
STERN - Cohn Pool
- UVA
ISOZAKI - Tsukuba
- MOCA
Hiroshi Oe - Noh Theatre
EL WAKIL - Island Mosque Jeddah
- Al Sulaiman Palace
VENTURI
- Gordon Wu
- Long Island Hse.
PELLI
- Petronas Towers
Ambasz - "fables"
- Banque Lambert
Ishii - Gable Bldg
PEI - Peking Hotel
Gough
CORREA
- Goa Hotel
SITE - Haas House
- Allsteel
JENCKS - LPMA
- Thematic House
PORTOGHESI
- Venice Biennale
- La Banca Popular
VANDENHOVE
- Delforge Hse.
- Blanche Hse.
- Hors-Chateau
JOHNSON & BURGEE
KAHN - Dacca Ass.
Moore, Ruble & Yudel - St Matthew's
Hoover Berg Desmond
- Douglas County Admin
Navarro
- Congress Hall
Hol
Purini & Thermes
STRAIGHT REVIVALISM
PORTMEIRION
WAR REBUILDING - WARSAW
TRUE VERNACULAR - FATHY
DISNEYLAND
REED
PASTICHE
SPOERRY - Port Grimand
LA POP
ERITH
Madonna Inn
PUERTO BANUS
Getty Museum
BOLOGNA
GAY ECLECTIC
INTERIOR DECORATION
HICKS
LUTENS REVIVAL
BEAUX-ARTS EXHIBITION
GREENBERG - Courthse.
- Hse.
PATTERN BOOKS
JAMESON
TERRY - Country Hses.
- Mosque
CASSON - Plunkett
VERNACULAR CLASSICISM
Aga Khan Awards
GASSON - Burrell
TERRY - Riverside
MIMAR
Kamal El-Kafrawi - Qatar Univ.
PELLI - World Finance Cntr.
- Rice Jones School
TIGERMAN - Anti-Cruelty
Boccara
MONTES - Cergy
Lion
Garay
Linazasoro
JONES - Mississauga City Hall
LEON KRIER
- Berlin-Tegel
- Completion of Washington
MYERS - Phoenix Group
Iniguez & Ustarroz
NEO-VERNACULAR
DARBOURNE & DARKE - Pimlico
- Islington
- Pershore
ABK - Chichester College
GUEDES
MAGUIRE & MURRAY
Esherick
REGIONALISM
MOORE - Sea Ranch
INSTANT COMMUNITIES
PORT GRIMAUD
ERSKINE
ARAU
BARNES - Haystack Mountain School
- St Paul's Sch.
VENTURI - Trubeck & Wislocki Hses.
CULLINAN - Leighton Crescent
DERBYSHIRE - Hillingdon Centre
RECYCLING
Lost New York
REHABILITATON
Fielden & Mawson
MOORE
- Church St. South Hsg.
Kresge College
VAN EYCK
- Zwolle Hsg.
- Hubertus Home
ARQUITECTONICA - Miami Hse.
- Skyscrapers
DIXON - St Marks Rd.
GLC POLICY
CRITICAL REGIONALISM
DUANY & PLATER-ZYBERG - Seaside
- Vilanova Hse.
Grassi
R.KRIER & KLEIHUES - IBA Berlin
COSENTINO
Bofinger
CONSTRUCTIVIST CLASSICISM
Porphyrios
- 'Classicism is not a style'
NATALINI - Computer Cntr. Bank
SHIN TOKI - Tsukuba Municipal Gym
TAKEYAMA - Nakamura Hosp.
Gibberd - Coutts Bank
GRAU
KLEIHUES
BLOM
MISSING LINK
KROLL - Louvain University
ROSSI - Gallaratese
- Modena Cemetry
- Fagnano Olona Sch.
ROWE - Collage City
Teatro del Mondo
STIRLING - Dusseldorf Mus.
- Meineke Strasse
- Staatsgalene Stuttgart
BOFILL - Arcades du lac
STIRLING
- Clore
- Mansion Hse.
- STUTTGART
UNGERS - Frankfurt Fair
- Frankfurt Tower
- ARCH AS THEME
- Bremerhaven
- DAM
TZONIS
FRAMPTON
Community Arch.
- Prince Charles' speech
- Rod Hackney
CAMPI - Casa Pollini
- Casa Maggi
CULOT - Exhibitions
URBAN CLASSICISTS
ROBERTSON - Hses
- Washington Office
ADHOC URBANIST
TOWNSCAPE
BOFILL
- Calle J.S. Bach
- S.Greg
- Barrio Gaudi
- Xanadu
GREENE
GUEDES
GOODMAN
DROP CITY
Les Halles
JOHANSEN
- Mummers Theater
- Johansen Hse
HANDMADE HOUSES
SELF-BUILD
TAKEYAMA
- Hsng.
WAMPLER
TURNER
OMA
L. KRIER - Echternach
- Roayal Mint Sq.
- La Villette
- Luxembourg
ERSKINE - Byker
SURRATIONALISM
CONTEXTUALISM
R.KRIER - Morphology
- Stuttgart
- Ritterstrasse
ADHOCISM
COLLINS - 'Sitte Revival'
URBAN PROTEST
UNGERS - Student Hostel
- Tiergarten Mus.
- Marburg
AMSTERDAM
BRUSSELS
AYMONINO
LA TENDENZA
Covent Garden
BOTTA - Morbio & Hses.
CIRIANI - Housing
MONEO - Museum
MONTES - Cergy-Pontoise
BATEY & MACK
METAPHOR METAPHYSICAL
UTZON
GOFF - Nicol House
SYDNEY OPERA HOUSE
LE CORBUSIER
RONCHAMP
Philip's Pavilion
BARRAGAN
SEMIOTICS
PIETILA
AIDA - Nirvana Hse
- House like a Die
LEO
MEANING IN ARCHITECTURE
TWA Terminal
NORBERG-SCHULZ
AULENTI
PICHLER
HIRAI
TAKEYAMA - Pepsi Plant
- Beverly Tom Hotel
HOWARD
ARQUITECTONICA
RANALLI
MACHADO
SILVETTI
PELLI - 'Blue Whale'
ANTHROPOMORPHISM
HARA - Hara Hse.
- Awazu Hse.
ITO - PMT Blg.
ISOZAKI - Fujimi Club
BOTTA - Hses.
MIYAWAKI - Blue Box Hse
- Akita Sogo Bank.
ISHIYAMA - Fantasy Villa
SCOLARI
ABRAHAM
GOUGH
FERRI
FACE HOUSES
VENTURI - Brant-Johnson Hse.
MACK
SITE - Peeling Project
- Indeterminate Facade
- Notch Project
TIGERMAN
- Hot Dog House
- Daisy Hse.
- Best Home of all
- Pensacola Place
KROLL - Alma Metro St.
TEAM ZOO
Domo con Kula
YAMASHITA - Face Hse.
- Dental-Clinic
- Tokyo office
MOZUNA
- Heaven Phase
- Yin Yang Hse.
- Zen Temple
- Yosue Hse.
GHYAMA & SUZUKI
- Sunflower
- Chohachi Art Mus.
- Egg Dome
OMA - Delirious New York
- Hotel Sphinx
HUMOR
ROMANTIC REVIVAL
ISHII - 54 Windows
- Naoshima
TREMAGLIO - Arena Hse.
TAKAMATSU
PELLI - Four Leaf Towers
ROKKAKU - Kouko Cl
TIGERMAN - Pompedour
YEANG
- Bioclimatic Skyscraper
RANKO RADOVIC
GRIMSHAW - Waterloo St
HIROSHI HARA - Yamato Int. B
ALBERTS - NMB Bank
POST-MODERN SPACE
SKEWS, DIAGONALS
KAHN - wrap around ruins
- Goldenberg Hse.
AALTO - Saynatsalo Town Hall
- Imatra
LAYERING & AMBIGUITY
SCHAROUN - Berlin Phil.
LE CORBUSIER - Carpenter Center
MEIER - Smith Hse.
- Douglas Hse.
NETSCH
REVERSE PERSPECTIVE
SUPERGRAPHICS
Hadrian's Villa
Hotel de Beauvais
PASENELLA - Dunbar Hse.
- Gray Hse.
HEDJUK - Diamond Series
- Wall Hses.
EISENMAN
- Houses I-XI
Frontality & Rotation
MOORE - Aedcules
- Moore Hse.
- Sea Ranch
- Santa Barbara
- Klotz Hse.
HHP
'Folly Farm'
MICHELS
WALKER
JOHANSEN
TURNBULL - Zimmermann Hse.
DISSONANT COLLAGE
DEMI-FORMS
COATE - Alexander Hse.
POSITIVE/NEGATIVE REVERSALS
KUPPER - Nilsson Hse.
MOZUNA - Anti-Dwelling Box
- Yin Yang Hse.
ELISION
ASYMMETRICAL SYMMETRY
GRAVES - Mezzo Hse
- Crooks Hse
- Warehouse Conversion
T.G.Smith - Matthews Street Hse.
- Long Hse.
MOORE - Burns Hse.
GEHRY - Gehry House
MEIER - Atheneum
SHIFTED AXES
LIBESKIND
End Space
GEHRY - Loyola
- Aerospace
- Wosk
- Winton
MORPHOSIS - Houses
ASPLUND REVIVAL - Villa Snell
JAN & JON - Oslo University Press
- Skogbrand
NOUVEL - Belfort Theatre
E.MOSS - 708 House
- Culver City
FOLDING
- Deleu
- Le Pli
MOORE, RUBLE & YUDELL
- Kwee Hse
Holzbauer - House for Art Coll.
DECONSTRUCTION
TSCHUMI
- Event Sp
DERRIDA
1960
1965
1970
1975
1980
1985
199

ESSAYS ESSAYS

CHARLES JENCKS

DIE META-ERZÄHLUNG DER POSTMODERNE

THE POST-MODERN METANARRATIVE

EINE VERSÄUMTE BEGEGNUNG

Wenige Monate vor seinem Tod arrangierte die BBC eine Telefondebatte zwischen Jean-François Lyotard und mir über die Frage der Postmoderne. Trotz mehrerer Versuche hatten wir zwei uns nie getroffen, unsere Differenzen nie besprochen. Seine »Postmoderne«, 1979 dargelegt in *La condition Postmoderne* (*Das postmoderne Wissen*), war ein Essay über den Skeptizismus gegenüber allen Meta-Erzählungen, während meine, ein paar Jahre zuvor erschienene *The Language of Post-Modern Architecture (Die Sprache der postmodernen Architektur)* die wohlwollende Aufnahme einer Meta-Erzählung war: der des entstehenden globalen Pluralismus und seiner hybriden Kultur.

Obwohl der Begriff Postmoderne seit 1875 im Spiel ist, waren dies die beiden ersten Bücher, die sich dem Thema umfassend widmeten. Und so weit ich weiß, trugen ihre voneinander abweichenden Ansichten dazu bei, dass der Terminus eine traurige Berühmtheit erlangte. Beide Abhandlungen wurden Bestseller und in viele Sprachen übersetzt. Aber die Ironie für Lyotard und mich war, dass erst diese Texte den grundsätzlichen Riss öffneten und jene Verwirrung stifteten, die den Begriff seitdem verfolgt hat. Bezog sich die Rede von der Postmoderne auf eine positive kulturelle Bewegung, wie ich behauptete, oder auf einen negativen gesellschaftlichen Zustand, wie Frederic Jameson später, 1983, in seinem Aufsatz *Postmoderne – Zur Logik der Kultur im Spätkapitalismus* schreiben würde? Handelte es sich um eine Form der Ultra- oder Extrem-Moderne, um die Logik von Nihilismus plus Konsumismus, wie viele französische und amerikanische Autoren auf der Linken annahmen? Oder war die Postmoderne die von Architekten, Künstlern und Schriftstellern gewählte Strategie, um mit entgegengesetzten Geschmackskulturen, hohen und niedrigen Wahrnehmungscodes umzugehen?

Im Rückblick scheint die Antwort klar: Sie war beides. Der Versuch, die Trennlinie zwischen Massen- und Hochkultur zu überschreiten, vereinte Autoren wie Leslie Fiedler und John Barth mit Popkünstlern wie Robert Rauschenberg und Richard Hamilton. Das Ziel bestand darin, die Grenzen und Snobismen von Beruf, Geschlecht, Klasse und Ethnie zu überwinden. Aber es gab ein Problem. Der Boden zwischen diesen Geschmackskulturen verwandelte sich rasch in einen Sumpf. Er wurde »midcult« und »globcult« genannt und erhielt als Echo auf den Vorwurf von Kitsch und Ersatz noch viel beleidigendere Schimpfnamen. So wie die Moderne ihre Schrecken – den Nationalismus und die Massenproduktion von Tod – hatte, hatte auch die Postmoderne ihre dunkle Seite, das Simulakrum und die Markenzeichen. Die Moderne hatte ihre Doppelgänger, ihre Aufklärung und ihre Todeslager; die Postmoderne hatte ihren Pluralismus und Jeff Koons.

Es war Lyotard, der in seinem Buch *Postmoderne für Kinder. Briefe aus den Jahren 1982-1985* die Meinung vertrat, Auschwitz sei ein Verbrechen, das die Postmodernität eröffnet habe. Die Rationalität der Aufklärung sei zur instrumentellen Vernunft verkommen, die zum Holocaust geführt habe und bis heute zu vielem anderen mehr. Diese Auffassung ist und bleibt schockierend. Ich habe sie nie akzeptiert, Jürgen Habermas und viele andere Verteidiger des »unvollendeten Projekts der Moderne« natürlich auch nicht. Aber man musste auf Lyotards Erklärungen hören;

A NON-MEETING

A few months before he died, the BBC set up a telephone debate between Jean-François Lyotard and me on the question of postmodernism. We had never met and talked through our differences, in spite of several attempts. His "Postmodernism", outlined in *La Condition Postmoderne*, 1979, was an essay on skepticism towards all metanarratives, whereas my coinage of a few years before, *The Language of Post-Modern Architecture*, with a hyphen, was the positive embrace of a metanarrative: the emergent global pluralism and its hybrid culture.

Although the term Post-Modernism had been in play since 1875, these were the first two books devoted to the subject and, for all I know, their divergent views helped to energize the runaway notoriety of the concept. Both tracts became best sellers and were translated into many languages. The irony for Lyotard and me was that they opened up the fundamental fissure (and confusion) that has beset the term ever since. Did the phrase refer to a positive cultural movement as I claimed, or a negative social condition, as Frederic Jameson was later to write, in *Postmodernism, The Cultural Logic of Late-Capitalism*, (1983)? Was it a form of ultra- or extreme modernism, the logic of nihilism plus consumerism, as many French and American writers on the left were assuming, or was it the chosen strategy of architects, artists and writers dealing with opposite taste-cultures, high and low codes of perception?

In retrospect, the answer seems obvious: it was both. The attempt to cross the divide between mass and high culture united writers, such as Leslie Fiedler and John Barth, with Pop artists such as Robert Rauschenburg and Richard Hamilton. The positive goal was to transcend the borders and snobbisms of profession, gender, class and race—but there was a problem. The ground between these taste-cultures was fast developing into a swamp. It was termed "midcult", "globcult" and much more insulting epithets, usually echoing *kitsch* and *ersatz*. Just as Modernism had its horrors of nationalism and mass-produced death, Post-Modernism had its dark side with the simulacrum and image branding. Modernism had its doubles, its Enlightenment and Death Camps—and Post-Modernism had its pluralism and Jeff Koons.

It was Lyotard who argued, in *The Postmodern Explained to Children*, that "Auschwitz is a crime opening up postmodernity" and that Enlightenment rationality became the instrumental reason that ran the Holocaust and much else today. The idea was (and remains) shocking. I didn't accept it. Neither, of course, did Jürgen Habermas and so many apologists of the "unfinished project of Modernity." Nonetheless, one had to listen to Lyotard's explanations, as they had some logic—hence our telephone call. It started with the usual Anglo-Saxon "Hello, how nice ..." versus a more convincing politesse, moved quickly onto the sadness of not meeting and then to the disputed subject, the end of metanarratives.

"It is not the extinction, but the multiplication of stories that characterize our time," I offered and, if I remember correctly, it was a point with which he somewhat agreed. However, he insisted, it was the major stories that had previously united cultures—religious, social and scientific ones—that were on the

sie hatten etwas Logisches, daher unser Telefonat. Es begann mit dem gewöhnlichen angelsächsischen »Hallo, wie schön, Sie zu ...« gegenüber der überzeugenderen französischen Politesse, ging schnell zu der Bemerkung über, wie bedauerlich es doch sei, einander nicht zu treffen, und kam dann zum Gegenstand der Debatte: dem Ende der Meta-Erzählungen.

»Es ist nicht die Auslöschung, sondern die Vervielfältigung von Geschichten, die unsere Zeit charakterisiert«, bot ich an. Und wenn ich mich recht entsinne, war dies ein Punkt, dem er irgendwie zustimmte. Aber, so insistierte er, es seien die großen, früher ganze Kulturen religiös, sozial und wissenschaftlich einigenden Geschichten, die an ihr Ende gekommen oder heute zumindest unglaubwürdig geworden seien. Der Holocaust und hundert Millionen Tote in zwei Weltkriegen hätten sämtliche erklärende Geschichten vertrieben: Gott, Fortschritt, Sozialismus, Nationalismus und die Vorzüge der Quantenphysik.

»Okay«, sagte ich, ihn auf halbem Wege treffend, »die Moderne kennt viele Tode. Und sie setzen sich heute fort: Ölpest-Verseuchungen durch Tanker wie die Torrey Canyon und die Exxon Valdez; Kernschmelze in Tschernobyl; Lügen über Bhopal; stets etwa 44 gleichzeitig geführte lokale Kriege, die, wie das Elend der Kurden, ihre Wurzel im modernen Nationalstaat haben. In der Architektur gab es die Sprengungen von Pruitt-Igoe und über hundert anderer modernistischer Wohnsiedlungen.« Lyotard und ich konnten uns über einige dieser Übeltaten, die in die Postmoderne geführt hatten, durchaus verständigen; ebenso über deren Verbindung zur instrumentellen Vernunft. Aber ich wollte ihn auf einen essentiellen Gedanken bringen.

»Trotz allem ist eine neue Meta-Erzählung im Entstehen, eine neue Sicht der Welt.« – »Was denn für eine?« – »Sie kommt aus der Kosmologie und den neuen Komplexitätswissenschaften und handelt vom Universum als dem einzig schöpferischen, werdenden Ereignis, einem Kosmos, der viel dynamischer und vitaler ist als alles, was die Modernisten voraussehen konnten. Und dieses sich immer noch ereignende Ereignis schließt uns in seinen Plot mit ein, versieht uns wie alle Narrative mit Identität.«

Als wir allmählich übereinstimmten und gemeinsames Territorium absteckten, platzte der Redakteur der BBC plötzlich ins Studio und stoppte das Interview, weil der Raum für ein anderes Ferngespräch verplant war. Obwohl wir versuchten, einen neuen Platz für die Aufnahme zu finden, haben wir diesen viel versprechenden Anfang nie zu Ende gebracht. Der Augenblick war verloren. Wegen Lyotards Tod, dachte ich später mit Bedauern, war unser Nicht-Treffen in mancher Hinsicht sehr postmodern. Es war fragmentarisch, medial und wurde durch die Medien zerstört. Obwohl unsere Begegnung nur Minuten gedauert hatte, war ich sicher, dass Lyotard diesen Gedanken durchaus ironisch gefunden hätte.

Nun also »Die Revision der Postmoderne«, und zwar nach Überschreiten ihres Zenits als lebendige Bewegung und gesellschaftlicher Zustand, wobei sie ihre Kleider und Namen gewechselt und ein anderes Alias angenommen hat, aber noch während sie sich auf verschiedene Weise weiterschleppt Ich nenne diese Etappe am liebsten »Architektur des Neuen Paradigmas«. Warum? Weil die meisten Bedeutungen der Postmoderne triviali-

way out, or at least incredible today. The Holocaust, and one hundred million dead in two World Wars, had seen off the explanatory stories: God, progress, socialism, nationalism and the virtue of quantum physics.

"OK", I was meeting him part of the way, "but there are many deaths of Modernism (and they continue today: oil spills, such as the Torrey Canyon and the Exxon Valdez; the nuclear meltdown at Chernobyl; the lies over Bhopal; the 44 local wars underway at any one time that have, like the plight of the Kurds, a root cause in the modern nation state. In architecture there was the blowing up of Pruitt-Igoe and over a hundred other modernist housing estates." We could agree on some of the virulence ushering in Post-Modernity and on its connection to instrumental reason, but I wanted to press him on a key idea.

"There is, nevertheless, a new metanarrative emerging, a new world view."—"What's that?"—"It's coming from cosmology and the new sciences of complexity and it concerns the view of the universe as a single, creative, unfolding event, a cosmos much more dynamic and alive than anything the Modernists could contemplate," I rolled out by rote, "and this event that is still occurring contains us in its plot and, like all narratives, provides our identity."

As we started to agree and stake out common territory, the BBC suddenly broke into the studio and stopped the interview, because the room was scheduled for another long distance encounter. Then, in spite of attempts to find a new quiet place for recording, we never finished this promising beginning. The moment was lost. With Lyotard's death, I later reflected ruefully, our non-meeting was in some ways very Post-Modern. It was fragmentary, mediated and then destroyed by the media. Although our encounter was only for minutes, I was sure he would find some ironic humour in the thought.

So, "Post-Modernism Revisited:" after its moment travelling towards the sun, after having been a live movement and social condition, but still while it drags on in several ways, having changed its clothes and pseudonyms and adopted another alias. At least for me, it is best framed in architecture, for the moment, under the rubric of »the new paradigm.« Why? Because most meanings of Post-Modernism have been trivialized and locked into one or another of its sectarian definitions. Borrowing Habermas' phraseology, we might speak of "the unfinished project of Post-Modernism" because this, no doubt, continues under various headings (and will last as long as the Modernist juggernaut rolls on).

Moreover, not only does it relate fundamentally to the metanarrative of the universe story, as I was trying to persuade Lyotard, but to its own narrative, its own history. Here I will simplify the story greatly in architecture as a linear development in six parts though, as my evolutionary tree shows, the pattern is really a complex web of competing traditions that run concurrently (Ill. on page 10/11). It starts, predictably, as an internal critique within modernism, a tradition that had become much too imperial, commercial and a sign of the corporate Pax Americana.

siert und in die eine oder andere sektiererische Definition gesperrt sind. In Anlehnung an Habermas' Terminologie könnten wir vom »unvollendeten Projekt der Postmoderne« sprechen, das zweifellos unter verschiedenen Etiketten fortgeführt wird (und sicher noch so lange andauert, wie der Dschagannath-Wagen des Modernismus rollt).

Ich beziehe mich im Folgenden nicht allein auf die Meta-Erzählung der Geschichte des Universums, von der ich Lyotard zu überzeugen versuchte, sondern zunächst auf das eigene Narrativ der Postmoderne, ihre eigene Historie. Dazu werde ich ihre Architektur stark vereinfachend als eine lineare Entwicklung in sechs Teilen darstellen, obwohl das in diesem Band veröffentlichte Entwicklungsdiagramm (auf Seite 10/11) zeigt, dass es sich in Wirklichkeit um ein komplexes Geflecht gleichzeitiger, miteinander im Wettbewerb stehender Traditionen handelt. Die Postmoderne begann, voraussehbar, als Kritik innerhalb der Moderne, einer Tradition, die viel zu imperial, kommerziell und zum Zeichen der korporierten Pax Americana geworden war.

ERSTE KRITIK: KOMPLEXITÄT STATT SIMPLIZITÄT

Zwangsläufig war das Anfangsstadium der Postmoderne, 1960 bis 1972, von der Reaktion auf die Zerstörung der historischen Stadt bestimmt. Jane Jacobs verfasste 1961 mit *Tod und Leben großer amerikanischer Städte. Das Versagen der Stadtplanung* die erste Attacke auf einen reduktiven Modernismus und damit das Programm der sich entwickelnden Bewegung. Wie bei Architekturmanifesten üblich, hatte die Publikation keine Bilder und endete als billiges Taschenbuch, das noch nach vierzig Jahren im Buchhandel erhältlich ist. Jacobs baute in ihrer Abhandlung auf Argumente der Systemtheorie und Beobachtungen darüber, wie Städte tatsächlich funktionierten. Sie wandte damit ein Prinzip an, das später zu dem der postmodernen Komplexitätswissenschaften werden sollte. Die Schlussfolgerung ihres Buchs war, dass die Stadt nicht nur ein statistisches Problem von »Simplizität« oder »desorganisierter Komplexität« sei, sondern auch – nach dem Vorbild der Humanwissenschaften – eines von »organisierter Komplexität«.

In dieser ersten Phase der Postmoderne – angetrieben durch eine Gegenkultur mit ihren Truppen aus Betroffenen-Planern, Feministinnen, Black-Power-Enthusiasten und Minderheiten jedweder Art – wurde die Moderne als Repräsentantin der Macht angesehen, einer blassen, kommerzialisierten Mittelklasse und Bürokratie. Anklagen kamen aus allen Lagern: Das kapitalistische Amerika habe die Innenstädte in modernistischer Weise verbaut, Walter Gropius mit seiner plumpen, klischeehaften Pan-Am-Zentrale die Integrität des Bauhauses verkauft und moderne Kunst sei zu einer nichtssagenden Kulisse, einem Lifestyle heruntergekommen. Die Anhänger der Moderne hätten die Schlachten der letzten hundert Jahre nicht für Lever-Seife und CBS geschlagen, auch nicht für ihre gestalterisch dürftigen Konzerngebäude, die typisch für die Architektur der fünfziger und sechziger Jahre wurden. Die Reaktion gegen minimalistische Hochhäuser kam also aus der modernen Bewegung selbst. So gesehen war »Postmoderne« stets nur ein anderer Ausdruck für kritische Moderne, das heißt für eine Moderne, die auf den eige-

FIRST CRITIQUE: COMPLEXITY NOT SIMPLICITY

Inevitably, the initial stage of Post-Modernism, from 1960 to 1972, was a reaction against the destruction of the historical city. Jane Jacobs wrote the first attack on reductive modernism and the manifesto of the nascent movement in 1961, entitled *The Death and Life of Great American Cities*, and subtitled *The Failure of Town Planning*. As architectural manifestoes go, it was non-visual and ended up as a cheap paperback, still in print after forty years. It relied on arguments coming from systems theory and on watching how cities actually worked. Here she stated a principle of what was later to become the "Post-Modern sciences of complexity" when she pointed out, in conclusion, that the city is not only a statistical problem of "simplicity," or "disorganized complexity," but also one of "organized complexity," like those of the life sciences.

In this first period of Post-Modernism, driven by the counterculture and its myriad battalions—advocacy planners, feminists, black power enthusiasts, minorities of all types—Modernism was seen as representing the power structure, a bland, commercialized middle class and bureaucracy. Accusations came from all quarters: corporate America had built the downtown in a Modernist mode; Walter Gropius had sold out the integrity of the Bauhaus and designed a squat, clichéd headquarters for the Pan Am corporation; and so much modern art had degenerated into a bland backdrop, a *genre-de-vie*. Modernists had not fought battles of the previous hundred years to make the world safe for Lever Soap and CBS—or for their reduced headquarter buildings that typified modern architecture of the 1950s and 1960s—and so the reaction against these minimalist towers came from within the Modern Movement itself. In that sense, Post-Modernism has always been another word for critical modernism: that is, Modernism looking back at its own success and the problems that this has caused. Inevitably, then, one cannot do justice to the idea of Post-Modernism without criticizing its shortcomings: irony is not an extra option.

In 1966, Robert Venturi wrote the second manifesto of the fledgling movement, *Complexity and Contradiction in Architecture* (Ill. 1). Here the argument was conducted like a slide lecture, which resulted in tiny photos being crammed into the margins. This cheap paperback, aimed at students, was launched with an introduction by the historian Vincent Scully as the worthy successor to Le Corbusier's *Vers une architecture*: as a gentle, not aggressive, manifesto. Instead of being analysed in any depth, buildings from different periods were used to illustrate a point such as "The Obligation Toward the Difficult Whole." From then on, different architectural histories—and in particular the Mannerist, Baroque, and Edwardian periods—were consulted to inform contemporary work. Historical consciousness returned to help the architect solve problems, among them the contrary pressures exerted by the interior function of a building and the exterior urban landscape. Venturi showed that Francesco Borromini and Edwin Lutyens had successfully resolved these contradictory forces, leading to buildings that are full of surprise, ambiguity, and wit.

For the next fifteen years *Complexity and Contradiction in Architecture* influenced students and nascent Post-Modernists. Its

nen Erfolg und die dadurch verursachten Probleme zurückschaut. Deshalb lässt sich der Idee der Postmoderne unmöglich gerecht werden, ohne auch ihre Mängel zu kritisieren: Ironie ist davon nicht ausgenommen.

1966 schrieb Robert Venturi das zweite Manifest der noch sehr jungen Bewegung: *Komplexität und Widerspruch in der Architektur.* (Abb. 1) Hier wurde der Gedankengang wie bei einem Diavortrag geführt und dazu winzige Fotos in die Randspalten gezwängt. Das billige Taschenbuch für Studenten enthielt eine Einführung des Historikers Vincent Scully und wurde als würdiger Nachfolger von Le Corbusiers *Ausblick auf eine Architektur* lanciert – allerdings als sanftes, nicht aggressives Manifest. Ohne tief gehende Analyse stellte Venturi Gebäude verschiedener Zeitalter zusammen, um beispielsweise »die Verpflichtung auf das schwierige Ganze« darzustellen. Von nun an zog man gern architekturgeschichtliche Werke – vor allem über den Manierismus, das Barock und die Epoche Eduards VII. – für die Gegenwart zu Rate. Historisches Bewusstsein kehrte wieder und half Architekten, unter anderem den Widerspruch von innerer Funktion eines Gebäudes und städtischer Umgebung zu lösen. Venturi zeigte, dass Francesco Borromini und Edwin Lutyens diese Gegenkräfte erfolgreich versöhnt und geistreiche Bauten voller Überraschung und Vieldeutigkeit geschaffen hatten.

In den nächsten fünfzehn Jahren formte *Komplexität und Widerspruch* Studenten und werdende Postmodernisten. Erst in den achtziger Jahren, als zu viele Bauten an zu vielen ironischen Anspielungen förmlich erstickten, wurde die problematische Seite des Buchs deutlich. Und da wir gerade bei »Ironie« sind: Ungefähr zu dieser Zeit begannen Venturi und seine Ehefrau Denise Scott Brown zu leugnen, irgendetwas mit der Postmoderne zu tun zu haben. Zweierlei muss dazu gesagt werden. Ihr Einfluss auf die Entfaltung von Ornament, Anspielung und geometrischen Innovationen war wesentlich für die Bewegung. Und wie Umberto Eco später ausführen sollte, war auch die Ironie wesentlich für die Postmoderne. Sie erlaubte ihren Anhängern, Geschichte in ihrer Architektur anzuwenden, sie aber gleichzeitig von unreflektiertem Revival zu unterscheiden. Ironie bedeutete die doppelte Botschaft des »Ja-Aber«, eine Taktik, die ich später »doppelte Kodierung« nannte.

RADIKALER PLURALISMUS GLEICH RADIKALER EKLEKTIZISMUS

Die zweite Phase der Postmoderne, 1972 bis 1978, beruhte auf den Protesten der sechziger Jahre und führte in eine Philosophie des kulturellen Pluralismus. Der von der Moderne verabscheute Eklektizismus strömte zurück in die Welt des Designs und der Künste, insbesondere in politisch ambitionierte Bereiche wie die feministische Kunst. In der Architektur reichte er von der Ad-hoc-Assemblage eines Lucien Kroll bis zum radikalen Eklektizismus eines James Stirling. Mischung, Mischform, Vielsprachigkeit, Collage, Nebeneinander, Inklusion waren die Schlüsselworte. Sie standen für eine grundlegende Veränderung globaler Kommunikation, für die Annahme, alle Kulturen und Epochen seien gleich wertvoll und sogar ihre Vermischung möglicherweise wichtig. Im Gegensatz zur Behauptung der Moderne

negative side only became apparent during the 1980s, in too many buildings that were smothered with too many ironic allusions—and speaking of irony, at about this time, Venturi and his wife, Denise Scott Brown, started denying they had anything to do with Post-Modernism. Two things should be said about this. Their influence on the emergence of ornament, allusion, and geometrical innovation was essential to the movement and, as Umberto Eco was to argue, irony itself was also essential to Post-Modernism. It allowed Post-Modernists to assert the inevitability of historical usage and, at the same time, distinguish their work from unreflective revivalism. Irony sent the double message—"yes-but"—and in this sense was one tactic of what I was to term "double-coding."

RADICAL PLURALISM = RADICAL ECLECTICISM

The second stage of Post-Modernism, from 1972 to 1978, was built on the protests of the 1960s, but it translated them into a philosophy of cultural pluralism. The eclecticism that modernists had deplored flooded back in the design and art worlds, especially with political movements such as Feminist art. In architecture it ranged from the ad hoc assemblage method of Lucien Kroll to the radical eclecticism of James Stirling. Hybrid, mixture, polyglot, mongrel, collage, juxtaposition, inclusion—these were the key words. They reflected a basic shift in global communication, the acceptance of all cultures and periods as equally valid and even their mixture as possibly relevant. Counter to the Modern Movement, there was no one true style for any period. Did that mean anything goes? Not quite: distinctions were to be made. These focussed on how suitable the chosen languages of architecture were to the local context, the building's function and the customary dialect of the people. Whatever the mode that they were talking in, one thing was obvious: it was not Esperanto. The International Style might be fine for international businessmen, but it was not deep enough in reference to engage a world media culture, now a richly diverse one.

In the Stuttgart Museum addition of 1977, Stirling juxtaposed several different styles, or "language games," as Jean-François Lyotard would call them: Classicism, Modernism, vernacular and high-tech—and some strident green paint and dayglo handrails that jarred the senses into action. Typically, the languages divided into low and high art forms: the double-coding that I had been writing about. This acknowledged the gaps between different groups of city-dwellers.

The next year, the American critic, Paul Goldberger, called the AT&T building the first "masterpiece" of Post-Modernism, but in important ways that building misunderstood what it was all about and Stirling's Stuttgart shows why. At his museum, the styles are not resolved into a synthetic totality, as they are at the AT&T. Rather they are placed in extreme ironic tension with each other to underscore the heterogeneity of society, the pluralism that acknowledges no single discourse as dominant (Ill. 2). The "tensed field" of juxtaposed styles was an idea shared with Post-Modern literature, especially the novels of Umberto Eco and Salman Rushdie, that were equally eclectic. A new understanding was thus reached. Oppositions between languages and

1

2

3

4

5

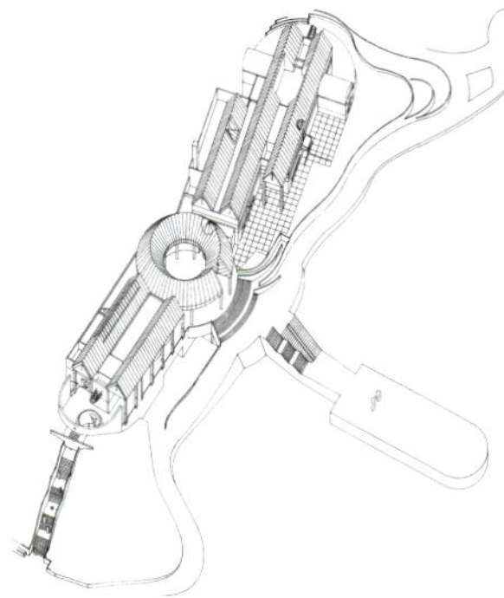
6

7

1 Robert Venturi, Denise Scott Brown: Gordon and Virginia MacDonald Medical Research Laboratories, University of California, Los Angeles, 1991

2 James Stirling, Michael Wilford: Neue Staatsgalerie Stuttgart, 1983

3 Deutsche Ausgabe von *Die Sprache der postmodernen Architektur*, 1981. Auf dem Einband Charles Moore, Piazza d'Italia, New Orleans, 1978
German Edition of *The Language of Post-Modern Architecture*, 1981. On the cover Charles Moore's Piazza d'Italia, New Orleans, 1978.

4 Aldo Rossi: Wohnbauten in der Friedrichstadt/Housing in Friedrichstadt, Berlin, 1985

5 Kisho Kurokawa: Museum für Zeitgenössische Kunst/Museum of Contemporary Art, Hiroshima, 1989

6 Museum für Zeitgenössische Kunst/Museum of Contemporary Art, Hiroshima, 1989, Axonometrie/Axonometric

7 Antoine Predock: Nelson Kunstmuseum/Nelson Fine Arts Center, Arizona State University, Tempe, 1989

gab es zu keiner Zeit den jeweils einen wahren Stil. Bedeutete dies, dass deshalb alles möglich war? Nicht ganz; Unterschiede mussten gemacht werden. Entscheidend war die Frage, ob die ausgewählte Architektursprache zum Ort, zur Funktion des Gebäudes und zur gewohnten Ausdrucksweise der Nutzer passte. Und wie auch immer sie sprachen: Es war kein Esperanto. Der International Style mochte für internationale Geschäftsleute gut und schön sein; aber er ging mit seinen Referenzen nicht weit genug, um einer weltweiten medialen, inzwischen reich diversifizierten Kultur zu genügen.

1977 stellte Stirling in seinem Entwurf für die Staatsgalerie Stuttgart mehrere verschiedene Stile – oder »Sprachspiele«, wie Lyotard gesagt hätte – einander gegenüber: Klassizismus, Moderne, Regionalismus und Hightech sowie ein paar grellgrüne, leuchtende Handläufe, die die Sinne in Aufruhr versetzten. Typischerweise umfassten seine Architektur-Sprachen niedere und höhere Kunstformen – die doppelte Kodierung, über die ich geschrieben hatte –, um unterschiedlichen Schichten der Stadtbevölkerung gerecht zu werden.

Im folgenden Jahr nannte der amerikanische Kritiker Paul Goldberger das neue Hochhaus der AT&T in New York das erste Meisterwerk der Postmoderne. Aber in Bezug auf wichtige Aspekte missverstand dieser Bau von Philip Johnson, worum es bei der Postmoderne ging. Stirlings Staatsgalerie zeigt warum. Bei seinem Museum sind die Stile nicht, wie beim Gebäude der AT&T, völlig in einer Synthese aufgegangen. Vielmehr werden sie in extreme ironische Spannung versetzt, um die Heterogenität der Gesellschaft und den Pluralismus – der keinen Diskurs als einzig dominanten anerkennt – zu unterstreichen. (Abb. 2) Die Idee vom Spannungsfeld entgegengesetzter Stile charakterisierte auch die postmoderne Literatur, zum Beispiel die Romane von Eco und Salman Rushdie. Dadurch brach sich ein neues Verständnis Bahn. Gegensätze zwischen Sprachen und verschiedenen Meinungen können tatsächlich eine besondere Art von Bedeutung schaffen; sie können sogar die eigentliche Bedeutung ausmachen. Man könnte sagen, das grundlegend Bedeutsame von Stirlings Neuer Staatsgalerie lag im neuen Epistem des Pluralismus. Das Stuttgarter Gebäude stellte die Aufsplitterung der Geschmackskulturen dar, wodurch »Konflikt« und – in erfreulicher Weise – »Differenz« zum Thema von Architektur wurden.

Meine eigenen Schriften, in denen ich 1975 die Postmoderne benannte und ihren Pluralismus definierte, mögen ebenfalls ein Katalysator des zweiten Stadiums gewesen sein; sie mögen Stirling sogar beeinflusst haben, mit dem ich damals in dauernder Diskussion stand. Ich hatte mehrere Artikel geschrieben, die zeigten, wie sein 1973 fertig gestelltes, spätmodernes Olivetti-Trainingszentrum im englischen Haslemere die intendierte Kommunikation verfehlte. Wir tauschten unsere Ansichten über die Notwendigkeit von Metapher und mehrfacher Kodierung aus; mit dem Ersten stimmte er nicht überein, akzeptierte jedoch das Zweite. Den eigenen Beitrag einzuschätzen ist schwierig. Für Stirling jedenfalls waren Colin Rowes' und Fred Koetters' Ausführungen über die Collage City von großer Bedeutung.

Mein Buch *Die Sprache der postmodernen Architektur* brachte es auf zahlreiche Ausgaben in vielen Sprachen. Die dritte Auflage von 1991 stellte einen anderen Ansatz des radikalen Eklekti-

different viewpoints can actually create their own particular kind of meaning—even be the meaning—and one could say that the fundamental significance of Stirling's Neue Staatsgalerie was the new episteme of pluralism itself. In effect, the building represented the fragmentation of taste cultures, with conflict and enjoyable difference becoming the subject of the architecture.

My writings, naming Post-Modernism in 1975 and defining this pluralism, may also have helped catalyse the second stage and even have influenced Stirling, with whom I was in constant discussion. I had written several articles showing how his Late-Modern Olivetti building failed to communicate as intended, and we exchanged views on the need for metaphor and multiple-coding. (He disagreed with the former, but accepted the latter.) It is hard to gauge one's own contribution and, in the case of Stirling, there is no doubt that Colin Rowe and Fred Koetter's writings on Collage City were of great importance.

The book *The Language of Post-Modern Architecture* went into multiple editions and many languages. Its third edition, in 1981, featured a different approach to radical eclecticism than Stirling's. Charles Moore's Piazza d'Italia of 1976-1979 was equally a collage of oppositions, again Classical and industrial, but it was more colorful, populist and oriented to street culture (Ill. 3). Here was an architecture meant to challenge other media, and to make use of several at once. Worked out in participation with its users—the Italian community of New Orleans—its modern version of the Five Italian Orders was both excessive and to the point. It was based on the local context and one of its lively subcultures, those energetic European immigrants competing with the three other main ethnic groups. The piazza centered on the place where the Italian mayor would address his community each year—hence the main but not exclusive language. At this stage the notion of architecture as communicative media competing with all the others became the focus of Post-Modernism, something I was to put in blank verse definitions:

Post-Modernism is revisiting the past—with quotation marks. / Post-Modernism is revisiting the future—with irony. / Post-Modernism is acknowledging the already said, as Umberto Eco has already said, in the age of lost innocence.

Charles Moore, a Yale professor, would probably not have had the bullishness to produce such hyper-Pop without a good deal of contemporary writing behind it. There was Pop Art itself, of course, but more important were Tom Wolfe's hysterical panegyrics on "electrographic architecture" (the neon sign artists of Las Vegas celebrated in *The Kandy-Kolored Tangerine-Flake Streamline Baby* and more particularly *Las Vegas (What?) Las Vegas (Can't Hear You! Too Noisy) Las Vegas!!!!*). This was the article that, placed by Robert Venturi's bedside, led to his, Denise Scott Brown's and Steven Izenour's *Learning from Las Vegas*, 1972.

In their book, another plea was made for learning from the past, as well as from Las Vegas, and for creating an architecture that would be inclusive, not just aimed at the professional elite, or "orthodox Modernists" as they were termed by this team of writers. Their research into the vernacular strip was commendable for opening up the architectural discourse and the first of subsequent sorties made, with the aid of architectural students, into the no-go area of sprawl, crime, sex, commercial vernacular

zismus als den von Stirling dar. Charles Moores Piazza d'Italia, zwischen 1976 und 1979 entstanden, war zwar ebenfalls eine Collage von Gegensätzen, auch mit klassischen und industriellen Formen, aber farbenfroher, volkstümlicher und auf das Straßenleben ausgerichtet. (Abb. 3) Hier zeigte sich eine Architektur, die andere Medien herausforderte und sich zugleich mehrerer bediente. Entstanden unter Teilnahme der Nutzer, also der italienischen Gemeinde von New Orleans, war ihre moderne Version der fünf Säulenordnungen zwar übertrieben, traf aber den Punkt. Sie erfasste den lokalen Kontext und die vitale Subkultur der temperamentvollen europäischen Einwanderer, die mit drei anderen ethnischen Gruppen der Stadt konkurrierten. Mittelpunkt der Piazza war die Stelle, an der der italienische Bürgermeister jedes Jahr zu seinen Landsleuten sprach – deshalb die direkte, aber anderes nicht ausschließende Bildsprache.

Zu diesem Zeitpunkt stand Architektur als kommunikatives und konkurriendes Medium im Brennpunkt der Postmoderne, etwas, das ich später mit folgenden Blankversen beschrieb: Die Postmoderne ist ein Wiedersehen mit der Vergangenheit – in Anführungszeichen. / Die Postmoderne ist ein Wiedersehen mit der Zukunft – mit Ironie. / Die Postmoderne ist Anerkennung des schon Gesagten, wie schon Eco gesagt hat, im Zeitalter der verlorenen Unschuld.

Charles Moore, Professor in Yale, hätte vermutlich nicht so locker einen solchen Hyper-Pop geschaffen, ohne eine Menge zeitgenössischer wissenschaftlicher Literatur im Hintergrund. Es gab natürlich die Pop-Art selbst; aber wichtiger waren Tom Wolfes irrsinnig komische Lobreden auf »elektrographische Architektur«, auf die Neonlicht-Künstler von Las Vegas, die er in *The Kandy-Kolored Tangerine-Flake Streamline Baby* (deutsch: *Das bonbonfarbene tangerinrot-gespritzte Stromlinienbaby*) und mehr noch in *Las Vegas (What?) Las Vegas (Can't Hear You! Too Noisy) Las Vegas!!!* feierte. Dieser Artikel lag auf dem Nachttisch von Robert Venturi und führte 1972 zu dem von ihm, Denise Scott Brown und Steven Izenour verfassten Buch *Learning from Las Vegas*.

Darin wurde ein weiteres Plädoyer für das Lernen aus der Vergangenheit gehalten und eben für ein Lernen von Las Vegas. Die Autoren propagierten außerdem eine inklusive Architektur, die sich nicht nur an eine professionelle Elite oder »orthodoxe Modernisten« richten dürfe. Die in dem Buch veröffentlichte Untersuchung der amerikanischen Main Street, des »vernacular strip«, verdiente Anerkennung, weil sie den architektonischen Diskurs aufbrach. Erstmalig wurde mit Unterstützung von Architekturstudenten eine Exkursion in die No-go-Gebiete des Sprawl, der Kriminalität, des Sex und der örtlichen kommerziellen Misch-Masch-Architektur thematisiert. Bernard Tschumi und Rem Koolhaas sollten diesen Ansatz bald ebenfalls verfolgen. Doch unglücklicherweise reduzierte das Team um Venturi das Symbolische in der Architektur auf den von ihnen so genannten »dekorierten Schuppen«, also den funktionalen Bau mit applizierten Zeichen.

Dies führte zu einer Spaltung innerhalb der Bewegung, weil die Theorie ganz falsch war, weil ein Symbol ja das glatte Gegenteil einer Applikation ist. Zeichen, wie zum Beispiel ein Stoppschild, sind denotativ, Symbole dagegen konnotativ. Während Zeichen also einen sachlich-direkten Bezug haben und eindeu-

and un-pedigreed architecture. Bernard Tschumi and Rem Koolhaas were to follow suit. Yet, unfortunately, the Venturi team reduced symbolism in architecture to what they called "the decorated shed," that is a functional shed with signs applied.

This led to a schism within the movement, because the theory was so wrong, because a symbol is the very opposite of appliquéd signs. Where the latter, like a "stop sign", are denotative, symbols are connotative; where they are superficial and single in meaning, symbols are complex and deep in resonance. A symbolic architecture is precisely the reverse of what they called it in *Learning from Las Vegas*. It is tied to many meanings in a multivalent way so that one cannot tell what generated the form: whether it was function, space, sign, ornament or technique. As I argued in *Towards a Symbolic Architecture*, 1985, their idea of the decorated shed produces "signolic," not symbolic architecture. Signs, like their recommended Las Vegas high flyers, are one-liners that do not engage the rest of the building; they force a dissociated architecture. Unfortunately too many Post-Modernists learned the wrong lessons from Las Vegas and produced an assemblage of clichés rather than a resonant symbolic architecture. They ushered in what came to be called "Po Mo;" but the movement continued to move on, in response to these problems.

POST-MODERN CLASSICISM

The third stage of the growing tradition, from 1978 to 1985, saw Post-Modernism go public with the Venice Architectural Biennale of 1980, then turn professional and, finally, corporate. During this period, the ironic classicism of Venturi, Stirling and Moore and countless others became more straightforward and urban. Its continued quotation marks acknowledged Eco's formulation of "the already said," but its inflation in scale showed that pm was going straight for mainstream culture and power. Michael Graves' Humana Tower for the large health benefit corporation in Louisville was one of its first corporate monuments, *pace* Goldberger, that embraced both Classicism and industrial society.

However, in becoming successful, this stage of the movement took on many of the problems that beset Modernism: above all, overproduction, inflation, and what is called "quick-build." Massive two billion dollar buildings were designed, as usual with leviathans, on the back of an envelope. Philip Johnson, who declared himself quite publicly a "whore" for architecture (he would do a lot to get the job done) was the fastest at work. Even Stirling had been proud of the conceptual sketch of Stuttgart, quickly conceived on the back of his airplane ticket. Cesar Pelli was no doubt the master of this restricted genre—most evident at the fifty-story Canary Wharf Tower in London's Docklands, a building that had, under construction, a progress of one story per week and that, finished, makes pleasing proportional rectangles out of a commission that is now fashionable to deplore. (The rectangles are more pleasing the farther one is away from them because of problems of parallax.)

Less speedy and more thoughtful Post-Modern classical structures were built around the planet, epitomizing the embrace of the corporate and civic worlds. These buildings are probably too

tig sind, haben Symbole einen metaphorisch-indirekten, assoziativen Bezug und sind komplex. Symbolische Architektur ist genau das Gegenteil von dem, was die drei Autoren in *Lernen von Las Vegas* so nannten. Sie ist mit vielen Bedeutungen auf vieldeutige Weise verknüpft, sodass sich nicht sagen lässt, was ihre Form erzeugt hat: die Funktion, der Raum, das Zeichen, das Ornament oder die Technik. Wie ich 1985 in *Towards a Symbolic Architecture* dargelegt habe, ließ die Idee des dekorierten Schuppens nur signalhafte, doch keinswegs symbolische Architektur zu. Zeichen, die Venturi, Scott Brown und Izenour empfahlen, zum Beispiel die von Las Vegas inspirierten, über den Bauten schwebenden Schilder, waren Gebilde für sich, die keinerlei Beziehung zum übrigen Gebäude hatten und eine losgelöste Architektur erzwangen. Unglücklicherweise lernten zu viele Postmodernisten die falschen Lektionen von Las Vegas und produzierten lieber eine Ansammlung von Klischees statt einer resonanzreichen, symbolischen Architektur. Das endete mit dem, was schließlich »PoMo« genannt wurde. Aber die Bewegung ging weiter und reagierte auf diese Probleme.

POSTMODERNER KLASSIZISMUS

Im dritten Stadium ihres wachsenden Traditionsbewusstseins, 1978 bis 1985, ging die Postmoderne mit der I. Architekturbiennale von Venedig 1980 in die Öffentlichkeit, setzte sich dann professionell durch und wurde schließlich für die *Corporate Identity* tauglich. Während dieser Zeit wurde der ironische Klassizismus von Venturi, Stirling, Moore und vielen anderen Architekten direkter und urbaner. Seine fortwährend in Anführungsstriche gesetzten Zitate bestätigten Ecos Formulierung des »Schon-Gesagten«. Doch es zeigte sich, dass die Postmoderne – aufgeblasen ins Maßstabslose – schnurstracks auf die Kultur des Mainstreams und der Macht zulief. Eines ihrer ersten Monumente – bei allem Respekt für Goldberger – war Michael Graves' Humana Tower für die große Gesundheits-Fürsorge-Organisation in Louisville, ein Gebäude, das Klassizismus und Industriegesellschaft vereinigte.

Mit dem Erfolg der Bewegung übernahm die Postmoderne viele Erblasten des Modernismus: vor allem Überproduktion, Inflation und das »Rasch-aus-dem-Boden-Stampfen«. Riesige Bauwerke im Wert von zwei Milliarden Dollar wurden – wie bei Giganten üblich – auf der Rückseite eines Briefumschlags entworfen. Philip Johnson, der sich in aller Öffentlichkeit als »Hure« der Architektur bezeichnete (er würde vieles tun, um den Job machen zu können), arbeitete am schnellsten. Sogar Stirling war stolz auf die konzeptionelle Skizze für Stuttgart, die er schnell auf die Rückseite seines Flugscheins geworfen hatte. Cesar Pelli war zweifellos der Meister dieses beschränkten Genres, besonders augenfällig bei dem fünfzig Geschosse hohen Canary Wharf Tower in den Docklands von London – ein Auftrag, zu dem man heute nicht mehr so leicht stehen würde. Das Gebäude wuchs während der Bauzeit in einer Geschwindigkeit von einem Stockwerk pro Woche. Nun, da es fertig ist, zeigt es angenehm proportionierte Rechtecke. (Wegen der Parallaxe sind die Rechtecke übrigens angenehmer, je weiter weg man von ihnen steht.)

well known to need summarizing. Suffice it to say that some of the lasting achievements of the third stage of Post-Modernism are evident at the IBA in Berlin, the International Building Exhibition that continued throughout the 1980s and employed some of the best Post-Modern architects, among them Charles Moore, Hans Hollein, Oswald Mathias Ungers and Rob Krier. If there was one text behind this European urbanism, it was Aldo Rossi's *L'architettura della città*, 1966, and so it was appropriate that Rossi's colourful toy-block classicism epitomized the planning (Ill. 4). The lessons of history drawn upon at IBA concerned not only previous Classical periods, but also the historical typology of the city, its streets, its squares, its contained open space and its common language. All of this was absorbed at IBA, which was certainly the best urbanism built in the 1980s. Later, Barcelona in the 1990s, under its mayor Pasqual Maragall, became the example of an enlightened Post-Modern urbanism and, because of the 1992 Olympics, financially viable as well.

The gathering argument of Post-Modernism thus mixed two related motives. First was the search for a viable urbanism that could pull the patterns of city growth into some kind of complex whole that did not destroy that of the past (Venturi's "difficult whole"). Second, the other side of the coin, was the search for a rich language of architecture that could communicate with the diverse population of the heteropolis—the direction in which all cities in the global market-place were evolving. Los Angeles took on the mantle as the most heterogeneous city, following New York City in that direction but having an even greater "diversity index" (as sociologists call the mixture of ethnic and lifestyle clusters). This cultural and social variety posed the greatest problems, as the race riots of 1993 were to point up, and architects were not equipped with the power to deal with them. However, the so-called Los Angeles School, led by Frank O. Gehry, Eric Moss and Thom Mayne, did forge a new heteroglot and informal language of architecture to deal with it on an urbanistic level. This was one valid response to the bland, corporate style of the ascendant Po Mo.

SMALL BLOCK PLANNING

In reacting to its own inflationary success, the fourth stage of Post-Modernism, starting around the middle 1980s, was also concerned with historical meanings. Instead of the huge corporate structure expressed as a single volume, the over-large office was now broken up into "small blocks" that were expressed with many articulations.

Jane Jacobs had recommended small-block planning in the 1960s, Léon Krier did likewise in the 1970s and, by the late 1980s, James Stirling, Hiroshi Hara, Kisho Kurokawa, and Antoine Predock (among many others) were looking to historical precedent for breaking up architectural volumes into discrete and grammatical units (Ill. 7). Seventeenth and eighteenth century cities were consulted, including a study of the perimeter blocks of Naples. The coherent juxtapositions of small classical units in ancient Greece were very persuasively demonstrated in the seductive drawings of Léon Krier. By the late 1980s, he had left Post-Modernism and his brother Rob and joined the

Weniger schnell realisierte, dafür aber rücksichtsvollere postmoderne klassische Bauwerke, die das Einvernehmen von kommerzieller und bürgerlicher Welt verkörpern, entstanden nun rund um den Globus. Sie sind wahrscheinlich zu bekannt, als dass sie noch eine zusammenfassende Beschreibung nötig hätten. Erwähnt sei aber, dass zu den bleibenden Errungenschaften des dritten Stadiums der Postmoderne Projekte der Internationalen Bau-Ausstellung Berlin (IBA) gehören. Die IBA dauerte fast die gesamten achtziger Jahre; für sie wurden einige der besten postmodernen Architekten engagiert, darunter Charles Moore, Hans Hollein, Oswald Mathias Ungers, Rob Krier und James Stirling. Wenn es einen Text gab, der diesem (europäischen) Urbanismus die Stichworte lieferte, war es Aldo Rossis Studie *Die Architektur der Stadt* von 1966, weshalb es angemessen ist, dass Rossis farbenfroher Spielzeug-Block-Klassizismus die Planungsphilosophie der IBA am besten verkörpert. (Abb. 4) Die von ihr beherzigten geschichtlichen Lehren betrafen nicht allein frühere klassische Epochen, sondern auch die historische Typologie der Stadt, ihre Straßen, Plätze, die gefassten offenen Räume und ihre gemeinsame Sprache. All dies wurde von der IBA aufgenommen; mit ihr entstand der sicherlich beste Städtebau der achtziger Jahre. Später, in den neunziger Jahren, wurde Barcelona unter seinem Bürgermeister Pasqual Maragall zum Paradebeispiel eines aufgeklärten postmodernen Städtebaus, der aufgrund der Olympischen Sommerspiele 1992 auch finanziell überlebensfähig war.

Was die Postmoderne an Argumenten zusammentrug, verband zwei verwandte Absichten: zunächst die Suche nach einem entwicklungsfähigen Urbanismus, der städtisches Wachstum einem komplexen Ganzen angliedern könnte, ohne Strukturen der Vergangenheit zu zerstören (Venturis »schwieriges Ganzes«). An zweiter Stelle stand die Suche nach einer reichen architektonischen Sprache, in der die verschiedenen Bewohnerschichten der Heteropolis – in die sich jede Stadt der Welt entwickeln wird – kommunizieren könnten. Los Angeles ist inzwischen wegen seines größeren Diversitätsindexes (wie Soziologen die Mischung der Gruppen von Ethnien und Lebensstilen nennen) noch vor New York die Rolle der am meisten heterogenen Stadt zugefallen. Die Rassenunruhen von 1993 zeigten jedoch, dass diese soziale und kulturelle Vielfalt das Zusammenleben vor größte Probleme stellte und Architekten keine Macht hatten, sie zu lösen. Schließlich entwickelte die so genannte Los Angeles School, geführt von Frank O. Gehry, Eric Owen Moss und Thom Mayne, eine heteroglotte und informelle Architektursprache für den Städtebau: eine gute Antwort auf das glatte Corporate Design der aufsteigenden PoMo.

KLEINE BLÖCKE PLANEN

Als Reaktion auf den eigenen inflationären Erfolg war das vierte Stadium der Postmoderne, das Mitte der achtziger Jahre begann, auch um historische Bedeutungen bemüht. Anstatt riesige Komplexe als Einzelvolumen zu errichten, wurden überdimensionale Bürogebäude nun in kleine Blöcke aufgebrochen, die sich sehr verschieden artikulierten.

Jane Jacobs hatte schon in den sechziger Jahren kleine Blöcke

Traditionalist camp; indeed, he had even managed to lead Prince Charles in his march backwards to a "Vision of Britain." Krier was the main theorist behind the new town of Seaside, Florida and much of what was now called the New Urbanism, but it was his pavilion planning and the breaking down of large megastructures into grammatical units that continued to inspire Post-Modernists.

By the late 1980s, however, they found themselves in a tricky situation. They had to veer between a reactionary traditionalism on the rise and some of their own heavy-handed symbolism on the decline. A typical Post-Modern monster was Michael Graves' decorative Swans at Disneyworld. Here were Giovanni Lorenzo Bernini's four foot high sculptural birds blown up nine times to perch on very heavy corner plinths. The Disney Corporation and its "Entertainment Architecture" did as much to destroy the third stage of post-modernism as New York's Sixth Avenue, with its row of dumb boxes, did to destroy its parent. The solution? To adopt a more abstract representation, an allusive symbolism.

This was evident in Kisho Kurokawa's Hiroshima Museum of Contemporary Art, 1989, which alluded to many previous eras of Japanese and Western architecture as well as to the recent destruction of Hiroshima. In the sense that modern technology and warfare produced the bomb and destroyed Hiroshima, her erasure is the ultimate Modernist attack on time and memory. While Kurokawa's building hints at this past (in the scorch-marks of the blast left on several stones incorporated into the building and in its mushroom cloud central space), it also signifies the future with veiled hints of a spacecraft and high-tech equipment (Ill. 5, 6). His Hiroshima museum manages to tie different periods and cultures together through this understated allusion. In a city that suffered total amnesia, Kurokawa has designed a healing amalgam of time: the cracked stone base alludes to Edo Culture and represents the past; the center of the building, with its white tiling, is reminiscent of modern structures, and the aluminum top has many overtones of the future, including space travel.

In a broad sense, the building could also be seen as part of the Post-Modern tradition that gave birth to several Holocaust museums that were begun in the early 1990s, first in the USA, then in Germany. Again, Post-Modern text and Post-Modern building marched in a two-step. As mentioned at the outset, Jean-François Lyotard had polemically declared »Auschwitz a crime open-ing up postmodernity" (the French edition of his argument in *The Postmodern Explained to Children* was published in 1986). Inevitably, Modernists denied this reproach and a furious debate started, as one-sided as the style wars that were dividing architects. The issues are too deep and important to discuss here, but one can follow the reasoning in further books, to my mind the most important being Zygmunt Bauman's *Modernity and the Holocaust*, 1989. This is the most chilling indictment of the connections between the two parts of his title (albeit indirect links), made more persuasive by the fact that he is a Holocaust survivor and the way in which he builds up the argument dispassionately.

The significant thing for architecture was that buildings such as Daniel Libeskind's Jewish Museum in Berlin, 1989-1999, were now dealing with important public content in a symbolic and

empfohlen, Léon Krier dann in den siebziger Jahren. In den späten achtziger Jahren sahen sich Stirling, Hiroshi Hara, Kisho Kurokawa und Antoine Predock – unter vielen anderen – nach historischen Vorbildern für das Aufbrechen riesiger architektonischer Volumina in kleinere, zurückhaltendere und verständlichere Einheiten um. (Abb. 7) Man beschäftigte sich mit dem Städtebau des siebzehnten und achtzehnten Jahrhunderts, untersuchte die Blockrandbebauung von Neapel. Die Kohärenz kleinteiliger klassizistischer Einheiten aus dem antiken Griechenland wurde auf sehr überzeugende Art in den verführerischen Zeichnungen Léon Kriers vorgeführt. In den späten achtziger Jahren hatte er die Postmoderne und seinen Bruder Rob verlassen und sich dem Lager der Traditionalisten angeschlossen. Es war ihm sogar gelungen, Prinz Charles auf seinem Marsch zurück zu einer »Vision of Britain« zu führen. Krier wurde auch der Haupttheoretiker der neu gegründeten Stadt Seaside/Florida und stand hinter vielem von dem, was nun »New Urbanism« genannt wurde. Aber seine pavillonartigen Bauten und das Aufbrechen von Megastrukturen in sinnvolle kleinere Einheiten inspirierten die Postmodernisten auch weiterhin.

Gegen Ende der achtziger Jahre befanden diese sich in einer vertrackten Lage. Denn sie mussten einerseits von einem reaktionären, im Aufwind befindlichen Traditionalismus abkommen und andererseits vom eigenen, grobschlächtigen Symbolismus abrücken, der sich im Niedergang befand. Ein typisches PoMo-Monster war Graves' Hotel Swan in Disneyworld, bei dem Berninis etwa einen Meter hohe Schwanskulpturen auf das Neunfache vergrößert und auf sehr schwere Ecksockel gesetzt wurden. Die Disney Corporation hat mit ihrer Unterhaltungsarchitektur ebenso viel zur Zerstörung des dritten Stadiums der Postmoderne beigetragen, wie die plumpen Kisten entlang der Sixth Avenue in New York es mit ihren Vorgängern taten. Die Lösung? Die Anwendung einer eher abstrakten Darstellung, eines lediglich allusiven Symbolismus.

Ein Beispiel dafür war Kisho Kurokawas Museum für Zeitgenössische Kunst in Hiroshima von 1989, das sowohl auf frühere Epochen der japanischen und westlichen Architektur als auch auf die Zerstörung der Stadt anspielt. Moderne Technologie und Kriegsführung hatten die Atombombe hervorgebracht und Hiroshima zerstört; gleichzeitig steht der ausgelöschte Ort auch für die ultimative modernistische Attacke auf Zeit und Gedächtnis. Kurokawa verweist mit seinem Bauwerk auf diese Vergangenheit (durch die Verwendung von Steinen mit Brandspuren des Feuersturms oder durch den einem Atompilz ähnlichen Zentralraum); er deutet aber auch Zukunft an mit versteckten Hinweisen auf ein Raumschiff und durch die Hightech-Ausstattung des Gebäudes. (Abb. 5, 6) Beim Museum in Hiroshima gelingt also die Verbindung verschiedener Epochen und Kulturen durch unaufdringliche Anspielungen. Kurokawa entwarf für eine Stadt, die unter totaler Amnesie litt, ein heilendes Amalgam von Zeit: Der geborstene steinerne Sockelbereich spielt auf die Endokultur an und repräsentiert die Vergangenheit. Das Zentrum des Gebäudes erinnert mit weißen Kacheln an moderne Architektur, während das Aluminiumdach Zukunft, zum Beispiel Raumfahrt, anklingen lässt.

In umfassenderem Sinn kann das Gebäude auch als Teil jener

convincing way (versus the decorated shed and Graves' swans) and were coming to terms with a part of modern history that had been suppressed. Cultural amnesia was again under attack (Ill. 8) and Libeskind has followed with further competition-winning schemes that are, I would argue, one fulfillment of the Post-Modern agenda. They bind past, present and future, if not into a continuum, then into a discussion.

COMPLEXITY IN ITS SECOND INCARNATION

The fifth stage of Post-Modern architecture started in the early 1990s and presents yet other ways of dealing with time and cultural pluralism. One way is through the broad architectural movement that I discussed in *The Architecture of the Jumping Universe*, 1995, based on complexity theory that sees time as the master builder. The most convincing example of this is DNA: molecules of memory that have taken more than three billion years to build up organizations complex enough to produce us, among other creatures. Architectural memory and complexity too are the work of long periods of destruction and restructuring. By the 1990s, with the aid of the computer and a new complexity theory coming from Ilja Prigogine and the Santa Fe Institute, the 1960s ideas of Jane Jacobs and Robert Venturi had taken on a new twist. Now one could understand emergence, self-organizing systems and how complexity arose over time. Secondly, and more particularly in architecture, the old standbys of collage and juxtaposition were no longer the only ways of dealing with pluralism.

One aspect of the new movement comes in the guise of Folding theory, which stems from Deleuze and his writings on Le Pli. Greg Lynn and Jeffrey Kipnis, among many younger architects, and Peter Eisenman and Daniel Libeskind, among a few older ones, have seen a way beyond discordant collage. Finding the oppositional methods of Stirling at Stuttgart and the ironies of Venturi in London too confrontational, they have fashioned a method of folding-in difference. Here, variety and pluralism are allowed, but are subsumed into a supple, continuously changing whole. As Kipnis argues, it is coherent and congruent, yet still inclusive of difference.

The recent work of Frank O. Gehry epitomizes both the folding and complexity theories without explicitly being based on either. Gehry is aware of the writings on both and respects them, but he is led more by his intuitive concerns. Nonetheless, his New Guggenheim Museum in Bilbao characterizes the supple, pliant, moving quality of the one and the notions of self-organizing systems and a fractal order of the other. For instance, the all-over titanium panels of the museum repeat endlessly as they fold into self-similar, fractal shapes of natural forms: the two most obvious are flower petals and the shimmering water of the Nervion River into which the building springs (Ill. 9).

Into these continuously changing curves, many types of space are poured—Gehry's pluralism is typological more than semantic. The interior galleries run the gamut through all the types: spaces that are long, thin, white, curved, and high; spaces that are small, squashed, square, colored, and low; and both abstract spaces and art-specific rooms. Furthermore, the hills,

postmodernen Tradition angesehen werden, die mehrere Holocaustmuseen hervorbrachte. Man begann mit ihrem Bau in den frühen neunziger Jahren, zuerst in den USA, dann in Deutschland. Wieder gingen postmoderne Thematik und postmoderne Architektur den gleichen Weg. Wie oben erwähnt, hatte Lyotard Auschwitz für ein Verbrechen erklärt, das die Postmodernität eröffnet habe (die französische Ausgabe seines Buchs *Postmoderne für Kinder*, das diesen Gedanken enthält, erschien 1986). Die Modernisten bestritten diesen Vorwurf und fingen eine wütende Debatte an, die so einseitig war wie die Grabenkämpfe um den richtigen Stil – und die Architektenschaft spaltete. Die Themen dieser Kontroverse sind zu tief und zu wichtig, als dass sie hier diskutiert werden könnten; aber man kann sich mit der Argumentation auch in anderen Büchern auseinandersetzen, unter denen meines Erachtens Zygmunt Baumans *Dialektik der Ordnung. Die Moderne und der Holocaust* von 1989 das bedeutendste ist. Bei diesem handelt es sich um die schärfste Anklage gegen die – wenn auch indirekten – Zusammenhänge zwischen den beiden im Titel genannten Phänomenen; und die Tatsache, dass der Autor ein Überlebender des Holocausts ist und seine Argumente sachlich vorträgt, macht das Werk umso überzeugender.

Für die Architektur war bedeutsam, dass Gebäude wie Daniel Libeskinds Jüdisches Museum in Berlin, zwischen 1989 und 1999 entworfen und errichtet, sich nun in einer symbolischen und überzeugenden Art wichtiger gesellschaftlicher Inhalte annahmen (im Gegensatz zum dekorierten Schuppen und den Schwan-Skulpturen von Graves) und sich einem bis dahin unterdrückten Teil der Geschichte der Moderne stellten. Wieder wurde kulturelle Amnesie attackiert. (Abb. 8) Und Libeskind folgte mit weiteren siegreichen Wettbewerbsentwürfen, die, wie ich meine, eine Erfüllung des postmodernen Programms darstellen. Denn sie verbinden Vergangenheit, Gegenwart und Zukunft, nicht zu einem Kontinuum, sondern zu einem Dialog.

DIE ZWEITE INKARNATION VON KOMPLEXITÄT

Das fünfte Stadium postmoderner Architektur begann in den frühen neunziger Jahren und erbrachte wiederum andere Arten des Umgangs mit Zeit und kulturellem Pluralismus. Eine Herangehensweise kommt aus der breiten Architekturbewegung, die ich 1995 in *Die Architektur des springenden Universums* diskutiert habe; sie fußt auf der Komplexitätstheorie, die den Faktor Zeit als »Baumeister« sieht. Das überzeugendste Beispiel dafür ist die DNA; sie besteht aus Erinnerungs-Molekülen, die mehr als drei Milliarden Jahre gebraucht haben, um Organismen aufzubauen, komplex genug, um uns Menschen – unter anderen Kreaturen – entstehen zu lassen. Architektonisches Gedächtnis und Komplexität sind ebenfalls das Werk langer Perioden von Zerstörung und Wiederaufbau. Mit Unterstützung des Computers sowie der Komplexitätstheorie von Ilja Prigogine und des kalifornischen Santa-Fe-Instituts nahmen die Ideen von Jane Jacobs und Robert Venturi aus den sechziger Jahren in den neunziger Jahren eine neue Wendung. Jetzt konnte man verstehen, was Emergenz und was selbstorganisierte Systeme sind und wie Komplexität im Lauf der Zeit entstand. Zweitens, eher spezifisch für die Architektur, zeigte sich: Nicht nur mit dem alten Beistand von Colla-

8

9

10

8 Daniel Libeskind: Jüdisches Museum Berlin/Jewish Museum Berlin, 1999
9 Frank Gehry, Guggenheim Museum Bilbao, 1997
10 Norman Foster: Swiss Re Headquarters, London, 2003

ge und Juxtaposition lassen sich Wege finden, mit dem Pluralismus umzugehen.

Ein Aspekt der neuen Bewegung entwickelte sich im Rahmen der Faltungstheorie, die von Gilles Deleuze und seiner Schrift *Die Falte* inspiriert ist. Greg Lynn und Jeffrey Kipnis, unter vielen jüngeren Architekten, und Peter Eisenman und Libeskind, unter wenigen älteren, erkannten darin eine Überwindung disharmonischer Collagen. Weil sie Stirlings Methode der Opposition in Stuttgart und Venturis Gebrauch von Ironie in London als zu konfrontativ empfanden, kamen sie auf das Prinzip der Faltung. Es gestattet Verschiedenheit und Pluralismus, die sich aber einem geschmeidigen, sich dauernd wandelnden Ganzen unterordnen. Es ist, wie Kipnis sagt, kohärent und kongruent und schließt doch die Differenz mit ein.

Die letzten Arbeiten von Gehry verkörpern sowohl die Faltungs- als auch die Komplexitätstheorie, ohne dass sie sich ausdrücklich auf eine von beiden bezögen. Gehry kennt und schätzt die Schriften über diese Theorien, lässt sich aber mehr von seinen intuitiven Interessen leiten. Nichtsdestotrotz steht sein neues Guggenheim Museum in Bilbao einerseits für das Geschmeidige, Sich-Faltende und Sich-Bewegende der Faltungstheorie und andererseits für selbstorganisierte Systeme und fraktale Ordnungen der Komplexitätstheorie. Zum Beispiel wiederholen sich die das Museum verkleidenden Titaniumpaneele endlos, indem sie sich zu selbstähnlichen Teilgebilden natürlicher Formen falten. Die beiden nächstliegenden Assozationen sind Blütenblätter und das glitzernde Wasser des Flusses Nervion, in den das Gebäude eintaucht. (Abb. 9)

Die sich ständig wandelnden Krümmungen des Museums enthalten viele Raumtypen, wobei Gehrys Pluralismus eher typologisch als semantisch ist. Die inneren Gallerien durchlaufen die ganze Skala: lange, dünne, weiße, gekurvte und hohe Räume; kleine, gedrückte, quadratische, farbige und niedrige Räume; neutrale wie auch für spezielle Kunst konzipierte Räume. Mehr noch: Hügel, Straßen und der Fluss von Bilbao sind in das Museum einbezogen und werden entweder durch schmale Ausblikke oder durch riesige, über 18 Meter hohe, schräge und gebogene Fenster zelebriert.

Am deutlichsten erscheint Gehrys Pluralismus in Bezügen auf das Grundstück. Das Gebäude rutscht zur einen Seite unter eine Autobahn und erweist durch seine industriell hergestellte Oberfläche den Zügen und dem Bahnhof zur anderen Seite Reverenz. Getreu dem fünften Stadium postmoderner Architektur, das sich – wie zuvor die vierte Phase – ebenfalls gegen expliziten Symbolismus wendet, sind diese Bezüge zurückgenommen, nur angedeutet; aber für die, die sich die Mühe des Hinschauens machen, sind sie offensichtlich.

Als das Gebäude 1997 eröffnet wurde, fanden die Basken es vielleicht zu amerikanisch, zu bombastisch, zu hegemonial. Bald aber schätzten sie die indirekte Art, mit der Gehry auf das Gelände und die frühere Fabriklandschaft reagiert und ein Gebäude geschaffen hatte, das eine sterbende Industriestadt wieder auferstehen ließ. Wieder einmal sollten wir zurücktreten, um das größere Ganze zu sehen. Wenn die Postmodernisierung je als quartärer Wirtschaftssektor existierte, der die moderne Produktion ersetzt, dann hier. Durch diese und andere Schöpfungen hat

streets, and river of Bilbao are very much pulled into the museum and celebrated, both with glimpsed views and with vast, sixty-foot-high, tilted and warped windows.

The pluralism is most apparent in references to the site. The building slides under an existing highway to one side and then, with its industrial surface, acknowledges the trains and the railroad station to the other. Following the fourth stage of Post-Modern architecture, which also reacts against explicit symbolism, these references are understated and oblique, but for those who care to look they are palpable.

When the building opened in 1997, the Basques may have found that the art and culture were too American, too bombastic, or too hegemonic, but they soon appreciated the way in which Gehry had implicitly responded to the site and the preexisting industrial landscape to create a building that resuscitates a dying rust-belt city. Again, we should step back to see the bigger picture. If ever post-modernization existed as a quaternary industry replacing modernized manufacturing, it is here. The cultural industry has, through this and other creations, revived Bilbao's economy and thus has created new links across time that would have surprised the Modernists and materialists.

Beyond its imagery that appeals to a diverse audience, its multiple-coding and warped curves, its revival of a post-industrial economy, what makes it particularly post-modern is the fact that, as in other Gehry buildings, its personal order has been enabled by computer production. This point should be emphasized. The computer is the instrument for understanding complexity in the natural and human worlds; it is to Post-Modernity what the telescope and microscope were to Modernity. In the first edition of *The Language of Post-Modern Architecture*, I foresaw a new crafted architecture that would be just as cheaply produced as the mass-produced elements of modern architecture. This was theoretically possible in the 1970s when factory robots programmed by different software manufactured differently shaped elements as quickly and easily as identical ones. Yet it was not until the early 1990s that the Post-Modern goal was generally available in architecture (and Gehry's Bilbao announced the fact to the world. It was as visible as shift in architecture beyond Modernism as the blowing up of the mass housing at Pruitt-Igoe had been in 1972.

THE NEW PARADIGM & ENIGMATIC SIGNIFIER

By the mid-1990s, as many anthologies on the subject appeared, post-modernism was starting to wane as a live movement, becoming diffuse as a concept and démodé as a term, even of abuse. Nevertheless, its *raison d'etre* continued, as did its practice. There had to be an opposition to the reigning economic and cultural reality of modernism—its boredom, commercialism, conformity, and cliché—and now it was the turn of those associated with Late-Modernism: they could be termed the loyal opposition. Because of this change in emphasis I used the phrase "the new paradigm in architecture" to signal the turn.

Several key buildings showed its promise—those by architects I have already mentioned, Frank Gehry, Peter Eisenman, and Daniel Libeskind—and those on the outskirts of the new

die Kulturindustrie die Wirtschaft von Bilbao wieder belebt. Sie hat so, über die Zeit hinweg, neue Verbindungen geschaffen, die Modernisten und Materialisten sicher überrascht hätten.

Was den Bau besonders postmodern macht – jenseits seiner Bildlichkeit, die ein breites Publikum attraktiv findet, seiner mehrfachen Kodierung und seiner wellenförmigen Krümmungen, jenseits auch seiner Wiederbelebung einer postindustriellen Ökonomie –, ist die Tatsache, dass seine individuelle Ordnung wie bei anderen Bauten Gehrys durch den Computer ermöglicht wurde. Das kann nicht stark genug betont werden. Der Computer ist das Instrument zum Verständnis der Komplexität in Natur und Gesellschaft; für die Postmoderne bedeutet er das, was Teleskop und Mikroskop für die Moderne waren. In der ersten Ausgabe von *Die Sprache der postmodernen Architektur* (1977) sah ich schon eine neue Baukunst kommen, die genau so preiswert hergestellt werden würde wie die massenproduzierten Fertigteile der modernen Architektur. Theoretisch war dies schon in den siebziger Jahren möglich, als speziell programmierte Roboter unterschiedlich gestaltete Bauteile genauso schnell und leicht wie identisch gestaltete produzierten. Aber erst in den frühen neunziger Jahren setzte sich dieses postmoderne Ziel auch unter Architekten durch, und Gehrys Bilbao-Projekt verkündete es der Welt. Der Architektur widerfuhr damit eine Verschiebung über den Modernismus hinaus, so sichtbar wie 1972 bei der Sprengung der Großsiedlung Pruitt-Igoe.

DAS NEUE PARADIGMA UND DER ENIGMATISCHE SIGNIFIKANT

Um die Mitte der neunziger Jahre, als viele Anthologien zur Postmoderne publiziert wurden, begann sie als lebendige Bewegung zu verblassen. Als Konzept wurde sie diffus; als Begriff – selbst als Schimpfwort – kam sie aus der Mode. Dennoch bestanden ihre *raison d'être* und ihre Praxis fort – als notwendiges Gegengewicht zur herrschenden ökonomischen und kulturellen Realität des Modernismus: zu seiner Langeweile, seinem Kommerzialismus, seiner Konformität und seinem Klischee. Nun waren die an der Reihe, die der »späten Moderne« zugerechnet werden. Man könnte sie auch als loyale Opposition bezeichnen. Um diesen Akzentwechsel, diese Wende zu verdeutlichen, sprach ich vom »neuen Paradigma in der Architektur«.

Einige Schlüsselbauten zeigten sein Versprechen: solche von Architekten wie Gehry, Eisenman und Libeskind, die ich schon erwähnte, und solche von Architekten an den Rändern des neuen Paradigmas, niederländischen Architekten, und zwar nicht allein von Koolhaas, sondern auch von Ben van Berkel und MVRDV. Es gab jene, die sich wie Zaha Hadid, Eric Owen Moss und Morphosis vom Dekonstruktivismus entfernt, und jene, die wie Norman Foster Hightech in Ökotech verwandelt hatten. Will Alsop, Coop Himmelb(l)au und japanische Architekten wie Kisho Kurokawa, Shoei Yoh, Masaharu Takasaki und Arata Isozaki engagierten sich zeitweise für diesen Ansatz, ebenso die australischen Büros ARM (Ashton Raggatt MacDougall) und LAB (Peter Davidson, Donald L. Bates), das ein maßgebendes Projekt der neuen Bewegung verwirklichte, den Federation Square in Melbourne. Warum kann man in den genannten Architekten

paradigm by the Dutch architects, not only Rem Koolhaas, but Ben van Berkel and MVRDV. There were some who had moved on from Deconstruction—Zaha Hadid, Eric Owen Moss and Morphosis—and others, such as Norman Foster, who had turned high-tech into eco-tech. Will Alsop, Coop Himmelb(l)au and Japanese architects such as Kisho Kurokawa, Shoei Yoh, Masaharu Takasaki and Arata Isozaki were intermittently engaged with the approach, as were the Australian architects ARM (Ashton Raggatt MacDougall) and LAB (Peter Davidson, Donald L. Bates), who completed a seminal work of the new movement, Melbourne's Federation Square. Why could they be seen as continuing the agenda of Post-Modernism? Because they developed the complexity paradigm (see above), because they produced sculptural iconic buildings that had some significance (the enigmatic signifier) and because they used the computer to personalize their mass production. Of course, they would avoid the pm moniker like a virus, but that didn't mean that they escaped the practice.

Since I have discussed this stage of post-modernism at length in several articles and the seventh edition of *The Language of Post-Modern Architecture* and since the reader can see the complexity of overlapping movements in the first diagram, published in this book, I will not rehearse the arguments or narrative. Rather, I will just mention two characteristic buildings that signal the shift and draw conclusions about the movement as a whole. The first is by the most prominent modern architect, Norman Foster; the second is Daniel Libeskind's design for the replacement of buildings at Ground Zero.

Stemming from Greg Lynn, Jeff Kipnis and the young university professors who I have mentioned above was a group of architects known affectionately as the Blobmeisters. They designed rounded buildings; they warped floor, wall and ceiling into a continuous curve and they argued that the blob is really a more developed form of the cube. It can handle more information than this Modernist archetype; its complexity and therefore sensitivity are potentially greater. Yet, at the beginning of this new tradition of building, when Modernists are moving into unchartered territory, their first steps can be hesitant and awkward. This is true particularly around the entrance to a structure and where it meets the ground or another building. Norman Foster's two giant blobs, one for the Mayor of London, the other for a new music centre in Newcastle, both have these problems. Their internal space and structure are more convincing than the way in which they relate to the city.

By contrast, Foster's Swiss Re Headquarters building is a perfected, stretched blob, conceived as a city landmark. It started off life as an egg shape and then, after wind and structural studies, re-emerged as other natural metaphors–not only the far-fetched gherkin of the tabloids, but a more plausible and welcoming pine cone and pineapple. The spiral skycourts and aesthetic refinements give further rationale to these metaphors, making them multivalent and enigmatic in a plausible way. Once again, the computer helped produce self-similar forms at an acceptable price. The entasis of this skyscraper, like that of a Doric column, leads to a new kind of propositional beauty, one worked out digitally (Ill. 10, 11).

die Fortsetzer des postmodernen Programms sehen? Weil sie das oben erläuterte Paradigma der Komplexität entwickelten, weil sie skulpturale ikonische Bauten mit Bedeutung (Signifikanz) – also enigmatische Signifikanten – schufen und weil sie den Computer nutzten, um ihre Architekturen persönlich zu gestalten. Natürlich würden sie das Etikett »Postmoderne« wie einen Virus meiden; doch das besagt nicht, dass sie sich von ihrer Praxis gelöst hätten.

Da ich dieses Stadium der Postmoderne in mehreren Artikeln und der siebten Auflage von *Die Sprache der postmodernen Architektur* ausgiebig diskutiert habe und der Leser die Komplexität einander überlagernder Bewegungen in dem Diagramm erkennen kann, das in diesem Buch abgebildet ist, will ich nicht weiter darauf eingehen. Lieber möchte ich zwei charakteristische Gebäude erwähnen, die diese Verschiebung signalisieren, und dann die Schlüsse über die Bewegung als Ganze ziehen. Der erste Bau stammt von dem derzeit wohl prominentesten modernen Architekten, von Norman Foster; beim zweiten handelt es sich um Daniel Libeskinds Entwurf für Ground Zero in New York.

Aus der Schule von Greg Lynn, Jeff Kipnis und den oben erwähnten jungen Universitätsprofessoren stammte eine Gruppe von Architekten, die unter der mit Zuneigung gebrauchten Bezeichnung »Blobmeister« bekannt wurden. Sie entwarfen gerundete Bauten (blobs); sie bogen deren Böden, Wände und Dekken zu einer durchgehenden Kurve und argumentierten, ein Blob sei in Wahrheit eine höher entwickelte Form des Kubus. Ein Blob könne mit mehr Informationen umgehen als der modernistische Archetyp, böte mehr Potenzial für Komplexität und folglich Sensibilität. Aber am Beginn einer neuen Bautradition, bei der sich die Neuerer noch auf unerforschtem Terrain bewegen, wirken die ersten Schritte mitunter zögerlich und unbeholfen. In unserem Beispiel gilt dies insbesondere für den Bereich rund um den Eingang eines Gebäudes oder dort, wo es den Boden berührt beziehungsweise auf ein anderes Gebäude trifft. Fosters zwei riesige Blobs, einer für den Bürgermeister von London, der andere für ein neues Musikzentrum in Newcastle, haben dieses Problem. Der Innenraum und die Konstruktion sind überzeugender als die Art, wie sich die beiden Bauten auf den Stadtraum beziehen.

Im Gegensatz dazu ist Fosters Hauptverwaltung der Swiss Re Company in London ein perfektionierter gestreckter Blob, der als städtisches Wahrzeichen konzipiert wurde. Erst war er eiförmig, dann verwandelte er sich, nach Windkraft- und Statikuntersuchungen, in andere Natur-Metaphern, nicht nur in die weit hergeholte »Essiggurke«, sondern auch eher einleuchtend und einladend in einen Pinienzapfen oder eine Ananas. Die spiralförmigen Innenhöfe und ästhetischen Raffinements begründen diese Metaphern, machen sie auf plausible Art vieldeutig und rätselhaft. Wieder half der Computer, selbstähnliche Formen zu annehmbaren Kosten zu produzieren. Die einer dorischen Säule ähnliche Entasis führt bei diesem Wolkenkratzer zu einer neuen, digital entworfenen Art, Schönheit zu behaupten. (Abb. 10, 11)

Der enigmatische Signifikant (das rätselhaft Bezeichnende) wurde der Weg schlechthin, um das Thema »Landmark Buil-

The enigmatic signifier became the way to deal with the landmark building. This architectural type and phrase, a telling euphemism for what used to be called a monument, developed for good and bad reasons. The chief negative motives are cultural. With the continual decline of the Christian and Modern belief systems, with the rise of consumer society and a celebrity system, architects are caught in a vicious trap. They have few, if any, credible public conventions and ideologies to build for; they lack any iconography beyond a debased machine aesthetic (or high-tech) and an ecological imperative that has yet to produce accepted symbols, so they are pushed and pulled in opposite ways. The absence of all beliefs leads them to a degree zero minimalism: a good expression of neutrality, but of course one that is totally absorbed into the reigning system.

By contrast, a competitive culture demands difference, significance and fantastic expression in excess of the building task. The enigmatic signifier responds to this conundrum. The injunction is: you must design an extraordinary landmark, but it must not look like anything seen before and it may not refer to any known religion, ideology or set of conventions. In the 1910s, the artist Giorgio de Chirico, faced with similar perplexities, was asked what he painted and replied, "the enigma."

The enigmatic signifier in the hands of Gehry can work well, because he labours over the sculptural aspects of the form and light and adopts multiple metaphors that relate, albeit loosely, to the building's role. Thus in his Disney Concert Hall, the overtones of music and cultural brio were interpreted with clashing petal forms, ship metaphors and symphonic images. At Bilbao, many critics found similar allusions to fishes, ducks, trains, clouds and the adjacent hills. One excited writer acclaimed the structure as a "Constructivist artichoke," another as a "mermaid in metallic sequins". Several of these organic overtones might be appropriate to the central place of art in the city today, the museum as cathedral; some might be subjective or accidental. Yet with the best work in the new paradigm, these metaphors are more than random projections, the outcome of a Rorschach test or automatic, unconscious creation. They are emergent, multivalent signifiers in search of an open interpretation: one related to the building task, the site and the language of the particular architecture.

The idea of the "open work" of art has been in the air since Umberto Eco proposed it as a typical response of artists and writers in the 1960s. Now, for social reasons, it has emerged more fully into architectural view. Since the monument has mutated into the landmark building, since architects have lost most conventional iconography, they now hope to find, through a process of search and invention, some emergent metaphors, ones that amaze and delight, but are not specific to any ideology.

I believe that it is the job of architects to take responsibility for the public and esoteric meanings of a civic building, whether enigmatic or not, but this is an especially difficult task in a global culture without a shared value system. The temptation is to hide behind social and technical requirements, to use supposed determinants to suppress symbolism. Perhaps the only architect of the new paradigm who admits to both larger spiritual concerns and a public symbolism is Daniel Libeskind. His

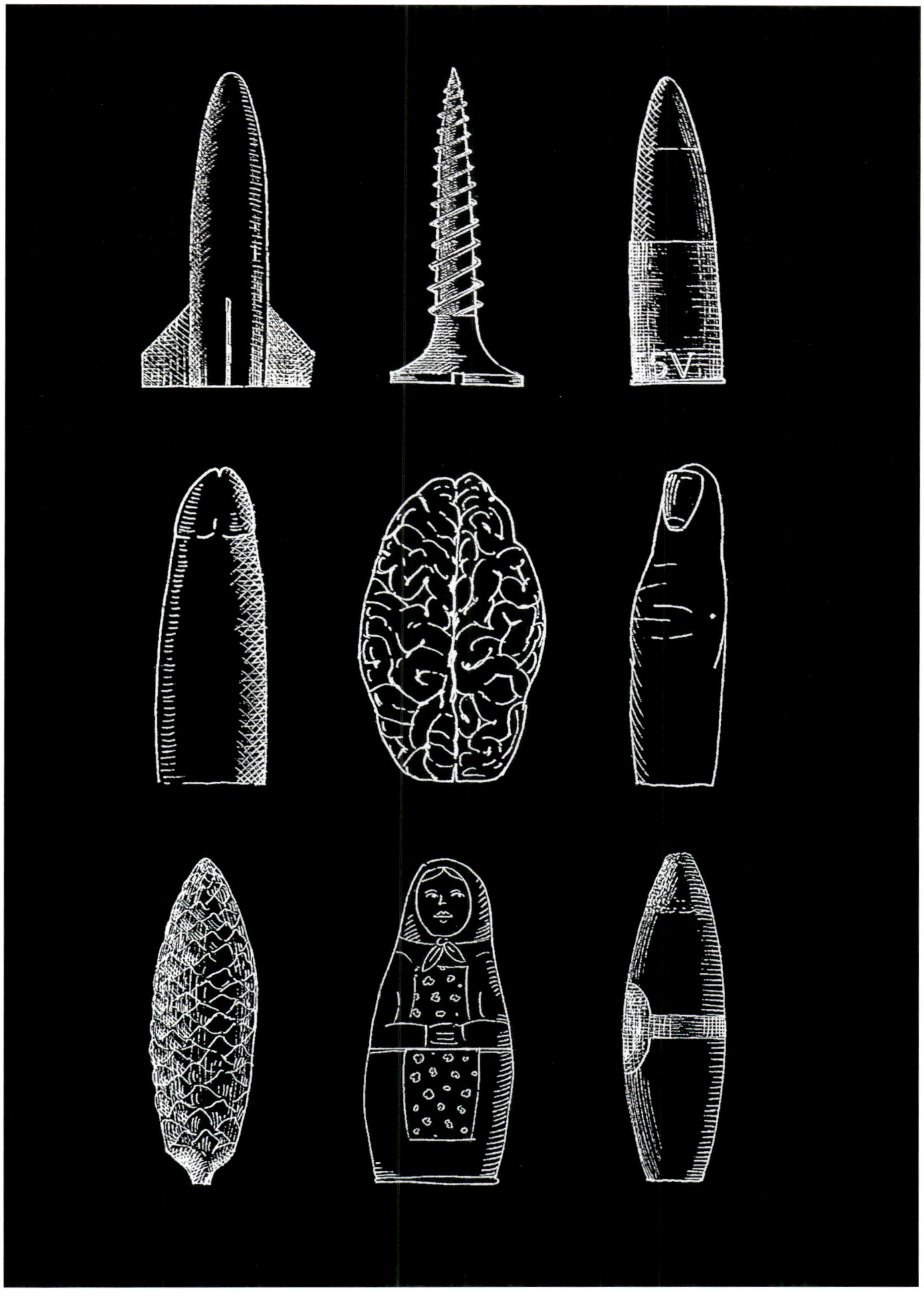

11

11 Formen ähnlich den Swiss Re Headquarters von Norman Foster
Shapes resembling Norman Foster's Swiss Re Headquarters

ding« zu behandeln. Dieser architektonische Typus mitsamt der Wortschöpfung – ein aufschlussreicher Euphemismus für das, was früher Monument genannt wurde – entwickelte sich aufgrund positiver und negativer Ursachen. Die wichtigsten negativen Anlässe sind kulturell bedingt. Infolge des andauernden Niedergangs der Glaubenssätze von Christentum und Moderne und des Aufkommens der Konsumgesellschaft sowie eines Starkult-Systems stecken Architekten in einer gemeinen Falle. Es gibt inzwischen, wenn überhaupt, nur wenige glaubwürdige, in der breiten Öffentlichkeit akzeptierte Konventionen und Ideologien, auf die sie bauen können. Jenseits einer diskreditierten Maschinen- oder Hightech-Ästhetik und eines ökologischen Imperativs, der akzeptable Symbole erst noch liefern muss, mangelt es ihnen an jedweder Ikonographie. So werden sie in entgegengesetzte Richtungen geschoben und gezogen. Die Abwesenheit allen Glaubens führt viele zu einem absoluten Minimalismus, gewiss einem guten Ausdruck von Neutralität, aber natürlich einem, der vom herrschenden System völlig absorbiert wird.

Eine auf Wettbewerb gründende Kultur dagegen verlangt zusätzlich zur Bauaufgabe Differenz, Signifikanz und extravagante Expressivität. Der enigmatische Signifikant reagiert auf die nebulöse Direktive: Du musst ein außerordentliches Wahrzeichen entwerfen; aber es darf nicht wie irgendetwas vorher Gesehenes aussehen und darf sich nicht auf eine bekannte Religion, Ideologie oder Konvention beziehen. Als um 1910 der Künstler Giorgio de Chirico, der sich mit ähnlichen Verwirrungen konfrontiert sah, gefragt wurde, was er male, antwortete er: »das Rätsel«.

Bei Gehry funktioniert der enigmatische Signifikant so gut, weil sich der Architekt mit den skulpturalen Erscheinungen der Form und des Lichts große Mühe gibt und multiple Metaphern wählt, die sich, wenn auch nur lose, auf die Rolle des Bauwerks beziehen. In seiner Walt-Disney-Konzerthalle in Los Angeles interpretierte er die Musik und das kulturelle Brio durch aneinander stoßende Blütenblattformen, Schiffssymbole und symphonische Mataphern. In Bilbao fanden viele Kritiker ähnliche Arten von Anspielungen auf Fische, Enten, Züge, Wolken und die Hügel der näheren Umgebung. Ein begeisterter Kritiker feierte das Gebäude als »konstruktivistische Artischocke«, ein anderer als »Nixe im metallischen Paillettenkostüm«. Manche dieser organischen Untertöne mögen für einen zentralen Kunstort in der Stadt von heute – das Museum als Kathedrale – angemessen sein; andere hingegen wirken subjektiv oder zufällig. Doch bei den besten Vertretern des neuen Paradigmas sind diese Metaphern mehr als bloß willkürliche Projektion, mehr als bloß Resultat eines psychologischen Rorschachtests, mehr als bloß automatische, unbewusste Schöpfung. Sie sind auftauchende, vieldeutige Signifikanten auf der Suche nach einer offenen Interpretation der Bauaufgabe, des Grundstücks und der Architektursprache.

Die Idee des »offenen Kunstwerks« liegt in der Luft, seit Eco sie in den sechziger Jahren als angemessene Strategie für Künstler und Autoren vorschlug. Nun ist es aus gesellschaftlichen Gründen auch klarer in das Blickfeld von Architekten getreten. Jetzt, da das Monument zum Landmark Building mutiert und

Imperial War Museum North, outside Manchester, explicitly symbolizes the various kinds of war (on land, sea and in the air) as well as a globe that is fragmented by strife. He constantly invokes the cultural and emotional plane of expression as the duty of the architect; he is not afraid of facing up to the fundamental issues of meaning and nihilism that silence other designers (Ill. 12-14). For all these reasons, he carries forward the PM agenda developed since the 1960s. Perhaps, like Gehry, some of his expressive grammar is too often repeated across projects, but one has to applaud his courage in confronting a major problem of the moment: spiritual crisis and the loss of a shared metaphysics.

Libeskind won the competition for Ground Zero in New York because he faced the symbolic and spiritual issues of the problem both specifically and with the more allusive enigmatic signifier. Rather than be an inadvertent metaphor of death (the "skeletons and hanging bodies" of Viñoly's solution) or an evasive techno-abstraction (as were some of the other entries), he was specific about certain memorial signs: for instance, the "wedge of light" and the "1776 Tower" (both an ascending spiral and sign of the Statue of Liberty). At the same time the slashes, spirals of crystals and abstract slurry walls were suggestive of related meanings of what happened. Nationalist references may have been overdone and in some cases over-simple. "Heroes Walk?"—in many cases, the firemen had no choice but to be heroes.

Yet these exaggerations are countered with a general grammar that keeps the eye and mind moving around the site, from one tower to the next, and down to their focus on the sunken ground plane: the slurry wall. This last blank canvas is a fitting receptacle for later memorialization. Balancing specific signs with enigmatic signifiers keeps his project from being read in either an exclusively chauvinistic or aberrant way. At least this seems to be the case at this design stage, before the final compromises have been made and the very long process of bartering and construction has started.

Whatever the architecture, the deeper conundrums for a Post-Modern age remain: those that Gauguin famously turned into a painting and an uncomfortable question: D'où venons-nous? Que sommes-nous? Où allons-nous? Many people (and some philosophers) would say that there are no adequate answers to these perennial queries and that disorientation in a global culture is inevitable and permanent. Yet other philosophers, notably Mary Midgely, argue that new credible, public concepts have emerged such as the notion of the earth as a self-regulating system, Gaia. The metaphor of a dynamic planet tuning itself through feedback is, of course, one of the insights of the new paradigm in science, but whether architects come up with a public iconography based on Gaia remains to be seen.

My belief, as I mentioned to Lyotard in our non-meeting, is that the universe story will become a shared metaphysics. I developed this idea in an extensive work, designed and built over the last twelve years and recently published as *The Garden of Cosmic Speculation.* This narrative of cosmogenesis, elaborated in different ways by scientists, philosophers and poets, obviously cannot be summarized here, but the argument is that this may

die konventionelle Ikonographie größtenteils obsolet geworden ist, hoffen sie, Metaphern aufzuspüren oder zu erfinden, die erstaunen und entzücken, aber nicht ideologisch determiniert sind.

Ich glaube, es ist die Aufgabe von Architekten, die Verantwortung für allgemein verständliche und künstlerische Bedeutungen eines öffentlichen Gebäudes zu übernehmen. Dies aber ist in einer globalen Kultur ohne gemeinsames Wertesystem eine besonders schwierige Aufgabe. Die Versuchung ist groß, sich hinter sozialen und technischen Notwendigkeiten zu verstecken und vermeintlichen Vorgaben zu genügen, um das Symbolische zu unterdrücken. Der vielleicht einzige Architekt des neuen Paradigmas, der für beides Raum hat – die größeren geistigen Belange und die öffentliche Symbolik –, ist Daniel Libeskind. Sein am Rand von Manchester gelegenes Imperial War Museum North symbolisiert explizit die verschiedenen Kriegsarten (zu Lande, zu Wasser, in der Luft) und einen durch Konflikte zerrissenen Globus. Immer wieder bezeichnet Libeskind es als die Pflicht des Architekten, die kulturelle und emotionale Ausdruksebene zu beachten. Er hat keine Angst, sich den fundamentalen Fragen von Bedeutung und Nihilismus zu stellen, die andere Entwerfer zum Schweigen bringen. Aus all diesen Gründen trägt er das seit den sechziger Jahren entwickelte Programm der Postmoderne weiter. (Abb. 12-14) Vielleicht wird, wie bei Gehry, manches Element seiner expressiven Grammatik von Projekt zu Projekt zu oft wiederholt; doch seinem Mut zur Konfrontation mit einem großen Problem unserer Zeit, nämlich der geistigen Krise und dem Verlust einer gemeinsamen Metaphysik, ist Beifall zu zollen.

Libeskind gewann den Wettbewerb für Ground Zero in New York, weil er sich den symbolischen und spirituellen Aspekten des Problems einerseits direkt, andererseits durch den eher anspielungsreichen enigmatischen Signifikanten stellte. Anstatt eine ungewollte Metapher des Todes (wie die »Skelette« und »hängenden Körper« der Lösung Rafael Viñolys) oder eine ausweichende technische Abstraktion anzubieten (wie bei einigen anderen Beiträgen der Fall), schlug Libeskind unmissverständliche Zeichen der Erinnerung vor: zum Beispiel den »Keil des Lichts« und den »Turm von 1776« (beide jeweils eine aufsteigende Spirale und ein Pendant der Freiheitsstatue). Zugleich suggerierten Schlitze, verdrehte Kristalle und abstrahierte Stützwände Bedeutungen, die dem verwandt sind, was am 11. September 2001 geschah. Mag sein, dass nationalistische Bezüge übertrieben und in einigen Fällen zu simpel waren, zum Beispiel der »Weg der Helden« – die Feuerwehrmänner hatten ja oft gar keine andere Wahl, als Helden zu sein.

Allerdings tritt diesen Übertreibungen eine allgemeine Grammatik entgegen, die dafür sorgt, dass sich Auge und Verstand ständig über das Gelände bewegen, dass sie von einem Turm zum nächsten und hinunter auf die versunkene Bodenplatte wandern, auf die Schutzwände. Diese letzte leere Textur ist eine Stelle, die später der Erinnerungstätigkeit dienen kann. Die Balance zwischen spezifischen Zeichen und enigmatischen Signifikanten hält Libeskinds Projekt sowohl von chauvinistischer als auch von abwegiger Lesart frei. Zumindest scheint das in diesem Stadium der Fall zu sein, bevor die letzten Kompromis-

12

13

14

Daniel Libeskind, Imperial War Museum North, Manchester, 2002
12 Luftaufnahme/Aerial view
13 Eingangsseite/Entrance side
14 Ausstellungshalle/Exhibition hall

se geschlossen worden sind und der sehr lange Prozess des Handelns und Schacherns und Bauens beginnt.

Wie auch immer die Architektur sein mag, die tieferen Rätsel des postmodernen Zeitalters bleiben. Jene, die Paul Gauguin in sein berühmtes Gemälde mit der unbequemen Frage verwandelte: »Woher kommen wir? Was sind wir? Wohin gehen wir?« Viele Menschen und manche Philosophen würden sagen, dass es auf diese ewigen Fragen keine adäquaten Antworten gebe und dass in einer globalen Kultur Orientierungslosigkeit unvermeidlich, ja dauerhaft sei. Andere Philosophen wiederum, besonders Mary Midgely, argumentieren, dass inzwischen neue glaubwürdige, das heißt auch öffentlich wahrgenommene Konzepte – zum Beispiel der Begriff von der Erde als dem sich selbst regulierenden System Gaia – entstanden seien. Das Bild eines dynamischen Planeten, der sich selbst in eine stimmige Verfassung bringt, ist natürlich eine der Einsichten des neuen Paradigmas in der Wissenschaft. Ob aber Architekten mit einer auf dem Bild der Gaia basierenden, allgemein anerkannten Ikonographie aufwarten werden, muss sich noch zeigen.

Wie ich Lyotard gegenüber in unserer versäumten Begegnung erwähnte, bin ich festen Glaubens, dass die Geschichte des Universums zur allseits akzeptierten Metaphysik werden wird. Ich habe diese Idee in einer ausgedehnten Arbeit entwickelt, sie im Lauf der letzten zwölf Jahre entworfen und gebaut und jüngst in dem Buch *The Garden of Cosmic Speculation* publiziert. Die Erzählung der Kosmogenesis, die auf verschiedene Arten von Wissenschaftlern, Philosophen und Dichtern entworfen wurde, kann hier natürlich nicht zusammengefasst werden; aber die These lautet, dass sie der Orientierungskurs für die Zukunft werden könne. Vielleicht kann diese Erzählung die einende Perspektive auf eine globale Kultur liefern und, im Kontext des oben diskutierten enigmatischen Signifikanten, die Quelle einer zeitgenössischen Ikonologie und Ikonographie werden. Die Geschichte des Universums hatte keinen Vergil oder Dante und noch weniger einen Steven Spielberg oder einen Woody Allen; aber schnell hebt sie frühere Antworten auf Gauguins ängstliche Frage auf. Da viele verschiedene Menschen diese Erzählung untersuchen, wird sie sicher Hinweise auf eine Richtung geben und genau jene Traditionen und Standards schaffen, an denen neue Architektur gemessen werden kann.

Lässt sich also anlässlich von »Die Revision der Postmoderne« nach dreißig Jahren Theorie und Praxis eine grobe Bilanz für Architektur und Urbanismus aufstellen? Auf der positiven Seite steht, dass Architektur heute routinemäßig alle Nuancen des postmodernen Programms aufnimmt: Ironie, Farbe, Humor, Kontext, lokale und historische Referenzen, gemischte Geschmackskulturen, Komplexitätstheorie, Computerproduktion individualisierter Elemente und eine Reihe von Ausdrucksweisen, die sich der Natur annähern (zum Beispiel fraktale Grammatiken, fremdartige oder chaotische Attraktoren, flüssige Morphologien etc.). Dass Architektur eine Sprache ist, ist heute ein akzeptierter Bestandteil der Praxis. Diese Elemente der postmodernen Agenda sind in der gesamten Profession inzwischen so verbreitet, dass es sich schon um stillschweigende Voraussetzungen handelt. Auf der negativen Seite steht, dass die Postmoderne – durch die Kombination von globaler kommerzieller Kul-

become the orientation point for the future. Possibly, it could provide that unifying perspective for a global culture and, in the context of the enigmatic signifier discussed above, become a locus for a contemporary iconology and iconography. The universe story has not had its Virgil or Dante, much less its Steven Spielberg or Woody Allen, but it is fast sublating previous answers to Gauguin's anxious question. As many different people investigate this narrative, it is bound to provide hints of a direction and create the very traditions and standards by which new architecture can be gauged.

So, "Post-Modernism Revisited:" after thirty years of theory and practice, can one fashion a rough balance sheet for architecture and urbanism? On the positive side, architecture now routinely incorporates all the traces of the pm programme—irony, color, humor, context, local and historical reference, mixed taste-cultures, complexity theory, computer production of individualized elements, and a series of languages closer to nature (eg. fractal grammars, strange or chaotic attractors, fluid morphologies etc.). Indeed, the view that architecture is a language is now an accepted part of practice. These parts of the PM agenda are now so diffused throughout the profession as to be tacit assumptions. On the negative side, Post-Modernity (the combination of a commercial global culture and mass mediation by the inventions of the electronic age) has destroyed much local culture, aided massive fraud at the Enron scale, amplified celebrity culture and turned *ersatz* into "business as usual." Given this mixed record, loyalty to Post-Modernism amounts to the critical opposition that it, in turn, has always directed to its parent, Modernism. As Umberto Eco long ago pointed out, Post-Modernism grew up in an age of lost innocence and this has still not been found.

Bibliography

Jacobs, Jane, The Death and Life of Great American Cities, New York 1961.
Jencks, Charles, The Language of Post-Modern Architecture, Sixth Edition, London/New York, 1991; seventh edition published as The New Paradigm in Architecture, London, New Haven 2002.
See also: The New Paradigm in Architecture, The Architectural Review, February 2003, pp. 72-77. Parts of the above article appeared in these sources as well as in: Post-Modernism and the Revenge of the Book, in: this is not architecture, edited by Kester Rattenbury, London 2002, pp. 174-197.
The Architecture of the Jumping Universe, Second Edition, London/New York 1997.
Mr. Jencks' Jumping Universe, 45 minute programme, BBC, 11.5.1997.
The Post-Modern Agenda, in: The Post-Modern Reader, ed. Charles Jencks. London/New York 1992, pp. 10-39.
The Garden of Cosmic Speculation, London/New York 2003.
Kipnis, Jeffrey, Towards a New Architecture, in: Architectural Design 63, 3/4 (1993), pp. 41-49.
Venturi, Robert, Complexity and Contradiction in Architecture. Museum of Modern Art Papers on Architecture, New York 1966.
Venturi, Robert, Denise Scott Brown, Steven Izenour, Learning from Las Vegas, Cambridge, Mass. 1972.

tur und Massenvermittlung durch Erfindungen des elektronischen Zeitalters – viel an lokaler Kultur zerstört, zum massiven Betrug auf Enron-Niveau beigetragen, den Starkult verstärkt, das Surrogat und die Simulation in ein ganz gewöhnliches Geschäft verwandelt hat. Angesichts dieser gemischten Bilanz läuft Loyalität gegenüber der Postmoderne auf kritische Opposition hinaus, mit der sie sich selbst stets gegen ihren Vorläufer, den Modernismus, gewandt hat. Wie Umberto Eco vor langem aufzeigte, wuchs die Postmoderne in einem Zeitalter verlorener Unschuld auf. Diese wurde übrigens noch immer nicht wiedererlangt.

Bibliographie
Jacobs, Jane, Tod und Leben großer amerikanischer Städte, Berlin 1963.
Jencks, Charles, The Language of Post-Modern Architecture, London/New York 1991.
Ders., The Post-Modern Agenda, in: Ders. (Hg.), The Post-Modern Reader, London/New York 1992, S. 10-39.
Ders., The Architecture of the Jumping Universe, London/New York 1997.
Mr. Jencks' Jumping Universe, Rundfunksendung der BBC, 11. Mai 1997.
Ders., Die Architektur des springenden Universums, in: Arch+, H. 141, 1998.
Ders., Post-Modernism and the Revenge of the Book, in: Rattenbury, Kester (Hg.), This is not architecture, London 2002, S. 174-197.
Ders., The New Paradigm in Architecture, London/New Haven 2002.
Ders., The New Paradigm in Architecture, in: The Architectural Review, H. 2/2003, S. 72-77.
Ders., The Garden of Cosmic Speculation, London/New York 2003.
Kipnis, Jeffrey, Towards a New Architecture, in: Architectural Design, H. 3/4/1993, S. 41-49.
Venturi, Robert, Komplexität und Widerspruch in der Architektur, Braunschweig/Wiesbaden 1978.
Ders., Denise Scott Brown, Steven Izenour: Lernen von Las Vegas. Zur Ikonographie und Architektursymbolik der Geschäftsstadt, Braunschweig/Wiesbaden 1979.

WOLFGANG WELSCH

WAS WAR DIE POSTMODERNE – UND WAS KÖNNTE AUS IHR WERDEN?

WHAT WAS POST-MODERNISM — AND WHAT MIGHT IT BECOME?

Die Frage, was die Postmoderne war, kann nicht allein aus dem Blick auf die Architektur beantwortet werden. Denn der architektonische Diskurs stellte weder den Anfang noch das Ende der Debatten, sondern nur ein – allerdings prominentes – Zwischenstück dar, und in ihm kam nur ein Teil der Argumente für oder gegen eine Revision bzw. Überwindung der Moderne zur Sprache.

KURZE GESCHICHTE DES TERMINUS »POSTMODERNE«

Nach sporadischen Verwendungen des Ausdrucks (die erste schon 1870) begann die Diskussion um die Postmoderne 1959 in der nordamerikanischen Literaturtheorie und -kritik.[1] Irving Howe konstatierte (und bald ist ihm Harry Levin darin gefolgt), dass die Literatur der Gegenwart im Vergleich mit der großen Literatur der Moderne (Yeats, Eliot, Pound, Joyce) weit weniger stark und innovatorisch sei; in diesem Sinn bezeichnete er sie als »post-modern«. Zehn Jahre später machte Leslie Fiedler (ähnlich auch Susan Sonntag) aus dieser Negativ- eine Positivdiagnose: Die zeitgenössische Literatur (Vian, Barth, Cohen, Mailer) ziele auf etwas anderes als die Klassische Moderne und besitze eigene Meriten. Fiedler sah diese vor allem in der neuartigen Verbindung von Elite- und Massenkultur. Er erklärte, »dass wir den Todeskampf der literarischen Moderne und die Geburtswehen der Post-Moderne durchleben. Die Spezies Literatur, die die Bezeichnung ›modern‹ für sich beansprucht hat (mit der Anmaßung, sie repräsentiere äußerste Fortgeschrittenheit in Sensibilität und Form und über sie hinaus sei ›Neuheit‹ nicht mehr möglich) und deren Siegeszug kurz vor dem Ersten Weltkrieg begann und kurz nach dem Zweiten endete, ist *tot*, das heißt, sie gehört der Geschichte an, nicht der Wirklichkeit.«[2] Unter der Überschrift »Cross the Border – Close the Gap« plädierte Fiedler für eine Verbindung von High und Low, Extravaganz und Trivialität, Mythos und Wirklichkeit, Traumwelt und Maschinenwelt. Den postmodernen Schriftsteller definierte er als »Doppelagenten«[3]: »gleichermaßen zu Hause in der Welt der Technologie und im Reich des Wunders«[4]. – Soziologisch wie semantisch ist also eine Doppelstruktur charakteristisch: die Verbindung von elitärem und populärem Geschmack bzw. von Fiktion und Wirklichkeit. Ein postmodernes Werk ist in sich plural, es erfüllt widersprüchliche Erwartungen.

1975 übertrug Charles Jencks den Begriff auf die Architektur.[5] Jencks war mit der nordamerikanischen Literaturdebatte vertraut, und sein architektonischer Postmoderne-Begriff stimmt mit dem literarischen Fiedlers überein. Er scheint geradezu mit Fiedlers Stift zu schreiben, wenn er erklärt: »Der Fehler der modernen Architektur war, dass sie sich an eine Elite richtete. Die Postmoderne versucht, den Anspruch des Elitären zu überwinden, nicht durch Aufgabe desselben, sondern durch Erweiterung der Sprache der Architektur in verschiedene Richtungen – zum Bodenständigen, zur Überlieferung und zum kommerziellen Jargon der Straße. Daher die Doppelkodierung, die Architektur, welche die Elite und den Mann auf der Straße anspricht.«[6] Das läuft auf »Cross the Border – Close the Gap« mittels Säule und Palmendekor hinaus; Jencks' »Doppelkodierer« sind die architektonischen Revenants von Fiedlers literarischen »Doppelagenten«. Ein postmoderner Bau muss Jencks zufolge mindes-

1 Umfassend habe ich die Geschichte des Ausdrucks »postmodern« dargestellt in: Wolfgang Welsch, Unsere postmoderne Moderne, Berlin[6] 2002, S. 9-43. Vgl. auch Wolfgang Welsch (Hg.), Wege aus der Moderne – Schlüsseltexte der Postmoderne-Diskussion, Berlin[2] 1994.

2 Leslie Fiedler, Cross the Border – Close the Gap, in: Playboy, Dez. 1969; dt. Überquert die Grenze, schließt den Graben!, in: Wege aus der Moderne, a.a.O., S. 57.

3 Ebd., S. 69.

4 Ebd., S. 73.

5 Jencks' seminaler Aufsatz war: The Rise of Post-Modern Architecture, in: Architecture – inner Town Government, Eindhoven 1975, sowie Architecture Association Quarterly, Nr. 4/1975. Zuvor

The question as to what Post-Modernism was cannot be answered solely from the point of view of architecture. Because the architectural discourse was neither the beginning nor the end of the debate but simply one—albeit prominent—interlude, and it articulated only some of the arguments for or against a move to revise or overcome Modernism.

A BRIEF HISTORY OF THE TERM "POST-MODERNISM"

Although the term had been used sporadically (the first time as early as 1870), the real discussion of Post-Modernism in North American literary theory and criticism began in 1959.[1] Irving Howe stated (and Harry Levin followed suit shortly afterwards) that contemporary literature was not nearly as strong and innovative as great Modernist literature (Yeats, Eliot, Pound, Joyce); it was in this sense that he called it "Post-Modern." Ten years later, Leslie Fiedler (and similarly Susan Sonntag) turned this negative diagnosis around and gave it a positive connotation: contemporary literature (Vian, Barth, Cohen, Mailer), he said, was aiming for something different from Classical Modernism and had its own merits. Fiedler saw this particularly in the new link between elite culture and mass culture. He declared that "we are living through the death throes of Modernism and the birth pangs of Post-Modernism. The kind of literature which had arrogated to itself the name 'Modern' (with the presumption that it represented the ultimate advance in sensibility and form, that beyond it newness was not possible), and whose moment of triumph lasted from a point just before World War I until one just after World War II, is dead, i.e., belongs to history not actuality."[2] Under the title *Cross the Border—Close the Gap*, Fiedler pleaded for a link between high and low, extravagance and triviality, myth and reality, dream world and machine world. He defined the Post-Modern writer as a "Double Agent"[3] who was "equally at home in the world of technology and the realm of wonder."[4] – Thus, both sociologically and semantically, there is a characteristic dual structure: the link between elite and popular taste, between fiction and reality. A Post-Modern work is in and of itself pluralistic; it fulfils contradictory expectations.

In 1975, Charles Jencks applied the term to architecture.[5] Jencks was familiar with the North American literary debate, and his concept of Post-Modernism in architecture concurs with Fiedler's literary concept. His sentiments echo those of Fiedler when he declares: "Modern architecture suffered from elitism. Post-Modernism is trying to get over that elitism not by dropping it, but rather by extending the language of architecture in many different ways—into the vernacular, towards tradition and the commercial slang of the street. Hence the double-coding, the architecture which speaks to the elite and the man on the street."[6]

This amounts to "crossing the border and closing the gap" with columns and decorative palms; Jencks' "double-coders" are the architectural reincarnations of Fiedler's literary "double agents." According to Jencks, a Post-Modern building must use at least two architectural languages simultaneously, such as traditional and modern, elite and popular, international and regional codes. Jencks saw the actual motor driving Post-Modern trends

1 I have described the history of the term "Post-Modern" in detail in: Wolfgang Welsch, Unsere postmoderne Moderne, Sixth Edition, Berlin 2002, pp. 9-43. See also Wolfgang Welsch (ed.), Wege aus der Moderne. Schlüsseltexte der Postmoderne-Diskussion, Second Edition, Berlin 1994.

2 Leslie Fiedler, Cross the Border – Close the Gap [first published in Playboy, Dec. 1969]; reprinted in: A Fiedler Reader, New York 1977, pp. 270-294, here p. 270.

3 Ibid., p. 288.

4 Ibid., p. 294.

5 Jencks' seminal essay was The Rise of Post-Modern Architecture, in: Architecture – Inner Town Government, Eindhoven 1975, and Architecture Association

tens zwei Architektursprachen gleichzeitig verwenden, etwa traditionelle und moderne, elitäre und populäre, internationale und regionale Codes. Jencks sah im tief reichenden Pluralismus der modernen Gesellschaften den eigentlichen Motor der postmodernen Tendenzen: »Die Diskontinuität der Geschmackskulturen ist es, die sowohl die theoretische Basis als auch die ›Doppelkodierung‹ der Postmoderne erzeugt.«[7]

1980 setzte Portoghesi mit der Ausstellung »Die Gegenwart der Vergangenheit« bei der Ersten Architektur-Biennale in Venedig einen anderen Akzent.[8] Moderne und Internationaler Stil haben Portoghesi zufolge ihr Monopol verloren, die Baugeschichte soll jetzt ins Zentrum architektonischen Denkens zurückkehren. Die Folge war, dass die architektonische Postmoderne fortan mit Antimodernismus, Traditionalismus und Neo-Historismus assoziiert werden konnte.

Heinrich Klotz störte sich an der Gleichsetzung von »Postmoderne« mit »populistischer Genussszene« sowie »Nostalgie-Historismus« und hat die Formel »nicht nur Funktion, sondern auch Fiktion«[9] vorgeschlagen. Das postmoderne Resultat sollten »nicht länger nur Funktionsbehälter und Konstruktionswunder, sondern Darstellungen von symbolhaften Gehalten und bildnerischen Themen«[10] sein. Klotz' Doppelformel »nicht nur Funktion, sondern auch Fiktion« bewegt sich ebenso wie Jencks' »Doppelkodierung« noch immer in Fiedlers Fahrwasser – schon dieser hatte für die Wiedereinführung der »Fiktion« plädiert.

Gemeinsamkeiten zwischen diesen unterschiedlichen Optionen sind offenkundig. Man wendet sich vom Alleingeltungsanspruch der modernen Architektur ab und verficht stattdessen Pluralität. Diese aber kann verschieden aufgefasst und in Szene gesetzt werden. Die einen meinen, nun sei alles erlaubt – der Weg zu Beliebigkeit und Potpourri stehe offen; dass auf diese Weise die Pluralität keineswegs bewahrt oder gar ausgedrückt, sondern durch Mischmasch und den Verzicht auf Wertzuweisung getilgt wird, wird oft zu spät erkannt. Andere hingegen wollen nur die Einbahnstraße in die Vergangenheit beschreiten. Eine dritte Richtung fordert mehr: dass in ein und demselben Bau *mehrere* Paradigmen zur Artikulation gelangen – aber nicht in einer Einheitssauce zur Unkenntlichkeit verrührt, sondern in ihrem Kontrast und Widerspruch vor Augen geführt. Der geheime Inspirator dieser Richtung scheint jemand zu sein, der sich selbst nie als »postmodern« bezeichnet hat: Robert Venturi, der 1966 für »Komplexität und Widerspruch in der Architektur« und damit für eine Architektur eintrat, »die von dem Reichtum und der Vieldeutigkeit moderner Lebenserfahrung zehrt«.[11] Seine damaligen Ideen stehen wie eine von fernher leitende Matrix hinter den postmodernen Tendenzen.

POSTMODERNE IN DER PHILOSOPHIE

Die philosophische Postmoderne-Diskussion setzte später als die literaturwissenschaftliche und architekturtheoretische ein und lief auf ein insgesamt anderes Bild hinaus. Maßstab setzend war Jean-François Lyotards *La Condition postmoderne* (dt. *Das postmoderne Wissen*) von 1979. Lyotard ging vom Unterschied modernen und postmodernen Wissens aus. Der moderne Wissensty-

hatte nur Joseph Hudnut den Terminus 1949 im Titel seines Aufsatzes »The postmodern house« verwendet (in: Architecture and the Spirit of Man, Cambridge 1949). Ferner fand sich der Terminus bei Nikolaus Pevsner (Architecture in Our Time. The Anti-Pioneers, in: The Listener, 29. Dez. 1966 u. 5. Jan. 1967).
6 Charles Jencks, Die Sprache der postmodernen Architektur. Die Entstehung einer alternativen Tradition [1977], Stuttgart 1980, S. 8.
7 Ebd., S. 6.
8 Vgl. auch das Begleitbuch Dopo l'architettura moderna [1980]; dt.: Ausklang der modernen Architektur, Zürich 1982.
9 Heinrich Klotz, Moderne und Postmoderne. Architektur der Gegenwart 1960-

as lying in the far-reaching pluralism of modern societies: "[I]t is this discontinuity in taste cultures which creates both the theoretical base and 'dual-coding' of Post-Modernism."[7]

In 1980, Portoghesi set a different accent at the First Architecture Biennale in Venice with the exhibition "The presence of the past."[8] According to Portoghesi, Modernism and the International Style had lost their monopoly and architectural thought should once more focus on architectural history. The consequence of this was that architectural Post-Modernism could from then on be associated with antimodernism, traditionalism and neo-historicism.

Heinrich Klotz took exception to "Post-Modernism" being equated with "populist taste" or "nostalgic historicism" and proposed the slogan "not just function, but also fiction."[9] The outcome of a Post-Modern approach should "no longer be just functional containers and miracles of structure but depictions of symbolic contents and artistic themes."[10] Klotz's double "not just function, but also fiction"—just like Jencks' "double coding"—is still following in Fiedler's wake—he too had pleaded for the reintroduction of "fiction."

The common ground shared by these different options is obvious: there is a move away from modern architecture's claim to universal validity and an emphasis instead on pluralism. However, pluralism can be interpreted and orchestrated in different ways. Some people believed that everything was now permitted—the way is open to potpourri and anything goes; the fact that pluralism is not preserved nor even expressed in this way, but is actually wiped out by hotchpotch and generations of indifference, is recognised by many too late. Others, by contrast, only want to recognise the one-way street that leads to the past. A third direction requires still more: that in one and the same building several paradigms are articulated—and not mixed together, so that none can be recognised but clearly displayed with all their contrasts and contradictions. The secret inspiration seems to be someone who never classified himself as Post-Modern: Robert Venturi, who in 1966 advocated "complexity and contradiction in architecture," thus an architecture, "based on the richness and ambiguity of modern experience."[11] His ideas from this time stand behind Post-Modernist trends like a remote guiding matrix.

POST-MODERNISM IN PHILOSOPHY

Post-Modernism in the philosophical discussion began later than in literary and architectural theory and centred around a completely different image. The seminal work was Jean-François Lyotard's *La Condition postmoderne* of 1979. Lyotard's starting point was the difference between Modern and Post-Modern knowledge. The modern type of knowledge aimed at "meta-narrative," i.e. at an overall idea that should embrace all individual knowledge and have a political and social aim; the principle example of this is the Enlightenment's model of emancipation. This modern expectation has since lost credibility: "Simplifying to the extreme, I define Post-Modern as incredulity toward metanarratives."[12] However, this change does not result from a diffuse atmosphere, but from a change in knowledge

Quarterly, no. 4, 1975. The only person to have used the term before that was Joseph Hudnut in 1949 in the title of his article The Post-Modern house, in: Architecture and the Spirit of Man, Cambridge 1949. The term was also used by Nikolaus Pevsner: Architecture in Our Time. The Anti-Pioneers, in: The Listener, 29 Dec. 1966 and 5 Jan. 1967.
6 Charles Jencks, The Language of Modern Architecture, London 1977, p. 8.
7 Ibid., p. 6.
8 Cf. also the book that accompanied the exhibition: Dopo l'architettura moderna, Rome 1980.
9 Heinrich Klotz, Moderne und Postmoderne. Architektur der Gegenwart 1960-1980, Braunschweig/Wiesbaden 1984, pp. 16

pus zielt auf eine »Meta-Erzählung«, d.h. auf eine Gesamtidee, welche sämtliches Einzelwissen umfassen und auf ein politisches und soziales Ziel ausrichten soll; Hauptbeispiel ist das Emanzipationsmodell der Aufklärung. Diese moderne Erwartung ist inzwischen unglaubwürdig geworden: »In äußerster Vereinfachung kann man sagen: ›Postmoderne‹ bedeutet, dass man den Meta-Erzählungen keinen Glauben mehr schenkt.«[12] Diese Umstellung resultiert aber nicht aus einer diffusen Stimmungslage, sondern aus dem Wandel des Wissens, wie ihn grundlegende Revisionen seit Beginn des 20. Jahrhunderts bewirkt haben, die mit Namen wie Heisenberg, Einstein und Gödel verbunden sind. Diesen neuen Wissenstypus des zwanzigsten Jahrhunderts, der nicht mehr auf Einheit, sondern auf Pluralität, Komplementarität und Unausschöpfbarkeit setzt, bezeichnet Lyotard als postmodern. Es geht also nicht um ein Abrücken von Errungenschaften des 20. Jahrhunderts, sondern um deren Realisierung. Lyotard zufolge zielten auch die künstlerischen Avantgarden des frühen 20. Jahrhunderts auf die Sprengung der altmodernen Totalitätshoffnungen: »Was seit einem Jahrhundert in der Malerei oder in der Musik geschehen ist, antizipiert gewissermaßen die Postmoderne, die ich meine.«[13] Philosophisch gesehen, kongruiert die Postmoderne also mit den Innovationen der wissenschaftlichen und künstlerischen Avantgarden des 20. Jahrhunderts.

Der postmoderne »Gemüts- oder Geisteszustand«[14] – der nicht mehr Einheitsobsessionen folgt, sondern sich dem irreduziblen Widerstreit der vielen Sprach-, Denk- und Lebensformen stellt – ist auch vor der Moderne und inmitten ihrer schon möglich gewesen. Aristoteles und Diderot sind Beispiele dafür. Lyotard befreit die Auffassung der Postmoderne von dem noch immer dem Innovationsgestus der Moderne folgenden (und insofern ganz modernistisch bleibenden) gängigen Verständnis derselben als einer neuen Epoche oder der neuesten Mode (»ab 1970« oder dergleichen).[15]

Aber nicht nur seiner zeitlichen Konturierung nach (Kongruenz mit den Avantgarden des 20. Jahrhunderts, Einstellungs- statt Epochenbegriff) unterscheidet sich das philosophische Postmoderne-Verständnis vom sonst verbreiteten, sondern es führt auch zu einer einschneidenden Kritik an den im Architekturdiskurs gängigen Kennzeichen der Postmoderne: Beliebigkeit, Relativismus, Eklektizismus, Nostalgie, Indifferenz, Bonbonstil. Kaum jemand dürfte diese Phänomene schärfer gegeißelt haben als Lyotard: Sie bedienen ihm zufolge nur »die Gewohnheiten des Illustriertenlesers« und befördern »den Geist des Supermarkt-Kunden«.[16] Gegenüber diesem konsumistischen und diffusen Postmodernismus[17] hat Lyotard für eine »achtenswerte Postmoderne«[18] plädiert, welche die unterschiedlichen Sprach-, Denk- und Lebensformen nicht bis zur Unkenntlichkeit verrührt, sondern in ihrer Heterogenität wahrt und insgesamt einer Perspektive der Gerechtigkeit verpflichtet ist.[19] Dieser philosophische Postmodernismus vertritt das Gegenteil von flotter Beliebigkeit und zynischer Ellbogenlizenz – das Gegenteil der Klischees, die den Blätterwald durchziehen. Die feuilletonistische Diskussion ist (nicht nur in Deutschland) weit unter dem Niveau des philosophischen Begriffs von Postmoderne geblieben.

brought about by a fundamentally new way of thinking since the beginning of the 20th century, associated with names such as Heisenberg, Einstein and Gödel. Lyotard labelled this new type of knowledge of the twentieth century—which no longer stresses unity, but pluralism, complementarity and inexhaustible potential—Post-Modern. It is thus not about disassociation from the achievements of the 20th century but about their realisation. According to Lyotard, the artistic avant-garde movements of the early 20th century were aiming to blow apart old-Modernism's hopes for totality: "What has been happening in painting or music for a century now anticipates to some extent the Post-Modernism I mean."[13] From a philosophical point of view, Post-Modernism is thus congruent with the innovations of the scientific and artistic avant-gardes of the 20th century.

The Post-Modernist "psychological or intellectual condition" as Lyotard calls it[14]—which is no longer obsessed with unity, but engages with the irreducible conflict between the many forms of language, thought and life—was always possible, both before and in the midst of the Modern Movement. Aristotle and Diderot are examples of this. Lyotard liberates Post-Modernism from the common understanding of it as a new epoch or the latest fashion ("from 1970," say) that still followed Modernism's innovative gesture (and thus remained rooted in Modernism).[15]

But the philosophical understanding of Post-Modernism differs not only in its temporal contours from the term as it is commonly used (congruence with the 20th century avant-gardes and with an attitude—rather than epoch-related definition), it also leads to a scathing criticism of the labels commonly used in the architectural discourse on Post-Modernism: an anything-goes approach, relativism, eclecticism, nostalgia, indifference, candy style. No-one can have censured these phenomena more acutely than Lyotard: in his opinion they serve only "the habits of the tabloid reader" and promote "the spirit of the supermarket shopper."[16] As a response to this consumer-oriented and diffuse Post-Modernism,[17] Lyotard pleaded for a "worthy Post-Modernism,"[18] which does not mix the different forms of living, thinking and speaking together until they are no longer recognisable, but preserves their heterogeneity and has an overall commitment to a perspective of equity.[19] This philosophical Post-Modernism represents the very opposite of a carefree anything-goes attitude and a cynical dog-eat-dog mentality—the opposite of all the clichés propagated by the tabloids. The discussion in the Sunday supplements remained (not only in Germany) way beneath the level of the philosophical concept of Post-Modernism.

With Lyotard too there is a veiled congruence with Venturi's approach, both in the starting point (complexity or pluralism and contradiction or conflict) and in the final form: Venturi had spoken of an "obligation to the whole"[20] and stressed that it "must embody the difficult unity of inclusion rather than the easy unity of exclusion," in other words it is a "difficult whole [that] includes multiplicity and diversity of elements in relationships that are inconsistent" and also does not preclude the unresolved. Lyotard's advocacy of plurality and incommensurability as well as justice within conflict is clearly close to this.

With hindsight, it seems appropriate to differentiate between two versions of Post-Modernism: one that takes pluralism

1980, Braunschweig/Wiesbaden 1984, S. 16 bzw. S. 423. Vgl. die im selben Jahr von Klotz konzipierte Eröffnungsausstellung des Deutschen Architekturmuseums »Die Revision der Moderne: Postmoderne Architektur 1960-1980« (Katalog Braunschweig/Wiesbaden 1984).

10 Ebd., S. 17.

11 Robert Venturi, Komplexität und Widerspruch in der Architektur [1966], hrsg. v. Heinrich Klotz, Braunschweig/Wiesbaden 1978, S. 23.

12 Jean-François Lyotard, La Condition postmoderne. Rapport sur le savoir, Paris 1979, S. 7.

13 Jean-François Lyotard u.a., Immaterialität und Postmoderne, Berlin 1985, S. 38.

14 Jean-François Lyotard, Philosophie

and 423. Published in English as: The history of postmodern architecture, translated by Radka Donnell, Cambridge/Mass./London 1988; Cf. the Deutsches Architekturmuseum's opening exhibition in the same year curated by Klotz "Die Revision der Moderne: Postmoderne Architektur 1960-1980," catalogue Braunschweig/Wiesbaden 1984.

10 Ibid., p. 17.

11 Robert Venturi, Complexity and contradiction in architecture, New York 1977, p. 23.

12 Jean-François Lyotard, The postmodern condition: a report on knowledge, Manchester 1984, p. xxiv.

13 Jean-François Lyotard et al., Immaterialität und Postmoderne, Berlin 1985, p. 38.

Auch bei Lyotard besteht eine untergründige Kongruenz mit Venturis Ansatz. Sie betrifft den Ausgangspunkt (Komplexität bzw. Pluralität und Widerspruch bzw. Widerstreit) und ebenso die Endgestalt: Venturi hatte von der »Verpflichtung für das Ganze« gesprochen und betont, dass es nicht um eine »Elimination des Mannigfachen«, sondern um »Einheit im Mannigfachen« gehen müsse, also um ein »prekäres Ganzes«, das mit einer »inkonsistenten« Beziehung der Glieder zu rechnen bereit ist und auch das »Ungelöste« nicht ausschließt.[20] Dem ist Lyotards Eintreten für Pluralität und Inkommensurabilität sowie für Gerechtigkeit im Widerstreit ersichtlich nahe.

Rückblickend bleibt die Unterscheidung zwischen zwei Versionen von Postmoderne anzuraten: zwischen einer, welche die Pluralität ernst nimmt, und einer anderen, die sie verspielt. Im öffentlichen Disput hat die letztere bzw. der Angriff auf sie dominiert. Was jedoch Standards heutiger Selbstverständigung angeht, hat die erstere (für die Venturis Leitworte »Komplexität« und »Widerspruch« paradigmatisch sind) gesiegt.

Das ist gerade an der Weise zu erkennen, wie die Apologeten der Moderne, welche die Postmoderne einst so vehement bekämpft hatten, heute ihre geliebte Moderne beschreiben. Sie tun es just mit postmodernen Kategorien. So hat bereits 1989 eine Sammelbesprechung neuerer Monographien zur Architektur der Moderne als deren Generaltendenz vermerkt: »Historiker des modernen Bauens entdecken Vielfalt und Widerspruch«[21]. Vielfalt und Widerspruch sollten den neueren Veröffentlichungen zufolge auf einmal die Essenz der Moderne ausdrücken. 1966, als Venturi diese Kategorien als Leitvokabeln eines anderen Bauens propagierte, hatte man ob dieses Verrats an der Moderne laut aufgeschrien. Gut zwanzig Jahre später erklärt man Venturis Kategorien zu Herzformeln schon der guten alten Moderne. So schnell hat sich die postmoderne Sichtweise in der Sache durchgesetzt. – Das gilt auch über die Architektur hinaus. Postmoderne Auffassungen sind zu selbstverständlichen Standards des zeitgenössischen Bewusstseins geworden.

AUSBLICK

Die Postmoderne war eine Erscheinungsform der Moderne. Zwar hatte sie sich von manchen Auflagen der Moderne befreit (in der Architektur exemplarisch von denen des Internationalen Stils), aber anderen Geboten folgte sie weiterhin getreulich: Die Potpourri-Version gab sich demokratisch, indem sie die konsumistisch-inszenatorischen Bedürfnisse der Erlebnisgesellschaft bediente, und die strenge Version berief sich auf die Maßstab setzenden Errungenschaften der wissenschaftlichen und künstlerischen Avantgarden des 20. Jahrhunderts. In beiden Fällen distanzierte man sich nur von dieser oder jener Ausprägung der Moderne, um stattdessen eine andere zu favorisieren. Von einer Verabschiedung der Moderne als solcher konnte keine Rede sein. Die Postmoderne blieb eine Spielart der Moderne.

Was aber zeichnet sich heute, nachdem wir die postmodernen Befreiungsexperimente und Lockerungsübungen absolviert haben, als künftige Tendenz ab? Kristallisiert sich ein neues Paradigma heraus, das sich von der Grundhaltung der Moderne entschiedener absetzt, als die Postmoderne es je tat?

seriously and the other that simply plays with it. In the public debate, the latter, or an attack on the latter, has dominated. However, in terms of contemporary self-understanding, the former (for which Venturi's keywords "complexity" and "contradiction" are emblematic) has won the day.

That can be seen in the way the apologists of Modernism, who once fought so vehemently against Post-Modernism, now describe their beloved Modernism: namely, using precisely the categories of Post-Modernism. For example, back in 1989, a review of recent monographs on the architecture of Modernism noted their general tendency as follows: "Historians of Modern architecture have discovered diversity and contradiction."[21] Suddenly, according to these recent publications, diversity and contradiction allegedly express the essence of Modernism. In 1966, when Venturi propagated these categories as axioms for a new kind of architecture, there were loud cries of indignation about this betrayal of Modernism. A good twenty years later and Venturi's categories are declared to be the cherished slogans of good old Modernism. That is how quickly the Post-Modernist view has established itself. That is also true beyond architecture: Post-Modernist attitudes are now an unquestioned part of contemporary consciousness.

PROSPECTS FOR THE FUTURE

Post-Modernism was one manifestation of Modernism. Although it freed itself from some of the constraints of Modernism (in architecture from those imposed by the International Style, for example), it nevertheless remained true to other precepts: the potpourri version liked to appear to be democratic by serving the ostentatious consumer needs of a society hungry for mass experience, while the more severe version sought its legitimacy in the seminal achievements of the scientific and artistic avant-gardes of the 20th century. In each case, they distanced themselves from only one variety of Modernism, instead leaning manifestly towards the other. There was no question of a departure from Modernism as such. Post-Modernism remained a variation on Modernism.

But what is emerging today as a trend for the future, now that we have finished with Post-Modernist liberation experiments and warm-up exercises? Is a new paradigm beginning to crystallize, which will distance itself more distinctly from Modernism's fundamental principles than Post-Modernism ever did?

What were Modernism's fundamental principles? They consisted in basing everything on human beings and relating everything back to human beings. Diderot formulated it thus in 1755: "Man is the only term of reference from which everything must begin and lead back to."[22] Evidently, he thought that it was the existence of mankind that made the existence of all other things interesting: without man, the "drama of nature is reduced to a sad and silent scene;" it only gains sense and meaning through man; he is to be seen as the "centre" of everything.[23]

This way of thinking became more firmly established through Kant's epistemic theory. According to Kant, we can only relate to objects that have already been determined a priori by our forms of cognition. Consequently, we are surrounded by

und Malerei im Zeitalter ihres Experimentierens, Berlin 1986, S. 97.
15 Ähnliche Argumente hat Gianni Vattimo vorgebracht: Das Ende der Moderne [1985], Stuttgart 1990.
16 Lyotard, Immaterialität und Postmoderne, a.a.O., S. 100. Vgl. ebd. S. 30 u. S. 38.
17 Allein auf diesen beziehen sich die Postmoderne-Diagnosen des Soziologen Jean Baudrillard.
18 Jean-François Lyotard, Der Widerstreit [1983], München 1987, S. 12.
19 Hinzu kommt das für Lyotard so wichtige Thema des »Undarstellbaren«. Es findet sich ähnlich bei Derrida und ist in dessen Diskussionen mit Architekten wie Eisenman oder Tschumi wichtig geworden.

14 Cf. Jean-François Lyotard, Philosophie und Malerei im Zeitalter ihres Experimentierens, Berlin 1986, p. 97.
15 Gianni Vattimo put forward similar arguments in: The end of modernity, Baltimore 1988.
16 Lyotard, Immaterialität und Postmoderne, op. cit., p. 100. Cf. ibid., p. 30 and p. 38.
17 The diagnoses of Post-Modernism by sociologist Jean Baudrillard refer only to this.
18 Jean-François Lyotard, Der Widerstreit, Munich 1987, p. 12.
19 Added to that is the theme of "that which cannot be depicted" which is so important to Lyotard. Derrida explores it in a similar way and it has gained

1

1 Tadao Ando: Kirche auf dem Wasser/Church on the Water, Hokkaido (Japan), 1988

2

2 Ieoh Ming Pei: Miho Museum, Shiga (Japan), 1997

3

3 Charles Jencks, Maggie Keswick: Garden of Cosmic Speculation, Dumfriesshire (GB)

Was war die Grundhaltung der Moderne? Sie bestand darin, in allem vom Menschen auszugehen und alles auf den Menschen zurückzubeziehen. Diderot hatte es 1755 formuliert: »Der Mensch ist der einzigartige Begriff, von dem man ausgehen und auf den man alles zurückführen muss.«[22] Offenbar sei es das Dasein des Menschen, welches die Existenz der anderen Dinge überhaupt erst interessant mache: Ohne den Menschen wäre das »Schauspiel der Natur nur eine traurige und stumme Szene«; erst der Mensch verleiht ihm Sinn und Bedeutung; er ist als der »Mittelpunkt« von allem anzusehen.[23]

Diese Denkweise wurde durch Kants epistemische Wende für die Folgezeit befestigt. Kant zufolge können wir uns immer nur auf Gegenstände beziehen, die a priori schon durch unsere Erkenntnisformen bestimmt sind. Folglich begegnen wir allenthalben mensch-geprägten Erscheinungen. Die Welt ist im Grunde ein gigantisches Humantheater. Letztlich haben wir es immer nur mit uns selbst zu tun. Das ist das grundlegende Axiom der modernen Denkweise. Noch die zeitgenössischen Konstruktivismen und Relativismen, die gegenwärtigen Human- und Kulturwissenschaften folgen ihm. Der Mensch gilt – mal mehr, mal weniger ausdrücklich – als das Maß der Welt.

Auch die moderne Architektur wollte dieser Maxime in ihrem Bereich zum Durchbruch verhelfen. Le Corbusier erklärte wiederholt, dass es im Unterschied zur älteren Architektur darauf ankomme, die Architektur als »ein rein menschliches Programm« aufzufassen, »das den Menschen wieder zum Mittelpunkt der baulichen Aufgabe macht« und alles nach »menschlichem Maßstab« einrichtet.[24]

Und gegen diese Grundmaxime der Moderne ist auch die postmoderne Architektur nicht angegangen, sie hat sie vielmehr ungebrochen fortgeführt. Ob man Hightech oder Poetik bevorzug-

phenomena that are determined by mankind. The world is basically a gigantic human theatre. Ultimately, we are only ever relating to ourselves. That is the fundamental axiom of the modern way of thinking. Even contemporary forms of constructivism and relativism follow it; the contemporary arts and humanities follow it. Mankind is considered to be the measure of all things—sometimes more, sometimes less explicitly.

Modernist architecture also sought to help this maxim achieve a breakthrough in its field. Le Corbusier repeatedly declared that by contrast with architecture from the past, architecture should now be understood as "[a] profoundly humanistic program [that] restores man to the central preoccupation of architecture" and that organises everything on "a human scale."[24]

And even Post-Modernist architecture did nothing to contest this fundamental maxim of Modernism; on the contrary, it continued it without a break. Whether you preferred hi-tech or the poetic—time and again, the legitimating formula was that it was a question of designing the world, the city, or the building "for people."

Today, however, signs of a radical revision are beginning to appear on the horizon, a revision that goes to the most profound premise of Modernism's human-centred view. This was based on the assumption that humans and the world were quite different kinds of being (res cogitans versus res extensa), that we humans in principle embody a quite different order from that of the world and that therefore all our attempts to forge links with the world are based only on our way of being and can only lead to a world that reflects human nature. Today, a change of paradigm is developing in contrast to the Modernist assumption that people are genuinely alienated from the world ("the individual

20 Venturi, Komplexität und Widerspruch in der Architektur, a.a.O., S. 24, 161, 136, 158.
21 Mathias Schreiber, Vom Programm zur Poesie. Historiker des modernen Bauens entdecken Vielfalt und Widerspruch, in: FAZ, Literatur, 16. September 1989.
22 Denis Diderot, Artikel »Enzyklopädie« [1755], in: Enzyklopädie. Philosophische und politische Texte aus der »Encyclopédie« sowie Prospekt und Ankündigung der letzten Bände, München 1969, S. 79-175, hier S. 121.
23 Ebd., S. 120.
24 Le Corbusier, An die Studenten der Bauhochschulen [1957], in: ders., An die Studenten – Die »Charte d'Athènes« [1957], Reinbek 1962, S. 7-52, hier S. 19,

importance in his discussions with architects such as Eisenman or Tschumi.
20 Venturi, Complexity and contradiction architecture, op. cit., p. 16, 21, 88.
21 Mathias Schreiber, Vom Programm zur Poesie. Historiker des modernen Bauens entdecken Vielfalt und Widerspruch, Frankfurter Allgemeine Zeitung, literature section, 16 September 1989.
22 Denis Diderot, article entitled "Enzyklopädie" [1755], in: Enzyklopädie. Philosophische und politische Texte aus der 'Encyclopédie' sowie Prospekt und Ankündigung der letzten Bände, Munich 1969, pp. 79-175, here p. 121.
23 Ibid., p. 120.
24 Le Corbusier, Le Corbusier talks with students from the schools of architecture,

te – immer lautete die legitimatorische Formel, dass es um eine Gestaltung der Welt, der Stadt, des Gebäudes »für die Menschen« gehe.

Heute aber scheint eine Revision stattzufinden, die an die Wurzel geht. Sie betrifft noch die tiefste Prämisse der menschzentrierten Auffassung der Moderne. Diese hatte auf der Annahme beruht, dass Mensch und Welt von ganz unterschiedlicher Seinsart seien (*res cogitans* versus *res extensa*), dass wir Menschen im Grunde eine andere Ordnung als die der Welt verkörpern und dass deshalb all unsere Brückenschläge zur Welt nur nach unserer Art erfolgen und nur zu einer Welt nach Menschenart führen können. Heute deutet sich gegenüber dieser modernen Annahme einer genuinen Weltfremdheit des Menschen (»der Mensch gegen den Rest der Welt«) ein Paradigmenwechsel an. Das Bewusstsein einer grundsätzlichen Verbundenheit des Menschen mit der Welt bricht sich Bahn.

Die wesentlichen Anstöße dazu kommen von Evolutionstheorie, Hirnforschung und Künstlicher Intelligenz. Sie gebieten eine radikale Revision der alten, auf Exklusivität und Zentralität des Menschen setzenden Anthropologie. Heute sehen wir, dass wir Menschen von weiter herkommen als vom Menschen und dass evolutionäre und prähumane Einschreibungen uns zum größten Teil ausmachen – noch unsere kulturellen Leistungen basieren auf ihnen.

Dadurch entzieht die neue Anthropologie jedem Anthropozentrismus den Boden. Sie sprengt den anthropozentrischen Kokon der Moderne. Das alte Bild einer Mensch-Welt-Opposition wird von dem neuen einer grundlegenden Weltzugehörigkeit des Menschen abgelöst. Nicht *homo humanus*, sondern *homo mundanus* ist die zutreffende Bestimmung des Menschen.[25]

Für das Denken und Planen in Sachen Architektur und Stadt ergeben sich daraus grundsätzliche Umstellungen. Wir sollten nicht zuerst von uns selbst und unseren Bedürfnissen ausgehen, sondern von dem, was uns umgibt und dem wir zugehören. Indem wir von anderem als Menschlichem abhängen, gilt es dieser Verbundenheit mit der Welt Rechnung zu tragen, damit wir uns als Menschen gut befinden können. Die Stadt sollte nicht als ausschließlich humaner Raum konzipiert werden – nur dann wird sie die menschliche Existenz in all ihren Dimensionen zu entfalten erlauben.

Wir sollten, kurz gesagt, nicht von innen nach außen, sondern von außen nach innen denken und planen. Transhumane Aspekte sollten nicht erst nachträglich zur Geltung gebracht werden, sondern von vornherein die Form der Architektur mitbestimmen.[26] Der planerische und gestalterische Blick sollte sich nicht zuerst und ausschließlich auf ein zu errichtendes Objekt richten, sondern dieses primär als etwas in seiner Umgebung, als Element in einem größeren Kontext sehen: als eine Modulation des Feldes, in dem es ein Faktor sein wird. (So wie ein jedes Stück Natur vom weiten Umfeld der Natur her seine Form und Eigenart gewinnt.)

In dieser Hinsicht scheint mir das Verfahren mancher japanischer Architekten vorbildlich. Wenn sie ein Gebäude konzipieren, fangen sie nicht damit an, sich auf den Bau zu konzentrieren, sondern sie denken zuallererst an die Umgebung: an die Landschaft, an den Fluss von Energien, an das Klima, den Wind,

against the rest of the world"). The consciousness that human beings are fundamentally connected with the world is making headway.

The major impetus for this is coming from evolutionary theory, brain research and artificial intelligence. These disciplines demand a radical revision of the traditional kind of anthropology that is based on the exclusivity and centrality of human beings. Today we realise that we come from much farther back than from mankind and that evolutionary and pre-human influences play a major part in making us what we are—even our cultural achievements are based on them.

With this, contemporary anthropology knocks the bottom out of any form of anthropocentrism. It shatters Modernism's anthropocentric cocoon. The old image of a man-world opposition is replaced by a new one in which humankind is fundamentally part of the world. Not homo humanus, but homo mundanus is the appropriate definition of human beings.[25]

This necessitates fundamental adjustments in the way we think about and plan architecture and the city. Our starting point should not be ourselves and our needs but that which surrounds us and that which we are part of. Since we are dependent on factors that are not exclusively to do with human beings, we must do justice to this connectedness with the world, so that we as human beings can feel good. The city should no longer be designed as an exclusively human space—only then will it allow human existence to develop in all its dimensions.

In brief, we should think and plan not from the inside outwards but from the outside inwards. Transhuman aspects should not be brought to bear as an afterthought, but should play a part in determining architectural form from the outset.[26] Planners and designers should not direct their attention initially and exclusively to the building they intend to construct but see it primarily as a part of its surroundings, an element in a larger context: as a modulation of the field in which it will be a factor. (Just as each piece of nature acquires its form and its peculiarities from the broader context of nature.)

In this respect, I find the approach of a number of Japanese architects exemplary. When they design a building, they do not begin by concentrating on the building itself. Instead, they think first of all about the surroundings: about the landscape, the flow of energies, the climate, the wind, the natural processes, about colours and elements—and about time. They look first at the conditions of the external, natural and also the cultural environment. They design the building from the outside rather from the inside and make it interact with that which is not the building. There are no fixed boundaries between outside and inside: outside is inside and inside is outside.

The position Charles Jencks has recently adopted is interes-ting here. He talks of "new paradigms in architecture" and sees the common link between them as being the "idea of a new urban order [...] that is based more closely on what nature shows us with its eternally changing manifestations."[27] Jencks pleads for a "new world view that sees nature and culture as equally rooted in the history of the universe."[28] Architects " are venturing cautiously into a world of organic or cosmic images that interprets cities as landscapes."[29]

bzw. Le Corbusiers »Charta von Athen« [1933]. Kritische Neuausgabe, hrsg. von Thilo Hilpert, Braunschweig/Wiesbaden 1984, S. 162 [§ 87].

25 Ich habe diese Perspektive erstmals 2001 beim XVth International Congress of Aesthetics in Tokyo-Makuhari entfaltet (Art Transcending the Human Pale – Towards a Transhuman Stance, International Yearbook of Aesthetics, Bd. 5, 2001, S. 3-23). (vgl. Ken-ichi Sasaki, Preface, ebd., III f.). Ausführlich werde ich meine Überlegungen in Jenseits der Anthropozentrik der Moderne präsentieren (2004).

26 Vgl. Wolfgang Welsch, Orte des Menschen?, in: Baukultur in Deutschland, hrsg. v. Bundesministerium für Verkehr, Bau- und Wohnungswesen, Berlin 2002,

New York 1999, p. 26.

24 Le Corbusier, The Athens Charter, New York 1973, § 87.

25 I developed this perspective for the first time in 2001 at the "XVth International Congress of Aesthetics" in Tokyo-Makuhari (Art Transcending the Human Pale – Towards a Transhuman Stance, in: International Yearbook of Aesthetics, vol. 5, 2001, pp. 3-23. I shall present my thoughts in detail in: Jenseits der Anthropozentrik der Moderne (2004).

26 Cf. Wolfgang Welsch, Orte des Menschen?, in: Baukultur in Deutschland. Documentation of a congress in Cologne, 3-5 December 2001, published by Bundesministerium für Verkehr, Bau- und Wohnungswesen, Berlin 2002, pp. 23-37.

die natürlichen Prozesse, an Farben und Elemente – und die Zeit. Sie nehmen zuerst das Außerhalb in den Blick, die natürlichen, aber auch die kulturellen Umweltgegebenheiten. Sie konzipieren das Gebäude eher von außen als von innen und gestalten es so, dass es mit dem, was nicht das Gebäude ist, interagiert. Es gibt keine feste Grenze zwischen Außen und Innen: Außen ist Innen und Innen ist Außen.

Aufschlussreich ist Charles Jencks' neuere Position. Er spricht von »neuen Paradigmen der Architektur« und sieht deren Gemeinsamkeit in der »Vorstellung von einer neuen städtischen Ordnung [...], die sich enger an das anlehnt, was uns die Natur mit ihren ewig wechselnden Erscheinungsformen vormacht«[27]. Jencks plädiert für »eine neue Weltanschauung, die Natur und Kultur gleichermaßen in der Geschichte des Universums verwurzelt sieht«[28]. Die Architekten »tasten sich in eine organische oder kosmische Bilderwelt vor, die die Städte als Landschaften interpretiert«[29].

Schon im 20. Jahrhundert hatte es, seit Frank Lloyd Wright, verschiedentlich Ansätze zu einer organischen Architektur gegeben. Auch Le Corbusier schlug zeitweise diesen Weg ein. Nur hat bei ihm letztlich der technologische Aspekt den organischen wieder aufgesogen; sein Lobpreis der Muscheln oder Wolken mündete schließlich doch in den des Flugzeugs.[30] Wenn seit kurzem wieder biomorphe Architekturvorstellungen Platz greifen, so kann man erneut ein solches Abgleiten feststellen (die Dominanz des Digital-Technologischen dementiert oftmals geradezu die organische Intention), aber diese Tendenzen sind doch ein Indiz dafür, dass viele nach einer Gestaltungsweise suchen, die unserem biologischen, motorischen und sensorischen In-der-Welt-Sein besser Rechnung trägt, als die dezidiert rationalistische Architektur dies je vermochte, die unsere Körperlichkeit und die damit verbundene Weltlichkeit bloß als *wetware* ansah und gering schätzte.[31]

Vielleicht sind wir auf dem Weg zu einer Architektur, die unser Sein in einer nicht einfachhin menschlich bestimmten Welt zur Geltung bringt. Für sie wären Kriterien wie Atmen-Können und Atmosphäre, Weite und Komplexität Leitkategorien. Das wahrhaft menschliche Maß ist nicht die Wohnschachtel, sondern die Welt.[32]

Man überwindet den Anthropozentrismus nicht, indem man den Menschen einfach hinter sich lässt und auf etwas anderes setzt, sondern indem man ein anderes Selbstverständnis entwikkelt, in dem der Mensch nicht mehr die erste Geige spielt, oder besser: in dem die erste Geige nicht schon für das ganze Orchester gehalten wird; wo vielmehr auch solches, was nicht der Mensch ist, zum Klingen kommt und zur Geltung gebracht wird.

Eine solche Veränderung würde über eine Fortschreibung oder Erneuerung der modernen Programmatik (etwa im Sinn einer »zweiten Moderne«) ebenso hinausgehen wie über die Revision, welche die Postmoderne ins Auge gefasst hatte. Die eigentliche »Revision der Moderne« dürfte uns erst noch bevorstehen. Die Postmoderne wird für den Weg dorthin ihre Verdienste gehabt haben; aber betreten hat sie das neue Terrain noch nicht.

Back in the 20th century, since Frank Lloyd Wright, there had been a number of different attempts at organic architecture. Le Corbusier also went down this road for a while. In his case, however, the fascination with technology soon absorbed the organic; his eulogy to shells or clouds ended ultimately in his veneration of the aeroplane.[30] Although biomorphic ideas of architecture have now begun to establish themselves, a new tendency to drift off in that way can also be noted (often the dominance of digital technology positively denies the organic intention). Nevertheless, these trends are an indication of the fact that many people are seeking a design approach that takes our biological, motor and sensory being-in-the-world better into account than the decidedly rationalist architecture which saw our physicality, and consequently our worldliness, as mere wetware and thus placed little value on it.[31]

Perhaps we are moving towards an architecture that will validate our being in a world that is not simply determined by humans. It would be guided by criteria such as atmosphere and space to breathe, by a sense of expanse and complexity. The truly human scale is not the proverbial "little box," but the world.[32]

It is not possible to overcome anthropocentrism by simply abandoning humankind and pinning our hopes on something else. Rather, we must develop a different understanding of ourselves in which we humans do not always play first fiddle, or rather, where the first fiddle is not mistaken for the entire orchestra, where those things that are not humankind have an opportunity to make themselves heard and be validated.

A change of this kind would go beyond a continuation or revamp of the programme of Modernism (for instance in the sense of a "Second Modernism") and beyond the revision that Post-Modernism had contemplated. A "Revision of Modernism" proper is probably still ahead of us. Post-Modernism will prove to have had its merits in taking us a step closer, but it has not yet broken new ground.

S. 23-37.
27 Charles Jencks, State of the Art, StadtBauwelt, 94. Jahrgang (2003), Heft 24, S. 36-41, hier S. 36.
28 Ebd., S. 37.
29 Ebd. Jencks weist vor allem auf Gehry hin. – Auch Portoghesi hat ähnliche Ansichten wie Jencks entwickelt.
30 Vgl. Le Corbusier, An die Studenten der Bauhochschulen, a.a.O., S. 42-44.
31 Auch das »ökologische Bauen« ist auf einem ähnlichen Weg, neigt aber oft dazu, Natur allzu humanistisch-funktionalistisch zu behandeln.
32 Vgl. Wolfgang Welsch, Räume bilden Menschen, in: Raumstationen, hrsg. von Egon Schirmbeck, Regensburg 2001, S. 12-24.

27 Charles Jencks, "State of the Art," in: StadtBauwelt, vol. 94 (2003), no. 24, pp. 36-41, here p. 36.
28 Ibid., p. 37.
29 Ibid. Jencks makes particular reference to Gehry. Recently Portoghesi has also developed views similar to those of Jencks.
30 Cf. Le Corbusier, Le Corbusier talks with students from the schools of architecture, 1999. op. cit., pp. 42-44.
31 "Ecological architecture" is going down a similar road, but often tends to treat nature in a way that is far too humanistic and functionalist.
32 Cf. Wolfgang Welsch, Räume bilden Menschen, in: Egon Schirmbeck (ed.), Raumstationen, Regensburg 2001, pp. 12-24.

PAUL NOLTE

VON DER KLASSISCHEN MODERNE ZUR REVISION DER POSTMODERNE?

DER WANDEL DER DEUTSCHEN GESELLSCHAFT IM 20. JAHRHUNDERT

FROM CLASSICAL MODERNISM TO A REVISION OF POST-MODERNISM?

CHANGES IN GERMAN SOCIETY IN THE 20TH CENTURY

Kann man eine Gesellschaft an ihren Behausungen erkennen? An den baulichen Formen, die sie ihren wichtigsten Funktionen gibt – dem Wohnen, dem Herrschen, dem Produzieren und Handeln, der religiösen und ästhetischen Reflexion? In Agrargesellschaften, in dörflichen Zusammenhängen scheint diese Gleichung relativ einfach aufzugehen. Soziale Strukturen bilden sich in der gebauten Landschaft ab: die Kirche im Mittelpunkt, daneben vielleicht ein kleines Rathaus oder Schulgebäude; repräsentative Höfe, in denen wirtschaftlicher Zweck und soziale Selbstdarstellung eine enge Verbindung eingehen; Hütten und Katen am Rande, die zugleich gesellschaftliche Marginalität ausdrücken. In komplexen Gesellschaften, in großen Städten, in der technischen und industriellen Moderne ist es schwieriger geworden, Architektur und Städtebau eindeutig auf soziale Strukturen, auf Eigenschaften der Bewohner und Nutzer gebauter Umwelt, zu beziehen. Versteckt sich hinter der Altbaufassade Armut, Verfall, soziale Bedürftigkeit? Oder ist sie eine Kulisse des Understatement für großzügige Yuppie-Kultur? Wird hinter den nüchternen Glasbändern eines dreistöckigen Flachbaus unterrichtet oder produziert oder verwaltet?

Und dennoch hat sich die Wechselbeziehung zwischen gesellschaftlicher Struktur und baulicher Verkörperung auch in der westlichen, urbanen Moderne des 20. Jahrhunderts nicht aufgelöst. In der flüchtigen Holzbauweise amerikanischer Vorstädte erkennen wir nicht nur historische Tradition, sondern auch die Gegenwart einer flüchtigen und immer zur Mobilität bereiten Gesellschaft. Die Stein auf Stein gemauerten Siedlungen mitteleuropäischer Städte dagegen erzählen von Bodenständigkeit und Sesshaftigkeit ihrer Bewohner. Moderne und Postmoderne haben eindeutige Zuordnungen häufig aufgelöst. Sie haben aber auch die Möglichkeiten der Differenzierung, der nuancierten Abbildung sozialer Verhältnisse, politischer Utopien, kultureller Erfahrungen enorm gesteigert: zum einen wegen eines gewachsenen Arsenals technischer Möglichkeiten – das Feld des Ingenieurs –, zum anderen wegen Steigerung und Differenzierung ästhetischer Ausdrucksmöglichkeiten – das Feld des Architekten. Die Überlagerung von Gesellschaftsstruktur und ästhetischer Repräsentation reicht auch im 20. Jahrhundert bis in die Grundbegriffe hinein. »Moderne« oder »Postmoderne« bezeichnen, wenn auch auf je diffuse Weise, Stadien der allgemeinen sozialen Entwicklung ebenso wie Phasen der Kunst- oder der Architekturgeschichte. Der Begriff der »Klassischen Moderne«, den Historiker gerne für die Zeit der vorletzten Jahrhundertwende und des beginnenden 20. Jahrhunderts verwenden, ist sogar als unmittelbares Lehnwort aus der Kunstgeschichte übernommen worden.

In dieser Zeit der Klassischen Moderne trat auch die Gesellschaft des 1871 gegründeten Deutschen Reiches in ein neues Zeitalter ein. Die erste, schmerzhafte Phase der Industriellen Revolution war abgeschlossen, Kohle und Stahl waren zur Selbstverständlichkeit geworden, ein dichtes Netz der Eisenbahn, das sich seitdem bis in die 1980er Jahre nur noch wenig veränderte, durchzog das Land. Es verband die Menschen in den großen städtischen Zentren, hierhin hatte sich um 1900 der Schwerpunkt der gesellschaftlichen Entwicklung verlagert. Berlin wuchs in rasantem Tempo, das die Zeitgenossen immer wieder mit der Dy-

Is it possible to recognise a society by its dwellings, by the architectural form it gives to its most important functions—living, governing, production and trading, religious and aesthetic reflection? In agricultural societies, in village settings, this equation seems to work relatively simply. Social structures are reflected in the built landscape: the church at the centre, next to it perhaps a small town hall or school building, prosperous farms, in which economic purpose and social self-representation go hand in hand, and cottages and shacks on the periphery, which at the same time express social marginality. In complex societies, in large cities, in technical and industrial Modernism, it has become more difficult to relate architecture and urban design so unequivocally to social structures, to characteristics of the inhabitants and users of the built environment. What is hiding behind the façade of that old building? Poverty, dilapidation, social deprivation? Or is it merely an understated front for affluent yuppie culture? What is going on behind the simple ribbon windows of a three-storey low-rise building? Teaching, production processes, or administration?

Nevertheless, the correlation between social structures and their architectural expression has not yet disappeared, not even in Western, urban Modernism of the 20th century. In the fleeting appearance of the timber-frame buildings of America's suburbs we recognise not only past traditions, but also the present of a fleeting society that is always prepared for mobility. By contrast, the settlements of Central Europe, towns built of stone painstakingly laid on stone, tell a story of settled people who have put down roots in a place. The borders between clearly defined categories often became blurred under Modernism and Post-Modernism. But, at the same time, the possibilities for differentiation, the subtly nuanced depiction of social conditions, political utopias, and cultural experiences, grew enormously: firstly because of the growing arsenal of technical possibilities—the field of the engineer—and secondly because of the increase in and differentiated range of possibilities for aesthetic expression—the field of the architect. The superimposition of social structure and aesthetic representation continued into the 20th century, affecting even its most fundamental concepts: "Modernism" or "Post-Modernism" describe, albeit in a diffuse way, stages of general social development just as much as they describe phases in the history of art or architecture. The concept of "Classical Modernism," which historians like to use for the period around the late 19th and early 20th century, is even a direct borrowing from art history.

In this age of Classical Modernism, the society of the German Empire that had been founded in 1871 also entered a new age. The first painful phase of the Industrial Revolution was over, coal and steel were now taken for granted, a dense network of railways that barely changed from then until well into the 1980s covered the country. It linked the people in the large urban centres, which was where the focus of social development had shifted to around 1900. Berlin grew at breakneck speed, which people at the time compared with the dynamics of Chicago, into a world metropolis, into Modernism's laboratory. Here it was possible to study modern class-based society in its purest form: middle-class residential areas in the West—in elegant

namik Chicagos verglichen, zu einer weltstädtischen Metropole heran, zu einem Laboratorium der Moderne. Hier konnte man die moderne Klassengesellschaft in Reinkultur studieren: Bürgerliche Wohnviertel im Westen, etwa im vornehmen Charlottenburg, standen der Enge und dem Elend in Quartieren der östlichen Innenstadt, der tief gestaffelten Mietskasernen und Hinterhöfe von Kreuzberg oder Friedrichshain schroff gegenüber. Migranten aus den agrarischen Ostprovinzen prägten das Bild in diesem Schmelztiegel des Umbruchs und Aufbruchs.

Aber neben die handwerkliche und industrielle Produktion trat immer mehr die Sichtbarkeit eines expandierenden Konsums und zeichnete das Bild der modernen Konsumgesellschaft vor. In den großen Warenhäusern wie Wertheim am Leipziger Platz oder dem 1908 eröffneten KaDeWe versuchte diese Konsumgesellschaft schon früh zu zeigen, dass sie auf eigenständige Weise zur Repräsentativität, ja zum Monumentalen in der Lage war. In ihrer Geburtsstunde vor dem Ersten Weltkrieg war die Moderne selber ein Faszinosum, und die deutsche Gesellschaft strotzte vor Selbstvertrauen und Zukunftszuversicht. Aber zugleich mischten sich Angst, Verunsicherung und Nervosität in die vorwärts drängende Dynamik, und man suchte Zuflucht in den Formen der Vergangenheit. Mit seiner Mischung aus Modernität und Historismus, aus bürgerlichem Anspruch und Schlossersatz brachte das in den 1890er Jahren fertig gestellte Reichstagsgebäude Paul Wallots diese Schwebelage sehr charakteristisch zum Ausdruck.

Der Erste Weltkrieg stellte die optimistischen Vorstellungen von einer friedlichen, fortschrittlichen und zivilisatorischen Moderne zum ersten Mal grundsätzlich in Frage Aber die Erfahrung von Krieg und Gewalt, von Inflation und Vermögensverlust hatte auch reinigende, ernüchternde Effekte. Zu keiner Zeit trat das Projekt der Moderne als ein Projekt der nüchternen Sachlichkeit, der kühlen Rationalität, der Reduzierung auf das funktional Notwendige klarer hervor als in den zwanziger Jahren. Aus Amerika kamen neue Organisationsprinzipien der Wirtschaft, die in Lebensbereiche weit jenseits von Produktion und Betrieb ausstrahlten: Taylor und Ford wurden zu Ikonen eines Lebensstils der Planung, des Managements, der Effizienz. Mehr als man lange Zeit glaubte, strahlte dieser Entwurf auch auf die nationalsozialistische Bewegung aus und verlieh ihr Attraktivität gerade bei Jüngeren. Überhaupt lässt sich der Nationalsozialismus nicht einfach als ein Atavismus, ein Fremdkörper, eine Widerstandsbewegung in der Moderne und gegen sie verstehen, sondern bildete selbst die Janusköpfigkeit der Moderne ab. Das gilt zum einen für das Spannungsverhältnis zwischen radikalem Fortschrittsentwurf und radikaler Ablehnung des Fortschritts, welches das »Dritte Reich« immer wieder kennzeichnete – von der Wissenschaftspolitik bis zu Architektur und Städtebau. Es gilt aber auch für die Spannungen innerhalb der technisch rationalisierten Moderne. Denn das Streben nach einer rational geplanten und effizient gesteuerten Gesellschaft konnte sich genauso gut auf eine antidemokratische Führer- und Expertenherrschaft richten oder gar auf die Vision einer völkisch und rassisch purifizierten Ordnung.

Euphorische und erlittene Moderne verquickten sich also in der ersten Hälfte des 20. Jahrhunderts auf enge und komplizier-

Charlottenburg, for example—stood out in stark contrast to the cramp-ed, squalid conditions in neighbourhoods of Kreuzberg or Friedrichshain in the Eastern inner-city with their tenements built deep into the blocks around dark, dingy backyards. Migrants from the agricultural Eastern provinces characterised this melting pot of radical change and new departures.

But alongside craft-based and industrial production, the visibility of an expanding consumerism emerged, prefiguring the modern consumer society. In Berlin's large department stores, such as Wertheim on Leipziger Platz or KaDeWe, which opened in 1908, this consumer society tried very early on to demonstrate that it was capable of expressing prestige, indeed monumentalism, in its own particular way. In the hour of its birth before the First World War, Modernism itself was fascinating, and German society was bursting with self-confidence and faith in the future. But, at the same time, the forward-surging dynamic became mixed with fear, uncertainty and nervousness, and people sought refuge in familiar forms from the past. With its mixture of modernity and historicism, bourgeois ambition and *ersatz* palace, Paul Wallot's building for the Reichstag, which was completed in the 1890s, epitomised this in-between state.

World War I questioned for the first time the optimistic ideas of Modernism as peaceful, progressive and civilising. However, the experience of war and violence, inflation and loss of wealth also had a purifying and sobering effect. At no time did Modernism appear more clearly than in the 1920s as a project of sober objectivity, cool rationality, a reduction to the functionally necessary. New principles for organising the economy came from America and impacted on areas of life that were far removed from production and the workplace: Taylor and Ford became the icons of a lifestyle centred around planning, management and efficiency. More than was thought for a long time, this blueprint also had an effect on the Nazi movement, making it appealing, particularly to younger people. In fact, National Socialism cannot simply be seen as an atavism, a foreign body, a movement of resistance within and against Modernism: on the contrary, it reflected the Janus-faced nature of Modernism. That applies, on the one hand, to the relationship of tension between the radical blueprint for progress and the radical rejection of progress that repeatedly characterised the "Third Reich"—be it in its scientific policies or its architecture and urban design. However, it also applies to the tensions within the Modern Movement and its technological rationalism: after all, the striving towards a rationally planned and efficiently run society could equally well be directed towards the anti-democratic rule of a führer and his »experts« or even towards the vision of a social order that was racially and ethnically cleansed.

The euphoric and agonising aspects of Modernism thus became closely intertwined in a complicated way in the first half of the 20th century in many parts of Europe and North America, but particularly strikingly and menacingly in Germany. The contrasts in the social structure, which had developed quickly and were far from being processed culturally, made a considerable contribution to this. The hyper-modernity of metropolitan centres stood alongside the backwardness of agricultural provinces, which were not able to join in this dynamic so rapidly.

te Weise – in vielen Teilen Europas und Nordamerikas, aber besonders auffällig und bedrängend in Deutschland. Die in kurzer Zeit entstandenen und kulturell noch lange nicht verarbeiteten Gegensätze in der sozialen Struktur trugen dazu erheblich bei. Hier die Hyper-Modernität großstädtischer Zentren, dort die Rückständigkeit agrarischer Provinzen, die an diese Dynamik so schnell keinen Anschluss fanden. Hier der bürgerliche Wohlstand, wenn auch psychisch verunsichert und teils materiell geschmälert durch die Folgen von zehn Jahren Inflation, dort die Enge und Entbehrung proletarischer Milieus, deren Situation sich angesichts von Weltwirtschaftskrise und Massenarbeitslosigkeit nicht durchgreifend verbessern konnte. War das die Moderne, in der zu leben sich lohnte, und wie konnte man diese schroffen Gegensätze auf Dauer aushalten? Je mehr Zeitgenossen diese Zweifel hegten und ihre Unzufriedenheit zugleich auf das politische System von Republik und parlamentarischer Demokratie projizierten, desto stärker wurde der Zulauf an den extremen Rändern des Parteiensystems. Die Kommunisten erhielten viel Zuspruch, wenn auch nur eine Minderheit der Deutschen, selbst der Arbeiter, noch an die Erfüllung der Moderne in einer großen sozialistischen Revolution glaubte. Weithin attraktiver erschien die Vision der Nationalsozialisten von der Glättung der Gegensätze. Vermeintliche »Fremdkörper« sollten ausgeschlossen, die Mehrheit der Gesellschaft in einer großen Volksgemeinschaft versöhnt werden, in der alte Konflikte still gestellt waren und Merkmale der sozialen Herkunft oder der Berufstätigkeit nicht mehr über das Prestige des Einzelnen entschieden. Das Ziel war eine Überwindung der modernen Gesellschaft – wenn man so will: eine Postmoderne *avant la lettre* –, aber das Ergebnis eher ein katastrophaler Irrweg der Moderne, der dennoch, auf sehr ambivalente Weise, Kontinuitäten in die Nachkriegsgesellschaft der Bundesrepublik wies.

In den fünfziger bis siebziger Jahren erreichte die Klassische Moderne in den westlichen Gesellschaften (aber nicht unähnlich auch im kommunistischen Osteuropa) ihren Höhe- und zugleich ihren Schlusspunkt. In dieser neuen Gründerzeit bestimmten wiederum Optimismus und Zukunftsvertrauen das Bild, getragen von einer lang andauernden ökonomischen Prosperität. Die wirtschaftliche Dynamik erleichterte es den Westdeutschen, die materiellen Folgen des Krieges zu verkraften, und sie beförderte obendrein, wie das auch anderswo der Fall war, den Übergang von einer gespaltenen Gesellschaft überwiegender Knappheit zu einer relativ wohlhabenden, relativ saturierten Mittelschichtgesellschaft. Die kleinbürgerliche Existenz wurde zu einer neuen Norm der Lebensführung, deren Erfüllung sich nicht zuletzt am Maßstab bestimmter Konsumgüter maß: in den fünfziger Jahren zunächst des Kühlschranks, dann immer mehr des privaten Automobils. Was die Nationalsozialisten mit Gewalt versucht hatten und die Sozialisten schon gar nicht mehr anzustreben wagten: Eine egalitäre Gesellschaft des materiellen Wohlergehens jenseits der Geschichte schien auf wundersame Weise naturwüchsig aus den Mechanismen des demokratisierten Kapitalismus hervorzugehen.

Das hieß nicht, dass man die Hände nur in den Schoß zu legen brauchte. Der Erfolg gebar auch neue Utopien für die Zukunft oder gab alten Utopien aus der Zwischenkriegszeit neue Nah-

Bourgeois prosperity, even if it was psychologically uncertain and to some extent materially diminished by the consequences of ten years of inflation, coexisted with the cramped conditions and deprivation of the proletarian milieu, whose situation was not able to improve radically because of the world economic crisis and mass unemployment. Was this the Modernism in which it was worth living, and how was it possible to tolerate these stark disparities in the long term? The more contemporaries harboured these doubts and at the same time projected their dissatisfaction onto the political system of republic and parliamentary democracy, the more popular the extreme margins of the party system became. The communists gained a great deal of support, despite the fact that only a minority of Germans—even amongst the working classes—still believed in the fulfilment of Modernism's dream in a grand-scale socialist revolution. The Nazis vision of smoothing out contrasts seemed far more attractive. Supposed "alien elements" were to be excluded, the majority within society was to be reconciled in one big national community, in which old conflicts would be quashed and markers of social origin or occupation would not longer decide the status of the individual. The aim was to supersede modern society; it was, if you like, a kind of Post-Modernism *avant la lettre*, but the result was more a case of Modernism taking a catastrophic wrong turn, which nevertheless showed up continuities in post-war West Germany in a very ambivalent way.

From the 1950s to 1970s, "Classical Modernism" reached both its culmination and conclusion in Western societies (and developments in Communist Eastern Europe were not entirely dissimilar). In this new phase of industrial expansion, optimism and faith in the future once more prevailed, underpinned by an economic prosperity that lasted a considerable time. The dynamics of the economy made it easier for West Germany to absorb the material consequences of the war and, as was the case in other places, they also promoted the transition from a split society of predominant scarcity to a relatively prosperous and satiated middle-class society. The middle-class way of life became a new social standard and matching up to it was measured by the yardstick of particular consumer goods: initially, in the 1950s, it was the refrigerator and then increasingly it became car-ownership. What the Nazis had tried to establish by force and what the socialists did not even dare to aspire to—an egalitarian society of material well-being outside the bounds of history—seemed in a wondrous way to have grown naturally out of the mechanisms of democratised capitalism.

That did not mean that people could just sit back and take things easy. Success gave birth to new utopias envisaged for the future and provided new nourishment to old utopias from the years between the wars. Technological progress seemed to know no bounds, and the target to strive for was rationally planned harmony. Architects and town planners cherished great hopes of reducing the density of the city with its social problem areas; town and country were to form a single entity and the people of the future would leave their living capsules and climb into helicopters to pursue needs that increasingly revolved around consumption and leisure. Now that Modernism's revolutionary promises of salvation had come to nothing, the conviction began to

rung. Grenzen der technischen Entwicklung schien es nicht mehr zu geben, und die Zielvorgabe hieß: rational geplante Harmonie. Architekten und Stadtplanern schwebte die Auflösung der verdichteten Großstadt mit ihren sozialen Problemzonen vor; Stadt und Land sollten eins werden, und die Menschen der Zukunft bestiegen von ihren Wohnkapseln aus private Helikopter, um ihren zunehmend von Konsum und Freizeit bestimmten Bedürfnissen nachzugehen. Nachdem die revolutionären Heilsversprechen der Moderne gescheitert waren, setzte sich eher die Überzeugung durch, die Gesellschaft der Zukunft durch effiziente und konkrete politische »Planung« und »Steuerung« – das waren Leitbegriffe vor allem der sechziger Jahre – erreichen zu können. Die Modernisierung der Verkehrsinfrastruktur im Autobahnbau gehörte ebenso dazu wie die Errichtung von Trabantenstädten aus gleichförmigen und vielgeschossigen Wohnmaschinen. Aber auch der soziale Ausgleich blieb ein wichtiges Ziel der gesellschaftlichen Planung und Steuerung. So versuchte man im Städtebau der Bundesrepublik häufig, herkömmliche Formen der sozialen Segregation zu überwinden, indem Zeilen von Reihenhäusern oder Flachdachbungalows zwischen die Geschosswohnungsblöcke eingezogen wurden. Das auffällige Bekenntnis zu einer Ästhetik des Funktionalen sollte auch die politische Botschaft unterstreichen: Die Gesellschaft der Bundesrepublik war endlich im demokratischen Westen angekommen, sie bekannte sich zu seinen Werten und profitierte von seinen materiellen Vorzügen.

Die Ernüchterung kam schnell und unerwartet, und sie hatte lang anhaltende Folgen. Die erste Ölkrise von 1973/74 markierte einen Bruch, der damals nur die Wirtschaft zu betreffen schien, doch schon bald auf die westlichen Gesellschaften und ihr kulturelles Selbstverständnis im Ganzen ausstrahlte. Die Erfahrung einer ersten, kleineren Rezession hatte es in der Bundesrepublik schon in den späten sechziger Jahren gegeben, doch dann kehrte noch einmal Normalität zurück. Nach 1973 war nichts mehr wie zuvor. Der Traum von der immer währenden Prosperität ging zu Ende und beendete auch die Vision vom allgemeinen Fortschritt und seiner politischen Steuerbarkeit. Gab es einen alternativen Fortschritt, wohin sollte man sich jetzt orientieren – gab es überhaupt noch den einen, den verbindlichen Weg in die Zukunft? Waren die Potenziale der Moderne nicht in den verschiedenen Perioden ihrer »klassischen« Ära ausprobiert und ausgereizt worden? Vielleicht konnte man jetzt nur noch wiederholen und zitieren, auf Verbindlichkeit verzichten, Vielfalt anerkennen – immerhin eröffnete das neue Chancen der Freiheit. Das war die Geburtsstunde der Postmoderne.

Da waren zunächst die Grenzen des Wachstums, die seit den frühen siebziger Jahren, befördert durch viel beachtete Expertengutachten wie diejenigen des »Club of Rome«, ins allgemeine Bewusstsein traten. Das Ende der Prosperität war kein Betriebsunfall, sondern es gab inhärente Grenzen einer Steigerung des Bruttosozialprodukts bei insgesamt begrenzten Ressourcen. Und darüber, das war die wichtige neue Botschaft, musste man weder entsetzt noch enttäuscht sein, denn das Leben jenseits der Wachstumsideologie gewann seine eigene normative Überzeugungskraft. Die natürliche Umwelt des Menschen, die Interaktion zwischen Gesellschaft und natürlicher Umwelt wurden ins

establish itself that it would be possible to create the societies of the future through efficient and concrete political "planning" and "control"—the key concepts of the time, in particular of the 1960s. The modernisation of transport infrastructure, which included building motorways, was just as much part of this concept as the creation of satellite towns made up of identical multistorey "machines for living." But social equity also remained an important goal of social planning and control. For example, urban design in West Germany often attempted to overcome conventional forms of social segregation by inserting rows of terraced houses or flat-roofed bungalows between the multistorey blocks of flats. The striking declaration of belief in an aesthetic based on what was functional was also intended to underline a political message: West German society had finally established itself as part of the Western democratic world; it believed in its values and benefited from its material advantages.

Disenchantment came quickly and unexpectedly, and it had long-lasting effects. The first oil crisis of 1973/74 marked a break in proceedings, which at the time seemed to affect only the economy, but soon began to impact on Western society and its cultural self-understanding in general. West Germany had experienced its first minor recession back in the late 1960s, but things had returned to normality. However, after 1973 nothing remained the same. The dream of permanent prosperity was shattered and with it the vision of progress and the ability to control it politically. Was there an alternative kind of progress? What direction should we now be following? Was there even a single »correct« path that would lead to a bright future? Had Modernism's potential not already been tried out and exhausted in the various periods of its »classical« era? Perhaps the only options now available were to repeat and quote from the past, abandon any notion of one truth, acknowledge diversity—after all, that would open up new opportunities for freedom. That was Post-Modernism's hour of birth.

First of all, came the recognition that there were limits to growth. Since the early 1970s this realisation had entered into the consciousness of the general public, promoted by numerous highly regarded expert reports, such as those published by the "Club of Rome." The end of prosperity was no freak accident: there are inherent limits to an increase in the gross national product due to the simple fact that resources are finite. And the important new message was that we should neither be outraged nor disappointed over that, since life beyond a growth-centred ideology acquired a normative persuasiveness of its own. Humankind's natural environment, the interaction between society and the natural environment, were suddenly included in the equation, and gave a lot of Classical Modernism's calculations a quite different complexion. The unity of human settlement and the landscape for example, as the great utopians of the time from Le Corbusier to Frank Lloyd Wright had designed them, were exposed as the one-sided subjugation of nature to the demands of human efficiency and replaced by completely different visions—the smaller grain designs of "ecological architecture." Complex technologies for energy generation or mobility were no longer seen as instruments of progress and increased wealth, but were discovered to be risks capable of threatening

1

2

3

4

1 Großsiedlung Märkisches Viertel, Berlin, 1962-1974
Märkisches Viertel, satellite town, Berlin, 1962-1974
2 Gentrifizierter Altbau: Gründerzeithäuser in Hamburg-Eppendorf
Example of gentrification: *Gründerzeit* houses in Eppendorf, Hamburg

3 Doris und Ralph Thut: Ökologische Reihenhausanlage, München-Perlach, 1978
Ecological terraced houses, Perlach, Munich 1978

4 Standardisierte Einzelwohnhäuser in Deutschland, Foto 1999
Standardised houses in Germany, photo: 1999

Kalkül gezogen, und damit sahen viele der Rechnungen, welche die Klassische Moderne aufgemacht hatte, auf einmal ganz anders aus. Die Einheit von menschlicher Siedlung und Landschaft etwa, wie sie die großen Utopisten dieser Zeit von Le Corbusier bis Frank Lloyd Wright entworfen hatten, wurde als einseitige Unterwerfung der Natur unter die Zwänge der menschlichen Effizienz entlarvt, und ganz anders geartete, auch kleinteiligere Entwürfe des »ökologischen Bauens« traten an ihre Stelle. Komplexe Technologien der Energieerzeugung oder der Mobilität waren nicht mehr Instrumente des Fortschritts und der Wohlstandsvermehrung, sondern entpuppten sich als Risiken, die sich nicht nur gegen die Natur, sondern sogar gegen die menschliche Existenz schlechthin richten konnten. Das Leben jenseits der Gewissheiten der Klassischen Moderne war ein Tanz auf dem Vulkan. Deshalb wurde der in den achtziger Jahren von dem Soziologen Ulrich Beck geprägte Begriff der »Risikogesellschaft« so populär.

Diesen Risiken konnte man sich nicht mehr mit dem Optimismus früherer Zeiten stellen. Sie konnten prinzipiell gar nicht überwunden, nicht in eine neue Harmonie aufgelöst werden, sondern mussten auf Dauer ausgehalten und irgendwie ausbalanciert werden. Der Zusammenbruch der klassisch-modernen Utopien ließ höchstens die Dystopien eine Zeit lang florieren, die Gegenbilder von einer schrecklichen, auf die finale Katastrophe zusteuernden Zukunft. Doch in der Postmoderne schrumpfte der Zukunftshorizont der westlichen Gesellschaften in jeder Hinsicht ein. Man konnte sich noch mit der Gegenwart arrangieren; eine prinzipiell andere Zukunft gewinnen zu wollen galt als vermessen. Wer hätte sich auch anmaßen wollen, die Richtung einer solchen Zukunft noch zu bestimmen? Dieser Grundhaltung korrespondierte ein Gefühl, das bald auf das Schlagwort vom »Ende der Geschichte« gebracht wurde: Die historische Entwicklung trat auf der Stelle, die Welt war in der Konfrontation zweier Blöcke wie eingefroren, auf eine Phase der extremen Dynamik schien nun eine Phase des Stillstands zu folgen. Wenn die Zukunft nicht mehr zur Verfügung stand, wandte man sich umso eher der Vergangenheit zu. Nicht zufällig waren deshalb die achtziger Jahre eine große Zeit der Historisierung, der Wiederentdeckung und »Aufarbeitung« von Geschichte in ganz unterschiedlichen kulturellen Formen. Da die Politik nicht mehr die Zukunft planen oder gar steuern konnte, entdeckte sie stattdessen die »Geschichtspolitik« und versuchte, über Erinnerungsbilder Identität zu stiften. In diesen Sog der Historisierung gerieten fast alle westlichen Gesellschaften, aber in Deutschland war er, wegen der Last der NS-Vergangenheit, besonders groß. Beide deutschen Staaten, die Bundesrepublik in der Ära Kohl wie die DDR in ihrer Spätphase, beteiligten sich daran.

Die ökonomische Krise nahm nicht nur den Glauben an die immer währende Prosperität, sie zerstörte auch, wie sich nach einigen Jahren herausstellte, das Projekt der großen und friedvollen sozialen Nivellierung. Wenn man um 1970 eigene Erfahrung in die Zukunft verlängerte, konnte man von einem weiteren Abschmelzen von Klassenunterschieden ausgehen, von einem fortschreitenden Aufstieg der Arbeitnehmer, vielleicht sogar einem Verschwinden derjenigen Reste der alten Armut, die der immer weiter ausgebaute Wohlfahrtsstaat bis dahin noch

not only nature but human existence per se. Life beyond the certainties of Classical Modernism was tantamount to dancing on a volcano. That is why the concept of the "risk society," coined in the 1980s by sociologist Ulrich Beck, became so popular.

It was no longer possible to confront these risks with the optimism of the past. It was not fundamentally possible to overcome them, nor to integrate them into a new harmony; they simp-ly had to be tolerated in the long term and somehow balanced out. The collapse of the utopia of Classical Modernism allowed the "dystopias" at most to flourish for a while—the counter-images of a terrible future heading for the ultimate catastrophe. Yet in Post-Modernism the future horizons of Western societies shrank in every regard. It was just about possible to come to terms with the present; but to seek to achieve a fundamentally different future was considered to be presumptuous. And who would have dared to try to determine the course that a future of that kind should take? This general attitude corresponded to a feeling that was soon embodied in the buzzword "the end of history:" historical progress was running on the spot, the world was frozen in the confrontation between the two political blocks, it seemed that a phase of extreme dynamism had been superseded by a phase of standstill. Since the future was no longer available, people turned all the more to the past. It was no coincidence that the 1980s was a time obsessed with history, when history was rediscovered and "processed" in quite different cultural forms. Since the world of politics was no longer able to plan, let alone control, the future, it turned to the past and tried to create a sense of identity through visual memories. Almost all Western societies were drawn into this historicism, but it was particularly predominant in Germany due to the burden of the Nazi past. Both German states participated: West Germany in the Helmut Kohl era and East Germany in its latter years.

The economic crisis not only shattered the faith in permanent prosperity, it also—as emerged several years later—destroyed the endeavour to level out social disparities on a peaceful and grand scale. If around 1970 people projected their own individual experience into the future, they could expect further dissolution of class differences, along with a continuing gain in importance of working people, and perhaps even the disappearance of whatever vestiges of the old poverty that the ever-expanding welfare state had not managed to eliminate. Ten years down the road, people's experiences suddenly looked very different. Old forms of poverty and marginality—poverty amongst the elderly, rural poverty—had continued to decline, but a "new social issue," with new forms of deprivation and exclusion was more than rivalling them. No-one had expected the new wave of mass unemployment, which even more so than fifty years previously was manifesting as a structural problem of society involving long-term exclusion from the labour market. Initially, it did not impact on the prosperity of a broad middle section of society, so the label "two-thirds society" hit the nail on the head, describing so aptly the rift between a prosperous majority and a poor minority. There was a greater polarisation of income in West Germany once more—albeit to a far lesser extent than in the USA or Britain. A trend that had lasted many years was reversed: income from paid employment could no longer keep abreast of

nicht hatte beseitigen können. Schon ein gutes Jahrzehnt später sahen die Erfahrungen ganz anders aus. Alte Formen der Armut und Marginalität – Armut im Alter, Armut auf dem Lande – hatten sich noch weiter zurückgezogen, aber eine »neue soziale Frage«, mit neuen Formen der Bedürftigkeit und Ausgrenzung, machte das mehr als wett. Mit neuer Massenarbeitslosigkeit, die sich mehr noch als ein halbes Jahrhundert zuvor als ein gesellschaftliches Strukturproblem dauernden Ausschlusses vom Arbeitsmarkt manifestierte, hatte kaum einer gerechnet. Den Wohlstand einer breiten Mitte traf das einstweilen nicht, sodass der Begriff der »Zweidrittelgesellschaft« auf den Punkt traf: die Trennung zwischen einer Wohlstandsmehrheit und einer Armutsminderheit. Wenngleich in weit geringerem Ausmaß als in den USA oder in England, nahm auch in der Bundesrepublik die Einkommenspolarisierung wieder zu, ein langjähriger Trend kehrte sich um: Die Einkünfte aus abhängiger Arbeit hielten mit denen aus Selbstständigkeit, Unternehmertätigkeit und Vermögen nicht mehr mit, erst recht nicht im kurzlebigen Boom der New Economy der neunziger Jahre.

Dem entsprach eine wieder wachsende soziale Segregation des Wohnens und Lebens. Der städtebauliche Anspruch auf soziale Durchmischung wurde kaum noch erhoben, Neubaugebiete erhielten wieder einen deutlicher schichtspezifischen Charakter – und die Mittelschicht zog sich aus den Wohnprojekten der sechziger und siebziger Jahre zurück, in denen die Unterschichten zurückblieben. In den Innenstädten entdeckte eine kaufkräftige Klientel die Vorzüge von Altbauwohnungen und Loftetagen, die Grenzen zwischen vernachlässigten und »gentrifizierten« Bezirken traten markanter hervor. Diese Spaltungen hatten viel mit einer schon länger anhaltenden Einwanderung in die Bundesrepublik zu tun, deren Dauerhaftigkeit man jedoch lange unterschätzt hatte. Migranten, zunächst aus Südeuropa, dann vor allem aus der Türkei, später auch aus Osteuropa, besetzten die weniger angesehenen beruflichen Positionen und bildeten eigene soziokulturelle und sozialräumliche Milieus, aus denen heraus ihnen Aufstieg und Integration jedoch nur ungenügend gelangen. Die postmoderne Gesellschaft war eine »multikulturelle« Gesellschaft und fand sich in dieser kulturellen und ethnischen Vielfalt bestätigt, weil sie dem Pluralitätsanspruch der Postmoderne, dem Verzicht auf eindeutige Vorgaben, entsprach. Wenn der Fortschritt überhaupt noch eine Richtung hatte, dann den der Differenzierung und zunehmenden Vielfalt.

Darin immerhin schienen die Unwägbarkeiten und Risiken der Postmoderne ihre Vorzüge zu haben: Sie schufen zugleich Chancen, vervielfältigten individuelle Optionen, eröffneten Freiheitsräume – auch wenn diese Freiheiten zunächst wie aus der Not geboren waren. Das Ende der klassischen Industrieökonomie und die schrumpfenden Horizonte der Erwerbsarbeit mussten ja so schlecht nicht sein, wenn man sie als günstige Gelegenheit begriff, das Leben in der nachklassischen Moderne an neuen, zum Beispiel »postmateriellen« Werten auszurichten. Eine gerechtere Verteilung des noch vorhandenen Arbeitsvolumens durch allgemeine Arbeitszeitverkürzung traf sich dann mit dem gesellschaftspolitischen Ziel einer Vermehrung von freier Zeit, von Zeit, die in selbstbestimmte und deswegen zunehmend individualisierte Lebensführung investiert werden

income from self-employment, entrepreneurial activity and capital, and most certainly not during the short-lived boom of the New Economy in the 1990s.

This was reflected in the return of social segregation—in housing in particular and life in general. Urban design's ambition to achieve a balanced social mix was scarcely even uttered any more; new-build areas once more took on a clear-cut class-specific character. The middle classes moved out of the housing projects of the 1960s and 1970, leaving them to be solely occupied by the lower social classes. In the inner cities, a clientele with high purchasing power discovered the appeal of living in old buildings and lofts, and the boundaries between run-down and gentrified areas became more conspicuous. These splits in society were closely connected with a wave of immigration into West Germany that had been going on for some time, the permanence of which had, however, been underestimated. Migrants—initially from Southern Europe, then Turkey, and later from Eastern Europe—occupied the low-status jobs and created their own social milieu both in the cultural and spatial sense, from which upward mobility and integration were possible to only a limited extent. Post-Modernist society was a "multicultural" society and saw itself reaffirmed in this cultural and ethnic diversity, which mirrored its pluralist ambitions: the abandonment of clear terms of reference. If progress took any particular direction at all it lay in differentiation and increasing diversity.

It was here that the imponderabilities and risks of Post-Modernism seemed to offer advantages: they also created opportunities, multiplied individual options, opened up scope for greater freedom—even if this freedom initially seemed to have been born out of necessity. The end of the classical industrial economy and the shrinking prospects for paid employment were perhaps not so bad after all, if they were seen as a good opportunity to organise life in post-Classical Modernism around new values, such as "post-material" values. Equitable distribution of the volume of work that was still available by across-the-board reductions in working hours coincided with the socio-political aim of increasing leisure time, time in which people could invest in self-determined and therefore increasingly individualised lifestyles. After the liberation from material deprivation, Post-Modernism now brought about emancipation from the deprivation of insufficient time. Freely disposable time, which until then had generally been the privilege of a small sector of the upper classes, now became common property and had to be filled with new forms of activity to prevent leisure from turning into boredom. Against this backdrop, an unparalleled commercialisation of leisure time has occurred since the 1980s, encompassing very different spheres ranging from event holidays to private television and other electronic media through to leisure and adventure parks. Some people have even been afraid that the entire country is turning into a gigantic leisure park.

Seen in that light, the time lost through paid employment in no way vanished beyond the reach of the economy—especially not if we think of the striking expansion and process of self-stylisation that consumption has gone through. It is only now that the Classical Modernist manufacturing society has totally

5

6

7

8

5 Sanierter Plattenbau vom Künstler Gustavo bemalt, Berlin-Lichtenberg, 2002
Refurbished concrete-slab building with art work by Gustavo, Lichtenberg, Berlin, 2002

6 Pei, Cobb, Freed & Partners: Atrium in Friedrichstadtpassage, Quartier/block 205, Berlin, 1996

7 Einkaufszentrum CentrO Oberhausen, Coca-Cola-Oase, 1996
CentrO Oberhausen shopping mall, Coca-Cola oasis, 1996

8 Standardisierter Lidl-Markt in Deutschland
Standardised Lidl supermarket in Germany

konnte. Nach der Befreiung aus der materiellen Not brachte die Postmoderne die Emanzipation von der Not der knappen Zeit. Frei verfügbare Zeit, bis dahin in fast allen Gesellschaftsformen ein Privileg einer schmalen Oberschicht, wurde zum Allgemeingut und musste mit neuen Formen der Betätigung gefüllt werden, damit Muße nicht in Langeweile umschlug. Vor diesem Hintergrund vollzog sich seit den achtziger Jahren eine beispiellose Kommerzialisierung der Freizeit in ganz unterschiedlichen Bereichen, vom Event-Urlaub über das Privatfernsehen und andere elektronische Medien bis zu den Freizeit- und Erlebnisparks. Manche befürchteten gar, das ganze Land verwandle sich in einen gigantischen Freizeitpark.

So gesehen wurde die der Erwerbsarbeit verloren gegangene Zeit keineswegs dem Zugriff der Ökonomie entzogen – und erst recht nicht, wenn man an die auffällige Expansion und Selbststilisierung des Konsums denkt. Erst jetzt wurde die klassisch-moderne Produktionsgesellschaft vollends zur postmodernen Konsumgesellschaft. Wenn der Reichtum, die ökonomische Potenz eines Landes, sich früher in qualmenden Schloten und vibrierenden Maschinenhallen manifestiert hatte, übernahmen jetzt glitzernde Shopping-Malls, häufig außerhalb der alten Innenstädte gelegen, diese symbolische Leitfunktion. Eine Zeit lang mochte man sich sogar der Illusion hingeben, im Konsum gelänge, was der Produktionsgesellschaft verwehrt blieb: die Erfüllung des Traums von Gleichheit und Gerechtigkeit – denn waren im Paradies des Güterüberflusses nicht alle Menschen gleich? Sehr bald zeigte sich jedoch, dass die Konsumwelt ihre eigenen Mechanismen etablierte, um soziale Hierarchie in der Postmoderne fortzusetzen und auch symbolisch zu markieren. Der Trend zur Polarisierung von Einkommen verlängerte sich mühelos in eine Polarisierung des Konsums zwischen Luxuspassagen und Discountmärkten.

Und schließlich, als ultimatives Versprechen der Postmoderne: die Auflösung herkömmlicher Bindungen und Abhängigkeiten des Einzelnen auch dort, wo Gemeinschaft und soziale Bindung bis dahin als unverzichtbar galten, nämlich im privaten Bereich, in der Familie. Seit mindestens zwei Jahrhunderten hatte der Liberalismus das Individuum hochgehalten, seine Emanzipation versprochen. Doch dieses Individuum gab sich bei näherem Hinsehen als männlicher Haushaltsvorstand in einem mehr oder minder patriarchalischen, auf lebenslangen, ja generationenübergreifenden Zusammenhalt berechneten Familienverband zu erkennen. Am Ende des 20. Jahrhunderts wurden auch diese vermeintlichen Selbstverständlichkeiten mit neuer Radikalität in Frage gestellt. Die »68er« hatten ideologisch und theoretisch bereits den Boden bereitet, doch seit den achtziger Jahren entwickelte sich – nicht untypisch für die Postmoderne! – ein ganz unideologischer Sog des praktischen Lebensvollzugs. Das königlich-preußische Gebot, ein jeder solle nach seiner Fasson selig werden, wurde auf elementare Weise ernst genommen. Die Entscheidung von Partnern für Kinder verlor ihre frühere Selbstverständlichkeit (auch in der Geburtenrate wurde die Bundesrepublik dezidiert »postmodern«!) ebenso wie die lebenslange Dauer von Beziehungen. Die Folge waren eine rasch zunehmende Zahl von Single-Haushalten und neue Beziehungsformen wie die »Patchwork-Familie« als frei geweb-

metamorphosed into the Post-Modernist consumer society. In the past, wealth, the economic potency of a country, manifested in smoking chimneystacks and vibrating machine shops; now glitzy shopping malls, often outside the old town centres, have taken on this symbolic function. For a time it was even possible to preserve the illusion that we have achieved through consumption what always remained beyond the reach of the manufacturing society: the fulfilment of the dream of equality and justice—for are not all human beings equal in this paradise with its cornucopia of goods? However, it soon became clear that the world of consumerism had established its own mechanisms to preserve the social hierarchy in Post-Modernism and to mark it symbolically. The trend towards polarisation of income extended itself effortlessly into a polarisation of consumption patterns, reflected in luxury shopping arcades at one end of the scale and cut-price supermarkets at the other.

And finally, as Post-Modernism's ultimate promise: the disintegration of traditional individual commitments and dependencies, including in those areas where in the past the community and social commitment had been considered indispensable, namely in the private sphere—the family. For at least two centuries, liberalism had upheld the status of the individual, promising his or her emancipation. But on closer examination, this individual turned out to be the male head of the household in a more or less patriarchal family structure, its cohesion calculated over an entire lifetime, indeed from one generation to another. At the end of the 20th century these things that had been taken for granted were questioned with a new radicality. The "68 generation" had already prepared the ground ideologically and theoretically, but since the 1980s—not atypically for Post-Modernism!—a totally unideological pull towards a practical way of life had developed. The royal Prussian dictate that everyone should seek happiness in their own way was taken seriously in a quite elementary way. The decision of partners to have children was no longer something that was taken for granted as before (West Germany was also decidedly "Post-Modernist" in its birth rate!) nor was the fact that relationships would last a lifetime. The result was a rapidly increasing number of single households and new forms of relationships such as the "patchwork family" made up of a random configuration of stepsiblings and their parents' partners from different phases of life.

One might think that a society of this kind would call for completely different forms of living, for new kinds of architecture for everyday living space, for comprehensive urban design schemes. But, in this respect too, the age of utopias and large-scale ideologically driven projects was over. The radical process of individualisation took place predominantly behind very conventional façades. New living communes or serviced residential complexes for singles? In the main, no! The classical single-family house, or three-bedroomed flat, simply became inhabited by a divorcee or a couple without children. Perhaps this trend towards increasing conventionality, indeed banality, of domestic architecture at the end of the 20th century also expressed a yearning to preserve convention in a world of unlimited possibilities.

Is Post-Modernist society a success story—or has it failed, run into a cul-de-sac, in need of revision? It would contradict the very

ter Flickenteppich aus Lebensabschnittspartnern und Stiefgeschwistern.

Man könnte meinen, dass eine solche Gesellschaft auch nach völlig anderen Formen des Wohnens, der baulichen Gestalt von alltäglichem Lebensraum, des großflächigen Städtebaus verlangte. Doch auch in dieser Hinsicht war die Zeit der Utopien und der ideologisch angetriebenen Großprojekte vorbei. Die radikale Individualisierung vollzog sich ganz überwiegend hinter sehr konventionellen Fassaden. Neue Wohnkommunen oder betreute Single-Wohnanlagen? – Überwiegend Fehlanzeige. Das klassische Einfamilienhaus oder die Vierzimmerwohnung wurden dann eben vom kinderlosen Paar oder dem Scheidungswitwer alleine bewohnt. Vielleicht drückte sich in dieser Tendenz zur Konventionalisierung, ja Banalisierung der Wohnarchitektur am Ende des 20. Jahrhunderts auch die Sehnsucht nach dem Halt der Konvention in einer Welt der beliebigen Möglichkeiten aus.

Ist die postmoderne Gesellschaft eine Erfolgsstory – oder ist sie gescheitert, in eine Sackgasse geraten, revisionsbedürftig? Es würde dem Selbstverständnis postmoderner Kultur geradezu widersprechen, sich selbst als die Bugwelle eines linear weiterlaufenden Fortschritts zu begreifen. Scherwellen, wechselnde Winde, sogar zeitweise Flauten gehören zu ihrem Grundbestand. Dennoch sind in den letzten Jahren aus unterschiedlichen Perspektiven immer häufiger Zweifel an dem postmodernen Modell gesellschaftlicher Entwicklung geäußert worden. War die Postmoderne nur ein schöner Traum, das Versprechen auf ein Paradies der Freiheit, das an den harten Realitäten kapitalistischer Dynamik ebenso wie an seinen eigenen Widersprüchen scheitern wird?

Die Postmoderne entsprang dem Geist der westlichen Gesellschaften vor der historischen Wende von 1989/90. In der Bundesrepublik Deutschland ist diese Zäsur, mit Lust und Last der Wiedervereinigung, bis heute mehr als in westlichen Nachbarländern eine sehr nachdrückliche Erfahrung. Das Modernitätsdefizit der neuen Bundesländer schien so gewaltig, dass eine Agenda der Klassischen Moderne nachholend erst zu ihrem Recht kommen musste. Die aus den achtziger Jahren ererbte ökonomische Strukturkrise hat sich im Gefolge der Deutschen Einheit nicht aufgelöst, sondern noch verstärkt, und es erscheint mehr und mehr zweifelhaft, dass diese Krise mit den Mitteln der Postmoderne gelöst oder auch nur übertüncht werden könnte. Die Kluft zwischen Arm und Reich ist weiter gewachsen und hat neue, regionalräumliche Dimensionen hinzugewonnen. Der Osten leidet unter Abwanderung zumal der Jungen, der Gebildeten und der Leistungswilligen, und solcher Wandel schlägt sich auch in der Materialität einer Gesellschaft nieder: in verlassenen Dörfern, leer stehenden Plattenbauten, im Rückbau statt Aufbau von Städten; Problemlagen, auf die postmoderne Konzepte – sei es der Architektur, sei es der Sozialpolitik – nicht recht eingestellt waren.

Der Wohlfahrtsstaat, ein Kind der Klassischen Moderne, stößt nun immer deutlicher an seine Grenzen. Seit den achtziger Jahren kannte man diese Grenzen sehr gut – etwa die Grenzen der demographischen Belastbarkeit in der Rentenversicherung. Doch es fehlte die Fähigkeit, kulturell und politisch umzusteuern. Im Gegenteil, der klassische Wohlfahrtsstaat musste in den

self-understanding of Post-Modernist culture to see itself at the forefront of linear progress. Shear waves, changing winds, even temporary calms are part of its stock in trade. Nevertheless, in recent years doubts about the Post-Modernist model of societal development have been increasingly voiced from different quarters. Was Post-Modernism just a pleasant dream, the promise of a paradise of freedom, which foundered both on the harsh realities of capitalist dynamics and its own contradictions?

Post-Modernism grew out of the spirit prevalent in Western societies prior to the events of 1989/90 that changed history. In West Germany, this caesura, with all the agony and ecstasy of reunification, has remained until today a very powerful experience, far more so than in other neighbouring countries of Western Europe. The modernity deficit of the former East Germany seemed so immense that it looked as if a programme of Classical Modernism would first have to be established in retrospect. The structural crisis in the economy inherited from the 1980s did not disappear in the wake of unification; on the contrary, it worsened and it seems more and more doubtful that it will be possible to solve this crisis, or even paper over the cracks, with the resources of Post-Modernism. The gap between rich and poor has continued to grow and has acquired new regional dimensions. The East is suffering from an exodus, in particular of young people, educated people and those willing to work, and a profound change of that nature is bound to be reflected in the material structure of a society: in abandoned villages, prefabricated blocks of flats standing empty, in cities losing instead of gaining population—problems, which Post-Modernist concepts in architecture and social policy were not really expecting to have to deal with.

It is becoming increasingly clear that the welfare state, a child of Classical Modernism, is coming up against its limits. We have been very familiar with these limits since the 1980s—for example, the limits of pension funds to cope with demographic trends. Nevertheless, the ability to change course culturally and politically was lacking. On the contrary, as we are now beginning to realise, over the last twenty years the classical welfare state had to absorb the burdens and risks associated with those options and liberties that accounted for the attraction of the Post-Modernist promise. Lower levels of paid employment came at a price: namely the increased use of redistributed funds. The same is true for the economic consequences of individualisation and increased diversity of family relationships, which not only lead to a pension gap, but far more directly to the need for mothers and children to receive social security benefits. We have now been invoiced for the long-forgotten costs of a pluralism that often seems to have remained on the surface. The crisis of "multi-culturalism" in terms of social segregation and ghettoisation, in terms of failed integration and an educational crisis for children of migrants is another example of this.

In order to be able to tackle these problem areas, a revision of Post-Modernism that includes the very principles of its cultural orientation is required. Mere historicist gestures are not getting us anywhere anymore. Since 1989 at the latest, we have known that the »end of history« is not yet upon us, but we are nevertheless still battling with the consequences of this insight. A

letzten zwei Jahrzehnten, wie wir zu erkennen beginnen, auch die Lasten und Risiken jener Optionen und Freiheiten auffangen, die den Glanz des postmodernen Versprechens ausgemacht haben. Weniger Erwerbsarbeit ließ sich nicht zum Nulltarif haben, sondern forderte erhöhten Einsatz von Transfermitteln. Ähnliches gilt für die ökonomischen Folgen von Individualisierung und Beziehungs-Patchwork, die nicht nur in eine Rentenlücke, sondern, viel unmittelbarer, auch in die Sozialhilfebedürftigkeit von Müttern und Kindern münden. Die lange Zeit vergessenen Kosten einer Pluralität, die oft vordergründig geblieben ist, erscheinen inzwischen auf unserer Rechnung. Die Krise des »Multikulturalismus« angesichts sozialer Segregation und Ghettobildung, gescheiterter Integration und Bildungsnotstands bei Migrantenkindern ist ein weiteres Beispiel dafür.

Um sich diesen Problemzonen stellen zu können, ist eine Revision der Postmoderne auch in den Grundlagen ihrer kulturellen Orientierung erforderlich. Der Gestus der Historisierung führt nicht mehr weiter. Spätestens seit 1989 wissen wir, dass das »Ende der Geschichte« noch nicht gekommen ist, aber mit den Konsequenzen aus dieser Einsicht tun wir uns immer noch schwer. Eine Rückkehr zu jenem optimistischen Fortschrittsglauben der Klassischen Moderne, der uns heute naiv erscheint, ist nicht möglich. Und doch steht so etwas wie eine Wiedergewinnung der Zukunft auf dem Programm; auch: eine Wiedergewinnung von Dynamik in einer Gesellschaft, die sich zu lange der eingefrorenen Bewegungsarmut, in der Veränderung nur ornamental war, hingegeben hat. Die gesellschaftlichen Problemzonen lassen sich nicht mehr länger mit einem Programm der größtmöglichen Beliebigkeit bearbeiten, sondern verlangen nach Präferenzen, nach der Diskussion und Implementierung von Werten.

So könnte es sein, dass eine revidierte Postmoderne sich durch eine Wiederkehr von sozialer Gemeinschaft als einem Gegengewicht zu radikaler Individualisierung auszeichnet. Das gilt für den Binnenraum privater Beziehungen in der Familie, im Generationenverbund ebenso wie für eine Gesellschaft im Ganzen, die sich verloren gegangener Solidarität neu vergewissern muss. Vielleicht stößt dann auch das glitzernde Lieblingskind der Postmoderne, die Welt des unbeschränkten hedonistischen Konsums, an neue Grenzen. Die Wiedergewinnung von Erwerbsarbeit und überhaupt eines produktiven Aktivismus könnte dann eher auf der Tagesordnung stehen. Gut möglich, dass in der Zukunft weniger Geld für Konsum zur Verfügung steht, weil die Menschen verantwortlich und selbstständig in die Nachhaltigkeit der Gesellschaft und ihrer eigenen Existenz investieren müssen: in Bildung oder Alterssicherung. Deswegen müssen in den Shopping-Malls noch nicht die Lichter ausgehen. Aber ohne Einfluss auf die gebaute Umwelt des Menschen wird diese Revision der postmodernen Gesellschaft kaum bleiben können. Die Kluft zwischen vielfachem privaten Reichtum und öffentlicher Armut muss neu überdacht werden. Die öffentliche Infrastruktur, die uns umgibt, die Schulen, Schwimmbäder, Rathäuser und Kirchen, stammen aus den fetten Jahren der Moderne und altern unaufhaltsam, mancherorts gibt es bereits Anzeichen des Verfalls. Diese Herausforderung an der Schnittstelle von Gesellschaft und Architektur, Politik und Städtebau könnte die nächsten zwei Jahrzehnte nachhaltig bestimmen.

return to Classical Modernism's optimistic faith in progress is not possible: it seems naïve to us today. And yet something of the nature of reclaiming the future seems to be on the agenda: an act of reclaiming dynamism in a society that has surrendered for too long to a frozen impoverishment of movement, in which change was merely ornamental. The problem areas of society can no longer be tackled with a programme that embraces an anything-goes philosophy to the highest degree; on the contrary, they demand choices, discussion and implementation of values.

Thus it might be possible that a revised Post-Modernism will be characterised by a return to a social community, as a counterbalance to radical individualisation. That applies to the personal realm of private relationships in the family, to the relationship between generations and to society as a whole, which has to reassure itself of the possibility of regaining lost solidarity. Perhaps Post-Modernism's glamorous favourite child, the world of unrestrained hedonistic consumption, will then come up against new limits. It would then be more possible to put the reclamation of paid employment, and in fact of a productive activism in general, on the agenda. It is quite possible that there will be less money available for consumerism in the future, because people will have to invest responsibly and autonomously in the sustainability of society and their own personal lives: in education or pension provision. That is no reason for the lights to go out in the shopping malls just yet. But, unless it influences people's built environment, this revision of Post-Modernist society will scarcely be able to have a lasting effect. The gap between manifold private wealth and public poverty needs re-thinking. The public infrastructure that surrounds us—schools, swimming pools, town halls and churches—dates back to the fat years of Modernism and is now aging inexorably; in some places, the signs of decline are already visible. This challenge to the interface between society and architecture, politics and urban design, could have a lasting impact on the next two decades.

ANTHONY VIDLER

ARCHITEKTUR NACH DER MODERNE: POSTMODERN ODER POSTHISTORISCH?

ARCHITECTURE AFTER MODERNISM: POST-MODERN OR POST-HISTOIRE?

»Mit dem Begriff ›posthistorisch‹ lässt sich offenbar gut beschreiben, was geschieht, wenn eine Institution oder eine kulturelle Errungenschaft aufhört, historisch relevant zu sein, sie keine neuen Qualitäten mehr produziert, sondern rein rezeptiv, eklektisch, imitativ wird. So verstanden würde der Begriff des Posthistorischen zur jetzigen Kulturepoche passen, die, nachdem sie ›mit Sinn erfüllt‹ war, nun ›ganz ohne Sinn‹ ist. Biologisch formuliert heißt dann die Alternative: Tod oder Mutation.«
Hendrik de Man, The Age of Doom, 1950

»Von jetzt an gibt es keine kunstimmanente Entwicklung mehr! Mit einer irgendwie sinnlogischen Kunstgeschichte ist es vorbei, selbst mit der Konsequenz der Absurditäten vorbei, die Entwicklung ist abgewickelt, und was nun kommt, ist bereits vorhanden: Der Synkretismus des Durcheinanders aller Stile und Möglichkeiten, das Posthistoire.«
Arnold Gehlen, Zeit-Bilder, 1961

"The term posthistorical seems adequate to describe what happens when an institution or a cultural achievement ceases to be historically active and productive of new qualities, and becomes purely receptive or eclectically imitative. Thus understood [the] notion of the post-historical would [...] fit the cultural phase that, following a 'fulfilment of sense,' has become 'devoid of sense.' The alternative then is, in biological terms, either death or mutation."
Hendrik de Man, The Age of Doom, 1950

"Now there is no longer any internal development within art! It is all up with art history based upon the logic of meaning, and even with any consistency of absurdities. The process of development has been completed, and what comes now is already in existence: the confused syncretism of all styles and possibilities—posthistory."
Arnold Gehlen, Zeit-Bilder, 1960

Die Moderne, so wurde gesagt, habe Geschichte abgelehnt und an ihre Stelle die Abstraktion gesetzt; ihre Versprechen von Funktionalität und ihr Technologie-Fetischismus seien nichts als verfehlte Utopien von Fortschritt gewesen; ihre Ideologie habe keine Verbindung mehr zu den Menschen gehabt, sei vielleicht sogar antihumanistisch gewesen; ihr formales Vokabular sei steril und unkommunikativ. Auf der anderen Seite stünde die Postmoderne zu all dem in direkter Opposition. Geschichte würde als Gegenpart zur Abstraktion wieder willkommen geheißen, jeder Anschein eines funktionalen Programms als viel zu deterministisch und kontrollierend aufgegeben. Die Sprache der Postmoderne, die aus den Wurzeln humanistischer Architektur und der expliziten Ikonographie der Werbung gewonnen sei, sei populär, wenn nicht gar populistisch. In letzter Konsequenz strebe sie – unterstützt von einem Sprössling der britischen Königsfamilie – danach, uns in eine bequemere Vergangenheit zurückzubringen, konfektioniert aus dem klassischen (oder besser: dörflichen) Stil. Die Postmoderne, heißt es, habe endlich wieder Verbindung zu den Menschen. Die Moderne dagegen stehe außerhalb von Geschichte und im Gegensatz zu ihr. Ihre radikalen, avantgardistischen Versuche, mit Geschichte zu brechen, seien nichts als der gescheiterte Fluchtversuch aus der Geschichte. Die Postmoderne dagegen akzeptiere Geschichte als Wert und Sprache und bestehe grundsätzlich auf der Kontinuität von Geschichte, die uns auf angenehme Weise wieder mit unseren humanistischen Wurzeln verbinde und menschlicher werden lasse.

Und dennoch – untersucht man das Geschichtsverständnis von Modernisten und Postmodernisten genauer, kommt eine irritierende Tatsache zum Vorschein: dass nämlich die Moderne weit davon entfernt war, Geschichte zu verwerfen, sie vielleicht sogar zu sehr respektierte. Auch wenn die Avantgarden der mo-

Modernism, we have been told, refused history in favour of abstraction; its functional promises and technological fetishism were nothing but failed utopias of progress; its ideology was out of touch with the people, if not anti-humanistic. Its formal vocabularies were sterile and uncommunicative. Post-Modernism, on the other hand, was its direct opposite. History was welcomed back as a counter to abstraction; any pretence of a functional programme was abandoned as over-deterministic and controlling; its language, drawn from the roots of humanistic architecture and the explicit iconography of advertising, was popular, if not populist. At its most extreme, as supported by a scion of the British royal family, it sought to return us to a more comfortable past rendered out of the whole cloth of classical (or better, village) style. It was, we were told, finally in touch with the people. In this formulation, Modernism appears out of history, against history, and, in its strident, avant-garde attempts to break with history, as nothing but a failed utopia of escape from history. Post-Modernism, on the other hand, seems to accept history as value and speech and insist on the fundamental continuity of history: a history that comfortably ties us back to our humanist roots and thereby renders us, once again, more human.

Yet a closer inspection of the historical stances of the Moderns and the Post-Moderns reveals a disconcerting fact: far from rejecting "history" as such, Modernism may have respected it too much. In asserting the need to break with the past, whether in Futurist or Constructivist terms, the Modernist avant-gardes in fact understood history as a fundamental force, an engine of the social world. Whether conceived in Hegelian or Marxian terms, as transcendentalist or dialectical, history moved and society did with it. If the avant-gardes had any illusions, they were that this movement might be anticipated, its force applied to new and anticipated ends. Even the abstraction of Modernist vocabulary

dernen Bewegung – ganz gleich ob Futuristen oder Konstruktivisten – die Notwendigkeit eines Bruchs mit der Vergangenheit behauptet haben, verstanden sie Geschichte als eine grundlegende Kraft, als Motor der sozialen Welt. Ob hegelianisch oder marxistisch, ob transzendental oder dialektisch aufgefasst, für sie war Geschichte stets in Bewegung und die Gesellschaft mit ihr. Wenn die Avantgarden irgendwelche Illusionen hatten, dann die, dass die Richtung dieser Bewegung voraussehbar sei und ihre Kraft auf neue, genau bestimmbare Ziele gelenkt werden könne. Selbst die Abstraktheit des Vokabulars der Moderne war abgeleitet vom tiefen Respekt, den die Moderne der Geschichte zollte. Es war der Respekt vor einem Verständnis von Geschichte, in der Ihre Erforscher – angefangen von Heinrich Wölfflin und Auguste Choisy bis zu Bruno Zevi und Colin Rowe – immer eher nach Wesenheiten und Strukturen als nach stilistischen Auswirkungen suchten. Deshalb wäre es durchaus richtig zu behaupten, Geschichte sei nie so lebendig gewesen wie zu Zeiten ihrer vermeintlichen Ablehnung durch die Moderne.

Und weiter lässt sich behaupten, dass auf der anderen Seite die Postmoderne eine tief gehende Verachtung für Geschichte an den Tag legt und stattdessen einem ahistorischen Mythos anhängt. Die alleinige Zuschreibung des »Humanismus« zur Renaissance ist doch nur abgedroschenes Zeug etablierter Fachgrößen, angefangen von Bernard Berenson bis hin zu Geoffrey Scott – wahrlich die letzten Zuckungen der Renaissance-Wiederbelebung. Und außerdem ist deren Renaissance nur die Erfindung vom glorreichen Italien, die ihrerseits auf den Legenden des 19. Jahrhunderts, von Jules Michelet oder Jacob Burckhardt, beruht. Die Bereitwilligkeit der Postmoderne, sich für die Bildung eines eigenen Vokabulars der Geschichte ebenso zu bedienen wie die Sprache der Werbung zu plündern, entlarvt ihre fundamentale Verachtung von Geschichte und ihre noch tiefere Verachtung der Gegenwart. Dass sich Prinz Charles die Wiederherstellung eines Dorfes auf dem Lande und sein Architekt die Wiederherstellung eines klassischen Atlantis vorstellen, ist Ausdruck derselben aristokratischen Illusion, die auf einer antidemokratischen, wenn nicht gar antisozialen Ideologie der nachromantischen Epoche fußt. Ob mit Bauern in der Pelerine oder mit Intellektuellen in der Toga, man stellt sich die Gesellschaft als stabiles Gebilde an einem sicheren Ort vor, ohne schmutzige, durch politische oder wirtschaftliche Konflikte ausgelöste Umbrüche. Tatsächlich kommt in postmodernen Modellen von Gesellschaft und Kultur »Konflikt« gar nicht vor; ihre »Geschichte« sei, wie Manfredo Tafuri argwöhnte, eine Geschichte »ohne Tränen«, während das genaue Gegenteil, von Le Corbusier deutlich als »Architektur oder Revolution« benannt, schließlich zu Gunsten der Architektur gelöst wurde.

Die Moderne zu denken hieße demnach, Geschichte als eine aktive, ungeheuer verstörende Kraft zu denken, sie zu ihren eigenen Bedingungen zu nehmen. Im realistischen wie im idealistischen Sinne hieße es, Geschichte durcheinander zu bringen, um ihre Gestalt zu ringen. Das genau ist mit historischem Denken gemeint. Im Gegensatz dazu hieße die Postmoderne zu denken alles zu ignorieren, was Geschichte zu Geschichte macht. Es hieße, dies und das herauszugreifen, was im jeweiligen Augenblick gut passt. In der Postmoderne wird Geschichte benutzt und

was derived from the deep respect Modernism evinced for history—a history that, from Heinrich Wölfflin and Auguste Choisy to Bruno Zevi and Colin Rowe, searched for essences and structures rather than stylistic affects. Indeed, it would be true to say that never was history more alive than in its so-called Modernist "rejection."

To continue in this vein, Post-Modernism, on the other hand, might be said to have a profound disdain for history, in favour of an a-historical myth. Its ascriptions of "humanism" to the Renaissance were, after all, nothing but the worn-out shards espoused by mandarin connoisseurs from Bernard Berenson to Geoffrey Scott: the very end-game of the Renaissance revival. Of course, the Renaissance was itself a fabrication based on mid-19th century myths of glorious Italy, from Jules Michelet to Jacob Burckhardt. Post-Modernism's willingness to ransack history, as well as billboards, for its vocabulary, revealed it indeed as fundamentally disrespectful of history and even more disrespectful of the present. For the Prince of Wales to imagine a restored country village and his architect to imagine a restored classical Atlantis illustrates two sides of an aristocratic illusion founded on an anti-democratic, if not anti-social, ideology of the post-Romantic period. Whether peasants in cloaks, or intellectuals in togas, society was imagined as stable and in place, with no untidy disruptions forced by industrial or political conflict. In fact, conflict was surprisingly absent from Post-Modern models of society and culture; its "history" was, as Manfredo Tafuri suspected, a history "without tears," where the opposition, bluntly stated by Le Corbusier as "Architecture or Revolution," was finally resolved in favour of architecture.

To think Modernism, then, would be to think of history as an active and profoundly disturbing force, to take history on its own terms, realistically or idealistically to tangle with history and wrestle it into shape. It is, indeed, to think historically. To think along Post-Modern lines, by contrast, would be to ignore everything that makes history history and to selectively pick and choose whatever authorizing sign fits the moment. History is used and abused in Post-Modernism, it is feared and confronted in Modernism.

Yet the counter-historical stance of Post-Modernism, however lauded as original by critics and followers in the 1980s, in fact takes its place within a much longer intellectual tradition that dates back to the late nineteenth century and which has seen many revivals and permutations to the present. Characterized by the philosopher and mathematician Antoine Augustin Cournot in the 1860s, this has become known as the tradition of Post-Histoire thought. For Cournot, history was neither everlasting, nor final. In his tripartite division, society passed through three periods: the pre-historical; the historical; and the "after" historical, later termed Post-Histoire. Pre-historical society was one that was closer to a natural organism than a human community: peoples, so to speak, "without history." Historical societies were those with institutions, traditions and great leaders, all subject to the "laws" of historical change, undergoing periods of growth and decline. Post-Historical societies, by contrast, had reached a stable and more or less unchanging state about which Cournot posited "history will be reduced to an

1

2

3

4

5

1 Otto Rudolf Salvisberg, Werksiedlung/Workers' housing in Piesteritz (D), 1915-1919
2 Paul Schmitthenner, Siedlung/Housing estate am Kochenhof, Stuttgart, 1933

3 Viktorianisches Reihenhaus Victorian terraced house, London, vor 1900/pre-1900
4 Venturi, Rauch & Scott Brown: Entwurf für die Strada Novissima Design for the Strada Novissima, Biennale, Venedig/Venice 1980

5 Léon Krier: Projekt Atlantis auf Teneriffa/Atlantis project in Teneriffe, 1988

missbraucht. In der Moderne wird sie gefürchtet, und man widersetzt sich ihr.

Aber die antihistorische Haltung der Postmoderne – mag sie von Kritikern und Anhängern in den achtziger Jahren noch so sehr als originell gepriesen worden sein – ist Teil einer viel älteren intellektuellen Tradition. Diese reicht bis in das späte neunzehnte Jahrhundert zurück und wurde bis in die Gegenwart häufig und in verschiedenen Erscheinungsformen wiederbelebt. Bereits um 1860 charakterisierte der Philosoph und Mathematiker Antoine Augustin Cournot das, was als posthistorisches Denken bekannt wurde. Für ihn war Geschichte weder ewig während noch zweckgerichtet. Die Gesellschaft durchlief seiner Vorstellung nach drei Perioden: eine prähistorische, eine historische und eine, die der historischen folgt und die Counot später posthistorisch nannte. Die prähistorische Gesellschaft schien ihm einem natürlichen Organismus ähnlicher als einer menschlichen Gemeinschaft – noch »ohne Geschichte«. Historische Gesellschaften nannte er jene mit Institutionen, Traditionen und großen Führern. Sie waren den »Gesetzen« geschichtlichen Wandels unterworfen und periodischem Aufstieg und Niedergang ausgesetzt. Posthistorische Gesellschaften hatten demgegenüber einen stabilen, mehr oder minder immer gleichen Status erreicht: Gesellschaften, so Cournot, in denen Geschichte auf ein amtliches Nachrichtenblatt beschränkt werden würde, nur dazu da, Gesetze, Statistiken, die Berufung von Staatslenkern und die Ernennung von Funktionären zu verzeichnen – also Gesellschaften, die in letzter Konsequenz keine Geschichte im gewöhnlichen Sinn des Wortes mehr hätten. Das Posthistoire denken heißt demnach, Geschichte als an ihr Ende kommend zu denken. Es heißt, Historie nicht als einen sozialen oder dialektischen Prozess, sondern als chronologische oder biologische Unvermeidbarkeit zu verstehen. Es heißt, sich das Leben nach dem Ende der Geschichte als endlose Wiederholung des immer Gleichen, als Stasis vorzustellen, wo nichts mehr erfunden, verwandelt oder sonstwie geändert werden muss. Im Sinne von Cournot wäre eine posthistorische Welt wie eine Bürokratie (er selbst gebrauchte den chinesischen Staatsapparat als Beispiel) oder wie Kafkas Schloss, um es mit einem literarischen Skeptizismus auszudrücken. Zu Beginn des zwanzigsten Jahrhunderts sahen Denker wie Raymond Ruyer im Posthistoire auch das Ende jedweder Entwicklung in den quasi darwinistischen Modellen des Finalismus und Neo-Finalismus. Die von deutschen Schriftstellern wie Ernst Jünger und dem Anthropologen Arnold Gehlen seit den fünfziger Jahren vorgenommene Neuinterpretation erkannte das Ende der Politik und den Triumph der Ordnung. In der Formulierung von Philosophen wie Hendrik de Man und Kunsthistorikern wie Hans Sedlmayr aus den fünfziger Jahren handelte es sich beim Posthistoire um eine Dystopie, ein Endspiel von Verlust und Verfall bar jeder Hoffnung. Erst in den neueren, postnietzscheanischen Begriffen eines Gianni Vattimo ist das Posthistoire einfach die Anerkennung der modernen Welt, wie sie ist: einer Welt von Veränderung ohne Veränderung, von möglicher Mutation ohne wirkliche Mutation.

Für Vattimo ist das Posthistoire ein Konzept, das ihm die Beschreibung dessen erlaubt, was er die Erfahrung des »Endes der

official gazette, serving to register the rule, statistical surveys, the appointment of chiefs of state and the nomination of functionaries, and will cease in consequence to have a history, in the sense that is normally given to the word." To think in terms of Post-Histoire is to think of history as coming to an end; it is to understand history, not as a social or dialectical process, but as a chronological or biological inevitability. It is to think of life, after the end of history, as an endless repetition of the same and as a state of stasis where no more invention, modification, or change need take place. In the sense outlined by Cournot, a Post-Histoire world would seem much like a bureaucracy (he gave the example of the Chinese state apparatus), or, in our more sceptical terms, like Kafka's Castle. As interpreted in the early twentieth century by thinkers such as Raymond Ruyer, Post-Histoire would be the end of evolution in quasi-Darwinian models of Finalism and Neo-Finalism. As reinterpreted by German writers such as Ernst Jünger and the anthropologist Arnold Gehlen from the 1950s on, it would signal the end of politics and the triumph of order. As reformulated by philosophers such as Hendrik de Man and art-historians such as Hans Sedlmayr in the 1950s, it was a pessimistic dystopia without hope, a pessimistic end-game of loss and decay. In the more recent post-Nietzschean terms of Gianni Vattimo, Post-Histoire is simply a recognition of the modern world as it is—a world of change without change, mutability without mutability.

For Gianni Vattimo, Post-Histoire is a concept that allows him to describe what he calls "the experience of the end of history." Here he takes his cue from Gehlen, who found the term useful to sum up the mentality that followed Post-Modern disillusionment in the great nineteenth-century narratives of historical progress—the moment, as Gehlen says, "when progress becomes routine." Vattimo sees such routinization in the developments of technology and consumerism that, while continuously renewed, nevertheless stay the same:

"There is a profound 'immobility' in the technological world which science fiction writers have often portrayed as the reduction of every experience of reality to an experience of images (no one ever really meets anyone else; instead, everyone watches everything on a television screen while alone at home). This same phenomenon can already be sensed in the air-conditioned, muffled silence in which computers work."

Flattened out, simultaneous, the world appears de-historicized. What made us "modern" (i.e. the experience of living every day in a narrative history of progress and development reinforced by the daily newspaper) now comes to a halt. The "master" narrative, once a secularisation of religious salvation, now fails and multiple other possible narratives rise up.

In the context of our argument, it is significant that Vattimo goes beyond other Post-Histoire thinkers in order to join the end of history argument to the emergence of Post-Modernism. He writes: "What legitimates Postmodernist theories and makes them worthy of discussion is the fact that their claim of a radical 'break' with modernity does not seem unfounded as long as these observations on the Post-Historical character of contemporary existence are valid."

Geschichte« nennt. Er greift hier ein Stichwort Gehlens auf, der den Begriff nützlich fand, um die Denkweise zusammenzufassen, die der postmodernen Desillusionierung über die großen, im neunzehnten Jahrhundert verfassten Erzählungen von historischem Fortschritt gefolgt war. Es war, wie Gehlen schreibt, der Augenblick, »als Fortschritt Routine wurde«. Vattimo wiederum erblickt die Zwangsläufigkeit von Routine in den Entwicklungen der Technologie und des Konsumismus, die immer gleich bleiben, während sie sich dauernd erneuern: »Es gibt eine tiefe ›Unbeweglichkeit‹ der technischen Welt, die von vielen Science-Fiction-Autoren als die Reduktion jeglicher Erfahrung der Wirklichkeit auf die Erfahrung der Bilder geschildert wird (niemand trifft mehr mit einem anderen Menschen zusammen, man betrachtet alles am Fernsehmonitor, den man vom Sessel in der eigenen Stube aus steuert) und wie sie sich, wirklichkeitsnäher, bereits in dem wattierten und klimatisierten Schweigen wahrnehmen läßt, das die Arbeit an Computern umgibt.«

Glatt geebnet und gleichzeitig in Echtzeit präsent erscheint die Welt geschichtslos. Was uns »modern« sein ließ – die von täglicher Zeitungslektüre noch verstärkte Erfahrung, in einer narrativen Historie immer weiter fortschreitender Entwicklung zu leben – hört nun auf. Die »Meistererzählung«, ursprünglich die säkularisierte Form religiöser Erlösung, wird unglaubwürdig. Dafür entstehen verschiedenste andere Erzählungen.

Für unseren Argumentationszusammenhang ist interessant, dass Vattimo über andere Denker des Posthistoire hinausgeht und den Gedanken vom Ende der Geschichte mit dem Entstehen der Postmoderne verknüpft. Er schreibt: »Was die Diskussion der postmodernistischen Theorien legitimiert und sie auch diskussionswürdig macht, ist die Tatsache, daß deren Anspruch auf eine radikale ›Wende‹ gegenüber der Moderne nicht unbegründet erscheint, falls die Feststellungen über den postgeschichtlichen Charakter der gegenwärtigen Existenz Geltung haben.«

So sind das Ende der Moderne beziehungsweise das Ende der Kunstgeschichte die logische Folge eines postmodernen Zustands. In dieser Hinsicht könnten wir die Postmoderne als ein besonderes Moment im posthistorischen Denken oder, besser noch, auf die Architektur bezogen als einen Sonderfall posthistorischen Denkens betrachten. Und so gesehen ist die Ausprägung der (architektonischen) Postmoderne seit dem späten neunzehnten Jahrhundert in unserer Welt kontinuierlich präsent: vom Hampstead Garden Suburb zum Dorf von Prinz Charles; vom nostalgischen Heimatstil der zwanziger zu den Siedlungen des New Urbanism der achtziger Jahre; von den englischen Renaissance Revivals unter Queen Anne und Eduard VII. zu den simulierten italienischen Piazzas von New Orleans; von den Straßen Camillo Sittes zur Strada Novissima des Paolo Portoghesi. Alle diese Antimodernismen nehmen folgerichtig ihren Platz in einer letzten Endes als geschichtslos aufgefassten Welt ein. Alles Historische ist dort zum leeren Zeichen seiner selbst geworden, seiner Kraft und unliebsamen Gewalt beraubt, verbunden mit der leuchtenden Vision einer Welt ohne Wandel. Dass diesem ikonographischen Mischmasch noch die Werbung der Las-Vegas-Welt beigegeben wurde, war nur ein kleiner Schritt, der vollständig zum Verständnis der Welt als Abbild ihrer Vergangenheit und Illusion ohne Zukunft passt.

6

7

Léon Krier
Musterstadt Poundbury, bei Dorchester, Planungsbeginn 1988, Baubeginn 1993
The new village of Poundbury, near Dorchester, planning began 1988, building began 1993

6 Markthalle/Market hall
7 Wohnbauten verschiedener Stilrichtungen/Housing in different styles

Dieses Verständnis posthistorischen Denkens in der Architektur schließt natürlich einen großen Teil der Bauten nicht aus, die – obwohl sie modern aussehen – dennoch einem ahistorischen Trend folgen. Das Posthistoire versteht ja »Modernität« selbst als schon abgeschlossenes, vollendetes Feld. Und oft genug wurden die verschiedenen Stile der Moderne auf dieselbe Art hervorgerufen, wie es die Postmoderne mit den Motiven des Klassischen tat. So kann zum Beispiel der »Konstruktivismus« mühelos als »Dekonstruktivismus« wieder auferstehen. Zugleich gibt es in jüngster Zeit reichlich Belege für einen Neoexpressionismus, der von Bruno Taut und Hans Scharoun oder Architekturen wie aus dem Film »Das Kabinett des Dr. Caligari« beeinflusst ist. Wir können sogar vermuten, dass auch die Hightech-Architektur, die in ihrer dreisten »Modernität« so unschuldig wirkt, in diese Kategorie fällt. Bei vielen dieser Bauten, die eine Kontinuität des Modernen zu repräsentieren scheinen, lässt sich stilistische Eigenheit und historische Referenz als bloße Wiederholung ausmachen und nicht als ein inneres Verstehen von grundlegender Veränderung und Dynamik historischen Denkens und Handelns.

Womit sich die Frage erhebt: Was bleibt denn außerhalb des politisch regressiven und mit Bildern angefüllten Posthistoire für das historische Denken und infolgedessen für eine historisch verstandene Modernität noch? Zuerst einmal, dank Jürgen Habermas und anderen, die Einsicht, dass wir auf besondere Weise noch immer tief in die als historischer Abschnitt verstandene Moderne verstrickt sind. Ganz gleich ob wir das Entstehen der Moderne mit den Akademien der Wissenschaften und der Künste im siebzehnten, mit dem philosophischen Denken im achtzehnten, mit den politischen und industriellen Revolutionen im neunzehnten oder mit den wissenschaftlichen Durchbrüchen im zwanzigsten Jahrhundert verknüpfen, klar ist, dass unsere historisch motivierte Reaktion all diese Phänomene grundsätzlich anerkennt; wir sehen uns eher in geistiger Verwandtschaft und nicht in geistiger Entfremdung zu ihnen. Ein Beispiel aus jüngerer Zeit wäre Peter Galison, Wissenschaftshistoriker an der Harvard Universität, der wichtige Lehren für global ausgerichtete Denksysteme unserer Zeit in den früheren Fragestellungen über »Zeit« fand, die Albert Einstein und Henri Poincaré untersucht hatten. Wenn das wirklich der Fall ist, dann wird auch klar, dass Modernität ein fortdauernder Prozess von Neubewertung und Erneuerung ist, der auf Experiment und Erforschung von Zusammenhängen basiert.

Bezogen auf die Architektur erhebt sich die Forderung, die architektonische Sprache aus sich heraus neu zu studieren und zu entwickeln, statt einen bereits existierenden Code oberflächlich zu zitieren. Als Alternative oder in Verbindung mit einem solchen Studium käme man auch zu einem rigorosen und produktiven Ansatz für ein grundlegendes Programm. Genau so haben Architekten, angefangen von Theo van Doesburg bis zu Peter Eisenman, den Charakter der Formensprache der Architektur auch aufgefasst; andere, von Le Corbusier bis Rem Koolhaas, kamen so zu einem Verständnis der Radikalität von Architektur. Wir sollten endlich anfangen, in diesem Sinne die Qualitäten der Moderne herauszuarbeiten und die quälende Stilfrage (die selbst ein Konzept des Posthistoire ist) beiseite zu lassen, um un-

Thus the end of modernity and the end of art history, respectively, as the immediate corollary of a Post-Modern condition. In this way we might see Post-Modernism as a special moment in Post-Histoire thought, or better as a special case of Post-Histoire thought in architectural terms. Indeed, seen in this context, (architectural) Post-Modernism has had a continuous presence in the modern world from the late nineteenth century on. From Hampstead Garden suburb to the Prince of Wales' village, from the nostalgic heimat style of the 1920s to the New Urbanist settlements of the 1980s, from the Queen Anne and Renaissance revivals of Edwardian England to the mock Italian piazzas of New Orleans, from the streets of Sitte to the Strada Novissima of Portoghesi: all these counter-modernisms and anti-modernisms take their logical place in a world conceived of as, finally, without history, a world in which all history has been transformed into an empty sign of itself, deprived of its force and discomforting violence, combined in a luminous vision of a world without change. The addition of advertising, of the world of Las Vegas, to this iconographic soup was then a simple step entirely consistent with a view of the world as image of its past and illusion without future.

Of course, this understanding of Post-Histoire thought in architecture does not exclude a great deal of work that, while it may look modern enough, nevertheless corresponds to a counter-historical trend. After all, Post-Histoire already understands "modernity" itself as a closed and completed historical field, while the different styles of the Modern have often enough been evoked in the same way as that in which Post-Modernism evoked Classical motifs. Thus "Constructivism" can easily enough be resurrected under the guise of "Deconstructivism," while we have seen ample evidence recently of a Neo-Expressionism drawn from the languages of Taut, Scharoun and the sets of movies such as Dr Caligari. We might suspect that even "hi-tech" itself, seemingly so innocent in its unabashed "modernity," to fall into this category also. In much of this work, which seems on the surface to represent a continuity of the Modern, we can detect stylistic conceit and historical reference as repetition, rather than an inner understanding of the transformation dynamics of historical thought and practice.

This opens the question of what, outside the politically regressive and image-filled frame of the Post-Histoire, is left for historical thought and thence for modernity conceived historically? In the first place, it is not difficult to understand, with Habermas and others, that we are still, in some way, deeply involved in the Modern, as historically defined. Whether we place the emergence of this tendency with the scientific and aesthetic academies of the seventeenth century, the philosophic thought of the eighteenth, the political and industrial revolutions of the nineteenth, or the scientific breakthroughs of the twentieth, it is clear that our historical response to all these phenomena is one of fundamental recognition, of affinity rather than estrangement. A recent example would be that cited by the Harvard historian of science, Peter Galison, who has found important lessons for contemporary global positioning systems in the temporal conundrums of Einstein and Poincaré. Secondly, if this is the case, it is equally clear that "modernity" is a continuing

8

8 Léon Krier: Poundbury,
bei/near Dorchester, seit/begun 1993

9

9 Rob Krier, Christoph Kohl:
Neues Haus auf dem Kirchplatz
von Noordzijde
New house on Noordzijde's church
square, Amsterdam, 1999

ser eigenes Empfinden von Modernität in einem historischen wie in einem dynamischen Sinn zu analysieren. Das würde auch eine Annäherung an die Geschichte der Moderne beinhalten, die sich dem Versuch, die Debatte zu schließen, und dem Finalismus verweigert und vielmehr sämtliche von ihr gestellten Fragen als noch immer offen betrachtet. Dann würde die Historiographie der modernen Architektur nicht weiter versuchen, Stile oder Bewegungen zu klassifizieren, auch wenn dies Teil der Bestandsaufnahme bliebe. Sie würde vielmehr die Stellen suchen, an denen unbequeme Fragen zur Form und zum Programm mit Blick auf die Gesellschaft und ihre politische Gestaltung gestellt wurden; wo eher Unentschiedenheit als Bestimmtheit an den Tag gelegt wurde; wo Projekte zwar begonnen, doch nicht beendet, sie gleichwohl nicht als Fehlschläge, sondern als noch nicht bewältigte, noch anstehende Herausforderungen betrachtet wurden; wo Störungen von außerhalb der Zunft zu unbequemen Fragen über etablierte Glaubenssätze führten; wo sogar die Formen, in denen wir Geschichte begreifen, hinterfragt wurden. Dies würde eine Neubewertung störender Momente und Persönlichkeiten einschließen, die nicht als etwas Seltsames und Peinliches, auch nicht als aufgewärmte Utopien (Utopie ist ein posthistorisches Konzept), sondern als Chancen für den Prozess und gegen den Schein von Modernität zu betrachten wären. Das würde auch eine ernsthafte Neueinschätzung der heiligen Kühe der Moderne erfordern, die allzu schnell kanonisch wurden. Die Ungereimtheiten und noch offenen Fragen, die hinter ihren Fassaden lauern, müssten geklärt werden. Schließlich würde es bedeuten, die nach dem Zweiten Weltkrieg vorherrschenden Auffassungen von »Modernismus« noch einmal zu hinterfragen – ihren Versuch zu prüfen, den schwankenden Boden der frühen Avantgarden zu festigen und für den Wiederaufbau Regeln für

project of re-evaluation and innovation, based on experiment and internal investigation.

In architectural terms, this would involve not the outward citation of an already formed language, but the internal study and development of architectural language in itself and, either alternatively or in conjunction, a similarly rigorous and productive approach to the fundamental programme of the work. It is in such a way that some architects, from van Doesburg to Peter Eisenman, for example, have understood the nature of the formal language of architecture and others, from Le Corbusier to Koolhaas, have understood the radicalism of the programme. We might indeed begin to characterize the qualities of the Modern in this way, thus bypassing the vexed question of style (itself a Post-Histoire concept) in order to construe historically and dynamically a sense of our own modernity. Such a task would involve an approach to modern history that refuses closure and finalism, rather seeing all of the questions posed by modernity as still open. In this formulation, the history of modern architecture would not seek to classify style or movement, even if this were a part of the historical record itself, but to look for places where the uncomfortable questions of form and programme with respect to society and its political formation were being asked: where irresolution rather than resolution was assumed; where projects were started but not finished (not as failures but as active and unresolved challenges); where disruptions from outside the field inconveniently questioned the verities of established practices; where the very forms in which we conceive of history itself have been put into question. This would involve a reassessment of disruptive moments and figures, neither as curiosities and embarrassments, nor as washed-up utopias (utopia is a Post-Histoire concept), but as

das Modernsein zu liefern. So müsste man, nur um ein paar Beispiele zu nennen, Bewegungen und Gruppen wie Archigram, Persönlichkeiten wie Friedrich Kiesler und Gordon Matta-Clark, Ikonen wie Le Corbusier und Ludwig Mies van der Rohe, schließlich auch Konzepte des Modernismus, die von Kritikern wie Clement Greenberg und Colin Rowe entwickelt wurden, allesamt von neuem gründlich erforschen. Ähnliches gilt für Historiker, etwa für Nikolaus Pevsner, Emil Kaufmann, Reyner Banham, Manfredo Tafuri, die alle versucht haben, Modernität im Einklang mit ihrer eigenen Vision der Zukunft zu deuten. Diese Historiker sollten dann nicht so sehr auf Grundlage ihres Beitrags zum geschichtlichen Verständnis früherer Phasen der Moderne beachtet werden – obwohl auch das wichtig ist –, sondern als Instanzen für die Prozesse der Selbstreflexion der Moderne. Diese Prozesse wären als noch offene Fragen erneut zu betrachten: zum Beispiel Kaufmanns formale Definitionen von Autonomie, die in der architektonischen Praxis von Philip Johnson über Aldo Rossi bis zu Peter Eisenman so mächtige Resonanz fanden; zum Beispiel Pevsners aufgeregte Feststellung der »Rückkehr des Historismus« schon im Jahr 1960 (was dazu führen könnte, die scheinbare Neuartigkeit der in den achtziger Jahren einbrechenden Postmoderne in Frage zu stellen); zum Beispiel Banhams eingehende Befragungen der Architekturmanifeste der Moderne, die nach einer neuen Beziehung zwischen Wissenschaft und Ästhetik riefen, wodurch die Experimente eines Cedric Price ungemein starken Antrieb erhielten; zum Beispiel Tafuris Redefinition der Moderne als durch die Ursprungsgeste der Renaissance konstituiert, ein Beitrag, der so viel für das Verständnis des Charakters der Moderne geleistet hat. Alle diese Geschichten sollten als modernistische Projekte an und für sich gedacht werden; sie sollten genutzt werden, um unsere vorgefassten Meinungen und unser historisches Bewusstsein zu hinterfragen.

Was nun könnte ein Modernismus – neu verstanden als ein Kontinuum, in dem eine posthistorische Postmoderne zeitweise und wiederkehrend ihren Platz einnimmt – für die gegenwärtige architektonische Praxis bedeuten? Zunächst einmal: keine Auferstehung des modernen Stils oder der modernen Stile, sondern eine beständige Resistenz gegenüber Stil an sich und die erneute Erkundung der Potenziale der Abstraktion, um eine kohärente Form des Ausdrucks zu entwickeln. Solche Abstraktion dürfte jedoch nicht auf den verschiedenen avantgardistischen Sprachen der zwanziger Jahre beruhen, sondern müsste sich an den heutigen programmatischen und technologischen Forderungen orientieren. Diese Forderungen würden eine Anerkennung der längst nicht mehr neuen digitalen Technologien einschließen; bislang dienten diese ja viel zu sehr einer Software-Ästhetik, die mit jedem neuen Programm aufkommt, ob nun »AutoCad«, »Rhino« oder »Maya«. Notwendig wären auch kritische Antworten auf die von der Moderne gestellten, aber bislang weder politisch noch architektonisch befriedigend gelösten Fragen: auf die Wohnungsfrage, die Architektur und Stadtentwicklung im globalen Maßstab noch immer beschäftigt; auf die Frage der Dichte, die sich, ebenfalls im globalen Maßstab, aufgrund der Bevölkerungsexplosion und der Flächenknappheit stellt; auf die ökologische Frage nach Ressourcen und Methoden des

openings into the process (rather than the appearance) of modernity; it would also involve a serious re-evaluation of the sacred cows of modernity, whose work has become, too quickly, canonical, in order to detect the internal inconsistencies, the still-open questions lurking behind their monographed façades; it would, finally, mean the opening up of those ideas of "Modernism," so prevalent after the Second World War, that were proposed in order to tidy up the erratic field of the early avant-gardes and provide rules for being modern in the era of reconstruction. Thus, to give some examples, movements and groups such as Archigram, figures such as Kiesler and Matta-Clark, icons such as Le Corbusier and Mies, and concepts of Modernism developed by critics such as Greenberg and Rowe would all come under renewed scrutiny, as would historians themselves, such as Pevsner, Kaufmann, Banham and Tafuri, all attempting to construe "modernity" according to their own particular vision of the future. Such historians should then be seen, not so much as contributing to our historical knowledge of earlier phases of the Modern (although this is important) but more as instances of the processes of modernity's self-reflection, themselves to be opened up as unanswered questions. Thus Kaufmann's formal definitions of "autonomy" which resonated so powerfully in the practice of architects from Johnson and Rossi to Eisenman; Pevsner's already nervous identification of the "return of Historicism" in 1960 (a phenomenon which might lead us to question the apparent newness of the Post-Modern irruption in the 1980s); Banham's interrogation of the "programme" as calling for a new relationship between science and aesthetics, which gave so strong an impetus to the experiments of Cedric Price; Tafuri's reinscription of modernity as constituted by the initial gesture of Renaissance, which did so much to open up the perceived nature of modernity itself: all these histories should be conceived as so many Modernist projects in and for themselves and should be used to challenge the preconceptions of our own historical consciousness.

What, then, might a Modernism reconceived as a continuum, within which a Post-Histoire Post-Modernism found its momentary and recurring place, mean for contemporary practice? In the first place, we would not expect to see a resurgence of modern style, or styles, but rather a consistent resistance to style and a re-exploration of the potentials for abstraction to develop acoherent form of expression. Such abstraction would, however, not be founded on the various avant-garde languages of the 1920s, but rather on the programmatic and technological demands of the present. These demands would include a recognition of the no-longer-new technologies of the digital; technologies that until now have been too subservient to the software aesthetic that arrives with every new programme, whether AutoCad or Rhino or Maya. They would also require a critical response to questions posed throughout by Modernism, but not yet satisfactorily answered in political or architectural terms: the housing question that still haunts architecture and development on a global scale; the question of density that is posed by population explosions and land scarcity, also on a global scale; the ecological question of resources and modes of conservation that, with radical shifts in climate and

Substanzerhalts, die wegen des radikalen Klimawandels und nachlassender Energiequellen das Bauwesen vor fundamentale Schwierigkeiten stellt, die weit mehr implizieren als die Frage nach dem richtigen Material oder »grüner« Architektur. Neue Anforderungen, die sich in früheren Stadien der Moderne noch gar nicht stellen konnten, werden den vollen Einsatz von Techniken verlangen, die alle möglichen Arten von Daten vernetzen und letztlich so gestalten könnten, dass die Konsequenzen programmatischer Entscheidungen messbar wären und damit alternative Entwürfe eingeschätzt und unterstützt werden könnten. Diese Alternativen wären nicht willkürlich ausgewählte oberflächliche Schönheiten oder gestaltete »blobs«, sondern stellten gebaute Argumente für politische, soziale und technologische Interventionen dar – gegen ein »business as usal«. Alles in allem müsste eine neue Moderne fortfahren, die Fragen der Gegenwart aus einer avantgardistischen Vorstellungskraft und Haltung heraus zu stellen, aber mit dem Vorteil der durch Studium vorangegangener Entwicklungen erlangten Weisheit und auf der langen Geschichte der Moderne aufbauend. Auf diese Art fände eine Bewegung, die angeblich mit der Zurückweisung alles Geschichtlichen begann, in der eigenen Geschichte ihre ideologischen und experimentellen Grundlagen.

Bibliographie
Belting, Hans, Das Ende der Kunstgeschichte?, München 1984.
Cournot, Antoine Augustin, Traité de l'enchaînement des idées fondamentales dans les sciences et dans l'histoire, Paris 1861.
Gehlen, Arnold, Zeit-Bilder. Zur Soziologie und Ästhetik der modernen Malerei, Frankfurt am Main/Bonn², 1965. Das Zitat findet sich in Teil XII/1, S. 206.
Ginzburg, Carlo, Mikro-Historie. Zwei oder drei Dinge, die ich von ihr weiß, in: Historische Anthropologie, H. 2/1993, S. 169-192.
de Man, Hendrik, The Age of Doom, in: Peter Dodge (Hg.), A Documentary Study of Hendrik de Man, Socialist Critic of Marxism, Princeton 1979. De Man wendet das Konzept von Cournot sogar auf die Geschichte der Kunst an: »Auf dieselbe Weise kann man die Tatsache erklären, dass bestimmte, zu einer gegebenen Kultur gehörenden Künste stets ein Stadium ihrer Entwicklung erreichen, wo sie unfähig werden, noch etwas auszudrücken; dies kann dann nur eine andere Kunst erreichen. Die europäischen Maler des trecento und quattrocento etwa begannen da, wo die Bildhauer der Kathedralen des dreizehnten Jahrhunderts aufgehört hatten; als Ausdruck für das ›Weltgefühl‹ des achtzehnten Jahrhunderts nahm die Musik den Platz der barocken Architektur ein, sobald diese ihre Archetypen hervorgebracht hatte.« S. 345 f.
Noever, Peter (Hg.), Architektur am Ende? Manifeste und Diskussionsbeiträge zur Wiener Architekturkonferenz. Mit einem Vorwort von Frank O. Gehry und Beiträgen von Coop Himmelb(l)au, Zaha Hadid, Steven Holl, Thom Mayne, Eric Owen Moss, Carme Pinós und Lebbeus Woods, München 1993.
Vattimo, Gianni, Das Ende der Moderne, Stuttgart 1990. Die beiden Zitate finden sich auf S. 12 und S. 16.

diminishing energy sources, poses fundamental problems for building that have much wider implications than materials and "green building." New demands, not fully posed by former modernities, would include the full use of modelling techniques for assimilating, integrating and ultimately forming data of all kinds in such a way that the consequences of programmatic decisions could be measured in terms that supported and evaluated design alternatives. These alternatives would not simply appear as random choices among beautiful surfaces or shaped blobs, but as arguments in form that proposed political, social, and technological interventions that implied a critique of 'business as usual.' In sum, a new modernity would continue to address the questions of the present with the imagination of an avant-garde stance, but now with the wisdom of hindsight and with a long history of the modern on which to rely. In this way, a movement that ostensibly began by rejecting "history" would now find its ideological and experimental sources in its own history.

Bibliography
Belting, Hans, The End of the History of Art?, Chicago 1987.
Cournot, Antoine Augustin, Traité de l'enchaînement des idées fondamentales dans les sciences et dans l'histoire, Paris 1861.
Gehlen, Arnold, Zeit-Bilder, Frankfurt am Main/Bonn 1960; quotation cited from Vattimo, p. 4.
Ginzburg, Carlo, Microhistory: Two or three things that I know about it, in: Critical Inquiry, vol. 20, no. 1 (Autumn 1993), pp. 10-35.
de Man, Hendrik, The Age of Doom, [1950] unpublished ms. in English, in: Peter Dodge (ed.), A Documentary Study of Hendrik de Man, Socialist Critic of Marxism, Princeton 1979.
De Man even applies Cournot's concept to the history of art: "In the same way, one can explain the fact that definite arts, belonging to a given civilization, always seem to reach a stage of development where they become unable to express more; this can then be done only by another art. So the European painters of the Trecento and Quattrocento started where the sculptors of the thirteenth-century cathedrals had stopped: as an expression of the "world feeling" of the eighteenth century, music took the place of baroque architecture as soon as the latter had produced its archetypes … ." ibid, pp. 345-346.
Peter, Noever, (ed.), The End of Architecture? Documents and Manifestos, Vienna Architecture Conference, foreword by Frank O. Gehry and contributions by Coop Himmelb(l)au, Zaha Hadid, Steven Holl, Thom Mayne, Eric Owen Moss, Carme Pinós, Lebbeus Woods, Munich 1993.
Gianni, Vattimo, The End of Modernity: Nihilism and Hermeneutics in Postmodern Culture, translated and with an introduction by Jon R. Snyder, Baltimore, 1988.

HUBERTUS ADAM

ZWISCHEN BANALITÄT UND EXTRAVAGANZ POSTMODERNE ARCHITEKTUR – UND IHRE (NACH-)WIRKUNGEN

BETWEEN BANALITY AND EXTRAVAGANCE POST-MODERN ARCHITECTURE— AND ITS (ONGOING) EFFECTS

Der Begriff »Postmoderne« sei inzwischen zur abgegriffenen Münze geworden, konstatierte Heinrich Klotz schon 1984.[1] Zwanzig Jahre später scheint der Terminus nicht nur verbraucht, sondern nachgerade zum Verdikt geworden zu sein. »Postmodern« zu sein, das ist im Sektor der Architektur alles andere als eine lobende Bestimmung, und kaum einer der seinerzeitigen Protagonisten möchte sich derzeit noch, und sei es selbst rückblickend, als ein Exponent der Postmoderne verstehen. Zeitlich zu nahe, um schon zum Gegenstand eines Retrokultes zu werden, aber so weit entfernt, dass von ihnen wenig Inspiration in das gegenwärtige Bauen einfließt, wirken viele der einstigen architektonischen Inkunabeln wie Relikte einer längst vergangenen Ära.

Die landläufige Vorstellung von der Postmoderne in der Architektur beschränkt sich auf das Stilistische und betrifft die – zum Teil ironisch verfremdete – Verwendung klassizierender und historisierender Elemente. Was als Befreiung vom funktionalistisch-puristischen Dogmatismus der Spätmoderne begann, erzeugte am Ende Überdruss, als Segmentgiebelchen Tiefgarageneinfahrten krönten und neckische postmoderne Elemente in das Repertoire von Fertigteilhaus-Anbietern eingegangen waren. Das ubiquitäre Applikationsdesign erzeugte neue Uniformität und widersprach damit den ursprünglichen Intentionen, spezifische Lösungen für einen konkreten Ort zu entwickeln. Gleichwohl deutet die Omnipräsenz postmoderner Versatzstükke darauf hin, wie erfolgreich und geschmacksbildend die Postmoderne gewirkt hat. Es gibt kaum einen Sektor menschlicher Aktivität, auf den der Begriff nicht angewandt worden wäre; seine eigentliche Karriere aber vollzog sich im Bereich der Architektur. Durch die Inkunabeln postmodernen Bauens – man kann in Deutschland vor allem an die Museen in Stuttgart, Mönchengladbach oder Frankfurt am Main denken – erlangte Architektur jenseits fachinterner Diskurse die Aufmerksamkeit und Akzeptanz einer breiten Öffentlichkeit, und dieses Interesse hält an. Ohne die damalige Trendwende, welche das Image des planenden Technokraten durch jenes des populären Raumkünstlers ersetzte, gäbe es keinen »Bilbao-Effekt« und kein Starwesen in der gegenwärtigen Architektur.

DEFINITIONEN DER POSTMODERNEN ARCHITEKTUR

Obwohl kein Begriff häufiger im Architekturdiskurs der vergangenen Jahrzehnte Verwendung gefunden hat als jener der Postmoderne, bleibt die Frage schwierig, was postmoderne Architektur ist und was nicht.

Bekanntlich lässt sich die Postmoderne begriffsgeschichtlich trotz früherem Auftauchen zuerst in der nordamerikanischen Literaturdebatte der Zeit nach dem Zweiten Weltkrieg fassen.[2] Als »postmodern« bezeichnete der Kritiker Irving Howe jene zeitgenössischen Autoren, welche auf die Neuerer vom Schlag eines Marcel Proust, James Joyce oder Ezra Pound folgten. Wusste sich Howe noch in der Tradition eines kulturpessimistisch grundierten Diskurses, demzufolge auf die Höhen der unausweichliche Niedergang folgt, so gelang es nachfolgenden Theoretikern, den Negativbegriff ins Positive zu kehren. Hinzuweisen ist hier auf Susan Sontag, vor allem aber auf den Aufsatz von

1 Heinrich Klotz (Hg.), Die Revision der Moderne. Postmoderne Architektur 1960-1980 (Katalog DAM Frankfurt), München 1984, S. 11.

2 Siehe hierzu vor allem: Wolfgang Welsch, Unsere postmoderne Moderne, Weinheim 1987, S. 12 ff.

Back in 1984, Heinrich Klotz pointed out that the term "Post-Modern" had become a worn-out cliché.[1] Twenty years later, it seems not only to be hackneyed, but also to have become a quasi-damning verdict. To be "Post-Modern" in the field of architecture is anything but a term of praise, and scarcely any of the protagonists of the time would like to be seen, even in retrospect, as an exponent of Post-Modernism. Still too close to become the object of a retro-cult, but nevertheless far enough away that they provide little inspiration to current architecture, many of the former architectural icons of their age now look more like relics of a bygone era.

The popular idea of Post-Modernism in architecture is confined to stylistic considerations and refers to the—to some extent tongue-in-cheek—use of pseudo-Classical and historicist elements. Once segmental gables started to crown the entrances to underground car parks and whimsical Post-Modern elements became part of the repertoire of companies selling off-the-peg buildings, what began as a liberation from the purist functionalism of late Modernism ended up engendering antipathy. The ubiquitous appliqué approach to design produced a new uniformity and thus contradicted the original intention to develop specific schemes for specific places. Nevertheless, the omnipresence of Post-Modern set pieces indicates just how successful Post-Modernism was and how it has influenced taste. There is scarcely a sphere of human activity to which the term was not applied, but it really shot to stardom in the field of architecture. Through the "icons" of Post-Modern architecture—in Germany we can cite above all the museums in Stuttgart, Mönchengladbach or Frankfurt am Main—architecture gained the attention and acceptance of a broad public, eliciting interest beyond the internal discourses within the profession, and this interest has not waned. Without the trend reversal at the time that replaced the image of the technocrat at a drawing board with that of a popular spatial artist, there would be no "Bilbao effect" and no stars in the firmament of contemporary architecture.

DEFINITIONS OF POST-MODERN ARCHITECTURE

Although no term has been used more often in the architectural discourse of recent years, what is Post-Modern architecture and what is not remains a difficult question.

It is well known that, historically speaking, the term Post-Modernism is generally identified as having first appeared in the North American literary debate in the years following World War II, although it had actually been used before that.[2] The literary critic Irving Howe described as "Post-Modern" those contemporary authors who followed innovators such as Marcel Proust, James Joyce or Ezra Pound. Although Howe still saw himself in the tradition of a discourse grounded in cultural pessimism, according to which any peak would inevitably be followed by decline, theoreticians after him nevertheless managed to turn the negative term into something positive. Susan Sontag must be mentioned here, and more particularly the article by Leslie Fiedler, which appeared in 1969 under the programmatic title *Cross the Border—Close the Gap* in an equally programmatic place, namely the December issue of the American *Playboy*.

1 Cf. Heinrich Klotz (ed.), The history of postmodern architecture, Cambridge/London 1988, p. 11.

2 Cf. especially: Wolfgang Welsch, Unsere postmoderne Moderne, Weinheim 1987, p.12 ff.

Leslie Fiedler, der unter dem programmatischen Titel »Cross the Border – Close the Gap« an einem ebenso programmatischen Ort, nämlich der Dezemberausgabe 1969 des amerikanischen *Playboy*, erschien. Fiedler erklärt die Epoche eines Proust, Joyce oder Mann endgültig für abgeschlossen, und zwar aufgrund eines eindimensionalen Intellektualismus und Elitarismus: »Die Vorstellung von einer Kunst für die ›Gebildeten‹ [...] und einer Subkunst für die ›Ungebildeten‹[...] bezeugt den letzten Überrest einer ärgerlichen Unterscheidung innerhalb einer industrialisierten Massengesellschaft [...], wie sie nur einer Klassengesellschaft zustünde.«[3] An diesem Zitat bemerkenswert: Zum einen zeigt es, in welchem Maße Fiedler von einem antielitären, antibürgerlichen Impuls der Jahre um 1968 geprägt war, und zum anderen – dies die zweite zeitliche Koinzidenz – entstand der Aufsatz zu einer Zeit, da der bürgerliche amerikanische Kunstbetrieb durch die Künstler der Pop-Art, allen voran Andy Warhol, grundsätzlich verändert worden war. Wenn Fiedler postuliert, die Kluft zwischen Künstler und Publikum, zwischen Professionalismus und Amateurhaftigkeit zu schließen, so lässt sich eine ähnliche Haltung erkennen wie in der These Warhols, jeder hätte das Zeug dazu, für einige Zeit ein Star zu sein.

Indem der postmoderne Autor für ein heterogenes Publikum schreibt und die gesellschaftlichen Zentrifugalkräfte zumindest im Akt der Rezeption aufhebt, bedarf es auch auf der Ebene des Formalen, also der Produktion, veränderter Strategien: Pluralismus, Doppelkodierung und Mehrdeutigkeit lauten die Stichworte. Bekanntestes Beispiel hierfür ist Umberto Ecos Buch *Der Name der Rose* (1980)[4], das man als historischen Roman, Detektivgeschichte und gelehrtes Traktat gleichermaßen lesen kann und das somit auf die Erwartungshaltungen unterschiedlicher Lesergruppen reagiert. In weitaus stärkerem Maße hatte James Joyce 1922 in seinem *Ulysses* textimmanent mit Polyfokalität und Polyperspektivität operiert, doch richtete sich sein Roman vornehmlich an ein gebildetes, dem Experimentellen gegenüber aufgeschlossenes Publikum.

Auf die Architektur übertragen wurde der Begriff der Postmoderne durch den Architekten und Architekturkritiker Charles Jencks. Jencks übernahm die Grundthesen des Aufsatzes von Leslie Fiedler und machte sie für den Sektor des Bauens fruchtbar, seit 1975 zunächst in einigen Aufsätzen, dann in diversen Büchern, vor allem *The Language of Postmodern Architecture* von 1977[5]. Die Publikation, zweifelsohne das wichtigste Überblickswerk zur Postmoderne, wurde mehrfach neu aufgelegt und dabei modifiziert und aktualisiert. In der fünften Auflage, die 1987 auf Englisch und ein Jahr später als dritte deutsche Auflage erschien, fügte Jencks ein neues Vorwort hinzu: »Die paradoxe Welt der Postmoderne«. Die moderne Welt habe sich schlicht als zu begrenzt, provinziell und verarmt erwiesen, und so sei die postmoderne erstanden: hybrid, doppelt kodiert und auf fundamentalen Dualitäten basierend. Manchmal entstehe der Stil aus der Gegenüberstellung von Alt und Neu wie bei Stirlings Stuttgarter Staatsgalerie, manchmal sei er eine erheiternde Umkehrung des Alten wie bei Venturi oder Hollein. Beinahe immer aber habe er etwas Merkwürdiges an sich: »Kurz gesagt, ein hochentwickelter Geschmack für das Paradoxe ist charakteristisch für unsere Zeit und unser Empfinden.«[6]

3 Hier zit. nach Welsch 1987, a.a.O. S. 15.
4 Umberto Eco, Der Name der Rose, München 1980.
5 Charles Jencks, The Language of Post-Modern Architecture, London 1977.
6 Charles Jencks, Die Sprache der postmodernen Architektur: Entstehung und Entwicklung einer alternativen Tradition, Stuttgart ^{3}1988, S. 6.

Fiedler declared the age of writers such as Proust, Joyce or Mann to be definitively over, due to its one-dimensional intellectualism and elitism: "The notion of one art for the 'cultured,' [...] and another subart for the 'uncultured,' [...] in fact represents the last survival in mass industrial societies [...] of an invidious distinction proper only to a class-structured community."[3] What is interesting about this quotation is that on the one hand it shows to what extent Fiedler was coloured by the anti-elitist, anti-bourgeois impetus of the years around 1968, and on the other—this is the second synchronous aspect—the article was written at a time when the bourgeois art industry in America had been radically changed by artists from the pop art movement, first and foremost Andy Warhol. Fiedler postulates closing the gap between artists and the public, between the world of professionals and amateurs; a similar attitude can be identified in Warhol's theory that everyone has what it takes to be a star for a time.

The fact that the Post-Modern author is writing for a heterogeneous public and eliminates the centrifugal forces of society—at least in the act of reception—means that different strategies are also required on the formal, i.e. the production, level: pluralism, double coding and ambiguity are the keywords. The most famous example of this is Umberto Eco's book *The Name of the Rose* (1980),[4] which can be read as a historical novel, detective story or scholarly tract and which thus responds to the expectations of different groups of readers. In 1922 in Ulysses, James Joyce had operated to a far greater extent with text-immanent polyfocality and polyperspectivity, but his novel was directed primarily at an educated audience open to experimental writing.

The term Post-Modernism was applied to architecture by the architect and architectural critic Charles Jencks. Jencks took up the basic theories set out in Leslie Fiedler's article and applied them to the sphere of architecture, from 1975 in various articles and essays, and then in a number of books, in particular *The Language of Post-Modern Architecture* of 1977.[5] The publication, without doubt the most important general survey of Post-Modernism, was reprinted several times and was both amended and updated. In the fifth edition, which came out in 1987 in English and a year later as the third German edition, Jencks added a new foreword, "The paradoxical world of Post-Modernism". The world of the Modern Movement, he wrote, proved simply too limited, provincial and impoverished, and thus Post-Modernism was born: hybrid, doubly-coded and based on fundamental dualities. Sometimes the style was created from the juxtaposition of old and new, as in Stirling's Staatsgalerie in Stuttgart, sometimes it was an amusing inversion of the old as seen in the works of Venturi or Hollein. Nearly always it has something strange about it: "In short, a highly developed taste for paradox is characteristic of our time and sensibility."[6] Paraphrasing Fiedler, although not quoting or mentioning him, Jencks proposes the following definition: "Post-Modern architecture is doubly-coded, half-Modern and half-conventional, in its attempt to communicate with both the public and a concerned minority, usually architects."[7]

The background against which this concept stands out is that of "Late-Modern architecture." Jencks contrasts the pragmatism

3 Leslie Fiedler, Cross the Border—Close the Gap, in: A Fiedler Reader, New York 1977, p. 287.
4 Umberto Eco, The Name of the Rose, San Diego 1983.
5 Charles Jencks, The Language of Post-Modern Architecture, London 1977.
6 Ibid, p. 6.
7 Ibid. p. 6.

1

2

3

4

5

6

7

1 Eero Saarinen: Stiles and Morse Colleges, Yale University, New Haven CT (USA), 1962
2 James Stirling, Michael Wilford: Neue Staatsgalerie Stuttgart, 1983. Belichtungsöffnungen der Tiefgarage im Sockelgeschoss/Light openings of the underground car park
3 Michael Graves: Portland Building, Portland OR (USA), 1983
4 Ricardo Bofill: Le Fond du Lac, Saint-Quentin-en-Yvelines (F), 1987
5 Adolfo Natalini: Kasteel Zwaenenstede, Haverleij (NL), seit/begun 1998, Foto/photo: 2003
6 Rob Krier, Sjoerd Soeters, Michael Graves: De Resident, Den Haag/The Hague, 2001
7 Rob Krier, Christoph Kohl: De Veste, Brandevoort (NL), seit/begun 1996, Foto/photo: 2003

Fiedler paraphrasierend, wenn auch nicht zitierend oder erwähnend, schlägt Jencks folgende Definition vor: »Die postmoderne Architektur ist doppelkodiert, zur Hälfte modern, zur Hälfte der Konvention verpflichtet, weil sie versucht, sowohl mit der Mehrzahl der Bevölkerung als auch mit einer beteiligten Minderheit, gewöhnlich Architekten, zu kommunizieren.«[7]

Die Folie, vor der sich dieses Konzept abhebt, ist jenes der »spätmodernen Architektur«. Jencks stellt dem Pragmatismus der Spätmoderne den Pluralismus der Postmoderne gegenüber, und dieser Pluralismus bedeutet ein Wiederanknüpfen an Kunst, Ornament und Symbolismus – Bestimmungen, welche die Baukunst über Jahrhunderte, gar Jahrtausende bestimmt hatten, aber während des Intermezzos der Moderne marginalisiert worden waren.

Der erste Teil des Buches gilt einer Auseinandersetzung mit der für tot erklärten Moderne. Dabei besteht der Hauptvorwurf in der »Univalenz« eines von Mies entwickelten und dann immer wieder aufgegriffenen und absolut gesetzten rationalen Systems, das universell gültig und ubiquitär applizierbar sei. Seinem Verdikt anheim fallen indes auch viele der bisherigen Versuche, Kritik an der kanonisierten Moderne zu üben – handele es sich dabei um die Positionen von den Smithsons und Team X, von Herman Hertzberger oder von Aldo Rossi. So konzediert Jencks zwar, dass Rossis Wohnquartier Gallaratese die klassischen Strukturen italienischer Städte aufgreift, fühlt sich jedoch an die faschistische Bautradition erinnert. Die semantischen Bedeutungen seien folglich irreführend und bedrückend und zeigten die »Unvereinbarkeit von populären und elitären Kodes«[8].

Diese Überlegungen werden auf abstrakterer Ebene im zweiten Teil des Buches weitergeführt, der mit Unterkapiteln über Metaphern, Wörter, Syntax und Semantik eine Abhandlung über Architektursemiotik darstellt. Gemäß dem »linguistic turn« in anderen Wissenschaften versteht Jencks Bauten als Medien der Kommunikation. Diese Auffassung läuft Gefahr, Architektur auf reine Bildlichkeit zu reduzieren und andere Aspekte, seien sie sozialer oder funktionaler Natur, zu missachten – und in der Tat bestanden darin die Hauptvorwürfe gegenüber der Postmoderne. Andererseits wächst der Architektur als symbolischem Kommunikationssystem neue gesellschaftliche Bedeutung zu.

Im dritten Teil des Buches versucht Jencks die Evolution der Postmoderne zwischen 1960 und 1980 zu strukturieren. Dabei argumentiert er vorwiegend stilistisch und verfolgt insgesamt sechs Tendenzen[9]: die Adaption historisierender Elemente (ob Saarinens mittelalterlich-pittoresk anmutende Stiles and Morse Colleges in New Haven oder Venturi und Rauchs Franklin Court in Philadelphia), die direkte Stilreproduktion (etwa im Werk von Quinlan Terry), die Wiederbelebung vernakulärer Architektur (zum Beispiel im Œuvre des englischen Teams Darbourne und Darke), den »Adhocismus«, das Reagieren auf den Kontext (in Ralph Erskines Byker Wall in Newcastle gleichermaßen wie in den urbanistischen Projekten von Léon Krier), die Arbeit mit Metaphern (etwa bei Stanley Tigerman oder Charles Moore) und schließlich den postmodernen Raum (in den Häusern von Robert Stern, Peter Eisenman und Charles Moore). An anderer Stelle arbeitet Jencks zehn Merkmale für postmoderne Architektur

of Late-Modernism with the pluralism of Post-Modernism, and this pluralism means re-embracing art, ornament and symbolism—features that had been an essential part of architecture over hundreds, even thousands, of years, but which had been marginalized during the intermezzo that was Modernism.

In the first part of the book, he pronounces Modern Architecture dead and then proceeds to dissect the corpse. His main reproach is what he calls the "univalence" of a system that claimed to be unerringly rational. Originally developed by Mies, it was then repeatedly taken up by others and was supposed to be universally valid and applicable everywhere and in all situations. In the process, many former attempts to criticise the canonised Modernism fall prey to his severe judgement—including the positions adopted by the Smithsons and Team X, Herman Hertzberger or Aldo Rossi. For example, Jencks does concede that Rossi's Gallaratese Neighbourhood continues the Classical structures of Italian cities, but he feels reminded of the Fascist architectural tradition. The semantic meanings, he says, are therefore misleading and oppressive and show the "disparity between popular and elitist codes."[8]

These reflections are continued on an abstract level in the second part of the book, which, with sections on metaphors, words, syntax and semantics, represents a discourse on architectural semiotics. Following the "linguistic turn" in other sciences, Jencks sees buildings as modes of communication. This view runs the risk of reducing architecture to the purely figurative and disregarding other aspects, be they social or functional in nature—which was, in fact, the principal reproach levelled against Post-Modernism. On the other hand, architecture as a symbolic communication system acquires new social significance.

Finally, in the third part of the book, Jencks attempts to structure the evolution of Post-Modernism between 1960 and 1980. In this, he argues mainly from a stylistic point of view and explores a total of six trends:[9] the adoption of historicist elements (whether Saarinen's interpretation of the medieval picturesque in Stiles and Morse Colleges in New Haven or Venturi and Rauch's Franklin Court in Philadelphia), straight revivalism of a particular style (as illustrated by the work of Quinlan Terry), neo-vernacular architecture (for example, in the work of the English team Darbourne and Darke), "ad-hocism," i.e. response to context (in Ralph Erskine's "Byker Wall" in Newcastle or equally in the urbanist projects of Léon Krier), work with metaphor (in the buildings of Stanley Tigerman or Charles Moore, for example) and finally Post-Modern space (in the work of Robert Stern, Peter Eisenman and Charles Moore). In a different publication, Jencks identified ten characteristics of Post-Modern architecture, of which he says at least six must be present: interest in popular and local codes of communication, in historical memory, urban context, ornament, representation, metaphor, participation, the public realm, pluralism and eclecticism.[10]

Post-Modernism became a truly widespread phenomenon around 1980. Charles Jencks classified the Portland Public Service Building by Michael Graves (1980-83) as an important milestone,[11] and Paolo Portoghesi brought together the European and American protagonists with the "Strada Novissima" at the first Architecture Biennale in Venice in 1980. In Germany, too, the

7 Ebd., S. 5.

8 Ebd., S. 21.
9 Siehe ebd., S. 81-132; einleitend auf S. 80 der »Evolutionary Tree« als Diagramm.

8 Ibid., p. 21.
9 Cf. ibid., pp. 81-132; introduced on p. 80 by the "Evolutionary Tree" diagram.
10 Cf. Charles Jencks, Late-Modern Architecture and other Essays, London 1980, p. 13. These characteristics are a summary of 30 criteria which Jencks uses to delineate Modernism, Late-Modernism and Post-Modernism (ibid., p. 32).

11 Cf. Charles Jencks, Post-modernism: The New Classicism in Art and Architecture, London 1987, p. 30.

heraus, von denen mindestens sechs vorliegen müssten: Interesse an populären und lokalen Codes der Kommunikation, an historischen Reminiszenzen, urbanem Kontext, Ornament, Repräsentation, Metapher, Partizipation, dem öffentlichen Bereich, Pluralismus und Eklektizismus.[10]

Zu einem Breitenphänomen wurde die Postmoderne um 1980. Charles Jencks hat das Portland Public Service Building von Michael Graves (1980-1983) als wichtigen Meilenstein eingestuft[11], und Paolo Portoghesi versammelte die europäischen und amerikanischen Protagonisten mit der Strada Novissima auf der ersten Architekturbiennale in Venedig 1980. Auch in Deutschland waren die achtziger Jahre das eigentliche Jahrzehnt der Postmoderne: 1982 eröffnete Hans Holleins Museum Abteiberg in Mönchengladbach, 1983 James Stirlings Neubau der Stuttgarter Staatsgalerie und noch ein Jahr später das Deutsche Architektur-Museum mit der Eröffnungsausstellung »Die Revision der Moderne«, in der die lange Inkubationszeit von 1960 bis 1980 bilanziert wurde. Wie schon Jencks einige Jahre zuvor, suchte auch Klotz mit den beiden anlässlich der Ausstellung erschienenen Büchern das Gesamtspektrum der frühen Postmoderne auszuloten. Dabei folgte er nicht der Rubrizierungsobsession von Jencks, sondern entwickelte den Grundgedanken einer »Fiktionalisierung«[12] der Architektur, bei welcher die stilistischen Reprisen lediglich Mittel zum Zweck sind. Ziel ist also das Wiedergewinnen poetischer Kraft, welche durch die Sachlichkeit des Funktionalismus nicht mehr vermittelt worden sei.[13] Bei seiner Suche nach den Werken des »Schönen Scheins« führt Klotz die von Robert Venturi und Charles Moore vertretene Idee einer Dekoration der Form mit der europäisch-rationalistischen Tradition typologischer Recherche zusammen, für die vor allem Aldo Rossi und O.M. Ungers stehen.[14] Trotz mancher Lücken – es fehlten die Spanier und Japaner, aber auch die Projekte von James Stirling – zeigte die Ausstellung ein breites Spektrum, das auch Projekte von OMA, Frank O. Gehry, Richard Meier, Peter Eisenman und Haus-Rucker-Co beinhaltete. Dieses umfassende Verständnis einer Postmoderne, welche die Moderne nicht vollständig zu ersetzen, sondern zu revidieren trachtete, bestimmte auch die Internationale Bauausstellung Berlin 1984/87 (IBA). Mit Jane Jacobs' Publikation *Tod und Leben großer amerikanischer Städte*[15]und Aldo Rossis *L'architettura della città*[16], deren Breitenwirkung erst mit den verspäteten Übersetzungen einsetzte, war das wohl wichtigste Themenfeld angesprochen, das eine Abkehr von der Ideologie der Moderne erforderte: der Städtebau. Gelangte die Postmoderne hierzulande auch mit den solitären Museumsbauten in Stuttgart, Mönchengladbach oder Frankfurt zum Durchbruch, so ist ihr bleibendes Verdienst doch im urbanistischen Sektor zu verorten, also im Suchen nach Typologien, um das Gewebe der historisch gewachsenen Stadt zu reparieren und fortzusetzen. Gewiss, architektonisch vermögen – aus heutiger Sicht – nicht alle Berliner IBA-Bauten zu überzeugen. Städtebaulich indes wurde die längst überfällige Abkehr vom Dogma der segregierten Stadt ins Werk gesetzt, das aus dem städtischen Raum suburbane Wüste hatte werden lassen. Neben die Neubaugebiete in Tegel, Tiergarten und der südlichen Friedrichstadt traten die Projekte der »behutsamen Stadterneuerung« in der Luisenstadt und in Kreuzberg SO 36.[17]

eighties were the decade proper of Post-Modernism: in 1982 Hans Hollein's Abteiberg Museum opened in Mönchengladbach, in 1983 James Stirling's new building for the Stuttgart Staatsgalerie, and just a year later came the Deutsches Architektur-Museum with its opening exhibition "Die Revision der Moderne," which evaluated the long incubation period between 1960 and 1980. Like Jencks some years earlier, Klotz also tried to take in the whole spectrum of early Post-Modernism with the two books that were published to accompany the exhibition. He did not follow Jencks's obsession with categorization, but developed the fundamental idea of the "fictionalisation"[12] of architecture, in which stylistic re-runs were simply means to an end. The aim was thus to regain the poetic power that the objectivity of functionalism had ceased to convey[13]. In searching for works representative of "keeping up appearances" Klotz brought together the idea of a decorated form put forward by Robert Venturi and Charles Moore and the rationalist European tradition of typological research, represented principally by Aldo Rossi and O. M. Ungers.[14] Despite some gaps—the Spaniards and Japanese were missing, as were James Stirling's projects—the exhibition showed a broad range including projects by OMA, Frank O. Gehry, Richard Meier, Peter Eisenman and Haus-Rucker-Co. This comprehensive understanding of a Post-Modernism that did not completely replace Modernism, but tried to revise it, was also a defining characteristic of the Internationale Bauausstellung Berlin 1984/87 (IBA). Jane Jacobs' publication *The Death and Life of Great American Cities*[15] and Aldo Rossi's *L'architettura della città*,[16] the widespread impact of which did not kick in immediately because of the delay in translating it, addressed what was probably the most important sphere in which a departure from the ideology of Modernism was called for: urban design. Although Post-Modernism here in Germany did achieve a breakthrough with the stand-alone museum buildings in Stuttgart, Mönchengladbach and Frankfurt, its lasting merit is without doubt in the sector of urban planning, in the search for typologies with which to repair and continue the texture of cities that had developed organically. Of course, seen from today's vantage point, not all the IBA buildings in Berlin are convincing architecturally. But, in urban design terms, the long overdue departure from the dogma of the segregated city, which had turned urban space into suburban wasteland, was set in motion. Alongside the areas designated for new building projects in Tegel, Tiergarten and Southern Friedrichstadt, were the refurbishment projects that made up the "careful urban renewal" programme in Luisenstadt and Kreuzberg's SO 36.[17]

POST-MODERNISM IN CRISIS

There are, of course, a number of extremely successful Post-Modern buildings, which have lost nothing of their original quality even after twenty years. The Neue Staatsgalerie in Stuttgart is an example of James Stirling playing successfully and intelligently with architectural tradition: the three-wing ensemble, which reflects the floor plan of the original Alte Staatsgalerie, encloses a rotunda, which can be interpreted as an allusion to Schinkel's rotunda in the Altes Museum in Berlin. While in

10 Charles Jencks, Spätmoderne Architektur. Beiträge über die Transformation des Internationalen Stils, Stuttgart 1981, S. 13. Diese Merkmale sind eine reduzierte Zusammenfassung von dreißig Kriterien, anhand derer Jencks Moderne, Spätmoderne und Postmoderne voneinander abgrenzt (ebd., S. 32).
11 Charles Jencks, Die Postmoderne. Der neue Klassizismus in Kunst und Architektur, Stuttgart 1987, S. 30.
12 Heinrich Klotz, Moderne und Postmoderne. Architektur der Gegenwart 1960-1980, Braunschweig/Wiesbaden 1984, S. 17.
13 Siehe ebd., S. 134.
14 Heinrich Klotz (Hrsg.), Die Revision der Moderne. Postmoderne Architektur

12 Heinrich Klotz, Moderne und Postmoderne. Architektur der Gegenwart 1960-1980, Braunschweig/Wiesbaden 1984, p. 17.
13 Cf. ibid., p. 134,
14 Cf. Heinrich Klotz (ed.), Die Revision der Moderne. Postmoderne Architektur 1960-1980 (Catalogue, DAM Frankfurt), Munich 1984, p. 9 ff.
15 Jane Jacobs, The Death and Life of Great American Cities, New York 1961.
16 Aldo Rossi, The Architecture of the City, Cambridge/Mass. 1982
17 An overview of all the IBA projects can be found in: Bauausstellung Berlin GmbH (ed.), Internationale Bauausstellung Berlin - Projektübersicht, Berlin-West 1987. Also: Senator für Bau- und

DIE POSTMODERNE IN DER KRISE

Es gibt überaus geglückte Bauten der Postmoderne, die auch nach zwanzig Jahren nichts von ihrer Qualität eingebüßt haben. Bei der Neuen Staatsgalerie Stuttgart gelang James Stirling ein intelligentes Spiel mit der Bautradition: Die Dreiflügelanlage, welche die Grundrissstruktur der Alten Staatsgalerie aufgreift, umschließt eine Rotunde, in der man eine Anspielung auf Schinkels Rotunde des Alten Museums in Berlin sehen kann. Fungierte die Rotunde mit den ausgestellten antiken Skulpturen in Berlin als ideelles Zentrum, so ist sie hier leer und aus dem Museumsrundgang ausgeschieden – die normative Ästhetik der Antike existiert nicht mehr. Ein ironisches Spiel mit dem Betrachter treibt der Architekt auch bei den beiden symmetrischen Lichtöffnungen der Tiefgarage im Sockel: Wie bei einer Ruine sind die Steine aus dem Mauerwerksverbund herausgebrochen und liegen auf dem Boden. Ironischerweise handelt es sich hier um die einzigen massiven Steinblöcke des Gebäudes, während sonst lediglich Natursteinplatten die Betonstruktur verkleiden. Richten sich Anspielungen wie diese an ein architektonisch und architekturhistorisch vorgebildetes Publikum, so referieren die pastellfarbenen Röhren und der Noppenfußboden des Foyers auf eine von der Popkultur beeinflusste Alltagsästhetik. High and Low, Pop und Pathos finden hier auf überzeugende Weise zusammen.

Allerdings ist festzuhalten, dass die Suche nach einer neuen Sprachfähigkeit der Architektur vielfach eher bescheidene Resultate zeitigte. Hintergründige Ironie und phantasievolle Oberflächengestaltung bilden die Ausnahmen von der Regel trivialen Applikationsdesigns und banaler Zeichenhaftigkeit. So sind Michael Graves' Hotels Dolphin und Swan (1987) für Disney in Florida banale, durch aufgeblähte Plastiken bekrönte Hotelgebirge, die dem Wunsch des Konzerns nach Einprägsamkeit entgegenkommen. Neueste Projekte, wie das unlängst realisierte Taba Heights Hotel in Ägypten, belegen, dass gerade seitens kommerzieller Auftraggeber weiterhin Interesse an einer derartigen Architektur besteht.[18]

Ein weiteres Krisenphänomen bestand darin, dass sich zu Beginn der achtziger Jahre die Tendenzen zu einer historisierenden Postmoderne verstärkten, bei welcher der intelligent-spielerische Umgang mit Versatzstücken der Tradition zugunsten der Inszenierung eines einheitlichen Bildes suspendiert wurde. Der wichtigste europäische Protagonist dieses Verständnisses war der Katalane Ricardo Bofill, der in der Banlieue von Paris sowie in Montpellier gewaltige Siedlungen des sozialen Wohnungsbaus realisieren konnte. Gewiss nutzte Bofill mit seinen präfabrizierten Betonelementen die Produktionsverfahren der Moderne, doch der ins Bombastische gesteigerte Neoklassizismus – wiewohl von sozialistischen oder gar kommunistischen Politikern in Auftrag gegeben – brachte dem Architekten seitens der Kritik den Vorwurf des Zynismus ein. Ähnlich verhielt es sich mit Léon Krier, der mit Verve die Moderne pauschal verdammte, in einer Luxusedition Albert Speer als größten Baumeister des 20. Jahrhunderts feierte und schließlich sein vom Prince of Wales favorisiertes Siedlungsideal mit dem Musterort Poundbury in der britischen Grafschaft Dorset realisieren konnte.

Publizistisch gestützt wurde diese Variante der Postmoderne

Berlin the rotunda was an symbolic centre for the Classical sculptures it exhibits, here it is empty and not part of the visitors' route around the museum—the normative aesthetics of Classicism no longer exist. With the two symmetrical light openings in the plinth for the underground car park, the architect is also playing an ironic game with the visitor: like in a ruin, the stones have broken out of the masonry and are lying on the ground. Ironically, they are the only solid blocks of stone in the entire building—all the others are natural-stone panels cladding the concrete structure. While allusions like this one are directed at a public with knowledge of architecture and architectural history, the pastel-coloured pipes and studded rubber flooring in the foyer make reference to an everyday aesthetics influenced by pop culture. High and low, pop and pathos come together here in a convincing way.

However, it must be said that the attempt to find a new language for architecture often produced rather mediocre results. Veiled irony and imaginative design of surfaces are the exception to the rule that consisted of a trivial appliqué approach to design combined with banal symbolism. For example, Michael Graves's Dolphin and Swan hotels (1987) for Disney in Florida are facile and gigantic structures crowned with oversized sculptures, which meet the corporation's desire to make a gesture that its audience will find memorable. The most recent projects, such as the Taba Heights Hotel completed not long ago in Egypt, prove that there is still interest in that kind of architecture, particularly on the part of commercial clients.[18]

A further phenomenon that is symptomatic of crisis consisted in the fact that, in the early 1980s, trends towards historicist versions of Post-Modernism intensified and the intelligent and playful treatment of traditional set pieces was suspended in favour of attempts to orchestrate a uniform image. The most important European protagonist of this approach was the Catalan Ricardo Bofill, who built gigantic social housing projects in the outer suburbs of Paris and in Montpellier. Certainly, with his prefabricated concrete elements Bofill made use of Modernism's production techniques, but the way he took Neo-Classicism to bombastic extremes—despite being commissioned by Socialist or even Communist politicians—elicited the accusation of cynicism from critics. The situation was similar in the case of Léon Krier, who vigorously condemned Modernism out of hand, wrote a luxury publication celebrating Albert Speer as the greatest architect of the 20th century, and finally got to build his ideal settlement, which was favoured by Prince Charles, in the model village of Poundbury in the English county of Dorset. This version of Post-Modernism was backed by the writings of Charles Jencks, who in his new publications drove the "radical eclecticism" of Post-Modernism into a neo-historicist straightjacket.[19]

There is no doubt that the revelling in historicist forms, which was sometimes associated with a conservative or escapist view of society, discredited the critical potential of Post-Modernism. The fact that hypertrophic Neo-Classicism led into a blind alley had in the meantime been recognised, even by Ricardo Bofill, who in his more recent projects made greater use of glass and sought to create a blend of Neo-Classicism and Modernism.[20] Nevertheless, in recent years we have seen a trend towards a

1960-1980, a.a.O. S. 9 ff.
15 Jane Jacobs, Tod und Leben großer amerikanischer Städte, Braunschweig/Wiesbaden 1963.
16 Aldo Rossi, L'architettura della città, Padova 1966.
17 Einen Überblick über sämtliche IBA-Projekte gibt: Bauausstellung Berlin GmbH (Hg.), Internationale Bauausstellung Berlin – Projektübersicht, Berlin-West 1987. Außerdem: Senator für Bau- und Wohnungswesen Berlin (Hg.), Idee – Prozess – Ergebnis: Die Reparatur und Rekonstruktion der Stadt, Kat. Martin-Gropius-Bau Berlin 1984, Berlin-West 1984.
18 Bauwelt 2003, H. 24, S. 26-31.

Wohnungswesen Berlin (ed.), Idee - Prozess - Ergebnis: Die Reparatur und Rekonstruktion der Stadt, Catalogue of an exhibition in the Martin-Gropius-Bau Berlin 1984, Berlin 1984.
18 Cf. Bauwelt 2003, no. 24, pp. 26-31.
19 Charles Jencks, Post-Modern Classicism, London 1980; ibid., Post-Modernism: The New Classicism in Art and Architecture, London 1987.
20 Cf. Bauwelt 2003, no. 24, pp. 20-23.

wiederum durch Charles Jencks, der in neuen Publikationen nunmehr den »radikalen Eklektizismus« der Postmoderne in die neohistoristische Engführung trieb.[19]

Ohne Zweifel hat das Schwelgen in historisierenden Formen, das mitunter mit einem konservativen oder eskapistischen Gesellschaftsbild verbunden war, das kritische Potenzial der Postmoderne diskreditiert. Dass der hypertrophe Neoklassizismus in eine Sackgasse führt, wurde inzwischen auch von Ricardo Bofill erkannt, der in seinen jüngeren Projekten verstärkt mit Glas baut und nach einer Legierung aus Klassizismus und Moderne sucht.[20]

Trotzdem ist in den letzten Jahren ein Trend hin zu einer neotraditionalistischen Architekturauffassung zu verzeichnen, in welcher der Neoklassizismus der Postmoderne wieder auflebt. Das Phänomen lässt sich in den postkommunistischen Staaten Osteuropas ebenso beobachten wie in den Siedlungen des »New Urbanism« der Vereinigten Staaten; in Deutschland mag man auf das Haus Bastian von Paul und Petra Kahlfeldt oder die Villa Gerl von Hans Kollhoff und Helga Timmermann verweisen[21], aber auch auf die zurzeit grassierende Rekonstruktionsmanie.[22] Am meisten mag erstaunen, dass das klassizistische Retro-Design gerade in den Niederlanden, dem bisherigen Musterland des Supermodernismus, auf überaus fruchtbaren Boden fällt. Sjoerd Soeters, Adolfo Natalini sowie Rob Krier und sein Partner Christoph Kohl sind Protagonisten einer Entwicklung, die mit dem innerstädtischen Projekt De Resident in Den Haag begann. Zwischen dem Zentralbahnhof und dem Stadthaus von Richard Meier ist seit dem Ende der neunziger Jahre nach einem Masterplan von Rob Krier und unter Mitwirkung von Soeters und Graves ein innerstädtisch verdichteter Büro- und Wohnkomplex in spätpostmodernen Formen entstanden. Außerdem sind Krier und Kohl derzeit mit einer Reihe von Siedlungsprojekten in den Niederlanden befasst. Das umfangreichste ist Brandevoort bei Helmond, eine vollständig neue Stadt, in deren Mitte eine von Wassergräben umgebene »Veste« mit sechshundert Wohnungen realisiert wird. Historisierende Ziegelsteinfassaden mit leicht variierender Traufhöhe, Tore und Türme sollen das Bild einer mittelalterlichen Kleinstadt in Brabant heraufbeschwören. Krier und Kohl sind auch beteiligt am Projekt De Haverleij nördlich von 's-Hertogenbosch: In der Wiesenlandschaft am Maasufer entsteht bis 2008 eine aus neun »Kastellen« und einer »Zitadelle« locker gefügte weitläufige Siedlung mit insgesamt 11 000 Wohneinheiten. Jedes der Kastelle wird von einem Architekturbüro realisiert, darunter Adolfo Natalini, Michael Graves, Claus en Caan und John Outram. Erklärlich sind derartige Bauvorhaben vor dem Hintergrund der Deregulierung des Wohnungsmarktes in den Niederlanden. Der vollständige Rückzug des Staates aus dem sozialen Wohnungsbau, die Zerschlagung der bisherigen Wohnbauträger und die Verwandlung bisheriger Mieter in Eigentümer lassen die Nachfrage nach Häusern und Wohnungen steigen, die Wertbeständigkeit simulieren.[23]

Hier ist die Postmoderne nicht mehr das intelligente Spiel mit Ironie, Fiktion und Realität. Man kann auch nicht mehr von Trash, von einer Vermengung von High and Low sprechen. Wie Werner Sewing ausgeführt hat, hat der New Urbanism mit Ro-

8

9

10

8 Peter Eisenman: Wexner Center for the Visual Arts, Columbus OH (USA), 1989
9 MVRDV: Costa Iberica, Verdichtung von Benidorm/Densification of Benidorm (E), Projekt/Project 1998
10 MVRDV: Niederländischer Pavillon/Dutch Pavilion, Expo 2000, Hannover

19 Charles Jencks, Post-Modern Classicism, London 1980; ders., Die Postmoderne. Der neue Klassizismus in Kunst und Architektur, a.a.O. 1987.
20 Bauwelt 2003, H. 24, S. 20-23.
21 Ulrich Brinkmann, Wohnen im Gestern, in: archithese 2001, H. 2, S. 18-25.
22 Eine Zusammenstellung der aktuellen Projekte in: Bauwelt 2004, H 1/2.
23 Siehe hierzu: Bart Lootsma, SuperDutch Afterthoughts, in: Post.Rotterdam, Kat. Porto 2001, Rotterdam 2001, S. 114-121.

bert Venturis *Learning from Las Vegas* nichts zu tun.[24] Und am Strip von Las Vegas stehen heute nicht mehr die »decorated sheds«, sondern die Hotelburgen des globalen Imagineering. Sie künden von einer Obsession der Ordnung, bei der sich hinter der Heterogenität der Bildsprache die Univalenz verbirgt, um auf den von Jencks gebrandmarkten Begriff zurückzukommen. Das ist keine Ironie mehr: das ist Ernst.

Dass mit historischen Gegebenheiten auch anders verfahren werden kann, zeigt der im Jahr 2000 fertig gestellte Umbau des Rathauses von Utrecht von Enric Miralles. Das Konzept des Architekten gefällt nicht allen, schon gar nicht jenen, die in der gebauten Umwelt des Menschen vor allem das Postulat der Ordnung verwirklicht sehen möchten. Doch in seiner Radikalität ist der Umgang des spanischen Architekten mit dem bestehenden Bau über Fragen des Geschmacks erhaben. Am Schein einer Harmonie zu kratzen, verborgene Schichten freizulegen, das ist selten mit solcher Obsession und doch zugleich so spielerisch versucht worden wie hier. Man kann über den Anteil an Bewusstheit, den Anteil an Zufälligkeit streiten, und doch offenbart das lustvoll-furiose, keineswegs zimperliche Vorgehen mehr Liebe zum Bestehenden als die Praxis jener Bewahrer des Alten, deren Geschichtsversessenheit sich als Geschichtsvergessenheit decouvriert.

DAS ENDE DER POSTMODERNE?

In Berlin lässt sich die Abkehr von der Postmoderne im engeren Sinne an zwei nahezu parallel geplanten Museumsprojekten exemplifizieren: Während Aldo Rossis aus einem Wettbewerb des Jahres 1988 hervorgegangener Neubau des Deutschen Historischen Museums[25] sich nach dem Mauerfall als obsolet erwies und unausgeführt blieb, wurde Daniel Libeskinds 1989 prämierter Entwurf für das Jüdische Museum[26] realisiert und ist ohne Zweifel als das herausragende Berliner Gebäude der neunziger Jahre einzustufen. Rossi hatte ein Pasticcio aus stereometrisch geprägten Baukörpern vorgelegt, deren assoziatives Potenzial sich wie eine Abbreviatur der abendländischen Bautradition verstehen ließ; Libeskind hingegen arbeitete mit einer durch verschiedene Transformationen versehrten und zum Teil ausgehöhlten plastischen Großform, welche sich als Metapher für Verlust und Zerstörung interpretieren lässt. Beide Entwürfe stellen die Frage nach der Relevanz von Kultur, kreisen um das Thema der Erinnerung und sind in starkem Maße semantisch aufgeladen. Sie nähern sich den Fragen jedoch von unterschiedlichen Seiten. Rossi konfiguriert Versatzstücke der Architekturgeschichte, um noch einmal von Synthese und Harmonie zu träumen, wenn auch das nachgerade melancholische Nebeneinander der Formen diese Vision in den Bereich der Utopie verweist und auf das von Manfredo Tafuri umrissene Grundproblem der Architektur Rossis verweist, dass es sich um letztlich inhaltslose Zeichen handelt, die nicht mehr mit dem kollektiven Gedächtnis korrelieren.[27] Libeskind hingegen zeigt sich antiutopisch, indem er im Fragmentarischen die Basis der gegenwärtigen Kultur sieht.

Für die neue, von Libeskind vertretene Stilrichtung, welche die Komplexität weniger in der Revitalisierung historischer For-

neo-traditionalist view of architecture, in which Post-Modernism's version of Neo-Classicism has been revived. The phenomenon can be seen equally in the post-communist countries of Eastern Europe or the "New Urbanism" housing estates in the U.S.A.; in Germany the Bastian House by Paul and Petra Kahlfeldt or the Gerl Villa by Hans Kollhoff and Helga Timmermann can be cited as examples,[21] but so can the reconstruction mania that is rife at the moment.[22] The most astonishing thing is that Neo-Classical retro-design fell on extremely fertile ground in the Netherlands of all places, formerly Super-Modernism's model country. Sjoerd Soeters and Adolfo Natalini, along with Rob Krier and his partner Christoph Kohl, are the protagonists of a development that began with the inner-city De Resident project in the Hague. Since the end of the nineties a high-density inner-city office and residential complex that draws upon late Post-Modern forms has been under construction on a site between the central station and Richard Meier's Stadthuis. The author of the master plan is Rob Krier and Soeters and Graves collaborated on the design. Krier and Kohl are also currently working on a series of urban development projects in the Netherlands. The largest of these is Brandevoort near Helmond, which is a completely new town, in the centre of which is a "Veste" with 600 flats, surrounded by a moat. Historicist brick façades with slight variations in eaves heights, gateways and towers are intended to evoke the image of a small Medieval town of Brabant. Krier and Kohl are also involved in the De Haverleij project to the north of Hertogenbosch: in the meadow landscape on the banks of the River Maas a low-density housing estate consisting of nine castles and a citadel is currently being built and is scheduled for completion in 2008. It will comprise a total of 11,000 living units. Each of the castles has been designed by a different architectural practice, including Adolfo Natalini, Michael Graves, Claus en Caan and John Outram. This kind of building project is understandable against the backdrop of the deregulation of the housing market in the Netherlands. The state's complete withdrawal from building social housing, the demise of the former housing developers and the transformation of tenants into home owners have increased the demand for houses and flats that simulate stable values.[23]

Here Post-Modernism is no longer an intelligent game with irony, fiction and reality. Nor is it possible to continue to speak of trash, of a mingling of high and low. As Werner Sewing has argued, New Urbanism has nothing to do with Robert Venturi's *Learning from Las Vegas*.[24] And the Las Vegas Strip is no longer lined with "decorated sheds," but with the colossal hotels that are the product of global imagineering. They speak of an obsession with order, in which univalence—to go back to the term denounced by Jencks—hides behind the heterogeneity of the visual language. It is no longer ironic: it is serious.

The fact that history can be treated differently is demonstrated in the extension to Utrecht's Town Hall by Enric Miralles, which was completed in 2000. Not everyone likes the architect's concept, especially not those people who would like to see the postulate of order reflected in the built environment. But, in its radicality, the Spanish architect's treatment of the existing building stands above questions of taste. Seldom has anyone so

24 Werner Sewing, No more Learning from Las Vegas, in: ders., Bildregie. Architektur zwischen Retrodesign und Eventkultur, Basel/Boston/Berlin 2003, S. 7-20.
25 Aedes Galerie für Architektur (Hg.), Aldo Rossi: Deutsches Historisches Museum 1989, Berlin 1989.
26 Senator für Bau- und Wohnungswesen Berlin (Hg.), Erweiterung Berlin Museum mit Abteilung Jüdisches Museum: Voraussetzung - Verfahren - Ergebnisse, Berlin 1990.
27 Manfredo Tafuri, The Sphere and the Labyrinth. Avant-Gardes and Architecture from Piranesi to the 70s, Cambridge/London 1987, S. 273 ff.

21 Cf. Ulrich Brinkmann, Wohnen im Gestern, in: archithese 2001, no. 2, pp. 18-25.
22 A compilation of current projects of this kind can be found in: Bauwelt 2004, no. 1/2.
23 Cf.: Bart Lootsma, SuperDutch Afterthoughts, in: Post.Rotterdam, Cat. Porto 2001, Rotterdam 2001, pp. 114-121.
24 Werner Sewing, No more Learning from Las Vegas, in: ibid., Bildregie. Architektur zwischen Retrodesign und Eventkultur, Basel/Boston/Berlin 2003, pp. 7-20.

men und Typologien als in der Fragmentierung suchte, war durch eine Ausstellung des MoMA 1988 ein passendes Etikett gefunden worden. »Deconstructivist Architecture«[28] hieß die Schau, nachdem der ursprünglich vorgesehene Titel »Violated Perfection« verworfen worden war.

Es stellt sich die Frage, ob die Postmoderne wirklich Ende der achtziger Jahre endete und ob die Architekten des Dekonstruktivismus – in der Schau des MoMA waren Coop Himmelb(l)au, Frank O. Gehry, Zaha Hadid, Rem Koolhaas, Daniel Libeskind, Peter Eisenman und Bernard Tschumi vertreten – tatsächlich den Bruch mit der Postmoderne vollzogen. Einige von ihnen waren in den Anthologien von Jencks und Klotz berücksichtigt worden, und in der Tat teilten Postmoderne und Dekonstruktivisten die kritische Haltung gegenüber der Moderne. Hinzuweisen ist hier besonders auf Rem Koolhaas, der in »What ever Happened to Urbanism?« konstatierte, dass die Ideen, ästhetischen Vorstellungen und Strategien der Moderne sich überlebt hätten.[29] Gegen die Monofunktionalität und die Obsession der Ordnung setzt er – anknüpfend an seine Gedanken über »Lobotomie« und die hybride Funktionsnutzung in den Wolkenkratzern New Yorks[30] – die Theorie der »Bigness«[31]: Riesige Strukturen bedeuten die endgültige Abkehr von der Form-follows-function-Ideologie, weil sie räumliche Potenziale für unterschiedliche Nutzungen bieten.

Auch im Œuvre von Peter Eisenman scheinen Themen auf, die gerade in der Postmoderne Virulenz erlangten (auch wenn der Architekt selbst die Postmoderne ablehnte[32]). Dies betrifft vor allem den Umgang mit der Geschichte: Immer wieder sind es fiktive Ausgrabungen, die – gleichsam analog einer Psychoanalyse – verborgene Tiefenschichten und denkbare Potenziale freilegen sollen. Beim Wexner Center for the Visual Arts in Columbus/Ohio beispielsweise überlagerte Eisenman die divergierenden städtebaulichen Raster der Stadt sowie der Universität und ließ überdies den Ziegelbau eines abgerissenen Zeughauses fragmentarisch wiedererstehen.

Es ist somit fraglich, ob ein Verständnis der Postmoderne als einer mit dem Dekonstruktivismus abgeschlossenen Stilepoche sinnvoll ist. Viel eher kann die Postmoderne als eine Epochenschwelle und als Resultat eines gesamtgesellschaftlichen Paradigmenwechsels verstanden werden. Dieser Paradigmenwechsel ließe sich im ökonomischen, sozialen und kulturellen Sektor verorten und ist an die spezifischen Umbrüche gebunden, die sich Ende der sechziger Jahre ergaben.

Die Kritik an der Moderne entstand zunächst in anderen Disziplinen. Zu nennen sind Michel Foucault und Theodor W. Adorno, die Psychoanalyse Lacans oder die Ethnologie von Michel Leiris als Beispiele einer Dezentrierung des Subjekts, die Dissens- und Sprachspieltheorie von Jean-François Lyotard und Hermann Lübbe mit seiner These eines Schwindens der Gegenwart angesichts einer Übermacht von kulturellen Sedimentierungen.

Erst durch die gesellschaftlichen Wandlungen der ausgehenden sechziger Jahre aber fand die zum Teil schon zuvor ausgebildete Kritik der Moderne zu einem spezifischen Rezeptionshorizont. Da die Postmoderne mit der Moderne brach und somit die Unschuld der Moderne nicht mehr behauptet werden kann, dauert die Postmoderne an, zumindest sind gewisse Stränge weiter-

obsessively, and yet so playfully, tried to scratch at the veneer of apparent harmony and uncover hidden layers. It is possible to argue the toss about just how much is deliberate and conscious and how much is random, but no matter, the sheer joy and fervour of the architect's approach—totally without qualms—testifies to greater love for the existing fabric than that of those architects who set about preserving the historic, but whose obsession with history turns out to be actual disregard for history.

THE END OF POST-MODERNISM?

In Berlin the abandonment of Post-Modernism in the stricter sense of the term is exemplified in two museum projects that were planned at virtually the same time: while Aldo Rossi's design for a Museum of German History, chosen in a competition in 1988,[25] became obsolete after the fall of the Berlin Wall and was shelved, Daniel Libeskind's design for the Jewish Museum, which won the competition held in 1989,[26] was built, and must without a doubt be classed as the most outstanding building of the 1990s in Berlin. Rossi had submitted a pastiche made up of stereometric volumes, whose associative potential could be interpreted as an abbreviation for Western architectural tradition; Libeskind, by contrast, worked with a sculptural megaform that was damaged and in places eroded by different stages of transformation and that can be interpreted as a metaphor for loss and destruction. Both designs question the relevance of culture, revolve around the theme of memory and are highly charged semantically. But they approach the questions from completely different sides. Rossi configures set pieces taken from architectural history in an attempt to recreate a dream of synthesis and harmony, but the virtually melancholic juxtaposition of forms relegates this vision to the realms of utopia and points up the basic problem with Rossi's architecture outlined by Manfredo Tafuri - that it is ultimately about signs devoid of content that no longer have any correlation in the collective memory.[27] Libeskind, on the other hand, is anti-utopian in that he sees the fragmentary as the basis of contemporary culture.

For the new style represented by Libeskind, which seeks complexity not so much in the revitalisation of historical forms and typologies as in fragmentation, an apt label was found through the exhibition at MoMA in 1988. The show was called "Deconstructivist Architecture,"[28] the original title "Violated Perfection" having been rejected.

The question arises whether Post-Modernism really did end at the close of the eighties and whether the architects of Deconstructivism—the MoMA show included Coop Himmelb(l)au, Frank O. Gehry, Zaha Hadid, Rem Koolhaas, Daniel Libeskind, Peter Eisenman and Bernard Tschumi—really did break fully with Post-Modernism. Some of them were included in anthologies by Jencks and Klotz, and it is true that Post-Modernism and Deconstructivism shared a critical attitude to Modernism. Particularly interesting in this context is Rem Koolhaas, who in *Whatever Happened to Urbanism?* observed that the theories, aesthetic ideas and strategies of Modernism were passé.[29] Against monofunctionality and an obsession with order, he set his theory of "Bigness"[30]—following up his ideas about "lobotomy" and

28 Philip Johnson/Mark Wigley, Deconstructivist Architecture, Kat. MoMA, New York 1988.
29 Rem Koolhaas, What ever Happened to Urbanism, in: ders., S, M, L, XL, Rotterdam 1995, S. 958-971.
30 Rem Koolhaas, Delirious New York (1976), Rotterdam 1994.
31 Rem Koolhaas, Bigness, in: ders., S, M, L, XL, a.a.O., S. 494-517.
32 Peter Eisenman, Postfunktionalismus, in: ders., Aura und Exzess. Zur Überwindung der Metaphysik in der Architektur, Wien 1995, S. 35-42. Außerdem: Charles Jencks, Dialoge mit Peter Eisenman, in: ders., Die neuen Modernen: Von der Spät- zur Neomoderne, Stuttgart 1990, S. 208-237.

25 Aedes Galerie für Architektur (ed.), Aldo Rossi: Deutsches Historisches Museum 1989, Berlin 1989.
26 Senator für Bau- und Wohnungswesen Berlin (ed.), Erweiterung Berlin Museum mit Abteilung Jüdisches Museum: Voraussetzung - Verfahren - Ergebnisse, Berlin 1990.
27 Cf. Manfredo Tafuri, The Sphere and the Labyrinth. Avant-Gardes and Architecture from Piranesi to the 70s. Cambridge and London 1987, p. 273 ff.
28 Philip Johnson/Mark Wigley, Deconstructivist Architecture, Cat. MoMA, New York 1988.
29 Rem Koolhaas, Whatever Happened to Urbanism, in: ibid., S, M, L, XL, Rotterdam 1995, pp. 958-971.

hin, wenn auch in Metamorphosen und Transformationen, virulent. Daher ist festzuhalten, dass Theoreme der Postmoderne weiterhin für das Verständnis des heutigen Architekturdiskurses von anhaltender Bedeutung sind.

In diesem Zusammenhang sei versucht, drei Grundgedanken zu extrahieren:

– Die Verbindung von High und Low Culture, die sich in der sämtliche kulturellen Bereiche berührenden Akzeptanz des Phänomens »Trash« äußert.
– Die Koinzidenz von Affirmation und Subversion, welche frühere Strategien der kritischen Praxis in Frage stellt.
– Ironie und Paradox als Haltungen gegenüber der bestehenden Realität.

Nicht die neohistoristischen Siedlungen von Rob Krier setzen diesem Verständnis entsprechend die Postmoderne fort, sondern Konzepte, wie sie beispielsweise von MVRDV entwickelt werden. Die Idee, die gesamte Schweineproduktion der Niederlande in 620 Meter hohen »Pig Towers« zu konzentrieren, ist eines der verstörendsten Projekte der niederländischen Architekten.[33] Elemente der ökologischen Landwirtschaft werden mit dem Konzept der industriellen Tierproduktion verbunden; synthetisiert sind somit zwei Haltungen, die bislang als antithetisch empfunden wurden. Der provokative Aspekt liegt insbesondere darin, dass in einer Zeit, in der das agrikulturelle System zunehmend in die Krise gerät, die Lösung nicht in einer grundsätzlichen Neuorientierung gesucht wird. Nicht die Alternativen zu den heutigen Produktions- und Konsumtionsgewohnheiten interessieren MVRDV, sondern die noch verbleibenden Potenziale der Optimierung. Ähnlich geht es in der Studie »Costa Iberica«[34] nicht darum, das spanische Ferienressort Benidorm durch Strukturverbesserungen verträglicher zu machen oder gar durch andere Tourismuskonzepte infrage zu stellen. Vielmehr entwickeln die Architekten zwei suggestive visuelle Szenarien: Während sie die *waterfront* von Benidorm durch megalomane Megastrukturen verdichten und damit die spätmoderne Ästhetik und Morphologie der Apartmentblocks potenzieren und ins Beklemmend-Absurde übersteigern, ergibt sich die Möglichkeit, weniger dicht besiedelte Küstenregionen von Bebauung zu befreien.

MVRDV haben die kritische Theorie verlassen, welche die Lösung außerhalb eines gegebenen Systems suchte. Ihre Haltung ist bis zu einem gewissen Grade affirmativ, weil sie die bestehenden Gegebenheiten akzeptiert. Indem Architektur als unausweichliches Resultat statistischer Analysen dargestellt wird, gewinnt sie scheinbare Objektivität. MVRDV nutzen die herkömmlichen analytischen Methoden des Urbanismus und entwickeln vorbehaltlos Vorschläge, als handele es sich um die Lösung einer mathematischen Gleichung. Nicht zuletzt die Renderings und Animationen tragen dazu bei, die Suggestivität der angebotenen Lösung zu verstärken. Dabei handelt es sich nicht eigentlich um Visionen, sondern um neue Formationen des Vorhandenen. MVRDV entstellen die Aporie des Realen zur Kenntlichkeit; aus der Affirmation wird Subversion.[35]

Deutlich vor Augen geführt wurde die Koinzidenz von Affirmation und Subversion beim Holländischen Pavillon für die Expo 2000, dem MVRDV den doppeldeutigen Titel »Holland

33 MVRDV, Pig City, in: archithese 2001, H. 6, S. 76-79.
34 MVRDV, Costa Iberica, Barcelona 1998.
35 Hubertus Adam, Stacking and Layering, in: El Croquis 111, MVRDV 1998-2002, Madrid 2002, S. 30-38.

hybrid use of functions in New York's skyscrapers.[31] Gigantic structures signal the definitive departure from the form-follows-function ideology, because they offer spatial potential for a range of different uses.

Themes also appear in Peter Eisenman's œuvre that had become extremely virulent in Post-Modernism (even though the architect himself protested against Post-Modernism).[32] This applies in particular to the treatment of history: again and again it is fictitious excavations that—as it were on an analogy to psychoanalysis—are intended to uncover hidden depths and endless potential. In the Wexner Center for the Visual Arts in Columbus/Ohio, Eisenman superimposed the divergent urban design grids of the city and the university, and over this resurrected in fragmentary form the brick building of a demolished arsenal.

Thus it is debatable whether it is useful to understand Post-Modernism as a style era that came to an end with Deconstructivism. Post-Modernism is far better understood as the transition between eras and the result of a shift in paradigm in society as a whole. This shift in paradigm can be located in the economic, social and cultural sphere and is associated with specific radical changes that occurred at the end of the 1960s.

The critique of Modernism originated in other disciplines. Michel Foucault and Theodor W. Adorno, Lacan's psychoanalysis or Michel Leiris' ethnology should be cited here as examples of a decentering of the subject, along with Jean-François Lyotard's theory of dissent and language games and Hermann Lübbe with his theory of the contraction of the present in the face of a predominance of cultural sedimentations.

However, it was only through the social changes that took place at the end of the sixties that the critique of Modernism that had already begun to crystallise found a specific reception framework. Since Post-Modernism represented a break with Modernism and thus the innocence of Modernism could no longer be asserted, Post-Modernism continued to be virulent, at least certain strands of it, albeit in metamorphosed and transformed ways. It is therefore important to bear in mind that theories on Post-Modernism continue to be important to the understanding of today's architectural discourse. In this context, I shall attempt to extract three fundamental ideas:

– The link between high and low culture, which throughout the cultural sphere is expressed in the acceptance of the phenomenon of "trash."
– The coincidence of affirmation and subversion, which calls into question earlier strategies of critical practice.
– Irony and paradox as attitudes to existing reality.

It was not Rob Krier's neo-historicist urban development schemes that continued Post-Modernism in line with this understanding, but concepts such as those developed by MVRDV.

The idea of concentrating the entire pig production of the Netherlands in 620-metre-high "Pig Towers" is one of the most disturbing projects Dutch architects have ever come up with.[33] It links elements of ecological farming with the concept of industrial animal production: a synthesis of two attitudes that had until then be felt to be antithetical. The particularly provocative aspect is the fact that at a time in which the agricultural system is sliding into an ever-greater crisis, the solution is

30 Rem Koolhaas, Bigness, in: ibid., S, M, L, XL, Rotterdam 1995, pp. 494-517.
31 Rem Koolhaas, Delirious New York (1976), Rotterdam 1994.
32 Cf. Peter Eisenman, Post-Functionalism, in: Oppositions, 1976, 6, pp. 1-4. Also: Charles Jencks, Dialogues with Peter Eisenman, in: ibid., The New Moderns: From Late-to Neo-Modernism, London 1990, pp. 208-237
33 MVRDV, Pig City, in: archithese 2001, H. 6, S. 76-79.

makes Space« gaben. Die spielerische Leichtigkeit, mit welcher MVRDV die Landschaften ihrer Herkunft übereinander türmten, knüpfte an die Follies an, die seit jeher zum festen architektonischen Inventar der Weltausstellungen gehörten; ein auf den Kopf gestelltes Haus beispielsweise amüsierte die Besucher im Jahr 1900 in Paris. Mit dem schwebenden Wald und dem See auf dem Dach bedienten sich MVRDV souverän des aus der Kunst- und Literaturgeschichte bekannten Topos einer »verkehrten Welt«. Eine Welt, bei der die Naturgesetze außer Kraft gesetzt wurden und das Unterste sich zuoberst kehrt, die Übereinanderschichtung von Landschaften, die üblicherweise nebeneinander zu finden sind: All dies widerspricht der Wahrnehmung. Aber das Bild, das wir uns von der Natur machen, entspricht schwerlich der Realität. Längst ist Natur operationalisiert und instrumentalisiert worden, urbar gemacht, menschlichen Bedürfnissen angeglichen. Gewissermaßen als Extrakt Hollands verwies das Projekt von MVRDV auf die Künstlichkeit der Landschaften, welche die heutigen Industriestaaten prägen.

Natürlich wirken Gedanken wie diese provozierend frech und entbehren nicht der Ironie. Aber wie hatte schon Friedrich Schelling formuliert: »Ironie ist die Form des Paradoxen. Paradox ist alles, was zugleich gut und groß ist.« Gerade die Ironie erlaubt es den Holländern, allseits bekannte Klischees noch einmal zu zitieren. Banalität und Extravaganz finden zu einer Synthese. Wenn es denn ein Erbe der Postmoderne gibt, so ist es ein Umgang mit Architektur, der zwischen Spiel und Pragmatismus, High and Low, Affirmation und Subversion oszilliert.

not sought in a fundamental re-orientation. MVRDV is not interested in alternatives to today's production and consumption habits, but in identifying what potential still remains to optimise them. Similarly, in the "Costa Iberica" study[34] it was not a question of making the Spanish holiday resort of Benidorm less of a blot on the landscape by making structural improvements or even questioning it and considering other concepts of tourism. Instead, the architects developed two suggestive visual scenarios: by increasing the density of Benidorm's waterfront with megalomaniac megastructures and thus potentiating the late-Modernist aesthetics and morphology of the apartment blocks, magnifying them to the oppressive and absurd, they created the possibility of keeping less densely populated coastal regions completely free of development.

MVRDV have abandoned the critical theory that seeks the solution outside a given system. Their attitude is to a certain degree affirmative, because they accept existing conditions. By depicting architecture as the inevitable result of statistical analyses, it acquires apparent objectivity. MVRDV use the conventional analytical methods of urbanism and develop proposals without any reservations, as if it were a question of solving a mathematical equation. Not least their renderings and animations contribute to enhancing the suggestivity of the solution put forward. And, in fact, they are not actually visions but new configurations of the pre-existing. MVRDV distort reality's aporia towards recognition; affirmation becomes subversion[35].

The coincidence between affirmation and subversion was clearly demonstrated in the Dutch Pavilion for Expo 2000, which MVRDV gave the ambiguous title "Holland makes Space." The playful lightness with which MVRDV piled up the landscapes of their home country on top of one another was reminiscent of the follies that have from time immemorial been a firm part of the architectural repertoire of world expositions; a house turned upside down, for example, amused visitors to the Paris expo in 1900. With the floating wood and lake on the roof MVRDV confidently used the theme of a "topsy-turvy world" so familiar to us from the history of art and literature. A world in which the laws of nature are annulled and the very lowest becomes the very top, the layering of landscapes on top of one another that are usually found next to one another—all this contradicts percept-ion. But the image of nature we create for ourselves does not really correspond to reality. For a long time nature has been operationalised and instrumentalised, cultivated, adapted to human needs. To a certain extent as an extract of Holland, the MVRDV project made reference to the artificiality of the landscapes that now dominate today's industrialised nations.

Of course, ideas like this make a provocative and impudent effect and are not without irony. However, as Friedrich Schelling put it: "Irony is the form of the paradox. Paradox is everything that is both good and great." Particularly irony allows the Dutch to quote universally familiar clichés one more time. Banality and extravagance form a synthesis. If a legacy of Post-Modernism does exist it is the way of dealing with architecture that oscillates between play and pragmatism, high and low, affirmation and subversion.

34 MVRDV, Costa Iberica, Barcelona 1998.
35 Hubertus Adam, Stacking and Layering, in: El Croquis 111, MVRDV 1998-2002, Madrid 2002, S. 30-38.

VICKY RICHARDSON

DIE ARCHITEKTUR DES REGIONALISMUS IM ZEITALTER DER GLOBALISIERUNG

REGIONAL ARCHITECTURE IN THE AGE OF GLOBALISATION

»Mittlerweile können wir akzeptieren, dass es wohl kaum einen Unterschied macht, ob man den Satz ›Einen Caffè Latte bitte; nein, nicht tall, sondern grande‹ in New York oder Tokio hört. Aber im Idealfall wird in Zukunft die gestaltete Umgebung, auf die wir beim Verlassen des allgegenwärtigen Coffee-Shops treffen – etwa ein Fahrkartenautomat mit überraschend gutem Graphikdesign oder ein traditionell errichtetes Bambushaus – die beiden Metropolen deutlich voneinander unterscheiden.« So begann im Januar 2000 ein Gegenangriff der New Yorker Design-Zeitschrift *Metropolis* auf das »global blanding«, das weltweite Gleichmachen und Weichspülen von Design im Zuge der Globalisierung.[1]

Die Haltung von *Metropolis* spiegelt die weit verbreitete Sorge wider, dass unsere Epoche von undurchschaubaren multinationalen Konzernen beherrscht wird und von den Gnaden einer labilen, stets unter Hochspannung stehenden Wirtschaft abhängt. Der Soziologe Anthony Giddens, Direktor der London School of Economics, charakterisiert diese Situation als eine »entfesselte Welt«, in welcher jeder Aspekt des Lebens – gleich ob politisch oder kulturell, ob ökonomisch oder technologisch – von unten nach oben gekehrt wird.[2] Die kanadische Journalistin Naomi Klein dokumentiert in ihrem Bestseller *No Logo! Der Kampf der Global Players um Marktmacht. Ein Spiel mit vielen Verlierern und wenigen Gewinnern* die Welt der Marken. Sie beschreibt, wie jede Sphäre des Lebens und des öffentlichen Raums einschließlich des Bildungswesens zum Opfer der Macht von Unternehmen geworden ist: »An fast jeder Universität in Nordamerika tauchen Werbetafeln auf dem Campus auf; es gibt sie an Fahrradständern, auf Sitzbänken, in Fluren zwischen Hörsälen, in Bibliotheken, ja sogar auf Toiletten.«[3]

Auch innerhalb der Architektenschaft gibt es das Gefühl, Globalisierung und Unternehmenskultur führten zu einer eigenschafts- und ortlosen Stahl-Glas-Architektur. Der in London tätige Architekt Andrew Houlton bemerkt: »Hightech-Architektur wird von großen Firmen gerne als gebautes Logo vereinnahmt.«[4]

Die für die Globalisierung charakteristische Architektur, welche die Forderungen von Developern und Marketingfachleuten pragmatisch reflektiert, scheint die der Shopping-Malls, der Gewerbeparks und der Geschäftsbüros zu sein. Für den voluminösen *Harvard Design Guide to Shopping* verfasste Rem Koolhaas einen pessimistischen Essay über Globalisierungsmüll und »Junk-Space«:

»Wenn Space-Junk – Weltraummüll – der von Menschen stammende Schrott ist, der das Universum zunehmend verschandelt, so ist Junk-Space das, was die Menschheit auf unserem Planeten hinterlassen wird. [...] Junk-Space ist das, was nach der Modernisierung übrig bleibt, oder, genauer gesagt, das, was gerinnt, während die Modernisierung stattfindet, ihr Fallout. Die Modernisierung hatte ein rationales Programm: den Segen der Wissenschaft universell zu verbreiten. Junk-Space ist ihre Apotheose oder Kernschmelze. [...] Obgleich ihre jeweiligen Teile das Ergebnis brillanter, hypertechnischer, mittels menschlicher Intelligenz und Phantasie sowie unaufhörlicher Berechnung präzise geplanter Erfindungen sind, bedeutet ihre Summe das Ende der Aufklärung, ihre Wiederauferstehung als Farce, ein minderwertiges Purgatorium.«[5]

1 Pilar Guzman, Going to Towns. Thirty-nine experts from six cities predict that international design can come home again, in: Metropolis, H. 1/2000.
2 Anthony Giddens, Entfesselte Welt. Wie die Globalisierung unser Leben verändert, Frankfurt am Main 2001.
3 Naomi Klein, No Logo! Der Kampf der Global Players um Marktmacht. Ein Spiel mit vielen Verlierern und wenigen Gewinnern, München 2001.
4 Andrew Houlton in: Public Views 3. Encounters. Between here and there, Ausstellungskatalog der Architecture Foundation, London 2001.
5 Rem Koolhaas, Junk-Space, in:

"At this point, we can accept that there is probably very little to distinguish a 'grande-no-not-tall-latte' experience in New York from one in Tokyo. Yet ideally, the designed environment that we will see in the future—a graphically striking ticket booth or a traditionally wrought bamboo house—when we step outside the omnipresent coffee shop will keep the two cities apart."[1] So began a counterattack on "global-blanding" (the worldwide homogenisation of design resulting from globalisation) in the January 2000 issue of *Metropolis*, the New York-based design magazine.

The stance taken by *Metropolis* reflects a wider assumption that our era is one that is dominated by unaccountable multinational corporations, at the mercy of an unstable electric economy. The sociologist Anthony Giddens, who is the Director of the London School of Economics, characterises it as the "Runaway World", in which every aspect of life—political, cultural, technological and economic—is being turned upside down.[2]

In her bestselling book, *No Logo*, the Canadian journalist Naomi Klein documents the landscape of branding. She describes how every area of life and public space has fallen victim to corporate power, including the educational sphere: "At almost every university in North America, advertising billboards appear on campus bicycle racks, on benches, in hallways linking lecture halls, in libraries and even in bathroom stalls".[3]

Within architecture too, there is a sense that globalisation and a corporate culture is leading to a characterless, placeless architecture of glass and steel. As the London-based architect Andrew Houlton remarks: "High-tech [architecture] has been absorbed by a corporate culture as a popular building logo."[4]

The characteristic architecture of globalisation, which pragmatically reflects the demands of developers and marketeers, seems to be that of shopping malls, business parks and commercial offices. In the *Harvard Design Guide to Shopping*, Rem Koolhaas pens a pessimistic essay about the detritus of globalisation and the landscape of "Junkspace:"

"If space-junk is the human debris that litters the universe, junk-space is the residue mankind leaves on the planet... Junkspace is what remains after modernization has run its course or, more precisely, what coagulated while modernization is in progress, is fallout. Modernization had a rational program: to share the blessings of science, universally. Junkspace is its apotheosis, or meltdown... Although its individual parts are the outcome of brilliant inventions, lucidly planned by human intelligence, boosted by infinite computation, their sum spells the end of Enlightenment, its resurrection as farce, a low-grade purgatory."[5]

Koolhaas is no advocate for particularism, yet his view, as glimpsed above, is shared by many who reach the conclusion that architecture needs to rediscover its roots in local climate, culture, tradition and landscape. What can loosely be described as regional architecture is backed up by sociologists such as Giddens, who argue that the flipside of globalisation is a return to the local with a revival of long forgotten cultural identities: "Globalisation not only pulls upwards, but also pushes downwards, creating new pressures for local autonomy."[6]

As well as the political pressure put by it on traditional nation states, it is also the case that the new communication tools

1 Pilar Guzman, Going to Towns. Thirty-nine experts from six cities predict that international design can come home again, in: Metropolis, New York, January 2000.
2 Anthony Giddens, Runaway World, London 1999.
3 Naomi Klein, No Logo, London 2001.
4 Andrew Houlton in: Public Views 3. Encounters. Between here and there, Architecture Foundation exhibition catalogue, London 2001.
5 Rem Koolhaas, Junkspace, in: Chuihua Judy Chung, Jeffrey Inaba,

Koolhaas ist kein Befürworter irgendeines Partikularismus; doch seine Ansicht, die wir hier nur kurz streifen können, wird von vielen geteilt, die zu dem Schluss kommen, dass die Architektur ihre Wurzeln im Klima, der Kultur, der Tradition und der Topographie ihres jeweiligen Ortes wieder entdecken muss. Was als regionale Architektur umschrieben werden kann, wird von Soziologen wie Giddens unterstützt. Sie argumentieren, dass die Kehrseite der Globalisierung eine Rückkehr zum Lokalen sei, die mit einer Wiederbelebung längst vergessener kultureller Identitäten einhergehe. Globalisierung »erzeugt nicht nur einen Sog nach oben, sondern auch einen Druck nach unten und wiederbelebt die Forderung nach lokaler Selbständigkeit«[6].

Vom politischen Druck auf den traditionellen Nationalstaat einmal abgesehen, muss man aber auch feststellen, dass die Kommunikationsinstrumente der globalisierten Welt – also vor allem Internet und E-Mail – kulturelle Mannigfaltigkeit durchaus erleichtern können. Eine Freundin von mir, die ihre Kindheit in Ostafrika verbracht hatte, nun aber in New York wohnte, wurde neugierig darauf, ihre Wurzeln wieder zu entdecken. Dazu wollte sie etwas über die Sprache Tschibemba herausfinden, die von Stämmen in Sambia gesprochen wird, wo sie aufwuchs. Bei ihrer Recherche im Internet fand sie eine amerikanische Website zum Thema Linguistik und dort einen Artikel, der den Namen eines Wörterbuchs enthielt, das sie dann online bei Amazon erwerben konnte. Diese Begebenheit demonstriert, dass globale Verbindungen – anstatt lokale Dialekte und Charakteristika auszulöschen – auch das Potenzial haben, ein breites Spektrum kultureller Formen am Leben zu erhalten.

KRITISCHER REGIONALISMUS

Vor gut zwanzig Jahren – das heißt unter ganz anderen politischen und sozialen Umständen – trat mit dem Aufsatz von Kenneth Frampton *Towards a Critical Regionalism* der Begriff »Regionalismus« in die architektonische Debatte. Vor dem Hintergrund des niedergehenden Sozialstaats hatte sich die Postmoderne zur beherrschenden stilistischen Kraft der internationalen Architektur entwickelt. Der »Kritische Regionalismus«, schrieb Frampton 1983, sei eine »Architektur des Widerstands« – ein Mittel zur »Wiederaneignung des im neunzehnten Jahrhundert entstandenen Gedankens der Tektonik, als Gegenwehr zur zeitgenössischen Tendenz, Architektur auf bloß szenische Effekte zu beschränken«[7].

Eigentlich wurde der Begriff »Kritischer Regionalismus« schon vorher geprägt. Erstmals gebrauchten ihn die beiden Architekten und Wissenschaftler Alexander Tzonis und Liane Lefaivre in ihrem 1981 publizierten Aufsatz *The Grid and the Pathway*[8]. Trotz verschiedener Differenzen mit Frampton in Bezug auf die präzise Definition benutzten auch Tzonis und Lefaivre das Adjektiv »kritisch«, um diese Variante des Regionalismus von früheren romantischen und bornierten Konzepten zu unterscheiden, vor allem natürlich vom »Heimatstil« im nationalsozialistischen Deutschland.

Frampton betonte, dass der Kritische Regionalismus durch die »indirekte Interpretation« charakteristischer Elemente eines besonderen Ortes entstünde. »Er mag die ihn leitende Inspi-

associated with the globalised world (namely the Internet and e mail) can facilitate cultural diversity. Consider the following recent experience of a friend of mine. Having spent the first few years of her life in East Africa, but now living in central London, she became interested in rediscovering her childhood. She decided to investigate the Chibemba language, spoken by tribes in Zambia, where she grew up. By searching the Internet, she found an American linguistics website and an article containing the name of a dictionary, which she was able to purchase via the online bookseller, Amazon. This surely demonstrates that instead of leading to a kind of 'blotting-out' of local dialects and characteristics, global interconnection has the potential to keep alive a diverse range of cultural forms.

CRITICAL REGIONALISM

Twenty years ago, under very different political and social circumstances, the term "regionalism" entered architectural debate with the publication of the essay *Towards a Critical Regionalism*[7] by Kenneth Frampton. Frampton saw regionalism as "an architecture of resistance." Against a background of declining welfare-state socialism, Post-Modernism was becoming the major stylistic force within international architecture. Critical regionalism, wrote Frampton, was a means of "recovering the 19th century notion of the tectonic in an effort to resist the contemporary tendency to reduce architecture to scenographic effects."

The term "critical regionalism" had actually been coined two years previously by the architects and academics Alexander Tzonis and Liane Lefaivre in their essay *The Grid and the Pathway.*[8] Despite certain differences with Frampton over the precise definition, both essays used the word "critical" in order to distinguish this variety of regionalism from romantic, parochial forms that had previously existed—particularly the *volkische* architecture of Nazis in Germany prior to the Second World War.

Frampton stressed that critical regionalism came about by "indirectly" interpreting elements from the peculiarities of a particular place. "It may find its governing inspiration in such things as the range and quality of the local light, or in the tectonic derived from a peculiar structural mode, or in the topography of a given site."[9]

It was "critical" because it needed to be self-conscious and questioning of other forms of regionalism, particularly those that mimicked local forms and construction techniques in a simplistic or kitsch manner. As Frampton explains: "It is necessary to distinguish between critical regionalism and simple-minded attempts to revive the hypothetical forms of a lost vernacular. In contradistinction to critical regionalism, the primary vehicle of populism is the communication or instrumental sign."[10] In this period, regionalism, also described by Tzonis and Lefaivre as "tropical architecture", was part of a reaction against the failure of the first wave of modern architecture in the developing world.

In his opposition to Post-Modernism, Frampton saw critical regionalism as a way of taking forward the Modernist project. To

Arch+, H. 149/150/2000, S. 55 ff.

6 Anthony Giddesn, a.a.O., S. 24.

7 Kenneth Frampton, Towards a Critical Regionalism. Six Points for an Architecture of Resistance, in: Hal Foster (Hg.): The Anti-Aesthetic. Essays on Postmodern Culture, New York 1998, S. 16 ff. Kenneth Frampton, Die Architektur der Moderne. Eine kritische Baugeschichte. Teil III./5 Kritischer Regionalismus, Stuttgart 1995, S. 263 ff.

8 Alexander Tzonis/Liane Lefaivre, The Grid and the Pathway, in: Architecture in Greece H. 5/1981. Hierbei handelt es sich um eine Einführung in das Werk der griechischen Architek-

Rem Koolhaas, Sze Tsung Leong (eds), The Harvard Design School Guide to Shopping, Colonge 2001.

6 Cf. Anothy Giddens, Runaway World, p. 13.

7 Kenneth Frampton, Towards a Critical Regionalism. Six Points for an Architecture of Resistance, in: Hal Foster (ed.), The Anti-Aesthetic. Essays on Post-Modern Culture, New York 1983.

8 Alexander Tzonis and Liane Lefaivre, The Grid and the Pathway, in: Architecture in Greece, no. 5, 1981.

9 Cf. Kenneth Frampton, Towards a Critical Regionalism.

1

2

3

4

5

1 Simon Conder Associates: Beach House, Dungeness (UK), 2003
2 Enric Miralles, Benedetta Tagliabue, RMJM: Schottisches Parlament/ Scottish Parliament, Edinburgh, 2004

3 Peter Zumthor: Thermalbad/ Thermal Baths, Vals, Schweiz/ Switzerland, 1996, Innenansicht/ Interior view
4 Thermalbad/Thermal Baths, Vals, 1996, Außenansicht/ Exterior view

5 Gion A. Caminada: Totenstube/ House of the Dead, Vrin, Schweiz/ Switzerland, 2002

ration aus Phänomenen wie der Qualität des örtlichen Lichts, der von eigenen Bauweisen abgeleiteten Tektonik oder der besonderen Topographie des Grundstücks beziehen.«[9]

Er hieß »kritisch«, weil er selbstbewusst sein musste und andere Arten von Regionalismus – besonders die simplifizierte oder sentimentale Mimikry lokaler Bauformen und Bauweisen – in Frage zu stellen hatte. Frampton erklärte: »Es ist notwendig, [...] zwischen Kritischem Regionalismus und naiven Versuchen einer Wiederbelebung von lediglich vermuteten Formen einer verlorenen Ortstypik zu trennen. Denn im Gegensatz zum Kritischen Regionalismus ist das primäre Vehikel des Populismus das direkt kommunikative oder instrumentelle Zeichen.«[10]

Während dieser Phase war der Regionalismus, den Tzonis und Lefaivre auch als »tropische Architektur« beschrieben, Teil einer Reaktion auf das Versagen der ersten Woge moderner Architektur in Entwicklungsländern.

In seiner Opposition zur Postmoderne sah Frampton den Kritischen Regionalismus als einen Weg, das Projekt der Moderne fortzusetzen. Andere hingegen zelebrierten mit ihm lediglich Differenz und die Abwehr von Universalismus. Der südafrikanische Architekt Leon van Schaik, der sich mit den Problemen herumschlug, die das deutlich wahrnehmbare Versagen des International Style in Afrika aufgeworfen hatte, verteidigte den Universalcharakter von Kultur gegen jede Art Regionalismus: »Ich finde das vor kurzem wieder eingeführte Gesellschaftsspiel namens Regionalismus höchst verdächtig. Es ist ein Spiel, bei dem auf miserabel definierter Grundlage einige Gebäude als ›regional‹, andere als ›international‹ beschrieben werden. Dabei scheint es, dass die Begriffe ›regional‹ und ›relevant‹ zusammengehören, während ›international‹ nur ein Schimpfwort ist, das keiner näheren Bestimmung bedarf.«[11]

Demgegenüber zeigte van Schaik auf, »dass in der Kultur alles Exzellente, wiewohl häufig im Besonderen wurzelnd, aus der Fähigkeit rührt, den lokalen Ursprung zu überschreiten und sich auf die Höhe des universalen Diskurses zu begeben, das heißt, sich an die Spitze des wachsenden Bewusstseins der Menschheit zu setzen«[12].

Im Rahmen der im Herbst 2003 an der Universität Cambridge gehaltenen Slade Lectures kritisierte der Architekturhistoriker William J. R. Curtis den Regionalismus als »verkappten Nationalismus«, als eine »Süßstoff-Sicht« auf Identität.[13] Curtis forderte dazu auf, das Wort »regional« zu vermeiden und lieber von »Gebiet« und »Identität« zu sprechen. Ähnlich irreführend findet auch die amerikanische Künstlerin und Schriftstellerin Lucy R. Lippard den Begriff Regionalismus, weil er die Repräsentation eines objektiv existenten geographischen Territoriums durch Architektur impliziere. Lippard weist darauf hin, dass eine Region gewöhnlich nicht durch ihre politischen und geographischen Grenzen zu fassen sei, sondern vielmehr durch ihre Geschichten, ihre innere Verbundenheit kraft gemeinsamer Erfahrungen, ihre oft nicht aufgezeichnete kollektive Historie. Bei »Region« sagt sie, handele es sich eher um einen mentalen Zustand als um einen physischen Ort auf der Landkarte.[14]

others, though, it represented the celebration of difference and the rejection of universalism. Grappling with solutions to the problems thrown up by the perceived failure of the International Style in Africa, South African architect Leon van Schaik defended the universality of culture against regionalism: "I am deeply suspicious of the recently reintroduced parlour game 'regionalism.' A game in which on ill-defined grounds some buildings are considered regional while others are described as 'international.' Here it seems that 'regional' and 'relevant' are terms that go together while international is an unaccompanied expletive."[11]

Van Schaik pointed out that although excellence in the sphere of culture is often rooted in the particular, "its excellence derives from its ability to transcend that local origin and peak in the universal conversation, which is the cutting edge of mankind's growing awareness."[12]

During the 2003 Slade lectures at the University of Cambridge, architectural historian William Curtis criticised regionalism as "nationalism in disguise—a saccharin view of identity."[13] Curtis claims to avoid the word "regional" in favour of terms such as "territory" and "identity". Similarly, for the American artist and writer Lucy Lippard the term "regionalism" is misleading, because it implies the representation of objective geographical area through architecture. Lippard points out that a region is "generally understood not as a politically or geographically delimited space, but as one determined by stories, loyalties, group identity, common experiences and histories (often unrecorded), a state of mind rather than a place on a map."[14]

THE FLUIDITY OF CULTURE

Research carried out by Paul Oliver, Chair of the Master's course in International Studies in Vernacular Architecture at Oxford Brookes University, makes it clear that ideas, building techniques and culture are not objective features of societies that are unique to particular geographical regions. All these features are in fact highly fluid and they alter over time with cultural shifts in society and changes in the means of production. In his three-volume *Encyclopaedia of Vernacular Architecture of the World*, Oliver shows that, throughout history, the migration of people seeking food, work and a better standard of living means that ways of building have travelled with them across the world.[15] A farm building from the nineteenth century in rural Ukraine may have striking similarities with one in the Canadian province of Manitoba.

For Curtis, the revival of interest in tradition and history is the product of a sense of dislocation in a fast-changing world. To Anthony Giddens, the "Runaway World" has created a sense (and a reality) of risk and insecurity. Key changes, such as the emergence and re-emergence of nation states in East and Western Europe, are paralleled by climatic change (global warming) that appears, rightly or wrongly, to call into question traditional environmental zones.

In this context, Lippard argues that identity and rootedness are becoming increasingly important ways for people to understand the world. In her book, *The Lure of the Local*, Lippard

ten Dimitris und Susana Antonakakis; Alexander Tzonis (u.a.), Die Frage des Regionalismus, in: Michael Andritzky (u.a. Hg.), Für eine andere Architektur. Erster Band. Bauen mit der Natur und in der Region, Frankfurt am Main 1981, S. 121 ff.
9 Kenneth Frampton, a.a.O.
10 Ebd.
11 Leon van Schaik, Against Regionalism, in: Architecture SA, H. 3/4/1986.
12 siehe Anmerkung 11.
13 William J. R. Curtis, Slade Lectures. 6th Lecture. Identity Territory Origins, unveröffentlichtes Manuskript einer Vorlesung an der Universität

10 Cf. Ibid.
11 Leon van Schaik, Against Regionalism, in: Architecture SA, March/April 1986.
12 Ibid.
13 William J. R. Curtis, Slade Lectures. 6th Lecture: Identity, Territory, Origins, 18 November 2003, University of Cambridge, unpublished manuscript.
14 Lucy R Lippard, The Lure of the Local. Senses of Place in a Multicentered Society, New York 1997.
15 Paul Oliver (ed.), Encyclopaedia of Vernacular Architecture of the World, Cambridge 1997.

FLIESSENDE KULTUR

Untersuchungen zufolge, die von Paul Oliver, dem Leiter der Meisterkurse für Internationale Studien zur Regionalen Architektur an der Brookes Universität Oxford geleitet wurden, sind Erfindungen, Baukultur und -technik keine objektiven gesellschaftlichen Charakteristika, die nur speziellen geographischen Regionen zu eigen sind. In Wirklichkeit sind solche Merkmale höchst fließend. Sie ändern sich im Lauf der Zeit aufgrund kultureller Verschiebungen und von Veränderungen der Produktionsmittel. In seiner dreibändigen *Encyclopaedia of Vernacular Architecture of the World* zeigt Oliver, dass in der gesamten Geschichte die Wanderungsbewegung der nach Nahrung, Arbeit und einem besseren Leben suchenden Menschen stets bedeutete, dass Bauweisen mit den Migranten durch die Welt zogen. Deshalb habe ein Bauernhof in der ländlichen Ukraine des 19. Jahrhunderts erstaunliche Ähnlichkeiten mit einem Farmhaus in der kanadischen Provinz Manitoba.[15]

Für Curtis ist das wieder auflebende Interesse an Tradition und Geschichte Produkt eines Gespürs für die Entortung des Menschen in einer sich rasch wandelnden Welt. Für Giddens hat diese »entfesselte Welt« ein nicht allein gefühltes, sondern auch wirkliches Risiko geschaffen. Entscheidende Veränderungen – etwa die Entstehung und das Wiedererstehen von Nationalstaaten in Ost- und Westeuropa –, die sich zur selben Zeit ereignen wie der durch die globale Erwärmung ausgelöste Klimawandel, scheinen, ob zu Recht oder nicht, die gewohnte Umwelt von Menschen in Frage zu stellen.

In diesem Zusammenhang behauptet Lippard, dass Identität und Verwurzelung für die Menschen immer wichtiger werden, um die Welt zu verstehen. In ihrem Buch *The Lure of the Local*, was so viel heißt wie »Die Verlockung des Örtlichen«, hinterfragt sie die abschätzige Verwendung des Begriffs Regionalismus als »sentimentale und hinterwäldlerische Kunst«. Sie schreibt, dass in unserer homogenen, nomadischen, elektronischen Kultur so etwas wie reiner Regionalismus nicht mehr existiere. Kunst könne aber zugleich universal und doch mit einem Ort befasst sein. »Wenn Kunst als universal definiert und die Form dem Inhalt aus Routine vorgezogen wird, dann werden Künstler dazu ermutigt, ihre unmittelbare geistige und räumliche Umgebung hinter sich zu lassen. Wenn man aber den Inhalt als primäre Komponente und die gelebte Erfahrung als primäres Material eines Kunstwerks betrachtet, dann ist Regionalismus keine Einschränkung, sondern ein Vorteil; er ist dann eine willkommene Grundlage, die nicht notwendig äußere Einflüsse ausschließt, sondern im Sieb des Lokalen filtert. Gute regionale Kunst hat stets beides: Wurzeln und Weite.«[16]

MODERNER REGIONALISMUS

Lippards Schrift stellt eine nützliche Erklärung für die starke Strömung innerhalb der zeitgenössischen Architektur dar, die in der Besonderheit des Ortes wurzelt, deren theoretische Grundlage gleichwohl die Moderne ist. Simon Conder, ein in London tätiger britischer Architekt, ist einer von etlichen Praktikern, deren Interesse sich in Richtung einer Architektur verschoben hat, die auf das lokale Idiom reagiert und doch strikt

6

7

6 Percy Thomas Partnership: Welsh Millennium Centre, Cardiff (GB), 2004

7 Sheila O'Donnell, John Tuomey: Furniture College, Letterfrack, Irland/Ireland, 2001

Cambridge am 18. November 2003.
14 Lucy R. Lippard, The Lure of the Local. Senses of Place in a Multicentered Society, New York 1997.
15 Paul Oliver (Hg.), Encyclopaedia of Vernacular Architecture of the World, Cambridge 1997.
16 Lucy R. Lippard, The Lure of the Local, a.a.O., 14.

8

9

10

11

12

Glenn Murcutt: House in the Southern Highlands, New South Wales, Australien/Australia, 2001

8 Nordansicht/North front
9 Detail Garage/Detail of tractor shed
10 Osteingang/Eastern entrance
11 Gesamtansicht/General view
12 Südansicht/South front

modern im Gebrauch minimalistischer Formen ist. Conders Strandhaus in Südostengland ist ein Beispiel, das gut in Lippards Charakteristik einer Architektur passt, die »äußere Einflüsse im Sieb des Lokalen filtert«. Ganz und gar mit Platten schwarzen Gummis verkleidet, ist das Haus eine Interpretation der benachbarten Fischerhütten, die sich an der allen Wettern ausgesetzten Küste von Dungeness in Kent reihen. Gewöhnlich waren diese Hütten selbst gebaut und mit schwarzem Teer gestrichen, um sie vor Sprühwasser, Wind und Regen zu schützen. Der Umriss des von Conder entworfenen Hauses gleicht dem seiner Nachbarn. Aber im Unterschied zu diesen besteht seine Besonderheit in dem künstlichen Gummi (einem Produkt namens »Prelasti«, das gemeinhin für Fließbänder und zur Abdichtung von Wasserbehältern verwendet wird); einem Material einer belgischen Firma, das durch eine Recherche im Internet gefunden wurde. Bauen im »Geist« von Dungeness hieß für Conder nicht, örtliche Baustoffe »ehrlich« zu nutzen, sondern etwas vom lokalen Charakter zu erfassen und dies dann in einer zeitgemäßen Weise umzudeuten.

Wie Conder sind auch die irischen Architekten Sheila O'Donnell und John Tuomey – die das Furniture College in Letterfrack im Westen Irlands entwarfen – nicht an der Authentizität von Material und Konstruktion interessiert. Während ihrer Arbeit an der Fachhochschule für Möbelhandwerk sammelten sie Steine am nahen Strand, um eine Farbe für den Putz des Colleges zu finden. Aber der Sand von Latterfrack passte nicht richtig, weshalb sie Sand aus einem anderen Landesteil beschafften. Sheila O'Donnell sagt: »Wir interessieren uns für das Verhältnis zwischen Baustoff und Landschaft. Daher kommen wir zu ähnlichen Schlüssen wie die Leute von früher. Aber es ist nicht so, dass wir im strikten Sinne ortstypische Baustoffe verwenden.«[17]

Der amerikanische Architekt William P. Bruder ist bekannt für seine hoch kontextuellen Arbeiten, die mit ihren örtlichen Gegebenheiten korrespondieren, obwohl für diese Bauten industrielle Materialien – deutlich gesagt: Fließbandwaren – verwandt werden. Bruder beschreibt Architektur als »Balance zwischen Poetik und Pragmatismus«[18]; oft benutzt er ganz gewöhnliche Baustoffe in ganz ungewöhnlicher Weise. Sein letztes Projekt ist dafür ein gutes Beispiel. Das Nevada Museum of Art in Reno, fertig gestellt im Juli 2003, wurde mit drei aufeinander lagernden Schichten aus schwarzem Stahl verkleidet. Sie erinnern an die Oberschichten von Basaltfelsen, welche die rauhe Landschaft der Black-Rock-Wüste 120 Meilen nördlich der Stadt wie dunkle Punkte markieren.

Der undogmatische Ansatz der hier erwähnten drei Architekturbüros zeigt, dass die Nutzung der Vorteile des weltweiten Markts für Baustoffe tatsächlich beim Entwerfen solcher Gebäude hilft, etwas vom Geist, wenn auch nicht der Bautradition eines Ortes zu erfassen.

Ironischerweise führt das wachsende Gespür einer Verbundenheit unter solchen Architekten, die in besonderen Gegenden überall auf der Welt tätig sind, derzeit zu einer Wiederbelebung des Interesses an Lokalität und Regionalität. Die Entstehung einer sehr distinkten Schule mit dem Namen »Schweizerischer Regionalismus«, konzentriert auf den Kanton Graubünden und vor allem auf das Werk von Peter Zumthor, hat großen Einfluss

17 Sheila O'Donnell in Vicky Richardson, Out of place, in: Riba journal, H. 11/2001, S. 16 ff.

18 William P. Bruder: unveröffentlichtes Manuskript einer Vorlesung an der Westminster Universität London am 26. September 2000.

challenges the pejorative use of the term "regionalism" in the art world to imply "corny backwater art." She writes that "in our homogenised, peripatetic, electronic culture" there is no such thing as regionalism. Art can be both universal and concerned with place: "If art is defined as 'universal' and form is routinely favoured over content, then artists are encouraged to transcend their immediate locales. But if content is considered the prime component of art, and lived experience is seen as a prime material, then regionalism is not a limitation but an advantage, a welcome base that need not exclude outside influences but sifts them through a local filter. Good regional art has both roots and reach."[16]

MODERN VERNACULAR

Lippard's writing is a useful way of explaining the strong current within contemporary architecture that is rooted in the specifics of place, yet whose theoretical basis is Modernism. Simon Conder, a British architect based in London, is one of a number of contemporary practitioners whose interest has shifted towards an architecture that is responsive to its locale, yet is strictly Modernist in its use of minimalist form. Conder's Beach House in southern England is an example that fits into Lippard's characterisation as "sifting outside influences through a local filter." Entirely covered with sheets of black rubber, the house is an interpretation of the neighbouring fisherman's cottages that line the weather-beaten coast of Dungeness in Kent. Conventionally these cottages were self-built and painted with black tar to protect them from sea spray, wind and rain. In silhouette the house is similar to its neighbours, but unlike them, its distinctive building component is an artificial rubber (a product called Prelasti that is commonly used for conveyor belts and for lining reservoirs) that was manufactured in a factory in Belgium and sourced via the Internet. For Conder, building in the spirit of Dungeness was not about authentically using local materials, but about capturing something of the local character and interpreting it in a contemporary way.

Like Conder, the Irish architects O'Donnell & Tuomey, who designed the furniture college in Letterfrack in the West of Ireland, are not dogmatic about the authenticity of materials or building techniques. For this project, the architect collected stones from the local beaches to find a colour for the render. However, the local sand was not a good match, so sand was sourced from another part of the country. Partner Sheila O'Donnell says: "We're interested in the relationship between building materials and the landscape, so we come to similar conclusions to people from the past, but we're not literally using local materials."[17]

The American architect William P. Bruder is known for highly contextual work that corresponds to its locale while using off-the-peg building products and materials. Describing architecture as a "balance between poetry and pragmatism"[18] Bruder often uses ordinary materials in extraordinary ways. His latest project is a case in point. The Nevada Art Museum in Reno, which was completed in July 2003, is clad in layers of black steel that are reminiscent of the basalt rock outcrops that dot

16 Cf. Lucy R Lippard, The Lure of the Local.
17 Sheila O'Donnell quoted in: Vicky Richardson, Out of Place, RIBA Journal, November 2001.

18 Lecture by William P. Bruder at University of Westminster, London, 26 September 2000, unpublished manuscript.

auf eine neue Generation von Architekten in Europa und außerhalb des Kontinents. Zumthors Thermalbad in Vals, fertig gestellt 1997, zeigt, dass regionale Charakteristika durch eine reine Form »moderner Bodenständigkeit« zum Ausdruck kommen können. Der Begriff »modern vernacular« wurde kürzlich von Steven Spier und Martin Tschanz benutzt, um neuere Arbeiten Schweizer Architekten zu beschreiben.[19]

Der einflussreichste Regionalist ist vermutlich der australische Architekt Glenn Murcutt. Nachdem er im Jahr 2002 den Pritzker-Preis gewonnen hatte und im Jahr 2003 zwei Monographien über ihn erschienen waren, wurden Murcutts Bauten – es sind ungefähr fünfhundert Wohnhäuser in Australien – in den Medien der ganzen Welt veröffentlicht. Obwohl tief in der einheimischen Tradition und Topographie Australiens verwurzelt, weicht Murcutts Werk der Moderne nirgends aus. Françoise Fromonot, Autorin eines der beiden jüngst publizierten Bücher über sein Schaffen, erklärt, bei einem typischen, von Murcutt in den achtziger Jahren entworfenen Wohnhaus treffe das Haus Farnsworth von Ludwig Mies van der Rohe auf die Logik des australischen Woolsheds (des Schuppens, in dem Schafswolle geschoren und gelagert wird).[20]

ARCHITEKTURPROPAGANDA

Obwohl sie wie die Verkörperung zeitgenössischer australischer Architektur wirken, haben Murcutts Bauten definitiv nichts mit Identität und Nationalität zu tun. Dennoch gibt es innerhalb des Regionalismus eine starke Strömung, die sich die Bestimmung und den Ausdruck von Identität zum Ziel gesetzt hat. Diesen Aspekt der Architektur beschreibt Curtis als »Sprache der Propaganda«.[21]

Der Gebrauch von Architektur zu politischen Zwecken ist gut dokumentiert. Man nehme nur das Gebäude der Nationalversammlung von Kuwait, 1972 von Jørn Utzon entworfen und ein Jahrzehnt später fertig gestellt. Die Elite von Kuwait – einem Staat, der 1961 seine Unabhängigkeit erlangte – beauftragte Utzon in den späten sechziger bzw. siebziger Jahren, eine monumentale Zitadelle zu entwerfen, welche die staatliche Identität stärken sollte. Das Charakteristikum des Gebäudes ist eine Reihe von Höfen, die durch mehrere kleinere Straßen mit einer Art Hauptstraße verbunden sind. Der Architekt sah darin eine Erinnerung an die traditionelle Architektur arabischer Basare.[22] Durch die Verbindung der neuen Nationalversammlung mit Jahrhunderte alten Traditionen sollte die Legitimität einer noch fragilen Nation gestützt werden.

Heute ist die Rolle der Architektur für die Legitimierung junger Nationalstaaten noch genauso wichtig. Allerdings wird sie nun weniger als Werkzeug der Eliten betrachtet; vielmehr erscheint sie als ein Mittel, das Selbstvertrauen der Bevölkerung zu wecken. Das Gebäude des schottischen Parlaments, das noch 2004 – zwei Jahre später als vorgesehen und mit einer Überschreitung der Baukosten um mehrere Millionen Pfund – eröffnet werden soll, ist ein gutes Beispiel für die Darstellung von Politik mithilfe der Architektur.

Die Dezentralisierung des Vereinigten Königreichs und die daraus folgende größere Eigenständigkeit Schottlands waren Er-

19 Steven Spier/Martin Tschanz, Swiss Made. New Architecture from Switzerland, London/New York 2003.
20 Françoise Fromonot, Glenn Murcutt. Buildings and Projects 1962-2003, London/New York 2003.
21 siehe William J.R. Curtis, Slade Lectures, a.a.O.
22 Françoise Fromonot, Jørn Utzon. Architetto della Sydney Opera House, Mailand 1998, S. 217 ff. Richard Weston, Utzon. Inspiration Vision Architektur, Kiel 2001, S. 300 ff.

the rugged landscape of the Black Rock Desert, 120 miles north of the city.

The undogmatic approach of these architects shows that taking advantage of the global market place in building materials can actually assist the process of designing buildings that capture the "spirit," if not the actual building traditions, of a place.

Ironically, the increased sense of connection between architects practising in particular locations around the world is currently leading to a revival of interest in regionalism and the vernacular. The emergence of a distinct school of Swiss regionalism, centred on the Canton of Graubunden and in particular the work of Peter Zumthor is a major influence on a new generation of architects in Europe and beyond. Zumthor's thermal bath in Vals (completed in 1997) demonstrates that regional characteristics can be expressed through a pure form of "modern vernacular"[19]—a term recently used to describe the work of Swiss architects.

The most influential regionalist is probably the Australian architect Glenn Murcutt. Since winning the Pritzker Prize in 2002 and following the publication in 2003 of two monographs, Murcutt's buildings (around 500 houses in Australia) have been featured in publications around the world. Despite being deeply rooted in the Australian vernacular tradition and landscape, Murcutt's work is inescapably modern. As Françoise Fromonot, the author of one of the recent books on his work, explains, a typical house designed by Murcutt in the 1980s is "Mies's Farnsworth House meets the logic of the Australian woolshed."[20]

ARCHITECTURAL PROPAGANDA

Although it has come to epitomise contemporary Australian architecture, Murcutt's architecture is definitely not about identity or nationalism. Nevertheless, there is a strong current within regionalism that is consciously aimed at expressing and defining identity. This is an aspect of architecture that William Curtis describes as the "language of propaganda."[21]

The use of architecture for political ends is well documented. Take the case of the Kuwait National Assembly, designed by Jørn Utzon in 1972 and completed a decade later. In the late 1960s and 1970s, the elite of Kuwait—a state created after a previous empire was carved up—commissioned Utzon to design a monumental citadel that was aimed at strengthening national identity. The building features a series of courtyards connected to a central street by a series of smaller streets, which the architect described as reminiscent of "traditional Islamic bazaar architecture,"[22] the idea being to reinforce the legitimacy of a fragile nation state by linking the assembly with centuries-old traditions.

Today, the role of architecture in legitimising "young" nation states is just as important. However, rather than being seen as a tool of elites, it is re-represented as a vehicle of the people. The Scottish Parliament in Edinburgh, which is due to be completed this year [2004] two years behind schedule and millions of pounds over budget is a good example of politics being played out in the arena of architecture.

19 Term used in: Steven Spier and Martin Tschanz, Swiss Made. New Architecture from Switzerland, London/New York 2003.
20 Françoise Fromonot, Glenn Murcutt. Buildings and Projects 1962-2003, London/New York 2003.
21 Cf. William J. R. Curtis, Slade Lectures.
22 Quoted in: Françoise Fromonot, Jørn Utzon. The Sydney Opera House, London 1998.

gebnis eines Referendums im Jahr 1997. Die neue Regierung machte sich gleich daran, einen Sitz für das erste schottische Parlament nach dreihundert Jahren zu realisieren. Den entsprechenden Wettbewerb gewannen die katalanischen Regionalisten Enric Miralles und Benedetta Tagliabue mit einem Entwurf, der schottische Nationalidentität und Landschaft verbindet. 1998 wurde das Büro EMBT dann mit der Planung des Regierungsgebäudes beauftragt. Von seinem Grundstück in der Altstadt Edinburghs weist der Bau in Richtung auf Arthur's Seat, einen durch vulkanische Erruption entstandenen Hügel. Das neue Parlamentsgebäude reagiert eher auf die Landschaft als auf die Stadt durch ein aus dem Boden geschnittenes, nach oben offenes Amphitheater, das die Partizipation des schottischen Volkes an der Demokratie bildlich darstellen, wenn nicht gar erleichtern soll.

Auch in Wales steht ein großes nationales Projekt – das Zentrum für Darstellende Künste – kurz vor seiner Vollendung. Das vom Büro Percy Thomas Partnership entworfene Wales Millennium Centre in Cardiff ist ein Beispiel dafür, wie sich die Architekten – aufgrund des Fehlens eines klaren nationalen Architekturidioms – lokaler Materialien sowie der kulturellen und symbolischen Formensprache bedienen, um der nationalen Identität Gestalt zu geben. Die Fassade bezieht ihre Inspiration aus den walisischen Kliffs und den für diese Region typischen geologischen Formationen. »Die Art, wie die Schichten von Fels lagern, scheint die Ausdauer unserer Nation beim Durchschreiten ganzer Zeitalter zu symbolisieren«, erklärt der Projektarchitekt Jonathan Adams.[23]

Freilich kommen solche Bauten einer Haltung gefährlich nah, die örtliche Baustoffe und Bauweisen um szenischer Effekte willen nutzt; dabei war es eben dieser Ansatz, den Frampton in den achtziger Jahren so lautstark kritisiert hatte. Eine andere Gefahr, wenn Identität in gebauter Form zum Ausdruck gebracht werden soll, besteht darin, dass etwas Fließendes und sich stets Veränderndes festgelegt und dogmatisch wird. Mit einiger Skepsis äußert sich daher der Architekt und Architekturtheoretiker Alan Colquhoun über den Regionalismus als ein »essentialistisches Modell«. Er schreibt: »Diesem Modell zufolge haben alle Gesellschaften einen Kern oder eine Essenz, die es lediglich zu entdecken oder zu erhalten gilt. [...] Das Konzept des Regionalismus hängt von seiner Möglichkeit ab, kulturelle Kodes und geographische Regionen in wechselseitige Beziehungen zu versetzen. Es beruht auf einem herkömmlichen System von Kommunikation, bei dem Klima, Geographie, handwerkliche Traditionen sowie Religionen absolut bestimmend sind.«[24]

Im Zeitalter der Globalisierung tritt das essentialistische Modell im Gewand des Radikalismus auf und ist eher nicht als Domäne konservativer Eliten zu sehen. Regionale und neue einheimische Architektur sind zu einem Gegenmittel gegen den Schmerz der Entortung geworden, während die Politik einer multikulturellen Identität längst Mainstream ist.

Die im Verlauf der letzten Jahre gewachsene Popularität der Prinzipien des amerikanischen »New Urbanism« ist ein anderes Beispiel für die breite Akzeptanz des Regionalismus. In Großbritannien etwa ist Prinz Charles – der in den achtziger Jahren für seinen Antimodernismus belächelt wurde – zu einer der Schlüs-

13

14

13 Black Rock Desert, USA

14 William P. Bruder: Nevada Museum of Art, Reno, 2003

23 Jonathan Adams auf der Tagung »Global Blanding« des Institute of Ideas London am 17. Juni 2000.

24 Alan Colquhoun, The Concept of Regionalism, in: Gülsüm Baydar Nalbantoglu/Chong Thai Wong (Hg.), Postcolonial Space(s), New York 1997, S. 13 ff.

selfiguren für die gegenwärtige Richtung neuer Wohnungsbauvorhaben aufgestiegen. Noch 1984 hielt man den Prince of Wales bloß für einen schlecht informierten Reaktionär, als er den im Architekturbüro Ahrends/Burton/Koralek verfassten Entwurf für die Erweiterung der Nationalgalerie in London als »monströses Furunkel auf dem Gesicht eines sehr geliebten und eleganten Freundes«[25] kritisierte. Daran änderte sich auch nichts, als Prinz Charles vier Jahre später seine architektonischen Visionen in die Realität umzusetzen begann, indem er Léon Krier den Auftrag gab, am Rande von Poundbury in der Nähe von Dorchester ein neues Dorf zu entwerfen. Doch was 1988 in der Grafschaft Dorset noch wie die Studie für ein romantisches Pasticcio aussah, ist inzwischen eines der Modelle für neue Ortschaften, welche die britische Regierung plant.

Die Grundsätze von Poundbury – darunter der Gebrauch traditioneller Materialien und Konstruktionen aus der Region, die Betonung des öffentlichen Raums für Fußgänger, schließlich der »menschliche Maßstab« – haben viel mit den Prinzipien des Congress for New Urbanism in den USA gemein. Diese Vereinigung hatte maßgeblichen Einfluss auf die Planung der Städte Seaside und Celebration im amerikanischen Bundesstaat Florida; auch dies Entwicklungen, die derzeit von der britischen Regierung favorisiert werden. Für den New Urbanism steht die Idee, dass die Architektur das feiern sollte, was einen Ort von anderen abhebt, im Mittelpunkt seiner Aktivitäten, weil innerhalb einer mehr und mehr globalen Kultur die regionalen Differenzen unter Beschuss geraten seien. Seine Vertreter behaupten dies übrigens ohne Rücksicht auf die Tatsache, dass das neotraditionalistische Denken, jedenfalls in Großbritannien und den USA, inzwischen die vermutlich einflussreichste Strategie zur Regenerierung und Entwicklung von Stadt ist.

GIBT ES EIN »GLOBAL BLANDING«, EINE WELTWEITE GLEICHMACHEREI?

Da die Gesellschaften der entwickelten Länder den Idealen der Aufklärung und dem sozialen Projekt der Moderne den Rücken kehren, ist alles, was übrig bleibt, eine Politik des Relativismus und der Diversität. In diesem Klima gibt es keine Debatte mehr über das Universale und das Partikulare, wie es noch in den achtziger Jahren der Fall war. Obwohl sich die Zeiten sehr verändert haben, meinen Tzonis und Lefaivre, die den Anspruch auf die Urheberschaft des Begriffs »Kritischer Regionalismus« erheben, dass die Konsolidierung der Globalisierung ihre Theorie von 1981 mehr denn je relevant mache. In ihrem letzten Buch *Critical Regionalism. Architecture and Identity in a Globalized World* – über zwanzig Jahre nach dem erwähnten Essay erschienen und mit sehr ähnlichem Inhalt – schreiben sie: »Das Konzept des Regionalismus ist immer noch da, der Begriff sogar noch bekannter als früher. Der Grund dafür hat mit dem omnipräsenten Konflikt in allen Bereichen einschließlich der Architektur zu tun – mit dem Konflikt zwischen Globalisierung und internationaler Intervention auf der einen, lokaler Identität und Sehnsucht nach ethnischer Insularität auf der anderen Seite.«[26]

Tzonis, Lefaivre und weitere selbst ernannte Regionalisten nehmen die Aussage von der weltweiten Gleichmacherei in Ar-

25 Prince Charles, RIBA Gala Speech. Extracts, in: Charles Jencks, The Prince, the Architects, and New Wave Monarchy, London 1988, S. 43.

26 Alexander Tzonis, Introducing an Architecture of the Present. Critical Regionalism and the Design of Identity, in: Liane Lefaivre/Alexander Tzonis, Critical Regionalism. Architecture and Identity in a Globalized World, München 2003, S. 10.

Scottish devolution from the UK took place in 1997, following a referendum, and the new Executive then set about finding a home for the first Scottish parliament for 300 years. After winning a competition with a scheme that linked Scottish national identity to the land, the Catalan regionalists Enric Miralles and Benedetta Tagliabue (EMBT) were commissioned to design the building in 1998. Reaching out from the site in Edinburgh's old town towards Arthur's Seat (an ancient volcanic mound), the new parliament responds to the landscape rather than the city and has an outdoor amphitheatre, carved out of the ground, to represent (if not actually facilitate) the participation of Scottish people in democracy.

In Wales too, a grand national project—this time a centre for performing arts—nears completion. The Wales Millennium Centre, designed by Percy Thomas Partnership, is an example of where (in the absence of a clear national architectural idiom) the architect has used local materials, culture and symbolic forms to give shape to national identity. The façade takes its inspiration from Welsh cliffs and stratified landforms typical of the region. "The layering of the strata of rock seems to symbolise the persistence of our nation through the passage of ages,"[23] explains the project architect Jonathan Adams.

Such buildings come dangerously close to using local materials, techniques and form as a scenographic effect—an approach criticised so vociferously by Frampton in the 1980s. Another danger is that by expressing identity in a built form, something that is fluid and constantly changing becomes fixed and dogmatic. The architect Alan Colquhoun writes with some scepticism about regionalism as an "essentialist model." "According to this model, all societies contain a core or essence, which must be discovered or preserved (the concept of regionalism depends on it being possible to correlate cultural codes with geographical regions. It is based on a traditional system of communication in which climate, geography, craft traditions and religions are absolutely determining."[24]

In the era of globalisation, the essentialist model has acquired the mantle of radicalism, rather than being seen as the preserve of conservative elites. Regional and new vernacular architecture has become an antidote to a sense of dislocation, while the politics of multiculturalism and identity are mainstream.

The growing popularity of New Urbanist principles during recent years is another example of the broad acceptance of regionalism. In Britain, for example, the Prince of Wales, who in the 1980s was derided for his anti-Modernism, has become one of the key influences on the direction of new housing provision. In 1984, the Prince was regarded as a badly informed reactionary when he criticised the competition entry for an extension to the National Gallery in London by Ahrends Burton and Koralek, describing it as a "monstrous carbuncle on the face of a much-loved and elegant friend."[25] Later on, in 1988, when the Prince put his vision for architecture into practice by commissioning Léon Krier to design a new village at Poundbury near Dorchester in Dorset, the attitude was much the same. However, what was initially seen as an exercise in romantic pastiche has become one of the models for new communities being planned by the British government. The principles of Poundbury—including the use of

23 Global Blanding seminar, Institute of Ideas, London 17 June 2000.

24 Alan Colquhoun, The Concept of Regionalism, in: Gülsüm Baydar Nalbantoglu and Chong Thai Wong (eds), Postcolonial Space(s), New York 1997.

25 The 150th anniversary of the Royal Institute of British Architects: a speech by the Prince of Wales, Royal Gala Evening at Hampton Court Palace, May 30, 1984.

chitektur und Produktdesign für bare Münze. Da die meisten Intellektuellen große Sympathie für den Gedanken hegen, dass Globalisierung eine schlechte Sache sei, gibt es für Kommentatoren wenig bis keinen Druck, einmal empirisch nachzuweisen, ob es wirklich einen Trend in Richtung auf eine Architektur gibt, die jeden lokalen Charakter verloren hat.

Ich vertrete allerdings den Standpunkt, dass eine regionale oder das Ortstypische zumindest ansprechende Architektur der einzige sozial und politisch akzeptable Ansatz im gegenwärtigen Klima ist. Der Gebrauch von Tradition und von heimischen Formen spricht die Forderung nach zeitlosen Lösungen an, im Gegensatz zu der raschen Folge von Ismen im gesamten zwanzigsten Jahrhundert. Regionalisten dürfen sich in einer Position sehen, die weit entfernt von jenem populären Pasticcio ist, das derzeit zum Beispiel in den USA groß in Mode ist. Wie dem auch sei, es lässt sich darüber streiten, ob nicht die Sehnsucht nach einer eher orts- als zeitverbundenen Architektur genauso romantisch ist. Wahrscheinlich werden künftige Generationen auf den Regionalismus von heute – auf die raffinierte schweizerische Moderne wie auf die stilistischen Imitate bei Wohnhäusern – mit Kopfschütteln zurückschauen und das Interesse am Lokalen als die romantische Obsession eines Zeitalters voller Unsicherheit betrachten.

regional building traditions and materials, the emphasis on public space and pedestrian access and a "human scale"—have much in common with those of the US-based Congress for New Urbanism, which influenced the planning of Seaside and Celebration in Florida (also developments that are currently in favour with the British government). With New Urbanism, the idea that architecture should celebrate what is different about a place takes centre stage. Its practitioners adopt the stance that regional differences are under attack within an increasingly global culture, regardless of the fact that such neo-traditionalist thinking (in Britain and the US) is probably the most influential force within urban regeneration and planning.

IS THERE REALLY A GLOBAL-BLANDING?

With societies of the developed world turning their backs on the ideals of the Enlightenment and the social project of Modernism, all that is left are the politics of relativism and diversity. In this climate, there is no longer a debate about the universal and the particular, as there was in the 1980s. Despite such changed times, Tzonis and Lefaivre—who claim authorship of the term "critical regionalism"—argue that the consolidation of globalisation makes their theory of 1981 even more pertinent. In their latest book, *Critical Regionalism, Architecture and Identity in a Globalised World* (published more than twenty years after their original essay, but with very similar content) they write: "The concept of regionalism is still with us and even more prominent as a term today. The reason for this has to do with the ubiquitous conflict in all fields—including architecture—between globalisation and international intervention, on the one hand, and local identity and the desire for ethnic insularity on the other."[26]

Tzonis, Lefaivre and other self-proclaimed regionalist architects take the idea of "global-blanding" at face value. Since most intellectuals feel broad sympathy with the idea that globalisation is "a bad thing", there is little or no pressure for commentators to establish whether there is indeed a trend towards architecture losing its local character.

I would argue, however, that regional, or at least locally responsive architecture, is the only socially and politically acceptable approach in the current climate. The use of tradition and the vernacular appeals to the demand for timeless solutions —in contradistinction to the twentieth century's sequence of 'isms.' Regionalist architects may see themselves as existing in a quite different vein to popularist pastiche (expressed, for example, by the current fashion in the United States for city dwellers to have, as their second home, a traditional log cabin). However the desire for an architecture that is connected with place rather than time, is arguably just as romantic. Future generations are likely to look back at today's regionalism—whether it is fine Swiss 'modern vernacular' or pastiche housing—and regard the interest in localism as the romantic obsession of an insecure age.

26 Alexander Tzonis, Introducing an Architecture of the Present. Critical Regionalism and the Design of Identity, in: Liane Lefaivre and Alexander Tzonis, Critical Regionalism. Architecture and Identity in a Globalized World, Munich 2003, p. 10.

HEINRICH WEFING

OHNE SÄULE FEHLT MIR WAS

ANMERKUNGEN ZUR FORTWIRKUNG DER POSTMODERNE IN DER AMERIKANISCHEN ALLTAGSARCHITEKTUR

I FEEL LOST WITHOUT COLUMNS

OBSERVATIONS ON THE CONTINUED INFLUENCE OF POST-MODERNISM ON AMERICAN EVERYDAY ARCHITECTURE

Nirgendwo hat sich die Postmoderne – oder das, was unter diesem Schlagwort in den achtziger Jahren populär wurde – so konkurrenzlos durchgesetzt wie an den Autobahnen Amerikas. Längs der Freeways und an den Ausfallstraßen der Metropolen reihen sich Einkaufszentren, Supermärkte und Autowaschanlagen aneinander, die allesamt aussehen, als hätten sie gleichermaßen von Las Vegas wie von Aldo Rossi gelernt. Lauter dekorierte Kisten, die zu Konsum-Städtchen zusammengeschoben werden, komplett mit Säulen, Brunnen und Piazza. Kaum eine »Mall«, die ohne Uhrenturm auskommt, der ebenso sehr als Urbanitätszitat funktioniert wie als architektonisches Ausrufezeichen an die Autofahrer, die auf dem Highway vorbeisausen und rechtzeitig bremsen müssen, um die Ausfahrt nicht zu verpassen. Tankstellen in gelbem Rauhputz, mit roten Ziegeln auf dem Dach, die vom spanischen Missionsstil inspiriert scheinen, stehen neben bonbonfarbenen Shopping-Dörfern mit Rundbögen und Pilastern, die von weitläufigen Parkplätzen umgeben sind wie ehedem die Bauerngehöfte Europas von Äckern und Wiesen.

Überall in Amerika findet man diese Ensembles in ungezählten Variationen, in Texas ebenso wie in Nevada, Florida oder Vermont. Jede Exkursion in die Vorstädte fördert dasselbe Ergebnis zutage, mit bestenfalls minimalen regionalen Unterschieden. Fährt man beispielsweise von San Francisco aus über die Golden Gate Bridge nach Norden, liegt gleich an der dritten Ausfahrt ein Einkaufsareal namens »Marin City«, eine Anlage cremefarbener Gebäude mit der Anmutung eines kalifornischen Kastells. Alle Baukörper, flache, holzverbretterte Kuben, sind weitgehend fensterlos; Gesimse, Rankgitter, Blendbögen und umlaufende Markisen aus grünem Metall sorgen allenfalls für eine dezente Massengliederung. Lediglich die Zugänge zu den Läden, Restaurants und Kaufhäusern sind stärker betont, durchweg mit Architekturelementen, die man im weitesten Sinne traditionell nennen könnte: Dreiecksgiebel, Tonnen- und Zeltdächer, turmartige Aufbauten. Den eigenartigen Eindruck eines Kavallerie-Forts, in dem man Videos ausleihen, Unterhaltungselektronik kaufen oder ein Steak essen kann, rufen die vier niedrigen, gleichfalls verbretterten Türme hervor, die beiderseits der beiden Zufahrten stehen – reine Schauarchitektur ohne Nutzwert: gedrungene Vierkante mit offenen Durchgängen unter Rundbögen im Erdgeschoss, darüber eine leere Turmkammer und ein flach geneigtes grünes Dach.

Eine Autobahnausfahrt weiter nördlich wirbt die nächste Anlage um Kunden, ein Komplex, der sich »Strawberry Village« nennt. Das Dörfliche, Überschaubare, Niedliche, das dieser Name verheißt, steht zwar in scharfem Gegensatz zu den Dimensionen des Einkaufszentrums, das sich über mehrere hundert Meter längs des Freeways hinstreckt; die Architektur aber löst das Versprechen ein. Alle Läden – überwiegend Einzelhandelsgeschäfte – sind in niedrigen Bauten untergebracht, die durch Arkadengänge miteinander verbunden werden. Deren Stützen und das weiße Holz-Gebälk sind von sorgsam gestutztem Efeu umrankt; auf den leicht geneigten Dächern liegen rote Mönch- und Nonnenziegel, und in regelmäßigen Abständen ragen geschweifte Ziergiebel auf, deren schlichte Putzflächen mit einigen dekorativen grünen Keramikfliesen geschmückt sind. Am südlichen Ende der Anlage gibt es einen Schnellimbiss, der in

Nowhere has Post-Modernism—or what became popular under that catchword in the 1980s—asserted itself with so little competition as along America's freeways. Along the freeways and main drags out of America's major cities, shopping malls, supermarkets and car washes line up beside one another, all looking as if they have learnt equally from Las Vegas and Aldo Rossi. Nothing but decorated boxes shoved together to make provincial consumer towns—complete with columns, fountains and a piazza. Scarcely a single mall that does not have its clock tower, which functions both as a quotation of urbanity and an architectural exclamation mark, attracting the attention of motorists speeding by on the highway so that they can brake in time to avoid overshooting the exit. Petrol stations in yellow rough-cast, with red-tiled roofs, seemingly inspired by the Spanish mission style, stand cheek-by-jowl with candy-coloured shopping villages with round arches and pilasters that are surrounded by sprawling car parks in the way that Europe's farms were once surrounded by fields and meadows.

Wherever you go in America, you will find these ensembles in countless variations, be it in Texas or Nevada, Florida or Vermont. Any excursion into the suburbs will turn up the same results, with at best minimal regional differences. For example, if you drive north out of San Francisco over the Golden Gate Bridge to the third exit off the freeway, you will find a shopping complex called "Marin City," an ensemble of crème-coloured buildings reminiscent of a Californian castle. All the buildings are low-rise, timber-clad cubes, largely without windows; cornices, trellises, blind arches and green metal awnings on all sides are the only features that provide some kind of subtle articulation to the massing of the building. Only the entrances to the shops, restaurants and department stores are given greater emphasis, with architectural elements throughout that could be called traditional in the broadest sense: triangular gables, barrel roofs and pyramid roofs, tower-like superstructures. The four low towers—also timber-clad—on either side of the two entrances evoke the strange impression of a cavalry fort in which it is possible to rent a video, buy home entertainment equipment or eat a steak—pure showpiece architecture without any real utility value: squat tetrahedrons with open passages or round arches on the ground floor and above that an empty tower chamber and a shallow-pitched green roof.

Drive one freeway exit further to the north and you will find the next complex touting for customers, a complex that calls itself "Strawberry Village." The dimensions of the shopping centre, which stretches along several hundred metres of the freeway, might be in sharp contrast to the village-like qualities that the name promises—manageable size, chocolate-box prettiness —but the architecture keeps the promise. All the shops are housed in low buildings linked by arcades. Carefully supported ivy grows round their columns and white timber beams; the shallow pitched roofs are covered in red mission tiles, and at regular intervals curved, ornamental gables tower up, their simple rendered surfaces decorated with green ceramic tiles. At the southern end of the complex is a snack bar, a pavilion in the same unspecified Mediterranean formal language, and to the north is a supermarket, parts of which are slightly higher and

derselben unbestimmt mediterranen Formensprache ausgeführt ist und lediglich als Pavillon freigestellt wurde, und im Norden befindet sich ein Supermarkt, der teils etwas höher aufragt und in seiner Gesamtanmutung an eine schlichte Missionskirche in Mittelamerika denken lässt. Die irgendwie südliche Atmosphäre des Ensembles wird noch unterstrichen durch den Uhrenturm im Zentrum des »Village«, gleich neben dem »Rain Tree Café«, einer offenen Betonpfeilerkonstruktion, an deren Fuß ein paar Bänke stehen, Terrakotta-Kübel mit saisonal wechselnder Bepflanzung und vier Löwenmasken auf grünen Fliesen, die Wasser in flache Brunnen speien.

Das nächste Konsumdorf liegt zwei Ausfahrten weiter an der Schnellstraße 101, und ungezählte andere folgen auf dem Weg nach Norden und Osten, eine fast ununterbrochene Kette bis hinüber in die Landeshauptstadt Sacramento. Bemerkenswert an dieser autogerechten Einkaufswelt ist freilich weniger die Dichte des Angebots als vielmehr die Dominanz eines bestimmten architektonischen Idioms. Längs der Highways sind die für Prestigeprojekte im Kulturbereich neuerdings gefeierten Biomorphismen ebenso ohne Chance wie die Explosionsästhetik des Dekonstruktivismus. An den Autobahnen finden sich mehr oder weniger transparente Kisten, wie man sie auch aus europäischen Gewerbegebieten kennt, sehr entfernte Nachfahren der Mies'schen Glashäuser; oder eben Varianten und Schwundstufen der Postmoderne. Gelegentlich kann man fast den Eindruck gewinnen, in den Einkaufszonen Amerikas sei die Zeit Ende der achtziger Jahre stehen geblieben, die Architekturgeschichte habe mit Aldo Rossi, James Stirling, Hans Hollein, Michael Graves und Charles Moore ihr Ende gefunden und neue Moden gäbe es seither nicht mehr.

Diese Dominanz hat natürlich viele Gründe. Architekturhistorisch mag eine Rolle spielen, dass die postmoderne Bewegung der siebziger und achtziger Jahre auch ihrerseits schon dezidiert wenig Berührungsängste mit dem Bauen für den Konsum hatte. Nicht zufällig hat Robert Venturi ja bereits in den sechziger Jahren für eine Übertragung kommerzieller Bildformen auf die Inhalte der Architektur plädiert; Hollein ist mit seinen feingearbeiteten Wiener Edelboutiquen bekannt geworden, Rossi wurde in ungewöhnlich breiten Kreisen populär mit Entwürfen für die Silberschmiede Alessi; und einige der fröhlichsten und intelligentesten Arbeiten der Architektengruppe SITE entstanden im Auftrag der amerikanischen Warenhaus-Kette Best.

Weitaus bedeutender noch als diese theoretischen Wurzeln aber dürfte ein anderer Umstand sein. Die Architektur der Einkaufsareale, entworfen von anonymen Baumeistern, die nie auf den Bilderseiten der Fachzeitschriften auftauchen werden, dient bestimmten Zwecken. Sie soll, darin der Gestaltung von Hotels oder Ferienclubs nicht unähnlich, eine angenehme Umgebung schaffen, in der sich die potenziellen Kunden wohl fühlen, ohne sich überhaupt Gedanken darüber machen zu müssen, wie das Wohlbefinden zustande kommt. Sie garantiert einen behaglichen, dabei unauffälligen Hintergrund für den Einkauf, sorgsam darauf bedacht, im besten Fall Konsumenten anzulocken, jedenfalls aber niemanden abzustoßen. Anders als es die vermeintliche oder tatsächliche Avantgarde gern für sich in Anspruch nimmt, will diese Shopping-Architektur deshalb gerade

which in its overall feel is reminiscent of a simple mission church in Central America. The ensemble's vaguely southern atmosphere is further underlined by a clock tower in the centre of the "village," right beside the "Rain Tree Café"—an open structure of concrete pillars, at the foot of which are a couple of benches, terracotta pots with seasonally changing planting and four lion masks on green tiles which spout water into shallow fountains.

The next consumer village is two freeway exits further on Interstate 101, and countless others are on the roads out north and east, an almost unbroken chain stretching beyond the state capital Sacramento. Admittedly, what is more remarkable about this car-friendly shopping world is not so much the density of what is on offer as the dominance of a particular architectural idiom. Along the highway, the biomorphisms recently celebrated in prestigious projects in the field of culture have as little chance as the explosion aesthetics of deconstructivism. The freeways are lined with the more or less transparent boxes we are familiar with from European industrial parks, very distant relatives of Mies's glass buildings, or with variations on Post-Modernism in varying stages of decline. Occasionally you could almost think that time has stood still since the end of the eighties in America's retail parks, almost believe that architectural history came to an end with Aldo Rossi, James Stirling, Hans Hollein, Michael Graves and Charles Moore, and that there have not been any new fashions since then.

There are, of course, many reasons for this dominance. In terms of architectural history, the fact that the Post-Modern movement of the seventies and eighties had decidedly few inhibitions about building for consumer purposes may play a part. It was no coincidence that as early as the sixties Robert Venturi had pleaded for commercial images to be transposed onto the contents of architecture, Hollein rose to fame with his finely detailed upmarket boutiques in Vienna, Rossi became popular in unusually broad circles with designs for the silversmith Alessi, and some of the most upbeat and intelligent works of the group of architects Site were commissioned by Best, an American chain of department stores.

However, a different set of circumstances is probably of far greater significance still than these theoretical roots. The architecture of retail parks, designed by anonymous architects, which will never appear in glossy architectural journals, serves very particular purposes. In this sense not unlike the design of hotels or holiday clubs, it is meant to create a pleasant environment in which potential customers feel at ease without having to think at all about what makes them feel at ease. It guarantees a comfortable and, at the same time, unobtrusive backdrop for the shopping experience, carefully intent at best on enticing consumers but in any case on not putting anyone off. Unlike the stated aim the would-be or actual avant-garde likes to embrace, this shopping architecture for that very reason does not break with "traditional ways of seeing things," does not provoke or undermine traditional expectations but, on the contrary, repeats precisely what people are used to and at most changes it very carefully, drawing upon handed-down expectations and traditions and continuing them wherever possible.

1

2

3

4

1 Woodbury, NY (USA): Kleinstädtisch angelegtes Einkaufszentrum
Village-like shopping mall

2 Clinton, CT (USA): Eingang zu einem Zentrum für Fabrikverkauf
Entrance to factory outlet shopping mall

3 Woodbury, NY (USA): »Stadtmitte« des Einkaufszentrums/Shopping mall: “village” centre

4 Houston, TX (USA): Hof des Einkaufszentrums/Courtyard of shopping mall

nicht mit »hergebrachten Sehgewohnheiten brechen«, provozieren oder traditionelle Erwartungen unterlaufen, sondern vielmehr im Gegenteil genau das Gewohnte wiederholen und höchstens behutsam verändern, überkommene Erwartungen bedienen und Traditionen, wo möglich, fortführen.

Der Witz, die Ironie, das Schalkhafte mancher Werke der Postmoderne ist den Einkaufsbauten der amerikanischen Vorstadt daher gänzlich fremd; sie kommen ohne Gags oder Schockelemente aus. Aber sie knüpfen, wie simplifiziert auch immer, an andere Theoreme und Absichten der unübersichtlichen Bewegung namens »Postmoderne« an. Die Abkehr vom dogmatischen Rationalismus spielt dabei natürlich eine Rolle, aber auch die Rückbesinnung auf die architektonische Überlieferung oder der Gedanke, Häuser und Stadtteile wie Städte *en miniature* zu organisieren.

Ein gutes Beispiel für diesen Versuch bietet »The Village at Corte Madera«, ebenfalls an der Interstate 101 nördlich von San Francisco gelegen. Dort ist das Konzept einer einheitlichen architektonischen Gestaltung zugunsten eines synthetischen Urbanismus wechselnder Formelemente aufgegeben worden. Kleine Giebelhäuschen, die jeweils nur einer Boutique, einer Bäckerei oder einer Goldschmiede Platz bieten, stehen in scheinbar zufälliger Folge neben einem Warenhaus mit doppelgeschossiger Sandsteinfassade und einem überdimensionalen Dreiecksgiebel aus Holz über dem Eingang, daneben wiederum befinden sich die riesigen Schaufenster einer Modekette oder der Phantasieklassizismus eines Möbelladens. Das Prinzip des gebremsten Kontrasts unterschiedlicher Stilzitate harmonisiert offenkundig mit dem Bemühen der Planer, der Anlage einen kleinstädtischen Charakter zu verleihen. Der Besucher betritt »The Village« von den ausgedehnten Parkplatzflächen her durch relativ schmale Ladenstraßen, die zu einer zentralen Achse führen, an der der größere Teil der Shops liegt, mit den beiden Warenhäusern an den entgegengesetzten Enden des Rückgrats. Die baumbestandene Fußgängerstraße verläuft allerdings nicht gerade, sondern knickt mehrfach sanft ab und formt dabei verschiedene Plätze, die mit Brunnen, Beeten, einem Uhrenturm, einem Kinderspielplatz und den Tischen diverser Restaurants und Cafés möbliert sind. Arkadengänge vor einigen Geschäften, Holzpavillons für Blumenläden oder Eisstände sowie aufwendig gestaltete Straßenlaternen verstärken noch den Eindruck, durch ein gewachsenes Städtchen zu schlendern.

Beherrscht wird die Architektur der Shopping-Malls erkennbar von dem Bemühen, das Ungeliebte zu verhindern, das Fremdartige, Ungewohnte, Spektakuläre zu meiden und stattdessen das Vertraute zu variieren. Man wird lange nach einem neueren Konsumquartier suchen müssen, das ganz in Sichtbeton ausgeführt ist oder dekonstruktivistisch wild herumwirbelt. Die Einkaufszentren sind errichtet, um möglichst viele Menschen anzusprechen. Der Rückgriff auf Traditionen, die in den Vereinigten Staaten durchweg robuster sind als in Deutschland, ist dabei geradezu ein Indikator für die architektonischen Vorlieben eines breiten Publikums. Zuverlässig und mit erstaunlicher Genauigkeit spiegeln die Konsumbauten denn auch Angebot und Nachfrage auf dem gigantischen amerikanischen Markt für Einfamilienhäuser und Wohnsiedlungen wider. Der

The wit, the irony, the playfulness of some mischievous Post-Modernist works is therefore completely alien to the shopping complexes of the American suburb; they manage perfectly well without "gags" or shock elements. But, in however simplified a form, they link into other theories and intentions of the impalpable movement called "Post-Modernism." Of course, the rejection of dogmatic rationalism plays a role, but so does the recollection of architectural tradition, or the idea of organising buildings and neighbourhoods as towns *en miniature*.

A good example of an attempt to do this is "The Village at Corte Madera," also situated on Interstate 101 to the north of San Francisco. The concept of a uniform architectural design has been abandoned in favour of a synthetic urbanism of changing formal elements. Small gabled buildings, each housing only one boutique, one baker's shop or one goldsmiths, stand in a seemingly random arrangement beside a department store with a two-storey sandstone façade and an oversized triangular wooden gable above the entrance; next to that are the enormous windows of a fashion chain or the fantasy Neo-Classicism of a furniture shop. The principle of subdued contrast between different stylistic quotations harmonises obviously with the planners' endeavours to give the complex a small-town character. The visitor enters "The Village" from its extensive car parks through relatively narrow parades of shops that lead to a central axis on which the majority of the shops are situated. The two department stores are at opposite ends of this spine. However, the shop-lined pedestrian street is not straight but bends gently at several points, creating squares furnished with fountains, flowerbeds, a clock tower, a children's playground and the tables of various restaurants and cafés. Arcades in front of some of the shops, wooden pavilions for flower shops or ice-cream stalls and elaborate street lamps further heighten the impression of wandering around a small town that has developed organically.

The architecture of the shopping malls is irrefutably marked by an endeavour to avoid anything that is unpopular, alien, unaccustomed, spectacular and instead to produce variations on the familiar. You would have to spend a long time looking for a recent "consumer neighbourhood" that is entirely in fair-faced concrete or is a wild frenzy of deconstructivism. Shopping centres are designed to appeal to as many people as possible and how they do that—making recourse to traditions that are far more robust in the United States than they are in Germany—proves to be an indicator for the architectural preferences of a broad sector of their clientele. Reliably, and with astonishing precision, the consumer buildings reflect the supply and demand on the gigantic American market for single-family homes and housing estates. This is dominated by every conceivable variation on the New England shingle house, Colonial Revival, Spanish style, Tudor, Regency, California ranch house et cetera—all of them created with the aim of replicating the atmosphere and appearance of an unspecified past. Beneath the academic discussion, beyond theoretical debates, derided or ignored by architectural critics, this everyday historicism dominates architecture in America and is simply reproduced in the shopping centres—only on a larger scale.

Das Deutsche Architekturmuseum stellt gleich in mehrfacher Hinsicht ein einzigartiges Dokument der Postmoderne dar: durch seine Entstehungsgeschichte als Teil des Museumsufers in Frankfurt am Main, durch die Architektur des von Oswald Mathias Ungers entworfenen Museumsgebäudes und durch die inhaltliche Arbeit, die das DAM unter der Leitung seines Gründungsdirektors Heinrich Klotz leistete. Und auch die weitere Geschichte des Hauses unter der Leitung erst von Vittorio Magnago Lampugnani, dann von Wilfried Wang und derzeit von Ingeborg Flagge kann als permanente Auseinandersetzung mit der Postmoderne beziehungsweise mit dem postmodernen Erbe gelesen werden, eine Auseinandersetzung, die vor dem Hintergrund der Entwicklung des Zeitgeistes im Allgemeinen und der Architektur im Besonderen, aber auch sehr konkret des weiteren Wegs der Stadt Frankfurt und ihrer Kulturpolitik zu betrachten ist.

FRANKFURT AM MAIN, ZENTRUM DER POSTMODERNE

Anfang der achtziger Jahre staunte die Öffentlichkeit über den von der Stadt Frankfurt bekundeten Anspruch, sich als ein Zentrum des kulturellen Lebens von nationaler Bedeutung profilieren zu wollen. Ausgerechnet Frankfurt! Angesichts der bis dahin in der überregionalen Wahrnehmung eher unauffälligen Kulturpolitik konnte man nur verblüfft sein. Für die Skeptiker wollten die ambitionierten Planungen – neben dem Wiederaufbau der Alten Oper war die Gründung von gut einem Dutzend Museen vorgesehen – so gar nicht in das Bild des abfällig als »Bankfurt« und »Krankfurt« bezeichneten Finanz-, Handels- und Verkehrszentrums passen. Doch die Visionäre sollten Recht behalten. Wo die Missstände am größten sind, so meinten sie, müsse man sich besonders hohe Ziele setzen. Und wie wenn nicht durch einen Kraftakt wollte man diese erreichen? In der Tat erscheint der damals in Frankfurt eingeschlagene Weg mit allen seinen Widersprüchen im Nachhinein als genau richtig für die zu jener Zeit noch immer von Krieg und Wiederaufbau schwer gezeichnete Stadt.

Nach den Luftangriffen des Zweiten Weltkriegs war von der alten Freien Reichsstadt mit ihrer so stolzen Geschichte wenig mehr übrig geblieben als Erinnerungen. Die Nachkriegsjahre waren durch die Präsenz der amerikanischen Streitkräfte geprägt, die sich in den zahlreichen Kasernen der Region niederließen, ihre europäische Kommandozentrale im Poelzig-Bau der IG Farben einrichteten und den Frankfurter Flughafen im großen Maßstab ausbauten. Auf dieser Grundlage florierten erst der Schwarzmarkt und das Bahnhofsviertel, dann auch die Börse, die Banken, die Messe und der Handel insgesamt. Frankfurt setzte auf wirtschaftlichen Erfolg und profilierte sich als bundesdeutsche Boomtown. Davon zeugen die ersten Hochhäuser des Bankenviertels, die sich allmählich zur ersten Skyline Deutschlands verdichteten. Als Symbol wirtschaftlicher Potenz und der Unwirtlichkeit der modernen Stadt in einem untermauerte diese Skyline den ambivalenten neuen Ruf Frankfurts als amerikanischstes aller deutschen Zentren.

Bis in die siebziger Jahre schien sich dieser Weg für »Mainhattan« auszuzahlen. Dann aber regte sich am Fuße der Türme der

Several factors make DAM, the German Museum of Architecture, a unique testimony to Post-Modernism: its genesis as part of the Museumsufer (museum mile on the river embankment) in Frankfurt am Main, the architecture of the building itself, designed by Oswald Mathias Ungers, and, in terms of content, the work done by DAM under its founding director Heinrich Klotz. The further history of the museum, under the directorship first of Vittorio Magnago Lampugnani, then Wilfried Wang, and currently Ingeborg Flagge, can also be seen as a permanent engagement with Post-Modernism or with the legacy of Post-Modernism, an engagement that must be viewed against the backdrop of changes in the zeitgeist in general and architecture in particular, but also in very concrete terms in the light of developments in Frankfurt and the city's cultural policy.

FRANKFURT AM MAIN, CENTRE OF POST-MODERNISM

In the early 1980s, the general public was amazed when the city of Frankfurt announced its wish to raise its profile to become a centre of cultural life of national importance. Frankfurt of all places! Considering that until then the city had always pursued a cultural policy that the rest of the country viewed as singularly unremarkable, amazement was the only response to be expected. To the sceptics, the ambitious plans—apart from rebuilding the historical opera house, the Alte Oper, there was also talk of founding a good dozen museums—just did not fit with the image of this city, which had become a centre for finance, trade and transport and had to put up with a number of derogatory nick-names along the lines of "Bankfurt" and "Krankfurt," "krank" being German for "ill." But the visionaries would be proved right. Where the malaise is greatest the goals must be highest, their theory went. And how were they going to achieve these goals if not through an act of supreme effort? In fact, with hindsight, the path Frankfurt embarked upon back then—with all its contradictions—seems to have been exactly right for the city, which at the time was still intensely marked by war and reconstruction.

Following the air raids of the Second World War, little other than memory remained of the city that was so proud of its history and tradition. The post-war years were characterised by the presence of the American military, who had taken over the numerous barracks in the region, set up their European Central Command in the IG Farben building designed by Poelzig and expanded Frankfurt Airport on a grand scale. Against this backdrop, first the black market and the red light district around the railway station flourished, followed by the stock exchange, the banks, trade shows and trade in general. Frankfurt set its sights on economic success and created an image for itself as *the* West German boom town. The first skyscrapers in the banking district, which gradually multiplied to form Germany's first high-rise skyline, bear witness to this development. As a symbol of economic power and the inhospitable nature of the modern city in one, this skyline underpinned Frankfurt's ambivalent new reputation as the most American of all German cities.

Until the early 1970s, this approach seemed to be paying dividends for "Mainhattan." But then an opposition movement

Widerstand. Immer mehr Bürger protestierten gegen die Einseitigkeit, mit der die Stadt die Interessen der Wirtschaft auch gegen Bürgerinteressen durchsetzte. Das ehemals noble Westend wurde zum Schauplatz eines Häuserkampfes zwischen Immobilienhaien und Stadtverwaltung auf der einen und den Bewohnern des Viertels und der kritischen, nicht zuletzt durch die Frankfurter Schule geprägten Studentenschaft auf der anderen Seite. Der Widerstand machte deutlich: Es sollte, durfte und konnte so nicht weitergehen.

Doch auch die Wirtschaft hatte ihre Schwierigkeiten. Sie beklagte die schlechte Reputation der Stadt – ihr negatives Image. Gerade den internationalen Unternehmen fiel es zunehmend schwer, ihre Mitarbeiter für einen Umzug an den Main zu begeistern. Zu unattraktiv präsentierte sich die Stadt, um in der Konkurrenz mit London, Paris oder Zürich bestehen zu können. Damit stieß Frankfurt zu einem Zeitpunkt an die eigenen »Grenzen des Wachstums«, als auch der Club of Rome der Weltöffentlichkeit die Folgen einseitiger wirtschaftlicher Entwicklung vor Augen führte. Im Kleinen spiegelte die Krise Frankfurts aktuelle Probleme globalen Maßstabs wider.

WALTER WALLMANN, HILMAR HOFFMANN UND DAS MUSEUMSUFER

Der Pragmatismus, mit dem sich die kriegszerstörte Stadt im Zeichen des »Wirtschaftswunders« rasch zu einem international bedeutenden Wirtschaftszentrum entwickelt hatte, prägte in den achtziger Jahren auch den Ausbau Frankfurts zu einem Ort der Kultur – wenngleich einer neuen, etwas anderen Art. Kulturpolitik wurde in Frankfurt in diesen Jahren als die Fortführung der Wirtschaftspolitik mit anderen Mitteln verstanden.

Sicherlich wurden die Chancen, die in der Krise der Siebziger steckten, von vielen erkannt. In die Tat umgesetzt wurden sie von einigen wenigen herausragenden Persönlichkeiten, allen voran von dem 1977 neu gewählten christdemokratischen Oberbürgermeister Walter Wallmann und seinem sozialdemokratischen Kulturdezernenten Hilmar Hoffmann. Für Hoffmann, der bereits vor Wallmann im Amt gewesen war, war klar, dass die Stadt, wollte sie nicht weiter an Anziehungskraft verlieren, ihr kulturelles Angebot deutlich würde erweitern müssen. Der von ihm angeführte Vergleich mit dem in dieser Hinsicht weit interessanteren Köln überzeugte und mobilisierte die Vertreter aller Parteien. In der Kommunikation mit den Bürgern hieß es populistisch »Kultur für alle«. Langfristig stand jedoch die Außenwirkung im Vordergrund. Es ging um die bessere internationale Positionierung Frankfurts; vor Ort wurden dafür *city marketing* und *city tuning* betrieben, wie man später sagen würde, und zwar mit einer für die damalige Zeit einmaligen Zielstrebigkeit und Professionalität. Ausgestattet mit dem höchsten Kulturetat der Republik, machte sich Frankfurt auf den Weg, seinem wirtschaftlich begründeten Ruf als weltweit kleinste aller *global cities* eine kulturelle Dimension zu verleihen.

Ein Schlüssel für den Erfolg dieses ehrgeizigen Vorhabens war das enge Miteinander von Wirtschaftspolitik, Kulturpolitik, Stadtplanung und Architektur. Angesichts der Perspektivlosigkeit späterer Zeiten muss der von Walter Wallmann und Hil-

began to form at the foot of the skyscrapers. More and more people protested against the city's biased support for the interests of business to the detriment of ordinary citizens. Frankfurt's once genteel Westend district became the arena for a battle between property sharks and the city council, on the one hand, and local residents and students whose critical stance was in part influenced by the Frankfurt School, on the other hand. The opposition they put up made it quite clear: things simply could not and would not be allowed to continue like this.

But business too had difficulties of its own. It bemoaned the city's bad reputation—its negative image. The international companies in particular found it increasingly difficult to convince their employees of the appeal of moving to Frankfurt. The image the city presented was not attractive enough to be able to compete with London, Paris or Zurich. In that, Frankfurt came up against its own "limits to growth" at the same time as the Club of Rome made the world aware of the consequences of one-sided economic growth. Frankfurt's crisis was a mirror image on the micro-scale of the problems facing the world on a global scale.

WALTER WALLMANN, HILMAR HOFFMANN AND THE MUSEUMSUFER

The pragmatism with which this city that had endured such severe destruction during the war had rapidly developed into a business centre of international significance under the star of Germany's "economic miracle" also influenced Frankfurt's development into a cultural centre in the 1980s—albeit of a new, rather different kind. Cultural policy in Frankfurt during these years was understood as a continuation of economic policy by other means.

No doubt many people recognised the opportunities that were latent in the crisis of the seventies, but only a very few outstanding public figures capitalized on them. First and foremost of these were the city's Governing Mayor, Walter Wallmann of the Christian Democrat Party that had been elected in 1977, and the Social Democrat head of the culture department Hilmar Hoffmann. For Hoffmann, who was already in office when Wallmann became mayor, it was clear that if the city was to avoid losing even more appeal, it had to significantly expand what it had to offer culturally. The comparison with Cologne, the city he cited as being far more interesting culturally, convinced and mobilised representatives of all parties. The populist slogan used in the city's PR communications was "culture for everyone." However, in the long term the focus was on making an impact on the outside world. The main concern was to improve Frankfurt's international positioning; "city marketing" and "city tuning" initiatives, as they would later be referred to in German, were launched—with a determination and level of professionalism that was unparalleled at the time. Equipped with the highest budget for culture in the country, Frankfurt set out to add a cultural dimension to its economically based reputation as the world's smallest global city.

One of the keys to the success of this ambitious project was the close cooperation between economic policy, cultural policy,

1

2

3

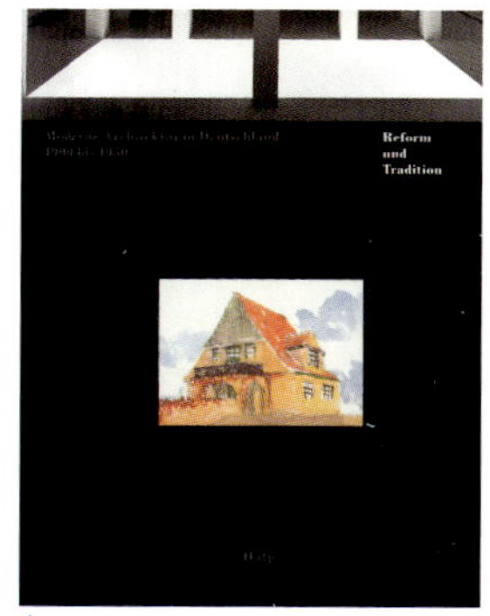
4

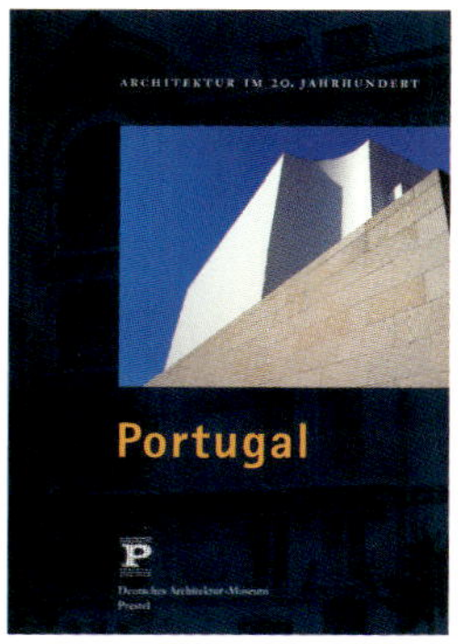

5

6

7

8

Ausstellungskataloge des DAM
DAM exhibition catalogues

1, 2
Ära Heinrich Klotz
Heinrich Klotz era
3, 4
Ära Vittorio Magnago Lampugnani
Vittorio Magnago Lampugnani era

5, 6
Ära Wilfried Wang
Wilfried Wang era
7, 8
Ära Ingeborg Flagge
Ingeborg Flagge era

mar Hoffmann gemeinsam mit dem Baudezernenten Hans-Eberhard Haverkampf eingeschlagene Weg als vorbildlich bezeichnet werden. Hier wurde nicht wie zuvor allein an der Substanz der Stadt gearbeitet, sondern zugleich an dem Bild der Stadt in den Medien und damit im Bewusstsein einer breiten überregionalen Öffentlichkeit. Mit viel Gespür für öffentliche Wirksamkeit wurden die Räume, in denen das Stadtleben stattfindet, neu definiert; punktuelle Neubauten reichten aus, um ganze Stadtbilder in ein neues Licht zu setzen. Diese Maßnahmen fanden nicht mehr am Stadtrand statt, sondern sie konzentrierten sich in der historischen Stadtmitte und prägten damit das Gesicht der Stadt selbst. Doch in einem solchen Ansatz steckten auch Gefahren, wie immer – in der Politik wie in der Architektur –, wenn es um Bilder geht und diese irgendwann wichtiger werden als die Inhalte. So gesehen stellte die Politik der Stadt in diesen Jahren eine riskante Gratwanderung dar.

Das von Walter Wallmann und Hilmar Hoffmann schließlich durchgeführte Programm sollte zur Gründung von dreizehn

urban planning and architecture. In the light of the lack of perspective of later times, the avenue taken by Walter Wallmann and Hilmar Hoffmann, in conjunction with the head of the building department Hans-Eberhard Haverkampf, has to be ranked as exemplary. They worked not as before solely on the fabric of the city, but also on its image in the media and thus in the awareness of the wider public on a national level. With a great feeling for what would make a positive impact on the public, the spaces in which urban life takes place were redefined; new buildings at carefully selected points were enough to cast entire areas of the cityscape in a new light. This kind of intervention was no longer carried out on the periphery of the city but in a concentrated form in the historical centre, thus shaping the face of the city itself. But there are also risks inherent in an approach of this kind, as there always are—be it in politics or architecture–when it is a question of images and when at some point those images become more important than content. Thus the city's policies during these years involved a risky tightrope walk.

Museen führen. Nicht alle befanden sich unmittelbar am Main, jedoch in ausreichender Nähe, um als Teil eines »Museumsufers« betrachtet werden zu können. Diese Begriffsschöpfung war so erfolgreich, weil sie einen lange vernachlässigten, aber dennoch fest im Bewusstsein der Bürger verankerten innerstädtischen Raum neu definierte: den Mainraum zwischen Alter Brücke und Friedensbrücke mit seinen Grünanlagen und großbürgerlichen Villen. Das Museumsufer wurde konzipiert, als nach dem Wegzug der alten Frankfurter Elite in den Taunus der Ausverkauf und Abriss dieser Villen drohte. Ihre Einbeziehung in das Konzept des Museumsufers sicherte also ihr Überleben. Dies war für die Stadt von unschätzbarem Wert. Zugleich war die Situation wie geschaffen, um das Bild einer Perlenkette mit den in lockerer Folge am Fluss aneinander gereihten Museen ohne allzu großen Aufwand überzeugend umsetzen zu können.

Mindestens so gut wie dieses städtebauliche Bild einer Perlenkette hatten wenig später auch die neu zu schaffenden architektonischen Bilder zu funktionieren, bestand das Museumsufer doch größtenteils aus Neugründungen ohne jede Sammlung und damit zunächst auch ohne Exponate. Es war klar, dass es Jahrzehnte brauchen würde, bis die neuen Museen Archive mit einer gewissen Bedeutung aufgebaut hätten, aus deren Bestand sie den Ausstellungsbetrieb bestreiten könnten. Vor diesem Hintergrund kam der visuellen Kommunikation eine außergewöhnlich große, für die Postmoderne offensichtlich typische Bedeutung zu.

So musste der spektakuläre Auftritt, der von den Museen erwartet wurde, teilweise von der Architektur geleistet werden. Dies erklärt die große Beachtung, die der baulichen Hülle geschenkt wurde. Mit einem enormen Aufwand wurden im damals architektonisch eher desinteressierten Frankfurt plötzlich große internationale Architektenwettbewerbe organisiert, aus denen regelmäßig nationale und internationale »Stararchitekten« als Sieger hervorgingen. Dies war Teil einer geschickten Inszenierung, die in der Architektur mündete, einer Architektur, der die Prägnanz ihrer Erscheinungsform mindestens so wichtig war wie die Schaffung guter Räume.

HEINRICH KLOTZ UND DAS DAM (1979-1989)

Die Idee, als Teil des Museumsufers auch ein Architekturmuseum zu schaffen, nahm bei einem von Peter Iden organisierten Treffen von Hilmar Hoffmann und Heinrich Klotz konkrete Formen an. Klotz, Kunsthistoriker und Professor an der Universität Marburg, versprach nicht zuletzt wegen seiner Erfahrung als Preisrichter bei Architekturwettbewerben der richtige Mann auf der Position des Gründungsdirektors eines Deutschen Architekturmuseums zu sein. Der Erfolg der ersten Aktionen von Heinrich Klotz aus dem Jahr 1979 bestätigte dies: Die Bereitschaft von Architekten, dem DAM Zeichnungen und Modelle zu überlassen, war überwältigend.

Mit der Eröffnung des von Oswald Mathias Ungers komplett in ein Museum transformierten Hauses am Schaumainkai im Jahr 1984 begann ein wahres Feuerwerk von Veranstaltungen. Zwischen 1984 und 1989, als Klotz als Gründungsdirektor des Zentrums für Kunst und Medientechnologie nach Karlsruhe

The programme Walter Wallmann and Hilmar Hoffmann initiated led to the foundation of thirteen museums. They were not all directly on the river but nevertheless near enough to allow them to be perceived as part of a Museumsufer. This name became so successful because it redefined an inner-city area that had been neglected for a long time but was nevertheless firmly anchored in the public consciousness: an area along the River Main between two bridges, the Alte Brücke and the Friedensbrücke, with its parks and bourgeois villas. The Museumsufer was conceived at a time when these villas were under threat of being sold off and demolished, Frankfurt's elite having moved out to the nearby Taunus hills. Incorporating the area into the concept of the Museumsufer guaranteed its survival. This turned out to be of inestimable value for the city. At the same time, it produced a situation that was just what was needed to create the convincing image of a string of pearls with a series of museums in an informal arrangement along the river.

Since the Museumsufer consisted in the main of newly founded museums without collections and therefore without exhibits, it was vital that the architectural metaphors that had to be created not long afterwards worked at least as well as this urban design metaphor of a string of pearls. It was obvious that it would take decades for the new museums to build up archives of any significance with which to put together exhibitions. Against this backdrop, visual communication took on exceptionally great significance—not untypical for Post-Modernism.

Thus to some extent the spectacular presence that was expected of the museums had to be provided by their architecture. This explains the great attention that was paid to the actual buildings. Suddenly, Frankfurt, a city that since the Second World War had shown no great interest in architecture, started to organise international architectural competitions on a grand scale and at vast expense. The winners of these competitions were usually national and international "star architects." This was all part of a skilful orchestration that culminated in the architecture of the buildings, an architecture in which the power of outer appearance was at least as important as the creation of good spaces.

HEINRICH KLOTZ AND DAM (1979-1989)

The idea of creating a museum of architecture as part of the Museumsufer took on concrete form at a meeting between Hilmar Hoffmann and Heinrich Klotz organised by Peter Iden. Not least because of his experience on the juries of architectural competitions, Klotz, art historian and professor at the University of Marburg, promised to be the right man for the post of founding director of a German museum of architecture. The success of Heinrich Klotz's first actions in 1979 reaffirmed this: the willingness of architects to donate drawings and models to DAM was astounding.

1984 saw the inauguration of the museum on Schaumainkai—the result of Oswald Mathias Ungers' total transformation of an existing building—and it also saw the start of a positive firework display of events. Between 1984 and 1989, when Klotz went to Karlsruhe as the founding director of the Centre for Art and

ging, präsentierte das DAM 57 Ausstellungen, bis zum Amtsantritt seines Nachfolgers im Jahr 1990 waren es gar 62. Dank der von der Stadt zur Verfügung gestellten, schier unbegrenzt anmutenden Mittel konnte für die Präsentationen ein hoher Aufwand getrieben werden. Das Publikum honorierte dies mit hohen Besucherzahlen: Das DAM profilierte sich effektiv als ein »Museum für alle«.

Auf den ersten Blick deckten die Ausstellungen ein breites Spektrum ab. Bei näherer Betrachtung sind aber doch deutliche Schwerpunkte zu erkennen. Hervorzuheben ist der Einsatz von Heinrich Klotz für die Architektur und die Architekten der Postmoderne. Ohne dass man ihm Einäugigkeit vorwerfen müsste, hat er in wesentlichen Situationen eindeutig Position bezogen, so bei der Entscheidung, Ungers mit dem Neubau des DAM zu beauftragen. Wie von Klotz intendiert, entwickelte sich dieser Bau rasch zu einer Ikone der Postmoderne, die von Anfang an mit dem DAM identifiziert wurde. Bei der offiziellen Eröffnung des Hauses im Jahr 1984 mit der Ausstellung »Die Revision der Moderne. Postmoderne Architektur 1960-1980« wirkten Architektur und Ausstellung zusammen als Gesamtwerk. Dementsprechend polarisierte die Präsentation: Die einen waren begeistert, die anderen entsetzt; gut unterhalten fühlten sich wohl alle.

Unter den Ausstellungen der nächsten Jahre ragten diejenigen heraus, die die Architektur der Gegenwart vorstellten, dabei die Vielfalt der zeitgenössischen Tendenzen hervorhoben, zugleich aber neue Wege im Umgang mit dem Erbe der Moderne, mit der Geschichte der Architektur und mit der historischen Stadt im Sinne der Postmoderne aufzeigten. Dazu zählten breit angelegte Schauen wie »Bauen heute. Architektur der Gegenwart in der Bundesrepublik Deutschland« von 1985 und punktuelle wie »Internationale Bauausstellung Berlin 87. Beispiele einer neuen Architektur« von 1986. Auf einer internationalen Ebene lieferte »Vision der Moderne. Das Prinzip Konstruktion« von 1986 die Gelegenheit, aktuelle Beiträge im Geiste der Moderne zu thematisieren. In »Architektur im 20. Jahrhundert« von 1989 wurden Zeichnungen, Modelle und Möbel aus der inzwischen durchaus ansehnlichen Sammlung des DAM präsentiert.

Diese Ausstellungen wurden von großformatigen Katalogen mit hohem dokumentarischen Wert begleitet, die sich an ein breites Publikum richteten. Dementsprechend waren sie sehr plakativ mit relativ kurzen Texten und umfassendem Bildteil ausgestattet. Analyse und Kritik erfolgten ganz wesentlich durch die Auswahl und Gegenüberstellung der Objekte. Wie in seinen Ausstellungen begnügte sich Klotz vielfach damit, seiner Zeit einen Spiegel vorzuhalten. Da das Bild in diesem Spiegel in den achtziger Jahren sehr oft ein faszinierendes war, eines, das sich durch Vielfalt und Komplexität auszeichnete, konnte das Publikum nur begeistert sein.

DAS HAUS UND ANDERE ERBSCHAFTEN DER POSTMODERNE

Überhaupt wirkte die gerade in der Nachkriegszeit vernachlässigte Idee, auch die Architektur der Gegenwart wie Kunst zu behandeln, sie in Verbindung zum Zeitgeist zu setzen, sie als Werk von Architektenpersönlichkeiten darzustellen und in ihrer Be-

Media Technology, DAM put on 57 exhibitions; by the time his successor actually took up his post in 1990 that number had risen to 62. Thanks to the funding provided by the city council, which seemed to be absolutely limitless, it was possible to lavish a great deal of expense on presentation. The public rewarded these efforts with high visitor numbers: DAM in effect created an image for itself as a "museum for everyone."

At first glance, the exhibitions seemed to cover a very broad spectrum. However, on closer examination it was possible to identify a number of distinct areas of emphasis. In particular, Heinrich Klotz's staunch commitment to the architecture and architects of Post-Modernism must be singled out. Without accusing him of being biased, it can safely be said that in crucial situations he took up an unequivocal position, for example in the decision to commission Ungers to design the building for DAM. Just as Klotz had intended, this building rapidly became an icon of Post-Modernism that was identified with DAM from the very start. At the official inauguration of the building in 1984 with the exhibition "Postmodern visions. Drawings, models and paintings in contemporary architecture," the architecture and the exhibition worked in harmony to form a *gesamtwerk*. The public response to the exhibition was polarised: some people were delighted, others appalled; but everyone felt well entertained.

The outstanding exhibitions of the years to follow are those that presented contemporary architecture in a way that emphasised contemporary trends while illustrating new ways of treating the legacy of Modernism, the history of architecture and the historical city in the spirit of Post-Modernism. They include broad-based shows such as "Building today. Contemporary architecture in West Germany" of 1985 and more specific ones such as "International Building Exhibition Berlin 1987. Examples of a new architecture" of 1986. On an international level, "The vision of Modernism. The structure principle" of 1986 provided the opportunity to focus on contemporary contributions influenced by Modernism. "Twentieth century architecture" of 1989 showed drawings, models and furniture from DAM's own collection, which had by now become thoroughly presentable.

These exhibitions were accompanied by large-format catalogues that had a high documentary value and at the same time were targeted at a broad public. Correspondingly, they were high-quality, but not particularly academic, publications with relatively short texts and extensive graphic sections. Analysis and criticism consisted essentially of the selection and juxtaposition of the exhibits. As in the exhibitions themselves, Klotz contented himself to a great extent in holding up a mirror to his times. Since the image in this mirror in the eighties was often a very fascinating one, one that was characterised by diversity and complexity, the public was bound to be enthusiastic.

THE BUILDING AND OTHER LEGACIES OF POST-MODERNISM

Generally speaking, the idea of treating not only historical but also contemporary architecture as art, which had been neglected above all in the post-war years, the idea of setting it in the

deutung für das öffentliche Leben zu präsentieren, zu diskutieren und zu fördern, auf das Publikum wie auf die Architekten berauschend. Die Erinnerung an diesen Rausch lebt auch heute noch weiter. Sie begründet den guten Ruf des DAM und setzte zugleich hohe Maßstäbe für seine Arbeit bis in die Gegenwart, und das obwohl sich die Rahmenbedingungen, unter denen das DAM zu arbeiten hat, seitdem drastisch verändert haben.

Heinrich Klotz verließ Frankfurt zur Zeit des Zusammenbruchs des Ostblocks und der Wiedervereinigung Deutschlands, beides Ereignisse von großen Auswirkungen auf das Bewusstsein der Menschen, aber auch auf die allgemeine Finanzlage. Im Nachhinein erscheinen die achtziger Jahre wie eine *belle époque*, die von dem in den Jahrzehnten zuvor erarbeiteten enormen Wohlstand profitierte. In diesem Wohlstand lag eine wesentliche Voraussetzung für die postmoderne Lockerung der materialistischen Denkweisen und die Aufwertung des Schöngeistigen. Von diesem Wohlstand profitierte auch das DAM in der Zeit von Heinrich Klotz. Dagegen hatten seine Nachfolger unter den seit den neunziger Jahren wachsenden finanziellen Nöten der Stadt Frankfurt und der damit verbundenen schleichenden Abkehr von einer Politik der »Kultur als Wirtschaftsfaktor« zu leiden.

Neben den leeren Kassen trug auch die wachsende nationale wie internationale Konkurrenz zur allmählichen Ernüchterung nach dem Höhenflug der ersten Jahre bei. Unter anderem durch das Frankfurter Beispiel angeregt, wurden in den neunziger Jahren mehrere öffentliche Institutionen, aber auch private Architekturgalerien gegründet. Seitdem kommt keiner Einrichtung mehr eine Sonderrolle zu, weder bei der Akquisition von Exponaten noch bei der Präsentation von Ausstellungen. Vielmehr stehen den Architekten inzwischen eine Vielzahl von Verlagen, Zeitschriften, Autoren, Werbeagenturen und dergleichen zur Verfügung, die sich um ihre Öffentlichkeitsarbeit kümmern können und dabei weniger wählerisch zu sein haben als ein Museum.

Angesichts der veränderten Stimmungslage wurde auch Ungers' Museumsbau am Schaumainkai in einem neuen Licht gesehen. Klotz hatte sich mit ihm identifiziert und selbstverständlich auch dort residiert. Die eigenwillige Architektur war für ihn Teil der Inszenierung. Je nach Bedarf erstreckten sich seine Wechselausstellungen über einzelne, mehrere oder alle Geschosse. Erst im Jahr 1990 kam es zur Einrichtung einer kleinen Dauerausstellung im zweiten Obergeschoss. »Von der Urhütte zum Wolkenkratzer. Eine Geschichte der gebauten Umwelt« stellte eine sehr figurative Präsentation ausgewählter historischer Situationen im Modell dar und richtete sich in erster Linie an jüngere Besucher und Laien.

Die Beziehung von Lampugnani zu dem Haus war eher distanziert. Die strenge Struktur des Gebäudes und die räumliche Verbindung der oberen Geschosse empfand er als problematisch. Um Ausstellungsfläche zu gewinnen, wurde die wissenschaftlich wenig überzeugende Dauerausstellung geschlossen; die Direktion zog weg vom Schaumainkai in die Nebenstelle an der Hedderichstraße, wo das DAM bereits seine Bibliothek, die Werkstätten, das Archiv und weitere Nebenräume unterhielt.

Erst unter Ingeborg Flagge fand die Direktion den Weg zurück ins Haupthaus. Mit diesem Schritt leitete sie eine »Versöh-

context of the zeitgeist, presenting it as the work of individual architects and demonstrating, discussing and promoting its importance for public life captivated the general public and architects alike. The memory of the euphoria still lives on. It is responsible for DAM's good reputation and at the same time set high standards for it that still apply—even though the background conditions within which DAM has to work have changed drastically since then.

Heinrich Klotz left Frankfurt at the time of the collapse of the Eastern Block and reunification of Germany, both events that had huge effects on people's consciousness but also on the general financial situation. In retrospect, the 1980s look like a *belle époque* that benefited from the enormous wealth generated in previous years. Inherent in this prosperity was an essential prerequisite for the postmodernist relaxation of materialist ways of thinking and an increase in the status of aesthetics. During Heinrich Klotz's time, DAM also enjoyed the fruits of this prosperity. By contrast, his successors have suffered from the city of Frankfurt's financial difficulties that have been growing since the 1990s and from the gradual move away from the policy of "culture as an economic factor" connected with that.

As well as empty coffers, growing national and international competition contributed to the gradual fall to earth after the euphoria of the early years. One of the effects of the example set by Frankfurt was that several public institutions as well as private architecture galleries were set up in the nineties. Since then no single institution has had special status, neither in terms of acquiring exhibits nor staging exhibitions. In fact, architects can now choose from numerous publishers, magazines, authors, advertising agencies and the like to take care of their PR work, with the advantage that these organisations do not have to be as selective as a museum.

The change in mood meant that Ungers' museum on Schaumainkai was also seen in a new light. Klotz had identified with the building and had, of course, also had his offices there. For him, the unconventional architecture was an integral part of the overall productions he staged. His temporary exhibitions would sometimes occupy individual floors of the building, or sometimes several or even all the floors in the building, as each situation dictated. It was not until 1990 that a small permanent exhibition was set up on the second floor. "From primordial hut to skyscraper: a history of architecture in 25 models" was a very figurative presentation of selected historical situations depicted by models and its target group was primarily younger visitors and non-specialists.

Lampugnani's relationship with the building was more distant. He found the structure of the building and the spatial connections between the upper floors problematic. To gain extra exhibition space, he closed the permanent exhibition, which was academically not very convincing; the management moved out of Schaumainkai to DAM's annex on Hedderichstrasse, where the museum already had its library, workshops, archives and other ancillary rooms.

It was only later under Ingeborg Flagge that the management made its way back into the main building. With this step she initiated a process of "reconciliation" with the Ungers building,

nung« mit dem Ungers-Bau ein, die als ein symbolisches Wiederanknüpfen an das Erbe von Heinrich Klotz betrachtet werden kann. In diesem Sinne sind auch die umfassende Restaurierung des Hauses, die Wiedereröffnung von »Von der Urhütte zum Wolkenkratzer« und auch die Präsentation der Ausstellung »Die Revision der Postmoderne« zum zwanzigjährigen Jubiläum des DAM im Herbst 2004 zu verstehen.

VITTORIO MAGNAGO LAMPUGNANI (1990-1995)

Obwohl beide von Hilmar Hoffmann berufen worden waren, konnten die Unterschiede zwischen Heinrich Klotz und seinem Nachfolger Vittorio Magnago Lampugnani kaum größer sein. Im Vergleich erscheint Klotz als eine barocke Persönlichkeit und als Meister der Kommunikation, in beiderlei Hinsicht sehr gut in die schrillen achtziger Jahre passend. Der leise Lampugnani wirkt dagegen puristisch und reduziert wie die Architektur, die für die neunziger Jahre auch typisch werden sollte. Aus Berlin und Mailand kommend, wo er als Berater der Internationalen Bauausstellung IBA Berlin 1987 und als Kurator tätig gewesen war beziehungsweise wo er sich für die Zeitschriften *Casabella* und *Domus* engagiert hatte, blieb er bis zu seiner Berufung an die ETH Zürich im Jahr 1995 am Main.

In dieser Zeit zeigte das DAM nicht mehr als zwanzig Schauen, reduzierte das Ausstellungsprogramm also drastisch. Diese Reduzierung begründete Lampugnani mit dem Ziel, die Ausstellungen wissenschaftlich gründlicher zu erarbeiten. Auch das zeigt, wie sehr das DAM unter Klotz eher als aktuelle Galerie arbeitete und wie sehr es sich unter Lampugnani zu einem Museum im konventionellen Sinn entwickelte. Machte das DAM unter Klotz Geschichte, sollte es sich nun mit der Geschichtsschreibung befassen. Letztendlich ging es Lampugnani um eine Revision der Geschichtsschreibung des zwanzigsten Jahrhunderts in Deutschland durch Einbeziehung bis dahin eher wenig gewürdigter konservativer Architekten und Architekturen. Mit diesem Ansatz sprach das DAM vielleicht ein Fachpublikum an, die breite Öffentlichkeit erreichte es damit weniger.

Doch auch die Zeit unter Lampugnani begann für das DAM mit einem Paukenschlag. Von der *Frankfurter Allgemeine Zeitung* publizistisch umfassend unterstützt, präsentierte »Berlin morgen. Ideen für das Herz einer Großstadt« städtebauliche und architektonische Visionen für den Ausbau von Berlin als Hauptstadt des wieder vereinigten Deutschlands und löste damit heftige Diskussionen aus.

Den wesentlichen Beitrag des DAM in den nächsten Jahren stellte die Trilogie »Moderne Architektur in Deutschland 1900-1950« dar. Der erste Teil mit dem Titel »Reform und Tradition« wurde 1992 eröffnet, der zweite »Expressionismus und Neue Sachlichkeit« 1994, der dritte »Macht und Monument« im Jahr 1998, also bereits unter der Leitung von Wilfried Wang. Beachtlich an diesen Ausstellungen war nicht zuletzt die exzellente Qualität der Exponate, hauptsächlich Originale, darunter zahlreiche Leihgaben, die mit großem Aufwand nach Deutschland geholt werden mussten. In der Tat wäre jede dieser drei Ausstellungen geeignet gewesen, als Dauerausstellung präsentiert zu werden.

which can be seen as a symbolic act of reconnecting with Heinrich Klotz's legacy. The extensive refurbishment of the building, the reopening of "From primordial hut to skyscraper" and the exhibition "Post-Modernism revisited" to mark DAM's twentieth anniversary in autumn 2004 are also to be seen in this light.

VITTORIO MAGNAGO LAMPUGNANI (1990-1995)

Although both men were appointed by Hilmar Hoffmann, the differences between Heinrich Klotz and his successor Vittorio Magnago Lampugnani could hardly be greater. Klotz was a master of communication with a Baroque public persona, in both respects fitting in very well with the brash eighties. By comparison, Lampugnani, with his quiet manner, seemed purist and reductionalist—like the architecture that would also characterise the nineties. He came to Frankfurt from Berlin and Milan, where he had been a curator and advisor to the Internationale Bauausstellung IBA Berlin and worked for the Italian magazines *Casabella* and *Domus*. He remained until 1995 when he was appointed to his current post at the ETH in Zurich.

During this time, DAM did not put on more than twenty shows; in other words, it reduced its exhibition programme drastically. Lampugnani explained this reduction by his goal of wanting the exhibitions to have a sounder academic foundation. That also illustrates the extent to which under Klotz DAM had worked more in the sense of a contemporary gallery and the extent to which it developed into a museum in the conventional sense under Lampugnani. While DAM made history under Klotz, it would now turn its attention to historiography. In the final analysis, Lampugnani was concerned with revising the historiography of the 20th century in Germany by incorporating conservative architects and architecture that had until then been little acknowledged. With this approach, DAM perhaps spoke to a specialist audience; it reached the general public to a lesser extent.

But DAM's time under the directorship of Lampugnani also began with a furore. Backed by extensive press coverage by the *Frankfurter Allgemeine Zeitung*, the exhibition "Berlin tomorrow. Ideas for the heart of a city" presented urban design and architectural visions for how Berlin could develop into the capital of a reunified Germany. It unleashed vehement discussions.

DAM's major contribution in the next few years was the trilogy of exhibitions "Modern Architecture in Germany 1900-1950." The first part, entitled "Reform and Tradition," opened in 1992, the second "Expressionism and Neue Sachlichkeit" in 1994, the third "Power and Monument" in 1998, the latter under Wilfried Wang. One of the remarkable things about these exhibitions was the exceptional quality of the exhibits, mainly originals, including numerous loans that were brought to Germany at great expense. In fact, each of these three exhibitions would have been suitable as a permanent exhibition.

Other major exhibitions of this period included "Heinrich Tessenow (1876-1950)" in 1991, "Antonio Sant'Elia. Architecture in drawings 1906-1916" in 1992 and "Peter Joseph Lenné. Landscape architect and town planner 1789-1866" in 1993. Shows on

Weitere größere Ausstellungen dieser Zeit waren »Heinrich Tessenow (1876-1950)« von 1991, »Antonio Sant'Elia. Gezeichnete Architektur 1906-1916« von 1992 sowie »Peter Joseph Lenné. Landschaftsarchitekt und Stadtplaner 1789-1865« von 1993. Zu den Schauen zu aktuellen Themen zählten »Ein Stück Großstadt als Experiment. Planungen am Potsdamer Platz« von 1995 und »Wohnen und Arbeiten am Fluss. Perspektiven für den Frankfurter Osthafen« von 1992.

WILFRIED WANG (1995-2000)

Bei allen Unterschieden wirkten Klotz und Lampugnani beide im Geiste der Postmoderne. Anders Wilfried Wang. Unter seiner Leitung setzte sich das DAM von dem für die Postmoderne typischen Lagerdenken und der Polemik der letzten Jahre ab und stellte sich auf die neuen, materiell wie inhaltlich sehr viel härteren Bedingungen der neunziger Jahre ein. Damit leitete er eine Konsolidierung der Arbeit des DAM und seiner Wirkung in der Öffentlichkeit ein.

Durch seinen Werdegang war der von Kulturdezernentin Linda Reisch berufene Wang dazu prädestiniert, die Tätigkeiten des DAM – und nicht nur seine Ausstrahlung – international zu erweitern. Der gebürtige Hamburger hatte in London Architektur studiert und die Zeitschrift *9H* mit herausgegeben; parallel dazu lehrte er an der Harvard University. In Frankfurt war er von Beginn an mit schwierigsten Bedingungen konfrontiert. Die Erwartungen hinsichtlich der öffentlichen Wirkung des Hauses waren gerade wegen der Stille der letzten Jahre hoch, doch die von der Stadt Frankfurt zur Verfügung gestellten Mittel sanken und sanken. In die Aufgabe, neue Finanzquellen zu erschließen, investierte Wang viel Energie – letztendlich mit Erfolg. Auf dieser Basis nahm die Zahl der Veranstaltungen wieder deutlich zu, sodass zwischen 1995 und 2000 rund fünfzig Ausstellungen durchgeführt werden konnten.

Unter diesen ragt die Reihe »Architektur im 20. Jahrhundert« deutlich heraus, mit der das DAM Europa für sich erschloss. Beginnend mit »Österreich« im Jahr 1996 wurden 1997 »Irland« und »Portugal«, 1998 »Schweden« und »Schweiz«, 1999 »Griechenland« und »Finnland« sowie 2000 »Deutschland« und »Spanien« präsentiert. Alle Einzelausstellungen dokumentierten in einer sachlichen Art und Weise die gesamte Architektur des Jahrhunderts in ihrer Vielfalt. Weil sie in Zusammenarbeit mit den führenden Wissenschaftlern und Architekten vor Ort realisiert wurden, stellen diese Ausstellungen eine historische Grundlagenarbeit von großer Konsistenz und Bedeutung dar.

Zu den Präsentationen zu Einzelthemen zählen »Weltbild Wörlitz. Entwurf einer Kulturlandschaft« von 1996, »Eine Architektur für alle Sinne: Die Arbeiten von Eileen Gray« von 1996, »Mart Stam. Architekt, Visionär, Gestalter« von 1997 und »Die Architektur von Heinz Bienefeld 1926-1995« von 1999. Große Beachtung fand »Die Neue Sammlung. Schenkungen und Akquisitionen 1995-1999« von 1999, die Neuerwerbungen von höchster Güte zeigte und damit die kontinuierliche Arbeit des DAM auf diesem Gebiet dokumentierte. Mit der Ausstellung »Maßstabssprung. Die Zukunft von Frankfurt am Main« von 1999 erzielte das DAM einen Publikumserfolg.

contemporary themes included "An Urban Experiment in Central Berlin. Planning Potsdamer Platz" in 1995 and "Living and working by the river. Prospects for Frankfurt's Osthafen" in 1992.

WILFRIED WANG (1995-2000)

Despite all the differences between them, Klotz and Lampugnani nevertheless both acted in the spirit of Post-Modernism. This was not the case with Wilfried Wang. Under his directorship, DAM distanced itself from the polarised thinking typical of Post-Modernism and from the polemics of preceding years and adapted to the new conditions of the nineties that were very much harsher—both materially and in terms of content. In this, he initiated a consolidation of DAM's work and its public impact.

His background made Wang, who had been appointed by head of culture Linda Reisch, predestined to expand DAM's activities—not just its public image—into the international arena. Born in Hamburg, Wang had studied architecture in London and been co-editor of the magazine *9H*; at the same time as that he had lectured at Harvard University. In Frankfurt, he faced extremely difficult conditions from the word go. In particular, due to the low-key role the museum had adopted in recent years, expectations with regard to its public impact were now high, and yet at the same time the funding provided by the Frankfurt city authorities dropped and dropped. Wang invested a great deal of energy in trying to find new sources of financing—ultimately with success. On that basis, the number of events rose again noticeably and around fifty exhibitions were staged between 1995 and 2000.

Amongst these, the series "Twentieth century architecture," with which DAM explored Europe, stands out clearly. The series began with Austria in 1996 and went on to showcase Ireland and Portugal in 1997, Sweden and Switzerland in 1998, Greece and Finland in 1999 and Germany and Spain in 2000. Each individual exhibition documented objectively the architecture of the century in all its diversity. Because leading academics and architects in the respective countries collaborated on these exhibitions, they represent a piece of thorough historical research of great significance.

The exhibitions on individual themes include "Landscape design and planning in Wörlitz: a worldview embodied" in 1996, "Eileen Gray. An architecture for all senses" in 1996, "Mart Stam. Architect, visionary, designer" in 1997 and "The architecture of Heinz Bienefeld 1926-1995" in 1999. "The new collection. Gifts and acquisitions 1995-1999" in 1999, which showed new acquisitions of outstanding quality and thus documented DAM's continuing work in this field, met with great acclaim. The exhibition "A leap of scale. The future of Frankfurt am Main" in 1999 was a huge success with the public.

INGEBORG FLAGGE (SEIT 2000)

Angesichts der weiterhin desolaten Finanzlage hatte auch die vom Kulturdezernenten Hans-Bernhard Nordhoff berufene Ingeborg Flagge, langjährige Geschäftsführerin des Bundes Deutscher Architekten BDA, Chefredakteurin der Zeitschrift *Der Architekt* und Professorin für Architekturgeschichte in Leipzig, zunächst die Existenz des Hauses zu sichern. Im Zuge dessen gelang ihr durch die Aktivierung der besonderen Potenziale des DAM eine institutionelle Konsolidierung im umfassenden Sinn.

Zu den in den neunziger Jahren vernachlässigten Ressourcen des DAM gehörte das von Oswald Mathias Ungers geplante Museumsgebäude. Die notwendige Renovierung wurde gleich zu Beginn von Flagges Amtszeit durchgeführt und lieferte den Anlass für publikumswirksame künstlerische Inszenierungen. Ingeborg Flagge machte möglich, was sich Ungers zur Einweihung des Gebäudes im Jahr 1984 gewünscht, aber nicht erhalten hatte: die öffentliche Präsentation des leeren Hauses als Exponat und museale Hülle in einem. Im Zuge der Renovierung wurde das Gebäude dem Originalzustand sehr nahe gebracht und zugleich punktuell technisch modernisiert.

Mit den Ausstellungen »Der Architekt Thomas Herzog« von 2002 und »leicht weit. Jörg Schlaich, Rudolf Bergermann« von 2004 setzte Ingeborg Flagge persönliche inhaltliche Akzente. Damit standen Einzelausstellungen zu lebenden und beruflich aktiven deutschen Architekten und Ingenieuren im Vordergrund der Arbeit des DAM. Beide Ausstellungen boten die Möglichkeit, zentrale Fragen der Gegenwartsarchitektur zu behandeln. Bei »Thomas Herzog« stand das energiebewusste Planen und Bauen mit neuen Baustoffen im Vordergrund, bei »leicht weit« die Beziehung zwischen Konstruktion und Gestalt. Weitere Werkpräsentationen kleineren Maßstabs folgten, darunter »Helmut Striffler« im Jahr 2002.

Die Themen der weiteren Schauen – insgesamt waren es von 2001 bis 2004 gut fünfzig – deckten wie unter Klotz ein breites Spektrum ab und behandelten so unterschiedliche Materien wie »digital real. blobmeister – erste gebaute Projekte« und »Helmut Jacoby. Meister der Architekturzeichnung« von 2001, »Das Geheimnis des Schattens« und »World Airports« von 2002, »Schönheit ruht in der Ordnung. Paul Schmitthenner 1884-1972« von 2003 und »Stanley Kubrick« von 2004.

Doch Ingeborg Flagge zeigte auch bei der Konzeption der Vortragsreihe »Große Architekten« viel Gespür für das, was das breite Publikum interessiert. Mit dieser Reihe, die durch private Sponsoren finanziert wird, gelang es erneut, *global players* regelmäßig an den Main zu holen. »Große Architekten« wird – ähnlich wie die Ausstellungen in den Anfangsjahren des DAM – von vielen Laien besucht. Zur weiteren Steigerung der Attraktivität des DAM im städtischen Alltag trugen die Einrichtung einer »Aktuellen Galerie« und die Wiedereröffnung der Dauerausstellung »Von der Urhütte zum Wolkenkratzer« bei. Doch auch die neue Cafeteria im Foyer mit schönem Blick auf die inzwischen sehr beliebte Frankfurter Skyline war für das neue Erscheinungsbild des DAM von großer Bedeutung. Das Haus, aus dem ein Museum geworden war, wurde nicht zuletzt durch solche Details wieder ein wenig ein Haus: ein Haus wenn nicht für alle, so doch für viele.

INGEBORG FLAGGE (SINCE 2000)

In 2000, Ingeborg Flagge, who had for many years been chief executive of the Bund Deutscher Architekten, Germany's main architects' association, editor-in-chief of its journal *Der Architekt* and professor of architectural history in Leipzig, was appointed by head of culture Hans-Bernhard Nordhoff. In view of the financial situation, which was still grim, her first priority was to safeguard the museum's survival. She succeeded by activating DAM's special potential to achieve an institutional consolidation in a broad sense.

One of DAM's resources that had been neglected in the nineties was the Ungers building itself. The necessary refurbishment was carried out right at the beginning of Flagge's term of office and provided an opportunity to stage artistic events that were very effective in PR terms. Ingeborg Flagge made possible what Ungers had wanted when the building was inaugurated in 1984, but did not manage to achieve: the public presentation of the empty building as an exhibition piece and shell of a museum in one. As part of the refurbishment, the building was returned virtually to its original condition and at the same time technical modernisation work was carried out at selected points.

With the exhibitions "Thomas Herzog. Architecture + technology" in 2002 and "Light structures. Jörg Schlaich, Rudolf Bergermann" in 2004, Ingeborg Flagge set her own personal keynotes in terms of content. DAM now focused on individual exhibitions on contemporary practising architects. These two exhibitions provided an opportunity to deal with central issues in contemporary architecture. With "Thomas Herzog," energy-efficient design and building with new materials was in the foreground, in the case of "Light structures" the focus was on the relationship between structure and form. Other smaller-scale presentations of the work of individual architects followed, including "Helmut Striffler" in 2002.

As under Klotz, the themes of the other shows—totalling over fifty between 2001 and 2004—covered a broad range of subjects and explored such different themes as "digital real. blobmeister—first built projects", "Helmut Jacoby. Master of architectural drawing" in 2001, "The secret of the shadow" and "World Airports" in 2002, "Beauty is based on order. Paul Schmitthenner 1884-1972" in 2003 and "Stanley Kubrick" in 2004.

However, in the conception of the series of talks on great architects, Ingeborg Flagge showed a good sense of what would interest the general public. With this series, financed by private sponsors, it became possible once more to entice global players to Frankfurt on a regular basis. Many non-architects have attended the "Great architects" series—as was the case with the exhibitions in DAM's early years.

The installation of a Contemporary Gallery and the reopening of the permanent exhibition "From primordial hut to skyscraper" also helped to increase DAM's attractiveness within the city's everyday life. The new café in the foyer, which offers a fine view of Frankfurt's now well-loved skyline, has also played a major role in DAM's new image. It is also thanks to details of this kind that the house that was turned into a museum has to some extent once more become a house: perhaps not a house for everyone, but nevertheless a house for many.

VOLKER FISCHER

SOVIEL WERDEN WAR NIE

HEINRICH KLOTZ UND SEIN ARCHITEKTURMUSEUM

A TIME OF UNPRECEDENTED DEVELOPMENT

HEINRICH KLOTZ AND HIS MUSEUM OF ARCHITECTURE

Es begann mit dem Besuch im Büro von Mies van der Rohe 1969 – kurz vor dessen Tod. Heinrich Klotz wollte ihn und andere bedeutende »Modernisten« für sein Buch *Conversations with Architects* interviewen. Zum Interview mit Mies kam es nicht mehr, auch nicht zum Gespräch mit Gropius, der im selben Jahr starb. Dass mit dem Tod von Mies van der Rohe eine Epoche zu Ende ging, war Klotz bewusst. Aber dass zeitgleich mit dem Verschwinden dieser Ära auch zahlreiche Modelle und andere Arbeitsmittel des großen Architekten vernichtet werden sollten, deprimierte ihn besonders.[1]

Heinrich Klotz (1935-1999) hatte schon früh seine Liebe zur Gegenwartsarchitektur entdeckt. Sie sollte sich während seiner Gastprofessuren in den Vereinigten Staaten durch enge Kontakte mit Paul Rudolph, Charles Moore, Robert Venturi und anderen vertiefen. Klotz ging in die Büros der Architekten, sprach mit ihnen und war immer mehr fasziniert von den Produkten künstlerischer Prozesse bei der Entstehung von Architektur – also den Zeichnungen und Modellen, die insbesondere nach Vollendung eines Baus so oft als nunmehr wertlos erachtet wurden. Die Protagonisten seines Buches *Conversations with Architects*, das er 1973 zusammen mit dem Architekturkritiker Vincent Scully veröffentlichte, kamen nun, anders als geplant, aus der Architektengeneration, die um 1960 angefangen hatte zu bauen.[2] Nach Deutschland zurückgekehrt, wurde Klotz 1972 Ordinarius für Kunstwissenschaften an der Universität Marburg. Neben seiner Tätigkeit als Hochschullehrer initiierte er in dieser Stadt einflussreiche Revitalisierungen historischer Bausubstanz durch zeitgenössische Architektureingriffe. In der *Frankfurter Rundschau* forderte er die Wertschätzung der Hochhaus-Skyline Frankfurts ein, zu einem Zeitpunkt, als dieses noch als »Bankfurt«, »Krankfurt« oder »Mainhattan« verteufelt wurde. Gleichzeitig warb er in mehreren deutschen Städten für die Gründung eines Deutschen Architekturmuseums. Klotz hatte eine Institution im Sinn, deren Schwerpunkt Ausstellungen sein sollten, Ausstellungen über lebende Architekten – damals, bis auf wenige Ausnahmen, ein Novum.

In Frankfurt am Main traf er auf eine außergewöhnlich günstige kulturpolitische Konstellation – zunächst (1976) auf den Baudezernenten Hans-Ehrhard Haverkampf und den Kulturdezernenten Hilmar Hoffmann (beide SPD). Damals existierten bereits Pläne für die Schaffung eines Museumsufers, und Heinrich Klotz überzeugte die Verantwortlichen, in diesem Rahmen auch ein Deutsches Architekturmuseum zu etablieren. Das sozialdemokratische Konzept wurde glücklicherweise von dem 1977 neu ins Amt gekommenen CDU-Oberbürgermeister Walter Wallmann übernommen. Die zusätzlichen Museen sollten in leer stehende, historistische Villen entlang des Mains einziehen, für die noch keine Nutzung gefunden war. Anfang 1979 entschieden Wallmann, Hoffmann und Klotz, das neu zu gründende Architekturmuseum in einer Gründerzeitvilla am Schaumainkai unterzubringen. Klotz setzte als designierter Direktor durch, dass auf eine Wettbewerbsausschreibung zur Neugestaltung des Altbaus verzichtet und der Architekt Oswald Mathias Ungers direkt engagiert wurde. Das geschah 1979. Es war der erste Auftrag für Ungers in Deutschland nach seinem langen Aufenthalt in den Vereinigten Staaten.

1 Vgl. In the Steps of Vasari. Charles Jencks interviews Heinrich Klotz, in: Architectural Design (AD), Nr. 3-4, 1985, S. 9-16.

2 John W. Cook, Heinrich Klotz, Conversations with Architects, New York 1973. Deutsch: Heinrich Klotz, John W. Cook, Architektur im Widerspruch. Bauen in den USA von Mies van der Rohe bis Andy Warhol, Zürich 1974.

It all began with a visit to Mies van der Rohe's office in 1969—not long before his death. Heinrich Klotz wanted to interview him and other prominent "Modernists" for his book *Conversations with architects.* The interview with Mies never happened, nor did the one with Gropius who died that same year. Klotz realised that Mies van der Rohe's death signalled the end of an era. But what he found particularly depressing was the fact that with the disappearance of this era numerous models and other working tools of the great architect were going to be destroyed.[1]

Heinrich Klotz (1935-1999) had discovered his love for contemporary architecture early on, a love that would deepen during his time in the United States as visiting professor through the close contact he enjoyed with Paul Rudolph, Charles Moore, Robert Venturi and others. Klotz went into architects' offices, talked with them and became all the more fascinated by the products of the artistic processes involved in the creation of architecture—in other words, the drawings and models that were so often thought to be worthless, particularly once a building had been completed. The protagonists of his book *Conversations with architects*, which he published in 1973 in conjunction with architectural critic Vincent Scully,[2] were of the generation of architects who had begun building around 1960, which was not what the authors had originally planned. On his return to Germany in 1972, Klotz became professor of art history at the University of Marburg. Apart from his teaching activities at the university, he also initiated an influential revitalisation of the historical building fabric in Marburg through contemporary architectural interventions. Writing in the *Frankfurter Rundschau*, he tried to convince people to appreciate Frankfurt's high-rise skyline at a time when it was still vilified as "Bankfurt," or "Mainhattan." At the same time, he tried to canvass support in several German cities for the foundation of a German Museum of Architecture. Klotz had an institution in mind that would focus on exhibiting the work of living architects—something which, apart from a handful of exceptions, was a novelty at the time.

In the sphere of cultural politics in Frankfurt am Main serendipity smiled on him—first of all (in 1976), in the form of Hans-Ehrhard Haverkampf, head of the city's building department, and Hilmar Hoffmann, head of its culture department (both Social Democrats). At the time, plans already existed to create an ensemble of museums on the south bank of the River Main, the Museumsufer as it was known in German, and Heinrich Klotz convinced them to include a German Museum of Architecture in these plans. The concept developed by the Social Democrats was fortunately adopted in 1977 by the city's new CDU Governing Mayor Walter Wallmann. The additional museums were to be accommodated in empty historicist villas near the Main for which no use had been found. In early 1979, Wallmann, Hoffmann and Klotz decided to put the Museum of Architecture in a late 19th century villa on the Schaumainkai. Klotz, who had been appointed director designate, managed to persuade people that it was not necessary to hold a competition for the conversion of the building and that the architect Oswald Mathias Ungers should be directly commissioned. This

1 Cf. In the Steps of Vasari. Charles Jencks interviews Heinrich Klotz, in: Architectural Design (AD), no. 3-4, 1985, pp. 9-16.

2 John W. Cook, Heinrich Klotz, Conversations with Architects, New York 1973.

Klotz und sein enger Freund, der Kulturkritiker Peter Iden, ebenfalls einer der Väter des Museumsufers, hatten für das neue Museum ein Konzept entwickelt, das sich der dialektischen Verbindung von aktueller Kunst und Architektur verschrieben hatte. Schnell wurde aber klar, dass in dem vorgesehenen Gebäude neben einem Architekturmuseum nicht auch noch ein Museum für Moderne Kunst unterzubringen sein würde, dessen Grundstock die Sammlung Ströher aus Darmstadt mit überwiegend großformatigen Pop-Art-Bildern und -Skulpturen bilden sollte. Als die Idee eines Architektur-/Moderne-Kunst-Museums publik wurde, entbrannte in Frankfurt ein »Kulturstreit«. Städel und Liebighaus befürchteten – wie sich später herausstellte, durchaus zu Recht – eine beträchtliche Einflussnahme des neuen Museumsdirektors auf das Gesamtkonzept des geplanten Museumsufers. Aber gerade durch Heinrich Klotz wurden die dann folgenden Wettbewerbe für das Museum für Kunsthandwerk, das Jüdische Museum, das Museum für Moderne Kunst, später das Postmuseum, das Museum für Vor- und Frühgeschichte und den Erweiterungsbau des Städel einem internationalen Niveau gerecht.

Die Programmatik, die Heinrich Klotz für das Architekturmuseum konzipierte, las sich so: »Wenn heute die Gründung von Architekturmuseen erneut in verschiedenen Ländern an Aktualität gewinnt, so geschieht dies unter dem ganz anderen Vorzeichen eines einsetzenden Bemühens um die Erhaltung und die ökologisch rücksichtsvolle Erneuerung unserer gebauten Umwelt. Das Verständnis von Architektur als reiner Bautechnik ging parallel mit dem Wiederaufbau der Nachkriegszeit. Nach der Erfüllung der Primärbedürfnisse im Bereich des Wohnens, Arbeitens und der städtischen Versorgung treten nun, ähnlich wie in anderen Lebensbereichen, die Ansprüche einer komplexer gewordenen Umwelt von Stadt und Dorf in den Mittelpunkt des Interesses. Damit stellt sich zugleich die Frage nach einer Architektur, der nicht nur die technische Erfüllung reiner Nützlichkeiten zugedacht wird, sondern der die baukünstlerische Aufgabe einer humanen Umweltgestaltung obliegen soll. Diese Thematik ist die aktuelle Arbeits- und Programmgrundlage des Deutschen Architekturmuseums.« Und er fährt fort: »Ein solches Museum hat gegenwärtig die bildungspolitische Aufgabe, den Gedanken einer umweltgerechten Architektur als baukünstlerisches Unternehmen zu verbreiten. [...] In diesem Wirkungszusammenhang verändert sich auch die herkömmliche Aufgabe eines Museums als einer Stätte bloßen Sammelns und Konservierens von Kunstobjekten. Die sterile Präsentation von architekturgeschichtlichen Gegenständen ist nicht zu befürchten, sofern das Museum seinen Auftrag als öffentliche Institution in einem publikumswirksamen Sinne richtig versteht.«[3]

1979, vor Beginn der Bauarbeiten am Architekturmuseum, bot Klotz mir an, mit ihm in Frankfurt die neue Institution aufzubauen. Zunächst war meine Hauptaufgabe, als Vertreter des Bauherrn – also des städtischen Kulturdezernats mit seinem Amt für Wissenschaft und Kunst – die zahlreichen, aufreibenden Bausitzungen durchzustehen. Bei jedem dieser Treffen brillierte das in Köln ansässige Büro von Oswald Mathias Ungers durch seinen Büroleiter Karl Otto Dietzsch mit präzisen Detail-

3 Heinrich Klotz, Das Deutsche Architekturmuseum in Frankfurt am Main, in: Jahrbuch für Architektur. Neues Bauen 1980/1981, Wiesbaden 1980, S. 179 f.

happened in 1979. It was Ungers' first commission in Germany after his long stay in the United States.

Klotz and his close friend, arts critic Peter Iden, who was also one of the founding fathers of the Museumsufer, had already developed a concept for the new museum, which was dedicated to exploring the dialectic link between contemporary art and architecture. However, it soon became clear that it would not be possible for the building envisaged to accommodate both a museum of architecture and a museum of modern art, the basis of which was to be the Ströher Collection from Darmstadt, consisting mainly of large-format pop art paintings and sculptures. When the idea of an architecture/modern art museum became public, a "cultural dispute" flared up in Frankfurt. The Städel and Liebighaus museums feared—and they would later be proved right—that the new museum director would have a considerable influence on the overall concept for the museum ensemble. But it was precisely thanks to Heinrich Klotz that the subsequent competitions for the Museum of Applied Arts, Jewish Museum, Museum of Modern Art and later the Post Museum, Museum for Pre- and Early History and the extension to the Städel Museum achieved the international standard they did.

The programme that Heinrich Klotz drew up for the Museum of Architecture, read as follows: "Although the founding of museums of architecture is becoming more widespread in different countries today, it is under completely new circumstances: there are signs that people are endeavouring to preserve and refurbish our built environment in a way that is respectful of ecological concerns. The understanding of architecture as pure building technology went hand in hand with the reconstruction work of the post-war years. Now that the primary needs have been fulfilled in the spheres of housing, work and public services our attention must shift, here as in other areas of life, to the needs of the environment in which towns and villages are situated, an environment that has become more complex. With this we must also look at the question of an architecture that is not only expected to technically fulfil purely utilitarian purposes, but should also be concerned with the architectural task of shaping the environment in a humane way. This theme is the current foundation of our work and programme development at the German Museum of Architecture." And he continues: "A museum of this kind has the educational remit to propagate the idea of environmentally sensitive architecture. [...] In this context the traditional role of a museum changes: it is no longer merely a place where art objects are collected and conserved. We need not fear the sterile presentation of objects of interest in terms of architectural history if the museum properly interprets its remit as a public institution that is intended to appeal to the public."[3]

In 1979, before construction work for the Museum of Architecture began, Klotz offered me the opportunity to work with him in setting up the new institution in Frankfurt. My main task initially—as representative of the client, the city's Office for Science and the Arts—was to survive the numerous and wearing construction meetings. At each of these meetings, Karl Otto Dietzsch, principal architect of Oswald Mathias Ungers' Cologne-based office, shone with the precise detailed and working

3 Heinrich Klotz, Das Deutsche Architekturmuseum in Frankfurt am Main, in: Jahrbuch für Architektur. Neues Bauen 1980/1981, Wiesbaden 1980, p. 179 f.

und Ausführungsplänen – nicht immer zur Freude der Vertreter des Hochbauamts und der anwesenden Sonderingenieure. Aber das zähe Ringen um die besten Lösungen war auch beglückend, zumal am Schluss alle am selben Strang zogen.

Während der Errichtung des Architekturmuseums arbeiteten wir in sehr bescheidenen Büros in der Frankfurter Innenstadt. Häufig kamen am Tag mehr als zehn Architekten, Architekturkritiker und Ausstellungsmacher, oft von weit her – aus New York, Melbourne, Toronto oder Tokio –, um Heinrich Klotz zu sprechen. In der dichten Folge solcher Gespräche war Heinrich Klotz in seinem Element: Unschlagbar eloquent in der Argumentation, eine Institution in allen Details vorstellend, die noch gar nicht wirklich existierte. Er schilderte die Bandbreite ihrer Aufgaben und ihre gesellschaftlichen Einflussmöglichkeiten mit einer Eindringlichkeit, die ihresgleichen suchte.

Oswald Mathias Ungers, von Heinrich Klotz wegen seiner humanistischen Architekturauffassung hoch geschätzt, ließ die Gründerzeitvilla völlig entkernen und eine Stahlbeton-Konstruktion einstellen. Herzstück wurde das »Haus-im-Haus«, das sich auf vier Stützen über drei Geschosse zunehmend verdichtet und seinen Abschluss in einer »Urhütte« erfährt, einem Symbol der Architektur schlechthin. Die strenge Quadratur des Raumgefüges, die ausschließliche Verwendung der Farbe Weiß und die Lichtdramaturgie aus Tages- und Kunstlicht entmaterialisieren den Raum und betonen das abstrakte Raumerlebnis: das Museum als Ort geistiger Vertiefung. Teil des architektonischen Konzepts ist die eingeschossige, gekuppelte Ausstellungshalle, die sich auf dem Gelände des ehemaligen Gartens hinter dem Altbau befindet. Ihr Zentrum ist wiederum ein exakter Würfel: ein offener Innenhof mit einem alten Kastanienbaum. Halle und Altbau sind von einer umlaufenden Glasgalerie gefasst, die sich zur Straße als Arkaden-Eingangshalle darbietet. Zwischen der Villa, der hinteren Halle und der Vorhalle entstehen kleine Straßen und Plätze. Die umlaufende hohe rote Sandsteinmauer nimmt den Charakter einer Stadtmauer an. So funktioniert das Museum wie die Miniaturisierung einer Stadt. Dieser Bau wurde also nicht nur ein Haus für die Architektur, sondern auch eines über die Architektur und mehr noch: ein gebautes Lehrstück geglückten Zusammenwirkens von Gegenwartsarchitektur und Denkmalpflege.

Als der Umbau nach dreieinhalb Jahren fertig gestellt war, erfolgte die Einrichtung der Eröffnungsausstellung. Gemeinsam mit mir, Hans-Peter Schwarz und Andrea Gleiniger konzipierte Klotz »Die Revision der Moderne«, eine aktuelle Bestandsaufnahme internationaler Architekturtendenzen von 1960 bis zur Mitte der achtziger Jahre. Ungers und Aldo Rossi, Venturi und Moore, Richard Meier und Peter Eisenman, Rob und Léon Krier, Mario Botta, Josef Paul Kleihues und Rem Koolhaas: Sie und uns einte das gemeinsame Bemühen, einem fiktional bedeutungslos gewordenen Funktionalismus eine neue inhaltliche, erzählerische Qualität von Architektur gegenüberzustellen. Zeitgleich mit der Vorbereitung der Eröffnungsausstellung und des Katalogs legte Heinrich Klotz mit seinem Werk *Moderne und Postmoderne* (1984) eine überwölbende Untersuchung der komplexen Bauauffassungen im 20. Jahrhundert und der Dialektik zwischen Moderne und Postmoderne vor.

drawings the firm consistently produced—not always to the delight of the representatives of Frankfurt's Department of Public Works and the consulting engineers. But the tough process of battling to find the best solutions was also very satisfying, particularly since in the end everyone pulled together.

During the construction phase of the Museum of Architecture we worked in very modest offices in the centre of Frankfurt. Often, over ten architects, architectural critics and exhibition curators would come in a day, mostly from a long way away—New York, Melbourne, Toronto or Tokyo—to speak to Heinrich Klotz. As one discussion followed hot on the heels of the one before, Heinrich Klotz was in his element: unbeatably eloquent in his argumentation, presenting an institution that did not yet actually exist down to every last detail. He described the breadth of its remit and its opportunities for influencing society with a vividness that remains unparalleled.

Oswald Mathias Ungers, whom Heinrich Klotz held in high esteem due to his humanistic view of architecture, completely gutted the 19th century villa and inserted a reinforced concrete structure inside it. The centrepiece was the "building-within-a-building," which rests on four columns and extends over three storeys, becoming more compact as it rises and terminating in a "primitive hut," thus in a symbol for architecture per se. The severe squareness of the spatial structure, the exclusive use of the colour white and the choreography of light with its interplay of daylight and artificial light dematerialise the space and emphasize the abstract experience of it: the museum as a place for deep intellectual absorption. The architectural concept also expresses itself in the single-storey, domed exhibition hall, which is on the site of the former garden behind the villa. Its centre is also an exact cube: an interior courtyard with an old chestnut tree. The hall and the original building are framed by a continuous glass gallery, which presents to the street as an arcaded entrance hall. Small streets and squares have been created between the villa, the hall to the rear, and the entrance hall. The high red sandstone encircling wall takes on the character of town walls. In this way the museum functions as a miniature town. This building thus became not just a building for architecture but also a building about architecture and, more than that, a built lesson in how contemporary architecture and conservation of historical buildings can engage in a successful dialectic relationship.

After three and a half years, the conversion was finished and the focus shifted to putting together an opening exhibition. In conjunction with Hans-Peter Schwarz, Andrea Gleiniger and me, Klotz created "The Revision of the Modern," which reviewed international architectural trends from the late 1960s until the mid-eighties. Ungers and Aldo Rossi, Venturi and Moore, Richard Meier and Peter Eisenman, Rob and Léon Krier, Mario Botta, Josef Paul Kleihues and Rem Koolhaas: what linked them and us was the mutual endeavour to juxtapose a functionalism that was thought to have become meaningless alongside a new narrative quality of architecture. At the same time as preparations for the exhibition opening and the catalogue were underway, Heinrich Klotz's book *The history of postmodern architecture* presented a wide-ranging exploration of the complex views of

Die Aneignung und das Einrichten des Architekturmuseums prägte ein großer Zauber. All die wunderbaren Zeichnungen, Modelle und Skizzen, die Heinrich Klotz größtenteils von den Entwurfstischen der Architekten für die Sammlung des Architekturmuseums erworben hatte, sollten nun angemessen präsentiert werden. Wir waren begeistert und hoch motiviert. Ungers aber schlug vor, sein Haus doch leer und die Ausstellung an einem anderen Ort stattfinden zu lassen. Niemand wollte sich an diesen Rat halten – wie übrigens auch nicht die Museumsleute der Staatsgalerie Stuttgart, denen der Architekt James Stirling ebensolches angetragen hatte.

Die Eröffnung des Deutschen Architekturmuseums fand am 1. Juni 1984 statt und wurde national und international enthusiastisch begrüßt. Es war die erste Institution in der Reihe von Architekturmuseen mit ähnlichem Anspruch, die folgen sollten. Gefeiert wurde vor allem auch die Kongenialität von Klotz und Ungers, wie folgende amerikanische Rezension verdeutlichen mag:

»Unter den immer wieder faszinierenden Meilensteinen der Architekturgeschichte gibt es jene seltenen Gebäude, bei denen Bauherr und Architekt zu einer solchen Kooperation fanden, dass ein Manifest ihrer je gemeinsamen architektonischen Überzeugungen entstand: Palladios Villa Trissino in Cricoli, Lord Burlingtons Villa in Chiswick oder Gropius' Bauhaus in Dessau. Die im Juni erfolgte Eröffnung von Oswald Mathias Ungers' neuem Gebäude für das Deutsche Architekturmuseum in Frankfurt am Main mit einer ›Die Revision der Moderne. Postmoderne Architektur 1960-1980‹ betitelten Ausstellung unterstrich die Bedeutung des von Ungers und dem Museumsgründer und -direktor Heinrich Klotz gemeinsam unterbreiteten Angebots, ein ebensolches Manifest triumphierender Postmoderne zu bauen. Kaum vorstellbar, dass es für einen Architekten, der mit Hingabe zwei Jahrzehnte verbrachte, um die wahre Natur der Architektur wie ihrer Repräsentation zu erforschen und um mit spitzem Stift einen ganzen Satz entwurflicher Strategien zu Papier zu bringen, eine willkommenere Aufgabe gibt als den Bau eines Architekturmuseums.«[4]

Die Existenz und der Erfolg des Deutschen Architekturmuseums gründeten ganz wesentlich auf dem zupackenden Charisma von Heinrich Klotz. Denn trotz der generellen politischen Entscheidung für diese neuartige Institution, die die Architektur (wieder) in den Rang von Kunst erheben wollte, bedurfte es eines Redekünstlers und Überzeugungstäters von hohem Grad, um zahlreiche Stadtpolitiker, einflussreiche Architekten, Geldgeber, Sponsoren, Banker und Wirtschaftleute zu überzeugen. Heinrich Klotz, durch seine Gremienarbeit in Marburg und im deutschen Denkmalschutz auch politisch und diplomatisch versiert, besaß diese Fähigkeiten. Er ging bei seiner Arbeit an die Grenzen seiner Leistungsfähigkeit, denn in der Gründungsphase des Museums hatte er ja noch seine Professur in Marburg inne.

Die inhaltlichen Positionen der Eröffnungsausstellung waren bereits 1980 im ersten von ihm herausgegebenen *Jahrbuch für Architektur* formuliert: »Neureichen-Barock und Prestige-Design, die sich von keinem Bauhaus-Dogma bändigen ließen, haben sich stets Geltung verschafft. Solange diese als Symptom-

4 Barry Bergdoll, Prototypes and archetypes, in: Architectural Record, August 1984, S. 106.

architecture in the 20th century and of the dialectic between Modernism and Post-Modernism.

The process of making the building into a museum and filling it with life had an extraordinary magic. All the wonderful drawings, models and sketches that Heinrich Klotz had acquired for the museum's collection, largely from the drawing boards of the architects, now had to be presented appropriately. We were fired up and highly motivated. But Ungers suggested leaving his building empty and holding the exhibition in a different place. No-one was willing to follow this suggestion—nor incidentally were the people responsible for the museum at Stuttgart's Staatsgalerie when its architect James Stirling made the same suggestion.

The German Museum of Architecture was inaugurated on 1 June 1984 and was greeted with great enthusiasm both nationally and internationally. It was the first institution in a series of subsequent museums of architecture that shared a similar ambition. One of the main aspects of it to be celebrated was the congenial collaboration of Klotz and Ungers, as the following American review typically illustrates: "Among the perennially fascinating milestones in the history of architecture are those rare buildings, in which patron and architect have collaborated to realize a manifesto of their mutually held architectural convictions: Palladio's Villa Trissino at Cricoli, Lord Burlington's Villa at Chiswick or Gropius's Bauhaus at Dessau. The inauguration in June of Oswald Mathias Ungers's new building for the Deutsches Architekturmuseum (German Museum of Architecture) in Frankfurt with an exhibition entitled 'Revision of the Modern: Postmodern Architecture 1960 - 1980' underscored Ungers's and museum founder and director Heinrich Klotz's joint bid to create just such a manifesto of triumphant Post-Modernism. For an architect who has dedicated two decades to investigating the very nature of architecture and its representation, and to honing a set of design strategies on paper, a more welcome brief than an architectural museum is scarcely imaginable."[4]

The existence and success of the German Museum of Architecture was due to a large degree to Heinrich Klotz's charisma that also exuded an unswerving sense of purpose. Because, despite the general political decision in favour of this new kind of institution that sought to elevate architecture (once more) to the ranks of art, it nevertheless needed a highly gifted orator who also had the courage of his convictions and could win over the numerous city politicians, influential architects, financial backers, sponsors, bankers and business people needed to actually get it off the ground. Heinrich Klotz was well versed in the ways of politics and diplomacy due to his work in committees in Marburg and in conservation of historic monuments in Germany, and he possessed these skills. He pushed himself to his absolute limits, particularly during the phase in which the museum was being set up when he still held the chair of architecture in Marburg.

The positions adopted in the opening exhibition had already been formulated in 1980 in the first *Jahrbuch für Architektur* edited by Klotz: "Nouveau-riche Baroque and prestige design, which do not allow themselves to be restrained by any Bauhaus

4 Barry Bergdoll, Prototypes and archetypes, in: Architectural Record, August 1984, p. 106.

Formen gesehen werden, die einen Mangel anzeigen, haben sie ihre Signifikanz. Sobald man sie jedoch wörtlich nimmt und sanktioniert, sind Surrogate zur Wahrheit geworden, zum adäquaten Mittel einer x-beliebigen Bedürfniserfüllung eines Bonbon-Bewusstseins oder einer Expander-Mentalität, nicht aber verbindliche Sprache. Warum also auf solche Irrtümer noch einschlagen?! Zwischen den Florida Hotels eines Morris Lapidus und den Bauten eines Robert Venturi besteht ein Unterschied. Blind ist die Kritik, die Lapidus schlägt und Venturi meint. Blind die Kritik, die den Eklektizismus geißelt und Ungers oder Rossi treffen will. Unfähigkeit zur Dialektik, Unfähigkeit zur Transformation kennzeichnen die Nostalgie und trennen diese von Architekten wie Venturi und Ungers. Das entscheidende Kriterium, Architektur von nostalgischer Ausstaffierung und geschmäcklerischer Bedürfnisbefriedigung zu unterscheiden, ist die Umdeutung des Vorgegebenen.«[5] Und nach einer Kritik des von Charles Jencks eingeführten Begriffs der »Postmoderne«, den Klotz dafür verantwortlich machte, dass Eklektizismus und Kitsch mit eben jener Umdeutung des Vorgegebenen unzulässig vermischt werden, zieht er den Schluss: »Und so wird am Ende das Las Vegas, das Venturi zum Studium empfahl, zu genau der Architektur, die Venturi angeblich auch baut. Und so wird die Geschichte, die Ungers als vorgegeben zum Ausgang nimmt, genau die Geschichte, die Ungers angeblich wiederholt. Alles Eklektiker, historische Formalisten! – so hört man die freiheitsbewussten und Technologie-Modernisten sagen, die sich allein an ihrem Genie orientieren und der Architektur zur Formenblähung verhelfen, damit überhaupt noch etwas aus dem modernistischen Darm, aus dem inhärenten Formenpotential hervordunsten mag.«[6]

Diese Sätze zeigen, wie sehr der Historiker auch zum Kämpfer geworden war. Sahen sich die Fachkollegen durch sie herausgefordert, wenn nicht angegriffen, reagierten an zeitgenössischer Architektur interessierte Menschen überwiegend positiv. Jene »Revision der Moderne«, deren Kraft gegenüber der matten Perpetuierung funktionalistischer Vor- und Nachkriegsarchitektur Heinrich Klotz nicht müde wurde zu reklamieren, hat dann insgesamt seine Arbeit am Deutschen Architekturmuseum geprägt. Die wirkungsmächtige Begeisterungsfähigkeit, die sich in eins wusste mit tatsächlichen Vorgängen, gab seinen Äußerungen und Arbeitsstrategien ihre Evidenz. Klotz hat die erwähnten Architekten über die Grenzen Deutschlands hinaus aktiv gefördert, nicht zuletzt durch entsprechende Voten in Architekturwettbewerben, an denen sie teilnahmen. Unvergessen auch die von ihm frei extemporierten Ausstellungseröffnungen im Architekturmuseum. Heinrich Klotz wusste das Wirken zeitgenössischer Architekten mit einer solch mitreißenden Kraft in eine historische und gesellschaftliche Perspektive zu stellen, dass die anwesenden Baumeister – ob Aldo Rossi oder Helmut Jahn, Charles Moore oder Rem Koolhaas, Frei Otto oder O.M. Ungers – sich emporgehoben und verstanden fühlten. Und das allgemeine Publikum vor allem verstand es auch.

5 Heinrich Klotz, Post-Moderne?, in: Jahrbuch für Architektur. Neues Bauen 1980/1981, a.a.O., S. 7.

6 Ebd., S. 8.

dogma, have always been able to achieve recognition. These approaches will retain their significance as long as they are seen as symptomatic forms that are indicative of a deficiency. But as soon as we take them literally and sanction them, they become a mere surrogate for the truth, an adequate means to fulfil any need you care to mention that is fed by a candy consciousness or iron-pumping mentality, but not a genuine universal language. So why should we even pay attention to errors of this kind?! Because there is a difference between the Florida hotels of Morris Lapidus and the buildings of Robert Venturi. The criticism that hits out at Lapidus when it actually means Venturi is blind. The criticism that slates eclecticism when its intention is to get at Ungers or Rossi is blind. The incapability to engage in dialectics, the incapacity to bring about transformation, is what characterises nostalgia and what separates architects such as Venturi and Ungers from any hint of nostalgia. The decisive criterion by which to distinguish true architecture from an approach that merely panders to taste and dresses up a building in nostalgic garb is whether it reinterprets what pre-exists."[5] And after a critique of the term "Post-Modernism" introduced by Charles Jencks, which Klotz held responsible for the fact that eclecticism and kitsch had become inadmissibly mixed up with that very reinterpretation of what pre-exists, he draws the conclusion: "And so, in the end, the Las Vegas Venturi recommends we study becomes precisely the architecture that Venturi allegedly builds. And so the history that Ungers takes as his pre-existing starting point becomes precisely the history that Ungers allegedly repeats. Eclectics all of them, historical formalists!—you hear the freedom-conscious and technology-centred Modernists exclaim, who base their work on nothing but their own genius and help architecture achieve a formal flatulence, without which nothing at all could still be emitted from the Modernistic intestines, from the inherent formal potential."[6]

These quotations show to what extent the historian had also become a fighter. While his colleagues in the profession felt themselves, if not exactly attacked, at the very least challenged, people interested in contemporary architecture reacted in the main positively. Heinrich Klotz tirelessly averred the power of "Revision of the Modern" to confront the jaded perpetuation of functionalistic pre- and post-war architecture and it characterised his entire work on the German Museum of Architecture. His ability to inspire enthusiasm to such effect—which was totally at one with actual events-made whatever he said, all his work strategies, totally convincing. Klotz actively promoted the architects mentioned beyond the borders of Germany, also by voting for them in the architectural competitions they took part in, and the impromptu speeches he made at exhibition openings in the Museum of Architecture will never be forgotten. Heinrich Klotz knew how to place the work of contemporary architects in a historical and social perspective with an energy that was so irresistibly infectious that the architects present—Aldo Rossi or Helmut Jahn, Charles Moore or Rem Koolhaas, Frei Otto or O. M. Ungers—felt singled out and understood. And above all the general public also understood.

5 Heinrich Klotz, Post-Moderne?, in: Jahrbuch für Architektur. Neues Bauen 1980/1981, Wiesbaden 1980, p. 7.

6 Ibid., p. 8

OSWALD MATHIAS UNGERS

WIR STEHEN AM ANFANG

WE ARE AT THE BEGINNING

Vor einiger Zeit, als Vittorio Gregotti noch Herausgeber von *Casabella* war, bat er mich um meine Ansicht zur Identität der europäischen Architektur. Die Frage war: Ist die europäische Architektur in einer Krise? Meine Antwort ist der Versuch einer Analyse des Autonomiegedankens in der Architektur.

Some time ago, when he was the editor of *Casabella*, Vittorio Gregotti asked me what I thought about the identity of European architecture. The question was: is European architecture in a crisis? This attempt to analyse the idea of autonomy in architecture is my response.

ÜBER DIE SITUATION DER ARCHITEKTUR HEUTE

Wie soll man auf die Frage nach der Identität der europäischen Architektur antworten? Natürlich gibt es eine Architektur, die an Ort und Zeit – den Zeitgeist –, die Tradition, an Zwecke, Nutzen und auch an das Nationalgefühl, die politische Macht und nicht zuletzt an ökonomische Bedingungen gebunden ist. Aber ist sie davon abhängig? Lässt sie sich ohne weiteres mit einer dieser Voraussetzungen rechtfertigen?

Man fragt sich: Europäische Architektur – was soll das sein? Ein Stil, ein Programm, eine Bewegung – womöglich eine Weltanschauung? Und dann gegen wen und für was? Die kontinentale Aufteilung der Kompetenzen in Nord und Süd, in Ost und West, europäisch gegen amerikanisch und den Rest der Welt. Das Programm einer regional begrenzten Architektur ist nicht mehr brauchbar in einer globalen Welt, in der Informationen mit Lichtgeschwindigkeit den Erdball umkreisen, in der Distanzen auf Nulldimensionen schrumpfen und in der Geschwindigkeit Identitätsansätze in Momentaufnahmen auflöst. Wie – so muss man sich heute fragen – wollen wir in dieser Welt bauen? Sollen es Zelte oder Häuser sein? Wollen wir als vagabundierende Nomaden leben, ständig herumfahren oder als Sesshafte an einem Ort bleiben, wollen wir Sauleber und Käse statt Griessuppe und Körner essen?

Es wird sich bald zeigen, ob aus dem kultivierten neolithischen Zustand der Architektur wieder der Rückfall in ein paläolithisches Nomadenleben heraufzieht und am Ende die in *Escape from New York* vorgezeichnete Horrorvision doch noch zur erschreckenden Wirklichkeit wird. Sollte uns das neue Jahrhundert aus der urbanen Sesshaftigkeit in ein archaisches Nomadisieren entlassen? Viele Anzeichen sprechen dafür, dass Begegnungen nicht mehr an Orten, sondern in Stationen, Flughäfen, Schnellbahnhöfen, Raststätten, Einkaufs- und sonstigen Zentren stattfinden.

Wir sind dabei, wie Jean Baudrillard meint, uns selbst zu überholen. Das heißt aber auch, dass wir aus der Architektur entlassen werden. Die vier Wände, die der Sesshafte braucht, um sesshaft zu sein, lösen sich immer mehr auf. Die Löcher in den Wänden vermehren sich. Es werden ständig neue Durchbrüche geschlagen, um Telefone, Televisionen, Telefaxe, Modems und das Internet einzulassen. Ein gigantischer kybernetischer Sturm trägt die Dächer ab und fegt die Wände hinweg. Dem Privaten wird allmählich der Garaus gemacht. In einem apokalyptischen Wirbel wird alles zu Staub zermahlen. Die objektive physikalische Welt zerfällt zu Partikeln, die Lebewesen darin zu Genen, unser Denken zerfällt zu Informationsbits und unsere Entscheidungen zu Dezidemen. Die Kultur, ein Staubhaufen des Kulturbetriebs. Das Gesetz der Entropie macht sich breit. Es gibt keinen Zweifel: Wir sind dabei, uns auf und davon zu machen (Vilém Flusser). Von der Erde zum

ON THE SITUATION OF ARCHITECTURE TODAY

How to go about answering the question of the identity of European architecture? Of course, there is a kind of architecture that is bound to time and place—to the *zeitgeist*—to tradition, to particular functions, uses and also to national identity, political power and, last but not least, economic conditions. But is it dependent on these factors? Can it be justified by just one of these preconditions?

The question is: European architecture—waht do we think it should be? A style, a programme, a movement, maybe even an entire worldview? And if that is true, against whom and for what? Responsibilities have been carved up across continents into North and South, East and West, European versus American and the rest of the world. The programme of a regionally limited architecture does not work in a globalised world in which information circumnavigates the earth at the speed of light, in which distances shrink to nothing and attempts to grasp at identity are dissolved by speed into mere snapshots of the moment. The question we have to ask today is how do we want to build in this world and what do we want to build? Tents or houses? Do we want to live as nomads, always on the move, or remain settled in one place? Do we want to eat pig's liver and cheese instead of grains and gruel?

We will soon see whether the cultivated neolythic state of architecture is drawing to a close and is about to give way to a relapse into a Palaeolithic nomadic life; we will soon see whether in the end the horror vision painted in *Escape from New York* is about to become terrifying reality after all. Is the new century going to release us from our settled urban existence into an archaic nomadic life? There are many indications suggesting that encounters no longer happen in real places but at railway stations, airports, bus stations, motorway service stations, shopping centres and other centres.

Baudrillard believes we are in the process of superseding ourselves. However, that would also mean that we are being released from architecture. The four walls which we need for a settled way of life are dissolving more and more. The holes in the walls are multiplying. We are constantly hammering new holes in our walls to let in telephones, televisions, fax machines, modems and the Internet. A gigantic cybernetic storm is ripping off the roofs and blowing down the walls. The private realm is gradually being routed. Everything is being reduced to dust in an apocalyptic whirlwind. The objective physical world is disintegrating into particles, the creatures in it into genes, our thoughts are being broken down into nothing more than information bytes and our decisions into OR gates. Culture is nothing but a pile of dust created by the culture industry. The laws of entropy are gaining ground. There is no doubt about it, we are in the process of getting up and going

Mond und dann zum Mars und wer weiß wo sonst noch hin.

Nachdem wir durch kalkulatorische Zerlegung, Zergliederung, Zersetzung, Zerfaserung und Zerstückelung alles verwüstet haben, wollen wir es zur Kompensation wieder zusammenbringen und vernetzen. Auflösung, Transparenz, Chaos und ständiger Wechsel als immanenter Prozess verhindern jedoch jeden Ansatz einer geschichtlichen Kontinuität. Wie aber soll es Identität geben, wenn es keine Geschichte gibt?

Architektur ist nicht für Nomaden gemacht Sie ist für die Sesshaften, für die Bleibenden und nicht für die Fahrenden. Sie ist gemacht für die Körnerfresser und nicht für die Milkshake-Fans, die Hip-Hop-Generation, die im Netz von einem Event zum anderen zappt. Wenn tatsächlich die Identität der Architektur im Begriff ist, sich aufzulösen, wie soll dann noch von einer Architektursprache, einer historischen Entwicklung, einer Bewusstseinsbildung die Rede sein? Die griffigen Formeln von Transparenz, Dekonstruktion, Simultaneität, von der direkten allzeitigen Verfügbarkeit aller Mittel und Bilder sind Strategien, die darauf abzielen, den Identitätsbegriff zu vernichten und durch Beliebigkeitsformeln zu ersetzen.

Neben den Visionisten beherrscht eine andere Gruppe die Szene: das Bricollage, die Bastler sind heute gefragte Leute. Sie sammeln zusammen, was ihnen opportun erscheint. Sie suchen nicht nach Strukturen, sondern nach dem, was gerade brauchbar ist. »Man könnte versucht sein zu sagen, der Ingenieur befrage das Universum, während der Bastler sich an eine Sammlung von Überbleibseln menschlicher Produkte richte, d.h. an eine Untergruppe der Kultur«, schreibt Lévi-Strauss. Mit anderen Worten: Der erste handelt mit Hilfe von Begriffen, letzterer mit Allegorien.

Die Metaphorik ist ein gewagtes Spiel und endet all zu oft in Ereignisparks und in Disneyland. Man denkt unwillkürlich an Charles Dickens Roman *Great Expectations* und an die – wie uns Lévi-Strauss erzählt – durch Beobachtung inspirierte Architektur des Vorstadtschlosses von Mr. Wemmick mit seiner Miniatur-Zugbrücke, seiner Kanone, die neun Uhr ankündigt, und seinem Salat- und Gurkenbeet, dank dessen die Verteidiger eine Belagerung aushalten könnten, wenn es nötig wäre ... Manch einer hat sich hinter Bildern verschanzt und glaubt, aushalten zu können mit seinem Salatbeet.

Die Frage, die sich heute stellt, ist: Hat Architektur überhaupt noch eine Bedeutung zwischen Visionismus auf der einen und dem Bricollage auf der anderen Seite? Ist sie zu einem Medium avantgardistischer Spekulationen mutiert, oder ist sie nur noch Mittel der Selbstdarstellung? Gibt es nicht trotz aller zerknäulten Exzesse doch noch Konstanten, die im Laufe der Geschichte unverändert geblieben sind?

Euphemistisch gesehen ist natürlich alles möglich in einer Welt, in der Werte konsumiert werden wie Produkte, die sich nach Angebot und Nachfrage richtet, in der sogar Städte nicht mehr nach einem Identitätsprinzip, einem Leitbild, sondern nach Opportunitäten gemacht werden, in denen das Einheitsprinzip dominiert und nicht die Vielfältigkeit der Widersprüche. Zufälligkeit, Austauschbarkeit, Beliebigkeit, nicht Struktur, Konzept und Kontinuität sind die Ressourcen, aus denen

(Vilém Flusser): from the earth to the moon and then Mars and who knows where else.

When, through our calculating dissection, dismantling, dismembering and analysis, we have wrought wholesale devastation, we shall no doubt try and compensate by linking everything up again, bringing it all together once more. However, dissolution, transparency, chaos and permanent change as an immanent process hinder any attempt at historical continuity. How can we have identity without history?

Architecture is not intended for nomads. It is for people leading a settled existence, for those who stay around not for those always on the move. It is intended for the muesli eaters and not for the milk shake fans, the hip-hop generation who zap around on the Net from one event to the next. If the identity of architecture truly is in the process of disintegrating, how can we possibly continue to speak of an architectural language, historical development, a formation of consciousness? The buzzwords transparency, deconstruction, simultaneity, the direct, constant availability of all media and images are pithy, but they are all strategies that aim at destroying the concept of identity and replacing it with a philosophy of anything goes.

Apart from the visionists, another group also dominates the scene: the bricoleurs, the DIY folk are very sought after today. They assemble whatever seems opportune. They do not look for structures but merely for what is useful at a particular moment. To quote Lévi-Strauss: "It might be said that the engineer questions the universe, while the bricoleur addresses himself to a collection of oddments left over from human endeavours, that is only a sub-set of the culture." In other words: the former deals in concepts, the latter in allegories.

The use of metaphor is a risky game and ends up all too often in theme parks and Disneyland. Charles Dickens's novel *Great Expectations* comes to mind, as does—recounted by Lévi-Strauss—the architecture of Mr. Wemmick's little suburban castle, inspired by observation, with its miniature drawbridge, its canon that signals 9 o'clock every evening and his lettuce and cucumber patch that would enable the defenders to sit out a siege if necessary. A number of people have barricaded themselves in behind images and believed they would be able to hold out with their lettuce patch.

The question that is raised today is whether architecture still has any meaning, caught as it is between visionism on the one hand and bricolage on the other? Has it mutated into a medium of pseudo-avant-garde speculations, or is it nothing more than a vehicle for self-representation? Are there not, despite all the tangled convoluted excesses, still constants that have remained unchanged throughout the course of history?

Seen euphemistically, everything is, of course, possible in a world in which values are consumed like products, which is based on supply and demand, and in which cities are no longer created on the principle of an identity, a paradigm, but are based on opportunism, in which, instead of the diversity of contradictions, the principle of uniformity dominates. Instead of structure, concept and continuity, randomness,

die Dinge, die Objekte, die aktuelle Architektur gebastelt werden. Wir erleben eine Zeit, in der die ehemals spezifischen Orte vertauscht und rücksichtslos überall benutzt und eingesetzt werden. Dabei verliert der reale Ort seine Gültigkeit genauso wie seine Identität. Kuala Lumpur ist überall – in London, New York, Paris, Lille, Setschuan – und warum nicht auch in Berlin. Sieht so die Demokratisierung der Architektur aus, die manche angeblich reinen Herzens forderten? Weltweit verbreitete Horrorvisionen? Blondel meinte, »dass Gott, um sein Volk zu bestrafen, ihm drohte, es seiner Architekten zu berauben.« – Mir scheint, der Zeitpunkt, dass sich die Prophezeiung erfüllt, ist nahe.

ÜBER DIE RATIO DER ARCHITEKTUR

In seinen ästhetischen Studien schreibt Wittgenstein: »Architektur verewigt und verherrlicht etwas. Darum kann es Architektur nicht geben, wo nichts zu verherrlichen ist.« Dieser Satz ist in meinen Augen die Grundthese für eine autonome Architektur. Die Architektur – so interpretiere ich Wittgenstein – hat ihre eigene Logik, ihre eigene Identität. Sie wird beherrscht von einer Gesetzlichkeit, die unabhängig von anderen Einflüssen existiert. »Sie verewigt und verherrlicht etwas.« Das meint: Sie ist von Dauer und nicht vergänglich. Sie ist nicht für den Alltag. Sie ist nicht Handwerk, sondern Kunst. Auch Aldo Rossi war der Auffassung, dass es heute noch die Aufgabe des Architekten sei, »Monumente« zu errichten. Er sagt: »Während Architekten jederzeit bereit sind, sich selbst, ihren Tätigkeitsbereich in Frage zu stellen, neigen sie zugleich dazu, die Grundvoraussetzung aller Gestaltung zu vergessen, die lautet: dass es immer etwas geben muss, auf das Architektur sich bezieht.«

Es geht im Wesentlichen um die Idee, um die Ratio der Architektur, um die Architektur an sich, um die elementaren Werte. Architektur bedarf keiner fremden Einflüsse und Anstöße, sie ist nicht nachrangige Funktion von etwas, sondern erfüllt sich in sich selbst als unabhängiges und ungebundenes Konzept. Architektur ist ein Kulturgut, das alle angeht und nicht nur die Eigenartigkeiten einzelner Gruppen, Religionen oder mystischer Vereinigungen. Der Geist der Architektur weht überall und entfaltet sich, wo er will. In Anlehnung an Ed Reinhard sage ich, seinen Satz »Kunst ist Kunst und alles andere ist alles andere« abwandelnd: »Architektur ist Architektur und alles andere ist alles andere!« Ich will damit sagen: Die Architektur als eine Identität, eine sich gleichbleibende Aussage, wechselt nicht mit den Zeitzonen und Nationalitäten, sie ist kein Sozialprodukt, noch hängt sie ab von zufälligen Launen und lustigen Events. Sie hat eine Beständigkeit, die sich in ihren Grundmodulen zyklisch wiederholt und nichts anderem verpflichtet ist als dem Denkvermögen des menschlichen Geistes.

In Sempers Buch *Der Stil der technischen und tektonischen Künste* fand ich einen Text über die Zeitlosigkeit der Architektur. Semper schreibt: »So, wie die Natur bei ihrer unendlichen Fülle doch in ihren Motiven höchst sparsam ist; wie sich eine stetige Wiederholung in ihren Grundformen zeigt, wie aber diese nach ihren verschiedenen Daseinsbedingungen tausendfach modifiziert, in Teilen verkürzt oder verlängert, in Teilen ausge-

interchangeability, anything goes are the resources from which things, objects, contemporary architecture are put together. We are living through a time in which what were once specific places are now swapped at will and used everywhere without a thought. Through this the authentic place loses all validity along with its identity. Kuala Lumpur is everywhere—in London, New York, Paris, Lille, and Szechwan—and, why not in Berlin too? Is this what the democratisation of architecture looks like, which some people allegedly called for with absolute sincerity? Horror visions throughout the world? Blondel said: "[...] that God, in order to punish his people, threatened to deprive them of their architects."—It seems to me the time when this prophecy will be fulfilled is nigh.

ON THE RATIONALE OF ARCHITECTURE

In his aesthetic studies, Wittgenstein writes: "Architecture immortalizes and glorifies something: hence where there is nothing to glorify there can be no architecture." This statement is in my eyes the basic prerequisite for autonomous architecture. Thus architecture—as I interpret Wittgenstein—has its own logic, its own identity. It is governed by inherent laws that exist independently of other influences. "It immortalizes and glorifies something." That means it is long-lasting, not transitory. It is not for everyday use. It is not a craft but an art form. Aldo Rossi also believed that the remit of architects today was still to erect "monumenti." He says: "While architects are always prepared to question themselves and their field of work, at the same time they tend to forget the basic prerequisite for all design, namely that there must always be something to which architecture relates."

What we are talking about here is the idea, the rationale of architecture, architecture per se, elemental values. Architecture has no need of outside influences and stimuli; it is not a subordinate function of something else, but rather finds fulfilment in and of itself as an independent and free concept. Architecture is a cultural asset that affects everything and not only the peculiarities of individual groups, religions or mystic associations. The spirit of architecture blows and acts wherever it pleases.

Adapting Ed Reinhard's slogan "Art is art and everything else is everything else," I would maintain: "Architecture is architecture and everything else is everything else!" What I mean by that is that architecture as an identity, an unchanging statement, does not vary from one time zone to another, one nationality to another; it is not a social product, nor does it depend on random moods and amusing events. It has a constancy, the basic modules of which repeat themselves in a cycle and are committed to nothing other than the intellectual capacity of the human mind.

In Semper's book *Style in the technical and tectonic arts* I came across a passage about the timelessness of architecture. He writes: "Just as nature with her infinite abundance is very sparse in her motives, repeating continually the same basic forms by modifying them a thousandfold according to the formative stage reached by living beings and their

bildet, in anderen nur angedeutet erscheinen; wie die Natur ihre Entwicklungsgeschichte hat, innerhalb welcher die alten Motive bei jeder Neugestaltung wieder durchblicken, ebenso liegen auch der Kunst nur wenige Normalformen und Typen unter, die aus urältester Tradition stammend in stetem Hervortreten dennoch eine unendliche Mannigfaltigkeit darbieten, und gleich jenen Naturtypen ihre Geschichte haben.« Anknüpfend an diesen Text behaupte ich, es gibt in der Architektur zwei Grundmodule, die immer wieder in unendlich vielen und andersartigen Variationen durchdekliniert wurden. Die beiden Grundmodule in ihrer höchsten Vollendung sind der Parthenon und das Pantheon. Zwischen diesen beiden Polen – Parthenon und Pantheon, Arche und Lade, Höhle und Zelt, Gestell und Masse – pendelt die Aussage der Architektur als intellektuelles Konzept. Das eine entsteht durch Induktion, das andere durch Deduktion. Das Hinzufügen und Zusammenstellen, das komponentenhafte Denken beim Parthenon steht dem Wegnehmen, dem Abtragen, dem Aushöhlen, dem deduktiven und ganzheitlichen Denken beim Pantheon gegenüber.

Ich wage zu behaupten, dass die Grundkonzepte der Architektur sich im Wesentlichen gleich geblieben sind. Ihre Grundmodule haben sich nicht verändert. Die Geometrie, die sie verbindet, die Denkkonzepte, die ihnen zugrunde liegen, sind identisch über Grenzen, Kontinente und Zeiträume hinweg. Sie gehören zur Architektur wie Arme und Beine, Kopf und Leib zum Körper.

Wenn die Frage nach der Identität der Architektur gestellt wird, dann gibt es dazu eine Geschichte aus dem Alten Testament, die ich hier einfüge: »Gott segnete Noah und befahl ihm und seinen drei Söhnen ›Seid fruchtbar und mehret euch und erfüllet die Erde.‹« (1. Mose 9, Vers 1) Das taten sie und bauten den Turm zu Babel. Dann aber sagte Gott: »›Lasst uns hernieder fahren und dort ihre Sprache verwirren, dass keiner des anderen Sprache verstehe.‹ So zerstreute sie der Herr in alle Länder, dass sie aufhören mussten, die Stadt zu bauen.« (1. Mose 11, Vers 7 + 8) Die Verwirrung der Sprache, die Eigenartigkeit, hatte den Bau gestoppt. Die Sprachverwirrung war die Ursache für das Scheitern des Projekts und die Zerstreuung die Folge. Einer verstand den anderen nicht mehr. Die Identität war verloren gegangen. Stellt man jedoch statt der Verse 7 und 8 des ersten Buches Mose 11 den vierten Vers der biblischen Erzählung in den Vordergrund, wie es der jüdische Gelehrte und Rabbiner Benno Jacob getan hat, dann liest sich die Geschichte ganz anders. Im vierten Vers heißt es: »Lasst uns eine Stadt und einen Turm bauen [...], denn wir werden sonst zerstreut in alle Länder.« Die Angst vor der Zerstreuung scheint das Motiv gewesen zu sein, Stadt und Turm zu bauen. Der Turm drückte nicht die Hybris der Menschen aus, sondern ihren Wunsch nach Identität. Der Turmbau zu Babel war nicht nur der Ursprung für eine gemeinsame Sprache, für den Urgrund des Denkens und Handelns, sondern auch für die Unmöglichkeit, die Grundmuster zu verlassen und Gott zu »dekonstruieren«. Gott wollte nicht ein Zentrum, sondern die ganze Welt. Er wollte nicht eine Einheit ohne Differenzierung und ohne Unterschiede, sondern die Vielheit des Unvollendeten. Deshalb hat er sein Volk in die Welt geschickt.

different conditions of existence, shortening some parts and lengthening others, developing parts which are only alluded to in others, just as nature has her history of development within which old motives are discernible in every new formation—in the same way art is also based on a few standard forms and types that stem from the most ancient traditions and that always reappear yet offer an infinite variety and like nature's types have their history." Following on from this text, I believe there are two basic modules in architecture, which are played out again and again in an infinite number of variations. These two basic modules in their highest state of perfection are the Parthenon and the Pantheon. Architecture's message swings as an intellectual concept between these two poles —Parthenon and Pantheon—ark and covenant, cave and tent, frame and mass. One is created through induction, the other through deduction. The process of adding things and assembling them—the component-based thinking behind the Parthenon—is in contrast to the process of dismantling and eroding—the deductive and integrative thinking behind the Pantheon.

I would even go so far as to claim that the basic concepts of architecture have remained essentially the same. Their basic modules have not changed. The geometry that links them, the intellectual concepts they are based on, are identical across national borders, continents and time frames. They belong to architecture as arms and legs, head and torso, belong to the body.

If the question of the identity of architecture is raised, there is an Old Testament story, which I shall quote here: "God blessed Noah and his three sons and said to them 'Be fruitful and multiply and fill the earth.'" (Genesis 9:1) They did that and built the Tower of Babel. But then God said: "'Come, let us go down and confuse their language there, so that they may not understand one another's speech'. So the Lord scattered them abroad from there over the face of all the earth, and they left off building the city." (Genesis 11:7-8) It was the confusion of language, individuality that stopped the building. The confusion of language was the reason the project failed and the scattering the consequence. People no longer understood each other. Identity had been lost. If, instead of verses 7-8, we focus on the fourth verse of Chapter 11, as the Jewish bible commentator and rabbi Benno Jacob did, the story reads very differently. The fourth verse says: "Come, let us build ourselves a city, and a tower [...], lest we be scattered abroad upon the face of the whole earth." The fear of being scattered seems to be the motive for building the city and the tower. The tower did not express the hubris of humankind but rather their desire for identity. The Tower of Babel was not only the origin of a common language, of the prime source of thought and action, but also of the impossibility of abandoning the basic exemplar and "deconstructing" God. God did not want a centre, but the whole world. He did not want a single unity without differentiation or variation, but the plurality of the unfinished. That is why He sent His people into the world.

In his *Reflections on World History*, Jacob Burckhardt writes: "Nothing leads so clearly as architecture to the awareness that

In den *Weltgeschichtlichen Betrachtungen* schreibt Jacob Burckhardt: »Nichts führt so deutlich wie die Architektur zum Bewusstsein, dass die Kunst eine eigene Welt neben der Welt der ›Wirklichkeit‹, aufzubauen vermag, mit Mitteln, die geistig sind.«

ÜBER DAS WESEN DER ARCHITEKTUR

In Verbindung mit dem Begriff der Identität ist gleichzeitig auch die Frage nach dem Wesen der Architektur an sich zu sehen. Nicht das Verhalten des einzelnen, der jeweilige Ausdruck, beschäftigte die Philosophen der Milesischen Schule. Die antiken Systeme fragten danach, was die Dinge ihrem Wesen nach sind, und nicht nach den abgeleiteten Erfahrungen. Ihre Antwort lautete: Die Dinge sind ihrem Wesen nach Ausdruck von Ordnung und Form. Zur Erläuterung dieser Frage übernehme ich aus dem Essay *Bezugssysteme* von Gottfried Benn einen kurzen Abschnitt über das Wesen der Dinge: »Ein Töpfer ist dabei, Ton zu kneten. Frage: Was für ein Ding macht er da? Eine Teekanne. Was ist eine Teekanne? Ein Gefäß mit einer Schnauze, um Tee hindurchzugießen, mit einem Deckel, um ihn warm zu halten, und einem Henkel, um die Kanne anfassen zu können. In diesem Fall begriff man das Wesen des Gegenstandes im Hinblick auf seinen Zweck, der ihm sein charakteristisches Gepräge gibt. Das Material spielt dabei keine Rolle: Man kann die Teekanne aus Ton, Silber oder sonst einem festen Stoff machen [...]. Das Wesen aber, das wirkliche Sein, die Substanz des Gegenstandes ist seine Form.«

Man stelle sich nur vor, die Welt sei – sofern sie planvoll geschaffen ist – nach Art der Teekanne geschaffen. Der Stoff wird dann um der Form willen da sein, die verwirklicht werden soll. Das Wesen alles Lebendigen wird in der vollendeten Form bestehen, in die es hineinwächst. Hieraus könnte man mit Benn schließen, dass die physikalischen Phänomene ästhetischen Charakters sind. Auf die Architektur übertragen heißt das: Die reine Form ist die Grundbedingung der Architektur. Ihre Dimension ist von ausschließlich ästhetisch-formalem Charakter. Das Wesen der Architektur ist demnach als ein strukturelles Konzept zu sehen und nicht als ein materielles. Es ist als ein Konzept zu verstehen, das den Regeln und Ordnungssystemen der Geometrie entspricht. Dieses Konzept ist ungebunden und richtet sich ausschließlich nach Gesetzmäßigkeiten von Maß, Zahl und Proportion. Es existiert über den Zeiten und Orten als eine Sprache mit eigener formal-ästhetischer Logik.

»Aus dem Widerspiel der Verhältnisse von Maßen und Zahlen bildet sich das Gerüst der abstrakten Sprache der Kunst; das gilt von Tönen, Farben, Bewegungen und Formen. Am deutlichsten aber tritt es hervor bei der Kunst, deren Ziel raumbildende Formung ist: der Architektur«, schreibt Fritz Schumacher in seinem *Lesebuch für Architekten*. In *Eupalinos oder der Architekt*, einem Text, den Valéry für Corbusier schrieb und den Rilke übersetzte, sagt Sokrates in einem fingierten Gespräch zu Phaidros: »Er sagte diesem unförmigen Haufen von Steinen und Balken, die um ihn herumlagen, ihre gestaltete Zukunft voraus. Er gab Ihnen nur Befehle und Zahlen.«

Als Mies van der Rohe bei der spektakulären Errichtung des

art has the capacity to construct a world of its own, alongside the world of 'reality' and it does that it by means that are of the mind."

ON THE NATURE OF ARCHITECTURE

In connection with the concept of identity, we must look at the question of the nature of architecture per se. It was not the behaviour of the individual, not the individual expression, that concerned the philosophers of the Milesian School. The systems of the Antiquity asked what the nature of things was, not what we deduced them to be on the basis of experience. Their answer was: things are by their nature the expression of order and form. To explain this question, I shall look at a short passage from Gottfried Benn's essay *Bezugssysteme*, on the nature of things: "A potter is kneading clay. Question: What sort of thing is he making there? A teapot. What is a teapot? A vessel with a spout through which to pour tea, with a lid to keep the tea warm and a handle to hold the pot by. In this case the nature of the object was understood by its purpose, which in turn gives it its characteristic appearance. The material is of no importance here: the teapot can be made of clay, silver or any other solid material [...] The nature of the object, its true being, its substance, is its form."

Let us imagine that the world—assuming it was created according to a plan—is made in the same way as the teapot. The material is then present for the sake of the form that is to be created. The nature of all living things will consist of the completed form into which they grow. From this we could conclude with Benn that physical phenomena are aesthetic in character. Applied to architecture that means: pure form is the basic condition for architecture. Its dimension is exclusively aesthetic and formal in character. The nature of architecture must thus be seen as a structural concept and not a material one. It must be seen as a concept that corresponds to the rules and ordering systems of geometry. This concept is independent and based exclusively on the laws of measure, number, and proportion. It exists beyond time and place as a language with its own formal-aesthetic logic.

"Out of the interaction of the relationships between measure and numbers the basic framework of the abstract language of art is formed: that applies to tones, colours, movement and form. But it emerges most clearly in the art which has as its goal to create form in a way that creates space: architecture," writes Fritz Schumacher in his compendium on architecture *Lesebuch für Architekten*. In *Eupalinos, or the Architect*, a text which Valéry wrote for Corbusier, Socrates says in a conversation with the fictitious Phaedrus: "He foretold their monumental future to the shapeless heaps of stones and beams that lay around us; [...] He gave them nothing but commands and figures."

When Mies van der Rohe held a short speech in the customary fashion during the spectacular erection of the roof of the New National Gallery in Berlin 1968, he said: "I like to keep things simple. Just consider this: a simple person is not a simpleton. I love simplicity, probably because I love clarity, not

Daches der Neuen Nationalgalerie in Berlin 1968 eine wie üblich kurze Rede hielt, sagte er: »Ich möchte die Dinge einfach haben. Bedenken Sie: Ein einfacher Mensch ist kein Einfaltspinsel. Ich liebe Einfachheit, wahrscheinlich weil ich Klarheit liebe, nicht weil es billig ist oder dergleichen. Wir denken nie daran, Kosten zu reduzieren, wenn wir arbeiten. Natürlich wollen wir neue Möglichkeiten finden, und ich suche nach ihnen. Aber wenn es nicht wirklich einen neuen Weg zu geben scheint, haben wir keine Angst, bei dem alten zu bleiben, d.h. bei dem, was wir vorher gemacht haben. Sehen Sie, ich entwerfe nicht jedes Gebäude anders. Überhaupt, wir suchen nicht nach neuen Effekten.« »Architektur«, sagt er, »ist kein Cocktail.« Von diesem Standpunkt aus betrachtet ist der Avantgardismus überholt. Denn wenn es Gesetzmäßigkeiten gibt, die unverändert fortbestehen, ist es müßig, nach ständig neuen, noch nie da gewesenen spektakulären Lösungen und Konzepten zu suchen.

Den zum Teil hilflosen Bestrebungen nach Neuem, noch nie Dagewesenem haftet zweifellos eine Infantilität an, die zwar kurzfristig Blendwerk zu erzeugen in der Lage ist, die allgemeine Problematik und die Kultur der Architektur aber unberührt lässt. Natürlich sind Bravourstücke wie Verknautschungen, Zerfaserungen und Zersplitterungen von höchster Attraktivität und breiten sich, wie man sehen kann, überall inflationär aus. Die Blob-Architektur ist angesagt. In Wirklichkeit aber ist zu befürchten, dass es sich um Tageserscheinungen mit relativ kurzer Verfallszeit handelt. Das Wesen der Architektur berühren sie kaum. Der Marktwert jedoch bringt scheinbar Vorteile demjenigen, der sich ihrer exzentrischen und exotischen Möglichkeiten bedient.

In *Der Kult der Avantgardekünstler* spricht Kuspit von der geometrischen Heilung: »Im Gegensatz [zur therapeutischen Kunsthaltung von Picasso und Duchamps, Anm. d. V.] verfügt die Geometrie von Mondrian und Malewitsch über substantiellere Rätselhaftigkeit: es ist die der elementaren Einfachheit. [...] Mondrian und Malewitsch wollen diese Epiphanie durch geometrische Kompositionen herbeiführen. [...] Damit wird die Geometrie zum magischen Prüfstein der Existenz. [...] Es scheint, als rette einem die göttliche Geometrie das Leben und gäbe einem sein Glück zurück, indem sie das Selbst auf eine höhere Ebene der Existenz erhebt, wo es von der Schuld erlöst wird, die unglückliche Objekt-Beziehungen erzeugen.«

ÜBER VIER THESEN ZUR ARCHITEKTUR

Nach dem, was ich bisher gesagt habe, möchte ich vier Thesen aufstellen, die meine Architekturauffassung belegen.

Meine erste These lautet: Die Avantgarde ist ein Auslaufmodell. Sie hat es nicht geschafft, die an sie geknüpften Hoffnungen und Versprechungen der Befreiung von den Zwängen der Form und Ordnung einzulösen. Der Avantgardismus ist überholt, was die immer schneller sich wiederholenden Geniestreiche zur Genüge beweisen. Die Avantgarde hat die Identität der Kunst geleugnet und gleichzeitig ausgelöscht. An ihre Stelle traten Algorithmen, Events und schnelle Gags, hemmungslose Selbstdarstellungen und das Chaos der Werte und Bezüge.

because it is cheap or anything like that. When we are working we never think about reducing costs. Of course, we want to find new possibilities and I do look for them. But if there really does not seem to be a new way, we are not frightened of sticking to the old one, i.e. to the one we have followed previously. You see, I do not design each building to be different. In fact, generally speaking, we do not look for new effects [...] Architecture is not a cocktail." Seen from this point of view, avant-gardism has had its day. Because if there are innate laws that remain constant, it is futile to constantly look for spectacular schemes and concepts that have never existed before.

To some extent helpless endeavours to find something new, something that has never existed before, no doubt have something to do with a certain infantile attitude, which is capable of producing an illusion in the short term, but does not touch the general problems and culture of architecture. Of course, virtuoso gestures of brilliance such as crumpled, disintegrated and fragmented compositions are extremely attractive and are spreading at an inflationary rate, as we can witness everywhere. Blob architecture is the order of the day. However, in reality, I fear we are looking at one-day wonders with a relatively short shelf life. They scarcely touch the essence of architecture. However, their market value does bring apparent advantages to those who make use of their eccentric and exotic possibilities.

In *The Cult of the Avant-Garde Artist*, Kuspit talks of the geometrical cure: "In contrast [to the therapeutic attitude of the art of Picasso and Duchamps], the geometry of Mondrian and Malevich has a more substantial mysteriousness: that of fundamental simplicity. [...] Mondrian and Malevich try to induce this epiphany through composing with geometry or making geometrical simplicity seem composed. [...] Geometry then becomes the magical touchstone of existence. [...] Indeed, divine geometry seems to redeem one's life and restore one to happiness by lifting one's self to a higher plane of existence where it is absolved of the guilt that comes of unhappy relations with objects."

ON FOUR HYPOTHESES ON ARCHITECTURE

To follow on from what I have said so far, I would like to put forward four hypotheses that support my view of architecture.

My first hypothesis is this: the avant-garde is a discontinued line. It has not managed to fulfil the hopes and promises that it would liberate us from the constraints of form and order. Avant-gardism is obsolete, and the strokes of genius that repeat themselves with ever-greater frequency provide ample proof of that. The avant-garde both denied and obliterated art's identity. In its place came algorithms, staged events and cheap gags that were uninhibited acts of self-representation and consisted of a chaotic jumble of values and references.

The second hypothesis: identity can only be created when both the time and space continuum form the basis of architecture. That includes both the conviction that the fundamental historical structures are indispensable and the recognition that not the outer shell but the core—i.e. the concept, the basic idea—forms the vocabulary of architecture. To put it in extreme

Die zweite These: Identität kann nur entstehen, wenn gleichzeitig das Zeit- und Raumkontinuum Grundlage der Architektur ist. Dazu gehört die Unverzichtbarkeit historischer Grundstrukturen, aber auch die Erkenntnis, dass nicht die äußere Hülle, sondern der Kern, d.h. das Konzept, die Grundidee, das architektonische Vokabular bildet. Extrem formuliert: Das Architekturkonzept der Antike ist auch das Konzept der Moderne. Architektur ist nicht Erfindung, sondern Entdeckung.

Die dritte These besteht in der Behauptung, die Architektur habe eine autonome Sprache, deren Entwicklungsstufen die gesamte Menschheit umfasse. Die Methode entspricht einem Deduktionsprozess, der vom Ganzen auf das Einzelne schließt, vom Allgemeinen auf das Besondere.

Die vierte These geht von der Erkenntnis aus, dass die Identität der Architektur eine eigene Gesetzmäßigkeit hat, die nicht dazu dient, einen realen, nationalen oder ethnographischen Raum zu spiegeln. Mit anderen Worten: Genauso wenig wie es eine europäische Mathematik, eine nationale Physik oder ortsabhängige Wissenschaft und Kunst gibt – ausgenommen das Kunsthandwerk, die Folklore oder politische und soziale Programme –, gibt es auch keine exklusive Architektur der Nationalitäten und Völker.

Die Volkskunst und die Kunst der »Primitiven« und ethnischer Gruppen sind Ausdruck von Mythen und Religionen und wirken deshalb durch ihre Gebundenheit einschränkend auf die freie Entfaltung der Form und eine aufgeklärte Vernunft. Kunstwerke sind keine Mythen mehr, sondern dienen dem Verstehen und der Bewusstseinsbildung. »Der, der baut oder schafft«, sagt Valéry, »da er es mit dem Rest der Welt zu tun hat und mit der Bewegung in der Natur, die immerfort bemüht sind, aufzulösen, zu verderben, umzustürzen, was er hervorbringt, – muss ein drittes Prinzip anerkennen und muss versuchen, dieses seinen Werken mitzuteilen als einen Ausdruck des Widerstands, den sie ihrem vergänglichen Geschick entgegensetzen sollen. Er sucht also den Bestand oder die Dauer.«

Die mathematische Regel und das geometrische Ordnungsprinzip waren das Fundament der Architektur der Antike. Der antike Schönheitsbegriff bezog sich nicht so sehr auf die Erscheinung als vielmehr auf die Vervollkommnung der Regeln und Proportionen. Es war ein stetiger Prozess der Verfeinerung und Idealisierung. Bei Platon heißt es: »Wenn jemand von allen Künsten die Lehre von Zahl, Maß und Gleichgewicht scheiden wollte, dann würde überall nur ein kümmerlicher Rest übrig bleiben.« Für den Neuplatoniker Augustinus, den auch Mies für seine Architekturkonzeption mit dem Satz »Schönheit ist der Glanz des Wahren« in Anspruch nahm, ist das Bauen eine Wissenschaft, die auf der Anwendung geometrischer Gesetze beruht. Es ist kein Zufall, dass die klassische Epoche der abendländischen Architektur mit den theoretischen Schriften der oberitalienischen Humanisten des Quattro- und Cinquecento, mit den *hommes des lettres* Alberti, Palladio, Scamozzi und deren Zeitgenossen, beginnt, basierend auf der Wiederentdeckung von Vitruvs berühmter Schrift *De architectura libri decem.* Wäre es deshalb nicht richtiger, von einer abendländischen, einer humanistischen Architektur zu sprechen statt von einer europäischen, um einen geistigen statt einen realen Raum adjekti-

terms: the architectural concept of the Antiquity is also the concept of Modernism. Architecture is not about invention but discovery.

The third hypothesis centres on the claim that architecture has an autonomous language and that its stages of development cover the whole of humankind. The method is a process of deduction that makes inferences about the individual from the whole, about the particular from the general.

The fourth hypothesis is based on the insight that the identity of architecture has its own innate laws, which do not have the purpose of reflecting real, national or ethnographic space. In other words: just as there is no such thing as European mathematics, national physics or local science and art—apart from folklore or political and social programmes—nor is there an exclusive architecture of nationalities and cultures.

Folk art and the art of primitive peoples and ethnographic groups are the expression of myths and religions and through this dependency they have a restrictive effect on the free development of form and on enlightened rationality. Works of art are no longer myths, but serve the purpose of understanding and formation of consciousness. “Since he who constructs or creates,” says Valéry, “has to deal with the rest of the world and with the movement of nature, which both tend perpetually to dissolve, corrupt, or upset what he makes, he must recognise and seek to communicate a third principle that expresses the resistance he wishes them to offer to their [transient] destiny, which is to persist. So he seeks solidity or lastingness.”

Mathematical rules and geometrical principles of order were the foundations of architecture in the Antiquity. The Classical idea of beauty was not so much concerned with appearance as with perfecting rules and proportions. It was a constant process of refining and idealising. Plato said: “If anyone tried to take the theory of number, measure and balance out of all the arts, miserable remnants would be all that was left.” For the Neo-Platonist Augustine, whom Mies drew upon for his architectural concept in his dictum that “Beauty is the splendour of truth,” architecture is a science that is based on the use of geometrical laws. It is no coincidence that the age of Classicism in Western architecture begins with the theoretical writings of the Northern Italian humanists of the Quattro- and Cinquecento, with the “hommes des lettres” Alberti, Palladio, Scamozzi and their contemporaries, inspired by the rediscovery of Vitruvius’ famous treatise *De architectura libri decem* or *Ten books on architecture.* Would it not therefore be more correct to speak of Western or humanist architecture rather than of European architecture, in order to describe an intellectual rather than an actual space? Western architecture by its very nature seeks the absolute, an image of the idea. It is based on Plato’s idea of the true, good and beautiful.

The clarity of geometry is more important than the expression of the material. The striving is for immateriality, the highest degree of perfection and simplicity. The ideal shape, the perfect volume, the reduction to basic forms is what underpins the nature of Western architecture and corresponds to Classical thought, for which the order of the world was reflected in regularity.

visch zu charakterisieren? Die abendländische Architektur will ihrem Wesen nach das Absolute, ein Abbild der Idee. Sie beruht auf der platonischen Vorstellung vom Wahren, Guten und Schönen.

Die Klarheit der Geometrie ist wichtiger als der Ausdruck des Materials. Das Streben ist die Immaterialität, der höchste Grad der Vollendung und Einfachheit. Die ideale Gestalt, der perfekte Körper, die Reduktion auf die Grundformen liegen dem Wesen der abendländischen Architektur zugrunde und entsprechen dem antiken Denken, für das sich in der Regelhaftigkeit die Ordnung der Welt darstellte.

»Chaos ist immer Zeichen einer Anarchie«, sagt Mies. »Anarchie ist immer eine Bewegung ohne Ordnung. Im Anschluss an die platonische Ideenlehre hat Augustinus die Grundidee der mittelalterlichen Weltanschauung gestaltet. In der Ordnungsidee des Mittelalters lebt, wenn auch in ganz neuen Dimensionen, jener Maßgeist, den Plato darstellte und begründete. Das edelste Erbe der Antike.«

ÜBER DAS DIALEKTISCHE PRINZIP ODER DIE COINCIDENTIA OPPOSITORUM

Etwa um 1450 – in der Epoche des Humanismus – wurden zwei entscheidende Gedanken formuliert. Der eine steht im Traktat *De re aedificatoria* von Leon Battista Alberti, der andere im Traktat *De docta ignorantia* von Nikolaus von Kues. Alberti spricht von der »Varietà in unitàs« und Cusanus von der »Coincidentia oppositorum«. Die Ideen von der »Vielfalt in der Einheit« und vom »Zusammenfall der Gegensätze« stehen am Anfang des Diskurses über das Denken nach der Antike und am Beginn der Neuzeit. »Die Vielfalt in der Einheit« gibt einen Hinweis auf die unbeschränkten Interpretationsmöglichkeiten der Architektur und weist damit auch auf äußere Einflüsse hin. Die Interpretationen sind unerschöpflich. Sie umfassen auch ethnologische, geographische, soziale und politische Komponenten, ohne jedoch die Einheit, die Einheit der Idee, in Frage zu stellen oder sogar aufzulösen. Auch Cusanus betont die Gegensätze, die Unterschiedlichkeiten, die Widersprüche, wenn er vom »Zusammenfall der Gegensätze« spricht. Es geht ihm aber nicht um die Auflösung der Gegensätze in ein einheitliches, in ein exklusives System, sondern um das Nebeneinander von These und Antithese, um das Ein- und Ausatmen, wie Goethe es metaphorisch nannte.

Hier wird ein Wesenszug des abendländischen Denkens sichtbar, das zwar hin und wieder nach Einheitlichkeit strebte, aber doch die Vielfalt und Unterschiedlichkeit akzeptiert und als System des Handelns praktizierte. Es gibt ein abendländisches Grundkonzept der Architektur, das unveränderlich ist, sich in rhythmischen Variationen durch Epochen und Zeiträume hindurchzieht. Es hat sowohl idealistische als auch realistische Züge. Mit anderen Worten: Es ist ein dialektisches Konzept. Beide, das Streben nach dem Ideal und die Anerkennung der Wirklichkeit, haben ihre Spuren im abendländischen Denken hinterlassen. Eines verbindet die beiden Gegensätze, die schon Cusanus und Alberti erkannten und programmatisch erfassten, und das ist der Widerspruch. Die Erkenntnis, dass trotz

"Chaos is always a sign of anarchy," said Mies. "Anarchy is always a movement without order. Following on from the Platonic theory of ideas, Augustine developed the fundamental idea underlying the Medieval worldview. In the Medieval concept of order lives the spirit of measure that Plato described and explained—albeit in completely new dimensions. It is the most noble legacy of the Antiquity."

ON THE DIALECTIC PRINCIPLE OR THE COINCIDENCE OF OPPOSITES

Around 1450—in the age of Humanism—two fundamental ideas were formulated. One appears in the tract *De re aedificatoria* (On Architecture) by Leon Battista Alberti, the other in a tract by Nicolas Cusanus *De docta ignorantia* (On Learned Ignorance). Alberti speaks of "varietà in unitàs" and Cusanus of "coincidentia oppositorum." Thus the ideas of "diversity in unity" and of the "coincidence of opposites" mark the beginning of the way of thinking after Antiquity and at the beginning of the modern age. "Diversity in unity" is a pointer to the unlimited possibilities for interpreting architecture and thus also points to other influences. The interpretations are inexhaustible. They include ethnological, geographical, sociopolitical components, but do not question or indeed resolve the unity of the idea. Cusanus also emphasized contrasts, differences, and contradictions when he spoke of the "coincidence of opposites." But he was not concerned with resolving opposites in a uniform, exclusive system, but in the coexistence of hypothesis and antithesis, with breathing in and breathing out, as Goethe metaphorically called it.

Here an immutable attribute of Western thought becomes visible that does occasionally strive for uniformity, but nevertheless accepts diversity and difference and practices it as a system of acting. There is a basic Western concept of architecture, which is unchanging and runs in rhythmic variations through different times and epochs. It has both idealistic and realistic features. In other words, it is a dialectic concept. Both these things—a striving for the ideal and the recognition of reality—have left their mark on Western thought. There is one thing linking the two contrasts that Cusanus and Alberti recognised and formulated in programmatic terms and that is contradiction, the recognition that, despite all our striving to perfect the imperfect, the breaks, the unattainable, contradiction, all contain life and reality.

Western architecture finds its actual fulfilment—or, seen from a different point of view, its failure—in fragments, the incomplete, the imperfect. Simple cultures strive for harmonisation, for the fulfilment of a single principle that governs everything and is bound to end in a cul-de-sac. It is important to understand that the ideal is unattainable because it originates in a deterministic way of thinking and thus has no sense of perspective.

The real world is like a palimpsest. Layers are erased and overlaid with new ones. The upper layer covers the ones beneath it. Patchwork lies on top of patchwork. Layer on layer. Hypothesis on antithesis. It is in a dialectic way of thinking, in

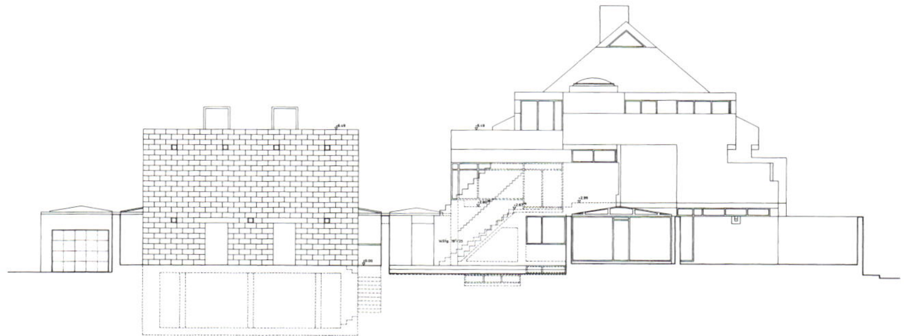
1

2

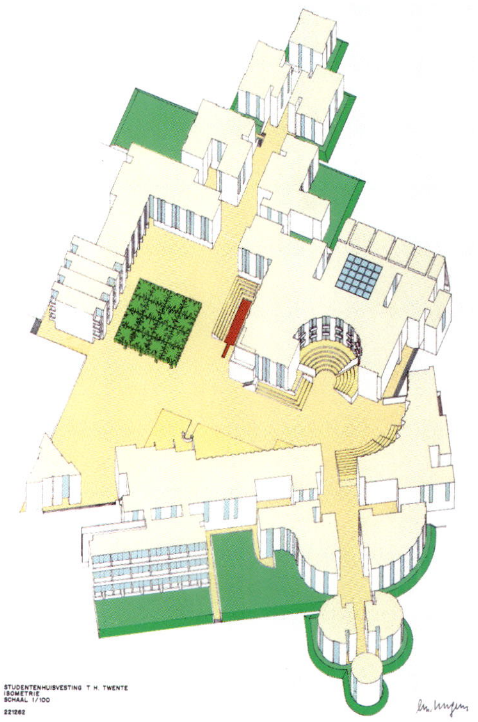
3

4

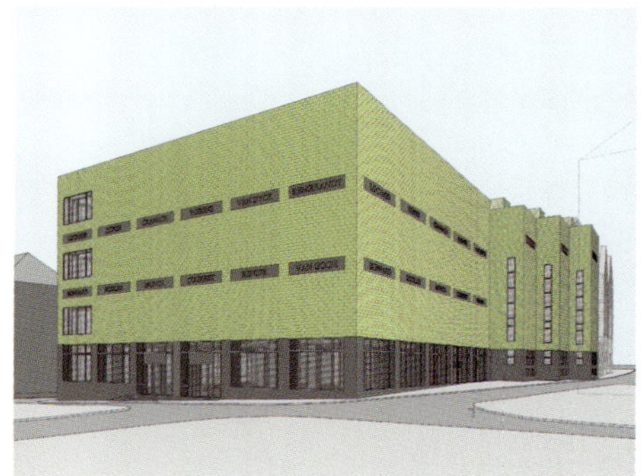
5

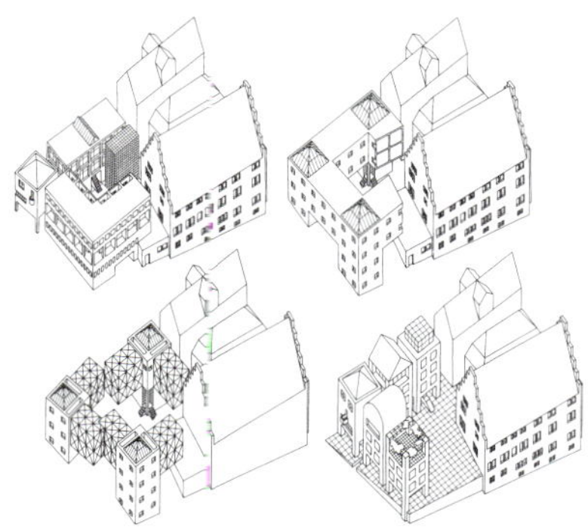
6

7

Bauten von/Buildings by
Oswald Mathias Ungers

1 Kubus Haus, Köln, 1989/90 mit altem Wohnhaus (1958/59)
Kubus House, Cologne, 1989/90, including old house (1958/59)
2 Haus Glashütte
Glashütte House, Bitburg (D), 1986-1988

3 Studentenwohnheim
Student hall of residence, Twente, bei/near Enschede (NL) 1964
4 Residenz Deutsche Botschaft
German Ambassador's Residence, Washington, 1987-1995
5 Wallraf-Richartz-Museum, Köln
Cologne, 1996-2000

6 Marburger Häuser
Houses in Marburg, 1976
7 Friedrichstadtpassage,
Quartier/block 205, Berlin, 1991-1995

des Strebens nach Vollendung das Unvollendete, die Brüche, das Unerreichbare, der Widerspruch Leben und Realität beinhalten.

Die abendländische Architektur findet ihre eigentliche Erfüllung oder – wenn man so will, den Punkt ihres Scheiterns – in den Bruchstücken, dem Fragmentarischen, dem Unvollendeten. Einfache Kulturen streben nach Angleichung, nach Erfüllung eines alles beherrschenden Prinzips, das zwangsläufig in eine Sackgasse führt. Man muss wissen: Das Ideal ist unerreichbar, weil es deterministischem Denken entspringt und deshalb perspektivlos ist.

Die reale Welt ist wie ein Palimpsest. Schichten werden ausradiert und neue darüber gelegt. Die jeweils obere überdeckt die darunter liegenden. Stückwerk liegt über Stückwerk. Schicht über Schicht. These über Antithese. In einem dialektischen Denken, in diesem antithetischen Übereinander und Gegeneinander der Widersprüche und Gegensätze, in dieser Vielfalt der Möglichkeiten und Unmöglichkeiten, in diesem Gewirr von ständig neuen Interpretationen und Widerlegungen, in dem von Popper bezeichneten Zustand von »conjecture and refutation«, von Vermutung und Widerlegung, im Zweifel der Gefühle und Gedanken liegen die Ansätze und Herausforderungen, sich in einer immer komplexer werdenden Realität zu bewegen.

Die abendländische Architektur an sich ist benennbar, ihre *varietà* jedoch, der Zusammenfall ihrer Gegensätze ist ungewiss und offen. Meine Antwort auf die eingangs gestellte Frage: Welche Identität für die europäische Architektur? ist deshalb: Sie lässt sich nicht identifizieren, die europäische Architektur. Es gibt sie nicht. Aber es gibt ein abendländisches, ein humanistisches Denken, das im Wesentlichen von Vernunft, Offenheit, Vielfalt und Freiheit geprägt ist. Das in seinen Grundzügen dialektischem Denken entspricht und daher unerschöpfliche Möglichkeiten bietet.

Aus diesem abendländischen Denken, das in der griechischen und römischen Antike seinen Ursprung hat, entwickelten sich die Scholastik, der Humanismus, die Renaissance, die Aufklärung, die moderne Wissenschaft. Es schuf im Laufe der Jahrhunderte eine Literatur, Kunst, Musik und Architektur. Es hat die Demokratie und den modernen Wirtschaftsstaat erfunden. Es hat Begriffe geprägt, die den Menschen in den Mittelpunkt stellten, und ethische und moralische Werte definiert. Es hat den Satz vom Menschen als dem Maß aller Dinge und der Nichtexistenz der Dinge, die nicht sind, erfunden. Es ist zur Grundlage der westlichen Zivilisation und Kultur geworden, die ihre Gültigkeit für die gesamte Menschheit trotz aller Rückschläge und teils erschreckender Fehlentwicklungen unter Beweis gestellt haben. Die abendländische Kultur lebt aus einem Kontinuum der ständigen dialektischen Auseinandersetzung mit der eigenen Lehre und Theorie. Diese ungeheuer komplexe Vielfalt, das ständige Wieder-in-Frage-Stellen der eigenen Position, diese geistige Vorurteilslosigkeit, die Grenzüberschreitung der eigenen Regeln haben im Laufe der Jahrhunderte ein Denken provoziert, das sich nicht in antagonistischen Kategorien des 19. Jahrhunderts, des Entweder-Oder, in ideologischen Grabenkämpfen oder deterministischer Zuversicht

this antithetical arrangement of contradictions and contrasts jostling for position, in this diverse range of possibilities and impossibilities, in this tangle of constantly new interpretations and counter-interpretation, in what Popper called "conjecture and refutation," in doubting feelings and thoughts, that the attempts and challenges to move in a reality of increasing complexity are found.

It is possible to describe Western architecture per se, but its varietà, the coincidence of its opposites, is uncertain and open. My answer to the question raised at the beginning—what is the identity of European architecture—is therefore: European architecture cannot be identified. It does not exist. But there is a Western, humanist way of thinking that differs from many other worldviews. It is a way of thinking that is essentially characterised by reason, openness, diversity and freedom. It is a way of thinking that in its essential features corresponds to dialectic thought and therefore offers inexhaustible possibilities.

Out of this Western way of thinking, which has its origins in Greek and Roman Antiquity, Scholasticism, Humanism, the Renaissance, the Enlightenment, and modern science developed. Over the centuries it created literature, art, music and architecture. It invented democracy and the modern economic state. It engendered concepts that placed human beings at the centre of things and defined ethical and moral values. It invented the theorem of humans as the measure of all things and of the non-existence of things that have no being. It became the foundation of Western civilisation and culture and proved its validity for the whole of humankind despite all the setbacks and sometimes horrific wrong turns. Western culture lives on the continuum of the constant dialectic examination of its own teachings and theories. This enormously complex diversity, the constant questioning of its own position, this intellectual impartiality, the willingness to transgress its own rules, have over the centuries provoked a way of thinking that went beyond the antagonistic categories of the 19th century, the either/or thinking, ideological trench warfare or deterministic confidence, that did not discredit itself in contrary positions, but reached its fulfilment in complementary complementarities. The recognition of morphological dependencies and interconnections comes from Western culture's worldview.

We are at the beginning of a process, not the end. Its cultural and civilizatory dimensions have not yet been exhausted. Western architecture, or, as it should more properly be called, humanistic architecture, has a potential of boundless breadth and intellectual depth, which is geared to renewal and—like nature—to a cyclical revival of basic concepts that always remain the same. We should be sceptical if the susceptibility of avant-gardism to being led astray mutates into the actual subject of architecture through distorted and to some extent degenerate messages. What we must fear is not the feeling of being outdated or passé, but the trivialisation of concepts, the commercialisation of values, the banal appropriation of ideas and thoughts, the ever greater ignorance of history and the negation of a cultural development that has shaped us for thousands of years.

erschöpfte, sich nicht in konträren Positionen diffamierte, sondern in komplementären Ergänzungen verwirklichte. Die Erkenntnisse der morphologischen Abhängigkeiten und Zusammenhänge entspringen dem Weltbild der abendländischen Kultur.

Wir stehen am Anfang eines Prozesses, nicht am Ende. Die kulturellen und zivilisatorischen Dimensionen sind noch nicht erschöpft. Die abendländische Architektur, oder wie es noch besser heißen müsste: die humanistische Architektur, hat ein Potenzial von unerschöpflicher Breite und geistiger Tiefe, das auf Erneuerung und – der Natur vergleichbar – auf eine zyklische Wiederbelebung der immer wieder gleichen Grundbegriffe angelegt ist. Es ist Skepsis geboten, wenn die Verführbarkeit des Avantgardismus durch entstellte und teilweise entartete Botschaften zum eigentlichen Thema der Architektur mutiert. Wir sollten uns nicht davor ängstigen, überholt zu werden oder veraltet zu sein, sondern vor der Banalisierung der Begriffe, der Kommerzialisierung der Werte, dem trivialen Gebrauch von Ideen und Gedanken, der immer geringer werdenden Kenntnis der Geschichte und der Negation einer Kulturentwicklung, die uns seit Jahrtausenden prägt.

Nietzsches Begriffspaar: das Dionysische und das Apollinische, sind Teil unseres Wesens und wirken im ständigen Wechsel bei der Suche nach Identität. In diesem Wechselspiel liegt – wie es scheinen mag – unsere Schwäche und Unentschiedenheit, unser Mangel an Lebendigkeit, aber auch die geistige Kraft, die den abendländischen Menschen, seine Kultur und seine Architektur geformt hat. So wie dieses Wechselspiel den Formenreichtum und die Mannigfaltigkeit der Vergangenheit erfüllte, liegt darin auch der Ansatz für das schöpferische Potenzial der Zukunft. Insofern charakterisiert die Identität der abendländischen Architektur ein Kreislauf, der sich ständig wiederholt, in seinen Grundzügen aber gleich bleibt. Nietzsche hat viel Aufhebens gemacht von der Lehre der »ewigen Wiederkehr«, die er in seinem *Zarathustra* verkündigt. Die Idee der in sich kreisenden Zeit, der Gedanke der ewigen Wiederkehr sind jedoch uralt.

Durch die Entwicklung einer humanistischen Kultur kam das enzyklopädische Denken in die Welt. Das morphologische Denken. Das Denken in ganzheitlichen und globalen Zusammenhängen, verbunden mit Toleranz und Menschlichkeit, wie sie in der Musik Bachs, Mozarts und Beethovens ihren höchsten Ausdruck fand. Diese Musik, ähnlich wie die Kunst und Architektur des Abendlandes, war nicht nur für den europäischen Raum komponiert und entworfen, sondern für die ganze Welt. »Seid umschlungen Millionen«, heißt es bei Schiller. Eine Vision, die Beethoven in einem symphonischen Höhepunkt in Töne umgesetzt hat, eine Botschaft, die an alle Völker und Kulturen gerichtet war. Das Gleiche tat Schinkel mit seiner Architektur, die über alle Stile und Epochen – von der Antike bis zur Neuzeit, vom Einfachen bis zum Komplexen, vom Schmucklosen bis zum Dekorativen – hinweg reichte. Hier zeigt sich die Identität der humanistischen Architektur als eine auf den Menschen und sein geistiges und kulturelles Erbe bezogene Kunst.

Nietzsche's paired concepts—the Dionysian and Apollonian—are part of our being and constantly interact in the search for identity. In this interplay lie—so it might seem—our weakness and indecision, our lack of vitality, but also the intellectual strength that has formed Western man, his culture and his architecture. Just as this interplay infused the wealth of forms and diversity of the past, it also contains the starting point for the creative potential inherent in the future. The identity of Western architecture is thus a cycle that constantly repeats itself, but which remains unchanged in its essential characteristics. Nietzsche made a great deal of ado of the theory of "eternal recurrence," which he proclaimed in his *Zarathustra.* However, the idea of cyclical time, of eternal recurrence is ancient.

Through the development of a humanist culture, encyclopaedic thinking was born, morphological thinking, thinking in integrated and global contexts, combined with tolerance and humanity, which found their highest expression in the music of Bach, Mozart and Beethoven, for example. This music, like the art and architecture of the West, was not composed and designed exclusively for Europe but for the whole world. "You millions I embrace you," Schiller writes. Beethoven converted this vision into sound in a symphonic climax, sending a message that was directed to all peoples and cultures. Schinkel did the same with his architecture, which went beyond all styles and ages—from Antiquity to the Modern Age, from the simple to the complex, from the undecorated to the ornamental. Here the identity of humanist architecture is seen to be an art form that relates to humankind and its intellectual and cultural legacy.

PROJEKTE PROJECTS

TEXTE VON TEXTS BY
Markus Jager (M. J.)
Elmar Kossel (E. K.)
Frank Schmitz (F. S.)
Romana Schneider (R. S.)
Wolfgang Welker (W. W.)
Christian Welzbacher (C. W.)

KULTUR ALS ERLEBNIS
CULTURE AS EXPERIENCE

Museumsbauten prägten insbesondere während der achtziger und neunziger Jahre das Spektrum zeitgenössischer Architektur. Das Deutsche Architekturmuseum gehörte ebenso wie das von Hans Hollein in der Eröffnungsausstellung des DAM präsentierte Museum in Mönchengladbach zu den wegweisenden Beispielen dieser Zeit. Bauten der Kultur sind weiterhin auch im internationalen Maßstab architektonische Trendsetter. Und nach wie vor regt diese Bauaufgabe die Architekten zu ihren attraktivsten Bauten und reizvollsten Raumschöpfungen an. Kultursponsoring und die touristische Verwertung der Hochkultur sorgen für einen anhaltenden Bauboom. Neue Kulturzentren werden zum Anziehungspunkt einer Stadt und befördern inzwischen auch maßgeblich die Konversion städtischer Brachen in hochwertige Areale. Bereits das Gebäude selbst garantiert manchmal einen so regen Publikumszuspruch, dass erste Besichtigungen stattfinden, noch bevor es seiner eigentlichen Bestimmung übergeben ist.

Bauten der Kultur stehen auch für eine Architektur, die zwischen Funktion und künstlerischer Freiheit pendelt. Es gibt spektakuläre Bauwerke dieser Gattung, die ihren musealen Zweck kaum erfüllen können, weil sie selbst ein Kunstwerk darstellen und bewusst die Grenzen von Funktionalität überschreiten. Andere nicht weniger attraktive Bauten sind entschieden auf die Bedürfnisse von Kunst, Wissenschaft und Kommunikation zugeschnitten. Den besten Exponenten ist gemein, dass in ihnen Flächen und Räume, Körper und Zwischenzonen variieren, die zu besonderen Raumerlebnissen führen. Unkonventionelle Verwendung von Materialien und Formen bedingt eine Architektur, die mittlerweile weit über das postmoderne Zitat hinaus neue Maßstäbe setzt und zum Ausdruck der Komplexität heutigen Bauens und Denkens wird. Wenn jedem Raum, jeder Fläche ein eigener Ausdruck zugedacht werden soll, sind auch besonders hohe Ansprüche an die technische Realisierung und Ausstattung des Bauwerks zu stellen. Dazu sind computergestützte Verfahren notwendig, wodurch auch die Möglichkeiten des konstruktionstechnisch Machbaren neu definiert werden.

Kritische Stimmen erkennen zwar an, dass mit spektakulären Kulturbauten die Popularität von Architektur wächst, befürchten aber, dass diese Werke ihrer wesentlichen Aufgabe und Bedeutung in sozialer und urbanistischer Hinsicht nicht gerecht werden können und wollen.

During the 1980s and 1990s it was museum buildings that stood out in the spectrum of contemporary architecture. The Deutsches Architekturmuseum, along with Hans Hollein's museum in Mönchengladbach, which was exhibited at DAM's inaugural exhibition, were amongst the groundbreaking examples of the time. Cultural buildings continue to be architectural trendsetters—on an international, as well as a national, scale. And it is this building type that still inspires architects to create their most attractive buildings and beautiful spaces. Arts sponsorship and tourism's marketing of high culture ensure that the building boom continues. New cultural centres have become a major attraction in cities and have also begun to stimulate the conversion of brownfield sites into high-quality locations. The buildings themselves are sometimes so popular that public viewings begin even before the building has opened for its actual purpose.

Cultural buildings also represent a kind of architecture that oscillates between function and artistic freedom. There are spectacular buildings of this genre that scarcely fulfil their function as museums because they are a work of art in themselves and deliberately push the bounds of functionality to the limit. Other, no less attractive, buildings are clearly tailored to the needs of art, science and communication. What the best examples have in common is that they include a variety of planes and spaces, volumes and transition zones, which create unusual experiences of space. The unconventional use of materials and forms has created an architecture that is now setting new benchmarks that far exceed the Postmodern quotation and are becoming an expression of the complexity of architecture and thought today. If every separate space, every plane, is to have its own singular expression, the building will have to meet particularly high standards of technical realisation and equipment. This is only possible using computer-aided methods, which also redefines the spectrum of what is feasible in structural terms.

Although critical voices acknowledge that spectacular cultural buildings increase architecture's popularity, they also fear that these works cannot—and indeed do not seek to—fulfil their principal purpose and importance in social and urban terms.

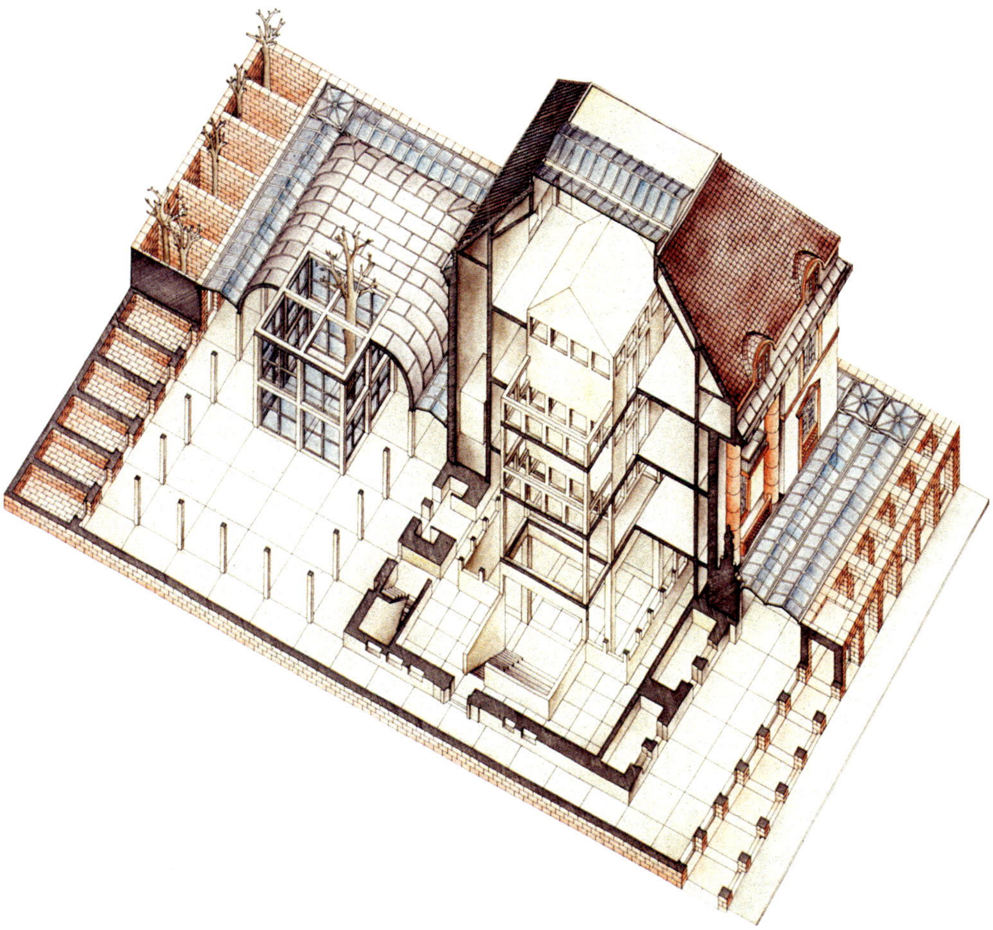

Oswald Mathias Ungers: Das Deutsche Architekturmuseum DAM, 1979-1984, Isometrie. Originalzeichnung, Sammlung DAM

Oswald Mathias Ungers: German Museum of Architecture DAM, 1979-1984, isometric view. Original drawing, DAM collection

HANS HOLLEIN

Städtisches Museum Abteiberg
Mönchengladbach, Deutschland, 1972-1982

Städtisches Museum Abteiberg
Mönchengladbach, Germany, 1972-1982

Was heutzutage als Guggenheim- oder Bilbao-Effekt bezeichnet wird, hat Hans Hollein mit dem Museum Abteiberg schon vor über zwanzig Jahren erreicht. So bemerkte der Architekturkritiker Wolfgang Pehnt bald nach Eröffnung: »Der Ort, der bislang eher die Anhänger des Traditionsvereins Borussia Mönchengladbach anzog, ist zum Ziel eines internationalen Kunst- und Architekturtourismus geworden.«

Hollein baute das Museum in den Abteiberg hinein, sodass ein Teil der Dachflächen ein öffentliches Forum bildet. Der Verwaltungsturm, ein Pavillon als Eingang in die museale Unterwelt sowie eine Gruppe von quadratischen Aufbauten, die den unterirdischen Ausstellungsräumen Nordlicht zuführen, bilden ein spannungsreiches Gebäudeensemble um den Platz und am Hang – eine städtische Silhouette *en miniature*. Die Vielfalt des Äußeren setzt sich im Inneren durch effektvoll gestaltete, abwechslungsreiche und überraschende Raumkonstellationen fort. Funktionale Schauräume, intime Kabinette und eine große Halle, die je nach Bedarf mit flexiblen Stellwänden bestückt werden kann, nehmen die Exponate auf. Die Architektur gibt keinen linearen Rundgang vor, sondern animiert den Besucher zum Flanieren durch die unterschiedlichen Raumlandschaften. Manche Stimmen hatten befürchtet, dass die Kunst angesichts einer so ausgeprägten Architektur zur Nebensache wird. Andere sehen ihre Vermutung bestätigt, dass sie erst in diesem unverwechselbaren Ambiente ihre größte Wirkung zu entfalten vermag. M. J.

Twenty years ago, Hans Hollein achieved what has since become known as the Guggenheim or Bilbao effect with the Abteiberg museum. Shortly after it opened, architectural critic Wolfgang Pehnt commented: "This town, which in the past was more likely to attract supporters of the old established football team Borussia Mönchengladbach, has now become a destination for international art and architectural tourism."

Hollein built the museum into the slope of the Abteiberg so that part of the roof creates a public forum. The tower housing the offices, a pavilion as an entrance into the underworld of museum culture and a group of square structures that feed northern light into the underground exhibition spaces form an exciting ensemble of buildings around the piazza and on the hillside—an urban silhouette *en miniature*. The diversity of the outside of the complex continues inside with exciting and surprising constellations of space designed to great effect. The exhibits are housed in functional exhibition rooms, intimate cabinets and a large hall in which flexible display panels can be installed as required. The architecture does not prescribe a linear route for visitors to follow around the museum, but instead inspires them to stroll through the different spatial landscapes. Some critics had feared that such distinctive architecture would relegate the art exhibits to the sidelines. Others see their belief confirmed that the art can only truly develop to full effect in this unmistakable ambiance. M. J.

1

2

3

1 Perspektivische Gesamtansicht. Plankopie, Sammlung DAM
2 Terrassen, über denen sich die Museumsaufbauten erheben
3 Rückwärtige Ansicht
4 Langgezogene Galerie mit Brücke und Lichttonne
5 Blick auf einen durch mobile Wände separierten Ausstellungsraum

1 Perspective view. Copy of a drawing from the DAM collection
2 Terraces and museum buildings above them
3 Rear view
4 Long gallery with walkway and barrel-shaped roof light
5 View of an exhibition space separated by movable partitions

4

5

ZAHA HADID ARCHITECTS

Rosenthal Center for Contemporary Art
Cincinnati, Ohio, USA, 1998-2003

Noch vor der Fertigstellung des Contemporary Arts Center wurde in den Medien immer wieder über Zaha Hadids erstes Bauwerk in den USA berichtet. Das CAC hat damit über Nacht eine internationale Bekanntheit erlangt, die es mit Kunstausstellungen allein kaum erzielt hätte.

Die Architektin war mit einem Grundstück konfrontiert, das so ziemlich alle Nachteile vereint, die man sich für ein Museum denken kann: klein und eingezwängt, sodass das Haus nur als Stockwerksbau zu entwickeln war. Um an einem solchen Ort einen kulturellen Leuchtturm zu errichten, bedarf es neben guter Architektur auch eines wirkungsvollen Leitbilds, das alle Widrigkeiten vergessen lässt. Hadids Leitbild ist der »urban carpet«, der Teppich, der für die Besucher ausgerollt wird. Dieser hat vom Erdgeschoss aus in zwei Richtungen seine Sogkraft zu entfalten. Zum einen soll er in den Stadtraum ausgreifen und die Besucher in das Haus ziehen, zum anderen als *promenade architecturale* für eine spannungsreiche Vertikalerschließung der acht Stockwerke sorgen. Aus diesem Grund sind die Geschosse nicht in identischer Folge übereinander gestapelt. Vielmehr besteht das Bauwerk aus einer Assemblage gestaffelter Körper. Jede Ausstellungsetage ist anders figuriert.

Im Zuge der Realisierung hat der Entwurf manche Purifizierungen erfahren. Auch der Charakter der Innenräume ist neutraler geworden. Für ein Haus, das über keine ständige Sammlung verfügt und nur mit Wechselausstellungen agiert, nicht unbedingt ein Nachteil. M. J.

Rosenthal Center for Contemporary Art
Cincinnati, Ohio, USA, 1998-2003

Even before completion of the Contemporary Arts Center, there was a great deal of media coverage of Zaha Hadid's first building in the USA. Thus overnight the CAC gained a degree of international fame that it would not have achieved with its art exhibitions alone.

The architect was confronted with a site that combined virtually all the disadvantages imaginable for a museum: so small and constricted that the only option was to design the museum over several storeys. Building a cultural beacon on a site like that needs not only good architecture but also a powerful metaphor that makes it possible to forget all the adversities. Hadid's metaphor is the "urban carpet" that is rolled out for visitors. This carpet has to unfurl from the ground floor in two directions to exert its power. On the one hand, it has to reach into the urban realm and attract visitors to the building, and, on the other hand, its role as a "promenade architecturale" is to create an exciting vertical circulation system to provide access to the eight storeys. For that reason, the storeys are not merely stacked one on top of the other in an identical sequence. Rather the building consists of an assembly of cantilevered volumes. Each exhibition floor is configured differently.

During the realisation process, the scheme went through several stages of purification. The character of the interiors also became more neutral. For an institution that does not have a permanent collection and works solely with temporary exhibitions, that is not necessarily a disadvantage. M. J.

1 Aufgeschnittene Außenperspektive mit Grundrissen, Ansicht und Lageplan. Gemälde von Zaha Hadid
2 Ansicht Ostseite
3 Gebäudedetail Südostecke
4 Innere Erschließung

1 Cutaway perspective of exterior with floor plans, elevation and site plan. Painting by Zaha Hadid
2 View of east façade
3 South-eastern corner: detail
4 Internal circulation

1

2

3+4

ATELIERS JEAN NOUVEL

Kultur- und Kongresszentrum
Luzern, Schweiz, 1995-2000

Cultural and Congress Centre
Lucerne, Switzerland, 1995-2000

Verblüffend ist, dass dieses Bauwerk – in der traditionsreichen Innerschweiz – trotz seiner avantgardistischen Architektur und seiner radikalen stadträumlichen Gebärde einhellige Begeisterung hervorruft.

Dass das Kulturzentrum überhaupt entstehen konnte und wirtschaftlichen Erfolg hat, ist in hohem Maße dem auch starken finanziellen Engagement von Bürgern der Stadt zu verdanken, die sich explizit für die Architektur Nouvels entschieden hatten. Im Prinzip besteht das Kultur-und Kongresszentrum (KKL) aus heterogenen Einzelbauten – Konzerthaus, Stadthalle mit Mehrzwecksaal, Kunstmuseum, Kongresszentrum und zwei Restaurants –, die von einem großen Flugdach zusammengehalten werden. Im Inneren unterscheiden sich die verschiedenen Gehäuse beträchtlich in ihren architektonischen Formen, Raumerlebnissen, Materialien, der Farbgebung und der Lichtregie. Die Palette reicht von einem farbenfroh-luxuriösen bis zu einem technisch-kühlen Ambiente. Das komplexe Wegenetz – im Erdgeschoss von Wasserläufen begleitet – knüpft an die Außenumgebung an und verbindet die autonomen Teile des Zentrums u.a. mit Brücken und Plätzen, als befände man sich in einer kleinen Stadt. Auch die architektonisch artikulierten Beziehungen zum einzigartigen Ausblick auf die Altstadt und den Vierwaldstätter See – Panoramafenster und Terrassen – ziehen den Besucher in den Bann. Natürlich profitiert das Bauwerk von seiner prominenten Lage. Doch ist es bisher keinem Architekten gelungen, diese Kulisse so großartig in Szene zu setzen. M. J.

It is astonishing that this building—located in the most deeply traditional heart of Switzerland—has attracted unanimous enthusiasm, despite its avant-garde architecture and radical gesture to the urban realm.

The fact that the Culture Centre was built at all and is financially successful is to a great degree thanks to local people, who invested personal commitment and financing and made an explicit decision in favour of Nouvel's architecture. In principle, the Cultural and Congress Centre consists of a juxtaposition of heterogeneous stand-alone buildings: a concert hall, a civic hall with multi-purpose space, an art museum, congress centre and two restaurants unified under a large canopy roof. The interiors of the different buildings vary greatly in terms of architectural form, spatial experience, materials, colour schemes and manipulation of light. The ambience in the different spaces ranges from colourful and luxurious to techno-cool. The complex network of pathways—interspersed with channels of water on the ground floor—links into the building's surroundings and connects the autonomous parts of the centre, using elements such as bridges and piazzas. It is like walking around a small town. The architecture—panoramic windows and terraces—creates relationships to the unique view of the old town and Lake Lucerne that captivate visitors. Of course, the building benefits enormously from its prominent position. But nevertheless, no architect to date has succeeded in dramatizing this backdrop so magnificently. M. J.

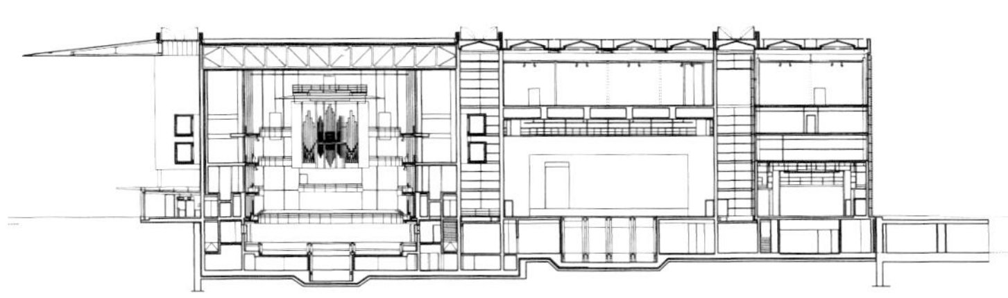

1

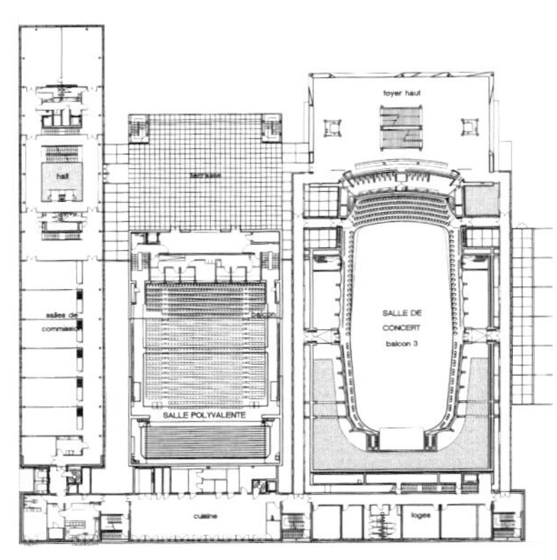

2

1 Längsschnitt, Grundriss Ebene 2
2 Ansicht vom See
3 Konzertsaal
4 Panoramafoyer Konzertsaal

1 Longitudinal section, plan of level 2
2 View from the lake
3 Concert hall
4 Panorama foyer in front of the concert hall

3

4

TOYO ITO & ASSOCIATES, ARCHITECTS

Mediathek
Sendai, Japan, 1995-2000

Zur Mediathek gehören eine Bibliothek, eine Kunstgalerie, eine audiovisuelle Bibliothek, ein Filmstudio und ein Café. Während des Planungsprozesses haben die künftigen Betreiber ihre Wünsche ständig modifiziert und erweitert. Um diesen wechselnden Ansprüchen gerecht zu werden, hat sich Ito für ein offenes und variables Raumkonzept entschieden, das auch nach der Fertigstellung weitere Änderungen erlaubt.

Mit seinem Kulturzentrum hat er eine Neu-Interpretation der Bauaufgaben »Bibliothek« und »Museum« gewagt. Nicht das Sammeln, Bewahren und Archivieren steht im Vordergrund, sondern vielfältige Formen der Nutzung und Kommunikation. Die Architektur des immateriell wirkenden Kubus ist auf die drei Grundelemente Stütze, Decke und Fassade reduziert. Sie macht ihren Nutzern keine starren Vorgaben, sondern bewegt sich mit ihnen.

Die dreizehn unterschiedlich dimensionierten, röhrenartigen Stützen, die teilweise Treppen und Aufzüge aufnehmen, scheinen beliebig im Raum zu stehen. Sie erinnern an Baumstämme, die in den Himmel wachsen, oder an Seegras, das schwerelos im Wasser treibt. Da sie als offene Fachwerkkegel ausgebildet sind, wirken sie leicht. Das Licht strömt und flutet durch sämtliche Etagen. Dieses Spiel wird durch die biomorphen und auf jeder Ebene anders konfigurierten Grundrisse begünstigt. Die Geschosse sind unterschiedlich hoch und mit jeweils anderen Materialien ausgelegt. Das ganze Haus ist im Grunde genommen eine große Medien-Lounge. Mehr als 2000 Menschen kommen in ihm täglich zusammen.

M. J.

Mediatheque
Sendai, Japan, 1995-2000

The Mediatheque includes a library, art gallery, audio-visual library, film studio and café. During the design process, the future operators constantly modified and added to their wishes. To respond appropriately to these changing demands, Ito chose an open and variable spatial concept, which would permit further changes even after completion.

With his cultural centre, he ventured a re-interpretation of the "library" and "museum" building briefs. The focus is not on collecting, preserving and archiving but on many different forms of use and communication. The architecture of this seemingly immaterial cube is reduced to the three basic elements of column, floor and façade. It does not prescribe rigid rules for its users but changes with them.

The thirteen different sized, pipe-like columns, some of which house stairs and lifts, seem to be positioned randomly. They evoke tree trunks reaching towards the sky, or seaweed drifting weightlessly in the water. Since they take the form of open latticework cones, they make an impression of lightness. Light streams in and floods several storeys. This play of light is enhanced by the biomorphic floor plans which are configured differently on each level. The storeys are of different heights and each has different floor coverings. The entire building is in principle a huge media lounge. Over 2000 people come together there each day.

M. J.

1 Stützensystem des Gebäudes. Skizze von Toyo Ito
2 Ansicht Hauptfassade
3 Café
4 Bibliothek

1 Building's column system. Sketch by Toyo Ito
2 View of main façade
3 Cafe
4 Library

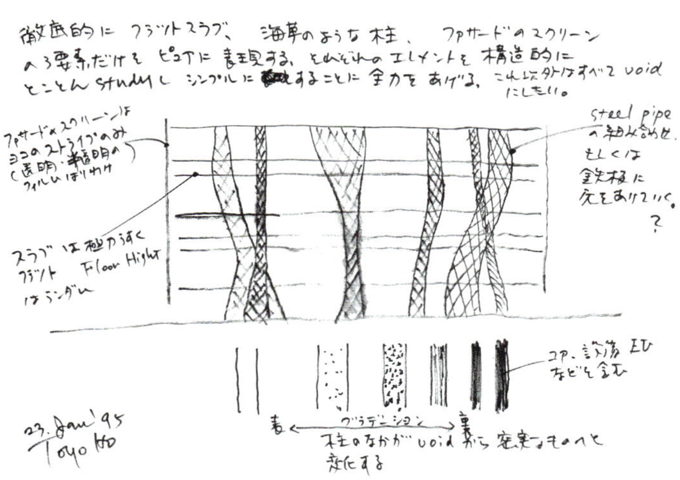

1

2

3

4

REORGANISATION DER STADT
RETHINKING URBANITY

Die Beseitigung der sprichwörtlichen »Unwirtlichkeit unserer Städte« durch die Reparatur der Innenstädte und Vororte gehörte zu den wichtigsten Städtebaumaßnahmen, die in den siebziger Jahren erdacht und seit den achtziger Jahren umgesetzt wurden. Symbol für die bewohnerfreundliche Neugestaltung eines baulich und sozial verwahrlosten städtischen Areals wurde die Piazza d'Italia von Charles Moore, die auch ein Highlight in der Eröffnungsausstellung des DAM war. Umfassendere städtebauliche Projekte wie die von Rob Krier sahen die Neubelebung des historischen Stadtgrundrisses vor und vor allem die Wiedergewinnung historischer Straßen- und Platzräume. Die »kritische Rekonstruktion« der Stadt von Josef Paul Kleihues – weiterhin aktuell, wie ein neueres Beispiel seines Büros zeigt – schloss ausdrücklich Neuinterpretation und Korrektur sowie die Integration neuer, unterschiedlicher Architekturen mit ein.

Eine nachhaltige und auf die innere Stadt fokussierte Weiterentwicklung vor allem von bereits existierender Bebauung bleibt weiterhin ein wichtiges Anliegen des Städtebaus. Ziel ist, der Verödung städtischer und der Ausuferung vorstädtischer Areale durch die Schaffung dichter und durchmischter Quartiere zu entgehen. Aber auch die Neuorganisation schrumpfender Städte ist eine zunehmend wichtige Aufgabe. Die Revitalisierung industriell gefertigter Großsiedlungen der ehemaligen DDR ist dafür ein Beispiel. Um ihrem monotonen Gesamteindruck entgegenzuwirken, wird versucht, durch schöpferischen Umgang mit standardisierter Plattenarchitektur mittels Weiterbau oder Rückbau (sprich Teilabriss) nachträglich eine differenzierte Stadtlandschaft entstehen zu lassen.

Eine weitere Herausforderung bilden städtische Brachen, meist verlassene Industrieareale. Unser Beispiel aus Wien zeigt nicht nur, wie historische Industriebauten neu genutzt werden können, sondern auch, welch wichtige Rolle dem Handel für die Stadtentwicklung hier zuerkannt wird. Um Urbanität in dem neu errichteten Wohngebiet zu erzeugen, wurden Erlebnisräume aus Shopping-Mall und Urban Entertainment Center (Kino, Kultur und Gastronomie) geschaffen, die allen Altersgruppen fast rund um die Uhr zur Verfügung stehen.

Wie städtische Zonen individuell, relativ ortsunabhängig und ohne massive Eingriffe nutzbar gemacht werden können, zeigen zwei Beispiele von jüngeren Architekturbüros.

Tackling the legendary "inhospitable nature of our cities" by repairing the inner cities and suburbs was one of the most important urban design measures of the late 20th century: conceived in the seventies and implemented since the eighties. A symbol of resident-friendly remodelling of an urban area that was scarred by both physical and social dereliction was the Piazza d'Italia by Charles Moore, which was also a highlight of DAM's inaugural exhibition. More comprehensive urban design projects, such as those undertaken by Rob Krier, aimed to re-establish the historical layout of cities and, in particular, reinstate historical streets and piazzas. Josef Paul Kleihues's philosophy of "critical reconstruction" of the city—which has lost none of its relevance, as a recent example built by his office shows—expressly included reinterpretation and correction and the integration of new and different kinds of architecture.

Sustainable development of existing building fabric, which above all focuses on the inner city, remains one of the key concerns of urban planners. The aim is to counter the depopulation of urban areas—and the increasing urban sprawl that accompanies it—by creating denser city neighbourhoods with a good mix of functions. But reorganising shrinking cities is also becoming an increasingly important task. The revitalisation of large housing developments in former East Germany that were built using industrially prefabricated construction methods is an example of this. To counter their overall impression of monotony, attempts are being made to treat the standardised concrete-slab architecture creatively and to produce a more diverse urban landscape by selectively demolishing some buildings and adding new ones.

Urban wastelands, usually derelict industrial sites, are another challenge. Our example from Vienna shows not only how historic industrial buildings can be converted for new uses but also how this project acknowledges the important role commerce plays in urban development. To generate urbanity in this newly developed residential area, experiential spaces were created, incorporating shopping malls and an Urban Entertainment Center (cinema, cultural facilities and restaurants and cafes) with facilities for all age groups that are open virtually 24 hours a day.

Examples of the work of two younger architectural offices demonstrate how urban zones can be used in a way that is individual, relatively independent of any particular place, and does not entail massive interventions.

Rob Krier: Projekt für die städtebauliche Korrektur der Tauentzienstraße, Berlin, 1980.
Original, Sammlung DAM

Rob Krier: Projekt for urban remodelling scheme on Tauentzienstrasse, Berlin, 1980.
Original, DAM collection

CHARLES MOORE

Piazza d'Italia
New Orleans, Louisiana, USA, 1975-1978

New Orleans gehörte Mitte der siebziger Jahre zu den landesweit bekannten sozialen Brennpunkten. Hieran hat sich auch durch gezielte Versuche, das Image der zerrütteten Kommune zu verbessern, wenig geändert. Dabei war die Piazza d'Italia Zeichen eines Aufbruchs gewesen. Moore wollte gemeinsam mit italienischstämmigen Bürgern in dem durch Abrisse zerstörten Zentrum ein Symbol für den Beitrag dieser Bevölkerungsgruppe zur ethnisch vielschichtigen Kultur der Stadt errichten.

Der Platz ist von fragmentierten Kolonnaden gefasst. Sie nehmen die fünf klassischen Säulenordnungen auf, interpretieren sie aber ironisch: Korinthische Kapitelle werden durch farbige Neonringe betont, bei anderen Säulen bilden herabfließende Wasserstrahlen die Kannelierung des Schafts. Zentrum der Anlage ist ein Brunnenbecken, das »Mittelmeer«, in das von den »Alpen« herab der Stiefel Italiens hineinwächst. Die Piazza stellt eine Bühne, einen Versammlungsraum unter freiem Himmel, eine Spiel- und Spaßkulisse dar. Die verfremdeten Accessoires der Heimat vermitteln zwischen alter und neuer Welt. Hier sollte »in erster Linie ein Fest der Sinne statt[finden], erst in zweiter Linie des Geistes und der Erinnerung«.

Dass das ambitionierte Projekt postmoderner Stadterneuerung von den Bewohnern nie wirklich angenommen wurde, war Grund für die im Herbst 2003 geplante Neuauflage des Neuanfangs: Die Anlage soll bald Entree eines Hotels werden, das in das umgebaute und erweiterte Hochhaus gleich hinter Moores Piazza einziehen wird. C. W.

Piazza d'Italia
New Orleans, Louisiana, USA, 1975-1978

In the mid-1970s, New Orleans was seen throughout the USA as one of the country's social flashpoints. Specific attempts to improve the wrecked community's image had done little to change things. The Piazza d'Italia was intended to represent a new departure in the city centre that had been destroyed by demolition. Moore worked with members of the Italian community to create a symbol of their contribution to the city's ethnically diverse culture.

The piazza is framed by fragmented colonnades. They take the motif of the five Classical orders of columns but interpret them ironically: Corinthian capitals are emphasised by brightly coloured neon rings, on other columns jets of water create the fluting on their shafts. The centre of the ensemble is a fountain—the "Mediterranean;" the boot of Italy descending from the "Alps" merges into it. The Piazza represents a stage, an open-air assembly space, a backdrop for fun and leisure. The accessories of the home country imported into a strange setting mediate between the old world and the new. This place is intended "primarily to celebrate the senses and only incidentally the intellect and memory." The fact that this ambitious Post-Modern urban renewal project was never truly accepted by the inhabitants prompted plans for a second attempt at this new departure in autumn 2003: the complex is to become the entrance for a hotel that will occupy a converted and extended skyscraper immediately behind Moore's piazza. C. W.

1-3 St. Joseph's Fountain auf der Piazza d'Italia, errichtet in Zusammenarbeit mit der Urban Innovations Group

1-3 St. Joseph's Fountain on the Piazza d'Italia, built in conjunction with the Urban Innovations Group

1

2

3

ROB KRIER

Projekt für die Neugestaltung der Stuttgarter Innenstadt
Deutschland, 1973/74

Im Gegensatz zu den Protagonisten einer »ironischen Postmoderne«, James Stirling oder Michael Graves, hat Rob Krier den Rückgriff auf den klassisch-akademischen Formenkanon immer ernst gemeint: »Es ist mein Ziel, die Architektur als entehrte und geschändete Kunstgattung zu rehabilitieren.« Seine seit Ende der sechziger Jahre formulierten architektonischen und städtebaulichen Visionen markieren das Paradox der Postmoderne: Die Kritik am International Style, dem angeblich zur Banalität verkommenen Baustil einer gewesenen Avantgarde, führt zum Rückgriff auf Typologien des 19. Jahrhunderts.

Kriers Projekt für Stuttgart, eines unter zahlreichen Anwendungsbeispielen der Postulate aus Aldo Rossis Manifest *L'architettura della città* (1966), sucht die Merkmale einer gründerzeitlichen Stadt dort zu beleben, wo Krieg und Nachkriegsplanung nur noch Rudimente übrig ließen. Hof, Vorhof und Platz sind die Vokabeln, mit denen Krier operiert. Die unscharfen Kreidezeichnungen zeigen überschaubare, autofreie Orte mit Menschen. Bilder dieser Art dienten dazu, jenseits des damals gängigen funktionalistischen Urbanitätsbegriffs, ein neues Lebensgefühl zu etablieren. Den hier formulierten Ansatz hat Krier inzwischen radikalisiert und seit Beginn der neunziger Jahre im großen Stil verwirklicht: In Den Haag entstand mit De Resident ein Innenstadtquartier, bei dem Geschichte nicht rekonstruiert, sondern neu erfunden wurde. C. W.

Project for the redesign of Stuttgart city centre
Germany, 1973/74

By contrast with the protagonists of "ironic Post-Modernism," James Stirling or Michael Graves, Rob Krier was always absolutely serious about making recourse to the Classical academic canon of forms: "It is my goal to rehabilitate architecture, which has become a dishonoured and discredited art form." The architectural and urban design visions he has been formulating since the end of the 1960s highlight the paradox of Post-Modernism: the criticism of the International Style, the architectural style of a former avant-garde that had allegedly degenerated into banality, leads to a return to typologies of the 19th century.

Krier's project for Stuttgart, one of numerous examples of the postulates set out in Aldo Rossi's manifesto *L'architettura della città* (1966), seeks to revive the features of a late 19th-century city in places where war and post-war planning policies had left in their wake nothing but rudimentary fragments. Courtyard, forecourt and piazza are the vocabulary with which Krier operates. His fuzzy-edged chalk drawings show human-scale, car-free places with people. Images of this kind seek to establish a new sense of vitality beyond the functionalist concept of urbanity that was common at the time. Krier has since made the approach he formulated here more radical and since the early 1990s he has been translating it into reality in grand style: in The Hague, the De Resident neighbourhood saw the creation of an inner-city district in which history was not reconstructed but replicated. C. W.

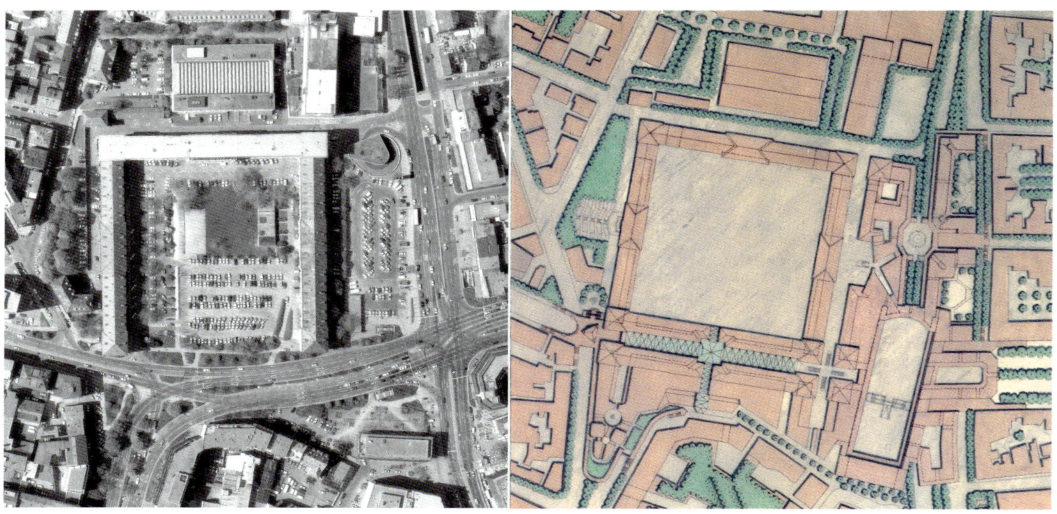

1

2+3

4

5

1 Der Rotebühlplatz im Jahr 1987 und Rob Kriers Vorschlag zur Umgestaltung
2 Ansicht des Rotebühlplatzes
3 Der kleine Vorhof am Österreichischen Platz
4 Rotebühlkaserne und Neubauten
5 Der große Hof am Österreichischen Platz

Ölkreide-Skizzen, Sammlung DAM

1 Rotebühlplatz in 1987 and Rob Krier's remodelling proposal
2 View of Rotebühlplatz
3 Small forecourt on Österreichischer Platz
4 Rotebühl barracks and new buildings
5 The large courtyard on Österreichischer Platz

Oil pastel sketches, DAM collection

KLEIHUES+KLEIHUES

Wohn- und Geschäftshaus Leipziger Platz
Berlin, Deutschland, 1998-2001

Commercial and residential building
Leipziger Platz, Berlin, Germany, 1998-2001

Die achteckige Figur des Leipziger Platzes geht als großzügiges Stadt-Entree auf das 18. Jahrhundert zurück. Was nach dem Fall der Mauer nur noch in Umrissen zu erahnen war, soll nach dem Willen des Senats als Stück historisches Berlin auferstehen. Doch der erste Neubau, das Mosse-Palais, bildete drei Jahre lang die von Ödnis umgebene Vorhut. Während am benachbarten Potsdamer Platz in kürzester Zeit gigantische Investitionen realisiert wurden, verharrte das Oktogon als prominenteste Stadtbrache von Berlin.

Seit dem Realisierungswettbewerb mehrerer Grundstückseigner beginnt sich der Kranz von Häusern zu schließen. Wie die übrigen Gewinner kommt auch Jan Kleihues der umstrittenen Gestaltungssatzung mit einem sechsgeschossigen Hauptkörper, einer Attika von drei Staffelgeschossen und einer klassischen Natursteinfassade nach. Diese wird konsequent über das Fassadenquadrat entwickelt, das sich aus den identischen Maßen von Grundstücksbreite und vorgeschriebener Traufhöhe ergibt. Das Ergebnis ist ein unprätentiöser, sich der Platzform unterordnender Bau mit Anspruch auf Elementarkraft und starkem Bezug zum Ort: So spielt der sachlich gehaltene Hinterhof auf den für Berlin typischen Block an.

Es ist allerdings ungewiss, ob sich der kommerzielle Erfolg des Potsdamer Platzes mit den im Sockel angebotenen Ladenlokalen und den Büroflächen hier wiederholen wird. Außerdem stehen strittige Besitzverhältnisse des angrenzenden Wertheim-Areals einer vollständigen Fassung des Platzes noch einige Zeit im Weg.
W. W.

The octagonal figure of Leipziger Platz as a grand entrance to the city dates back to the 18th century. Berlin's city government would now like to see resurrected as an example of historical Berlin what could only vaguely be discerned in outline after the fall of the Wall. But for three years the first new building, the Mosse-Palais, formed a lone vanguard surrounded by wasteland. Whilst gigantic investments were being made within the shortest space of time on neighbouring Potsdamer Platz, the octagon persistently remained Berlin's most prominent urban wasteland.

Since the design-and-build competition organised by the owners of a number of plots, the planned garland of buildings is beginning to connect up. Like the other winners, Jan Kleihues also adheres to the controversial design specification dictated by Berlin's urban planning authorities with a six-storey main volume, an attic with three levels which are set back and a Classical façade in natural stone. This is continued consistently across the square façade, which takes its shape from the fact that the width of the plot and the prescribed eaves height of the building are equal. The result is an unpretentious building that subordinates itself to the octagonal shape of Leipziger Platz and aims for elemental power and a strong relationship with the place. The rationalist rear courtyard is an allusion to the typical Berlin configuration of the block.

However, it is uncertain whether the commercial success of nearby Potsdamer Platz with the shops in the plinth and the office space will be repeated here. Furthermore, disputes over ownership of the adjacent Wertheim site will continue to block any attempt to frame the Leipziger Platz in its entirety. W. W.

1 Lageplan Leipziger Platz
2 Innenhof
3 Hauptfassade Leipziger Platz
4 Panorama Leipziger Platz (links Potsdamer Platz)

1 Site plan of Leipziger Platz
2 Courtyard
3 Main façade on Leipziger Platz
4 Panoramic view of Leipziger Platz (on the left: Potsdamer Platz)

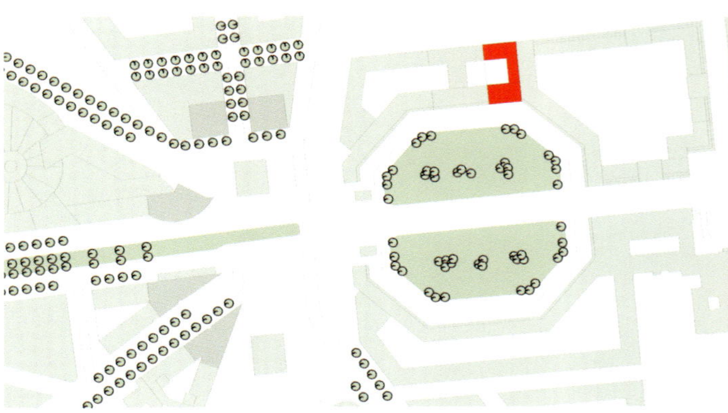

1

2

3

4

MEIER-SCUPIN & PETZET, MAYR, HEHENBERGER

Rehabilitation des Physikerquartiers
Leinefelde, Deutschland, 1998-2002

Das thüringische Leinefelde, inmitten des früheren Eichsfelder Industriegebiets gelegen, gehört zu den späten Neustädten der DDR. Nach der Wiedervereinigung litt Leinefelde wie fast alle ostdeutschen Städte unter einer hohen Arbeitslosigkeit und Einwohnerschwund. Als Reaktion darauf verfolgte die Stadt unter ihrem Bürgermeister Gerd Reinhardt systematisch und erfolgreich den Umbau des gesamten Ortes, sodass Leinefelde als »Zukunftswerkstatt Plattenbau« zum Außenstandort der Expo 2000 wurde. 2003 wurde die Stadt mit dem Deutschen Städtebaupreis ausgezeichnet.

Muck Petzets Umgestaltungsplan für das »Physikerquartier« reiht sich in das vorbildliche Gesamtkonzept ein. Seine Interventionen dienen der Weiterentwicklung der industriell gefertigten Siedlung und stellen eine Kombination von Sanierungs-, Modernisierungs-, Neubau- und Rückbaumaßnahmen dar. Von den ursprünglich 770 Wohneinheiten blieben 560. Sechs unterschiedliche Haustypen mit veränderten Grundrissen und neu gestalteten gemeinschaftlichen Grünräumen charakterisieren heute das Physikerquartier, das mit relativ bescheidenen Mitteln realisiert wurde. Der üblichen Sanierung der Wohnblocks folgten weitere Maßnahmen, die von den kostengünstigsten Kategorien »Minimal« und »Low« über die aufwendigeren Modelle »Mäander« und »Laubengang« bis zum Neubau reichten. Rund einhundert Wohneinheiten wurden abgerissen. Ein bis auf das Erdgeschoss rückgebauter Wohnblock dient nun als pavillonartiges Mieterzentrum. C. W.

Rehabilitation of the Physikerquartier
Leinefelde, Germany, 1998-2002

Leinefelde, a small town in the middle of the former Eichsfeld industrial region in Thuringia, was one of the last new towns to be built in East Germany. After reunification, Leinefelde, like virtually all East German towns, suffered from high unemployment and a dwindling population. In response, the town, under its mayor Gerd Reinhardt, launched a wholesale and systematic remodelling programme, which was so successful that Leinefelde was incorporated into Expo 2000 as an off-site exhibit under the title "Plattenbau Workshop of the Future." In 2003, the town was awarded the Städtebaupreis, Germany's prestigious urban design prize.

Muck Petzet's scheme for remodelling the "Physikerquartier" or "Physicists Quarter" fits into the exemplary master plan to upgrade this *Plattenbau* development, which was a construction method popular in East Germany that used industrially prefabricated concrete slabs. His interventions combine refurbishment, modernisation, new build and measures to reduce density. Of the 770 original dwellings, 560 remain. Today, six different types of building, in which the floor plans have been changed and the communal green spaces redesigned, characterise the Physikerquartier, which was realised at a relatively modest cost. The standard refurbishment of the housing was followed by other schemes which range from low-cost housing described as "Minimal" and "Low" through more expensive models such as "Meander" and "Gallery access," to new-build projects. Approximately one hundred dwellings were demolished. A block of flats that was remodelled so that only the ground floor remains is now used a pavilion-like residents' centre. C. W.

1 Lageplan Ausgangssituation 1997
2 Lageplan Zustand 2002

1 Site plan, original situation in 1997
2 Site plan, situation in 2002

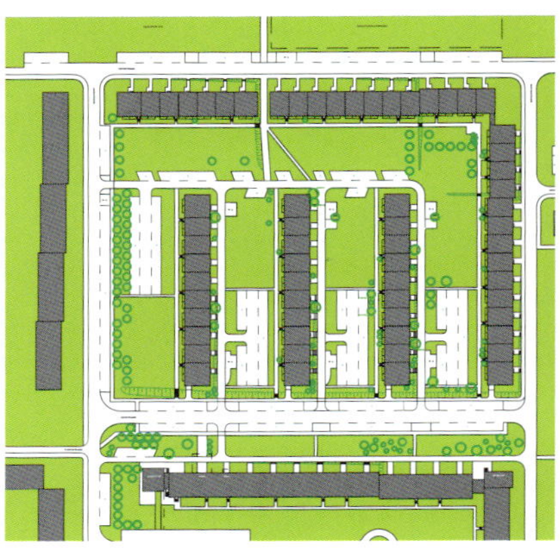
1

2

3 Typ »Neubau« zur Eckschließung, gefolgt vom Typ »Laubengang« mit Maisonettewohnungen, anschließend Typ »Minimal« und Typ »Low«
4 Rückbau: Mieterzentrum aus dem Erdgeschoss eines fünfgeschossigen Wohnblocks

3 Different types of intervention: "New build" closing the corner, followed by "Gallery Access" with duplex flats, "Minimal" and "Low"
4 Density reduction: a five-storey block of flats is partially demolished, leaving the ground floor intact to house a residents' centre.

3

4

5

6

5 Ein Prinzip der Revitalisierung war, die vorhandenen, bis zu einhundert Meter langen Wohnblöcke in visuell ansprechender Weise neu zu gliedern und mit Hilfe verschiedener Haustypen in unterschiedliche Bereiche aufzulösen. Für die Neugestaltung im Innern wurde ein Baukastensystem mit 68 unterschiedlichen Wohnungstypen entwickelt. In den neuen Grundrissen wurden z.B. enge Bäder oder innen liegende Küchen beseitigt. Die Realisierung der Grundrissänderungen (ca. 20 Prozent) erfolgte nach Mieterwunsch in leer stehenden Wohnungen innerhalb des bewohnten Hauses.
6 Typ »Mäander«. Änderung der Ausrichtung der Wohnungen. Jede zweite kann dank eines zusätzlichen Balkons auch zur Straße orientiert werden.
7 Haustyp »Low«. Zur Hofseite sind Gebäude dieser Kategorie mit neuen durchgehenden Balkonen ausgestattet.

5 One of the principles of the revitalisation scheme was to create new divisions in the blocks of flats, some of which were one hundred metres long, to make them more attractive and to use different types of building in different areas to make them less monotonous. The interiors of the buildings were redesigned using a modular system with 68 different types of dwelling. In the new floor plans, problems such as cramped bathrooms and internal kitchens were eliminated. The changes in layout (approx. 20 per cent) were carried out, in line with the tenants' wishes, in empty flats in otherwise inhabited buildings.
6 "Meander" type. The orientation of the flats was changed. A second balcony was added to every other flat, so that they also face onto the street.
7 "Low-cost" type. New communal balconies facing the courtyard were added to buildings in this category.

7

8

8 Rückbau eines Wohnhauses in ein eingeschossiges Gebäude im großen zentralen Hof des Quartiers, Sitz des Mieterzentrums und der Leinefelder Wohnungsbaugesellschaft. Im Bereich der ehemaligen Treppenhäuser wurden dem Pavillon Oberlichter aufgesetzt, die der zusätzlichen Belichtung und Belüftung dienen.
9 Gemeinschaftliche Freifläche im Innern des Physikerquartiers. Es gibt auch weiterhin keine Privatgärten in der Siedlung. Die Balkone haben eine nutzbare Tiefe von mindestens 1,5 Metern und sind gegen Einblick geschützt.

8 Partially demolishing a block of flats to create a single-storey building in the quarter's large central courtyard. It now houses the residents' centre and offices for the Leinefelde housing association. Rooflights were installed where the stairwells had once been, giving the pavilion extra daylight and natural ventilation.
9 Communal open space in the interior of the Physikerquartier. The estate has no private gardens. The balconies have a usable depth of at least 1.5 metres and are designed to protect people's privacy.

9

COOP HIMMELB(L)AU, ATELIER HOLZBAUER, ATELIERS JEAN NOUVEL, MANFRED WEHDORN

Revitalisierung der ehemaligen Gasbehälter
Wien, Österreich, 1999-2001

Revitalisation of former gasometers
Vienna, Austria, 1999-2001

Die Speicherbauten des Gaswerks Simmering, vier im Inneren hohle, ursprünglich durch Glaskuppeln überdeckte Backsteinkonstruktionen mit einer Höhe von 75 und einem Durchmesser von 62, 8 Metern stammen aus dem Jahr 1899. Nach der Schließung des ehemals größten Gaswerks in Europa wurde das Ensemble 1978 unter Denkmalschutz gestellt. 1989 erarbeitete der Wiener Architekt Manfred Wehdorn eine Machbarkeitsstudie für die Neubelebung des Areals, die 1996 in das Vorhaben der Stadt Wien einfloss, die Revitalisierung der vier Gebäude mit dem Schwerpunkt Wohnen in Angriff zu nehmen. Das Areal sollte mit einer Mischung aus Stadtfunktionen zum Musterbeispiel dafür werden, wie brachliegende Gewerbe- und Industrieflächen in Wohn-, Arbeits- und Erholungsraum verwandelt werden können. Außerdem erwartete man von dem Projekt Impulse für die Entwicklung des unmittelbaren Umfelds.

Neben insgesamt rund 600 auf die vier Gasometer verteilten neuen Wohnungen, dem Archiv der Stadt Wien und einem Studentenwohnheim beleben 11000 Quadratmeter Büros und vor allem Nutzungsangebote der konsumorientierten Freizeitgestaltung den Ort mit eigenem U-Bahn-Anschluss. Eine mehrgeschossige Shopping-Mall zieht sich unter den Gasometern hindurch. Ein vorgelagertes Urban Entertainment Center, das vom Architekturbüro Rüdiger Lainer stammt, ist ebenfalls mit dem Komplex verbunden. C. W.

The storage buildings of Simmering gasworks, four hollow brick structures, originally with glass domes, each 75 metres high and 62.8 metres in diameter, were built in 1899. After what was once the largest gasworks in Europe closed, the ensemble was included in the schedule of historic monuments in 1978. In 1989, Vienna-based architect Manfred Wehdorn prepared a feasibility study for the regeneration of the site, which in 1996 was incorporated into the city of Vienna's project to revitalise the four buildings with an emphasis on housing. The intention was to bring together a mix of urban functions and make the site a model example of how derelict brownfield sites can be transformed into spaces for living, working and recreation. There were also expectations that the project would stimulate the development of the immediate surroundings.

Along with a total of some 600 new dwellings distributed across the four gasometers, the archives of the city of Vienna and a student hall of residence, life was injected into the area by a further 11,000 square metres of office space and in particular by consumer-oriented entertainment facilities and a specially built Underground station. A multi-level shopping mall runs beneath all the gasometers. An urban entertainment centre, designed by Rüdiger Lainer's architectural practice, was built in front of the complex and is connected to it. C. W.

RÜDIGER LAINER: Urban Entertainment Center
1+2 Außen umhüllt ein farbiger, blickdurchlässiger Glassockel den so genannten Pleasure Dome, in dem zwölf Kinosäle wie Felsen aufgetürmt sind. Weiträumige Foyers sorgen hier wie auch in dem dreigeschossigen Shopping- und Vergnügungsbereich in der östlichen Gebäudehälfte für interessante Raumwahrnehmungen. Das vielschichtige Gebäude enthält auch reichlich Parkraum; eine mögliche Umnutzung wurde bei seiner Konzeption bereits berücksichtigt.

RÜDIGER LAINER: Urban Entertainment Center
1+2 A plinth of translucent, coloured glass envelops the so-called "Pleasure Dome," in which twelve cinema auditoria tower up like cliffs. Here, as in the three-storey shopping and amusement area in the Eastern half of the building, spacious foyers create opportunities for interesting experiences of space. The complex building also has ample parking space; the possibility of converting this space for a new use was taken into account when the complex was conceived.

1

2

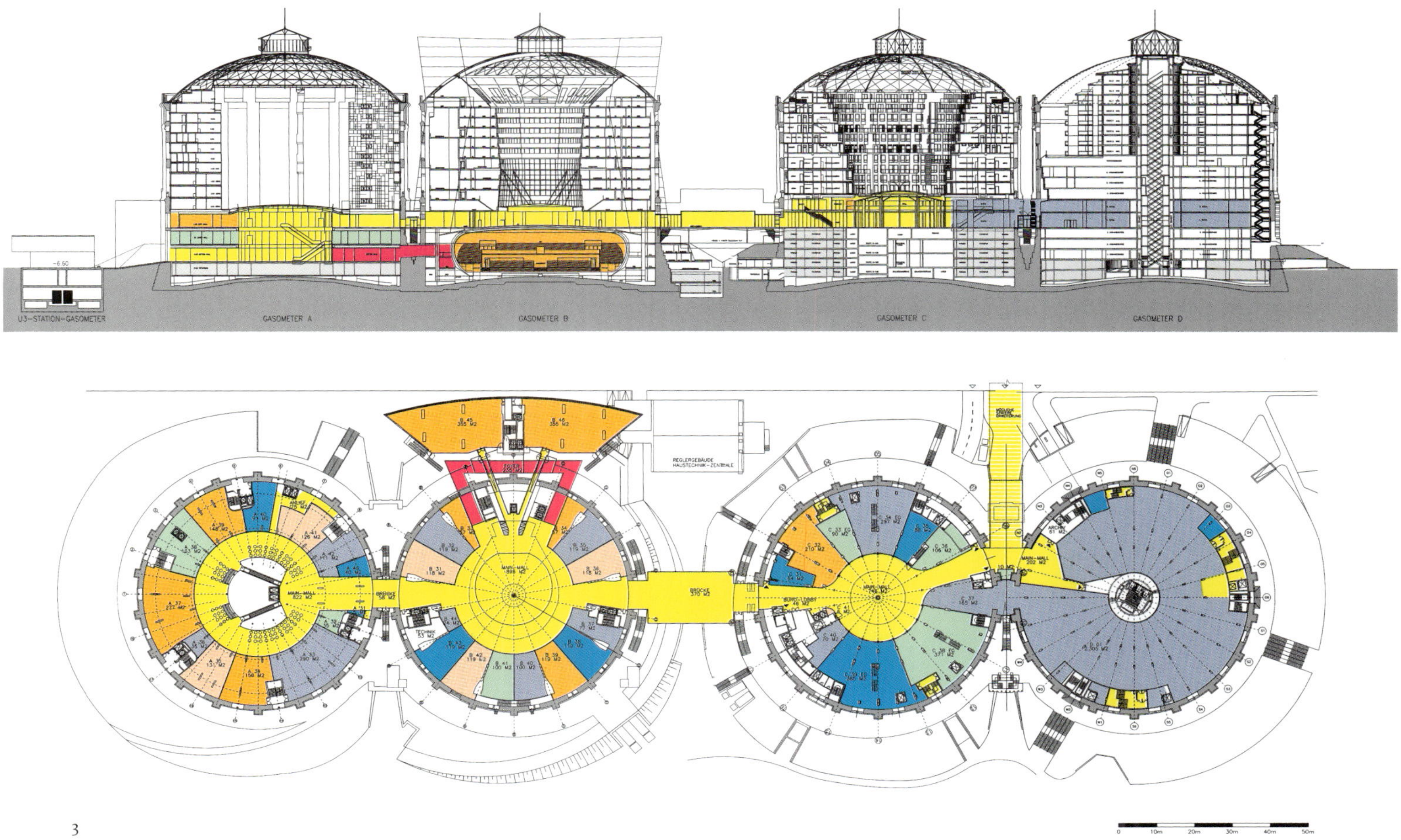

3

4

3 Schnitt durch die Gasometer. A: Nouvel, B: Coop-Himmelb(l)au, C: Wehdorn und D: Holzbauer (von links nach rechts). Darunter: Grundriss der Shopping-Mall-Ebene.
4 Eine gläserne Brücke führt vom Gasometer D in das Urban Entertainment Center von Rüdiger Lainer.

3 Section through the gasometers. A: Nouvel, B: Coop-Himmelb(l)au, C: Wehdorn and D: Holzbauer (from left to right). Beneath that: plan of the shopping mall level.
4 A glazed walkway leads from gasometer D into the Urban Entertainment Center designed by Rüdiger Lainer.

5

6

MANFRED WEHDORN: Gasometer C

5 Über fünf Garagengeschossen, die jeweils die gesamte Grundfläche ausfüllen, liegen zwei Shopping-Mall-, drei Büro- und sechs Wohnebenen, die auf den zentralen Hof hin orientiert sind. Ein Oberlicht trennt die Mall-Ebene von den oberen Etagen. Die terrassenartig gestaffelte kreisförmige Anlage mit den für Wien typischen Laubengängen wird durch vier Einschnitte gegliedert, in denen sich Treppenhäuser oder begrünte Höfe befinden. Die 92 Wohnungen verfügen teilweise über Balkone und Terrassen entweder zum Hof oder nach außen.

MANFRED WEHDORN: Gasometer C

5 On top of five parking levels, each covering the entire footprint of the building, are eleven more storeys organised around a central courtyard: two of them housing a shopping mall, three with offices and six with flats. There is a roof light between the mall and the storeys above it. The circular complex has setback terraces with access galleries typical for Vienna. Articulation is created by four cut-outs containing stairwells or planted courtyards. A number of the 92 flats have balconies and terraces, facing either the courtyard or outwards from the building.

COOP HIMMELB(L)AU: Gasometer B

6 Markant ist der nördliche Anbau in Form eines siebzig Meter hohen Schilds, der auf vier Stelzenpaaren ruht und durch zwei Übergänge mit dem Gasometer verbunden ist. Die 140 Wohnungen im Gasometer – darunter 73 Wohnungen eines Studentenwohnheims mit 247 Zimmern – sind ringförmig entlang der Hülle angelegt. Sie beginnen erst ab ca. dreißig Metern Höhe und bieten Ausblicke in den Hof und nach außen. Der Neubau enthält auf 17 Geschossen 116 Wohnungen. In den Untergeschossen befindet sich eine schallisolierte Veranstaltungshalle für 4000 Besucher.

COOP HIMMELB(L)AU: Gasometer B

6 The striking feature of this gasometer is a 70-metre high building that has been added on and forms the shape of a shield. It stands on four pairs of pilotis and is connected to the gasometer by two walkways. The 140 flats—of which 73 make up a 247-room student hall of residence—are arranged in a circle around the envelope of the building. The lowest level of flats is at thirty metres; they have views of either the courtyard or the city. The new building has 116 flats on 17 storeys. The underground levels of the building house a soundproof events venue with seating for 4000.

JEAN NOUVEL: Gasometer A
7 Neun als Ring angeordnete Türme, die durch Laubengänge verbunden sind, enthalten im unteren Bereich drei Büroebenen und in den oberen neun Geschossen 128 Wohnungen. Die Mitte wird von einem riesigen Bullauge – dem Oberlicht der Mall – überdacht. Damit der Eindruck architektonischer Leichtigkeit gesteigert wird, dominieren Glas und Stahl. Verspiegelte Wandflächen optimieren den Lichteinfall. Es war Nouvels Idee, die alte Kuppelkonstruktion der Gasometer zwar beizubehalten, jedoch unverglast als Metallskelett gegen den Himmel zu öffnen.

JEAN NOUVEL: Gasometer A
7 Nine towers, arranged in a ring and connected by access galleries, have three storeys of office space at the bottom with nine storeys above containing 128 flats. The centre of the gasometer is covered by a gigantic bull's eye—the mall's roof light. Glass and steel dominate, enhancing the impression of architectural lightness. Reflecting wall surfaces optimise the available daylight. It was Nouvel's idea to retain the old dome structure of the gasometers but to leave it unglazed, opening it up to the sky in the form of a metal skeleton.

7

WILHELM HOLZBAUER: Gasometer D
8 Über den beiden Shopping-Mall-Ebenen ist auf sechs Geschossen das Wiener Stadt- und Landesarchiv untergebracht. Die acht Wohngeschosse darüber sind in drei gleich lange Flügel gegliedert, die sich im Zentrum des Gasometers treffen und auf diese Weise in einer Höhe von 32 Metern drei begrünte Höfe bilden. Alle 114 Wohnungen sind auf diese Höfe orientiert. Die unteren zwölf Wohnungen besitzen einen eigenen Garten, während die der oberen Etagen mit Balkonen und Dachterrassen ausgestattet sind. Die Fenster des Gasometers sind unverglast.

WILHELM HOLZBAUER: Gasometer D
8 Vienna's city and state archives are housed on six storeys above the two shopping mall levels. The eight storeys of flats above are divided into three wings of equal length, which meet at the centre of the gasometer and create three planted courtyards 32 metres above ground level. All 114 flats face these courtyards. The 12 lowest flats have their own gardens; the flats on the upper storeys have balconies and roof terraces. The windows of the gasometers are unglazed.

8

KORTEKNIE STUHLMACHER ARCHITECTEN

Parasite Las Palmas
Rotterdam, Niederlande, 2001

»Prototypes for advanced ready-made amphibious small scale individual temporary ecological houses«, kurz Parasite. So nennen Mechthild Stuhlmacher und Rien Korteknie die kleinen Bauten, die sie als neues Werkzeug der Nachverdichtung anbieten. Ihren Blick richten die Architekten dabei auf die Randlagen (Para-Sites), die vernachlässigten und vergessenen Winkel in der Stadt: Industriebrachen, Dachlandschaften, Wasserflächen.

Parasiten sind Lebewesen, die sich für eine bestimmte Zeit auf Kosten eines Wirts ernähren. Analog dazu besetzt auch der Parasite einen vorübergehend verfügbaren Bauplatz und dockt sich an vorhandene Infrastrukturen an.

Eine erste Bewährungsprobe erlebte die Idee im Jahr 2001 auf dem als Ausstellungszentrum genutzten Lagergebäude Las Palmas von Bakema und van den Broek, als Rotterdam »Kulturhauptstadt Europas« war. In nur vier Tagen wurde auf einem stillgelegten Aufzugsschacht ein erster giftgrüner Prototyp errichtet. Möglich machte dies ein komplett in Deutschland vorgefertigter Bausatz aus verleimten Fichtenholzplatten. Der Grad an Vorfertigung ist derart hoch, dass die Technik eine Alternative zu den Standardprodukten der Einfamilienhaus-Industrie darstellt. Um die Konstruktion vor Augen zu führen, wurden sämtliche Holzoberflächen unverkleidet belassen. Das Ergebnis ist ein unkonventionelles Modellhaus, das dem Anspruch der Architekten an zeitgemäße Nachverdichtung, skulpturale Präsenz und Mobilität entspricht. W. W.

Las Palmas Parasite
Rotterdam, Netherlands, 2001

"Prototypes for advanced ready-made amphibious small scale individual temporary ecological houses," or Parasites for short. That is the name Mechthild Stuhlmacher and Rien Korteknie have given to the small buildings they are proposing as the new tool for increasing density. The architects focus their attention in this on fringe locations (para-sites), the neglected and forgotten nooks and crannies of the city: industrial wastelands, roofscapes, floating sites.

Parasites are creatures that feed themselves for a certain time at the expense of their host. These architectural parasites are analogous to this in that they occupy a site that is temporarily available and connect to the existing infrastructure.

The idea was first put to the test in Rotterdam when the city was cultural capital of Europe: in Las Palmas, the warehouses used as an exhibition centre designed by Bakema and van den Broek. In just four days, the first Day-Glo green prototype was erected on a decommissioned lift shaft. This was possible due to a completely prefabricated kit of glued spruce panels from Germany. The degree of prefabrication was so great that this method represents a real alternative to the standardised products used in the single-family home industry. To make the structure visible all the wooden surfaces were left unclad. The result is an unconventional model house which meets the architects' ambitions for a building that was contemporary, provided higher density, a sculptural presence and mobility. W. W.

1

1-3 Ansichten des Parasite auf dem Lagergebäude Las Palmas von Jacob Berend Bakema und Johannes Hendrik van den Broek

1-3 Views of the parasite on the Las Palmas warehouses by Jacob Berend Bakema and Johannes Hendrik van den Broek

2

3

NETZWERKARCHITEKTEN MIT RALF FLECKENSTEIN

Floating Homes
Berlin, Deutschland, 2002

»Vorne Wellen, hinten Weltstadt«. So wirbt die Wasserstadt GmbH auf ihrer Homepage um Investitionen. Und tatsächlich liegt die Halbinsel Stralau an der Rummelsburger Bucht, einer der Planungsschwerpunkte des Entwicklungsträgers, nur fünf S-Bahn-Stationen vom Alexanderplatz entfernt. Eingebettet in gründerzeitliche Gebäudesubstanz entsteht an der Spree ein Quartier, in dem Erholung groß geschrieben wird.

Die neueste Entwicklung zielt darauf ab, nicht nur Wohnen am, sondern auch auf dem Wasser anzubieten. Zu diesem Zweck wurde ein Wettbewerb unter Teams von Investoren und Architekten ausgeschrieben, der zum Ziel hatte, entsprechende Wohnformen zu entwickeln.

Fleckenstein und die Gruppe Netzwerkarchitekten, die den ersten Preis gewannen, setzen auf eine von Pontons getragene zweigeschossige Box, die individuelle Raum-, Wohn- und Nutzungskonstellationen zulässt. Möglich wird dies durch eine Grundkonstruktion aus Massivholzelementen, die nur die kompakte Hülle definiert, während der Innenausbau in Eigenregie erfolgen kann. Der Kunde bestimmt den Grundriss also weitestgehend selbst. Das Floating Home ist an den Längsseiten mit einer mattierten Einfachverglasung gedämmt. Eine Luftschicht speichert daraus resultierende Wärme oder kühlt den Innenraum durch Temperaturausgleich mit dem Wasser.

Bislang ist die Idee nur ein Wohntraum für Besserverdienende. Doch nach dem Willen der Planer soll sie sich bald auch dort durchsetzen, wo nur Wasserstraßen eine weitere Urbanisierung zulassen. W. W.

Floating Homes
Berlin, Germany, 2002

"Waves in front, world metropolis behind"—that is how Wasserstadt GmbH try to entice investors on their home page. And indeed the Stralau peninsula in Rummelsburg Bay, one of the key areas targeted by developers, is only five stops from Alexanderplatz on the S-Bahn, the suburban rail network. Surrounded by historical building fabric from the late 19th century, a neighbourhood will be created here on the River Spree in which recreation will feature strongly.

The latest development is aiming to create housing not only by the water but on the water. To this end a competition was organised for teams of architects and investors with the stated aim of developing appropriate forms of housing to make this possible.

Fleckenstein and Netzwerkarchitekten, who won the first prize, have set a two-storey box on pontoons, allowing spaces for different ways of living and different uses to be individually customized. This is made possible by the fact that the basic structure consists of elements of solid wood which defines the compact shell only; the interiors can be designed completely from scratch by the individual. The customers therefore decide on the layout themselves. The Floating Home is insulated on the long sides with matted single glazing. A layer of air stores the heat produced by this or cools the indoor space through a system of heat exchange with the water.

So far, the idea represents the possibility of a dream home for the affluent only. But the planners have indicated that they would also like to see it become reality in places where waterways offer the only possibility for urbanisation. W. W.

1

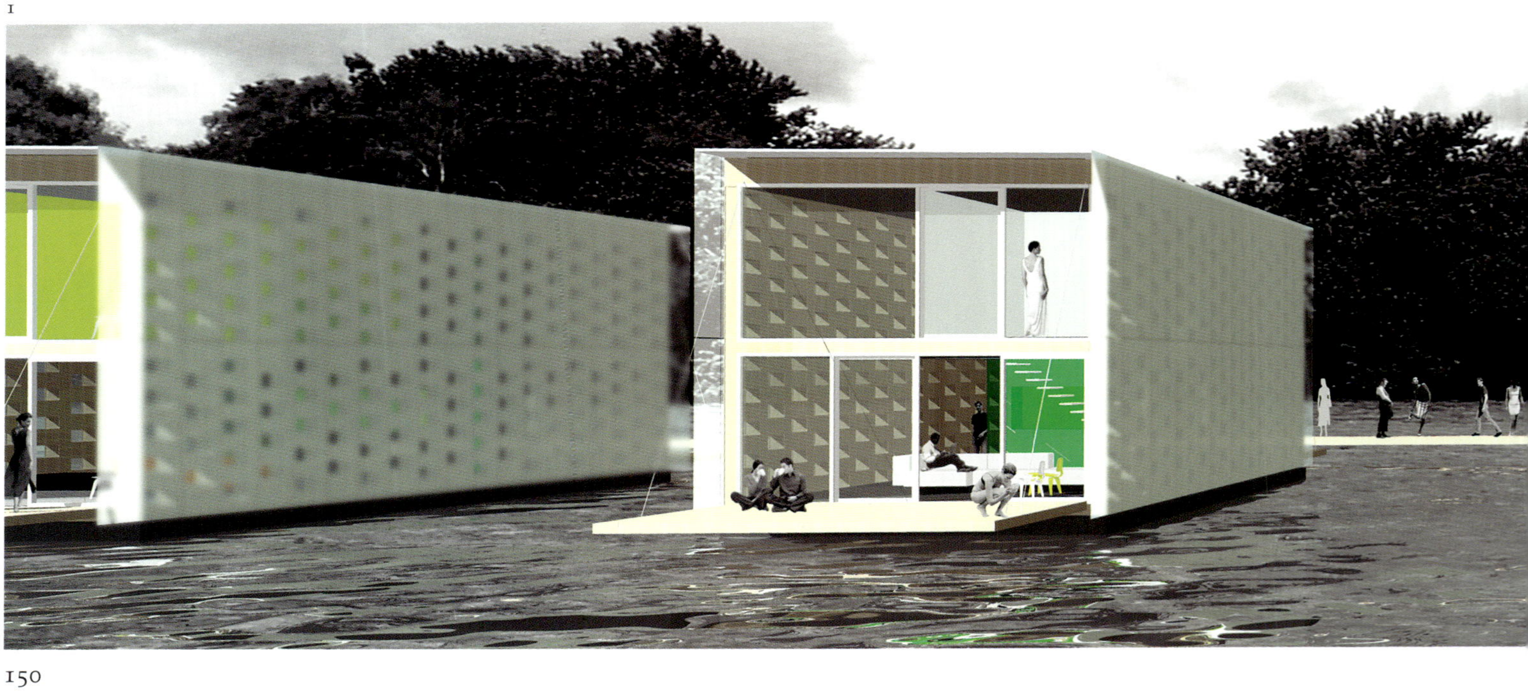

2

3

1 Ansicht vom Wasser
2 Nachtansicht vom Ufer
3 Innenperspektive in Richtung Wasser
4 Beispielhafte Grundrisslösung und Schnitt

1 View from the water
2 View by night from the river bank
3 Interior perspective view looking towards the water
4 Examples of possible floor plan and section

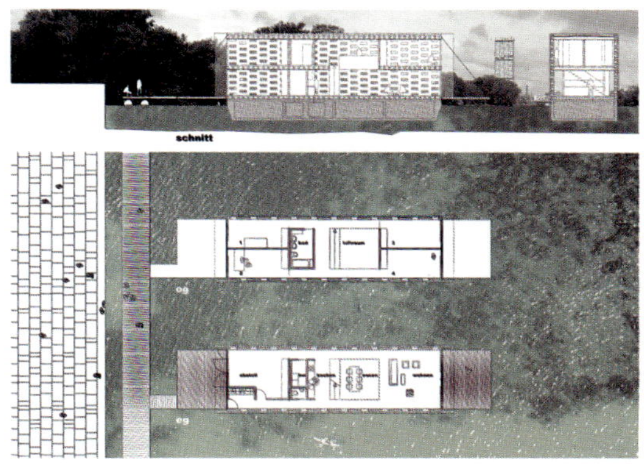

4

ÖKO ALS INVESTITION
ECOLOGY AS INVESTMENT

1987 wurde die International Netherlands Bank in Amsterdam fertig gestellt. Ein singuläres Beispiel, denn das Gebäude für diese einflussreiche Institution wurde nach den Kriterien »grüner Solararchitektur« errichtet. Bemerkenswert daran war, dass sich die Kosten für die Bewirtschaftung des großen Gebäudes durch diese Bauweise beträchtlich verminderten – ganz abgesehen vom gesteigerten Wohlbefinden der Beschäftigten. Das damals sich verbreitende Wissen um eine drohende Klimakatastrophe bewirkte aber nicht sofort ein allgemeines Umdenken. Einige wenige Architekten, die in der Eröffnungsausstellung des DAM vertreten waren, reagierten zwar mit alternativen Projekten oder mit apokalyptischen Szenarien auf Papier, um auf die Umweltzerstörung aufmerksam zu machen, aber ernsthafte Experimente (vor allem bei Einzelwohnhäusern) fanden in der Architektenschaft erst allmählich Beachtung. Zu sehr schien die ökologische Bauweise mit baukünstlerischen Standards unvereinbar.

Bei der Umweltmusterstadt SolarCity wurde versucht, einen hohen architektonischen Anspruch umzusetzen. Für diese Siedlung mit einer gleichfalls nach ökologischen Zielvorgaben konzipierten Infrastruktur gab es kein einheitlich bindendes, sondern ein am Markt orientiertes Ökokonzept, das dennoch eine große finanzielle Herausforderung für die beteiligten Wohnungsbaugesellschaften darstellte. Dass dieses Projekt nachhaltigen Bauens nur mit beträchtlichen EU-Fördermitteln realisiert werden konnte, zeigt auch, wie schwierig es noch immer ist, ökologischen Wohnungsbau in diesem Umfang unter normalen Bedingungen zu realisieren.

Aber nicht nur weitere umfassende Strategien zur Minimierung des Energiebedarfs (exemplarisch ist das von Rolf Disch entwickelte Plusenergiehaus) und die Schaffung regenerativer Energiequellen sind vonnöten. Auch Experimente mit recycelbaren Baustoffen – für die wir Shigeru Ban stellvertretend nennen – oder der effektive Umgang mit Wasserressourcen gewinnen in der heutigen Architektur an Bedeutung. Die Renaturierung des verseuchten Areals der riesigen Ford-Produktionsstätte mit (scheinbar) einfachsten Mitteln, nämlich durch gezielten Pflanzenwuchs und Regenwassernutzung, ist bemerkenswert – und schließt unseren Kreis: Die Gruppe SITE hatte vor über zwanzig Jahren bereits eine ähnliche Idee, die in der Eröffnungsausstellung des DAM erstmals präsentiert wurde.

The International Netherlands Bank in Amsterdam was completed in 1987: a singular example because the building for this influential institution was designed around “green solar architecture” criteria. The remarkable thing about the project was that this construction method has resulted in significantly lower running costs for this large building—not to mention enhancing the wellbeing of the people who work in it. However, knowledge of the threat of a climate disaster, which was becoming more widespread at the time, did not bring about an immediate or universal rethink in this field. A handful of architects who were represented at DAM’s inaugural exhibition responded with alternative projects or with apocalyptic scenarios on paper with the intention of drawing attention to the destruction of the environment, but serious experiments—particularly in individual houses—only gradually attracted the attention of the architectural profession. It simply did not seem possible to reconcile ecological building methods with architectural standards.

The environmental model town SolarCity was an attempt to create something that was of a high architectural standard. Although this development, the infrastructure for which was also conceived around environmental criteria, was not based on a single, binding ecological concept but on one that was geared to the market, it nevertheless represented a huge financial challenge for the housing corporations involved. The fact that it was only possible to realise this sustainable architecture project with the help of considerable EU funding also shows how difficult it still is to build ecological housing on this scale under normal conditions.

Green architecture is not confined to using regenerative sources of energy or developing comprehensive strategies for minimizing energy requirements. An outstanding example of the latter is the “surplus energy house” developed by Rolf Disch, in which the solar energy generated exceeds the house’s needs. Experiments with recyclable building materials—Shigeru Ban can be cited as an example here—or the efficient use of water resources are gaining importance in architecture today. The renaturalisation of the contaminated site of the gigantic Ford manufacturing plant with (apparently) very simple means, namely landscaping with specific plants and the use of rainwater, is remarkable—and brings us back full circle: over twenty years ago, the SITE group had a similar idea that was presented for the first time at DAM’s inaugural exhibition.

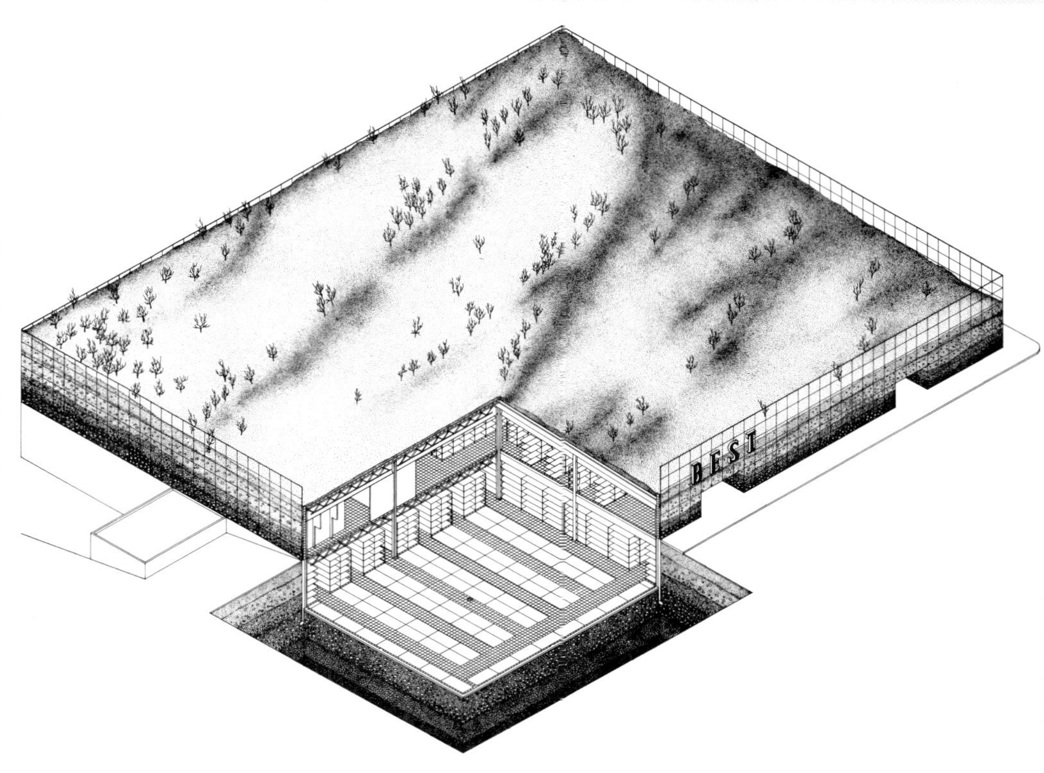

SITE: Terrarium Showroom, San Francisco, 1978. Lichtpause, Sammlung DAM

SITE: Terrarium Showroom, San Francisco, 1978. Tracing, DAM collection

HAUS-RUCKER-CO

Umweltmaschinen
1967-1971

Environmental machines
1967-1971

Mit der englischen Gruppe Archigram zog Ende der fünfziger Jahre das Happening in den architektonischen Entwurfs- und Präsentationsprozess ein. Italienische (Superstudio; Archizoom) und österreichische (Zünd-up; Coop Himmelb(l)au) Planer erweiterten ihre »Pop-Architektur« durch Performances.

Eine vergleichbare Vereinigung, die den Glauben an einen unendlichen Fortschritt parodierte und die zunehmende Umweltverschmutzung kritisierte, war die seit 1967 in Düsseldorf ansässige Gruppe Haus-Rucker-Co., bestehend aus Manfred und Laurids Ortner und Günther Zamp Kelp. Ihre »Leisuretime-Explosion« – entstanden während eines Aufenthalts in New York – stellt überdimensionierte Glaskugeln dar, die wie Parasiten die Hafenanlagen Manhattans besetzen. Die Gebilde haben die Gestalt gigantischer Glühbirnen, in denen Menschen vor der lebensfeindlichen Umwelt geschützt überleben sollen. Der »Air-Fountain« – zu einem Haltestellensystem in der Stadt erweiterbar – ist ein Luftbrunnen, aus dem die Bewohner bei Smog Sauerstoff tanken können.

Während die Brüder Ortner mit materialbewussten Bauten zur an der Tektonik orientierten Praxis zurückgekehrt sind (Sächsische Landesbibliothek, Dresden), gelang es Zamp Kelp, die fragile Ästhetik seiner frühen Visionen in ausgeführten Projekten umzusetzen. Vor allem der »Jahrtausendblick«, eine riesige, in die Bergwerkslandschaft des Lipperlands gebaute Treppe, deren Aussichtskorb von hintereinander geschichteten Glasplatten eingefasst wird, zeigt Verwandtschaft mit Arbeiten der sechziger Jahre.

C. W.

The English group of architects Archigram introduced the "happening" to the architectural design and presentation process at the end of the 1950s. Italian (Superstudio, Archizoom) and Austrian (Zünd-up, Coop Himmelb(l)au) designers expanded their "pop architecture" through performances.

A comparable group, who parodied blind faith in unlimited progress and criticised the growing pollution of the environment, was Haus-Rucker-Co., consisting of Manfred and Laurids Ortner and Günther Zamp Kelp, who had been based in Düsseldorf since 1967. Their "Leisure time explosion"—which they developed while they were in New York—consists of oversized glass spheres occupying the docklands of Manhattan like parasites. The structures are in the shape of gigantic light bulbs in which people would be able to seek refuge and survive the life-threatening environment. The air fountain—that could be extended to form a system of stations throughout the city—enables inhabitants to fill up with oxygen during smog.

While the Ortner brothers with their materially conscious buildings have gone back to a design practice based on tectonics (Saxon State Library in Dresden), Zamp Kelp has managed to translate the fragile aesthetics of his early visions into built projects. In particular, the Millennium View, a huge flight of stairs built into the mining landscape of the Lipperland region (near Dortmund), with its viewing cage enclosed by layer after layer of glass panels, is clearly related to his work of the sixties. C. W.

1 Air Fountain, 1971. Collage, Sammlung DAM
2 Leisuretime-Explosion, 1967. Collage, Sammlung DAM

1 Air Fountain, 1971. Collage, DAM collection
2 Leisure time Explosion, 1967. Collage, DAM collection

1

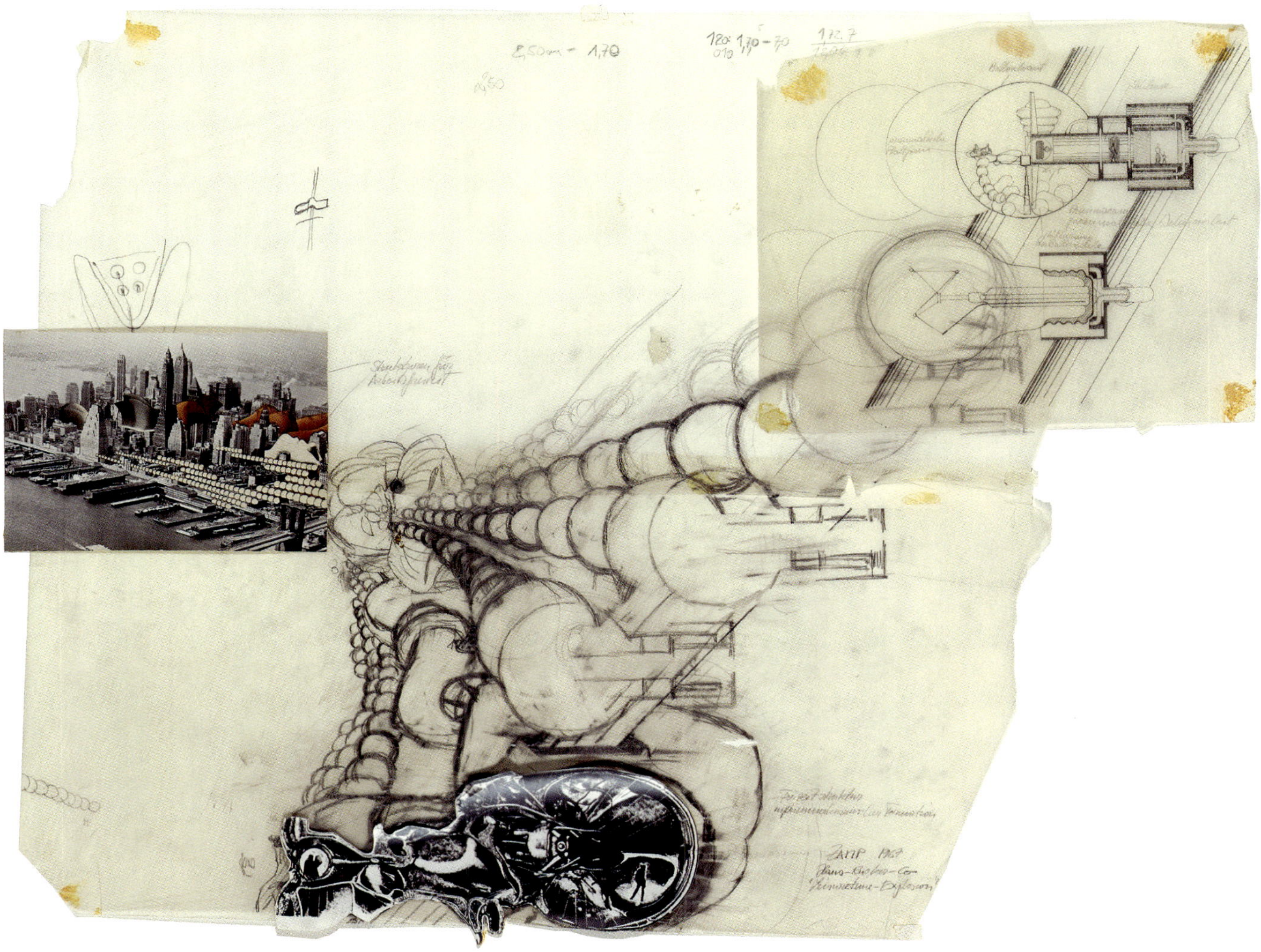

2

NORMAN FOSTER AND PARTNERS, HERZOG + PARTNER, RICHARD ROGERS PARTNERSHIP, AUER + WEBER + ARCHITEKTEN

SolarCity, Linz-Pichling, Österreich, 1995-2005

Das neue Wohnquartier der oberösterreichischen Landeshauptstadt, als ein EU-weites Musterbeispiel für nachhaltige Stadtentwicklung initiiert, soll bis zum Jahr 2005 mit 1317 Wohnungen samt Infrastruktur fertig gestellt sein. Der Masterplan stammt von Roland Rainer. Mit der städtebaulichen und architektonischen Realisierung wurden die READ-Gruppe (Renewable Energies in Architecture and Design), der die Büros Foster, Rogers, Herzog und Norbert Kaiser (Energietechnik) angehören, sowie der Solararchitektur-Spezialist Martin Treberspurg betraut. Insgesamt sind an der Errichtung der Siedlung zwölf Bauträger und 19 Architekturbüros beteiligt.

Die als Solararchitektur in Niedrigenergiebauweise ausgeführten Wohnhäuser folgen einer Gartenstadtstruktur. Radial vom Zentrum ausstrahlende Hauptalleen geben die Unterteilung des Ensembles vor. Das Straßen- und Wegenetz ist so geführt, dass Fußgänger und Radfahrer Priorität genießen. Bei der Abwasserbeseitigung werden neue ökologische Verfahren angewandt. Weitere wichtige Programmpunkte sind eine ausgewogene soziale Mischung der Bewohner und die landschaftsplanerische Gestaltung in und außerhalb der Siedlung.

Das Ortszentrum, das Geschäfte sowie soziale und kulturelle Einrichtungen vereinigt, wurde von Auer + Weber geschaffen. Die streng geometrische Anlage zu beiden Seiten der Hauptverkehrsader mit Straßenbahnhaltestelle besteht aus zweigeschossigen kompakten Modulen, deren Zwischenräume – Wege und Höfe – von einer filigranen Gerüststruktur überspannt werden.

C. W.

SolarCity, Linz, Austria, 1995-2005

This new residential area in the Pichling district of Linz, the regional capital of Upper Austria, was initiated as a model estate within the EU for sustainable, ecological urban development. The infrastructure and 1317 living units are scheduled for completion by 2005. The original master plan was drawn up by Roland Rainer. The READ Group (Renewable Energies in Architecture and Design), whose members include Foster, Rogers, Herzog and Norbert Kaiser (energy technology), was commissioned to oversee the urban development and architectural realisation, along with solar architecture specialist Martin Treberspurg. A total of twelve developers and nineteen architecture practices are involved in building the estate.

The housing is designed as low-energy solar architecture. The development follows the structure of a garden city with avenues radiating out from the centre dividing up the ensemble. The network of roads and paths is designed to give priority to pedestrians and cyclists. New ecological methods are used in the sewage treatment. Other important aspects of the programme are a balanced social mix of residents and an emphasis on landscape design within and around the development.

The centre of the estate, which has both shops and cultural and social facilities, was designed by Auer + Weber. The strictly geometrical complex on either side of the main traffic artery with tram stops consists of compact, two-storey modules. The spaces between them—paths and courtyards—are covered by a filigree structural framework.

C. W.

Luftfoto SolarCity, 2004
1 Auer+Weber: Zentrum
2 Richard Rogers: Wohnbauten
3 Thomas Herzog: Wohnbauten
4 Norman Foster: Wohnbauten

Aerial view of SolarCity, photo: 2004
1 Centre by Auer+Weber
2 Residential buildings by Richard Rogers
3 Residential buildings by Thomas Herzog
4 Residential buildings by Norman Foster

1

2

3

AUER + WEBER: Zentrum SolarCity
2 Marktplatz im Süden
3 Passage in Richtung Wohnbauten Foster

AUER + WEBER: SolarCity centre
2 Market place in the south
3 Passage looking towards Foster's residential buildings

4

NORMAN FOSTER: Dreigeschossige Wohnanlage
4 Jede Wohnung ist mit einem Südbalkon ausgestattet. Warmwasser wird mit der Aufbereitung durch Solarenergie gewonnen.

NORMAN FOSTER: Three-storey residential complex
4 Each living unit has a southfacing balcony. Hot water is provided by a solar energy system.

RICHARD ROGERS: Zweigeschossige Wohnanlage
5 Die Ausrichtung nach Süden garantiert eine optimale passive Solarenergienutzung.

RICHARD ROGERS: Two-storey residential complex
5 South facing to ensure optimal use of passive solar energy

5

6

THOMAS HERZOG: Dreigeschossige Wohnbauten
6 13 Meter tiefe Häuser im westlichen Teil enthalten je sechs Wohnungen, die von einem gemeinsamen Atrium erschlossen werden, das in Form eingehängter Loggien einen thermisch geschützten Freibereich für die Wohnungen bietet. Aufgrund der kompakten Bauweise, der guten Wärmedämmeigenschaften und der Solarenergienutzung kann der Niedrigenergiestandard unterschritten werden.
7 Wohnbebauung im östlichen Teil. Wegen der geringen Gebäudetiefe von nur einem Raum ist direkte Solarenergienutzung und einfache Querlüftung möglich.

8 Radfahrer- und Fußgängerbrücke über den kleinen Weikerlsee als Verbindung zum Landschaftspark und zu den Donauauen

HERZOG + PARTNER: Three-storey residential buildings
6 The housing to the west of the centre consists of a series of 13-metre-deep blocks, each containing six dwellings accessible from a common atrium. Overlooked by loggias attached to the façade, the atrium provides a thermally sheltered open space for the dwellings. The compact form of construction, the good thermal insulation and exploitation of solar energy mean that the low-energy standard required in the brief can be undercut.
7 Housing in the eastern area. The slenderness of the block (one room deep) means that direct solar energy and a simple cross-ventilation are possible.

8 Bridge for cyclists and pedestrians over a small lake, the Weikerlsee, linking the nature park and Danube meadows

7

8

WILLIAM MCDONOUGH + PARTNERS

Ford-Autowerke River Rouge
Dearborn, Michigan, USA, 2000-2004

Ford's River Rouge Truck Plant
Dearborn, Michigan, USA, 2000-2004

In den dreißiger Jahren arbeiteten auf dem fast 450 Hektar großen Werksgelände bis zu 100 000 Arbeiter in der Kohle-, Stahl- oder Autoteileproduktion. Nach dem Rückgang des Produktionsumfangs wurde auch das Ausmaß der Umweltzerstörungen deutlich. Ford entschied sich für ein Offensivprogramm, das den Standort in ein ökologisch wirkungsvolles und ökonomisch rentables Konzept überführen soll: Rückbau und Renaturierung werden als Teil einer gewandelten Firmenphilosophie inszeniert. Bis 2020 soll das Büro McDonough mit zwei Milliarden US-Dollar das Industrieareal in einen Naturpark mit integrierter Fabrikation verwandeln.

Das rektangulär angelegte Areal aus Lieferstraßen und Fertigungshallen wurde zunächst mit Hecken, Bäumen und Wasserläufen versehen, die verschmutzten Brachen mit indigenen Pflanzen begrünt, die Verunreinigungen als Nährstoffe absorbieren können. Auch die neuen Hallen für LKW-Montage und Lackierung fügen sich in den gewaltigen Naturierungsplan ein: An ihren Wänden wachsen Rankpflanzen, auf den Dächern Sedum. Somit entsteht das mit rund 43000 Quadratmetern größte begrünte Dach Nordamerikas; das Nutzwassersystem wird durch gesammelte Niederschläge gespeist.

Für Besucher bietet die zentrale Miller Road einen Geschichtsparcours, der mit Henry Ford und seinem Architekten Albert Kahn beginnt und am Visitors' Centre und mit einer Ausstellung zur ökologisch motivierten Planung endet. C. W.

In the 1930s, as many as 100,000 people worked on this almost 450-hectare factory site in the coal, steel or car parts industry. Once production had been scaled down, the extent of the environmental destruction became clear. Ford decided to tackle the problem head on and launched a programme to transform the site in a way that would be both economically profitable and ecologically beneficial: reconversion and renaturalisation will feature as part of a new corporate philosophy. McDonough's firm are scheduled to transform the industrial site into a nature park with integrated manufacturing by 2020 at a cost of 2 billion US dollars.

The first step involved adding hedges, trees and watercourses to the rectangular site with its service roads and production halls and to green the polluted brownfield sites with indigenous plants that can absorb the contaminants as nutrients. The new halls where trucks will be assembled and spray-painted also fit into the immense ecological redevelopment scheme: climbing plants grow up their walls; the roof is covered with sedum. The largest green roof in North America will be created covering an expanse of 454,000 square feet; runoff rainwater will be collected and fed into the service water system.

Miller Road which runs through the centre of the site offers visitors the opportunity to enjoy a walk through history—a history that began with Henry Ford and his architect Albert Kahn and ends at the Visitors' Centre with an exhibition on ecologically inspired design. C. W.

1 Begrünte vier Hektar umfassende Dachlandschaft der LKW-Fabrik, Foto 2004
2 Lageplan im Kontext von Dearborn
3 Blick auf Besucherzentrum. Im Vordergrund künstlich angelegter Teich für die Regenwasseraufbereitung, im Hintergrund LKW-Fabrik mit begrüntem Dach

1 10-acre habitat roof on the truck plant, photo: 2004
2 Site plan showing Dearborn
3 View of the visitors' centre. In the foreground an artificial pond for stormwater management. In the background truck plant with habitat roof

1

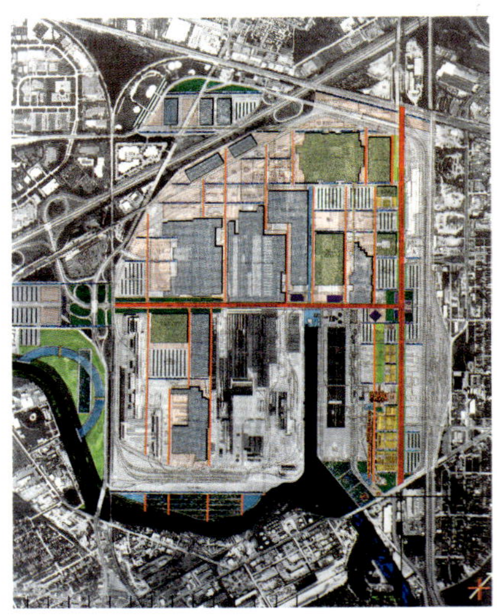
2+3

SHIGERU BAN ARCHITECTS

Japanischer Pavillon
EXPO, Hannover, Deutschland, 2000

Japanese Pavilion
EXPO, Hanover, Germany, 2000

Der japanische Architekt ist vor allem durch seinen Umgang mit »weichen« Baumaterialien bekannt geworden. 1986 begann er, mit Papprollen als Ersatz für Holz zu experimentieren. Nach dem verheerenden Erdbeben in Kobe 1995 nahm Ban diese Ideen wieder auf und schuf für obdachlos gewordene Bewohner leicht montierbare (später von der UN auch in anderen Krisengebieten eingesetzte) Papprollen-Blockhäuser als Notunterkünfte. Ban errichtete aber auch luxuriösere Wohnbauten, Kirchen und Ausstellungsräume aus dem ungewöhnlichen Baustoff.

Der japanische Pavillon, eine gewellte, gitternetzartige Tonnenschale aus Pappröhren, Karton und Papier, stellte einen Höhepunkt von mit vergänglichen Materialien hergestellter Architektur dar – auch wegen seiner Größe von 72 Metern Länge, bis zu 15,5 Metern Höhe und 35 Metern Spannweite. Diese bisher nicht gekannten Ausmaße führten allerdings zur Auflage deutscher Baubehörden, die ursprünglich geplante reine Papierkonstruktion mit einem Holzgerüst auszusteifen – in den Augen der Planer, darunter Frei Otto, eine unnötige Beschränkung. Die Hülle des Pavillons besteht aus einer speziell entworfenen, recycelbaren Papiermembran, die Wasser und Feuer abweist und Licht durchlässt. Das Fundament des Pavillons bilden – neben wenig Beton – im Wesentlichen mit Sand gefüllte Holzkisten. Nach dem Ende der Expo, die unter dem Motto »Mensch – Natur – Technik« stand, wurden die Materialien des spektakulären Baus wie geplant der Wiederverwertung zugeführt. C. W.

The Japanese architect became famous particularly for his use of "weak" building materials. In 1986 he started to experiment with cardboard tubes as a replacement for timber. The earthquake in Kobe in 1995 prompted Ban to revive these ideas and he created easy to assemble cardboard "log" houses as temporary shelters for people who had lost their homes. They were later used by the UN in other crisis areas. But Ban has also built more luxurious housing, churches and exhibition spaces from this unusual construction material.

The Japanese Pavilion, an undulating lattice arch made of cardboard tubes, cardboard and paper, represents a high spot of architecture from temporary materials—not least because of its dimensions: 72 metres long, up to 15.5 metres high and 35 metres wide. However, these previously unknown dimensions caused the German building authorities to insist that the structure, which was originally designed to be purely of paper, be reinforced by a timber scaffold—in the eyes of the designers, including Frei Otto with whom Ban collaborated on this project, an unnecessary measure. The skin of the pavilion consists of a specially designed, recyclable paper membrane that is resistant to water and fire and lets light through. The foundations of the pavilion were, apart from a small amount of concrete, mainly wooden boxes filled with sand. At the end of the exposition, which had "Man—Nature—Technology" as its slogan, the materials of this spectacular building were recycled as planned. C. W.

1 Luftaufnahme des Pavillons auf der EXPO 2000
2 Innenansicht mit Blick auf Konstruktion aus Pappröhren
3 Seitenansicht mit Blick auf Papiermembran

1 Aerial view of the pavilion at EXPO 2000
2 Interior view showing structure made of cardboard tubes
3 Side view showing paper membrane

1

2

3

HIGHTECH ALS FORTSCHRITT
HI-TECH AS PROGRESS

In der Eröffnungsausstellung des DAM waren Entwürfe utopischer Megastrukturen vertreten, die nur unter Einsatz von Hochtechnologie hätten realisiert werden können. Die futuristischen Visionen gaben sich dabei völlig autark. In den Zeichnungen existierte entweder gar keine Umgebung wie bei der »Megabridge« von Raimund Abraham, oder aber Stadt und Natur wurden rücksichtslos mit gigantischen Anlagen überzogen wie in den Fotomontagezyklen der Gruppe Superstudio.

Waren diese Projekte noch der damaligen Technikbegeisterung ergeben, oder waren sie Ausdruck einer Zivilisationskritik? Für die letztere Vermutung spricht, dass beispielsweise die technikbejahenden Arbeiten der Gruppe Archigram nicht in der Eröffnungsausstellung vertreten waren, obwohl sie seinerzeit schon zur Sammlung des DAM zählten. Sie wurden erst zwei Jahre später in »Die Vision der Moderne. Das Prinzip Konstruktion« gezeigt. Diese Ausstellung bildete eine Ergänzung zur »Revision der Moderne«, denn sie thematisierte den von Heinrich Klotz schon im Katalog der Eröffnungsausstellung betonten Grundsatz: »Wir setzen voraus, das eine Fülle von Errungenschaften der Moderne weiterhin gilt, und wir setzen voraus, dass eine Fülle von dogmatisch erstarrten Lehrsätzen der Moderne hinfällig ist.« Architektur, die von neuen Konstruktionsweisen und Materialien bestimmt war, wurde 1986 so in einem der »reduktionistischen Moderne« gegenüber kritischen Kontext präsentiert. Dazu wurden bedeutende europäische, amerikanische und japanische Architekten aufgeboten, deren Bauten oder Projekte unmissverständlich technische Innovation in den Vordergrund stellten.

Heute scheint die »Banalität eines Entweder-Oder« (Klotz) zwischen Baukunst und Hightech weitgehend überwunden. Es ist selbstverständlich geworden, neue Technologien nicht zu fürchten, sondern sie einzusetzen, um eine leistungsfähige, energie- und Ressourcen sparende Architektur zu schaffen. Modernste Computersysteme und fortgeschrittenste, für die menschlichen Sinne immer weniger wahrnehmbare Technik ermöglichen darüber hinaus Experimente, die noch vor kurzem undenkbar waren. Die Bandbreite reicht von Norman Foster, der glaubt, es sei inzwischen möglich, den ersten energieneutralen Wolkenkratzer zu bauen, bis zu jenen Architekten, die ihre Bauten nicht mehr aus der Wirklichkeit, sondern ganz aus dem Computer generieren.

DAM's inaugural exhibition included designs for Utopian megastructures, which could only have been realised using hi-tech methods. The futuristic visions appeared to be completely self-reliant. The drawings either showed no surroundings at all as in Raimund Abraham's "Megabridge" or gigantic complexes ruthlessly swamped the existing city and nature as, for example, in Superstudio's photomontage cycles.

Were these projects still riding the wave of enthusiasm for technology prevalent at the time, or were they expressing a criticism of civilisation? The fact that the work of Archigram, the group of architects who so strongly affirmed technology, was not included in the inaugural exhibition, although they were part of DAM's collection, would speak in favour of the latter assumption. It was not until two years later, in 1986, that they were exhibited in "The vision of Modernism. The structure principle." This exhibition complemented "Modernism revisted," in that it focused on the principle emphasised by Heinrich Klotz in the catalogue to the inaugural exhibition: "We assume that a multitude of Modernism's achievements continue to be valid, and we assume that a multitude of Modernism's principles that have fossilized into dogma are no longer valid." Thus architecture that was governed by new methods of construction and materials was presented in 1986 in a context that was critical of "reductionist Modernism." To that end, the work of renowned European, American and Japanese architects was assembled to focus on what was unmistakeably technologically innovative about their buildings or projects.

Today, the "banality of an either/or" (Klotz) between architecture and hi-tech has been largely overcome. It is now taken for granted that new technology is not something to be feared but something to use in order to create an architecture that is efficient and saves energy and resources. The latest computer systems and the most advanced technology, which is increasingly impossible to perceive through the human senses, are also making experiments possible that even recently were inconceivable. The spectrum ranges from Norman Foster, who believes it is now possible to build an energy-neutral skyscraper, to those architects who do not create their buildings on the basis of reality but generate them entirely with computers.

Raimund Abraham: Megabridge, 1965. Collage, Sammlung DAM

Raimund Abraham: Megabridge, 1965. Collage, DAM collection

HELMUT JAHN

One South Wacker Drive
Chicago, Illinois, USA, 1979-1982

One South Wacker Drive
Chicago, Illinois, USA, 1979-1982

Jahns Hochhaus wurde seinerzeit nicht wegen, sondern trotz seiner Hightech-Struktur gefeiert. Weil der Architekt sie hinter einer Fassade in der Tradition amerikanischer Art-déco-Hochhäuser verbarg, galt er fortan als Überwinder der funktionalistischen Hochhausarchitektur und des geschichtslosen Skelettbaus.

Das vierzigstöckige Gebäude ist in drei Zonen gegliedert, die durch die »Kolossalordnung« der farbigen Glasfassade und die Rücksprünge der jeweiligen Baukörper betont werden. Der Art-déco-Charakter setzt sich auch in den Innenräumen fort. Während der Bauzeit verfasste Jahn sein Manifest *Sky-Scrapers*. Sein künstlerisches Programm lautete, modernste Materialien und Techniken zu verwenden, diese jedoch mit traditionellem Formenvokabular zu verbinden. Er wollte keine Maschinenarchitektur unter dem Banner des technologischen Fortschritts, sondern eine »Synthese aus moderner Architektur und populärer Kultur«.

Diese Auffassung hat Jahn mittlerweile hinter sich gelassen. An Stelle verhüllender Fassadenkleider sind transparente Glasbauten im Sinne einer Skin-and-Bone-Architektur getreten. Seit er seine Projekte gemeinsam mit dem Bauingenieur Werner Sobek realisiert, zielt sein Schaffen auf eine enge Verschmelzung von Ingenieurwesen und Baukunst, die er mit dem Begriff »archineering« umschreibt. M. J.

Jahn's skyscraper was celebrated at the time not because of, but in spite of, its hi-tech structure. Because the architect hid the structure behind a façade in the tradition of American Art-Deco skyscraper, he was considered from then on as someone who had overcome functionalist skyscraper architecture and a-historical frame construction.

The fourty-storey building is divided into three zones, each emphasised by the "colossal order" of the coloured glass façade and the setback of each building volume. The Art-Deco character is continued in the interiors. Whilst the building was under construction, Jahn wrote his manifesto entitled *Sky-Scrapers*. His artistic credo centres on using the most modern materials and methods but linking them to traditional formal vocabulary. He did not want to create a machine-based architecture under the banner of technological progress, but a "synthesis of modern architecture and popular culture."

Jahn has since moved on from this view. Facades as "clothing for buildings" have been replaced by transparent glass buildings subscribing to the skin-and-bone theory of architecture. Since he began collaborating with structural engineer Werner Sobek, Jahn's work has been seeking a close fusion of engineering and architecture which he calls "archineering." M. J.

1

1 Skizze aus *Sky-Scrapers*, 1980/1981. Sammlung DAM
2 Schnitt, Ansichten und Grundrisse der Obergeschosse der 1. und 3. Stufe. Originalzeichnung, Sammlung DAM
3 Hochhaus im städtischen Kontext
4 Eingangslobby

1 Sketch from *Sky-Scrapers*, 1980/1981. DAM collection
2 Section, elevations and plans of steps 1 and 3. Original drawing, DAM collection
3 Skyscraper in urban context
4 Entrance foyer

2

3

4

FOSTER AND PARTNERS

Swiss Re Headquarters
London, Großbritannien, 2001-2003

Das Hochhaus – schon vor seiner Fertigstellung mit Spitznamen wie Gurke, Tannenzapfen oder Patronenhülse belegt – verbindet ökologische Leitbilder mit technischer Innovation. Es ist sowohl den Gesetzen der Natur als auch denen des Auto- und Flugzeugbaus verpflichtet. Das klingt zunächst wie ein Widerspruch. Weshalb sollte ein Gebäude nach aerodynamischen Kriterien entworfen sein? Die Antwort ist dieselbe wie beim Autobau: Um weniger Luftwiderstand zu bieten und damit Ressourcen zu sparen. Die kreisrunde, sich oben und unten verjüngende Grundrissfigur minimiert den Winddruck. Das erlaubt nicht nur schlankere, materialsparende Konstruktionen. Es verringert auch Verwirbelungen und vermeidet Bodenwinde in der Sockelzone des Gebäudes. Die schlanke Konstruktion ermöglicht zudem einen hohen Grad an natürlicher Belichtung und Klimatisierung. Die Fassade ist als atmungsaktive Membran konstruiert.

Konstruktiv ruht das Gebäude auf einem Mittelstrang, der den Großteil der Stützlast abfängt. Die Aussteifung erfolgt über die Fassadenkonstruktion aus einem Gitternetz diagonaler Stahlstreben. Die Geschossflächen bleiben dadurch stützenfrei und sind in ihrer Aufteilung variabel.

Mit dem Swiss-Re-Tower hat Norman Foster Ideen des »climatrophic design« aufgegriffen, die Buckminster Fuller vor über dreißig Jahren formulierte. Damals waren die Projekte wegen der komplizierten und nicht standardisierungsfähigen Elemente aus wirtschaftlichen Gründen nicht zu realisieren. Dank der Computertechnik bestehen diese Hemmnisse heutzutage nicht mehr.

M. J.

Swiss Re Headquarters
London, Great Britain, 2001-2003

The skyscraper—even before it was completed people were giving it nicknames such as gherkin, pinecone or giant bullet—combines ecological principles and technical innovation. It is indebted both to the laws of nature and those of automotive and aviation engineering. Initially that sounds like a contradiction. Why design a building around aerodynamic criteria? The answer is the same as in the field of automotive engineering: in order to offer less air resistance and thus save resources. The round plan form, tapering both downwards and upwards, minimises wind pressure, which makes it possible to use a more slender, material-saving structural system. It also reduces turbulence and prevents ground winds at the base of the building. The slender structure also facilitates a high degree of daylight and natural ventilation. The façade is a double skin that "breathes."

Structurally the building is carried on a central core, which carries the greater part of the column load. The façade structure, consisting of a steel diagrid, provides bracing. This means that the floors are column-free and can be flexibly divided up.

With the Swiss Re Tower, Norman Foster has taken up the ideas on "climatrophic design" that Buckminster Fuller first came up with over 30 years ago. Back then, economic considerations prevented the projects from being built because the elements were complicated and not possible to standardise. Thanks to computer technology, these obstacles no longer exist. M. J.

1 Lageplan mit Grundriss
2 Schnitt
3 Ansicht

1 Site plan with floor plan
2 Section
3 Perspective view

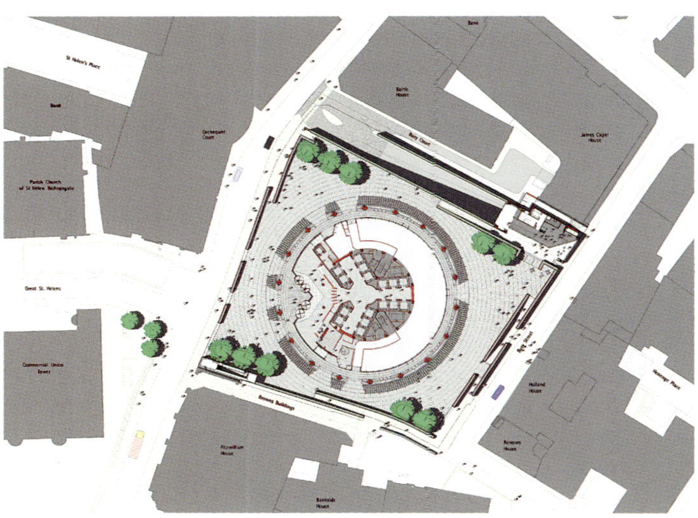

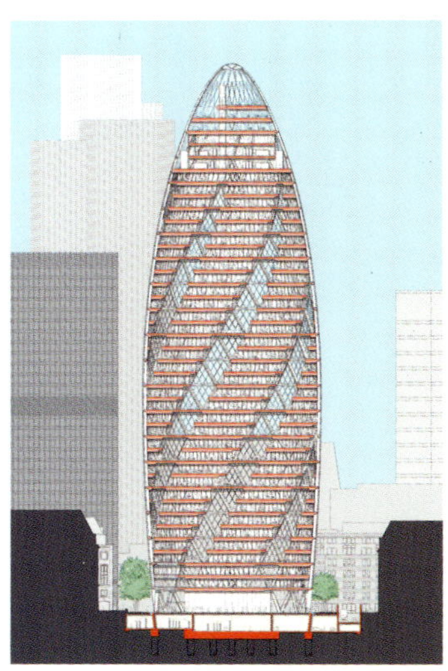

1+2

3

KOLATAN/MAC DONALD STUDIO

Resi-Rise-Skyscraper
New York, N.Y., USA, seit 1999

Resi-Rise skyscraper
New York, N.Y., USA, from 1999

Das Projekt wirkt wie das Update einer Idee aus den sechziger Jahren: biomorphes Design, Plug-in-System, nutzerdefiniertes Bauen, aber um »intelligente« Hightech-Materialien ergänzt und neu kommuniziert. Was einst Megastruktur hieß, nennt sich nun »vertical urbanism«.

Am südlichen Rand des New Yorker Central Parks soll das Gebäude mit fünfzig Stockwerken in den Himmel ragen – aber nicht gerade, sondern wie eine verwachsene Wirbelsäule. Daran können unterschiedlich große Wohn- und Bürokapseln andocken, die hinsichtlich Lage, Form und Ausstattung auf individuelle Wünsche zugeschnitten sind. Wenn ein Mieter oder Eigentümer auszieht, hinterlässt er keine leere Raumhülle, sondern einen Steckplatz. Die alte Kapsel wird entsorgt. Der nächste Nutzer erhält eine neue, auf seine Bedürfnisse zugeschnittene Kapsel.

Der Erfolg des Projekts von Sulan Kolatan und William Mac Donald wird davon abhängen, ob es gelingt, ein intelligentes Ressourcenmanagement zu gewährleisten. Die plastische Struktur des Erschließungsstrangs erfordert komplexe Konstruktionen und überproportionale Verkehrsflächen. Auch der Verbrauch an Raumkapseln steht auf den ersten Blick nicht im Einklang mit einer nachhaltigen Entwicklung. Zwar sollen sie aus recycelbaren Kunststoffen bestehen. Doch ob sich auch die Hightech-Ausstattung (Smart-Glas, das auf Licht- und Wetterbedingungen reagiert; klimakontrollierende Innenwände etc.) kosten- und ressourcensparend wiederverwenden lässt, bleibt abzuwarten – zumal auf Standardisierungen zu Gunsten von Individuallösungen verzichtet wird.

M. J.

The project looks like an update on an idea from the 1960s: biomorphic design, plug-in system, user-defined building, but with the addition of "intelligent" hi-tech materials and a new communications policy. What was once known as megastructure, now calls itself "vertical urbanism."

The building will stand on the southern edge of New York's Central Park, its 50 storeys towering skywards. But it will not stand up straight but resemble more a deformed spine. Residential and office pods of different sizes can dock into the spine, each tailored to the wishes of the individual in terms of position, form and interior fittings. When a tenant or owner moves out, they do not leave an empty space behind but a slot. The old pod is disposed of. The next user gets a new pod tailored to his or her needs.

The success of this project by Sulan Kolatan and William Mac Donald will depend on whether it is possible to guarantee intelligent resource management. The plastic structure of the circulation core requires complex structures and disproportionately large circulation areas. Furthermore, the consumption of the pods does not at first glance seem compatible with the idea of sustainable development. True, they are intended to be made of recyclable plastic. But whether the hi-tech features (smart glass, that responds to light and weather conditions, internal walls that regulate internal climate etc.) can be reused in a way that will save costs and resources, remains to be seen—particularly since standardisation was rejected in favour of individual solutions.

M. J.

1 Wohn- oder Bürokapsel
2 Detail des Hochhauses im Stadtraum von New York
3 Gebäudehülle

1 Living or office pod
2 Detail of the skyscraper and New York surroundings
3 Building skin

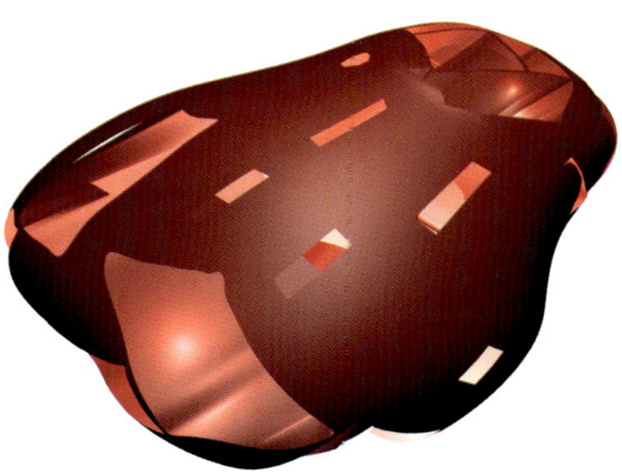

1

2

3

INGENHOVEN OVERDIEK ARCHITEKTEN

Hauptbahnhof Stuttgart
Deutschland, 1997-2008

Stuttgart railway station
Germany, 1997-2008

Innovative Lösungen müssen sich nicht immer spektakulär gebärden. Dem Team um Christoph Ingenhoven ist es in Zusammenarbeit mit Frei Otto gelungen, ein städtisches Großbauwerk zu projektieren, das gar nicht als solches wahrgenommen wird. Man hat den Entwurf für den neuen Stuttgarter Hauptbahnhof deshalb auch begeistert und anerkennend als »Nicht-Architektur« bezeichnet.

Die Idee basiert auf einem Modul, das sich durch Addition zu einem Bauwerk fügt. Die Form des filigran konstruierten Licht-Stütze-Elements, eine druckbeanspruchte Gewölbeschale aus Beton, wurde in zahlreichen aufwendigen Modellversuchen optimiert. Sie ermöglicht eine unterirdische Hallenkonstruktion, die acht Tiefbahnsteige mit Tageslicht versorgt. An der Oberfläche öffnen sich – als unverwechselbares Merkmal des Tragwerks – so genannte Lichtaugen, die in den Stuttgarter Schlossgarten eingebettet sind. Durch die sensible Einpassung des Hauptbahnhofs in die vorhandene Situation gelingt das ungewöhnliche Paradox, dass kein Bauland verbraucht, sondern vielmehr ein neuer Stadt- und Landschaftsraum erschlossen wird. Neben seinen urbanistischen und ökologischen Vorzügen überzeugt das Projekt auch durch die Eleganz seiner Konstruktion. Als raumgreifendes Schalenwerk besitzt es zugleich eine eigenwillige Plastizität und fasziniert durch das »Spiel der Körper im Licht«. M. J.

Innovative solutions do not necessarily have to look spectacular. In collaboration with Frei Otto, the team led by Christoph Ingenhoven has succeeded in designing a major urban structure that is in no way perceived as such. That is why the scheme for Stuttgart's new railway station has been called "non-architecture" in a gesture of enthusiastic recognition.

The idea is based on a module that is repeated to create a single structure. The form of the filigree columns, which also let in light, and the concrete shell roof subject to compression were optimised in numerous complex model experiments. They permit an underground hall structure and provide daylight to eight underground platforms. At ground level, the columns open up into so-called "light eyes" which have been sunk into Stuttgart's Schlossgarten, the gardens of its former palace. They are the structure's most striking feature. The sensitive way the railway station has been integrated into the existing context has made an unusual paradox possible: no building land was used; instead a new natural urban space was created. Apart from its urban design and ecological benefits, the project is also captivating through the elegance of its structure. This three-dimensional shell has a plasticity of its own and is fascinating because of the "play of volumes in light." M. J.

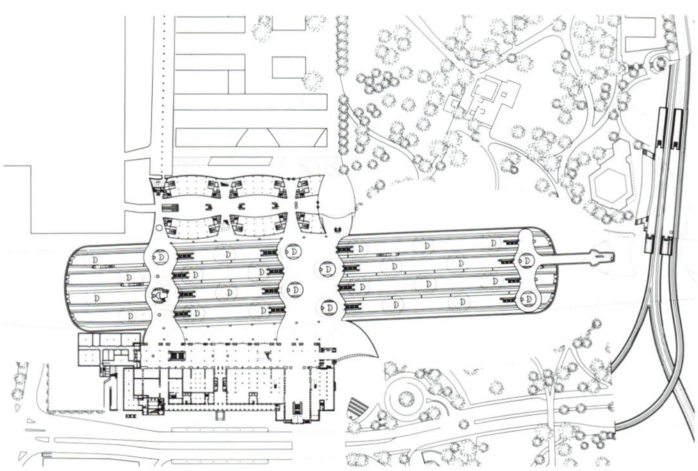

1

2

3

1 Grundriss Verteilerebene, 1:2500
2 Unterirdische Bahnhofshalle mit Tageslichtöffnungen. Modellfoto
3 Querschnitt durch das Lichtauge. Computersimulation
4 Luftansicht des neuen Bahnhofs. Modellfoto

1 Plan of circulation level in station, 1:2500
2 Subterranean hall with openings providing daylight. Model photo
3 Cross section of the "light eye." Computer animation
4 Bird's eye view of the new station. Model photo

4

LEBEN OHNE NOSTALGIE
LIFE WITHOUT NOSTALGIA

Die Suche nach Alternativen zur Eintönigkeit und Uniformität der Nachkriegsmoderne bedeutete keineswegs bei allen Architekten das Umschwenken auf eine gänzlich »unmodern« wirkende Architektur. Wie Beispiele aus der Eröffnungsausstellung des DAM zeigen, gab es auch nüchterne Tendenzen, kritisch auf den International Style zu antworten. Bei dem Altenwohnheim Guild House von Robert Venturi, einem Gründungsbau der Postmoderne, ging es nach seinem Prinzip des »dekorierten Schuppens« nur um eine äußerliche Relativierung und Ironisierung des Modernismus bei einem ansonsten recht schlichten Bau mit konventionellem Grundriss. Wie eine Kulisse ist ihm eine zeichenhafte Fassade vorgestellt, die dem ästhetischen Empfinden der Bewohner entsprechen sollte.

Rem Koolhaas hat sich schon früh mit verfallenden städtischen Gebieten auseinander gesetzt und hier mit einer Formensprache der avantgardistischen Moderne versucht, neuen Herausforderungen an den Ort, die Tradition und die Architekturgeschichte zu begegnen. Beweggrund seines Agierens ist dabei ebenfalls nicht eine visionäre Programmatik, sondern die Akzeptanz, wenn nicht gar die Überhöhung der Verhältnisse, wie sie sind.

Die neuen Beispiele muten radikal modern und global einsetzbar an. Auch bei ihnen lässt sich keine Idealvorstellung über Zukunft oder Gesellschaft erkennen, wohl aber das Bestreben, aufgrund der spezifischen Analyse im Rahmen realer Gegebenheiten zu unschematischen Lösungen zu kommen. Sentimentalität oder eine konventionell aufgefasste Behaglichkeit haftet diesen Architekturen nicht an. Sie sind vielmehr von einem Pragmatismus geprägt, der bis zur Ruppigkeit geht. Auf engstem Raum und zu niedrigen Kosten verweisen die Architekten mit ihren Wohnbauten auf verschiedene Möglichkeiten der nichtstandardisierten Standardisierung. Bei FOBA geht es um die Konzeption von Häusern, die sich serienmäßig herstellen, zugleich aber dem individuellen Geschmack des jeweiligen Käufers anpassen lassen. Die Architektinnen der hier vorgestellten Siedlung strebten sowohl mit traditionellen als auch mit modernen Mitteln die Individualisierung von Wohnungen im kollektiven Wohnblock an. Damit in Zusammenhang stand die Aufgabe, Erfordernisse des öffentlichen Raums mit privaten Bedürfnissen in Einklang zu bringen und architektonisch in Form einer gemeinschaftlichen Gartenanlage zu artikulieren.

The search for alternatives to the monotony and uniformity of post-war Modernism did not by any means cause all architects to suddenly change tack and start building a kind of architecture that looked completely "unmodern." As examples from DAM's inaugural exhibition show, there were also sober attempts to respond critically to the International Style. Guild House home for the elderly by Robert Venturi, one of Post-Modernism's seminal buildings, was—based on the "decorated shed" principle—simply an attempt to treat Modernism with irony and relativise it on the exterior at least; it was otherwise a very simple building with a conventional floor plan. A symbol-laden façade, intended to accommodate the aesthetic sensibilities of the residents, was placed in front of it like a stage set.

Rem Koolhaas engaged early on with run-down urban areas and tried to use the formal language of avant-garde Modernism to meet the new challenges of place, tradition and architectural history. The motive behind this is not visionary or programmatic zeal, but an acceptance or even exaggeration of the way things are.

The new examples look radically modern and globally feasible. Similarly, they bear no trace of any ideal vision of the future or of society, but they do show signs of an endeavour to find non-schematic solutions based on a specific analysis of a given situation and working within the constraints of reality. This kind of architecture bears no trace of sentimentality or conventional views of comfort. Rather it is marked by a pragmatism that sometimes borders on roughness. In the smallest space and at low cost, the architects illustrate different possibilities of non-standardised standardisation in their residential buildings. FOBA's concern is to design houses that can be mass-produced, yet at the same time can be adapted to the needs of the individual purchaser. The four women architects responsible for the housing development presented here were striving to create individualised living units within a collective housing block using both traditional and modern means. Connected with that was the brief to harmonise the requirements of the public realm with private needs and to express them architecturally in the form of a communal garden.

Robert Venturi: Guild-House, Philadelphia, 1960-1963, perspektivische Ansicht der Straßenseite. Bleistiftzeichnung, Sammlung DAM

Robert Venturi: Guild House, Philadelphia, 1960-1963, perspective view of the street side. Pencil drawing, DAM collection

OMA

Wohn-Hochhausprojekt
Rotterdam, Niederlande, 1982

Der Entwurf des von Rem Koolhaas 1975 gegründeten Office for Metropolitan Architecture hatte die Revitalisierung des brachliegenden Hafenviertels von Rotterdam zum Ziel. Zwei Elemente, ein Wohnhochhaus und ein Aussichtsturm, markieren die Hafeneinfahrt. Die Hochhausscheibe ist durch ihre Farbgestaltung und turmartige Vorsprünge vielfältig differenziert. »Durchgesteckte« Maisonettewohnungen ermöglichen in zwei von drei Stockwerken den Verzicht auf Erschließungskorridore. Unweit des Wohnhauses sollte das Segment einer funktionslos gewordenen Stahlbrücke aufgerichtet werden und mit Aussichts- und Restaurantplattform eine neue Bestimmung erhalten. Hierbei berief sich Koolhaas explizit auf El Lissitzkys Entwurf einer Rednertribüne für Lenin (1924), spielte aber gleichzeitig auf die für die Niederlande typischen Zugbrücken an.

Koolhaas verwendete die damals umstrittene Bauform des Wohnhochhauses, um hochwertigen, verdichteten und innenstadtnahen Wohnraum zu schaffen. Als Autor hatte er sich wenige Jahre zuvor in der berühmt gewordenen Studie *Delirious New York* (1978) ebenfalls damit auseinander gesetzt. Obwohl die Wiedergewinnung urbaner Räume ein zentrales Anliegen der Postmoderne war, stieß Koolhaas mit dem Projekt für Rotterdam ebenso wie mit seinem Entwurf für Scheibenhochhäuser in der Berliner Friedrichstadt (1980/81) auf Ablehnung. Beide Entwürfe ließen das Fragmentierte des Stadtraums deutlich sichtbar und bemühten sich nicht um die häufig favorisierte Stadtreparatur mit historischen Bautypen. F. S.

Project for a high-rise block of flats
Rotterdam, Netherlands, 1982

This scheme, developed by the Office for Metropolitan Architecture, which was set up in 1975 by Rem Koolhaas, aimed at revitalising Rotterdam's derelict docklands. Two elements, a high-rise block of flats and an observation tower, mark the entrance to the docks. The use of colour and tower-like projections adds variation and differentiation to the slab high-rise. Dual-aspect maisonette flats made it possible to dispense with circulation corridors on two out of three floors. Not far from the block of flats, a segment of a steel bridge that no longer served any purpose was to be erected with an outlook and restaurant platform added to give it a new use. In this Koolhaas is making explicit reference to El Lissitzky's design for a speaker's platform for Lenin (1924), but at the same time it alludes to the drawbridges typical of the Netherlands.

Koolhaas used the high-rise block of flats, a controversial form of building at the time, in order to create high quality, high-density living space close to the city centre. As a writer he had engaged with the same theme a few years earlier in his famous study *Delirious New York* (1978). Although reclaiming urban space was a central concern of Post-Modernism, Koolhaas met with rejection both for his project for Rotterdam and his scheme for slab high-rises in Berlin's Friedrichstadt (1980/81). Both schemes left the fragmented nature of the urban realm visible and made no attempt to indulge in the kind of urban repair so favoured at the time, which was based on historical building types. F. S.

1

2

3

4

1 Wohnung mit Dachterrasse
2 Innenansicht des Cafés
3 Gesamtansicht mit historischem Speicher- und Kontorgebäude
4 Innenansicht eines Appartements mit Blick auf die Stadt

Kolorierte Lichtpausen, Sammlung DAM

1 Apartment with roof terrace
2 Interior view of the cafe
3 Overall view with historical warehouse and office building
4 Interior view of an apartment with a view of the city

Coloured tracings, DAM collection

COOK & HAWLEY ARCHITECTS, DILLER + SCOFIDIO, KAZUYO SEJIMA + RYUE NISHIZAWA, AKIKO + HIROSHI TAKAHASHI, MARTHA SCHWARTZ INC.

Kitagata Garden City, Gifu, Japan, 1994-1998

Die Siedlung, von Arata Isozaki initiiert und koordiniert, wurde als sozialer Wohnungsbau errichtet und hat in Japan Modellcharakter. Vier Architektinnen waren eingeladen, jeweils einen Wohnblock zu entwerfen, der ca. 107 nicht standardgemäße Wohneinheiten enthalten sollte. Die Gebäude bilden durch ihre unterschiedlichen Formen einen unregelmäßig konturierten, lang gestreckten Hof.

Die Amerikanerin Elizabeth Diller entschied sich als einzige für einen gebogenen Grundriss ihres Blocks, der sich durch Parallelverschiebung der einzelnen Wohneinheiten um jeweils 1,40 Meter ergab. Mit diesem Kunstgriff verlieh sie der Fassade Plastizität. Der lang gezogene, zehngeschossige Bau von Kazuyo Sejima ist mehrfach geknickt. Alle Wohnungen haben eine Terrasse, die als Löcher in der nur sieben Meter breiten Hochhausscheibe wahrgenommen werden. Die Hofseite des Gebäudes ist durch Laubengänge und Feuertreppen gekennzeichnet. Ähnlich wie der Block von Sejima ist auch der Wohnblock der britischen Architektin Christine Hawley abgewinkelt und bildet zum Zentrum der Gesamtanlage einen unregelmäßig geschnittenen Platz. Die zehngeschossige Hochhausscheibe von Akiko Takahashi scheint aufgrund der gleichmäßigen Verteilung der Balkons im Vergleich zu den Nachbarbauten konventionell gestaltet zu sein. Dennoch enthält der Bau fünf verschiedene Wohnungstypen, die wie bei den benachbarten Wohnblöcken durch Laubengänge erschlossen werden. Die Freiflächen innerhalb und außerhalb des Ensembles wurden von der amerikanischen Landschaftsarchitektin Martha Schwartz gestaltet. F. S.

Kitagata Garden City, Gifu, Japan, 1994-1998

The development, initiated and coordinated by Arata Isozaki, was built as a social housing project and is intended to be a prototype for Japan. Four women architects were invited to design a block of flats, each containing approximately 107 non-standard dwellings. The different shaped buildings create long courtyards with irregular contours.

The American architect Elizabeth Diller was the only designer to choose a curved plan for her block which she created by setting back each individual living unit by 1.40 metres each. With this trick she gave the façade a certain plasticity. The long, ten-storey building by Kazuyo Sejima has several kinks. All the flats have terraces that look like holes in the slab high-rise, which is only seven metres deep. The courtyard side of the building is characterised by access galleries and fire stairs. The block of flats by British architect Christine Hawley similarly has an "elbow-joint" and forms an irregularly shaped piazza in the centre of the whole complex. Akiko Takahashi's ten-storey block with the regular arrangement of balconies makes a conventional appearance by comparison with the neighbouring buildings. However, the building in fact contains five different types of flat, and has access galleries like the neighbouring blocks. The open spaces within and around the ensemble were designed by American landscape architect Martha Schwartz. F. S.

1 Gesamtplan
1 Master plan

1 Elizabeth Diller
2 Kazuyo Sejima
3 Christine Hawley
4 Akiko Takahashi
5 Martha Schwartz

1

2 Blick auf die Gartenanlage von Martha Schwartz, im Vordergrund der Mieterpavillon von Emi Fukuzawa, links die Gebäude von Takahashi und Diller, rechts der Block von Sejima

2 View of the gardens designed by Martha Schwartz. In the foreground the residents pavilion by Emi Fukuzawa; on the left the buildings by Takahashi and Diller, on the right the block designed by Sejima

2

3

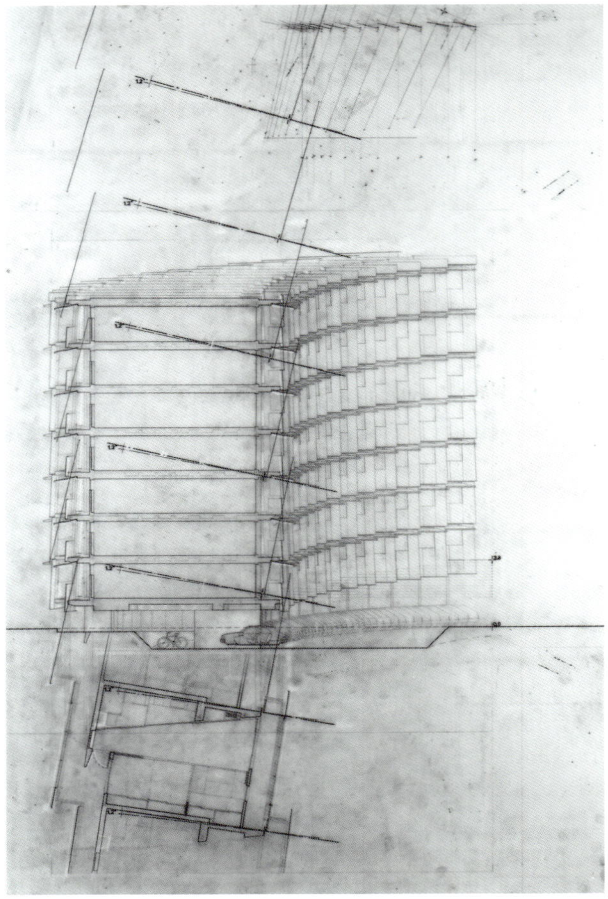

4

5

ELIZABETH DILLER: Slither Building
3-5 Wegen der Parallelverschiebung der einzelnen Wohnungen erhalten die Balkone durch die Rücksprünge größere Abgeschiedenheit. Die Wohnungen sind außerdem um einen Höhenunterschied von zwanzig Zentimetern gegeneinander versetzt, sodass die Laubengänge vor jeder Wohnung in ihrer Achse verspringen und nie in voller Länge zu übersehen sind. Von der Wohnungstür gelangt man unmittelbar in den großen Wohnraum jedes Apartments, der sich durch flexible Trennwände in kleinere Bereiche aufteilen lässt.

ELIZABETH DILLER: Slither Building
3-5 The setback of the individual flats means that the balconies are also set back and more separate from each other. The flats are also slightly staggered vertically, with a height difference between them of twenty centimetres, so that the access galleries project in their axis in front of each flat and it is never possible to see the entire length of the galleries. The front door of each flat opens immediately into the large living space, which can be divided up into smaller areas using flexible partitions.

6

7

8

KAZUYO SEJIMA: Kitagata-Wohnblock
6-8 Die Südfassade ist großflächig verglast und lässt die zweigeschossigen Wohn- und Essräume der Maisonettewohnungen erkennen. Innerhalb des strengen Rasters von tragenden Zwischenwänden organisierte Sejima höchst flexibel nutzbare Wohnungen. Jeder einzelne Raum ist vom öffentlichen und von einem wohnungsinternen, verglasten Laubengang erschlossen. Manche Zimmer sind untereinander durch Schiebetüren verbunden, sodass sich ein komplexes Raumgefüge ergibt. Die meisten Wohnungen verfügen über einen mit Tatami-Matten ausgelegten Raum.

KAZUYO SEJIMA: Kitagata block of flats
6-8 The south façade is glazed throughout, revealing the two-storey living and dining rooms of the duplex flats. Within the strict grid of load-bearing interior walls, Sejima has organised highly flexible flats. Access to each room is from a public access gallery and from an interior glazed gallery inside the flat. Some rooms are connected by sliding doors creating a complex spatial structure. Most of the flats have one room with Tatami mats as a floor covering.

9

10

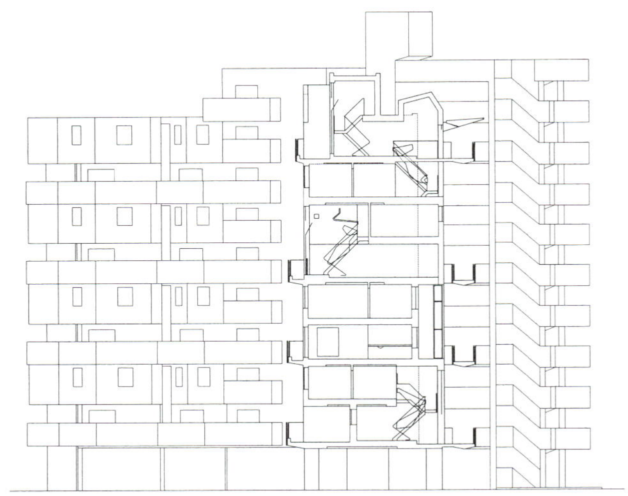

11

CHRISTINE HAWLEY: Kitagata-Wohnblock

9-11 Die wichtigste Gelenkstelle des zweiteiligen Baukörpers ist ein hoher Treppenturm. Zusätzlich sind die beiden Bauteile voneinander abgerückt und nur in einigen Geschossen durch kurze Brücken miteinander verbunden. Ein Bauteil ist eine Hochhausscheibe, deren Wohnungen durch Laubengänge erschlossen werden. Die Maisonettewohnungen erlauben in einigen Stockwerken den Verzicht auf Erschließungsgänge. Der zweite Bauteil ist durch eine fächerförmige Anlage der Grundrisse gekennzeichnet. Wohnräume treten als einzelne Baukörper vor die Bauflucht.

CHRISTINE HAWLEY: Kitagata block of flats

9-11 The principal "hinge" of the two-part building is a tall stair tower. The two parts of the building are not connected to each other except by short bridges on only a few storeys. One part of the building is a slab high-rise with access galleries in front of the flats. As the flats are maisonette, access galleries are not needed on some storeys. The striking feature of the second part of the building is the fan-shape of its floor plans. Living spaces project in front of the building line as separate volumes.

12

13

14

AKIKO TAKAHASHI: Kitagata-Wohnblock
12-14 Die unteren Stockwerke beherbergen eingeschossige Wohnungen, die oberen vier Etagen enthalten Maisonettewohnungen mit einem doppelgeschossigen Essbereich. Alle Wohnungstypen haben eine Breite von drei Achsen innerhalb des regelmäßigen Stützenrasters und sind durch offene Grundrisse gekennzeichnet. Jede Wohnung enthält einen großen, mit Tatami-Matten ausgelegten Raum, der in seiner Bestimmung nicht determiniert ist. Durch verschiebbare Trennwände lassen sich die Wohnungen in unterschiedliche Bereiche teilen.

AKIKO TAKAHASHI: Kitagata block of flats
12-14 The lower storeys contain flats on one level; on the top four storeys, the flats are duplex with a two-storey dining area. All types of flats occupy a width of three modules within the regular grid of columns and are characterised by open-plan layouts. Each unit has a large room with Tatami mats covering the floor, which does not have a specified function. Movable partitions enable the units to be divided up into separate areas.

MARTHA SCHWARTZ: Gartenanlage Kitagata, 2000
15-17 Die Anlage, die sich auf einem Plateau erhebt, dient nicht nur der Erholung, sondern ist auch für die Aufsicht aus den umliegenden Wohnhäusern konzipiert. Aktive Bereiche wie Spielplätze wechseln mit kontemplativen Zonen wie Bambusgarten oder Wasserbassin ab. Der »Garten der vier Jahreszeiten« besteht aus vier Würfeln mit farbigen Glaswänden – jeder eigens gestaltet und bepflanzt und mit Sitzmöbeln ausgestattet. Die Parkplätze vor den aufgeständerten Erdgeschossen der Wohnblöcke sind dem Blick der Gartenbesucher entzogen.

MARTHA SCHWARTZ: Kitagata communal garden, 2000
15-17 The complex garden layout, which rises up on a plateau, is used not only for recreation but is also intended to be legible from above, particularly from the surrounding blocks of flats. Activity areas, such as playgrounds, alternate with meditative zones like the bamboo garden or pool of water. The Four Seasons Garden consists of four cubes with coloured glass walls—each designed and planted differently and fitted out with seating. The parking spaces in front of the ground floors of the blocks of flats, which stand on pilotis, are hidden from the view of visitors to the garden.

15

16

17

MVRDV

Seniorenwohnhaus »WoZoCo«
Amsterdam, Niederlande, 1997

WoZoCo housing project for the elderly
Amsterdam, Netherlands, 1997

Auffälligstes Merkmal der achtgeschossigen Gebäudescheibe mit einhundert Wohneinheiten sind die wie Schubladen aus der Fassadenfront herausgezogenen Bauelemente. Während auf der holzverschalten Südseite lediglich Balkone in unregelmäßiger Verteilung hervortreten, kragen auf der gegenüber liegenden Front ganze Baukörper frei aus, die jeweils eine bis vier Wohnungen enthalten. Laubengänge erschließen die Apartments, die größtenteils zwei spiegelsymmetrischen Grundrisstypen folgen. Die Standardwohnung besteht aus anderthalb Zimmern auf rechteckigem Grundriss und enthält neben dem Wohn- und Schlafraum Küche, Abstellkammer, Bad und WC. Die ungewöhnliche Form des Gebäudes resultiert daraus, dass nur 87 Kleinwohnungen dieser Art im Block selbst untergebracht werden konnten und Raum für die darüber hinaus geforderten geschaffen werden musste.

Das Büro MVRDV (Maas, van Rijs, de Vries) versuchte, den für viele Wohnblocks typischen Eindruck der Gleichförmigkeit durch die unregelmäßige Platzierung und die verschiedene Größe der vorkragenden Bauteile zu vermeiden. Der Wechsel von Stahlstäben, Lochblech und verschiedenfarbigem Glas bei den Balkonbrüstungen soll ebenfalls dazu beitragen. Die vorgehängten, separaten Baukörper geben den darin befindlichen Wohnungen einen autonomen Charakter. Insofern gelang dem niederländischen Architekturbüro zumindest, die ökonomisch erforderliche konventionelle Reihung gleicher oder verwandter Grundrisse nicht in eine Monotonie der Fassaden münden zu lassen. F. S.

The most striking feature of this eight-storey slab building with one hundred living units are the elements that project from the façade of the building like drawers in a cabinet. While on the southern side of the building the only projecting elements are irregularly distributed balconies, the opposite side of the building has entire volumes cantilevering out, each containing between one and four apartments. Open galleries provide access to the apartments, most of which have one of two types of symmetrical floor plan. A typical apartment is rectangular in plan and consists of a living room, bed-sitting room, kitchen, storeroom, bathroom and toilet. The unusual shape of the building stems from the fact that only 87 small apartments of this kind could be accommodated in the block itself and that extra space had to be found for the remaining 13 apartments required by the brief.

MVRDV (Maas, van Rijs, de Vries) tried to avoid the impression of uniformity so typical for many apartment blocks by spacing the cantilevered elements at irregular intervals and making them different sizes. The balcony railings use steel rods, perforated sheet metal and different colours of glass for the same reason. The separate volumes suspended in front of the façade give the apartments they contain an autonomous character. In this way, the Dutch architectural practice at least managed to prevent the conventional series of identical or similar floor plans from producing monotonous façades. F. S.

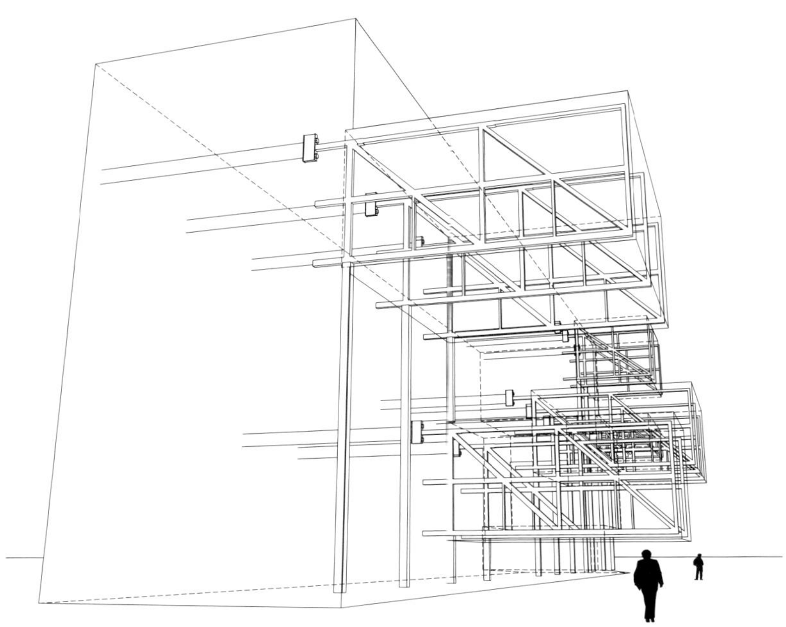

1

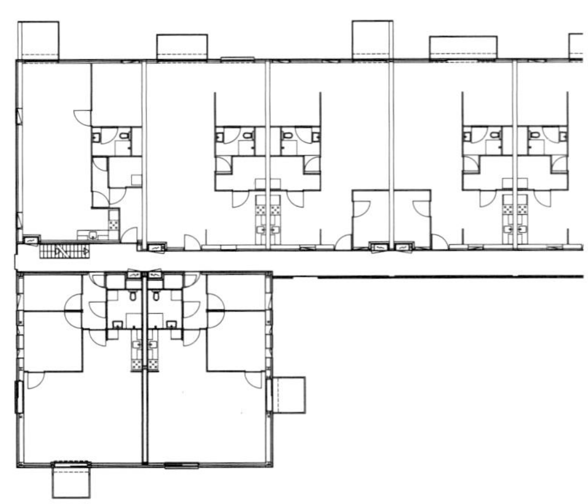

2

3

1 Tragwerk-Isometrie der angehängten Wohnkuben
2 Detail-Grundriss 5. Obergeschoss
3 Auskragende Wohnungen auf der Nordseite
4 Gesamtansicht Nordseite
5 Gesamtansicht Südseite

1 Isometric view showing structure of the projecting elements
2 Detail of 5th floor plan
3 Cantilevered flats on the northern side
4 View of the north side
5 View of the south side

4

5

FOBA

Einfamilienhaus »Aura«
Tokio, Japan, 1994-1996

"Aura," a single-family house
Tokyo, Japan, 1994-1996

Das kleine, dreigeschossige Haus auf einer Grundfläche von 3 x 20 Metern besteht aus zwei parallelen Sichtbetonscheiben mit geschwungenem Umriss, zwischen die eine Membran aus beschichteter Glasfaser gespannt ist. Beide Betonscheiben werden durch Zylinder aus Stahlbeton gegeneinander abgestützt. Durch die großflächige Dachhaut stellte der Architekt Katsu Umebayashi eine optimale Belichtung des zwischen zwei bestehende Bauten platzierten Stadthauses sicher, ohne Einblicke ins Gebäudeinnere zu ermöglichen.

Neben der ungewöhnlichen äußeren Erscheinung liegt die Besonderheit des Hauses in seinem offenen Grundriss, der auf Funktionsräume weitgehend verzichtet. Das Haus hat kein Badezimmer und nur eine sehr kleine Küche mit Waschbecken und Platz für einen Kühlschrank. Die Bewohner müssen zum Essen in nahe gelegene Restaurants gehen, zur Körperreinigung in öffentliche Badeanstalten, zur Unterhaltung in Kinos, was wegen der Nähe zum Tokioter Zentrum kein Problem darstellt. Nur in einer Stadt, die ihren »Nomaden« einen 24-Stunden-Service bieten kann, ist dieses Gebäudekonzept möglich.

Dadurch, dass nahezu die gesamte Geschossfläche von 122 Quadratmetern als Wohnraum frei verfügbar ist, lässt sich – trotz der beschränkten Grundfläche – jeder Eindruck von Kleinteiligkeit vermeiden.

Die Aufgabe, ein Wohnhaus auf schmalem, innerstädtischem Baugrund anzulegen, hat in den kleinteilig parzellierten Wohngegenden Tokios Tradition und resultiert nicht nur aus den in den letzten Jahren gestiegenen Grundstückspreisen. F. S.

This small, three-storey house, which has a footprint of only 3 x 20 metres, consists of two parallel curved slabs of fair-faced concrete with a membrane of coated fibreglass between them. The two concrete slabs are buttressed against each other by cylinders of reinforced concrete. The large expanse of roof enabled the architect Katsu Umebayashi to ensure optimum daylighting of this town house, which sits between two existing buildings, while at the same time protecting privacy.

Apart from its unusual appearance, the special character of this house lies in its open plan design that avoids any strict designation of functional space. The house has no bathroom and only a very small kitchen with a sink and space for a refrigerator. The inhabitants have to go to nearby restaurants to eat, to public baths to wash, and to the cinema for entertainment—all of which is not a problem due to the house's proximity to the centre of Tokyo. This concept for a building is only possible in a city that can provide round-the-clock services for its "nomads."

The fact that almost all of the building's 122 square metres of floor area are freely available as living space means that, despite its limited footprint, the house does not seem in any way small.

The brief to design a house on a narrow inner-city site has a long tradition in Tokyo's residential districts, which are divided up into small plots of land, and is not simply the result of rising real estate prices of recent years. F. S.

1 Das Wohnhaus in seiner Tokioter Umgebung
2 Eingangsseite
3 Gebäudeelemente

1 The house in its Tokyo setting
2 Entrance side
3 Elements of the building

1

2

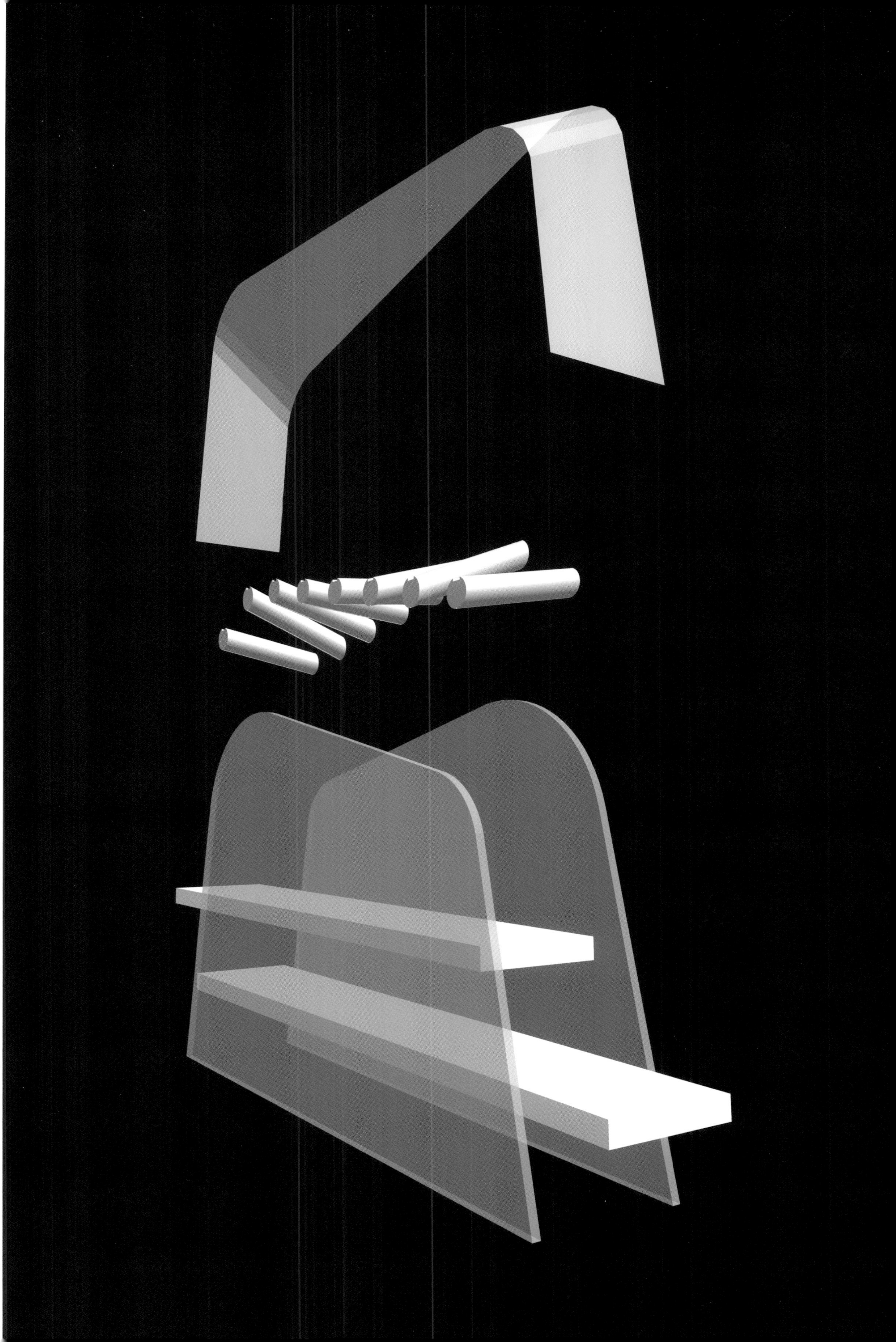

BESONDERHEITEN DES ORTES
GENIUS LOCI

Inspiriert von Heideggers Vortrag »Bauen Wohnen Denken« (1951), hat vor allem Christian Norberg-Schulz mit seiner 1976 verfassten Publikation über den »genius loci«, die 1979 in Italien, 1980 in den USA und 1982 in Deutschland erschien, eine Alternative zum weltweit gleichförmigen Funktionalismus des International Style aufgezeigt. Seine durch zahlreiche Fotos gestützte phänomenologische Untersuchung von Architektur beschrieb an unterschiedlichen Beispielen den jeweiligen Geist des Ortes, der allein Menschen Identifikation und Halt geben könne. Es sei Aufgabe des Architekten, auf den »Ruf« des Ortes zu hören, ihm Gestalt zu geben, ihn zu ergänzen und zu verbessern.

Aus der Eröffnungsausstellung des DAM ist Mario Botta hier vertreten, ein wichtiger Repräsentant der so genannten Tessiner Schule, die mit ihren Untersuchungen über die Bezüge zwischen einem Bauwerk und seinem städtebaulichen oder landschaftlichen Umfeld international große Beachtung fand. Seine Casa Rotonda ist ein mächtiges Zeichen in der Landschaft, das sich nicht unterordnet, sondern sich aus der Umgebung heraushebt – wie die abgebildete Skizze eindrücklich zeigt. Bottas Auffassung zufolge ist der Genius Loci nicht primär vorhanden, sondern wird erst durch den künstlerischen Eingriff des Architekten geschaffen. Um den einmaligen Charakter eines Ortes herauszustellen, muss der Architekt der vorhandenen Umgebung deshalb ein außergewöhnliches Bauwerk entgegensetzen. Die Besonderheit des Ortes kann sich erst durch eine solche Architektur enthüllen.

Dies trifft auch auf die neuen Beispiele zu. Den Architekten ist dabei die jeweilige kulturelle Tradition des Umlandes, in die ihre Bauten hineingesetzt sind, von großer Wichtigkeit. Renzo Piano steigert eine phantastische geographische Situation durch ein Gebäudeensemble, das eine eigenständige Interpretation der Baukultur des Landes darstellt. Entstanden ist ein sensibles, dabei kraftvolles Monument von enormer Ausstrahlung, das gleichzeitig höchst funktional ist und sich hinsichtlich seiner Konstruktion und Ausstattung fortgeschrittenster Technologien bedient. Benedict Tonon verbindet, bei gleichzeitiger Integration vorhandener landschaftlicher Qualitäten, zwei Aspekte der Tradition von Stadterweiterung: die organische Siedlung mit der formalen Strenge einer am sozialen Wohnungsbau der Moderne orientierten Architektur, ohne heimattümelnd zu sein.

Inspired by Heidegger's essay "Building Dwelling Thinking" (1951), Christian Norberg-Schulz's book written in 1976 on the *genius loci*, which was published in 1979 in Italy, in 1980 in the USA, and in 1982 in Germany, explored an alternative to the International Style's functionalist buildings that look the same the world over. His phenomenological analysis of architecture, underpinned by numerous photos, used different examples to describe the spirit particular to a particular place, which he said was the only thing that could give people a sense of identification and security. It was the responsibility of the architect, he concluded, to listen to the "call" of a place, give it physical shape, complete it and improve it.

The example from DAM's inaugural exhibition that we have chosen here is by Mario Botta, an important representative of the Ticino School, which attracted great international attention with its studies on the relationship between a building and its urban or natural surroundings. Botta's Casa Rotonda makes a powerful mark on the landscape; it does not subordinate itself, but stands out clearly from its surroundings—as the sketch reproduced here clearly shows. In Botta's opinion, the *genius loci* is not something pre-existing, but something that has to be created by the artistic intervention of the architect. To draw out the unique character of a place, the architect therefore has to build an extraordinary building to contrast with the surroundings. Only that kind of architecture is able to reveal the genius loci.

This also applies to the new examples in this category. The cultural traditions of the context their buildings are set in are of great importance to the architects. Renzo Piano heightens a fantastic geographical situation with an ensemble of buildings that represents an independent interpretation of the country's architectural culture. What emerged was a sensitive yet powerful monument that has enormous presence and is at the same time highly functional and uses the latest technology both in its structure and equipment. Benedict Tonon integrates the qualities of the landscape, while linking two different aspects of the tradition of city extensions, without falling into the trap of twee vernacularism. He combines an organic development pattern with the formal severity of an architecture based on Hamburg's social housing tradition of the 1920s.

Mario Botta: Casa Rotonda in Tessiner Landschaft, 1981. Tuschezeichnung, Sammlung DAM

Mario Botta: Casa Rotonda in the Ticino countryside, 1981. Pen and ink drawing, DAM collection

MARIO BOTTA

Casa Rotonda
Stabio, Schweiz, 1980-1982

Casa Rotonda
Stabio, Switzerland, 1980-1982

Der Solitär hebt sich deutlich von den traditionell gestalteten Einfamilienhäusern der Umgebung ab. Trotz seiner zylindrischen Form ist das Gebäude aus Betonformsteinen streng in Nord-Süd-Richtung ausgerichtet. Mit großen Einschnitten wird der Baukörper geöffnet und gegliedert. Im Norden verringert sich die Öffnung mit treppenartigen Sprüngen geschossweise nach oben. Der Treppenturm in der Mitte ist wie eine überdimensionierte Säule gestaltet.

Die Casa Rotonda oszilliert mit ihrer Mischung aus rundem Volumen, das sich einer Richtung zunächst verweigert, und fassadenartig artikulierten Seiten, zwischen Allansichtigkeit und Achsialität. Nicht nur mit dem Zitat der Säule, sondern auch mit der Namensgebung sucht Botta die Verankerung des Gebäudes in der Architekturgeschichte sinnfällig zu machen. Kritiker brachten die Casa Rotonda auf Grund ihrer Kreisform auch mit mittelalterlichen Wohntürmen, mit Palladios Villa Rotonda bei Vicenza (1566-1580) und dem Doppelzylinder des Hauses von Konstantin Melnikov (Moskau 1927) in Verbindung. Die Casa Rotonda und andere Villenbauten Bottas dokumentieren mit ihren elementaren geometrischen Formen und ihrer Monumentalität ebenfalls die Nähe zur Architektur Louis I. Kahns, auf die er sich immer wieder bezieht. Trotz des Rückgriffs auf traditionelle Bauformen und Motive wurzelt Bottas Formensprache, ähnlich wie die Richard Meiers, letztlich in der Moderne und steht postmodernen Tendenzen eigenständig gegenüber. E. K.

This discrete building is strikingly different from the traditional houses in the neighbourhood. Despite its cylindrical form, the building, which is of cast stone, has a strict north-south orientation. There are large cut-outs in the building to open up and articulate the volume. To the north the stepped cut-out becomes—by a floor at a time—narrower towards the top of the building. The stairwell in the centre is designed like an oversized column.

With its mixture of a round volume that initially refuses to face any particular direction and its façade-like sides, the Casa Rotonda oscillates between an equal view from all sides and axiality. Both with the column quotation and the name, Botta is trying to make the building's specific place in architectural history obvious. Due to its round shape, critics associated the Casa Rotonda with Medieval tower houses, with Palladio's Villa Rotonda near Vicenza (1566-1580) and the double cylinder of Konstantin Melnikov's house (Moscow 1927). With their elemental geometric forms and their monumentality, the Casa Rotonda and other villas designed by Botta also document the proximity to the architecture of Louis I. Kahn, to whom Botta repeatedly refers. Despite the return to traditional building forms and motifs, Botta's formal language, like that of Richard Meier, is ultimately rooted in Modernism and makes an autonomous stand against Post-Modern trends. E. K.

1

1 Südfassade
1 South façade

2

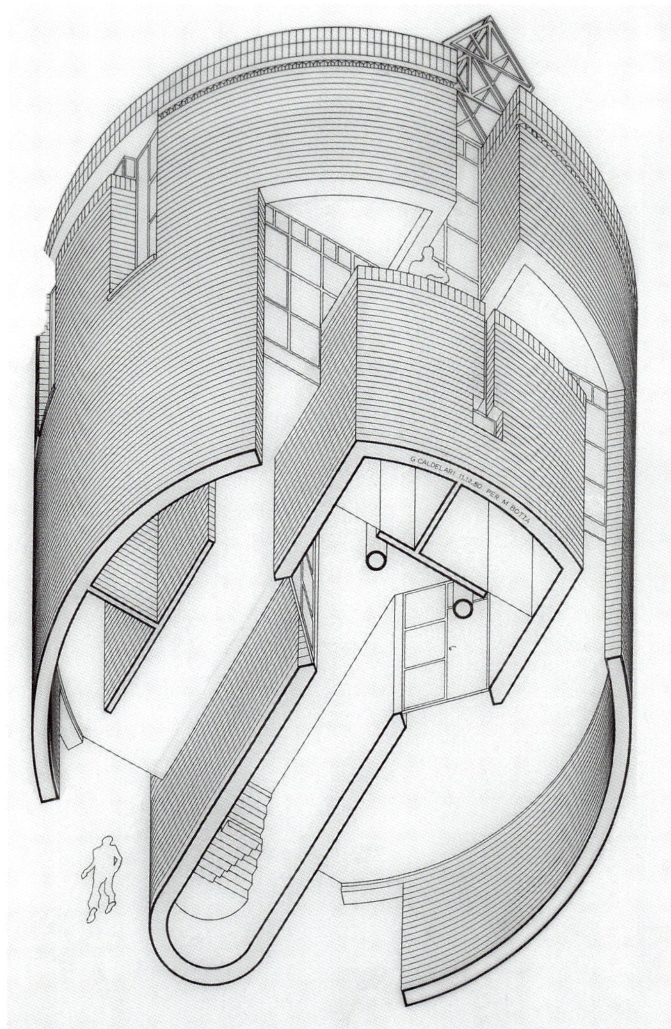

3

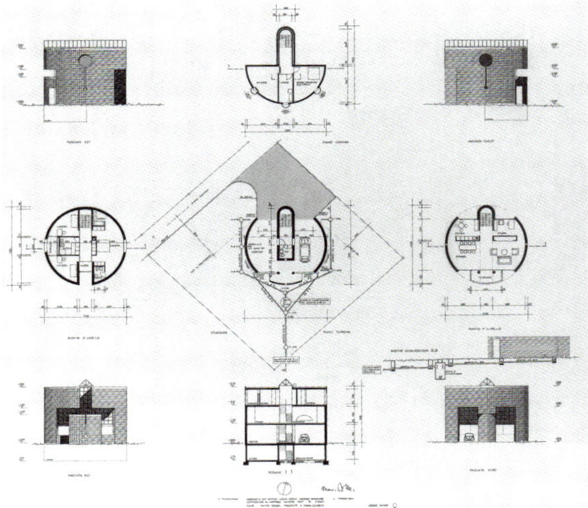

4

2 Isometrie Nordseite
3 Isometrie Südseite
4 Grundrisse, Ansichten, Schnitt

Tuschezeichnungen, Sammlung DAM

2 Isometric view of north side
3 Isometric view of south side
4 Plans, elevations, section

Pen and ink drawings, DAM collection

RENZO PIANO BUILDING WORKSHOP

Kulturzentrum Jean-Marie Tjibaou
Nouméa, Neukaledonien, 1991-1998

Das Ensemble aus zehn unterschiedlich großen Pavillons ist der Kultur der Kanaken, der Ureinwohner Neukaledoniens, gewidmet. Es ist ein Geschenk Frankreichs an seine ehemalige Kolonie – 1991 von François Mitterand in die Grands Projets der französischen Regierung eingereiht, zu denen auch der Grand Louvre (I. M. Pei) und die Bibliothèque National (Dominique Perrault) in Paris zählen.

Die Außenhaut der Pavillons wird von einer doppelschaligen Holzkonstruktion mit stählernen Querverbindungen gebildet. Eine schildartige Überhöhung der korbartigen Pavillons nach Norden – Sonnenseite auf der Südhalbkugel – schirmt sie gegen die Mittagssonne ab. Die Pavillons sind entlang einer überdachten, 230 Meter langen Straße angeordnet und zu drei lockeren Gruppen zusammengefasst. Hang abwärts, zur anderen Straßenseite, schließen sich schlichte Flachbauten an, in denen die Ausstellungs- und Verwaltungsräume sowie das Auditorium untergebracht sind.

Piano lehnt sich in der Gestaltung des Kulturzentrums an die traditionelle Flechtbauweise der Dörfer Neukaledoniens an und verbindet diese mit seiner eigener Konstruktionsweise und Architektursprache. Die Anlage, die sich sowohl in den kulturellen als auch in den exponierten landschaftlichen Kontext einordnet, bildet trotz ihrer Dimension keinen Fremdkörper wie noch Pianos Centre Pompidou (zusammen mit Richard Rogers, 1971-1977), das als gewaltige Kulturmaschine das umgebende Paris überragt und sich ausdrücklich von seiner Umgebung absetzt. E. K.

Jean-Marie Tjibaou Cultural Center
Nouméa, New Caledonia, 1991-1998

The ensemble of ten pavilions of different sizes is dedicated to the culture of the Kanak people, the indigenous inhabitants of New Caledonia. It was a gift from France to its former colony; in 1991 François Mitterand included it in the French government's series of *grands projets*, alongside other works such as the Grand Louvre (I. M. Pei) and the Bibliothèque National (Dominique Perrault) in Paris.

The outer skin of the pavilions is created by a double-layered timber structure with diagonal tie-rods of stainless steel. The basket-like pavilions are higher on the northern side—the sunny side in the Southern hemisphere—creating shell shapes that shade them from the midday sun. The pavilions are arranged along a 230 metre long covered street in three informal groups. Lower down the slope, facing the other side of the street, simple low buildings adjoin the pavilions. They house offices, exhibition spaces and an auditorium.

Piano has based the design of the Cultural Centre on the traditional thatchwork of New Caledonian village huts, and linked that with his own building techniques and architectural language. Despite its size, the complex fits both into its cultural context and its exposed natural setting, and in this is very different from Piano's Centre Pompidou (designed with Richard Rogers, 1971-1977), which is a gigantic "culture machine" towering above and standing out distinctly from its Parisian surroundings like a foreign body. E. K.

1

2

3

4

1 Entwurf »Dorf 3« mit Ateliers für Kulturerbe, graphische Künste, Tanz und Musik, Eingangsseite
2 Gesamtansicht vom Meer
3 Traditionelle Flechtbauweise
4 Bibliothek

1 Design study for "Village 3" with studios for cultural heritage, graphic arts, dance and music, entrance side
2 Overall view from the sea
3 Traditional thatchwork building method
4 Library

BENEDICT TONON

Siedlung Buchenkamp
Hamburg, Deutschland, 2000, 2004

Die Anlage gliedert sich in zwei städtebauliche Elemente. Eine halbkreisförmige »Raumschale« markiert die Trennung zum alten Wohngebiet und zur Bahntrasse. Sie öffnet sich nach Süden und gibt Zeilenbauten Raum, die sich in die Landschaft hinein erstrecken. Die Siedlung ist eingebettet in alte Baumbestände, Rükkstaustufen und kleine Fließgewässer. Damit gelingt es Tonon, ein Siedlungs-Idyll zu schaffen, das weder von Mülltonnen noch von Parkplätzen gestört wird. Alle Gebäude verfügen über Tiefgaragen und spezielle Einrichtungen für die Müllentsorgung.

Die Wohnanlage besteht aus fünf verschiedenen Haustypen: Die Häuser der »Raumschale« sind mit bandartigen Balkonen, kubischen Erkern und Wintergärten gestaltet. Zeilenbauten mit wellenförmigen Dachkanten, die ihre Flucht über den geschwungenen Weg hinweg fortsetzen und durch Sichtbeziehungen miteinander verbunden sind, enden in halbrunden, eingeschossigen Wohnungen, die für Behinderte reserviert sind. Kubische Stadtvillen scheinen mit ihrer quadratischen Fassade und dem zentralen Erker von Adolf Loos inspiriert. Im Nordosten der Siedlung entstehen Einfamilienhäuser mit prismatisch gefalteten Dachformen, die, je nach Standpunkt, sowohl die Interpretation als »Einzelhaus« als auch als »Wohnblock« zulassen. Form und Organisation der Siedlung betonen sowohl Individualität als auch Gemeinschaft.

Der Architekt stellt Buchenkamp zwar in die Hamburger Siedlungstradition der Moderne, aber Elemente wie die Wellenform, die Typologie des Einfamilienhauses und nicht zuletzt die Verbindung mit dem Ort weisen darüber hinaus, drängen aber weder eine eindeutig funktionalistisch-moderne noch semiotisch-postmoderne Lesart auf. E. K.

Buchenkamp housing estate
Hamburg, Germany, 2000, 2004

The complex is divided into two urban design sections: a semicircular ensemble tracing a shell shape marks the boundary to the existing residential area and the railway line. It opens to the south and creates space for rows of mid-rise blocks of flats, which reach out into the countryside. Set amongst established stands of trees, backwaters and small streams, Tonon succeeds in creating an idyllic housing estate which is disturbed neither by dustbins nor car parking: all the buildings have underground car parks and special facilities for refuse disposal.

The housing complex consists of five different types of building: the buildings that make up the "shell shape" have ribbon like balconies, cube-shaped bay windows and conservatories. Midrise blocks of flats with wavy roof edges, the line of which continues beyond the curved pathway and are visually connected with each other, terminate in semi-circular single-storey buildings with flats for disabled people. Cubic urban villas with square elevations and a central bay seem to have been inspired by Adolf Loos. In the northeast of the estate, single-family houses are being built. Their prismatic folded roofs can be read as "house" or "block of flats," depending on where they are seen from. The form and organisation of the estate emphasise both individuality and community.

Although the architect places Buchenkamp in the tradition of Modernist Hamburg estates elements such as the wave shape, the single-family house and not least the place, point to something else. Nevertheless, neither a clear-cut functionalist Modernist interpretation nor a semiotic Post-Modern interpretation is evoked. E. K.

1 Grundrisse, Ansichten und Schnitte der verschiedenen Haustypen
2 Luftbild von 2001

1 Floor plans, elevations and sections of the different types of building
2 Aerial view, 2001

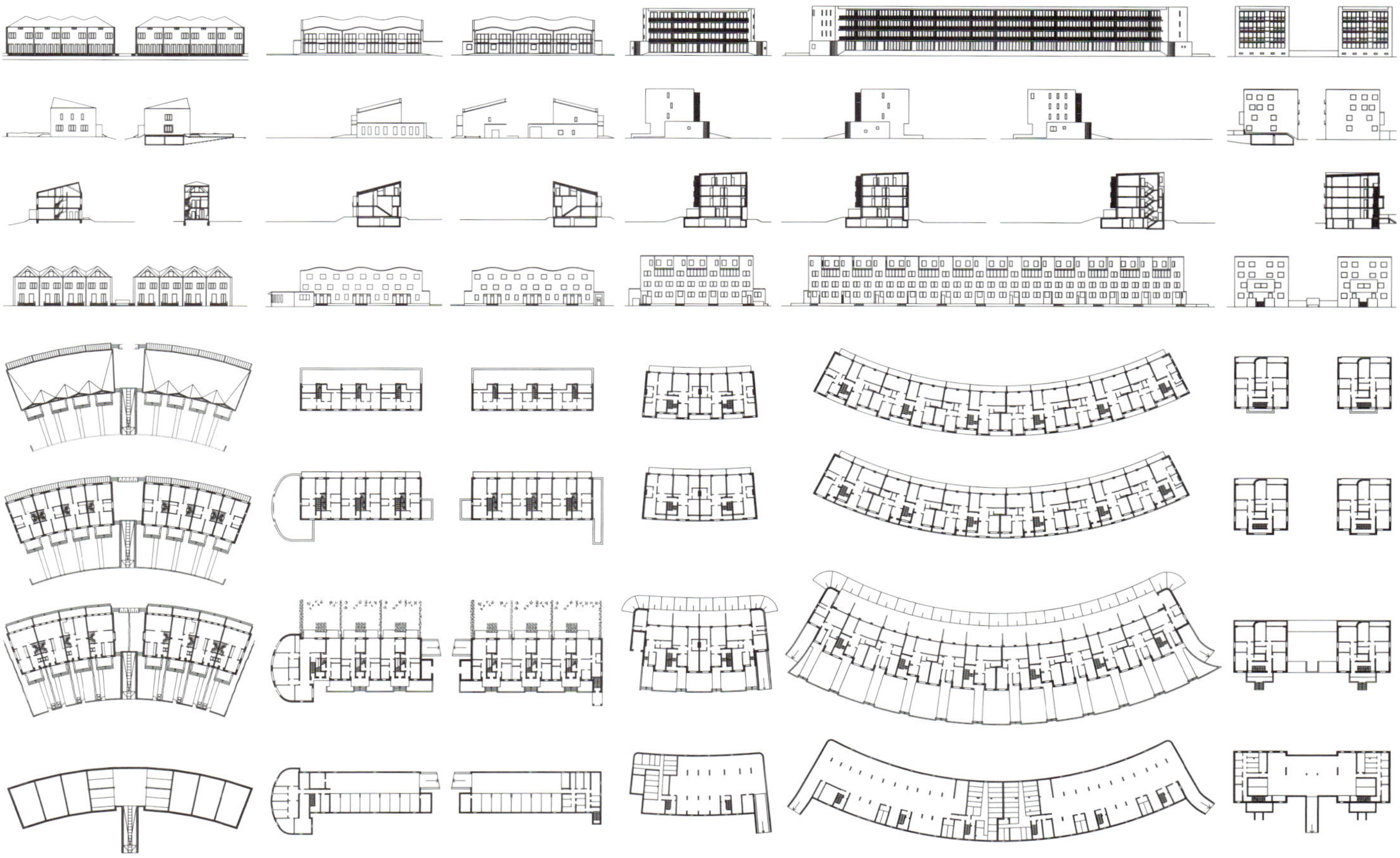

I

2

3

4

5

6

3 »Gartenhaus« mit Rundbau für eine integrative Wohngemeinschaft am südlichen Siedlungsrand
4 Öffentlicher Grünzug mit Retentionsfläche für den ökologischen Wasserhaushalt
5 Eingangstor mit Sitzbank, vom Bahnhof aus
6 Häuser vom Typ Villa mit Erker als gemeinsamer Treffpunkt für die Bewohner

3 "Garden house" with round building for an integrated living project on the southern edge of the development
4 Public green space with retention surface for an ecological water management system
5 Gateway with bench, coming from the station
6 Villa-type houses with projecting bays as communal areas for residents

NEUVERWENDUNG DER SÄULE
COLUMNS REDISCOVERED

In der Eröffnungsausstellung des DAM gab es eine Fülle von Beispielen für den Einsatz klassischer Bauelemente wie den der Säule – mal wörtlich zitiert, mal in der Manier der Pop-Art banalisiert, mal individuell verfremdet – und auch als expliziter Protest gegen die architektonische Armut funktionalistischer Architektur. Ein Beispiel dafür ist der Entwurf »Parasitenhaus« von J. J. Poli – eine idyllische Kleinarchitektur, die wie eine Außenbefahreinrichtung für die Fensterreinigung vor der eindimensionalen Rasterfassade eines maßstabslosen Hochhauses schwebt. Bei dieser Arbeit geht es allerdings eher um eine symbolische Geste und einen allgemeinen Traditionsbezug zum Klassizismus.

Thomas Gordon Smith dagegen, der mit einem Wohnhaus aus der Eröffnungsausstellung vertreten ist, verwendet klassisches Vokabular »wortgetreu« und vermischt dabei verschiedenste Elemente des architektonischen Formenschatzes aus mehreren Epochen gleichzeitig in einem Bau. Eine derartig unbekümmerte und willkürliche Adaption der klassischen Architektur steht in diametralem Gegensatz zu den Auffassungen der Architekten, die hier mit neueren Arbeiten vertreten sind.

Petra und Paul Kahlfeldt beanspruchen, die historischen Entwicklungslinien der klassischen Tradition aufzunehmen, von der auch die Moderne beeinflusst war. Ihre Philosophie ist, dass die Grundelemente des Bauens anhand der klassischen Architektur über Jahrhunderte wissenschaftlich erforscht worden sind und in Regeln über die architektonische Konstruktion resultieren, die a-historisch und deshalb grundsätzlich anwendbar sind. Es geht ihnen nicht um die Rezeption klassizistischer Bauformen, sondern darum, dass die geometrische Entwurfsmethode, die einem Gebäude zugrunde liegt, eine zeitlose Gültigkeit beanspruchen kann. Dies will auch der neue Stadtplatz von Kollhoff und Timmermann. Die Antwort der Architekten auf die von ihnen verabscheute Shopping-Mall-Ästhetik ist ein strenger von Häuserreihen gebildeter großstädtischer Raum, den sie bewusst von »biedermeierlichem Schmukkbedürfnis« freihalten wollten. Bei den neuen Beispielen, die sich als Raumgefüge aus überzeitlich anzuwendenden klassischen Elementen verstehen, hat die Säule wieder eine Ordnungsfunktion übernommen und stellt sich gegen die geistlose Vielfalt baulicher Umgebung. Sie bedeutet auch Protest gegen ein stilistisches Dogma bei zeitgemäßer Architektur, das klassizistische Elemente verbietet.

DAM's inaugural exhibition included many examples of the use of Classical architectural elements such as the column—sometimes quoted literally, sometimes given a banal appearance in pop-art style, sometimes individually defamiliarized, and sometimes used explicitly to protest against the poverty of functionalist architecture. An example of this is the design for the "parasite house" by J. J. Poli—idyllic small-scale architecture, which hovers in front of the one-dimensional modular façade of an out-of-scale tower block like a window-cleaning cradle. However, the main concern of this scheme was to make a symbolic gesture and a general reference to the tradition of Classicism.

By contrast, Thomas Gordon Smith, whose work was also represented in the inaugural exhibition with a scheme for a private house, uses Classical vocabulary with word-for-word authenticity and combines the most different elements of architectural formal vocabulary of several eras in a single building. That kind of completely uninhibited and arbitrary adaptation of Classical architecture is diametrically opposed to the architects represented here with more recent work.

Petra and Paul Kahlfeldt aim to incorporate the historical lines of development of the Classical tradition that also influenced Modernism. Their philosophy is that Classical architecture was academically studied for centuries to analyse architecture's basic elements and that the outcome was rules about architectural structure that are a-historical and therefore universally applicable. They are not concerned with the reception of neo-Classical architectural forms but with the geometrical design method that buildings are based on and that have timeless validity. This is also the aim of the new urban square designed by Kollhoff and Timmermann. The architects' response to the shopping-mall aesthetics they despise is a severe space on a scale appropriate to a major city. The space, which they expressly wanted to keep free of any "decorative frills and flounces," is simply framed by rows of buildings. In the new examples, which see themselves as spatial structures composed of timeless Classical elements, the column has once more taken on an ordering function and opposes the senseless miscellany of the built environment. It is also tantamount to a protest against the stylistic dogma in contemporary architecture that prohibits the use of Classical elements.

J. J. Poli: Parasitenhaus, 1980. Originalzeichnung, Sammlung DAM

J. J. Poli: Parasite house, 1980. Original drawing, DAM collection

THOMAS GORDON SMITH

Projekt für das Wohnhaus Richard und Sheila Long
Carson City, Nevada, USA, 1977-1979

Alle drei Entwurfsvarianten des Landhauses zeigen deutlich die eingehende Beschäftigung sowohl mit der Architektur der Renaissance und des Barock als auch mit antiken Villen. Das Ergebnis der Unbefangenheit, mit der Smith das historische Vokabular verwendet und dessen Elemente miteinander verbindet, mutet heute skurril und kitschig an. Auch drängen sich Assoziationen zu Hollywood-Villen auf, die ebenfalls – jedoch ohne ironische Brechung – mit Stilzitaten und Pathosformeln arbeiten. Während die erste Entwurfsvariante, das mehrfach gestaffelte Landhaus, noch wenig historisierenden Schmuck aufweist, häufen sich die Zitate zunehmend. Erst sind es nur dezente renaissancehafte Fensterumrahmungen und eine antikisierende Pergola, dann nehmen überstehende Dächer und rustizierte Säulen zu.

Der Living Room, der im Grundriss aus zwei sich überschneidenden Ovalen gebildet wird und dessen barocker Schwung sich über die Decken fortsetzt, stellt eine Bühnenarchitektur dar, die das wörtliche Zitat einer pompejischen Wandmalerei des späten II. Stils aufnimmt. Absurd scheint hier die Kombination mit schweren Polstermöbeln. Als wolle die Architektur Werte wie Dauerhaftigkeit und Gediegenheit, repräsentiert durch Versatzstücke von »Old Europe«, einer Upper-Middle-Class-Klientel verkaufen.

Trotz angestrebter Zeitlosigkeit wirkt das Haus zeitgeistig-postmodern und somit unzeitgemäß und überholt. E. K.

Project for a house for Richard and Sheila Long
Carson City, Nevada, USA, 1977-1979

All three schemes for the country house clearly demonstrate the architect's intense interest in the architecture of the Renaissance and Baroque and Classical villas. The result of the uninhibited way Smith uses and combines historical vocabulary looks today quirky and kitschy. Associations to Hollywood villas also come to mind, which also work with stylistic quotations and emotive clichés—albeit without irony. Whilst the first scheme, the country house with multiple setbacks, has very little historicist ornament, the stylistic quotations increase with each scheme. First they take the form of subtle renaissance-like window surrounds and a would-be Classical pergola, but then overhanging roofs and rusticated columns begin to proliferate.

The living room, which on plan is two intersecting ovals, has a Baroque curve which is continued in the ceiling shape. It is in effect a stage-set, a literal reference to a Pompeian fresco of the Late Second Style. That, in combination with heavy upholstered furniture, creates an absurd effect. It is as if the architecture is trying to sell values such as permanence and solidity, represented by set pieces from the "Old World," to an upper middle class clientele.

Although it is aiming at timelessness, the house appears to embody the spirit of Post-Modernism and thus seems outmoded and passé. E. K.

1 Grundriss Erdgeschoss, 1. und 2. Obergeschoss, 2. Entwurf. Zeichnung, Sammlung DAM
2 Innenansicht Wohnzimmer, 2. Entwurf. Aquarell, Sammlung DAM
3 Perspektivische Ansicht von Süden, 2. Entwurf. Aquarell, Sammlung DAM

1 Ground floor plan, 1st and 2nd floor plans, 2nd design. Drawing, DAM collection
2 Interior view of living room, 2nd design. Water colour, DAM collection
3 Perspective view from the south, 2nd design. Water colour, DAM collection

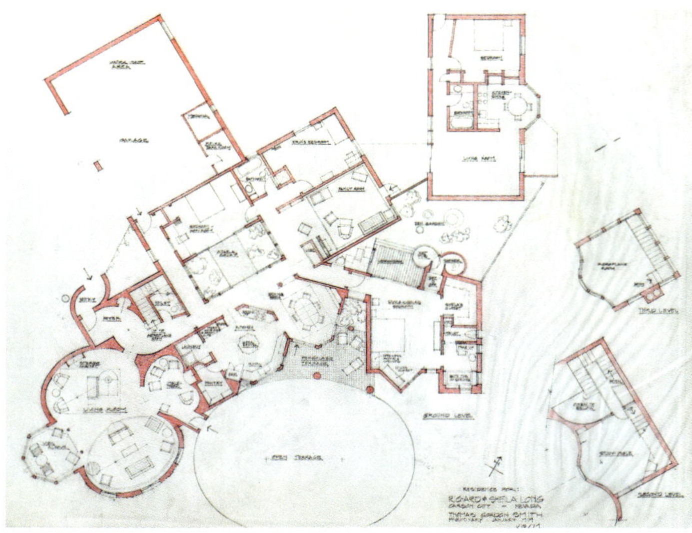

1

2

3

KAHLFELDT ARCHITEKTEN

Villa Bastian
Berlin, Deutschland, 1992-1994

Gegenüber Entwürfen und Bauten der Postmoderne, die durch Ironie und Verspieltheit beeindrucken, geriert sich die Architektur des Hauses in Berlin-Zehlendorf gänzlich streng und kühl. Sein Stil und damit das in einem von manchen Kritikern als unzeitgemäß empfundenen Formenkanon artikulierte Selbstverständnis einer gehobenen Klientel sowie deren Wunsch nach Repräsentation lösten heftige Kontroversen aus.

Zunächst als Umbau eines Hauses aus der Zeit vor dem 1. Weltkrieg geplant, wuchs sich der Auftrag fast zu einem Neubau aus. Zwar drängen sich bei der Villa Assoziationen zu Palladio und Gilly auf, jedoch verwendeten Petra und Paul Kahlfeldt das klassische Vokabular weder ironisch noch akademisch, sondern frei. Entstanden ist ein architektonisch minutiös durchgearbeitetes und handwerklich perfekt realisiertes Wohnhaus, das die Architekten nicht als »historistisch« verstanden wissen wollen, sondern als Beispiel für die Aneignung einer Architektursprache von zeitloser Gültigkeit – und damit als einen Ausweg aus der degenerierten, konsumbestimmten Postmoderne. Gleichzeitig plädieren Petra und Paul Kahlfeld mit ihrem Gebäude für die Überwindung einer klischeehaft angewandten Moderne und wenden sich gegen die Forderung, nur in einem modernen Stil zu bauen.

Deutlich zurückhaltender als bei der Villa Bastian geht das Büro mit dem klassischen Vokabular bei zwei später realisierten Villen an der Hamburger Elbchaussee um, die ebenfalls für eine wohlhabende Klientel geplant und errichtet wurden. E. K.

Villa Bastian
Berlin, Germany, 1992-1994

By comparison with Post-Modern designs, and buildings that impress with irony and playfulness, the architecture of this house in Berlin's Zehlendorf is severe and cool. Its style, and thus the self-image of a sophisticated clientele wishing to demonstrate prestige, articulated here in a canon of forms that some critics felt was old-fashioned, sparked intense controversy.

What was originally a commission to convert a house dating from before the First World War virtually took on the proportions of a new build. Although looking at the villa inevitably brings to mind associations to Palladio and Gilly, Petra and Paul Kahlfeldt use Classical vocabulary neither ironically nor academically, but freely. The result is a house with beautiful architectural detailing and perfect craftsmanship, which the architects want to be interpreted not as "historicist" but as an example of how to appropriate an architectural language of timeless validity—and therefore as a way out of a Post-Modernism that has become devalued and merely panders to consumerism. At the same time, Petra and Paul Kahlfeldt use this building to make a case for overcoming the clichéd use of Modernism and opposing the demand to build in an exclusively Modern style.

The architects use Classical vocabulary with far greater reserve in two villas they built later on Hamburg's Elbchaussee, similarly designed for affluent clients. E. K.

1 Blick auf Eingangsseite, Ostfassade
2 Innenraum Obergeschoss
3 Details Portikus
4 Grundrisse Keller-, Erd- und Obergeschoss

1 View of entrance side, east façade
2 Upper storey, interior
3 Details of portico
4 Plans of basement, ground floor and upper floor

1

2

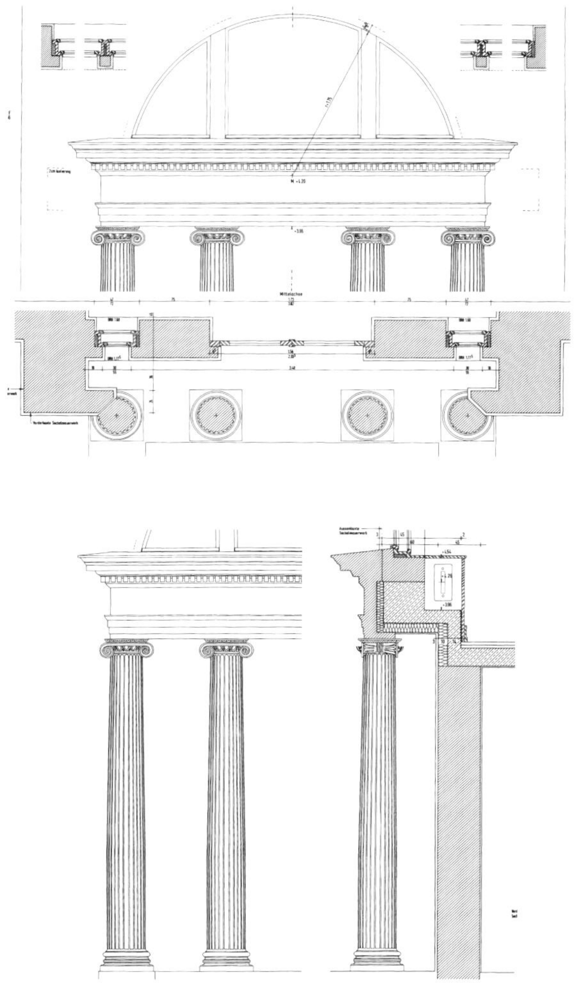

3

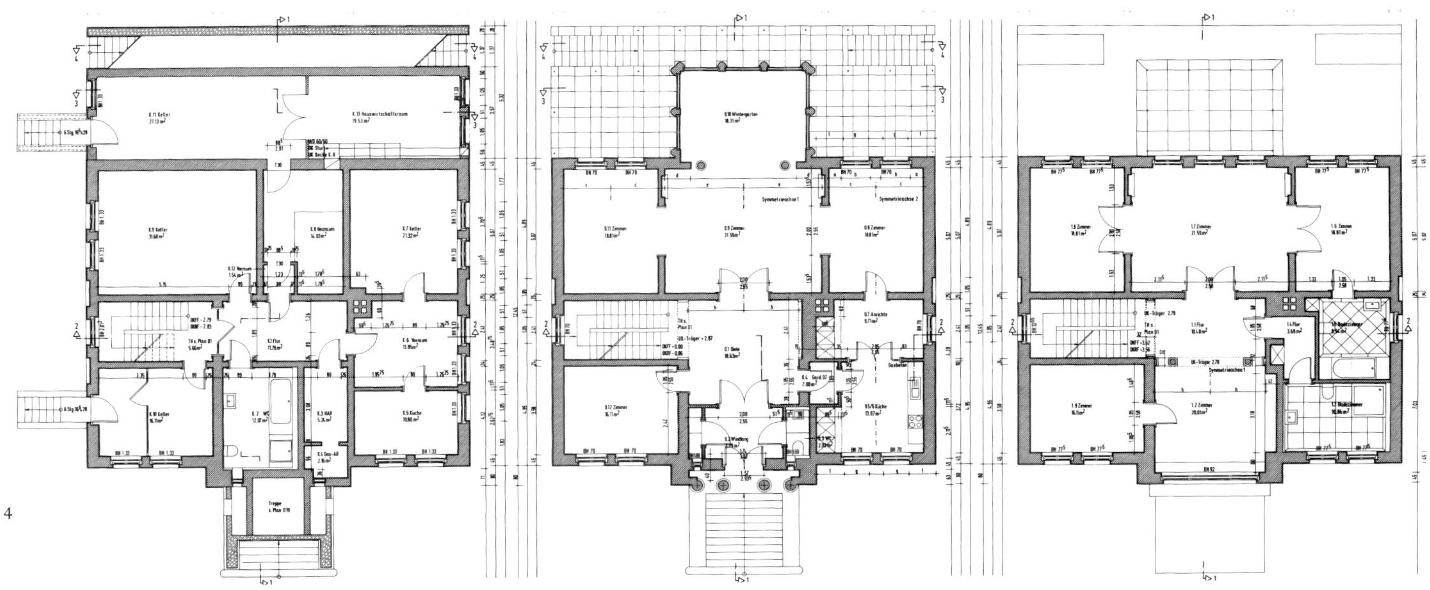

4

ARCHITEKTEN KOLLHOFF UND TIMMERMANN

Leibnizkolonnaden
Berlin, Deutschland, 2000-2001

Hans Kollhoff hat der gemäßigt modernen Formensprache, wie sie in der Wohnbebauung am Luisenplatz in Berlin-Charlottenburg (1982-1988) zum Ausdruck kommt, radikal abgeschworen und sich einer tektonischen, an Klassizismen orientierten Architektur zugewandt.

Die beiden U-förmigen Baukörper der Leibnizkolonnaden stehen einander spiegelbildlich gegenüber, schließen zwei angrenzende Baublöcke und fassen den so neu entstandenen Walter-Benjamin-Platz (vorher eine als Parkplatz genutzte Innenstadtbrache) zwischen Wieland- und Leibnizstraße. Der mit grauem Sandstein verkleidete Stahlbetonskelettbau beherbergt neben Wohnungen, Läden und Büros auch ein Hotel sowie Arztpraxen. Unter dem Platz, der vor allem bei schönem Wetter sehr belebt ist, befindet sich eine zweigeschossige Tiefgarage.

Kollhoff selbst begreift den Walter-Benjamin-Platz nach dem Gendarmenmarkt als die zweite »italienische« Piazza Berlins und stellt ihn in die Tradition barocker Schmuckplätze. Das Italienische, wie der Architekt es interpretiert, drückt sich zunächst in der Großform des Baus aus, die sich deutlich an einheitlich gestalteten Stadtplätzen des Barock wie etwa in Turin, aber auch der Plaza Mayor in Madrid orientiert, von denen Kollhoff die Dreiteilung der Gebäude übernimmt.

Die Schäfte der Gusssteinsäulen in den Kolonnaden sind mit Entasis gearbeitet; solche Elemente und der Detailreichtum des verwendeten klassizistischen Vokabulars bestimmen die Architektur Kollhoffs derzeit zunehmend. E. K.

Leibnizkolonnaden
Berlin, Germany, 2000-2001

Hans Kollhoff has radically rejected the moderate Modernist formal language, reflected for example in the block of flats he designed for Luisenplatz in Berlin-Charlottenburg (1982-1988), turning instead to a tectonic architecture rooted in Neo-Classicism.

The two U-shaped buildings that make up the Leibniz-Kolonnaden face each other like mirror images. They close up two adjacent blocks and thus create and frame a new square between Wielandstrasse and Leibnizstrasse, Walter-Benjamin-Platz (previously an inner-city wasteland used as a car park). The reinforced concrete frame building clad in grey sandstone contains flats, shops and offices as well as a hotel and medical centre. Beneath the square, which is very busy especially in nice weather, is a two-level underground car park.

Kollhoff himself sees Walter-Benjamin-Platz as Berlin's second "Italian" piazza after the Gendarmenmarkt, and places it in the tradition of Baroque ornamental squares. The Italian element, as the architect interprets it, is expressed in the building's megaform, which clearly takes it cue from the uniform design of town squares of the Baroque age, such as the one in Turin or the Plaza Mayor in Madrid, from which Kollhoff adopts the division into three of the buildings.

Entasis has been used on the cast-iron columns in the colonnades; Kollhoff's architecture is currently displaying more and more elements of that kind, along with the wealth of detail of Neo-Classical vocabulary. E. K.

I

1 Zentralperspektive des Walter-Benjamin-Platzes von der Leibnizstraße aus in Richtung Wielandstraße
2 Platzwand
3 Details
4 Perspektive Kolonnade
5 Fassadendetail

1 Central perspective of Walter-Benjamin-Platz seen from Leibnizstrasse looking towards Wielandstrasse
2 Building creating one side of the square
3 Details
4 Perspective view of colonnade
5 Façade detail

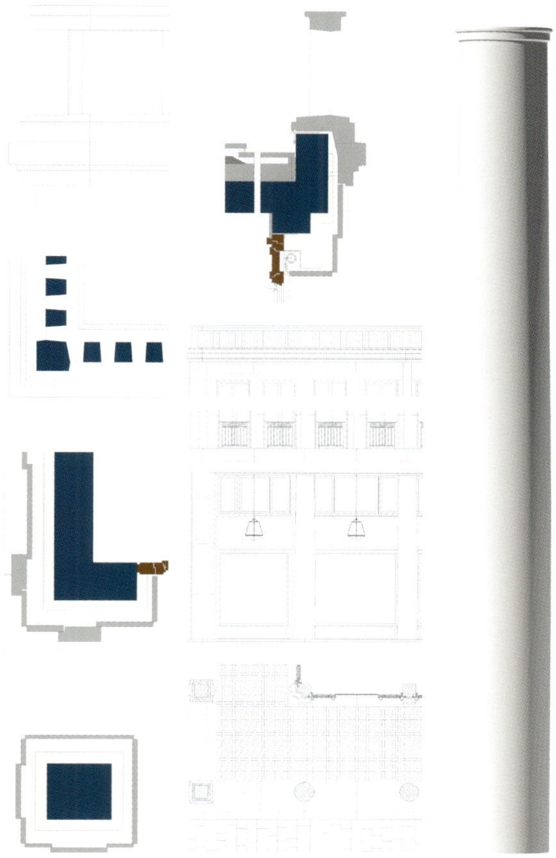

3

2

4

5

ANKNÜPFEN AN GESCHICHTE
CREATING HISTORICAL CONTINUITY

Der Vorwurf an die Moderne, für den Verlust von Tradition und Geschichtsbewusstsein verantwortlich zu sein, erhob sich besonders vehement angesichts einer weit verbreiteten Abrisswelle nach dem Zweiten Weltkrieg. Vor diesem Hintergrund wurde 1975 das Europäische Jahr des Denkmalschutzes unter dem Motto »Eine Zukunft für unsere Vergangenheit« ausgerufen. Die bald darauf einsetzenden Forschungen über die neuere Architekturgeschichte und das Engagement von Bürgern und Architekten führten zu einer Wende in der Beurteilung und Behandlung historischer Bausubstanz. Negativ beleumdete Bauwerke des 19. Jahrhunderts, politisch brisante Zeugnisse der NS-Zeit oder umstrittene Exponenten der fünfziger Jahre konnten vor dem Abbruch gerettet werden. Auch Industrieareale und Arbeitersiedlungen wurden nun als »Ressource Architektur« erkannt und unter Schutz gestellt. Die Umnutzung historischer Bauten für neue Inhalte geriet zur Zukunftsaufgabe.

Die beiden Beispiele aus der Eröffnungsausstellung des DAM von Giorgio Grassi und Josef Paul Kleihues erweitern bestehende Ensembles um Neubauten, die sensibel, aber selbstbewusst und ohne einen bestimmten Stil verwirklichen zu wollen, ganz aus der Aufgabe heraus zu einer überzeugenden Form gelangen. Als ähnliche Herausforderungen stehen aus jüngerer Zeit Bauten des Büros Neutelings/Riedijk, von Nicola Fortmann-Drühe und David Chipperfield zum Vergleich, die ebenfalls das Bestehende fortschreiben, ohne sich ihm unterzuordnen oder es zu übertrumpfen.

In der Eröffnungsausstellung waren auch Projekte von Reichlin/Reinhart vertreten, die den palladianischen Villentyp mit konstruktiven Mitteln und Materialien der Gegenwart neu entstehen ließen. Ihre Casa Tonini stellt eine Transformation der Villa Rotonda dar, ohne das Original zu kopieren. Werte wie Authentizität und Eigenständigkeit zeichnen dieses Experiment aus. Dagegen bedienen Fälschung und Simulation eher das allgemeine Empfinden. Skrupel, Gebäude originalgetreu zu rekonstruieren, obwohl die Geschichte bereits über sie hinweggegangen ist, scheinen in weiten Teilen der Bevölkerung verschwunden. Dafür ist der Wiederaufbau des Berliner Stadtschlosses ein heftig umstrittenes Beispiel. Wir erweisen mit einer Auswahl von Wettbewerbsprojekten den Architekten Reverenz, die sich für eine Neudefinition des Areals und einen zeitgenössischen Bau eingesetzt haben.

The accusation that Modernism is responsible for the loss of tradition and awareness of history was levelled with particular vehemence in the wake of the widespread spate of demolition after the Second World War. It was against this background that 1975 was proclaimed the European Year for the Conservation of Historic Buildings and Monuments under the slogan "A future for our past." This, combined with research into recent architectural history and the commitment of both the general public and architects, brought about a radical change in the evaluation and treatment of historic building fabric. 19th century buildings that had a bad reputation, politically embarrassing testimonies to the Nazi era, or controversial examples of fifties architecture were rescued from demolition. Industrial sites and workers' housing also began to be seen as an architectural resource and were listed as protected monuments. Converting historical buildings for new uses became a promising field of work for the future.

The two examples from DAM's inaugural exhibition by Giorgio Grassi and Josef Paul Kleihues extend existing ensembles by adding new buildings that are sensitive but self-confident and, without attempting to represent any particular style, evolve from the brief itself to create a convincing form. Recent buildings by Neutelings/Riedijk, Nicola Fortmann-Drühe and David Chipperfield are presented by way of comparison. They are examples of similar challenges and, like them, they continue what is already there without either subordinating themselves to it or out-trumping it.

The inaugural exhibition also included projects by Reichlin/Reinhart, which created a reincarnation of the Palladian villa using contemporary construction methods and materials. Their Casa Tonini is a transformation of the Villa Rotonda, without being a mere copy of the original. Values such as authenticity and autonomy are the hallmarks of this experiment. By contrast, the sensibilities of the general public seem best served by fakes and simulations. Large sections of the public appear to have lost all scruples about creating faithful reconstructions of buildings, despite the fact that history has already made them obsolete. A highly controversial example of this is the reconstruction of Berlin's Stadtschloss, or Imperial Palace. With a selection of projects submitted for competitions we have acknowledged the architects who advocate redefining the site and creating a contemporary building.

Bruno Reichlin, Fabio Reinhart: Casa Tonini, Torricella bei Lugano, Schweiz, 1972-1974, Grundrisse, Ansichten, Schnitte und Dachaufsicht. Original, Sammlung DAM

Bruno Reichlin, Fabio Reinhart: Casa Tonini, Torricella near Lugano, Switzerland, 1972-1974, Floor plans, elevations, sections and roof plan. Original, DAM collection

JOSEF PAUL KLEIHUES

Projekt für das Stadtarchiv Solingen
Deutschland, 1979

Project for the Stadtarchiv Solingen (near Wuppertal)
Germany, 1979

Die Neuorganisation von vier kulturellen Einrichtungen auf dem Gräfrather Klosterberg (Deutsches Klingenmuseum, Gräfrather Kirchenschatz, Bergische Galerie und Stadtarchiv) sollte vor allem dazu dienen, durch Umnutzung der vorhandenen Gebäude das historisch gewachsene Ensemble zu sichern. Raumnot führte dann im Plan zur Auslagerung des Stadtarchivs in einen Neubau.

Die »kritische Ergänzung« des historischen Bestands vollzog Kleihues mit zwei volumengleichen Türmen. Auf quadratischem Grund sind sie über eine gemeinsame Basis verbunden, die die Topographie des Klosterbergs aufnimmt und die beiden Türme als historisch folgerichtig entstandene Elemente erscheinen lässt. Der eine, der das eigentliche Archiv beherbergt, erwächst massiv aus der steinernen Sockelzone und erinnert an einen mittelalterlichen Wehrturm. Sein in Stahl und Glas gehaltener Gegenpart ist ganz dem Jetzt verpflichtet und nimmt die Arbeitsräume auf. Erschlossen wird der Bau über einen schmalen Spalt zwischen den Körpern.

Die Doppelung der Baukörper soll das Bewahren der vorhandenen Archivalien und deren ständige Ergänzung symbolisieren. Der mit dem Namen des Architekten verbundene »Poetische Rationalismus« offenbart sich am augenscheinlichsten in einer Konstruktion in Form eines stilisierten Blattes auf dem Dach des Stahlturms.

Kleihues konnte das Stadtarchiv nicht realisieren, errichtete jedoch 1990 das Deutsche Klingenmuseum, wie ursprünglich vorgesehen, im ehemaligen Klostergebäude. W. W.

The main aim behind the reorganisation of four cultural institutions on the Klosterberg in Gräfrath (Deutsches Klingenmuseum, Gräfrather Kirchenschatz, Bergische Galerie and Stadtarchiv) was to safeguard the historical ensemble by finding new uses for the existing buildings. A shortage of space meant that this plan included moving the municipal archives into a new building.

Kleihues implemented his idea of "a critical approach to additions" to the existing historical buildings using two towers with identical volumes. Both towers are square in plan and linked by a single foundation slab that follows the topography of the hill, the Klosterberg, and gives the towers the appearance of historically appropriate elements. One of the towers, which houses the archives proper, grows as a solid block out of the stone plinth and is reminiscent of a Medieval fortified tower. Its counterpart in steel and glass is totally contemporary in spirit and houses the offices. Access to the building is through a narrow slit between the two volumes.

The duplication of the volumes is meant to symbolise the preservation of the existing archives and their constant updating. The "poetic rationalism" associated with this architect's name manifests most clearly in a structure in the shape of a stylised leaf on the roof of the steel tower.

Kleihues was not allowed to build the Stadtarchiv, but he did complete the Deutsches Klingenmuseum in 1990—in the former monastery, as originally planned. W. W.

1 Stadtarchiv im Kontext des Gräfrather Klosterbergs
2 Fassadenabwicklung der beiden Türme
3 Normalgrundriss offene Verwaltungsebene und Archiv

1 Stadtarchiv in the context of the Gräfrather Klosterberg
2 Façades of the two towers
3 Typical floor plan for open-plan offices and archives

1

2

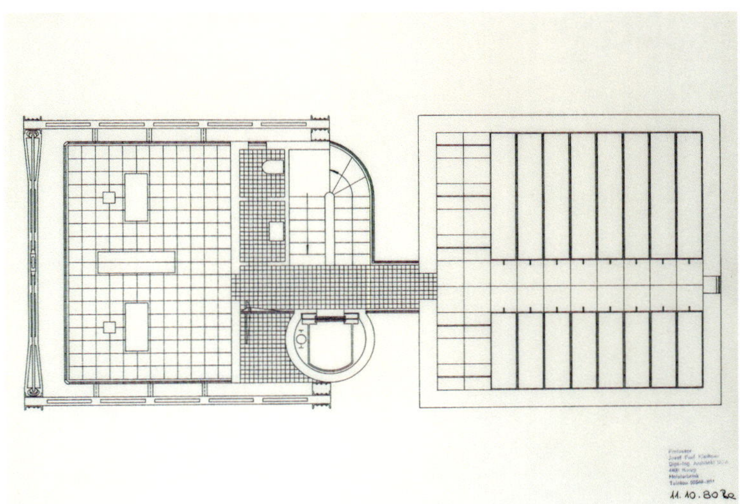

3

GIORGIO GRASSI

Umbau und Erweiterung des Visconti-Kastells
Abbiategrasso bei Mailand, Italien, 1970

Conversion and extension of the Visconti castle
Abbiategrasso near Milan, Italy, 1970

Die drei Baukörper des Kastells werden durch neue Bautrakte zu einer Vierflügelanlage erweitert. Während die historischen Außenfassaden nahezu unberührt bleiben, entsteht im Innern ein neuer Hof. Eingefasst wird er von einem Kolonnadenportikus, der die Arkade des Altbaus überblendet. Die Architektur des Kolonnadenhofs entspricht einem Typus, den Grassi mehrfach – auch bei Neubauprojekten – angewandt hat. Einen spezifischen Bezug zur Architektur des Kastells hat er nicht.

Es ist ein harter Kontrast, der sich sowohl in der Materialwahl (Ziegel gegen Naturstein) als auch im Formenvokabular (Spitzbogenarkade versus Pfeilerkolonnade) äußert. Das Alte bleibt zwar erhalten, tritt aber deutlich hinter dem Neuen zurück.

Bei der Erläuterung des – unausgeführt gebliebenen – Projekts hat Grassi zwischen der kunsthistorischen Bedeutung des Kastells und seiner künftigen Nutzungsbestimmung unterschieden. Ohne den historischen Wert des Bauwerks in Frage zu stellen, misst er der intendierten Nutzung einen höheren Stellenwert bei. Was auf den ersten Blick als sorgsame Bewahrung und Ergänzung des Alten erscheint, läuft de facto auf dessen architektonische und semantische Überformung hinaus. Im Fall des Visconti-Kastells heißt das: Die einstige Zwingburg der Feudalherren soll künftig als Stadt- und Gemeindezentrum genutzt werden. Grassis Umbau ist ein Plädoyer für die aktive Aneignung des historischen Erbes. M. J.

The three buildings that make up the castle are being extended and new sections added to create a four-wing composition. While the historical exterior façades will remain virtually untouched, a new courtyard will be created inside the castle. It will be framed by a colonnaded portico superimposed over the arcade of the historical building. The architecture of the colonnaded courtyard corresponds to a type which Grassi has used frequently—including in new-build projects. It does not specifically relate to the architecture of the castle.

There is a stark contrast reflected both in the choice of materials (brick next to natural stone) and the formal vocabulary (pointed arch arcade versus pillar colonnade). The existing buildings remain intact but are clearly subordinate to the new buildings.

In his comments on the project—which was never built—Grassi differentiated between the castle's significance in terms of art history and its future use. Without questioning the historical value of the building, he attaches greater importance to the future use. What seems at first glance to be careful conservation and extension of the existing building, amounts de facto to its architectural and semantic transformation. In the case of the Visconti castle that means that what was once the citadel of feudal lords will in future be used as a civic centre. Grassi's conversion is a plea for the historical legacy to be proactively appropriated. M. J.

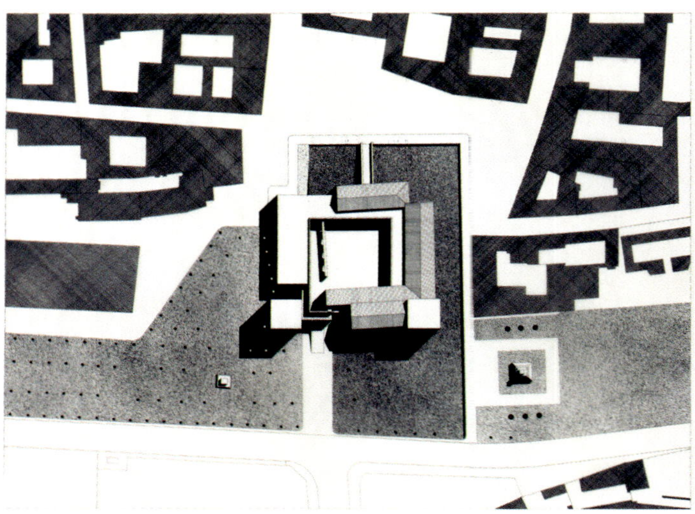

1

1 Lageplan mit Dachaufsicht
2 Ostansicht mit Schnitt des Treppenhauses
3 Westansicht
4 Hofansicht gegen Westen

Tusche und Spritztechnik auf Transparentpapier, Sammlung DAM

1 Site plan and roof plan
2 East elevation with section thorough the stairwell
3 West elevation
4 Courtyard elevation towards the west

Original drawings, DAM collection

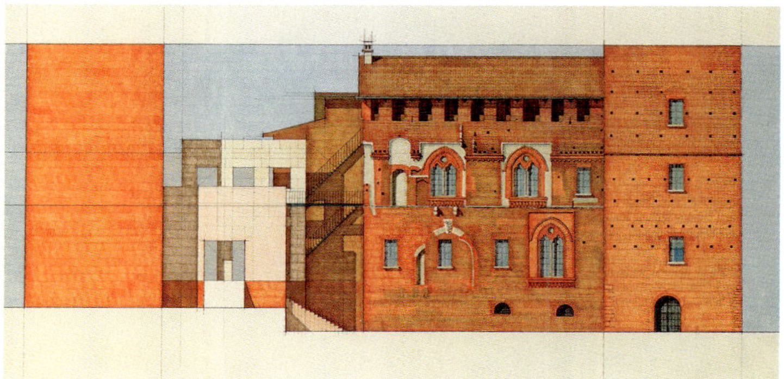

2+3

4

NICOLA FORTMANN-DRÜHE

Wohn- und Geschäftshaus
Potsdam, Deutschland, 2001-2002

Commercial and residential building
Potsdam, Germany, 2001-2002

Die barocke Fassung des Potsdamer Neuen Marktes geht auf den Wunsch Friedrichs II., der die meiste Zeit im Schloss Sanssouci lebte, zurück, auch in einer ihm angemessenen Stadt zu residieren. Seinerzeit wurden der vorhandenen, einfachen Platzbebauung deshalb prächtige Schauseiten vorgesetzt. Für das in einer Sichtachse liegende Gebäude Am Neuen Markt 5 sah der König eine Fassade im Stil Andrea Palladios vor. So diente bis zur Zerstörung des Gebäudes im Zweiten Weltkrieg eine Adaption des Palazzo Thiene in Vicenza als Point de vue.

Im Wettbewerb zur Schließung der Baulücke setzte sich Nicola Fortmann-Drühe mit einem ebenso einfachen wie schlüssigen Konzept durch. Analog zur benachbarten Kulissenarchitektur des 18. Jahrhunderts verkleidete sie das Gebäude zum Platz hin mit einer zweiten Schale, die den Vorgängerbau zitiert. Abstrahiert werden die wesentlichen Architekturelemente in Betonwerkstein wieder aufgenommen: Sockel, Kolossalordnung, Fensterrahmung und Hauptgesims. Ab der Sockelzone entfallen die Wandflächen und der Blick fällt auf das dahinter liegende Gebäude, das sich durch eine Glasfassade klar als Produkt unserer Zeit zu erkennen gibt.

Die Sockelzone ist für Läden und Büros vorgesehen, darüber liegen fünf schmale Maisonette-Wohnungen, die sich auf das Achsmaß der Kolossalordnung beziehen. Erschlossen werden sie über ein hofseitiges System von Treppen und Laubengängen, das ebenfalls als zweite Schicht dem eigentlichen Gebäude vorgesetzt ist und somit das Pendant zur Fassade am Platz bildet. W. W.

The Baroque setting of Potsdam's Neuer Markt is a result of Friedrich II's desire that not only his palace of Sanssouci but also the neighbouring town be appropriate. To accommodate his wishes, magnificent show façades were added to the show sides of the simple buildings around the square. For the building Am Neuen Markt 5, which stood on a visual axis, the King envisaged a façade in the style of Andrea Palladio. Thus, until it was destroyed in the Second World War, an adaptation of the Palazzo Thiene in Vicenza functioned as a point de vue.

In the competition held to close the gap in the buildings, Nicola Fortmann-Drühe's concept was convincing in its simplicity and logic. Following the analogy of the neighbouring stage-set architecture from the 18th century, she added a second skin to the side of the building facing the square, a quotation of the building that had stood there before. The most important elements of its architecture are repeated in an abstract form in cast stone: plinth, colossal order, window framing and main cornice. Above the plinth, the façade of the original building was not reconstructed, so that it is the building behind that catches the eye, its glass façade marking it clearly as a product of our time.

The plinth is destined to house shops and offices; above it are five narrow maisonette flats, which relate to the spacing of the colossal order. Access is from a system of staircases and access galleries on the courtyard side which are also placed in front of the actual building as a second layer and thus form a counterpoint to the façade to the square. W. W.

1 Fassadenelemente aus Betonfertigteilen
2 Platzansicht
3 Hofansicht
4 Detail der offenen Fassadenkulisse, Bereich Wohnhaus

1 Pre-fabricated concrete façade elements
2 View from the square
3 View from the courtyard
4 Detail of open façade, residential part of the building

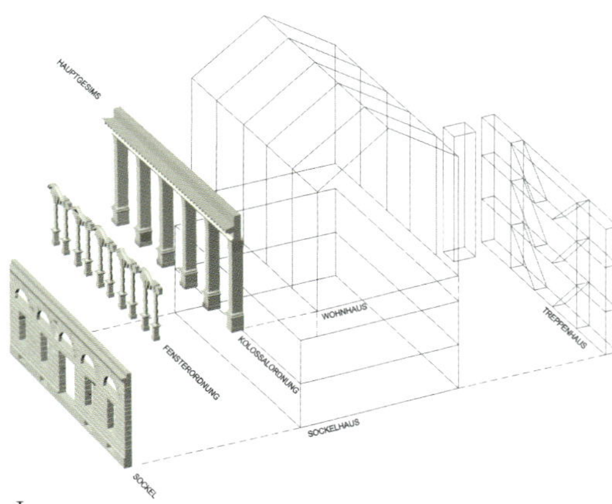

1

2

3

4

NEUTELINGS RIEDIJK ARCHITECTEN

Kunst- und Kulturzentrum STUK
Leuven, Belgien, 1998-2002

Die Umwandlung eines ehemaligen Chemielaboratoriums in ein Kulturzentrum war für Willem Jan Neutelings und Michiel Riedijk eine ungewohnte Herausforderung. Bekannt geworden durch »exzentrische« bzw. »modernistische« Gewerbebauten auf der grünen Wiese, waren sie hier, in der Altstadt von Leuven, mit einer Bauaufgabe konfrontiert, die denkmalpflegerische Behutsamkeit und architektonisches Einpassungsvermögen erforderte.

Mit einem vergleichsweise schmalen Budget konnte auf 10 000 Quadratmetern eine Kulturinstitution untergebracht werden, die zwei Theater- und Tanzsäle, einen Kammermusiksaal, ein Kino, einen Ausstellungsraum, Tanz- und Musikstudios, Werkstätten, Büros und ein Café-Restaurant beherbergt.

Um die verschiedenen Funktionen auf der relativ kleinen Fläche unterzubringen, wurde das hintere Areal des Grundstücks völlig neu organisiert. Entstanden ist ein attraktiver Hofraum, der den Mittelpunkt des Ensembles bildet. Um diesen Hof gruppieren sich alle wichtigen Räumlichkeiten. Im Querflügel und im linken Seitenflügel sind die neuen Säle untergebracht. Sie sind im Inneren individuell und modern gestaltet. Die Hoffassaden sind hingegen schlicht und unaufdringlich gefasst, sodass die vielteilige Struktur eine angemessene Einheitlichkeit gewinnt. Alt und Neu werden miteinander verzahnt, ohne jedoch ihre Eigenständigkeit zu verlieren. So wurden die Altbauten – das Vordergebäude und der Hörsaal im rechten Seitenflügel – kaum verändert und lediglich instand gesetzt. M. J.

Art and Cultural Centre, STUK
Leuven, Belgium, 1998-2002

The transformation of a former chemistry laboratory into a cultural centre was an unaccustomed challenge for Willem Jan Neutelings and Michiel Riedijk. They had become famous for their "eccentric" and "modernistic" industrial buildings on greenfield sites and were now confronted with a brief that required a careful approach to historically valuable buildings and sensitive integration skills.

With a relatively small budget, they managed to accommodate a cultural centre on 10,000 square metres, which included two auditoria for theatre and dance performances, a chamber music auditorium, a cinema, exhibition space, dance and music studios, workshops, offices and a café/restaurant.

In order to house the different functions within this limited floor space, the rear area of the site was completely reorganised. What emerged was an attractive courtyard that forms the focal point of the ensemble. All the important spaces are grouped around this courtyard. The new auditoria are housed in the cross wing and left wing. Their interiors are individual and modern in character. The façades to the courtyard are simple and reserved, giving a sense of coherence to the different parts of the complex. Old and new are intermeshed without losing their individuality. The existing buildings—the front wing and auditorium in the right wing—were scarcely changed, and simply repaired. M. J.

1

2

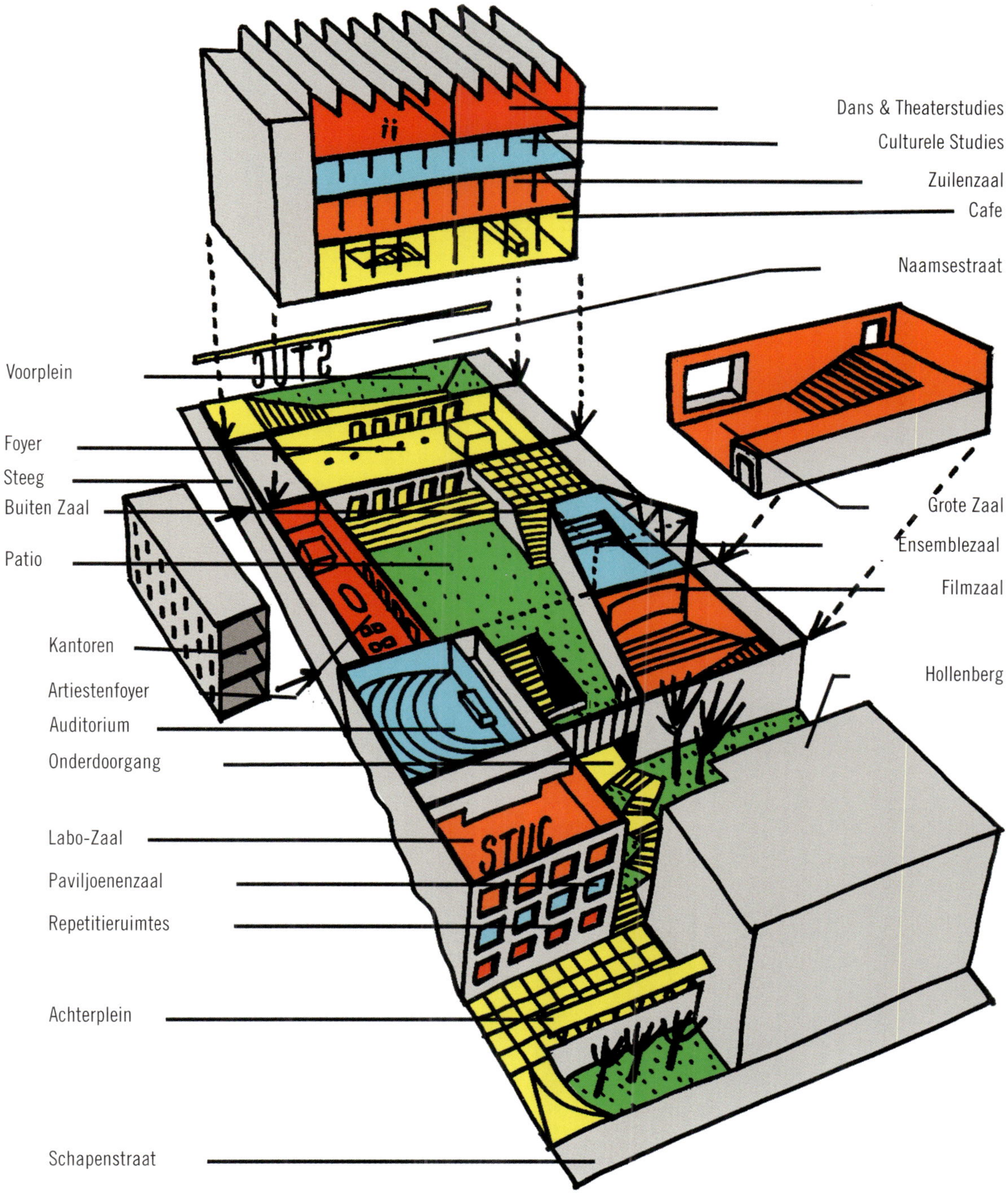

3

1 Eingangsseite von der Naamsestraat
2 Zentraler Innenhof
3 Überblick über das Kulturzentrum mit seinen Funktionen

1 Entrance side from Naamsestraat
2 Central courtyard
3 General view of the culture centre showing its functions

DAVID CHIPPERFIELD ARCHITECTS

Galerie an der Museumsinsel
Berlin, Deutschland, 2003-2005

Gallery on the Museumsinsel
Berlin, Germany, 2003-2005

Es ist einer der erlesensten Bauplätze, die Berlin zu vergeben hat. Das Grundstück »Hinter dem Gießhaus 1« gehört zu den letzten freien Arealen in direkter Nachbarschaft zur Museumsinsel. Wer hier baut, begibt sich in direkte Konkurrenz zu Schinkel, Stüler, Messel und Pei.

Entsprechend vornehm ist die Bauaufgabe. Im Auftrag des Kunsthändlers Heiner Bastian entsteht ein Galerie- und Ausstellungsgebäude, dessen Raumhöhen üppige sechs Meter betragen und natürliches Seitenlicht erhalten. Darüber hinaus werden im obersten Geschoss auch zwei Wohnungen Platz finden. Der Bauherr hatte im Vorfeld einen Wettbewerb veranstaltet, zu dem fünf renommierte Architekten geladen wurden, die bereits an anderen prominenten Stellen Berlins gebaut haben. Die Wahl fiel auf den Entwurf von David Chipperfield, der auch das benachbarte Neue Museum wieder herrichten wird.

Chipperfields Projekt vermeidet historische Anbiederungen und modernistische Attitüden. Es ist ein zeitlos-modernes Gebäude, das die Gliederungen und Proportionen der Nachbarbauten aufnimmt, aber eine eigenständig-schlichte Fassade aus sächsischem Sandstein besitzt, die durch große Fensterflächen akzentuiert wird.

Heiner Bastian hat sich nach eigenem Bekunden vor allem deshalb für den Entwurf entschieden, weil er das »rechte Maß zwischen Anonymität und Individualität« bewahrt. Das Gebäude drängt sich nicht in die erste Reihe seiner berühmten Nachbarn. Es begnügt sich mit einem souveränen Auftritt in deren Umfeld.

M. J.

It is one of Berlin's prime sites for development: the plot of land "Hinter dem Giesshaus 1" is one of the last undeveloped pieces of land in the immediate vicinity of Berlin's Museumsinsel or Museum Island. Any architect building here will find himself or herself in direct competition with Schinkel, Stüler, Messel and Pei.

The brief is correspondingly upmarket. Art dealer Heiner Bastian has commissioned a gallery and exhibition centre with six-metre high rooms, lit from the side by natural light. There will also be two apartments on the top floor. The client had organised a competition inviting five distinguished architects who had already designed buildings for other prominent sites in Berlin. The scheme selected was that submitted by David Chipperfield, who will also restore the neighbouring Neues Museum.

Chipperfield's project avoids any hint of sycophantic historicism or attempts to strike a modernistic pose. It is a timeless, modern building, which adopts the articulation and proportions of the neighbouring buildings but has a simple façade of Saxon sandstone, accentuated by large expanses of window.

Heiner Bastian himself stated that his main reason for choosing this particular scheme was that it held the "right balance between anonymity and individuality." The building does not elbow its way into the front row alongside its famous neighbours. It is content to be part of the overall context, yet separate and independent.

M. J.

1 Galerieraum im 2. Obergeschoss
2 Ansicht von der Bodestraße
3 Ansicht vom Lustgarten

1 Gallery on 2nd floor
2 View from Bodestrasse
3 View from Lustgarten

1

2

3

FRIDERICV

STEPHAN BRAUNFELS ARCHITEKTEN, FOSTER AND PARTNERS, SAUERBRUCH HUTTON ARCHITEKTEN, AXEL SCHULTES ARCHITEKTEN, VON GERKAN, MARG UND PARTNER

Entwürfe für das Schlossareal
Berlin, Deutschland, vor 2001

Nachdem das Berliner Stadtschloss, zu DDR-Zeiten im Ostteil der Stadt gelegen, 1950 gesprengt wurde, entstand dort der Palast der Republik, Sitz der DDR-Volkskammer. 1990 musste das Gebäude wegen Asbestgefahr geräumt werden und stand seitdem leer. Seit der Wiedervereinigung wirbt der Förderverein Berliner Schloss für die Rekonstruktion des Hohenzollernsitzes.

Mehrere Wettbewerbe zur Neugestaltung des hochsensiblen Areals förderten zahlreiche Vorschläge zutage. Die einen wollen den Palast erhalten und in einen neuen Schlossbau integrieren. Andere gehen vom Erhalt des Palastes aus, um ihn mit moderner Architektur zu ergänzen. Wieder andere plädieren für ein zeitgenössisches Bauwerk, das sich in seinen Abmessungen und Fassadenproportionen an dem einstigen Schloss orientiert.

Unterdessen hat die Asbestsanierung des Palasts der Republik dazu geführt, dass von ihm nur noch das Traggerüst übrig geblieben ist. Ende 2001 wurde ungeachtet heftiger öffentlicher Kontroversen von der so genannten Schlossplatz-Kommission entschieden, ein neues Gebäude in den Kubaturen des ehemaligen Schlosses zu errichteten, dessen Außenfassaden – mit Ausnahme der Spreeseite – originalgetreu rekonstruiert werden sollen. Dieser Beschluss wurde im Jahr 2002 vom Deutschen Bundestag bestätigt.

Die Palast-Ruine soll nun endgültig 2005 verschwinden, um einer provisorischen Begrünung des Schlossareals den Weg zu ebnen, bis die Gelder für die Rekonstruktion des Stadtschlosses vorhanden sind. R. S.

Schemes for the site of Stadtschloss
Berlin, Germany, pre-2001

In 1950 Berlin's Stadtschloss or Imperial Palace, which at the time was in East Berlin, was demolished and the Palast der Republik built in its place to house the East German parliament. In 1990, the building had to be closed because of asbestos contamination and has remained empty ever since. After reunification an association was formed to canvass support for the reconstruction of the Stadtschloss, which was the former residence of the Hohenzollern dynasty.

A series of competitions for the redevelopment of this highly sensitive site produced numerous proposals. Some sought to keep the Palast der Republik and integrate it into a reconstruction of the historic palace, others to keep it but complement it with modern architecture. Yet others make a case for building a contemporary building with dimensions and façade proportions based on the original palace.

One of the results of removing the asbestos from the Palast der Republik is that only the structural frame of the building remains. At the end of 2001, despite vehement public controversy, a specially set up commission, the "Schlossplatz Commission," decided to erect a new building with the same volume of the historic palace with its façades—with the exception of the façade facing the River Spree—faithful reconstructions of the original. This decision was reaffirmed by the German Parliament in 2002.

The shell of the Palast der Republik is now definitively set to be demolished in 2005 to make way for provisional landscaping of the site, until funds are available to reconstruct the Stadtschloss.

R. S.

1

1 Blick auf das Stadtschloss und den Berliner Dom mit Lustgarten. Zeppelin-Aufnahme von 1916

1 View of the Stadtschloss and the Berliner Dom and Lustgarten. Photo taken from a Zeppelin in 1916

2

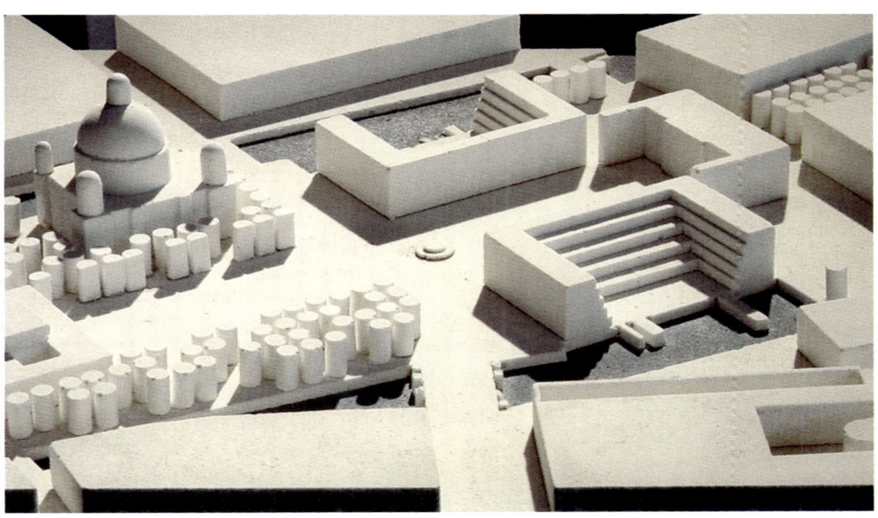

3

AXEL SCHULTES, 1996/2000
2+3 Der Entwurf zeigt eine neue städtebauliche Lösung. Statt eines zentralen Gebäudes soll eine Platzanlage in Fortsetzung des Lustgartens entstehen. Eingefasst wird dieser Platz von drei Bauten (»drei Schlösser«), deren Platzfassaden Kopien der ehemaligen Hoffassade des Schlüter-Schlosses bilden. An den Rückseiten verfügen die dreiflügeligen Bauten über offene Hofräume zur Spree und zum Kupfergraben. Damit verändert der Architekt die ursprünglich von kubischen Solitären geprägte Stadtlandschaft.

AXEL SCHULTES, 1996/2000
2+3 This scheme develops a new urban design solution. Instead of a central building, it envisages a piazza to continue the Lustgarten. The piazza would be framed by three buildings ("three palaces"); the façades to the piazza would be copies of the former courtyard façades of the original palace designed by Schlüter. At the rear, the three-wing buildings would have semi-enclosed courtyards opening to the River Spree and the Kupfergraben. In this way, the architect proposes changing the cityscape once characterised by cuboid standalone buildings.

4

5

NORMAN FOSTER, 1996
4+5 Nach Auffassung des Architekten sollte auf der Spreeinsel gar kein Gebäude stehen, stattdessen das Areal als öffentlicher Veranstaltungsplatz genutzt werden. Zu diesem Zweck sieht er die Errichtung von versenkbaren Schirmen vor, die eine Höhe von dreißig Metern und eine Kantenlänge von bis zu fünfzig Metern haben. Auf diese Weise könnte der Platz bei Bedarf vollkommen überdeckt werden.

NORMAN FOSTER, 1996
4+5 In the architect's opinion, there should be no buildings at all on the Spreeinsel; instead the site should be used as a venue for public events. With this in mind, he proposes erecting thirty-metre high canopies that can be lowered into the ground, each of their sides up to fifty metres in length. This would make it possible to completely cover the piazza if necessary.

SAUERBRUCH HUTTON, 2000
6+7 Der Entwurf sieht vor, wieder verwendbare Teile des Palastes der Republik, insbesondere den Volkskammersaal und eventuell den großen Kongress-Saal, zu belassen. Außerdem sollen die noch vorhandenen Keller des Schlosses integriert werden. Als Ergänzung des Vorhandenen dienen gläserne Pavillonbauten als öffentliches »Foyer«.

SAUERBRUCH HUTTON, 2000
6+7 This scheme proposes leaving certain reusable parts of the Palast der Republik intact, in particular the former chamber of the East German parliament and possibly the conference hall. The cellars of the historic Schloss would also be integrated. Glazed pavilions would form a public foyer and complement the existing buildings.

6

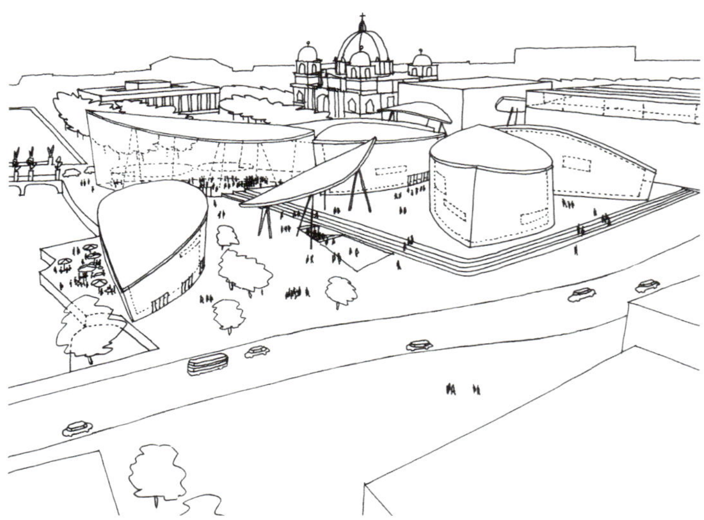

7

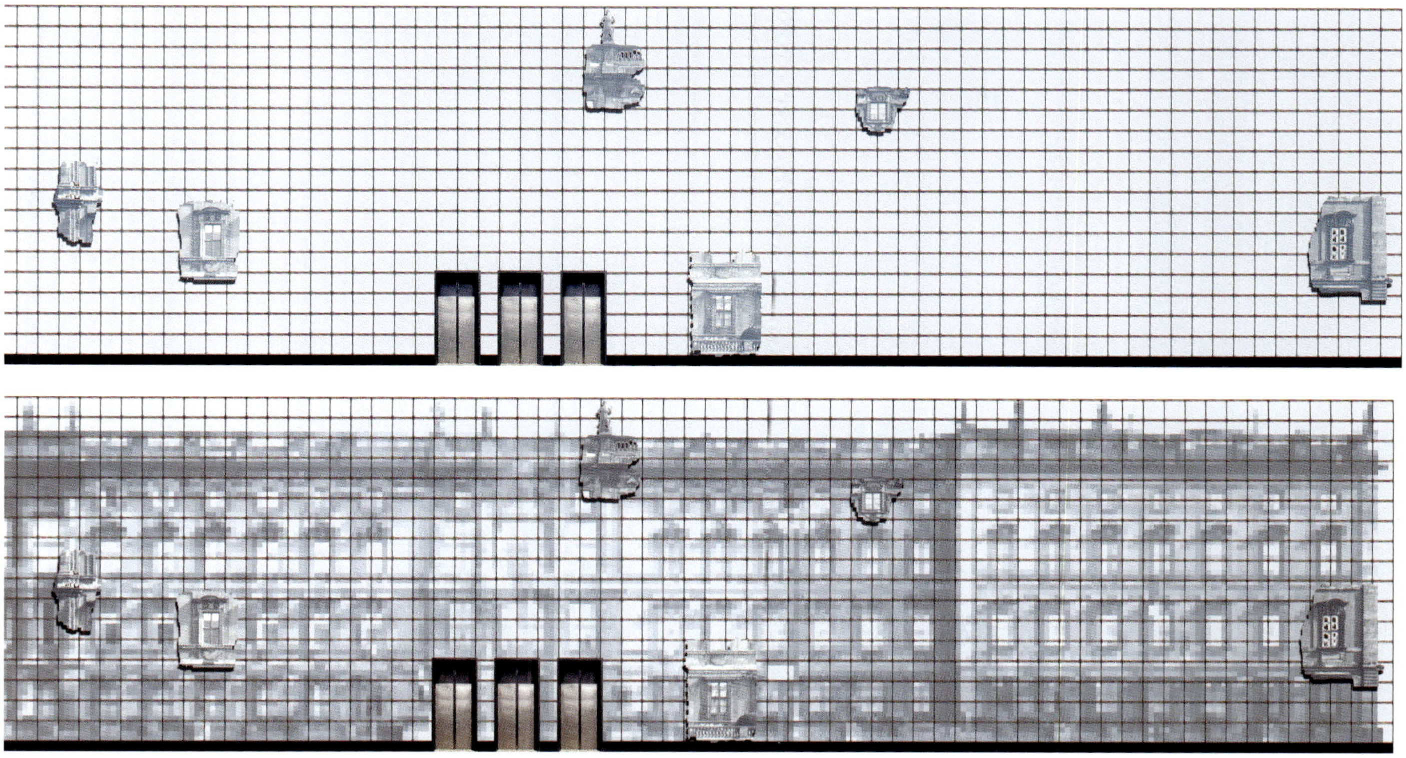

8

MEINHARD VON GERKAN, 2000
8 Der Entwurf sieht ein modernes Gebäude vor, das sich in den Abmessungen und Fassadenproportionen am Stadtschloss orientiert und das Bild des historischen Bauwerks simuliert. Die Glasfassade des »Janus-Schlosses« soll so bedruckt werden, dass von weitem der Eindruck des früheren Schlosses entsteht. Je näher man kommt, desto unschärfer werden die Konturen. Die Vision entpuppt sich als Illusion. Aus der Nähe treten lediglich die erhaltenen Fragmente des Schlosses hervor, die an ihren ursprünglichen Stellen in die Fassade eingepasst sind.

MEINHARD VON GERKAN, 2000
8 The scheme proposes a modern building, its dimensions and the proportions of its façades based on the Stadtschloss to simulate the appearance of the historic building. The "Janus Palace" would have a printed glass façade so that from a distance people would think they were looking at the historic palace. However, the closer they get to the building, the more blurred the contours become until finally the vision turns out to be an illusion. From close up, all that remains are the fragments of the original building, which have been fitted into the façade in their original positions.

9

STEPHAN BRAUNFELS, 1996
9 Dieser Vorschlag sieht einen neuen Schlossbau vor. Der Architekt öffnet jedoch den ehemaligen Schlüterhof zur Spree und zum Stadtraum am Alexanderplatz. Dadurch entsteht eine neue Achse, die ein Pendant zur westlich gelegenen Straße Unter den Linden bildet.

STEPHAN BRAUNFELS, 1996
9 This scheme proposed building a new palace. However, the architect opens up the courtyard of the former Schlüter Schloss to the River Spree and to the urban space at Alexanderplatz. This creates a new axis, a counterpart to the avenue Unter den Linden to the west of the site.

POPULISMUS ODER BAUKUNST
POPULISM OR HIGH ART

Dieses Kapitel soll eine Kontroverse andeuten, die auch im Zusammenhang mit der Eröffnungsausstellung des DAM entstand, als etliche Rezensenten in der Postmoderne den Niedergang von Architektur sahen. Ähnlich scharf wird heute der New Urbanism kritisiert. Eine wichtige Leitfigur dieser aus den USA stammenden Bewegung ist Léon Krier, der ausnahmsweise nicht mit einem Projekt aus der Eröffnungsausstellung zitiert wird, sondern mit einem städtebaulichen Entwurf, der 1986 in der DAM-Ausstellung »Internationale Bauausstellung Berlin 87. Beispiele einer neuen Architektur« gezeigt wurde.

Die Vertreter des New Urbanism – eines heterogenen Verbunds aus unterschiedlichen Akteuren des Bauens – sind mittlerweile weltweit aktiv. Erstmals trat er ungefähr 1980 in Erscheinung und wurde vor allem durch seine romantisierenden Kleinstadt-Neugründungen – in diesem Buch werden Seaside und Poundbury erwähnt – bekannt. Der New Urbansim versteht sich als Gegenbewegung zur Architektur der Moderne, der er anlastet, für den Verfall der innerstädtischen Zentren und die hemmungslose Ausbreitung gleichförmiger, hässlicher Vorstädte verantwortlich zu sein. Die Gegenstrategie des New Urbanism besteht darin, mit Hilfe eines traditionalistischen Städtebaus urbanes Leben zurückzugewinnen und die wuchernde Suburbia durch kleinstädtisch geprägte neue Siedlungen in historischem Stil einzudämmen. Von einer geheilten Stadt verspricht sich der New Urbanism auch eine geheilte Gesellschaft. Er propagiert einen ganzheitlichen Städtebau und fordert all jene Maßnahmen zur Reparatur der Stadt, die mittlerweile in Europa zum selbstverständlichen Repertoire des Stadtumbaus gehören.

Die Kritik am New Urbanism entzündet sich also nicht hier, sondern in erster Linie daran, dass er unkritisch und Geschichte missachtend auf historische Architektur zurückgreift, um sie zu einem gefälligen Städtebau zu komponieren, der keine Widersprüche oder Brüche zulässt. Damit in Zusammenhang steht der weitere Vorwurf, dass sich die Sehnsucht des New Urbanism nach einer heilen Welt sehr oft mit den Marktinteressen von Großinvestoren deckt, die durch ihre konzentrierte wirtschaftliche Macht öffentliches und privates Leben bestimmen – vor allem da, wo staatliche Instanzen Planungshoheit abgegeben haben. Die Gegner des New Urbanism befürchten, dass diese Bewegung ein kulturelles Klima befördert, das mit einem »Zurück in die Vergangenheit« zur kulturellen Stagnation führt.

This chapter is intended to allude to the controversy that also arose in connection with DAM's inaugural exhibition, when numerous critics viewed Postmodernism as the demise of architecture per se. Today, "New Urbanism" is at the centre of similarly acerbic criticism. A leading figure in this movement, which started in the USA, is Léon Krier. We have included one of his schemes that was also exhibited in 1986 in DAM's "International Building Exhibition Berlin 87. Examples of a new architecture."

The advocates of New Urbanism—a heterogeneous association made up of different actors within the architectural world—are now active throughout the world. The group first emerged around 1980 and achieved fame mainly through the new towns it built in a Romantic style—Seaside and Poundbury are mentioned in this book. New Urbanism sees itself as a countermovement to Modernism, which it holds responsible for the decay of the inner cities and the unchecked spread of uniform, ugly suburbs. New Urbanism's counter-strategy consists of using traditionalist urban design to revive urban life and attempting to halt the prolific sprawl of suburbia by building new developments in historical styles to look like archetypal small towns. New Urbanism has high hopes that "healing" the city will also heal society. It propagates holistic urban design and concurs with all the means of repairing the city that are now unquestionably part of the urban remodelling repertoire.

Thus it is not actually that aspect of New Urbanism that has attracted criticism. The main point of contention is that it makes recourse to historical architectural styles in a way that is uncritical and actually disregards history and uses them to create pleasing urban design compositions that permit neither contradictions nor discontinuities. Connected with that is the further accusation that New Urbanism's endeavours to create an ideal world very often concur with the market interests of large investors who are able to use their concentrated economic power to determine public and private life, particularly in cases where the state has abrogated its planning authority. The opponents of New Urbanism fear that this movement—with its "back to the past" philosophy—is fostering a cultural climate that will engender cultural stagnation.

Seaside, Florida. Standbild aus dem Film »The Truman Show« von Peter Weir

Seaside, Florida. Still from Peter Weir's film "The Truman Show"

LÉON KRIER

Städtebaulicher Entwurf Tegeler Hafen
Berlin, Deutschland, 1980

Urban design scheme for Tegel Harbour
Berlin, Germany, 1980

Das Projekt entstand im Rahmen eines der ersten Wettbewerbe der Internationalen Bauausstellung Berlin (IBA). Aufgabe war, ein Freizeitzentrum und ein städtebauliches Konzept für die Verzahnung der an das Wettbewerbsgebiet grenzenden Wohnbebauung zu entwickeln. Léon Krier hielt sich nicht an diese Vorgaben und schlug stattdessen vor, einen neuen, autarken Stadtteil zu errichten.

Seine Planung reiht sich ein in eine Fülle von Vorschlägen, mit denen der Architekt seit Anfang der siebziger Jahre gegen den modernistischen Städtebau mit seiner Funktionstrennung von Wohnen, Arbeiten, Erholen und Verkehr und für die Rettung der »europäischen Stadt« kämpft. Der Zerstörung gewachsener Strukturen durch anonyme und maßstabslose Architektur setzt er die Rekonstruktion der vorindustriellen Stadt – mit einer handwerklich orientierten Baukunst – entgegen, deren einzelne Quartiere alle für das tägliche Leben notwendige Funktionen erfüllen sollen.

Auch sein neues Viertel für Tegel ist bestimmt von dichten Blöcken, einem beziehungsreichen Netz von Straßen und Plätzen mit architektonisch herausgehobenen öffentlichen Bauten. Maßstab ist der Mensch, der in überschaubaren malerischen Stadträumen möglichst fußläufig alle für ihn wichtige Orte sozialer Interaktion erreichen kann.

Kriers Entwurf wurde trotz seiner Missachtung des Programms mit einem Sonderankauf geehrt, aber nicht realisiert. R. S.

This project was the result of one of the first competitions organised by the Internationale Bauausstellung Berlin, or International Building Exhibition (IBA). The brief called for a leisure centre and an urban design concept that would integrate the existing housing into the competition area. Léon Krier did not adhere to the brief and instead proposed building a new, completely self-related neighbourhood.

His plan fits in with the many proposals he had put forward since the 1970s as part of his battle against Modernist-style urban design with its segregation of residential, work, recreation and transport functions and his endeavours to rescue the "European city." He uses a crafts-based architecture to counter the destruction of established structures by anonymous, out-of-scale architecture, and attempts to reconstruct the pre-industrial city, each individual neighbourhood containing all the functions needed for daily living.

His new neighbourhood for Tegel is characterised by dense blocks, a close-knit network of streets and piazzas, and public buildings that display a more prominent kind of architecture. Everything is on a human scale and the picturesque urban spaces are laid out in such a way that people would be able to walk to all the important places of social interaction.

Although it disregarded the competition brief, Krier's scheme received a special award but was never built. R. S.

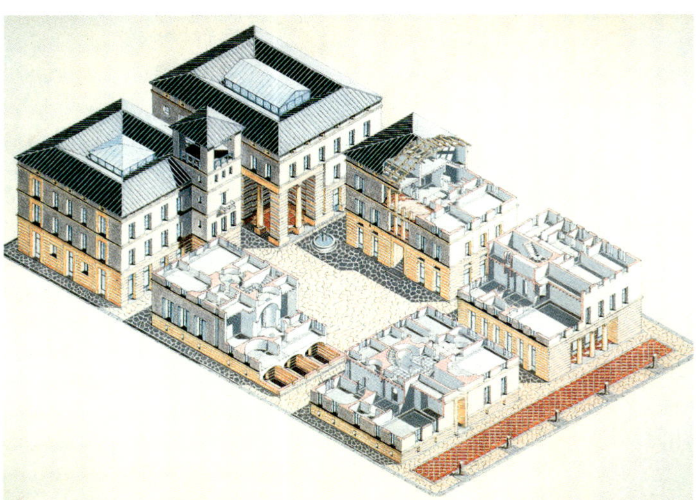

1

1 Insula Tegelensis, Isometrie, 1:200, Zeichnung 1982
2 Ansicht vom Wasser
3 Touristenplan, 1:2000, Zeichnung 1982

1 Insula Tegelensis, isometric view, 1:200, drawing: 1982
2 View from the water
3 Tourist plan, 1:2000, drawing 1982

2

3

LÉON KRIER

Haus des Architekten
Seaside, Florida, USA, 1985-1987/1999-2003

The architect's house
Seaside, Florida, USA, 1985-1987/1999-2003

In der ersten Stadt des New Urbanism hat Léon Krier auch sein erstes Haus verwirklicht: eine zunächst im Umfang bescheidenere Turmvilla, die seiner Lehre entsprechend auf klassischen architektonischen Prinzipien beruht.

»Architektur kann nichts anderes zum Ausdruck bringen als ihre eigene konstruktive Logik, also ihren Ursprung in den Gesetzen der Natur und der menschlichen Arbeit und Intelligenz.« Diese grundsätzliche Haltung konnte Krier an diesem Wohnhaus verwirklichen. Dabei kam ihm zu Hilfe, dass das Gebäude 1999 von einem Ehepaar gekauft wurde, das wegen der geplanten Erweiterung Kontakt zum Architekten aufnahm. Die neuen Eigentümer ließen sich auf Kriers Vorschlag ein, ein exemplarisches Bauwerk von höchster handwerklicher Qualität zu schaffen, das zeitlos schön, solide, wohnlich und elegant ist. Zunächst wurde das ursprüngliche Haus einer grundsätzlichen und sehr aufwendigen Überarbeitung unterzogen, dann um mehr als das Doppelte erweitert. Die neuen Bewohner hatten in engster Zusammenarbeit mit dem Architekten selbst die Bauleitung übernommen.

Krier schuf im frühen Stadium nur sehr einfache Skizzen, die dann sukzessive detailliert wurden. Tausende Faxe und hunderte Telefonate zwischen Architekt und Eigentümern waren notwendig, um jedes Detail des Holzhauses minutiös zu entwickeln. Auch die gesamte Innenausstattung vom Einbaumöbel bis zur Türklinke wurde (bis auf wenige Ausnahmen) von Krier entworfen; die Schreinerarbeiten führte ein Schweizer Handwerksmeister aus. R. S.

In the first town built as an example of "New Urbanism" Léon Krier also built his first building ever: originally a relatively modest-sized tower-shaped villa, which, in line with his theories, was based on Classical architectural principles.

"Architecture can express nothing but its own constructive logic; that is, its origin in the laws of nature and human labour and intelligence." Krier was able to give expression to this fundamental philosophy in this building. He was helped by the fact that the house was bought in 1999 by a married couple who contacted the architect to discuss plans to extend it. The new owners went along with Krier's proposal to create an exemplary building of the highest-quality craftsmanship, a building of timeless beauty, solidly built, comfortable and elegant. First of all, the house was fundamentally overhauled at great cost and then extended to more than twice its original size. The new owners took charge of the site supervision themselves, working closely with the architect.

In the early stages of the process, Krier produced only very simple sketches, which he then successively worked up into detailed drawings. Thousands of faxes and hundreds of telephone calls between the architect and the owners were required to make sure every last detail of this wooden house was meticulously correct. Krier was also responsible for every aspect of the interior design (with only a few exceptions)—from the built-in furniture to the door handles. A Swiss master craftsman was hired to do the joinery. R. S.

1 Entwurfsskizze Altbau mit neu angefügten Baukörpern
2 Eingangsseite
3 Gebäudedetail mit Erker
4 Grundriss-Skizze Erdgeschoss
5 Innenraum mit Ausstattung von Léon Krier

1 Design sketch of original building and new additions
2 Entrance side
3 Detail of building showing bay windows
4 Sketch of ground floor layout
5 Interior with furniture and fittings by Léon Krier

1

2

3

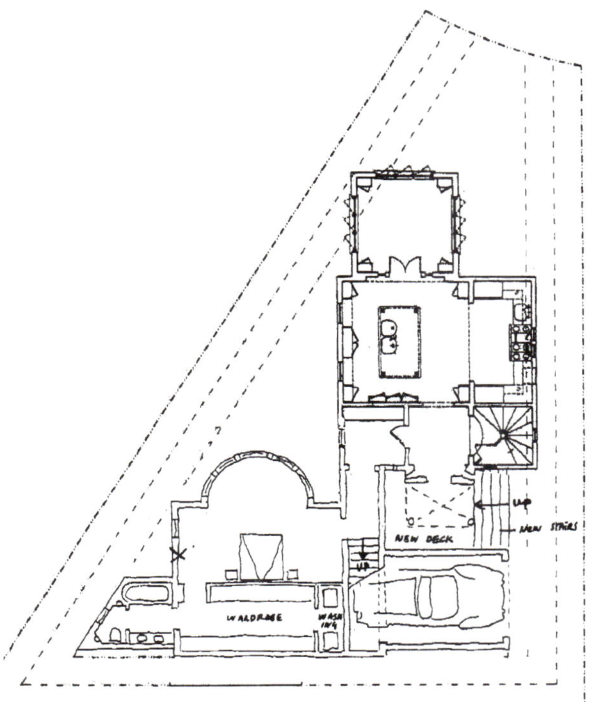

4

5

GEGEN DIE KONVENTION
KICKING AGAINST CONVENTION

Die postmoderne Befreiung vom funktionalen Determinismus bedeutete, außerhalb der gängigen Maxime »form follows function« Räume zu schaffen, die auf eine unübersichtliche und widersprüchliche Realität antworten sollten. Die meisten Architekten setzten dabei in je unterschiedlicher Weise auf Geschichte, Tradition und Konvention. Eine andere, ebenfalls uneinheitliche Strömung wendete sich dagegen, eine allgemeine und kohärente Realität zu konstruieren, und entschied sich für eine die etablierten Regeln überschreitende Architektur, die das Flüchtige und Widersprüchliche symbolisieren sollte. »Thema dieser Architektur ist«, so Heinrich Klotz, »die Gefährdung des Ganzen, das schwierige Zustandekommen einer problematischen Einheit. Die Brüche, die Sprünge, die Splitter, das Spiel mit statischen Gesetzen und den dynamischen Kräften.«

Das Projekt aus der Eröffnungsausstellung des DAM von Frank O. Gehry (sein eigenes Haus), das existentielle Instabilität beispielhaft inszeniert, wurde ein Schlüsselbau des Dekonstruktivismus. Gehrys Architektur aus antithetisch gefügten Fragmenten, die gewohnte Tektonik und Raumgrenzen missachtete, bot auch keine Quelle mehr für architektonische Referenzen. Die Gruppe Coop Himmelb(l)au, die hier mit dem Wissenschaftsmuseum für Lyon als neues Beispiel vertreten ist, sprengte ebenfalls schon vor Jahrzehnten die konventionelle Geometrie, etablierte das Spiel mit Ambiguität und die Manipulation von Architekturelementen, um latente, unterdrückte oder unbewusste Inhalte zum Ausdruck zu bringen.

In der Eröffnungsausstellung war Hans Hollein auch mit einer Auswahl von Fotocollagen vertreten, bei denen die Differenz zur bestehenden Stadt künstlerisch thematisiert wurde. Diese Blätter mit amorphen Gebilden über den Gebäuden reklamierten auch die Wiedereinführung des Monumentalen in die Stadtlandschaft. Das neue St. Petersburger Theater von Dominique Perrault, das sich wie eine goldene Wolke inmitten imposanter historischer Bauten niedergelassen hat, wird als zukünftiges Wahrzeichen der Stadt eine solche Forderung erfüllen.

Von den beiden neuen Beispielen, die auf konzeptionell unterschiedliche Weise mit architektonischen und städtebaulichen Konventionen brechen, bei ihrer Architektur aber ganz von den Interessen des Publikums geleitet sind, verspricht man sich auch den so genannten Bilbao-Effekt.

Post-Modernism's emancipation from functional determinism meant creating spaces beyond the widely held maxim of "form follows function" to respond to an unruly and contradictory reality. To do this, most architects drew upon history, tradition and convention in different ways. Another, equally heterogeneous, movement refused to build a universal, coherent reality and decided in favour of an architecture that went beyond established rules, an architecture intended to symbolise the transitory and contradictory. "The theme of this architecture," said Heinrich Klotz, "is the whole in jeopardy, the difficult creation of a problematic unity: the discontinuities, the disjointedness, the shards, the play with laws of structure and dynamic forces."

The project from DAM's inaugural exhibition by Frank O. Gehry (a house he designed for himself), which is a built example of existential instability, became one of the seminal buildings of Deconstructivism. Gehry's architecture, consisting of fragments in a relationship of antithesis that disregard the customary conventions of tectonics and spatial limitations, offered no further source for architectural references. The group of architects Coop Himmelb(l)au, who are represented here with their museum of science for Lyon as an example of recent work, similarly went beyond the constraints of conventional geometry several decades ago, established a play with ambiguity and manipulated architectural elements in order to express latent, repressed or unconscious contents.

Hans Hollein was also represented in the inaugural exhibition with a selection of photocollages, in which he gave artistic expression to his diverging view of the existing city. The graphic works showing amorphous structures over the buildings also called for the reintroduction of the monumental into the cityscape. Dominique Perrault's new theatre for St. Petersburg, which has settled in the city like a golden cloud amidst the imposing historic buildings, will fulfil this demand and is set to become one of the city's future landmarks.

There are great hopes that the two new examples, both of which break with architectural and urban design conventions in different conceptual ways but whose architecture is driven by the needs of the users, will create the so-called Bilbao effect.

Hans Hollein: Stadtgebilde über Wien, 1960

Hans Hollein: Urban figures over Vienna, 1960

FRANK O. GEHRY

Haus des Architekten
Santa Monica, Kalifornien, USA, 1978/79

Architect's own house
Santa Monica, California, USA, 1978/79

Der Altbau aus den zwanziger Jahren wurde an drei Seiten durch eingeschossige Teile ergänzt. Gehrys – genauestens konstruierte – Anbauten aus unregelmäßig geschnittenen, schräg gegeneinander gesetzten Flächen in Glas, Wellblech, Sperrholz und Maschendraht stehen in scharfem Kontrast zum herkömmlichen Kernbau und verleihen dem neuen Ensemble einen unfertigen Charakter, den der Architekt selbst als »open-ended composition« beschrieben hat.

Die neuen Raumgebilde um den Altbau vergrößern vor allem den Wohn- und Küchenbereich. Sie durchbrechen und stören gewohnte Raum- und Sichtbeziehungen, zum Beispiel wenn eine frühere Außenwand (mit Fenstern) zur Innenwand mutiert. Auch unterschiedliche Bodenniveaus in Alt- und Neubau tragen zur Dynamik einer komplexen Raumlandschaft bei, die voller Spannung ist. Und nicht allein Gartenmauer oder Freitreppe irritieren durch widersprüchliche Eigenschaften.

Das Haus, das sich konventionellen Erwartungen und Erfahrungen mit Architektur widersetzt, bildet den größtmöglichen Gegensatz zu den spätmodern-funktionalistischen Wohnhäusern der sechziger und siebziger Jahre. Dieser Schlüsselbau des Dekonstruktivismus nahm Anleihen sowohl bei Bauten Rudolph M. Schindlers als auch bei Installationen des Bildhauers Gordon Matta-Clark. Das Haus war für Zeitgenossen so unkonventionell, dass selbst Fachleute ihn manchmal als Architekten-Scherz verstanden. 1991/92 baute Gehry sein Haus wieder um und trug dem Konzept des Offenen und Unfertigen dabei erneut Rechnung. F. S.

New single-storey parts were added to three sides of the existing house built in the 1920s. Gehry's extensions—constructed with great precision—of irregular shaped planes of glass, corrugated iron, plywood and chainlink fencing, set in angular relationship to one another, are in stark contrast to the conventionality of the core building and give the new ensemble an unfinished character which Gehry himself described as an "open-ended composition."

The new three-dimensional structures around the original building extend in particular the living and kitchen areas. They pierce and disturb the usual spatial and visual relationships: for example, what was formerly an exterior wall (complete with windows) mutates into an internal wall. Different floor levels in the old and new buildings also contribute to the dynamics of a complex spatial landscape that is full of tension. And it is not only the garden wall or exterior staircase that irritate with their contradictory characteristics.

The house, which flies in the face of conventional expectations of and experiences with architecture, is the greatest possible contrast to the Late-Modern functionalist houses of the 1960s and 70s. This seminal building of Deconstructivism borrowed both from buildings by Rudolph M. Schindler and installations by the sculptor Gordon Matta-Clark. It was so unconventional at the time that even some people in the architectural world saw it as an architect's joke. In 1991/92, Gehry remodelled his house again, once more working with the idea of the open-ended and unfinished. F. S.

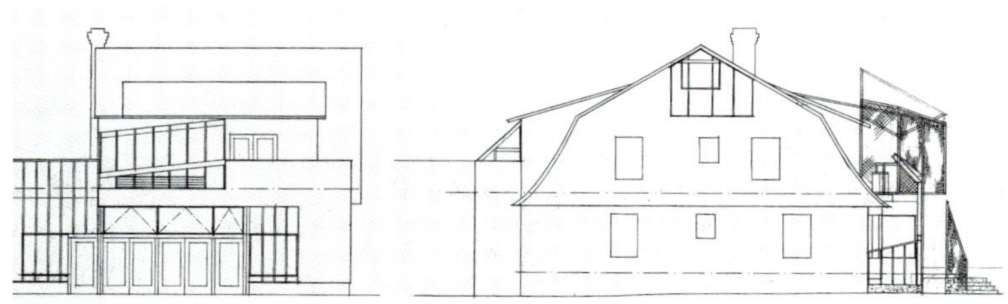

1

1 West- und Südansicht. Bleistiftzeichnung, Sammlung DAM
2 Fenster vom Altbau im Badezimmer
3 Küche, Blick nach Osten
4 Blick von Norden auf Eingangsseite

1 West and south elevations. Pencil drawing, DAM collection
2 Original window from the old building in current bathroom
3 Kitchen, looking east
4 View from the north towards the entrance side

2

3

4

COOP HIMMELB(L)AU

Musée des Confluences
Lyon, Frankreich, 2001-2007

Das Wissenschafts- und Kulturmuseum verdankt seinen Namen seiner Lage auf einer Halbinsel am Zusammenfluss von Rhône und Saône. Der als »Kristallwolke« bezeichnete Entwurf ist eine komplexe Assemblage aus unterschiedlichen Elementen wie Kegeln, Pyramiden, Pfeilspitzen. Materialien wie Glas, Beton und Blechverkleidungen sowie der Kontrast zwischen geraden und gebogenen Linien und Flächen verstärken den vielschichtigen Charakter des Gebäudes. Der Eingangsbereich ist großflächig verglast; darüber scheinen die weitgehend fensterlosen Ausstellungsräume zu schweben. Ein gläserner Doppelkegel mit einer spiralförmigen Rampe durchstößt den Bau von der Tiefgarage bis zur obersten Ausstellungsebene.

Das Lyoner Museum, ganz in der Tradition der dekonstruktivistischen Arbeiten von Coop Himmelb(l)au, nimmt auch Anleihen bei früheren Museumsbauten. So lässt die Glaspyramide an I.M. Peis Eingangshalle des Louvre denken, die Spiralrampe an Frank Lloyd Wrights Guggenheim Museum in New York. Zusammen mit der Stahlkonstruktion des Doppelkegels, die vom russischen Konstruktivismus inspiriert ist, verschmelzen diese Elemente zu einer neuen Gestalt, die an einen Vogel oder ein exotisches Flugobjekt erinnert.

Das Musée des Confluences ist eines der zahlreichen interaktiven Museen, die auf spielerische Wissensvermittlung und Information ausgerichtet sind. In den neunziger Jahren entstanden europaweit ähnliche Wissenschaftsmuseen, unter anderem in Wolfsburg (Zaha Hadid), Amsterdam (Renzo Piano) und Valencia (Rafael Moneo).

F. S.

Musée des Confluences
Lyon, France, 2001-2007

This museum of science and culture owes its name to its position on a peninsula at the confluence of the rivers Rhône and Saône. The scheme, which has been described as a "crystal cloud," is a complex assemblage of different elements such as cones, pyramids, arrowheads. Materials such as glass, concrete and metal cladding and the contrast between straight and curved lines and planes increase the complex character of the building. The entrance area is fully glazed; above it the largely windowless exhibition spaces seem to hover. A glazed double cone with a spiral ramp penetrates the building from the underground car park right through to the top exhibition level.

This museum in Lyon, totally in the tradition of deconstructivist works by Coop Himmelb(l)au, also borrows from earlier museum buildings. For example, the glazed pyramid is reminiscent of I. M. Pei's entrance foyer to the Louvre, the spiral ramp of Frank Lloyd Wright's Guggenheim Museum in New York. Along with the steel structure of the double cone, which is inspired by Russian Constructivism, these elements merge to form a new shape, evoking a bird or an exotic flying object.

The Musée des Confluences is one of many interactive museums designed to convey knowledge and information in a playful way. Similar science museums were built throughout Europe in the 1990s, including in Wolfsburg (Zaha Hadid), Amsterdam (Renzo Piano) and Valencia (Rafael Moneo).

F. S.

1

2

3

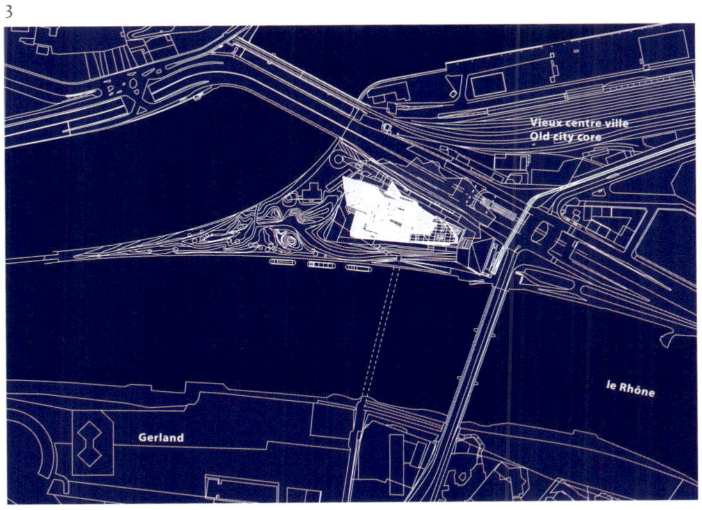

1 Blick von der Saône
2 Eingangsfoyer
3 Situationsplan
4 Längsschnitt
5 Ansicht von der Autobahn

1 View from the Saône River
2 Entrance foyer
3 Site plan
4 Longitudinal section
5 View from the motorway

4

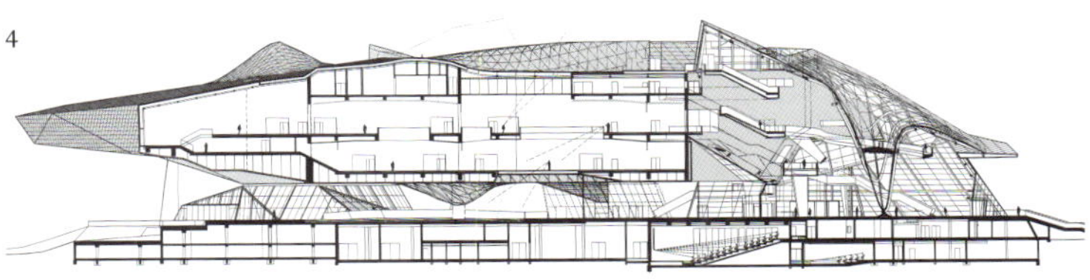

5

DOMINIQUE PERRAULT

Erweiterung des Marinski-Theaters
St. Petersburg, Russland, 2003

Extension to the Mariinsky Theatre
St. Petersburg, Russia, 2003

Das Marinski-Theater gehört zu den berühmtesten Opernhäusern der Welt, bleibt jedoch in technischer Ausstattung und Komfort hinter westlichem Niveau zurück. Mit einer Erweiterung um zwei Säle mit 2000 bzw. 350 Plätzen für Oper-, Ballet- und Konzertaufführungen sowie neuen Funktionsräumen soll der Anschluss an die Spitzen-Bühnen vollzogen werden.

Perrault unterscheidet in seinem siegreichen Wettbewerbsentwurf zwischen der eigentlichen Spielstätte, einem funktional organisierten Kubus aus schwarzem Marmor, und einer davon unabhängigen kristallinen Netzstruktur. Diese umkleidet den durch einen Kanal vom Altbau getrennten Neubau fast vollständig und orientiert sich farblich an den zahlreichen goldenen Kuppeln und Dächern der Stadt. Die Distanz zwischen Gebäude und Hülle begreift der Architekt als zeitgemäße Neuinterpretation des Foyers, das den öffentlichen Raum in das Gebäude hineinführt.

Der große Zuschauerraum ist klassisch gehalten und trägt mit seiner opulenten Ausstattung in den Farben Rot und Gold der Erwartung des Publikums Rechnung. Neu ist Perraults Konzept der offenen Oper: Tag und Nacht, selbst bei laufendem Spielbetrieb, soll sie jedermann zugänglich sein und nach Art einer überdachten Galerie mit Hilfe von Cafés, Restaurants, Boutiquen und Ausstellungsräumen, die auf den oberen Ebenen vorgesehen sind, soziale und intellektuelle Barrieren abbauen. Der Baubeginn ist für 2006 geplant, das Haus soll 2009 fertig gestellt sein. W. W.

The Mariinsky Theatre is one of the most famous opera houses in the world, yet it lags behind Western standards in terms of technical equipment and comfort. An extension consisting of two auditoria with 2000 and 350 seats respectively for opera, ballet and concerts and new functional spaces is designed to bring it up to the level of the world's top stages.

In his prize-winning competition design, Perrault makes a distinction between the actual performance venue, a functionally organised cube of black marble, and a crystalline net-like structure which is completely independent of it. This almost completely envelops the new building which is separated from the existing building by a canal and takes its orientation in its colour scheme from the city's numerous golden domes and roofs. The architect sees the distance between the building and its golden shell as a contemporary reinterpretation of the foyer which draws the public realm into the building.

The large auditorium is Classical in style and with its opulent fittings in red and gold fulfils the audience's expectations. By contrast, Perrault's concept of the open opera is new: he envisages it being accessible to everyone, day and night even during performances. Built in the style of a covered gallery, he hopes the cafés, restaurants, boutiques and exhibition spaces planned for the upper storeys will dismantle social and intellectual barriers. Construction is due to start in 2006 and completion is scheduled for 2009. W. W.

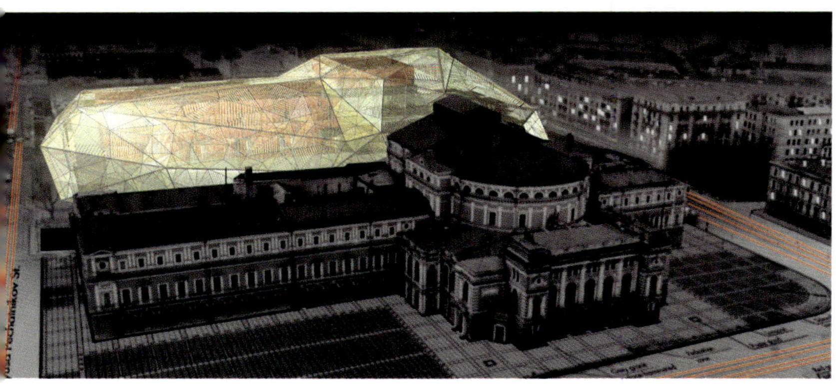

1

1 Alt- und Neubau im städtischen Kontext
2 Blick über den Krykov-Kanal auf das alte und neue Theater
3 Foyer mit öffentlichen Balkonen
4 Schnitt durch Neu- und Altbau (oben), Längsschnitt Neubau (unten)
5 Blick von Balkon in östliche Richtung

1 Old and new building in the context of the city
2 View over the Krykov canal to the old and new theatre
3 Foyer with public balconies
4 Section through the new and old buildings (top), longitudinal section through the new building (bottom)
5 View from a balcony looking eastwards

2

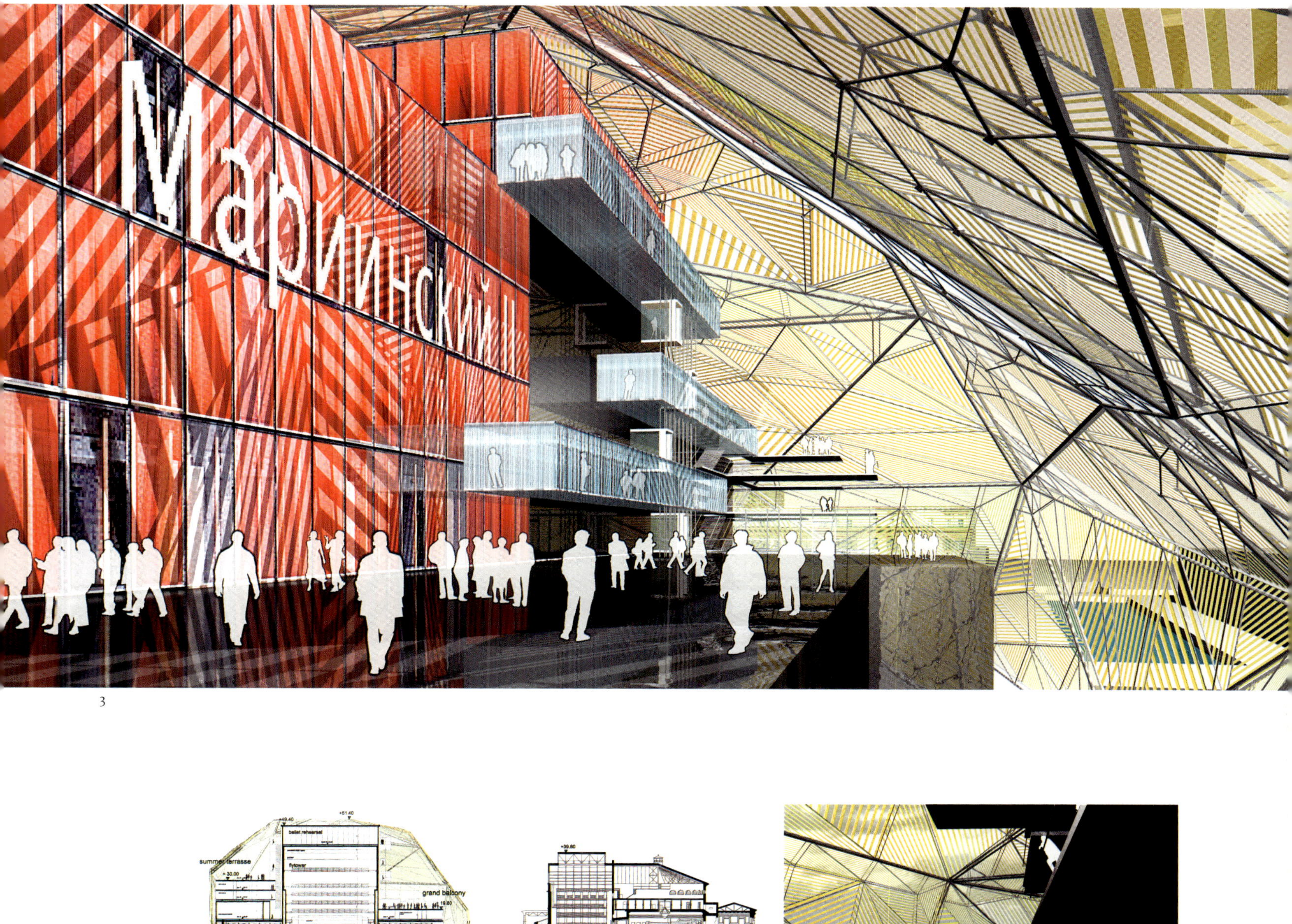
Мариинский II

3

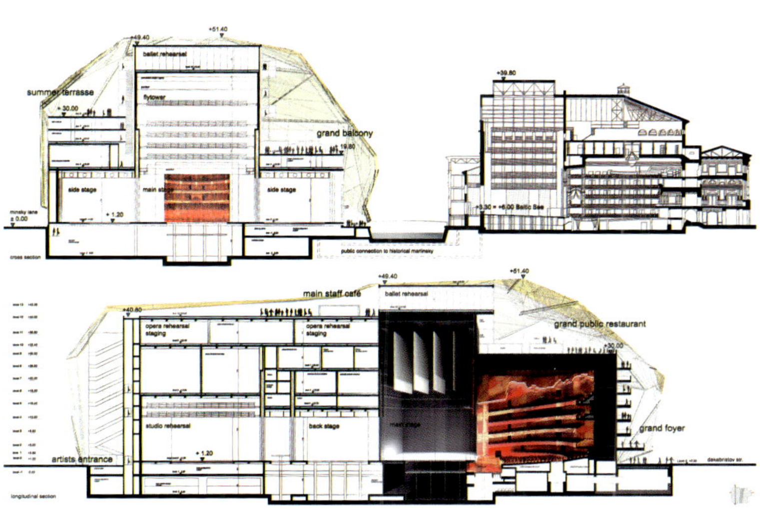
+51.40
+49.40
ballet rehearsal
summer terrasse
flytower
+ 30.00
grand balcony
19.80
side stage
main stage
side stage
minsky lane
± 0.00
+ 1.20
cross section
public connection to historical mariinsky
+39.80
+3.30 = +6.00 Baltic See
+49.40
+51.40
main staff café
ballet rehearsal
+40.80
opera rehearsal
staging
opera rehearsal
staging
grand public restaurant
+30.00
studio rehearsal
back stage
main stage
grand foyer
artists entrance
+ 1.20
dekabristov str.
longitudinal section

4

5

HÄUSER FÜR INDIVIDUALISTEN
HOMES FOR INDIVIDUALISTS

Wir schätzen das private Haus um unserer individuellen Freiheit und Autonomie willen, nicht nur als Ort von (familiären) Beziehungen, sondern auch als Ort des Rückzugs. Von einem Haus erwarten wir, dass es unsere Identität schützen und entwickeln kann. Es sind existentielle Erfahrungen, die wir mit dem privaten, dem häuslichen Leben verbinden.

Drei Wohnhäuser sind aus der Eröffnungsausstellung des DAM vertreten, die jeweils programmatische Experimente mit Architektur darstellen. Venturis Haus ist in seinem Ausdruck von »Complexity und Contradiction« zu einem paradigmatischen Bauwerk der Postmoderne geworden. Peter Eisenmans Villa verkörpert eine abstrakte architekturtheoretische Studie und lässt nicht erkennen, dass sich der Architekt mit der eigentlichen Bauaufgabe des Wohnens beschäftigt. Richard Meier baute ein elegantes Haus, das eine Auseinandersetzung mit der Tradition des Neuen Bauens darstellt. Auffallend ist bei diesen Häusern, dass jeweils der Architekt mit seinen Auffassungen dominiert und der Nutzer im Hintergrund bleibt.

Bei den neuen Beispielen, die wir ausgewählt haben, wird ein konzeptioneller Unterschied deutlich. Obwohl sie architektonisch nicht weniger markant in Erscheinung treten, haben Bauherren und Architekten offenbar gemeinsam individuelle Formen für das Wie des Wohnens entwickelt. Besonders beeindruckt es, wenn gegensätzliche Bedingungen des privaten Lebens räumlichen Ausdruck erhalten. Um Wohnen und Arbeiten zusammenfinden zu lassen, nimmt sich Ben van Berkel die endlose Möbiusschleife zum Vorbild. Der Weg durch dieses Haus ist immer ein Rundgang; fest gefügte Räume gibt es nicht. Auch beim Maison à Bordeaux von Rem Koolhaas ist die Überwindung räumlicher Begrenzungen entscheidend. Hier waren mehrere sehr verschiedene Leben zu koordinieren, das eines berufstätigen Mannes im Rollstuhl und seiner Familie. Man wollte kein Haus für einen Behinderten, sondern eines, das ihm größtmögliche Autonomie in einem privaten Universum bot.

Sich in einer außergewöhnlichen Umgebung einrichten zu können ist ein Privileg. So kann keines der hier gezeigten luxuriösen Häuser als Prototyp verstanden werden. Aber bei den einzelnen Bauten werden gedankliche und architektonische Konzeptionen verfolgt, die vielleicht auch bei Bauaufgaben mit eingeschränktem Programm und Etat umgesetzt werden könnten.

We value our houses because of the individual freedom and autonomy they provide; they are not just places in which (family) relationships take place but also places of privacy. We expect a house to provide a space in which our identity is protected and can develop. The experiences we associate with our life within the home are existential in nature.

Three private houses from DAM's inaugural exhibition are included here, each representing programmatic architectural experiments. Venturi's house, expressing "complexity and contradiction" as it does, has become one of Post-Modernism's paradigms. Peter Eisenman's villa is the embodiment of an abstract architectural study and shows no evidence that the architect has engaged with the actual brief of making a building for people to live in. Richard Meier built an elegant house that represents an engagement with the tradition of Neues Bauen. What is striking about all three houses is that the architect and his ideas dominate, while the needs of the user remain in the background.

A conceptual difference can be clearly seen in the new examples we have chosen here. Although their architecture is just as powerful, it is obvious that the clients and architects have worked together to develop forms to suit the individual clients' lifestyles. What is particularly impressive is when contrasting circumstances within an individual's life are given spatial expression. Ben van Berkel uses the endless Möbius strip for inspiration in his attempt to reconcile working and living needs. The route through this house is always circular; there are no fixed spaces. In Rem Koolhaas's Maison à Bordeaux, overcoming spatial constraints is also a decisive issue. Here the challenge was to coordinate several very different lifestyles: those of a professional man who is a wheelchair user and his family. The client did not want a house in the normal style of a building for the disabled but rather one that would give him the greatest possible autonomy in his private world.

People who have the opportunity to make a home for themselves in extraordinary buildings are in a privileged position. The luxurious houses shown here cannot therefore be seen as prototypes. But the intellectual and architectural ideas these individual buildings pursue can perhaps be integrated into other building projects with more restricted programmes and budgets.

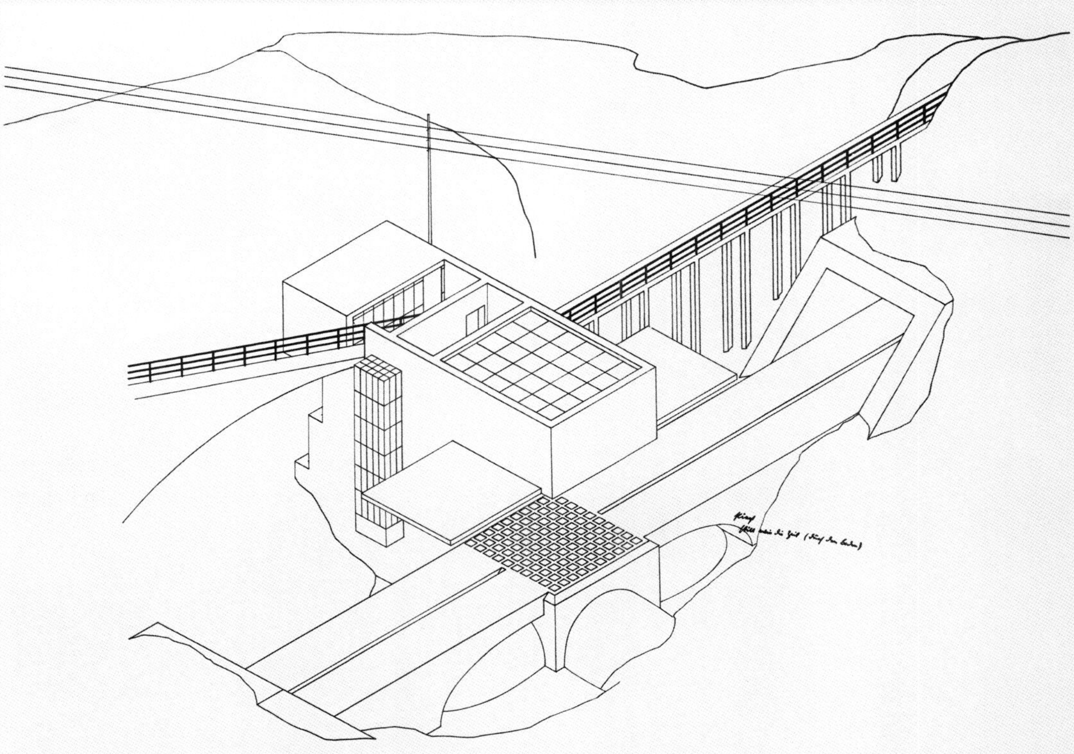

Wolf Meyer-Christian: Haus im Felsengrund, 1964, Isometrie.
Tuschezeichnung, Sammlung DAM

Wolf Meyer-Christian: House in a rockbed, 1964, isometric view.
Pen and ink drawing, DAM collection

ROBERT VENTURI

My Mother's House
Chestnut Hill, Pennsylvania, USA, 1962-1964

Es gibt Literatur, die Weltbilder zum Einsturz zu bringen vermag. *Komplexität und Widerspruch in der Architektur* von Robert Venturi ist eines dieser Bücher, weil es die Architektur aus einer sozial motivierten Einbahnstraße herausgeführt hat. Zeitgleich mit der Fertigstellung des Manuskripts plante Venturi dieses Haus, das als Umsetzung der theoretischen Ansätze für Furore gesorgt hat.

Übertrieben und respektlos zieren klassische Würdeformeln den verhältnismäßig kleinen Bau, dessen Fassaden entgegen der herrschenden Doktrin autonom sind und nichts von der Organisation der Räume preisgeben. Auf der Schauseite überschneiden sich ein massiver Türsturz und ein ihn krönendes Rundbogenmotiv. Dieses wiederum wird von einem tiefen Einschnitt in der Giebelfläche unterbrochen. Darüber hinaus konterkarieren unterschiedliche Fensterformate und ein leicht aus der Achse gerückter Schornstein den regelmäßigen Fassadenaufbau.

Spannungen ziehen sich auch durch das Innere. Die vorgebliche Achsensymmetrie des Grundrisses erweist sich bei näherem Hinsehen als nichtig, und die Treppe ändert beständig Richtung und Breite. Es ergibt sich ein Reichtum an unterschiedlichen Räumen, analog zur Komplexität des Raumprogramms.

Von der Postmoderne und der unreflektierten Anwendung historischer Formen hat sich der Architekt immer distanziert. Ironischerweise schuf er mit dieser Umsetzung architektonischer Symbolik ein Gebäude, das zum oft und schlecht kopierten Leitbild der Postmoderne wurde.

W. W.

My Mother's House
Chestnut Hill, Pennsylvania, USA, 1962-1964

Certain works of literature are capable of shattering established views of the world. *Complexity and contradiction in architecture* by Robert Venturi is one of these books because it has led architecture out of a socially motivated one-way street. At the same time as writing the book, Venturi caused a great furore when he designed this house which is a translation into reality of the theories of the book.

Classical symbols of status decorate the relatively small building in a way that is both completely exaggerated and lacking in respect. The facades, flying in the face of the prevailing doctrine of the time, are autonomous and reveal nothing about the organisation of the spaces. On the show side a massive door lintel and a rounded arch motif intersect. This in turn is broken by a deep incision in the plane of the gable. In addition to that, different types of window and the slightly off-centre chimney contradict the regular organisation of the façade.

Tensions continue inside the house. The seemingly axial symmetry of the plan proves on closer examination to be an illusion and the staircase constantly changes direction and width. A wealth of different spaces is created, reflecting the complexity of the domestic brief.

Venturi always distanced himself from Post-Modernism and the unthinking use of historical forms. It is ironic that, in translating architectural symbolism into reality, he created a building that would become a paradigm of Post-Modernism so frequently and badly copied.

W. W.

1

1 Wohnzimmer
1 Living room

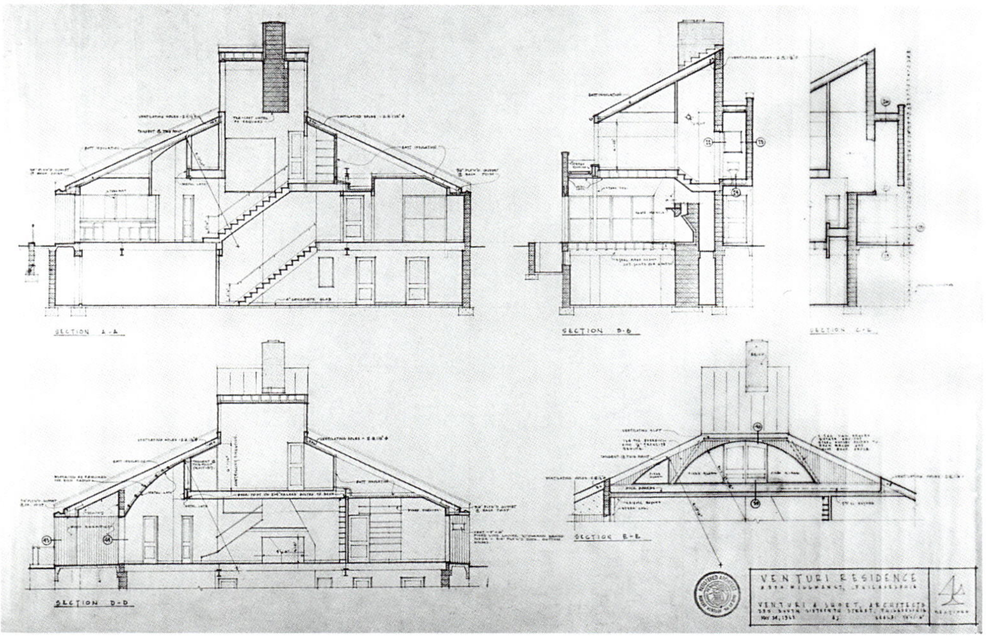

2

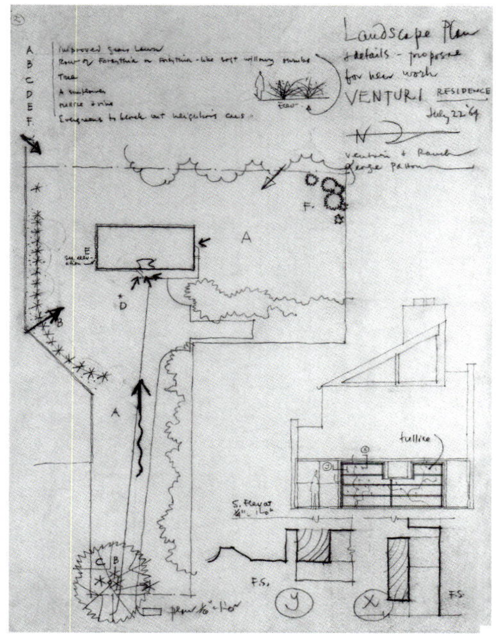

3

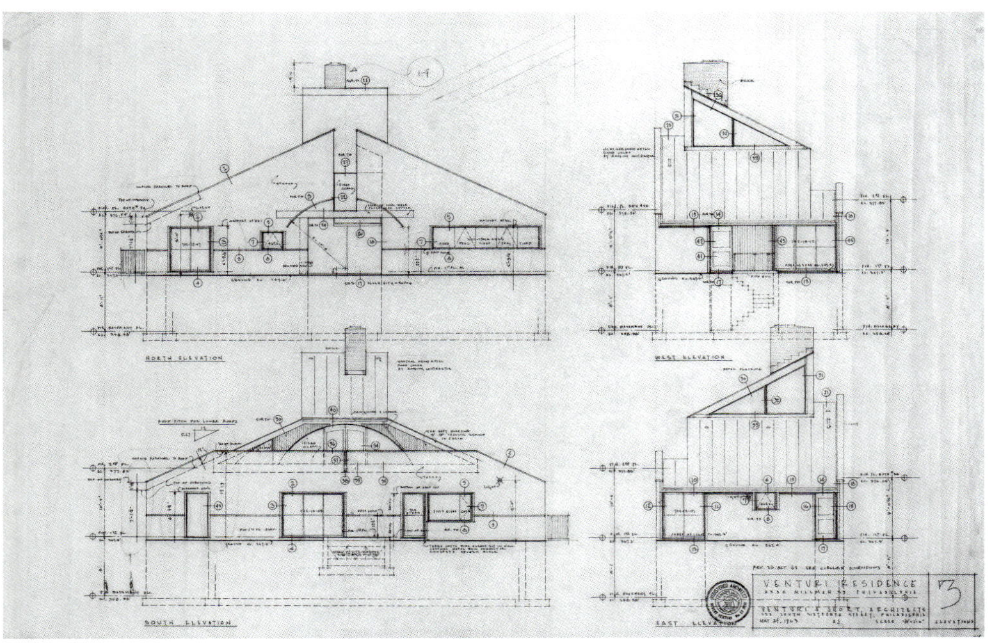

4

2 Schnitte
3 Lageplan
4 Ansichten

Bleistiftzeichnungen, Sammlung DAM

2 Sections
3 Site plan
4 Elevations

Pencil drawings, DAM collection

PETER EISENMAN

Haus Falk
Hardwick, Vermont, USA, 1969/70

Falk House
Hardwick, Vermont, USA, 1969/70

Vom spärlich bewachsenen Hügel setzt sich der weiße, zweigeschossige Betonbau deutlich ab. Das Gebäude besteht aus einem regelmäßigen Stützenraster, in das Wandelemente frei eingesetzt sind. Dabei formen die Wandscheiben nicht immer einzelne Zimmer, sondern stehen frei oder schneiden in Räume ein. Eisenmans »Transformationszeichnungen« zur Genese des Entwurfs, die mit den Konturen des Hauses und dem Stützenraster beginnt, sich dann über fragmentierte Wände immer weiter differenziert, verdeutlichen die »gesetzmäßige« Deduktion aus einfachen Grundelementen. Ähnlich konzeptuell ist eine Reihe von Einfamilienhäusern angelegt. Während das House I noch kubisch-geschlossen war, beginnt mit dem House II – dem Haus Falk – eine Aufbrechung des Baukörpers, die sich im House III durch ineinander gesteckte und gegeneinander verdrehte Bauteile weiter verkompliziert.

Eisenman bezog sich beim Haus Falk vor allem auf sein Vorbild Giuseppe Terragni und dessen Casa del Fascio in Como (1932-1936). Neben den Proportionen des Baukörpers war die Hauptfassade, die in ein Raster aus Vierkantstützen aufgelöst ist, der wichtigste Anknüpfungspunkt für Eisenman. Erschienen die Öffnungen und Lufträume beim Terragni-Bau jedoch wie aus einem Kubus herausgeschnitten, legte Eisenman das Stützenraster des Hauses Falk als zweite Schicht vor die Fassaden. Bei dem für die Architektur Eisenmans typischen komplexen Entwurfssystem ist der realisierte Bau nur als letzter Schritt, als Teil eines aufwendigen Konzepts zu verstehen. F. S.

The white two-storey concrete building stands out starkly from the sparse vegetation of the hillside. The building consists of a regular column grid, into which wall elements have been added at random. The walls do not always create separate rooms but are free standing or intersect spaces. Eisenman's "transformation drawings" on the genesis of the design, which begin with the contours of the house and the column grid and becomes gradually more differentiated due to the fragmented walls, illustrate his process of "natural" deduction from simple basic elements. An entire series of single-family houses is conceptual in this way. While House I was still cubic and closed, with House II—the Falk House—the volume begins to break up, and then in House III elements are inserted into one another and turned against one another making it more complicated.

With the Falk House, Eisenman was making reference to the work of Giuseppe Terragni and his Casa del Fascio in Como (1932-1936). Apart from the proportions of the volume, the main façade, which is broken down by a grid of rectangular pillars, is Eisenman's most important point of reference. However, while in Terragni's building the openings and voids look as if they have been cut out of a cube, Eisenman laid the column grid of the Falk House as a second layer over the facades. In the complex design system typical of Eisenman's architecture, the completed building has to be seen merely as the final stage, as part of a complex concept. F. S.

1 Planungsprozess letzte Stufe. Axonometrie
2 Ansicht von Süden
3 Detailansicht von Nordosten
4 Ansicht von Norden

1 Last stage of the planning process. Axonometric view
2 View from the south
3 View from the north-east, corner detail
4 View from the north

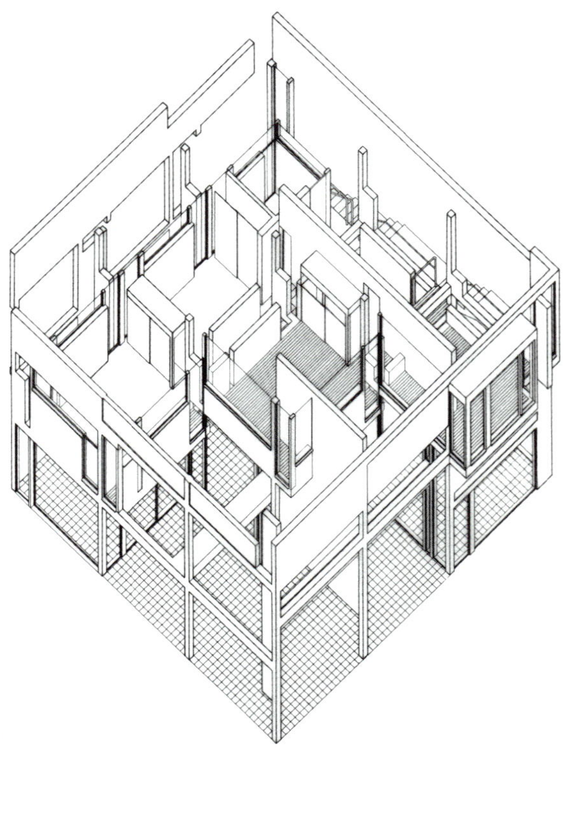

1

2

3

4

RICHARD MEIER

Haus Saltzman
East Hampton, New York, USA, 1967-1970

Saltzman House
East Hampton, New York, USA, 1967-1970

Das weiße, scharfkantig geschnittene Wohnhaus – ein holzverschalter Baukörper mit gerundeter Ecke – ist durch ein komplexes Spiel von Vor- und Rücksprüngen gekennzeichnet, insbesondere aber durch den Kontrast zwischen der massiven, beinahe fensterlosen Nordseite und den beiden großformatigen Fenstern auf der Süd- und Südostseite. Zu ebener Erde befinden sich Wirtschaftsräume und das Esszimmer, dessen Luftraum die gesamte Höhe des Hauses einnimmt. Im ersten Stock folgt der zweigeschossige Wohnbereich, der sich nach außen durch die hohen Fenster abzeichnet. Seine Struktur erhält der Raum durch ein Raster von Rundstützen. Die Raumhöhe ist außerdem durch eine eingezogene Empore differenziert. Über eine aufgeständerte Brücke ist der Hauptbau mit einem kleinen Gästehaus verbunden.

Meier knüpft an die »weiße Moderne« an. In Details wie den Brüstungen, die an Le Corbusier erinnern, Fensterbändern und Außentreppe sah Charles Jencks allerdings einen »Mangel an Ironie« im Umgang mit den Vorbildern. Meier wandte das Vokabular der klassischen Moderne jedoch nicht nur virtuos an, sondern entwickelte es weiter. Schon in der komplexen Gesamtform weicht die Villa deutlich von modernistischen Kuben ab.

Das Haus Saltzman steht in engem Zusammenhang mit Arbeiten anderer Mitglieder der 1969 gegründeten Architektengruppe New York Five (Peter Eisenman, Charles Gwathmey, Michael Graves, John Hejduk, Richard Meier), die wegen ihrer Anknüpfung an die klassische Moderne auch »Whites« genannt wurden.
F. S.

The crisp-edged white house—a timber-clad building with rounded corners—is characterised by a complex interplay of receding and projecting planes, and even more so by the contrast between the solid, almost windowless northern side and the two large-scale windows on the south and southeast side. At ground level are the utility rooms and dining room which is the full height of the house. On the first floor is the double-height living area, which is identifiable from outside by its tall windows. A grid of round columns structures the space. The height of the room is also differentiated by the addition of a gallery. A raised walkway links the main building with a small guesthouse.

Meier is working in the tradition of "white Modern architecture." However, Charles Jencks saw a "lack of irony" in Meier's treatment of models from the past in details such as the balustrades, which are reminiscent of Le Corbusier, ribbon windows and exterior stairs. However, Meier not only used the vocabulary of Classical Modernism with absolute virtuosity, he took it a step further. Even in its complex overall form, the villa is clearly different from Modernist cubes.

The Saltzman house is closely connected to the works of other members of the group of architects founded in 1969, the New York Five (Peter Eisenman, Charles Gwathmey, Michael Graves, John Hejduk, Richard Meier), who were also known as the "Whites" because of their allegiance to Classical Modernism. F. S.

1 Isometrische Gesamtansicht von Süden. Tuschezeichnung, Sammlung DAM
2 Ansicht von Südwesten
3 Ansicht von Osten
4 Innenansicht

1 Isometric view from the south. Pen and ink drawing, DAM collection
2 View from the south-west
3 View from the east
4 Interior view

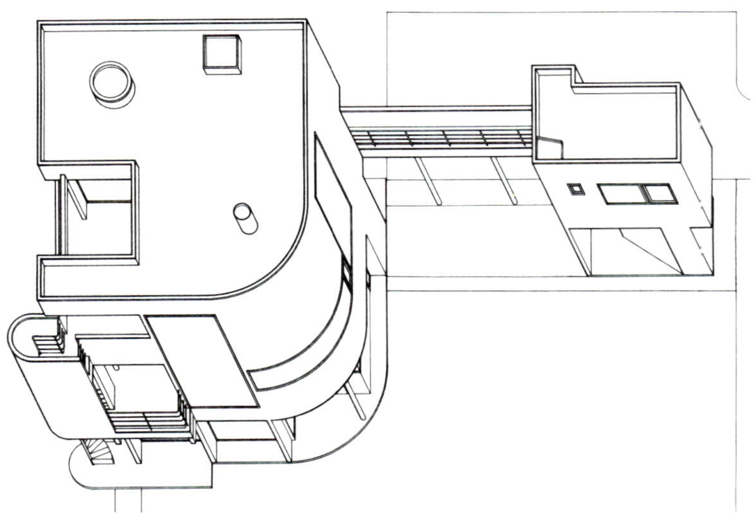

1

2

3

4

ALDO ROSSI ASSOCIATI

Villa Alessi
Suna di Verbania, Italien, 1992-1997

Die schöpferische und undogmatische Verbindung architektonischer Elemente verschiedener Epochen war ein wichtiges Prinzip in Aldo Rossis Schaffen. Spürbar ist dies auch in einem der letzten Werke des 1997 verstorbenen Architekten, dem Haus für den Design-Unternehmer Stefano Alessi.

Typologisch knüpft das Gebäude an die herrschaftlichen Feriendomizile an, die sich die wohlhabende Gesellschaft des 19. Jahrhunderts am Lago Maggiore errichten ließ. Naturstein, ein Tonnendach und Schmuckelemente aus Terrakotta bestimmen die asymmetrische Komposition kubischer Baukörper und verleihen der Villa ganz verschiedene Gesichter. Zwei gedrungene Granitsäulen monumentalisieren die spärlich durchfensterte Eingangsseite. Die eigentliche Schaufront orientiert sich zum Wasser hin, wo in drei Reihen geschichtete Säulen mit großer Geste dem Repräsentationsbedürfnis der Bewohner entgegenkommen.

Die klassische Anmutung des Hauses wird jedoch immer wieder gebrochen. So nimmt ein grün gestrichener Stahlträger anstelle des zu erwartenden schweren Sturzes der Eingangssituation den Ernst und ironisiert die Anspielung des Architekten auf die französische Revolutionsarchitektur. Das gleiche Element tritt noch an anderen Stellen exponiert in Erscheinung. So enden auf der Gartenseite beispielsweise auch die Geschosshöhen in Stahlträgern. Der im Innern des Hauses über der Bar sichtbare Stahlträger steht in Kontrast zum traditionell gehaltenen Interieur, für das Rossi ebenfalls verantwortlich zeichnete. W. W.

Villa Alessi
Suna di Verbania, Italy, 1992-1997

The creative and undogmatic linking of architectural elements from different eras was an important principle in Aldo Rossi's work. It can also be seen in one of the last works of the architect who died in 1997, a house for the design entrepreneur Stefano Alessi.

Typologically the building continues the tradition of the grand holiday residences which affluent society of the 19th century had built on the Lago Maggiore. Natural stone, a barrel roof and ornamental elements of terracotta determine the asymmetrical composition of cubic volumes and give the villa a number of quite distinct faces. Two squat granite columns monumentalise the entrance side of the villa with its sparse fenestration. The actual show front faces the water, where three rows of columns make a grand gesture to satisfy the residents' need for the building to reflect their social standing.

However, the Classical appearance of the house is repeatedly broken. For example, a steel girder painted green over the entrance where a heavy lintel would have been expected detracts from the seriousness and gives the architect's allusion to the French "revolutionary architecture" an ironic overtone. The same element appears at other places around the building. For example, on the garden side of the villa each floor terminates with a steel girder. The steel girder visible above the bar inside the house contrasts starkly with the otherwise traditional interior, which Rossi also designed. W. W.

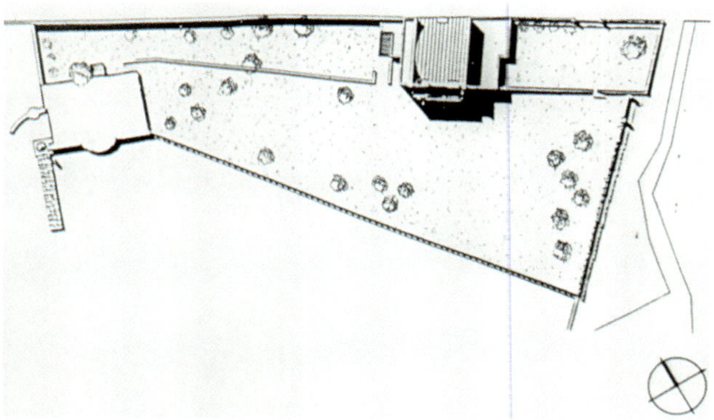

1

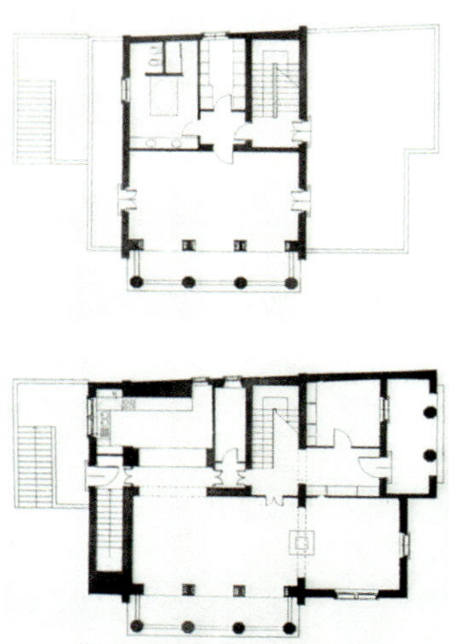

2

3

1 Lageplan
2 Grundrisse Erd- und Obergeschoss (oben)
3 Perspektivische Ansichten
4 Eingangsseite
5 Ansicht vom See
6 Wohnzimmer mit Bar

1 Site plan
2 Floor plans: ground floor and upper floor (top)
3 Perspective views
4 Entrance side
5 View from the lake
6 Living room with bar

4

5

6

JOHN PAWSON

Haus in Telluride
Colorado, USA, 1999-2001

Telluride House
Colorado, USA, 1999-2001

In seinem Aufsatz *Ornament und Verbrechen* (1908) schreibt Adolf Loos, dass der kultivierte Mensch den Drang nach Einfachheit habe. Demselben Gedanken ist auch dieses Ferienhaus in den Rocky Mountains verpflichtet. Außen passt es sich in Form und Material der denkmalgeschützten Nachbarbebauung an. Mit Zedernholz verkleidet, ruht es auf einem Sockel aus Naturstein und findet seinen Abschluss in einem mit Stahlblech gedeckten Satteldach. Hinter der traditionellen, streng gehaltenen Fassade verbirgt sich ein auf das Äußerste reduzierter Wohnraum.

Ein langer, schmaler Flur erschließt die ebenerdig liegenden, asketisch wirkenden Schlafräume und Badezimmer und mündet in einer Betontreppe, die nach oben führt. Schattenfugen lösen die Stufen von den nüchternen, weißen Wänden und betonen den Weg in den Wohn- und Essbereich, der unter der offenen Dachschräge die gesamte Etage einnimmt. Nach Osten hin schließt eine Terrasse an, unter der sich die Garage befindet.

Indirekte Beleuchtung, eine vor der Wand schwebende Bank und die parallel dazu laufende Küchenzeile, die den Raum zur Treppe hin abgrenzt, unterstreichen die große Linienführung. Die Faszination des über fünf Meter hohen Raums beruht des Weiteren auf natürlichem, durch Stoffjalousien gefiltertem Licht und dem Verzicht auf Farbe. Einfachheit als Lebensqualität; dafür stehen auch die ebenfalls von Pawson entworfenen kompromisslos modernen Möbelstücke aus Ahorn und der strenge Betonfußboden. W. W.

In his essay *Ornament and Crime* (1908), Adolf Loos writes that the cultivated person has an urge for simplicity. This holiday home in the Rocky Mountains is based on that very same idea. On the outside it fits in—both in terms of form and material—with the listed buildings around it. Clad in cedar, it rests on a plinth of natural stone and terminates in a gable roof of sheet steel. The austere, traditional façade conceals a living space that is reductionist in the extreme.

A long narrow corridor, which provides access to the ground floor bedrooms and bathroom, ascetic in style, leads into a concrete staircase to the upper floor. Shadow gaps separate the stairs from the sober white walls and emphasise both the walls and the way into the living and dining area which occupies the entire floor beneath the exposed roof slope. A terrace adjoins to the east under which a garage is situated.

Indirect lighting, a bench seemingly suspended in front of the wall and a galley kitchen running parallel to it, which divides the space off from the staircase, emphasise the strong linearity. Natural light filtered through fabric blinds and the deliberate absence of colour also add to the fascination of the space, which is over five metres high. Simplicity as a quality of life: this principle is also reflected in the uncompromisingly modern maple furniture, also designed by Pawson, and in the austere concrete floor. W. W.

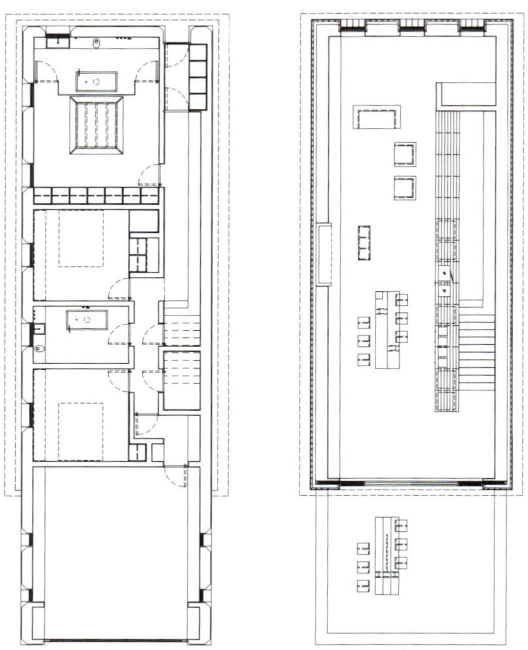

1

2

1 Grundrisse Erd- und Obergeschoss
2 Haus im örtlichen Kontext
3 Treppe zum Wohn- und Essbereich
4 Badezimmer im Erdgeschoss
5 Kamin im Wohnbereich
6 Fuß der Treppe

1 Ground and first floor plans
2 House in its local context
3 Stairs to living and dining area
4 Bathroom on ground floor
5 Fireplace in living area
6 Foot of the stairs

3

4

5

6

UN STUDIO VAN BERKEL & BOS

Möbius-Haus
Het Gooi (bei Amsterdam) Niederlande, 1993-1998

Möbius House
Het Gooi (near Amsterdam), The Netherlands, 1993-1998

Wie ineinander geschobene Eisschollen wirken die einzelnen Bauteile des lang gestreckten, zweigeschossigen Sichtbetonbaus. Vom Entree im Sockelgeschoss führt eine Treppe in den Wohnbereich des Hauptgeschosses. Die Garage im Zentrum des Gebäudes ist der einzige rechtwinklige Raum, ansonsten ist das abwechslungsreiche Raumkontinuum durch stumpfwinklige Ecken und einen unregelmäßigen Grundriss gekennzeichnet. Treppenpodeste, eingebaute Sitzbänke aus Beton, Vor- und Rücksprünge untergliedern den großen Innenraum, der von keinem Punkt aus vollständig zu überblicken ist. Als geschlossene Räume wurden lediglich zwei Büros, die Schlafzimmer und die Kinderzimmer konzipiert.

Für diese Wohnlandschaft, in der die Funktionen Schlafen, Arbeiten und Wohnen fließend ineinander übergehen, ließ sich Ben van Berkel vom Möbiusband anregen, dessen um 180 Grad verdrehte Enden so miteinander verbunden sind, dass sich eine Endlosschleife ergibt. Dieses Motiv, das keine Unterscheidung zwischen oben und unten kennt, findet seinen Ausdruck etwa in der Umkehrung der Materialien von Boden und Decke des Hauses.

Die ideengeschichtlichen Wurzeln von Berkels Konzept liegen in der klassischen Moderne, etwa im Organischen Bauen Hugo Härings, vor allem aber in den Raumlandschaften Hans Scharouns, der in seinen Einfamilienhäusern offene Wohnbereiche mit vielgestaltigen Grundrissen anlegte, die unterschiedliche Wegeführungen und stets neue Ansichten eröffneten. F. S.

The individual parts of this long two-storey building in fair-faced concrete look like interlocking ice floes. From the entrance at ground level, a staircase leads up to the living area of the main floor. The garage in the centre of the building is the only rectangular space, everywhere else the varied spatial flow is characterised by obtuse corners and an irregular floor plan. Landings, built-in seats of concrete, recessed and projecting planes divide up the large interior space, which cannot be seen in its entirety from any point. The only separate rooms are two studies, the main bedrooms and the children's bedrooms.

Ben van Berkel took his inspiration for this "living landscape," in which the transitions from sleeping, working and living areas are fluid, from the Möbius strip, the ends of which are turned around 180 degrees and connected to each other to produce a continuous loop. This motif, in which there is no difference between top and bottom, is reflected in the reversal of the materials used for the floors and ceilings of the house.

The ideological roots of Berkel's concept are to be found in Classical Modernism, for example in Hugo Häring's organic architecture, and above all in the spatial landscapes Hans Scharoun created in his houses for individual families with open-plan living areas and complex layouts, and unusual circulation systems giving new and surprising views. F. S.

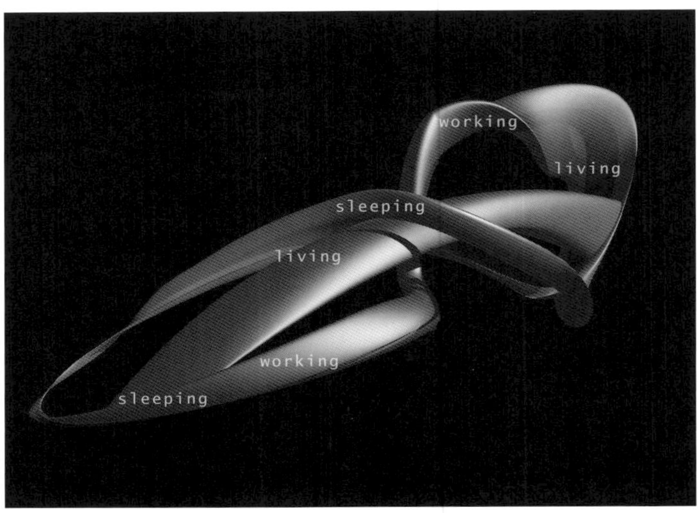

1

1 Verbindung der verschiedenen Lebensbereiche, Diagramm
2 Detail der Betonkonstruktion
3 Durchblick in östliche Richtung
4 Blick von Südwesten
5 Blick vom Wohnzimmer in Richtung Treppe und Veranda

1 Diagram showing relationships between the different living areas
2 Detail of concrete structure
3 Looking eastwards
4 View from the south-west
5 View from the living room towards the stairs and veranda

2+3

4

5

OMA

Maison à Bordeaux
Frankreich, 1998

Maison à Bordeaux
France, 1998

Das Haus ist ganz auf die Bedürfnisse des Bauherrn ausgelegt, der seit einem Autounfall auf den Rollstuhl angewiesen ist. Die drei Ebenen sind für ihn durch eine drei mal 3,5 Meter große Plattform erreichbar, die mit Hilfe eines hydraulischen Kolbens durch alle Geschosse herauf- und heruntergefahren werden kann. Das in den Berg eingegrabene Erdgeschoss, in dem sich neben dem Eingangsbereich die Küche befindet, ist von einem umschlossenen Hof aus zugänglich. Das allseitig verglaste Hauptgeschoss mit dem Wohnraum nimmt nur etwa die Hälfte der Grundfläche ein und ist zur Talseite durch eine große Terrasse ergänzt. Der scheinbar schwebende Betonkubus des Obergeschosses ist weitgehend geschlossen und nur durch unregelmäßig verteilte, kleine Rundfenster belichtet sowie durch eine kreisrunde Wandscheibe, die um ihre eigene Achse gedreht werden kann.

Im Obergeschoss befinden sich die Schlafräume und Kinderzimmer, die vom Erdgeschoss aus durch eine separate Wendeltreppe zugänglich sind. Im Hauptgeschoss durchstößt die Treppe in einem verchromten Zylinder die Terrasse. Rem Koolhaas spielt hier auf Philip Johnsons Glass House in New Canaan, Connecticut (1947-1949) an, in das ebenfalls ein Zylinder eingestellt ist. Beim Haus in Bordeaux hat der Metallzylinder tragende Funktion für eine Stahlkonstruktion, von der die Betonwände des Obergeschosses abgehängt sind.

Mit der Maison à Bordeaux gelingt Koolhaas die Fortschreibung eines zentralen Anliegens der Moderne: das wandelbare Haus.
F. S.

The house is completely tailored to the needs of the client, who has to rely on a wheelchair since a car accident. The three levels are designed so that he can reach them with a 3 by 3.5 metre platform that works by means of a hydraulic piston. The ground floor is set into the mountain and houses the entrance area and kitchen which is also accessible from a courtyard. The principal storey is glazed on all sides. The living room occupies about half the floor space, the remainder being a large terrace overlooking the valley. The concrete cube of the top floor seems to hover. Its only sources of daylight are small round windows at irregular intervals and a round shear wall which can turn on its own axis.

The top floor has the bedrooms and children's rooms that are also accessible from the ground floor by a separate spiral staircase. This staircase penetrates the terrace of the main floor in a chrome-plated cylinder. Rem Koolhaas is alluding here to Philip Johnson's Glass House in New Canaan, Connecticut (1947-1949), which also has a cylinder running through it. In the house in Bordeaux the metal cylinder also functions as a load-bearing element for a steel structure from which the concrete walls of the top floor are suspended.

In the Maison à Bordeaux Koolhaas has succeeded in continuing one of Modernism's principal concerns: the transformable house.
F. S.

1 Schnitt
2 Blick vom Hof auf die drei Geschosse des Hauses
3 Blick von Südwesten
4 Aufzugsplattform, Büro des Hausherrn

1 Section
2 View from the courtyard of all three storeys of the house
3 View from the south-west
4 Elevator platform, home owner's office

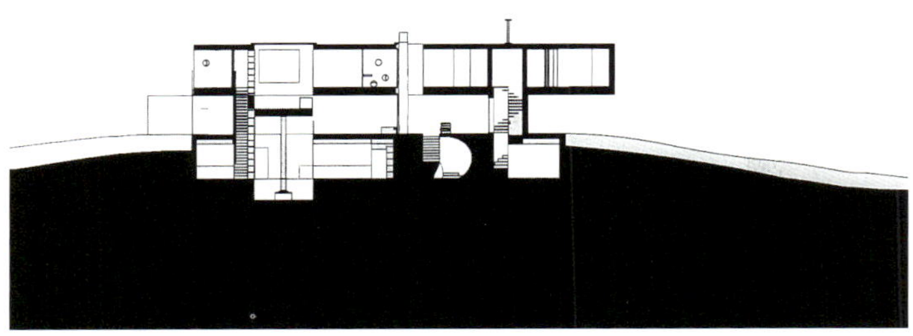
1

2

3

4

STEVEN HOLL ARCHITECTS

Oceanic Retreat
Kauai, Hawaii, USA, 2001-2003

Der unausgeführte Sichtbetonbau besteht aus zwei L-förmigen Bauteilen. Das kleinere Haus nimmt vor allem Räume für Gäste auf, das größere ein Büro sowie die Wohnräume der Bewohner. Dazwischen befindet sich eine Terrasse mit Schwimmbecken. Durch die zurückgesetzte Tür des Haupthauses wird das großzügige, zweigeschossige Entree betreten, das mit dem angrenzenden, um einige Stufen erhöhten Wohnbereich eine Einheit bildet. An den Wohnraum schließt sich eine Empore an, auf der ein Essbereich und ein Arbeitsraum untergebracht sind. Die Flachdächer sind von Solarzellen bedeckt und teilweise als Terrasse nutzbar. Trotz mehrfacher Vor- und Rücksprünge und unregelmäßig angeordneter Fenster erscheint die Gesamtform der beiden Hauskörper äußerst schlicht. Die Betonwände wachsen ohne Sockelbildung aus dem Boden, die Dachkante ist nicht akzentuiert. Die Bauten erscheinen wie monumentale Betonplastiken.

Ihre Silhouette mit vorkragenden, unten angeschrägten Enden erinnert entfernt an Schiffsmotive. Die Gestaltung der vorgeschobenen Empore des Haupthauses lässt an eine Kommandobrücke denken. Damit knüpft Holl an zwei berühmte Dichterhäuser an, die auch durch ihre Lage an einem Steilufer als Vorläufer des Oceanic Retreat gelten können. Das eine ist das Schiff Puglia, das sich Gabriele d'Annunzio 1925 am Comer See als Wohnhaus aufstellen ließ, das andere – in seiner schlichten Formensprache, mit angeschrägten Bauteilen und Flachdach – die Casa Malaparte auf Capri (1938-1943) von Adalberto Libera. F. S.

Oceanic Retreat
Kauai, Hawaii, USA, 2001-2003

This design in fair-faced concrete, which was never built, consists of two L-shaped buildings. The smaller one houses mainly guest rooms, the larger one an office and living spaces for the residents. In between the two is a terrace and swimming pool. The recessed door of the main building opens into a spacious, double-height entrance area which forms a single unity with the adjacent living area which is raised by a few steps. A gallery with dining and workspaces adjoins the living area. The flat roofs have photovoltaic cells and can in parts be used as a terrace. Despite the many recessed and projecting planes and irregularly placed windows, the overall form of the two volumes is extremely simple. The concrete walls "grow" directly out of the ground without any kind of plinth and the roof edge is not accentuated. The buildings look like monumental concrete sculptures.

Their silhouette with cantilevered ends sloping downwards is vaguely reminiscent of naval motifs. The shape of the gallery of the main house looks like a command bridge. Here Holl is making reference to two houses belonging to famous poets, which in their positions on a steep bank can be seen as forerunners of Oceanic Retreat. One is the Puglia Ship, which Gabriele d'Annunzio had chosen for himself as a residence in 1925 on Lake Como, the other—with its simple formal language, sloping elements and a flat roof—Casa Malaparte on Capri (1938-1943) designed by Adalberto Libera. F. S.

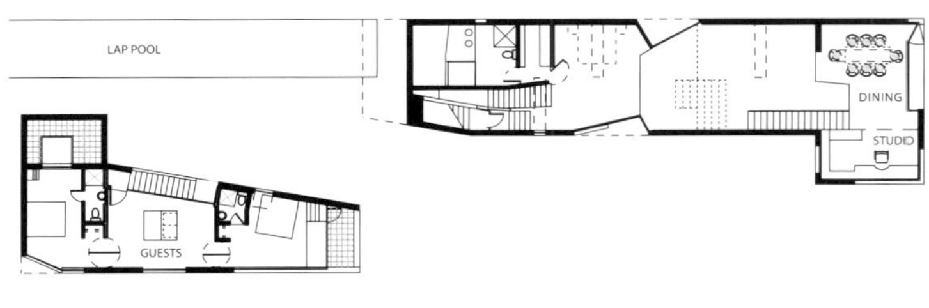

1

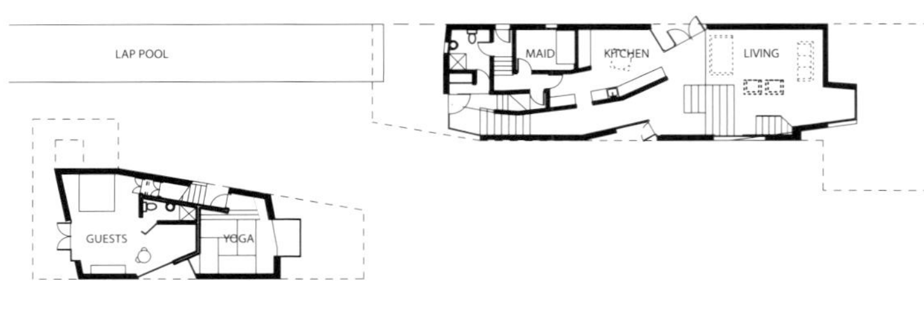

2

3

4

1 Grundrisse Obergeschoss
2 Grundrisse Erdgeschoss
3 Ansicht vom Strand
4 Blick auf das Ensemble

1 Upper floor plans
2 Ground floor plans
3 View from the beach
4 View of the ensemble

SHOPPING DER EXTRAKLASSE
EXCLUSIVE SHOPPING

Einkaufen ist ein wesentliches Element des öffentlichen Lebens. In der Eröffnungsausstellung des DAM gab es zwei Tendenzen zu diesem Thema. Einerseits die architektonisch ironische Überformung der typischen Kaufhalle für den alltäglichen Konsum durch die Gruppe SITE, zum anderen die prachtvoll gestalteten Läden und Reisebüros von Hans Hollein mit ihrer Aura des Nicht-Alltäglichen. In beiden Fällen stellten sich die Architekten einer über den Entwurf von Verkaufsstellen weit hinaus reichenden Aufgabe. Die Projekte von SITE transportierten zusätzlich systemkritische und ökologische Botschaften. Bei Hollein wurde der Konsum inszeniert. Zu diesem Zweck schuf der Architekt eine Atmosphäre mit Verweisen auf eine hedonistische Lebenskultur, die den Kunden in Bann ziehen sollte.

Die Versandhaus-Läden von SITE konnten zwar nicht überleben, aber ihr Vorbild wirkt fort wie in unserem neueren Beispiel einer Supermarkt-Filiale, deren Architektur von ökologischen Prinzipien bestimmt ist. Auch das von uns gewählte Fremdenverkehrsbüro von Hollein existiert nicht mehr. Vielleicht verhinderte es mit seinen allzu eindeutigen Anspielungen ein flexibles Reagieren auf veränderte Kundenansprüche. Dennoch ist der New Yorker Prada-Shop, für den Rem Koolhaas verantwortlich zeichnet, von ihm inspiriert, auch wenn das Modegeschäft im Gegensatz zu Holleins Interieur die auratische Schlichtheit einer vornehmen Galerie ausstrahlt, in der jedes Verkaufsstück wie ein wertvolles Kunstwerk positioniert ist.

Das Prada-Beispiel steht außerdem für die von Star-Architekten global konzipierten Edelboutiquen luxuriöser Marken, die seit den neunziger Jahren als besondere Attraktionen die großen Städte der Welt erobern. Auch der elegante gläserne Autosalon von Manuelle Gautrand wird Menschen anziehen, die nicht nur ein Produkt, sondern auch ein Image kaufen wollen.

Das Vergnügungsbedürfnis einer größer werdenden Klientel, für die das Einkaufen ein Mittel der Freizeitgestaltung ist und daher mit dem besonderen Erlebnis verbunden sein soll, wird nicht nur durch Scheinwelten aus populären architektonischen Versatzstükken erfolgreich bedient, sondern auch mit Hilfe anspruchsvoller Architektur, an der mitunter Modeschöpfer und Künstler beteiligt sind. Luxuskaufhäuser locken, unterhalten und animieren ihre Kundschaft inzwischen auch vermehrt mit ambitionierten Kunstausstellungen.

Shopping is a major part of public life. DAM's inaugural exhibition highlighted two trends on this topic: on the one hand, the SITE group's architecturally ironic transformation of a typical store for ordinary consumer goods, and, on the other, the sumptuous shops and travel agents by Hans Hollein with their definite aura of the extra-ordinary. In both cases, the architects rose to the challenge of a brief that went way beyond designing simple retail outlets. SITE's projects also convey messages about ecology and contain criticism of the system. Hollein, by contrast, makes consumerism the star feature of his designs. To this end, he uses references to a hedonistic lifestyle to create an atmosphere that is meant to captivate customers.

SITE's catalogue stores did not survive, but the example they set continues to have an influence in the more recent example of a supermarket whose architecture is governed by ecological principles. Similarly, the tourist information office by Hollein which we selected for the exhibition no longer exists. Perhaps its all too clear allusions hindered a flexible response to the changing needs of its clientele. Be that as it may, the Prada shop in New York, designed by Rem Koolhaas, was inspired by it, although this fashion boutique, in contrast to Hollein's interiors, radiates the simple aura of an upmarket gallery in which each article for sale is carefully positioned like a valuable work of art.

Prada is also an example of the upmarket boutiques designed by star architects that have since the 1990s become special attractions in the major cities around the world. Similarly, Manuelle Gautrand's elegant glazed car showroom will attract people who want to buy not just a product but an entire image.

The entertainment needs of an ever-growing clientele, for whom shopping is a leisure activity, which they therefore expect to be connected with a particular experience, are being served not only by fantasy worlds created by popular architectural set pieces but also with the help of more sophisticated architecture in which fashion designers and artists are also involved. Luxury department stores entice, amuse and animate their clientele, making increasing use of ambitious art exhibitions.

Archigram: Galerieprojekt für Bournemouth, 1970. Collage, Sammlung DAM

Archigram: Shopping arcade project for Bournemouth, 1970. Collage, DAM collection

SITE

Showrooms der Firma Best
USA, 1971-1984

Showrooms for Best Products Inc.
USA, 1971-84

Ein Jahr nach ihrer Gründung erhielt die von dem New Yorker Architekt James Wines geleitete Gruppe SITE (Sculpture in the Environment) den Auftrag, mehrere Shops des US-weit agierenden Versandhauses zu gestalten. Gemäß ihrem Ziel, Architektur, Kunst, Skulptur und Raum ganzheitlich zu verschmelzen, schlugen die Planer eine Reihe von ironischen, dabei konsumkritischen Gesamtkunstwerken vor, die immer vom Urtypus der Shopping-Architektur, der geschlossenen Kiste, ausgingen und deren amorphes Äußeres in geformte Gestalt zu überführen suchten. Beim frühen »Peeling-Projekt« (Richmond, Virginia, 1971/72) etwa löste sich an der rechten oberen Ecke die vorgeklebte Ziegelfassade und erinnerte damit an Venturis Feuerwache in New Haven (1970-1974). Für die kalifornische Stadt Sacramento entwickelte SITE das sogenannte »Notch-Projekt« (1977), bei dem die scheinbar herausgebrochene Eingangsecke des Kubus durch einen Motor herausgefahren werden konnte.

Während bei diesen und anderen Projekten wie »Indeterminate Façade« (1975) oder »Tilt-Showroom« (1978) noch mit Verweisen auf die Fragilität von Architektur gespielt wird, zeichnet sich später eine eindeutigere Hinwendung zu den Themen Umwelt und Natur ab. Beim »Forest Building« (1980), das in einen Eichenhain integriert wurde, durchschneiden die Bäume, die sich bereits auf dem Gelände befanden, den Bau. Als die Firma Best Mitte der neunziger Jahre einging, ereilte die Showrooms bald dasselbe Schicksal. SITE aber engagiert sich bis heute für eine kommunikative, sozial und ökologisch verantwortungsbewusste Architektur. C. W.

In 1970, one year after setting up, the SITE group (Sculpture in the Environment), headed by New York architect James Wines, was commissioned to design a number of stores for Best, a catalogue retailer with operations throughout the USA. Reflecting their declared aim to merge architecture, art, sculpture and space, the designers came up with a series of ironic *gesamtkunstwerke*, which were all based on the basic typology of shopping architecture—the closed box—and sought to transform their amorphous outer appearance into a deliberately designed shape. For example, in the early "Peeling Project" (Richmond, Virginia, 1971/72), the brick façade that had been stuck onto the building appeared to be peeling away in the upper right hand corner, reminiscent of Robert Venturi's fire station in New Haven (1970-1974). For the Californian city of Sacramento, SITE developed the so-called "Notch Project" (1977), in which the entrance corner of the show room, which appeared to have been broken out of the cube, could be moved in and out of the box by a motor.

While in this and other projects such as the "Indeterminate Façade" (1975) or "Tilt Showroom" (1978) the designers still play with references to the instability of architecture, by 1980 a more explicit trend towards environment and ecology begins to appear. In the "Forest Building"(1980), which was integrated into a copse of oaks, a number of trees that were on the site bisect the building. The company folded in the 1990s, and the showrooms did not survive for much longer. However, SITE is still actively involved in promoting communicative and socially and ecologically responsible architecture. C. W.

1

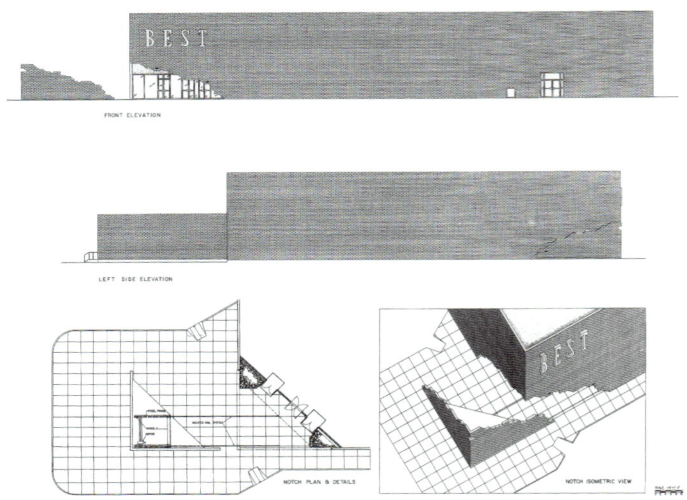

2

3

4

1 Peeling Project, Richmond
2 Notch Project, Sacramento. Hauptfassade, Seitenansicht, Konstruktionsdetails. Tuschezeichnung, Sammlung DAM
3 Notch Project mit ausgefahrener Eingangsecke
4 Notch Project mit geschlossener Eingangsecke

1 Peeling project, Richmond
2 Notch project, Sacramento. Main façade, side elevation, structural details. Pen and ink drawing, DAM collection
3 Notch Project with entrance corner moved out
4 Notch Project with entrance corner moved in

HANS HOLLEIN

Österreichisches Verkehrsbüro
Wien, Österreich, 1976-1978

Office for the Austrian Tourist Board
Vienna, Austria, 1976-1978

Seine Fähigkeit, werbewirksame Ideen in bildhafte Architektur und suggestive Ausstattung zu überführen, haben den Architekt, Designer und Künstler frühzeitig zu einem vielbeauftragten Gestalter von Messepavillons und besonders von Geschäften werden lassen. Nach den spätmodernen Höhepunkten dieser Gattung, dem Kerzenladen Retti und dem Juwelier Schullin (beide in Wien), die noch ganz der Ausstrahlungskraft von Materialien wie Aluminium und poliertem Granit vertrauten, arbeiten die späteren Interieurs mit theatralischen, zu sinnlich reizvollen Parcours kombinierten Requisiten und versetzen mit ihren Eindeutigkeit die Kunden in die Welt ihrer Träume. Für die Hauptstelle des Österreichischen Verkehrsbüros im Opernringhof setzte Hollein Metallpalmen, Säulenstümpfe und einen Strandpavillon ein, Accessoires, die leitmotivisch bei zwei weiteren Wiener Filialen benutzt und mit »antiken« Mauerresten und Wandbildern »idealer« Landschaften ergänzt wurden. »I have always considered architecture as an art. To me architecture is not primarily the solution of a problem, but the making of a statement«, erklärte Hollein anlässlich der Entgegennahme des Pritzker-Preises im Jahr 1985.

Das Verkehrsbüro wurde 1987 zerstört. Der Architekt selbst hat sich – angefangen mit dem 1985 projektierten Haas-Haus gegenüber dem Stephansdom – einer gemäßigten, dennoch formenreichen Moderne zugewandt, ohne seiner Freude an Sinnlichkeit, Ironie und am Zitat abzuschwören. C. W.

His ability to translate effective PR ideas into striking architecture and evocative fixtures and fittings, meant that the architect, designer and artist received many commissions early on in his career to design trade show pavilions and shops. After the late-Modernist high points of this genre, the Retti Candle Shop and Schullin Jewellery Store (both in Vienna), which still demonstrated complete confidence in the allure of materials such as aluminium and polished granite, the later interiors use theatrical props, combined to create sensuous appeal and in their total explicitness transport the customers to the world of their dreams. For the Austrian Tourist Board's main office on Opernringhof, Hollein used metal palm trees, stumps of columns and a beach pavilion, accessories which continue as a *leitmotif* in two other branch offices in Vienna and are complemented by "Classical" ruined walls and murals to create "ideal" landscapes. "I have always considered architecture as an art. To me architecture is not primarily the solution of a problem, but the making of a statement," Hollein declared in his acceptance speech on being awarded the Pritzker Prize in 1985.

The tourist information office was destroyed in 1987. The architect—starting with the Haas House designed in 1985 for a site opposite the Stephansdom, Vienna's Gothic cathedral—has now turned to a kind of Modernism that is more moderate and rich in form, yet without losing his joy in sensuous appeal, irony and quotations. C. W.

1 Tresenbereich
2 Blick auf Sitzgruppe
3 Blick auf Pavillon
4 Isometrische Gesamtdarstellung

1 Counter area
2 View of seating area
3 View of pavilion
4 Isometric drawing of project

1

2

3

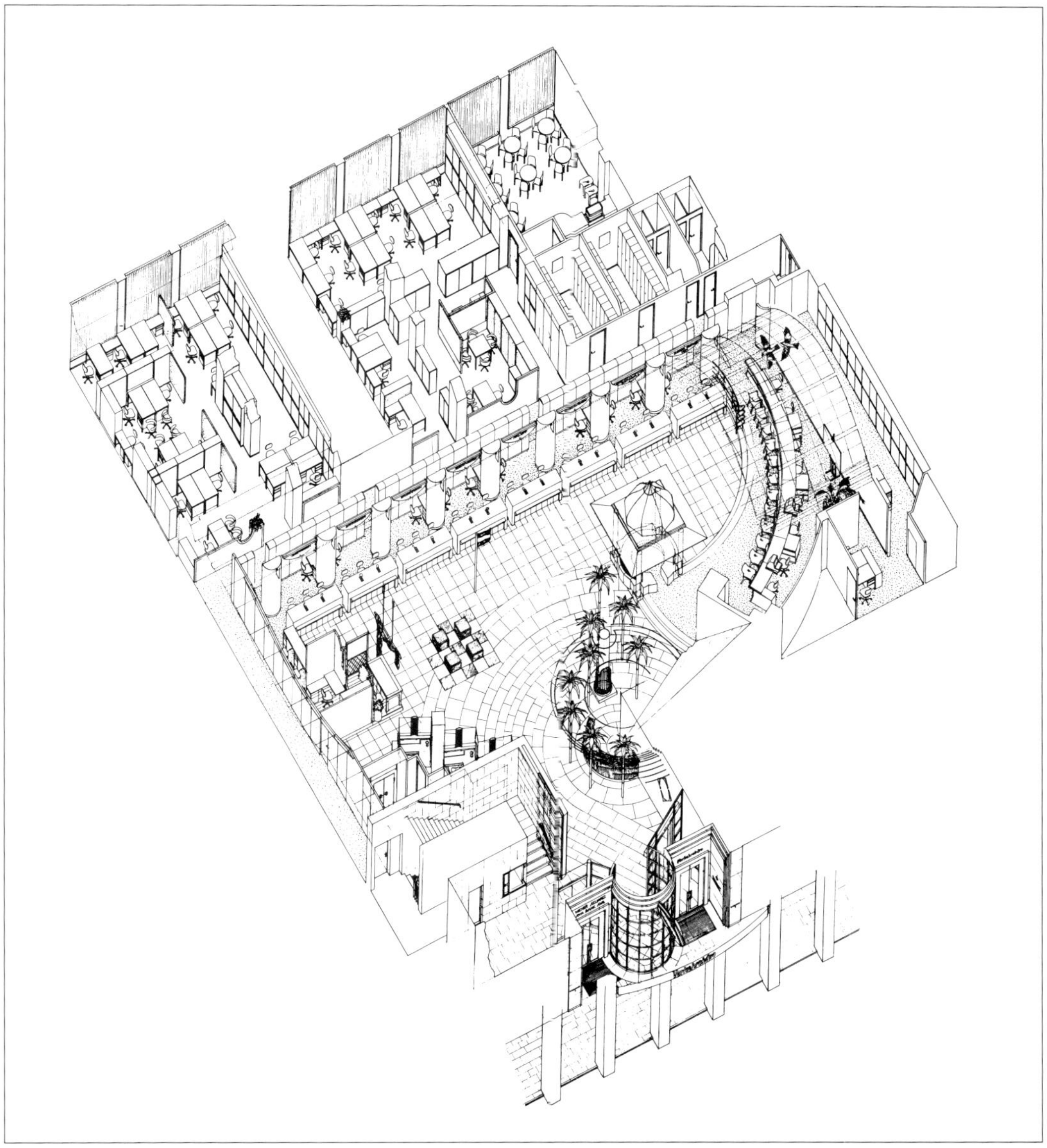

4

OMA

Prada, New York Epicenter
New York, USA, 2001

Prada, New York Epicenter
New York, USA, 2001

Im Jahr 2000 rief Rem Koolhaas an der Harvard School of Design das »Project on the city« ins Leben, das die Veränderung der Stadt im beginnenden 21. Jahrhundert untersuchte. Das Phänomen des Shopping bildete dabei einen eigenen Forschungskomplex. Koolhaas' Hauptthese ist, dass die Institutionen des zweckentbundenen Einkaufs sich krakenhaft ausbreiten und alle anderen Stadtfunktionen durchdringen, mit ihnen interagieren und zu einer untrennbaren Einheit verschmelzen; der Museumsshop, der Kultur und Geschäft amalgamiert, mag hierfür das plausible Beispiel sein.

Mit seinem ersten Laden für den Modehersteller Prada, der Ende 2001 am Broadway eröffnet wurde, kehrt Koolhaas das System um: Die Verkaufsfläche ist wandelbar und kann für kulturelle Veranstaltungen genauso genutzt werden wie für den Handel mit Kleidung. Dazu wurden Erd- und Kellergeschoss zusammengefasst. Die Kunden gelangen hinter dem Eingangsbereich in eine Senke, die auf der einen Seite aus Stufen besteht. Von dort aus lässt sich das Geschehen auf einer Bühne gegenüber beobachten, die aus dem Parkettboden herausgefahren werden kann. Wenn an dieser Stelle nicht tatsächlich Kunst stattfindet, werden Modeaccessoires wie Kunst präsentiert. Erst am Fuß der monumentalen Bodenwelle gelangt man in die daran anschließenden konventionellen Verkaufsräume im Untergeschoss. Die Erdgeschossfront des Altbaus, in der sich die Prada-Filiale befindet, beließ Koolhaas; im Inneren wird die Reihe gusseiserner Säulen durch quadratische Pfeiler in die Höhe gestemmt. C. W.

In 2000, Rem Koolhaas instigated the "Project on the city" at the Harvard School of Design with the intention of looking at how the city was changing at the beginning of the 21st century. The phenomenon of shopping was a separate area of research. Koolhaas' central theory is that shopping as an institution in its own right is spreading virulently and permeating all other urban functions, interacting with them and merging into a single unity. The museum shop, which amalgamates culture and business, is a plausible example of this.

With his first shop for the fashion retailer Prada, which opened on Broadway at the end of 2001, Koolhaas reverses the system: the retail space is flexible and can be used either for cultural events or fashion retailing. To this end, the ground floor and basement are joined together. Customers walk through the entrance area down to a sunken area with steps on one side. From there spectators have a good view of what is happening on a stage opposite which can be rotated out of the parquet floor. If actual art events do not take place here, fashion accessories are presented as if they were art objects. The stairs and stage together form a monumental "wave." It is only at the bottom of the wave, at basement level, that customers reach the conventional sales spaces. Koolhaas left the façade of the ground floor of the existing building in which Prada is located untouched; inside the row of cast-iron columns is raised onto square pillars. C. W.

1 Gestaltungselement Tapete mit Blumenmotiven
2 Rundraum in der Nähe der Bodenwelle
3 Mit Aluminiumgewebe verkleidete Stellagen
4 Treppe zum Erdgeschoss
5 Isometrische Gesamtansicht mit geöffneter Bühne
6 Isometrische Gesamtansicht mit System der herabhängenden Stellagen

1 Flowered wallpaper as a design element
2 Circular space near the floor wave
3 Display system covered in aluminium mesh
4 Stairs to the ground floor
5 Isometric view with open stage
6 Isometric view showing display system

1

2

3

4

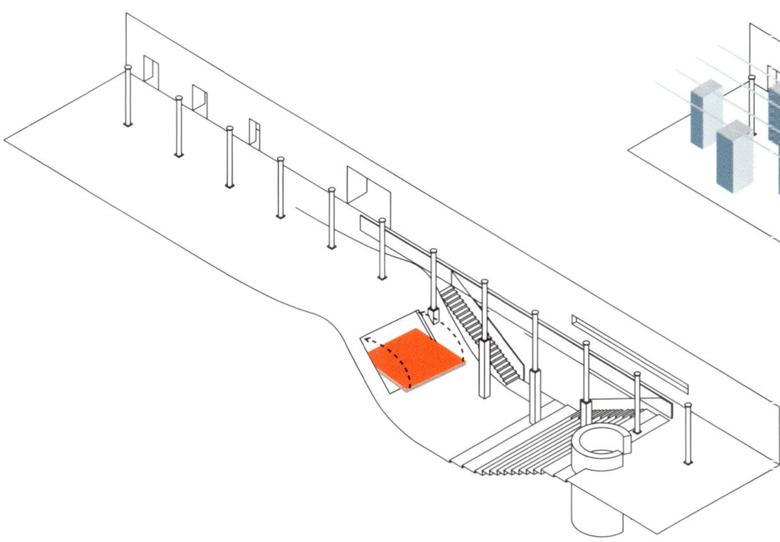

5

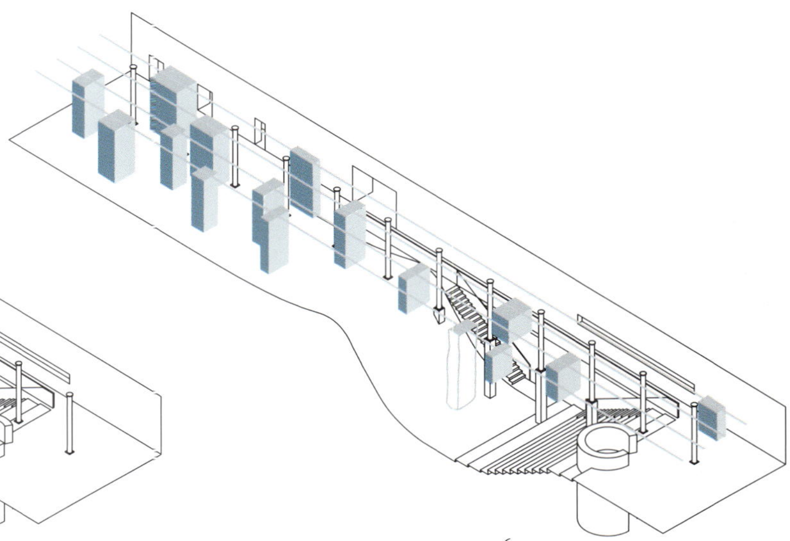

6

MANUELLE GAUTRAND ARCHITECTES

Citroën Showroom
Paris, Frankreich, 2004

Citroën showroom
Paris, France, 2004

Seit den zwanziger Jahren ist Citroën auf den Champs-Elysées mit einem Autosalon vertreten, den sich die Firma jedoch in jüngerer Zeit mit einem Fast-Food-Restaurant teilte. In einem Wettbewerb zur Neugestaltung der Verkaufsräume wurde nun ein ästhetisch und technologisch Aufsehen erregendes Gebäude prämiert. Es wirbt mit den Mitteln der Architektur für den hohen Standard der Marke.

Eine facettenartige Glasfassade umhüllt das gesamte Volumen, macht es zu einer Vitrine und spiegelt mit raffiniert integrierten roten Chevrons die Marke wider. Mit zunehmender Gebäudehöhe häufen sich die Prismen, das Firmensignet verliert an Eindeutigkeit und geht in der Gesamtskulptur auf. Der Inspiration und der Form einer Karosserie folgend, gibt es keine klare Trennung mehr zwischen Vorder- und Rückseite sowie dem Dach. Alles ist im Fluss.

Innen umschließen über Rolltreppen erschlossene Ebenen spiralförmig einen ebenfalls in der roten Hausfarbe gehaltenen Mast, an dem sieben Plateaus für die Exponate schweben. Die kleinen Bühnen drehen sich und sind in der Höhe variabel, um den Raum offen für alle Arten von Inszenierung zu halten. Eine Seite ist mit einer textilen Oberfläche verkleidet, auf der Projektionen möglich sind. Das allgegenwärtige Weiß gewinnt durch einen in die Verglasung eingebauten Farb- und Lichtfilter an Intensität und macht den Salon zu einem Ereignis für die Marke und für den Kunden, zu einer echten Citroën-Architektur. W. W.

Since the 1920s, Citroën has had a car showroom on the Champs-Elysées. Recently, however, the company shared the space with a fast-food restaurant. A scheme that attracted attention both for its aesthetic and technological qualities won a competition to remodel the showrooms. It uses architecture as a means to promote the high standard of the brand.

Facetted glass envelops the entire volume, making it into a display case which, with cleverly integrated red chevrons, reflects the brand. The density of prisms increase towards the upper part of the building, and the corporate logo becomes less distinct and dissolves into the overall sculpture. Inspired by the shape of a car body, there is no clear distinction between front and back or roof. Everything is fluid.

Inside the building, different levels that are accessible by escalator form a spiral surrounding a mast—also in the corporate red—from which seven small platforms for exhibition pieces are suspended. The platforms revolve and are of variable height to allow for all kinds of performance. One side has a textile covering, which can be used for projections. The ubiquitous white becomes more intense due to a colour and light filter built into the glazing and makes the showroom an experiential space for the brand and customer alike: true Citroën architecture. W. W.

1 Grundriss Erdgeschoss
2 Von Autokarosserie inspirierte Gesamtform. Modellfoto
3 Showroom im städtischen Kontext
4 Straßenansicht bei Nacht
5 Innenraumperspektive

1 Ground floor plan
2 Form inspired by car body. Photo of model
3 Showroom in the context of the city
4 View from the street at night
5 Interior perspective

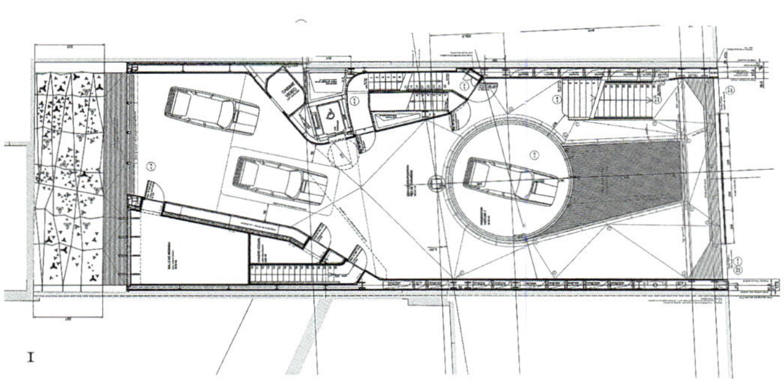

1

2

3

4

5

CHETWOOD ASSOCIATES

Sainsbury's Supermarkt
London, Großbritannien, 1999-2001

Seit Mitte der neunziger Jahre wurde – außerhalb Deutschlands – die Bauaufgabe Supermarkt zum Thema der Architektur. Massimiliano Fuksas errichtete 1996 einen Spar-Markt in Salzburg; Dominique Perrault entwickelte 2001 ein Projekt für M-Preis im Tiroler Ort Wattens, Diener und Diener bauten einen Migros-Markt in Luzern (2002). Auch der englische Marktführer Sainsbury entschloss sich – ähnlich wie die Ketten Dixon und Selfridges – zu einer Imagekampagne. Den Auftrag erhielt das Büro Chetwood Associates, das, vergleichbar mit dem Utrechter Team UN Studio, Architektur in den Kontext von Städtebau, Umweltplanung, Technik, Design und Soziologie stellt und computergeneriert mit erwarteten Daten- und Kundenströmen abgleicht.

Ein Jahr nach der Einweihung des Millennium Dome im Stadtteil Greenwich eröffnete die Sainsbury-Filiale ebenfalls auf der Halbinsel. Ästhetik und Anspruch orientieren sich am kühlen britischen Hightech. Das Versprechen umweltschonenden Bauens wird zunächst durch den Gebrauch von Aluminium eingelöst. Wegen des Einsatzes von natürlicher Energie, Tageslichtnutzung und dem Verzicht auf eine künstliche Klimaregulierung versteht der Projektarchitekt Paul Hinkin das Projekt zudem als vollständige Revision der Supermarktarchitektur. Solaranlagen, Windturbinen, Warmluft- und Regenwasserspeicher, recycelte Materialien gehören ebenfalls zum Programm. Das Haus soll lediglich die Hälfte der Energie eines vergleichbar großen Supermarkts (rund 33000 Quadratmeter) verbrauchen. C. W.

Sainsbury's supermarket
London, Great Britain, 1999-2001

Since the mid-nineties the supermarket has—outside Germany, at least—become a major theme in architecture. In 1996, Massimiliano Fuksas built a Spar supermarket in Salzburg; in 2001, Dominique Perrault developed a project for M-Preis in the Tyrolean town of Wattens, Diener and Diener built a Migros Market in Lucerne (2002). The English market leader Sainsbury's also decided—like the chains Dixons and Selfridges—to launch an image campaign. Chetwood Associates were commissioned, a firm of architects who like the Utrecht-based team UN Studio, places architecture in the context of urban design, environmental planning, technology, design and sociology and uses computer-generated models to match it to expected data and customer flows.

This branch of Sainsbury's opened on the Greenwich peninsula a year after the Millennium Dome. Both the aesthetics and the ambitions of the building were based on cool British hi-tech. The promise of ecological building is firstly fulfilled by the use of aluminium. Furthermore, with its use of natural energy, daylight and a deliberate decision not to use air conditioning, the project architect Paul Hinkin sees the project as a completely new approach to supermarket architecture. Solar energy systems, wind turbines, heat storage and rainwater storage, recycled materials are also part of the building programme. The building claims to use only half the energy of a conventional supermarket of comparable size (around 33,000 square metres). C. W.

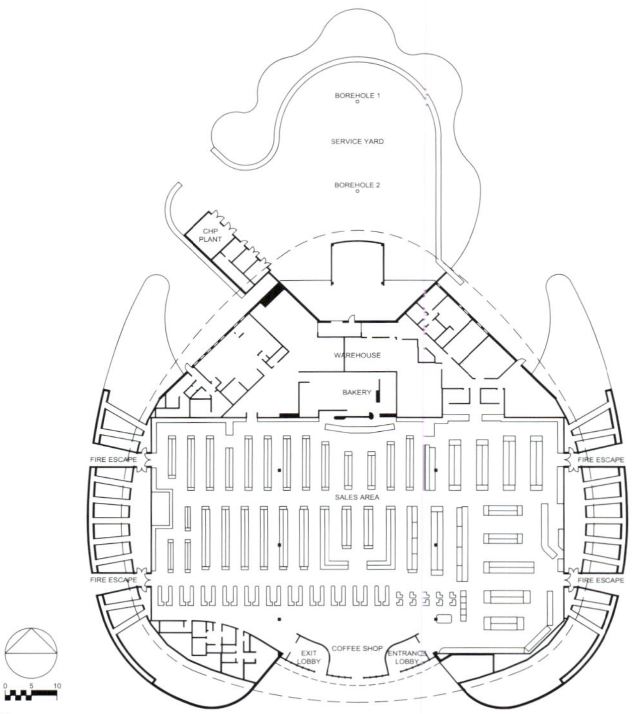

1

1 Grundriss
2 Innenansicht der Verkaufshalle
3 Rückwärtige Ansicht
4 Eingangssituation

1 Floor plan
2 Interior view of the supermarket
3 Rear view
4 Entrance situation

2

3
4

ORTE DER STILLE
PLACES OF TRANQUILLITY

In der Eröffnungsausstellung waren nur wenige Bauten vertreten, die Inseln des geistigen Rückzugs und der religiösen Besinnung darstellen. Bei den meisten Entwürfen handelte es sich um realisierte oder realisierbare Architekturen. Die Arbeit von Massimo Scolari (die er für die erste Architektur-Biennale 1980 in Venedig schuf) hingegen zieht sich melancholisch auf das Medium der Malerei zurück. Ein riesiges, dabei fragiles Tor in totem Felsen verankert, öffnet den Blick auf eine entfernte einsame sonnenbeschienene Insel mit einem Urbild von Haus. Auch der Friedhof von Aldo Rossi strahlt durch seine strenge Anlage und die archetypischen Baukörper eine erhabene Atmosphäre aus. Aber die Stadt der Toten ist den Lebenden nicht entrückt. Der Konus erinnert an einen Fabrikschornstein, die Umfassung des Friedhofs an das lombardische Bauernhaus und die zeilenförmige Anlage der Grabkammern an sozialen Wohnungsbau. Trotz seines menschlichen Maßstabs wirkt der Friedhof monumental. Gottfried Böhms Wallfahrtskirche dagegen ist ein Monument und überragt als gewaltiger kristalliner Baukörper die Stadt.

Die neuen Beispiele grenzen sich mit ihrer abstrakten Architektur als spirituelle Enklaven deutlich von der Alltagswelt ab. Ihre Standorte sind weder privilegiert noch attraktiv. Allesamt in städtischen, wenig kohärenten Arealen angesiedelt, haben sie neben ihrer eigentlichen Funktion auch die Aufgabe, zur Hebung der Qualität ihrer Umgebung beizutragen. Sie tun das nicht, indem sie sich in Szene setzen. Andos asketisches Museum für die Zwiesprache mit der Kunst repräsentiert seine grundlegende Haltung, »eine spirituelle Welt zu schaffen, einen Raum, der so stark und tief ist, dass er zu den Menschen drängt, die ihn besuchen«. Die Kirchen von Siza und Moneo sind ebenfalls Resultat eines sehr individuellen ästhetischen Empfindens, das ethisch begründet ist. Kein Detail- und Materialkult wird hier betrieben, jegliche formale Übersteigerung fehlt. Die Sakralbauten deuten architektonische Vorbilder an, die transformiert Bezüge zur Tradition und zum Ort herstellen. Die Bauten sind nicht glamourös, meiden alles Überflüssige, sind durchdrungen von Leere und Licht. Mit ihrer Ethik der Schlichtheit, Klarheit, Ordnung, Stille und Reduktion stemmen sie sich gegen eine Architekturszene der Superlative, der Übertreibung, der Eitelkeit und des visuellen Lärms.

The inaugural exhibition included only a handful of buildings that represented islands of spiritual retreat and religious contemplation. Most of the schemes were examples of architecture that had been built or could be built. By contrast, Massimo Scolari's work created for the first Architecture Biennale in Venice in 1980 withdraws melancholically into the medium of painting. A huge yet fragile gate anchored in a bleak cliff, reveals a view of a remote and sunny desert island and an archetypal house. Aldo Rossi's cemetery with its severe layout and archetypal buildings exudes a solemn atmosphere. However, the city of the dead is not totally removed from the world of the living. The conical tower is reminiscent of factory chimneys, the cemetery's boundary wall recalls a farmhouse in Lombardy and the arrangement of the tombs in rows recalls a social housing project. Despite its human scale, the cemetery makes a monumental impression. By contrast, Gottfried Böhm's pilgrimage church is a true monument and towers above the town as an immense crystalline structure.

The new examples with their abstract architecture see themselves as spiritual enclaves and clearly dissociate themselves from mundane life. The sites they stand on are neither privileged nor attractive. All of them are in urban areas with little coherence, and part of their remit, beyond their actual function, is to help improve the quality of their surroundings. They do not achieve that by placing themselves centre stage. Ando's ascetic museum, built to facilitate a dialogue with art, represents his fundamental attitude: "My intention is to create a spiritual world, to make a space which is so strong and deep it will penetrate to the people who contact that space." The churches by Siza and Moneo are also the result of a very individual aesthetic sense emanating from ethical principles. No cult of detail or materials is pursued here; there is no trace of formal excess. The sacred buildings make reference to architectural exemplars, which create links in a transformed form to tradition and place. The buildings are not glamorous; they are flooded with light and emptiness and avoid the superfluous. With their ethos of simplicity, clarity, order, stillness and reduction, they staunchly oppose an architectural scene dominated by superlatives, exaggeration, vanity and visual noise.

Massimo Scolari: Porta per città di mare, 1979-1982

GOTTFRIED BÖHM

Maria, Königin des Friedens
Velbert-Neviges, Deutschland, 1964-1968

1960 wurde der Entschluss für eine neue Wallfahrtskirche gefasst, da der spätbarocke Bau den Pilgerströmen nicht mehr gewachsen war. Nachdem Böhms Entwurf in der ersten Wettbewerbsstufe als »manieristisch« abgelehnt worden war, konnte er sich im zweiten Wettbewerb mit einer überarbeiteten und reduzierten Version durchsetzen.

Zur Kirche, die 2000 Gläubigen Sitzplätze bietet und damit kathedralenartige Ausmaße erreicht, führt eine breite, von flachen Stufungen unterbrochene Prozessionsstraße den Hang hinauf. Im Osten wird sie von kleinteilig gestaffelten Pilgerherbergen mit runden Erkern auf Rundstützen und einem gedeckten Gang begrenzt. Krönung der Anlage ist die Kirche selbst, ein vielfach kristallin gebrochenes expressives Sichtbetonmassiv, das Böhm als »Zeltstadt der Pilger« bezeichnete. Auch im Inneren dominieren die mächtigen Faltwerke, Betonpfeiler und Emporen, die sich hart gegen das Licht der Westfassade abzeichnen. Im Osten befinden sich die Durchgänge zu den Kapellen; dort wird in der Gnadenkapelle das Bildnis der Immaculata verwahrt. Schon zur Erbauungszeit ließ die Zahl der Pilger merklich nach, sodass die weiträumige Anlage zusehends verwaiste.

Böhm konzipierte die Wallfahrtskirche als Gesamtkunstwerk. Auch die Fenster gestaltete der Architekt selbst. Bei diesem herausragenden Kirchenbau setzte er sich sowohl mit Le Corbusiers skulpturaler Wallfahrtskapelle in Ronchamp (1950-1955) als auch mit der Architektur seines Vaters Dominikus auseinander.
E. K.

Mary, Queen of Peace
Velbert-Neviges, Germany, 1964-1968

In 1960, the decision was taken to build a new pilgrimage church because the late-Baroque building could no longer cope with the streams of pilgrims. Böhm's design was rejected in the first stage of the competition as being "mannerist," but was successful in the second competition in a revised and simplified version.

A processional path interrupted by broad shallow steps leads up the hill to the church, which can accommodate 7,000 worshippers, thus reaching cathedral-like proportions. In the east, it is flanked by small hostels for pilgrims with round oriels on columns and a covered walkway. The high point of the ensemble is the church itself, an expressive monolith in fair-faced concrete with a multiplicity of crystalline fragments, which Böhm described as "a tent city for pilgrims." The interior of the church is also dominated by powerful folded plates, concrete pillars and galleries, which stand out harshly against the light of the west façade. In the east are entrances to the chapels; the statue of the Immaculate Conception is kept in the Grace Chapel. Even at the time of its construction, the numbers of pilgrims dropped considerably so that the spacious complex became increasingly deserted.

Böhm designed the pilgrimage church as a *gesamtkunstwerk*. He also designed the windows. In this outstanding church building, he engaged both with Le Corbusier's sculptural pilgrimage chapel at Ronchamp (1950-1955) and with the architecture of his father Dominikus.
E. K.

1

2+3

4+5

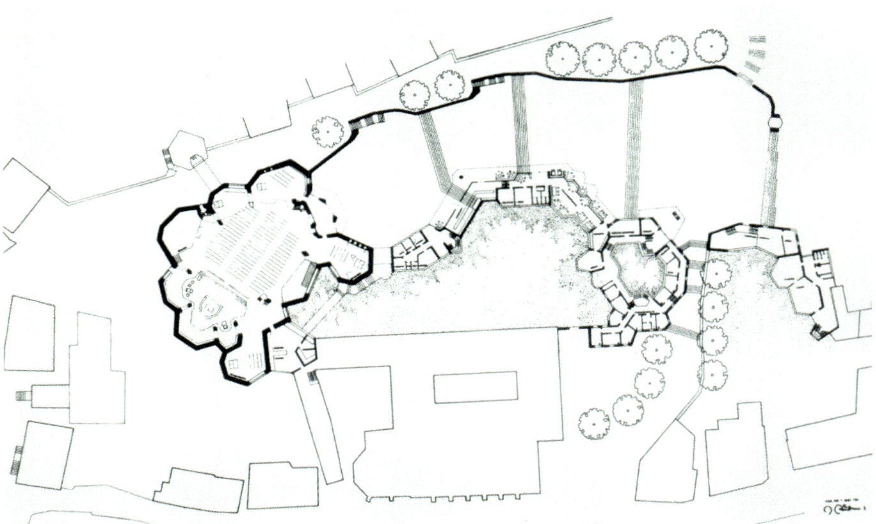

1 Pilgerweg mit Wallfahrtskirche. Bleistiftzeichnung, Sammlung DAM
2 Kirche im städtischen Kontext
3 Innenansicht
4 Grundriss des Ensembles
5 Pilgerweg

1 Pilgrims way with pilgrimage church. Pencil drawing, DAM collection
2 Church in the context of the town
3 Interior view
4 Layout of the ensemble
5 Pilgrims way

ALDO ROSSI

Friedhof San Cataldo
Modena, Italien, 1971

San Cataldo cemetery
Modena, Italy, 1971

Die Erweiterung des alten neoklassizistischen Friedhofs bot Rossi die Möglichkeit, seine Forderung zur Hinwendung an die traditionellen Werte und Typen der Architektur, die er in seinem Manifest *L'architettura della città* (1966) formuliert hatte, in großem Stil umzusetzen. Rossi ging dabei von Erinnerung, Geschichte und Ordnung sowie einer Typologie der architektonischen Formen aus, mit Hilfe derer er Erinnerung als normativen und konstituierenden Wert, auf dem Kultur und Gesellschaft basieren, evozieren will.

Die Anlage des Friedhofs setzt sich aus strengen geometrischen Körpern zusammen. Das erste der an einer zentralen Mittelachse aufgereihten Häuser ist das Ossarium, mit leeren quadratischen Fensterhöhlen, ein verlassenes Haus der Toten. Ihm folgt eine parallele Reihung von Zeilenbauten, die die Grabkammern enthalten. Die Zeilen sind insgesamt auf einer dreieckigen Grundfläche angeordnet, deren Basis dem Beinhaus zugekehrt ist, zur Spitze des Dreiecks hin steigen die Zeilenbauten in der Höhe an und weisen auf einen konischen Turm, der ein Massengrab enthält. Als letztes Element ist ein offener Arkadengang angefügt, der die Grabkammern weiträumig umfängt. Die Grundfigur erinnert an ein Fischskelett, eine Deutung, die Rossi selbst auf Skizzen formulierte.

Wie um die Allgemeingültigkeit seiner Typologie zu beweisen, verwendet Rossi dieselben geometrischen Grundformen und auch die Schottenwände der Arkaden bei dem zeitgleich realisierten Projekt des Wohnblocks Gallaratese in Mailand (1969-1973).

E. K.

The extension of this old Neo-Classical cemetery gave Rossi the opportunity to implement in grand style his demand for a return to traditional values and types in architecture, which he articulated in his manifesto *L'architettura della città* (1966). Rossi based his design on memory, history and order and on a typology of architectural forms, which he used to evoke memory as a normative and constituting factor on which culture and society are based.

The cemetery is composed of severe geometrical volumes. A series of buildings lines the central axis, first the ossuary, with its square glassless windows, a deserted house of the dead. It is accompanied by a parallel row of buildings, which contain the burial chambers. The rows are arranged on a triangular plan, the base of which faces the ossuary, the buildings increase in height towards the apex of the triangle and point to a conical tower containing a communal grave. The last element is an open arcade, which loosely frames the burial chambers. The ground plan is reminiscent of a fish skeleton, an interpretation that Rossi formulated in sketches.

As if to prove the universal validity of his typology, Rossi uses the same basic geometric shapes and the "cross walls" of the arcades in the Gallaratese housing complex in Milan which dates from the same time (1969-1973).

E. K.

1

2

3

1 Detailaufnahme der realisierten Anlage, im Vordergrund Beinhaus
2 Skizze Gesamtanlage, im Hintergrund Stadtarchitektur. Collage, Sammlung DAM
3 Beinhäuser und Konus, im Hintergrund Fabrik- und Stadtarchitektur. Collage, Sammlung DAM
4 Perspektivische Aufsicht der Gesamtanlage mit angrenzendem jüdischen und einem neoklassizistischen Friedhof. Original, Sammlung DAM

1 Photograph of a section of the cemetery as built, ossuary in the foreground
2 Sketch of the ensemble, in the background city architecture. Collage, DAM collection
3 Ossuaries and conical tower, in the background factory and city architecture. Collage, DAM collection
4 Perspective view of the cemetery from above, showing adjacent Jewish cemetery and Neo-Classical cemetery. Original, DAM collection

4

TADAO ANDO ARCHITECT & ASSOCIATES

Pulitzer Foundation for the Arts
St. Louis, Missouri, USA, 1997-2001

Die Idee, ein Museum für ihre hochkarätige Privatsammlung mit Werken von Rodin, Monet, Picasso, Miró, Modigliani und Warhol zu errichten, hatten Emily und Joseph Pulitzer jr. bereits zu Beginn der neunziger Jahre. Schon damals war Ando als Architekt im Gespräch – für den Umbau eines alten Fabrikgebäudes. Nach dem Tod ihres Mannes 1993 verfolgte Emily Pulitzer das Vorhaben alleine weiter und beauftragte Ando mit dem Neubau eines Museums.

Andos Sichtbetonbau, sein erstes Projekt in den USA, präsentiert sich nach außen geschlossen und konzentriert. Es entstand in Zusammenarbeit mit den Künstlern Ellsworth Kelly und Richard Serra, die auch Auftragsarbeiten für das Museum fertigten. Ando gruppiert zwei unterschiedlich hohe rechteckige Gebäudeteile um ein Wasserbecken. Der niedrigere Flügel besitzt neben einem Dachgarten einen Pavillon, dessen massive Deckenplatte aus Beton über der Glashaut der Fassade zu schweben scheint. Verglichen mit Andos zahlreichen anderen Museumsbauten ist dieses Haus durch die glückliche Ergänzung von Bauherrin und Architekt vielleicht sein intimstes und kompromisslosestes Werk.

Die Pulitzer Foundation, die in der Tradition kleiner Privatmuseen, wie etwa der Barnes Collection bei Philadelphia oder de Menill in Fort Worth (von Louis I. Kahn), steht, wendet sich entschieden gegen einen kommerzialisierten Museumsbetrieb. Das Haus soll allein der intensiven Auseinandersetzung mit Kunst dienen. So wird man auch ein Café und einen Museumsshop vergeblich suchen. E. K.

Pulitzer Foundation for the Arts
St. Louis, Missouri, USA, 1997-2001

Back in the early 1990s Emily and Joseph Pulitzer jr. first had the idea of building a museum to house their high-calibre private collection including works by Rodin, Monet, Picasso, Miró, Modigliani and Warhol. Even then Ando was under discussion as the architect—for the conversion of an old factory. After the death of her husband in 1993 Emily Pulitzer pursued the project on her own and commissioned Ando to build a new museum.

This was Ando's first project in the USA. From the outside, the building, which is in fair-faced concrete, appears closed and concentrated. It was designed in collaboration with the artists Ellsworth Kelly and Richard Serra, who were commissioned to produce permanent works for the museum. Ando groups two rectangular wings of different heights around a pool of water. The lower wing has a roof garden and a pavilion, its solid roof slab of concrete seemingly floating above the glass skin of the façade. The fortunate complementarity of client and architect has meant that this building, by contrast with his many other museums, is perhaps his most intimate and uncompromising work.

The Pulitzer Foundation, which is part of the tradition of small private museums such as the Barnes Collection near Philadelphia or de Menill in Fort Worth (by Louis I. Kahn), resolutely rejects any kind of commercialised museum business. The building is intended to be used solely for intensive engagement with art. Visitors will thus search in vain for a café or museum shop. E. K.

1

1 Museum im städtischen Kontext, rechts Skulptur von Richard Serra
2 Eingangsbereich
3 Innenhof mit Wassergarten
4 Treppenhaus mit einer Installation von Ellsworth Kelly

1 Museum in its urban context, on the right a sculpture by Richard Serra
2 Entrance area
3 Courtyard with water garden
4 Stairwell with an installation by Ellsworth Kelly

2

3

4

ÁLVARO SIZA

Santa Maria
Marco de Canaveses, Portugal, 1995

Die strenge Formensprache sowie eine eingeschränkte Material- und Farbwahl machen diese Kirche zum Fixpunkt in einer suburban anmutenden, zu schnell gewachsenen Stadt. Noch steht der Bau als Solitär auf einem Plateau. Dieser soll jedoch in naher Zukunft von Nebengebäuden gefasst werden und traditionelle portugiesische Kirchenvorplätze zitieren.

Schon von außen betrachtet fällt neben der Betonung der Vertikalen ein hoher Grad an Abstraktion auf. So wird über eine Aussparung im Kirchenvolumen eine Eingangssituation definiert, die an klassische Zweiturm-Fronten erinnert. Eine der sich ergebenden Flanken nimmt das Baptisterium auf, die andere dient als Glockenturm und erlaubt werktags den Einlass. Das monumentale, zehn Meter hohe Tor, das die Westfassade dominiert, öffnet sich hingegen nur an hohen Feiertagen.

Laut eigener Aussage sah der Architekt seine Aufgabe nicht darin, einen »demokratischen«, sondern einen der Meditation verpflichteten Raum zu schaffen. Deshalb griff er auf das liturgische Konzept der Wegkirche zurück. Der formale Bezug auf die Architektur der zwanziger Jahre ist in Sizas Werk eine allgegenwärtige Konstante. Im Gegensatz zu kastenförmigen Räumen wie der Aachener Fronleichnamskirche von Rudolf Schwarz (1928-1930) wird hier das Innere durch zwei umgekehrte Apsiden im Chor sowie durch die konvex gebogene Nordwand dynamisiert und die Architektur mittels raffinierter Lichtführung virtuos in Szene gesetzt. W. W.

Santa Maria
Marco de Canaveses, Portugal, 1995

The severe formal language and restricted choice of materials and colours make this church a fixed point in a town that is growing too fast and feels suburban. This building still stands alone on a plateau. However, in the near future it will be flanked by ancillary buildings in a way reminiscent of traditional Portuguese squares in front of churches.

What is striking even from outside is not only the vertical emphasis but also the high degree of abstraction. For example, a recess in the volume of the church defines an entrance reminiscent of classic two-tower fronts. One of the towers created accommodates the baptistery; the other is used as bell tower and is the main entrance on weekdays. The monumental, ten metre high main door which dominates the west façade, is only opened on high holidays.

In the architect's own words, he did not see his brief as being about creating a "democratic" space but one dedicated to meditation. That is why the space has the horizontal directionality associated with the hierarchical concept of the liturgy. Siza's work constantly makes formal reference to 1920s architecture. However, by contrast with the box-like spaces, found for example in Rudolf Schwarz's Church of Corpus Christi in Aachen (1928-1930), a sense of dynamics is added to the interior here by two reversed apses in the choir and by the convex curve of the north wall. The architecture is choreographed with virtuosity by the sophisticated way the light is manipulated. W. W.

1

2

3

1 Skizze zur Gesamtplanung
2 Rückseite auf Sockel mit Vorhof zur Kapelle
3 Hauptfront
4 Blick zum Altarraum
5 Blick vom Altarraum

1 Sketch for the overall design
2 Rear of church with forecourt in front of the chapel
3 Main façade
4 View towards the sanctuary
5 View from the sanctuary towards the entrance

4

5

JOSÉ RAFAEL MONEO

Our Lady of the Angels
Los Angeles, Kalifornien, USA, 1997-2002

Our Lady of the Angels
Los Angeles, California, USA, 1997-2002

Überlegungen, für die größte katholische Erzdiözese der USA mit 4,1 Mio. Gläubigen eine neue Kathedrale zu errichten, reichen bis in das Jahr 1904 zurück. 1994 erhielt das Projekt wieder Auftrieb, da die bisher genutzte Hauptkirche bei einem Erdbeben schwer beschädigt wurde. Die Behörden untersagten den Umbau und die Vergrößerung der Kirche, sodass die Planungen für einen Neubau endgültig Gestalt annehmen konnten.

Die neue Kathedrale erhebt sich auf einem ehemaligen Parkplatz in Downtown Los Angeles, entlang des Hollywood Freeways. Das Gotteshaus soll auch zur Belebung des Civic Centers der Stadt beitragen. Auch der Neubau der Walt Disney Concert Hall von Frank O. Gehry, die sich nur wenige Blocks weiter südlich befindet, dient, als weltliches Gegenstück zur Kathedrale, diesem Zweck.

Das Bauwerk, das 3000 Gläubige aufnehmen kann, spiegelt das Selbstbewusstsein der katholischen Bevölkerung von Los Angeles wider, deren größte Bevölkerungsgruppe lateinamerikanischer Herkunft ist. Moneo verbindet in seiner Kirche Elemente der lateinamerikanischen Tradition mit denen der Moderne. Der Schrein für die mexikanische Heilige Unsere Liebe Frau von Guadeloupe ist in die Umfassungsmauer des Komplexes eingelassen. Der Bau selbst besteht aus ockerfarbenem Sichtbeton. Die pfeilerartigen Schotten im Inneren sorgen in Verbindung mit den Alabasterfenstern für eine sublime Lichtwirkung. Aus Gründen der Erdbebensicherheit ruht der gewaltige Bau auf Fundamenten mit Gummidämpfern. E. K.

The idea of building a new cathedral for the largest Catholic archdiocese in the USA with 4.1 million believers dates back to 1904. In 1994, the project received new impetus when the church that had been used in the past suffered severe damage in an earthquake. The authorities would not allow the church to be remodelled or extended, so that plans for a new building finally began to take shape.

The new cathedral rises up on the site of what was a car park in downtown Los Angeles, on the Hollywood Freeway. However, it is used not only as a place of worship, but is also intended to contribute to reviving the city centre. The new Walt Disney Concert Hall by Frank O. Gehry, just a few blocks to the south, also serves this purpose as the cathedral's secular counterpart.

The building, which can accommodate 3,000 worshippers, reflects the self-image of the Catholic population of Los Angeles, whose largest ethnic group is of Latin American origin. Moneo combines elements from this tradition with elements of Modernism in this church. The shrine for the Mexican patron saint, Our Lady of Guadeloupe, is set into the complex's boundary wall. The building itself is in ochre-coloured fair-faced concrete. The pillar-like cross-walls inside the church and the alabaster windows create a sublime light effect. To make it earthquake-proof, the immense building is isolated from its foundations by rubber bearings. E. K.

1 Grundriss Erdgeschoss
2 Mittelschiff
3 Ansicht von Nordwesten
4 Ansicht von Nordosten vom Hollywood Freeway

1 Ground floor plan
2 Nave
3 View from the north-west
4 View from the north-east from Hollywood Freeway

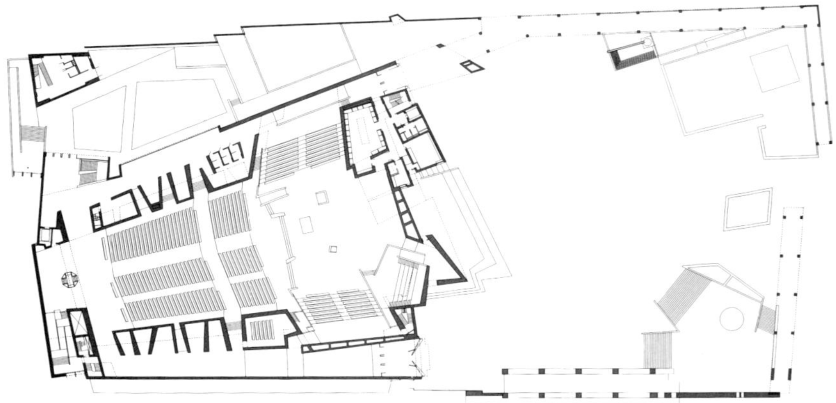

1

2

3

101
Hollywood Fwy
Ventura
Harbor Fwy
110
San Pedro
Pasadena Fwy
Pasadena
NO TRUCKS

4